W9-BNI-445

Content Area Reading

Content Area Reading
Literacy and Learning Across the Curriculum
SIXTH EDITION

Richard T. Vacca

Jo Anne L. Vacca

Kent State University

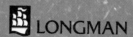 LONGMAN

An Imprint of Addison Wesley Longman, Inc.

New York • Reading, Massachusetts • Menlo Park, California • Harlow, England
Don Mills, Ontario • Sydney • Mexico City • Madrid • Amsterdam

Photo Credits

Page 1: John Eastcott/YVA Momatiuk/Stock Boston; page 169: © Spencer Grant/Stock Boston; page 312: © Elizabeth Crews/The Image Works; and page 463: © Chris Sheridan/Monkmeyer.

Acquisitions Editor: Virginia L. Blanford
Development Manager: Arlene Bessenoff
Development Editor: Nancy Crochiere
Marketing Manager: Renée Ortbals
Project Manager: Ellen MacElree
Design Manager and Text Design: Wendy Ann Fredericks
Cover Design and Illustration: Tina Vey
Art Studio: ElectraGraphics, Inc.
Photo Researcher: Mira Schachne
Prepress Services Supervisor: Valerie A. Vargas
Electronic Production Specialist: Heather Peres
Print Buyer: Denise Sandler
Electronic Page Makeup: Ruttle, Shaw & Wetherill, Inc.
Printer and Binder: RR Donnelley & Sons Company
Cover Printer: The Lehigh Press, Inc.

Library of Congress Cataloging-in-Publication Data

Vacca, Richard T.
Content area reading : literacy and learning across the curriculum
     / Richard T. Vacca. Jo Anne L. Vacca. — 6th ed.
Includes bibliographical references (p.) and index.
     ISBN 0-321-00363-2
     1. Content area reading.   I. Vacca, Jo Anne L.   II. Title.
LB1050.455.V33   1998
428.4'3—dc21   98-27313
                                                          CIP

Copyright © 1999 by Addison-Wesley Educational Publishers Inc.

All rights reserved. No part of this publication may be reproduced, stored in a retrieval system, or transmitted, in any form or by any means, electronic, mechanical, photocopying, recording, or otherwise, without the prior written permission of the publisher. Printed in the United States.

Please visit our website at **http://longman.awl.com**

ISBN 0-321-00363-2

3 4 5 6 7 8 9 10–DOC–010099

To Pauline and William Vacca

One was a seamstress,
The other a painter.
They were the gold of immigrants,
Masters of the dance.
They knew about patterns and scaffolds
And how to rise above circumstance.

They made a life
Stitch by stitch,
Brush stroke by brush stroke.
And all the while,
Scrimping and saving,
Laughing and loving,
Not letting limited means
Limit their dreams.

We know them as Mom and Dad.
Supportive, loving, steadfast—
Who could ask for more?

Brief Contents

Detailed Contents

PART 2   **CONTENT LITERACY CONNECTIONS 169**

Chapter 5   **Bringing Students and Texts Together   170**

Chapter 6   **Talking to Learn   212**

Chapter 7   **Writing to Learn   256**

Preface

When we began writing *Content Area Reading* 20 years ago, we wrote our chapter drafts in longhand on lined yellow legal pads using No. 2 pencils. Drafting chapters with paper and pencil wasn't easy. The physical demands alone were enough to make us wonder whether the endeavor was worth the effort. To this day, vestiges of a "writer's bump," the callus that builds on the edge of the middle finger where flesh rubs against the hard surface of the pencil, remind us of how it was then and what it's like now. Computers, loaded with sophisticated word processing software, have made writing this edition of *Content Area Reading* much less demanding physically, although the process is as challenging as ever intellectually and emotionally.

The changes that we have experienced as writers over the past two decades, however, pale in comparison to the changes that have occurred in the classroom. One such change involves how teachers relate to text. The traditional practice of "assigning and telling"—teachers assign texts to be read and then tell students what they have read about—is no longer considered appropriate practice in today's classroom. Teaching and learning in content classrooms involve far more than transmitting knowledge from teacher to student. Instead, *constructivist* views of learning position teachers as the architects of active learning environments and place students at the center of meaning-making in content classrooms.

Our students are not the same either. There is greater student diversity in our classrooms today than at any time in our nation's history. Teaching with texts is all the more challenging in today's classroom, where the range of academic, linguistic, and cultural diversity has been increasing steadily since the 1960s. Traditional approaches to content area instruction aren't reaching diverse learners in ways that support their academic development. Even though students today exhibit differences in academic achievement and come from all linguistic and cultural backgrounds, a "one size fits all" instructional mentality has persisted in content area classrooms. Instructional practices that involve mostly lecture and recitation often result in passive learning and nonparticipation by students. "Assign and tell" practices aren't working well with students of diverse backgrounds, nor have they worked well with mainstream students, because they are neither culturally nor academically appropriate.

Even notions of what constitutes an appropriate text for content area learning are changing. Twenty years ago, the textbook was the canon. Today, it is not surprising to see content area teachers integrating trade books into units of study, and highly interactive and engaging electronic texts are quickly becoming an integral part of today's classroom. A new chapter in this edition emphasizes the integration of electronic texts and trade books into curricular study.

The changing world of the classroom requires teachers to rethink business as usual, just as we find ourselves rethinking, rewriting, and fine-tuning a vision of learning and teaching with texts. We're told that the sign of a good book, one that has staying power, is that it's never finished saying what it has to say. We'll let you judge for yourself whether this is a good book or not, one that meets your professional needs, but when we compare the first edition to the present one, we're both delighted and surprised at how much the book has changed while maintaining its core beliefs and assumptions. What began as a modest attempt to show how reading can become a workable and sensible part of content area learning and teaching has expanded into an ambitious exploration of *content literacy*—the ability to use reading, writing, talking, and listening processes to learn subject matter across the curriculum.

HOW CONTENT AREA READING HAS CHANGED

Engaging in a revision of a textbook is often as challenging as writing a book from scratch. Throughout the rethinking process for this edition, we faced tactical decisions: What should be deleted from the previous edition? What should be deemphasized or expanded on? What should be added to reflect the changing nature of learners, teachers, and texts in today's content classrooms? The knowledge base related to content literacy and learning has changed dramatically in the past 20 years. And so has thinking about what constitutes best practice in learning with texts across the curriculum. Nevertheless, in making decisions related to changes in this edition, we followed the same functional criteria that guided the writing of the first edition. *Workable* and *sensible* remain the watchwords of this sixth edition. Influenced by the roles that language, cognition, culture, and social context play in using literate processes such as reading, talking, and writing to learn, the goal of this edition is as true as it was 20 years ago: to inspire teachers, whether novice or veteran, to examine instructional strategies and practices in light of what is known about the powerful bonds that exist between literacy and learning.

In this book, we define *content literacy* as the ability to use language to learn. Language is a predominant tool whereby teachers, students, and authors communicate. Yet it's easy to lose sight of or underestimate the many roles that language plays in classroom learning. One of the exciting changes in this edition is to highlight in Part 2 of the book the content literacy connections that exist among various modes of language. Talk is at the heart of classroom communication and has the potential to shape students' thinking and learning in powerful ways. Verbal interactions between teacher and students and between students and other students serve learning well. In Part 2, we emphasize the interrelatedness of reading, writing, talking, and listening as tools for subject matter learning.

Texts, whether printed in typesetter's ink or viewed electronically on a computer screen, are pivotal tools in the development of strategic, independent learners. Yet texts often remain silent and neglected in content area classrooms. The reality of text use in content areas is that many students, for reasons that we explore in this book, are disengaged from the process of learning with texts in their classrooms. Yet caring and knowledgeable teachers can make a difference in the way students use texts to learn. In this book, we explore how to create active learning environments in which students—alone and in collaboration—know *how, when,* and *why* to use all modes of language to learn with texts.

Underlying our beliefs about content literacy and learning is the idea that students learn *with* texts, not necessarily *from* texts. Learning from texts suggests that a text is a body of information to be mastered by readers rather than a tool readers use to construct meaning. Learning with texts underscores the transaction that takes place between reader and text rather than the transmission of knowledge from one party (the text) to another (the reader). Learning with texts implies that students have much to contribute to their own learning as they interact with texts to make meaning and construct knowledge. Active, engaged learners are strategic in their interactions with text; they know how to search for meaning in everything they talk about and listen to and read and write about. Engaged readers also know how to use what they know about a subject to make sense out of what they are reading and learning about. Furthermore, when students are engaged with texts, they aren't ambivalent about reading or their own reading processes. They're confident and competent with texts.

WHAT REMAINS AT THE CENTER OF THIS EDITION

This edition retains all of the features of the previous editions—a wealth of practical activities, a focus on content literacy—while making improvements in organization and overall coverage of teaching and learning strategies. Strategic learning, collaborative and cooperative grouping practices, the role that prior knowledge plays in comprehension and learning, learning with literature and technology, talking about texts, writing to learn, and instructional scaffolding before, during, and after reading represent major threads woven throughout the book, as well as topics for individual chapters.

As in previous editions, each chapter begins with a quotation to help you reflect on the theme of the chapter; a chapter overview, in which the relationships among important ideas are graphically depicted; a set of questions that serve as a frame of reference; and an organizing principle. At a glance, these organizing principles capture the major themes of this edition:

◆   Teachers play a crucial role in helping students learn with text.

◆   One important way that teachers respond to classroom diversity is to scaffold instruction so that students become aware of and competent with learning strategies.

◆   Trade books and electronic texts extend and enrich the curriculum.

◆   Instructional assessment is a continuous process of gathering multiple sources of relevant information for instructional purposes.

◆   Bringing students and texts together involves plans and practices that result in active student engagement and collaboration.

◆   Talking to learn helps students explore, clarify, and think deeply about ideas they encounter in reading and writing.

◆   Writing facilitates learning by helping students explore, clarify, and think deeply about ideas and concepts encountered in reading.

◆   Teaching words well means giving students multiple opportunities to learn how words are conceptually related in the materials they are studying.

◆   Piquing interest and raising expectations about the meaning of texts create a context in which students will read with purpose and anticipation.

◆   Looking for and using text structure helps students "do something" with texts in order to process and think more deeply about ideas encountered during reading.

◆   Study guides provide the kind of instructional support that allows students to interact with and respond to difficult texts in meaningful ways.

◆   Participating in planned, reflective, and inquiry-based professional development leads to professional growth and improved instruction.

As in previous editions, end-of-chapter activities encourage students to think about what they have read ("Minds-On") and to apply information and new ideas ("Hands-On"). Many of the Minds-On and Hands-On activities encourage group interaction and collaborative learning.

NEW TO THIS EDITION

While we have worked to retain the strengths that previous readers have found in this book, we have also added new material and features and reorganized the content of the book in ways that reflect the most current concerns and directions in the field.

Organizational Changes

The sixth edition of *Content Area Reading* is divided into four parts. Part 1, "The Changing World of Classrooms," reflects the challenges that content area teachers face as they deal with a myriad of changes in their classrooms. The four chapters in this part include a new chapter on integrating electronic texts and trade books into classrooms (Chapter 3) and an extensively revised chapter on teaching and learning in diverse classrooms. The chapter on assessment, previously found toward the end of the book, has been moved forward to reflect the new emphasis on assessment as an ongoing part of planning and implementing instruction. Part 2, "Content Literacy Connections," consists of three chapters that explore how lessons and thematic units bring learners and texts together, as well as the connections among reading, talking, and writing across the curriculum. Part 3, "Instructional Strategies: Integrating Literacy and Learning," offers four chapters that examine a multitude of theory-based, practical teaching strategies designed to scaffold instruction in ways that guide and support content literacy and learning.

New to this edition, Part 4, "Professional Development," focuses on ways in which teachers may examine their own beliefs and practices through a process of self-reflection and inquiry-based professional development. Many teachers today find themselves in a process of change and transition as they reconsider instructional beliefs related to literacy and learning. They are eschewing traditional approaches to text-related instruction in favor of strategies that reach all learners and support content literacy in their classrooms. Reflective teachers who inquire into what they do, how they do it, and why they do it find that they are more likely to take risks and experiment with the kinds of instructional alternatives described in this book.

Features

In addition to those features that have proved helpful in earlier editions—various pedagogical aids at the beginning and end of each chapter—the sixth edition of *Content Area Reading* includes a new boxed feature, "Nothing but Net." The Nothing but Net boxes which appear in Chapters 2, 3, and 12, guide readers in finding and using Internet resources in the content area classroom.

Content Area Reading is now also accompanied by a unique Web site *(http://longman.awl.com/vacca)* designed for use by both students and instructors. The Web site presents the most current reading tools and Internet resources, additional activities and exercises to accompany each chapter, and a variety of "hot links" and other resources that should prove invaluable in exploring topics and issues in content area literacy.

ACKNOWLEDGMENTS

We thank the following reviewers of this edition's manuscript for their encouragement and useful responses in shaping our thinking:

Nancy S. Bailey, Metropolitan State College of Denver

Robert S. Burroughs, University of Cincinnati

Chris A. Cherrington, Bloomsburg University

Karen Ford, Ball State University

Joan B. Elliot, Indiana University of Pennsylvania

Janis Harmon, University of Texas at San Antonio

Debra Houser, University of Texas at San Antonio

Alexandra G. Leavell, University of North Texas

B. Malcolm Lively, The University of Georgia

George I. Martin, Montclair State University

Marian J. McKenna, University of Montana at Missoula

Leeanna Morgan, Ohio University

Sarah S. Pate, University of Alabama

Jenny Piazza, University of Southern Colorado

Victoria Gentry Ridgeway, Clemson University

V. Frank Stone, University of Virginia

Taylor E. Turner, Marshall University

E. Lynne Weisenbach, University of Indianapolis

Kathleen G. Weiss, University of Houston

Jayne White, Drury College

Linda Wise, Montclair State University

Liliana Zecker, DePaul University

A special thanks goes to Sarah Nixon-Ponder of Southwest Missouri State University for the revision of our Instructor's Manual, and to Gary Moorman and Susan Nelson of Appalachian State University for developing the accompanying Web site. We also thank Ginny Blanford and Arlene Bessenoff, our editors at Longman, for keeping us on task by gently reminding us that we were not revising with paper and pencil anymore; Nancy Crochiere, our excellent development editor; and Wendy Fredericks and Ellen MacElree, who are responsible for the elegant design and production values of this edition.

R. T. V.
J. L. V.

PART
1

The Changing World
of Classrooms

Teaching and Learning with Texts

I was desperate to keep my brain alive.

—Terry Anderson, the last of 13 American hostages to be set free in Lebanon

Organizing Principle

Throughout his 2455 days in captivity, Terry Anderson waged an inner struggle with his worst fear: that he "would lapse into some kind of mental rot." As horrendous as his experience was, Anderson kept his brain alive through the sustaining power of language. His ordeal did not prevent him from communicating with fellow hostages—first by teaching them a sign language that he half-invented and then by developing a system of taps against the wall. And throughout his captivity, he fought to keep his brain alive by badgering his captors for books, and more books, until they were eventually delivered by the boxload. Terry Anderson knew all too well that the mind matters.

His experiences as a hostage dramatize that the real value of language lies in its uses. It is not an exaggeration to suggest that texts helped keep Anderson's mind and spirit alive, even that they kept his brain from mental and physical decay. *Brain* and *mind,* two terms often used interchangeably, explain what humans do best: thinking. Whereas the brain is a physical organ with its own intricate chemistry and physiology, the mind has a life of its own. To read is to engage the mind in thinking. Reading is a powerful means of putting language to use purposefully—whether it is to learn, to imagine, or to enjoy. Using language to teach and learn with texts—this is what content area reading is all about.

Although texts are routinely assigned in content area classrooms, showing students how to learn with texts enters into the plans of teachers only infrequently. When students become too dependent on teachers, not their own minds, as their primary source of learning, they are rarely in a strategic position to learn how to learn or to keep their minds alive. This need not be the case. How students interact with texts, other students, and the teacher is reflected in the organizing principle of this chapter: **All teachers play a critical role in helping students learn with texts.**

Study the chapter overview. It's your map to the major ideas that you will encounter in the chapter. The overview shows the relationships that exist among the concepts you will study. Use it as an organizer. What is the chapter about? What do you know already about the content to be presented in the chapter? What do you need to learn more about?

In conjunction with the chapter overview, take a moment or two to study the "Frame of Mind" questions. This feature uses key questions to help you think about the ideas that you will read about. Our intent is to create a mental disposition for learning, a critical "frame of mind," if you will, so that you can better interact with the ideas that we, as authors, have organized and developed in the chapter. When you finish reading, you should be able to respond fully to the "Frame of Mind" questions.

Chapter Overview

TEACHING AND LEARNING WITH TEXTS

BEYOND ASSIGNING AND TELLING

LAUGUAGE, CONTENT LITERACY, AND LEARNING

Content Literacy ← → Using Language to Learn

CONSTRUCTING MEANING

Schema → Comprehension → Learning

INSTRUCTIONAL SCAFFOLDING

1. Why do "assigning and telling" stifle active learning and deny students responsibility for learning on their own?

2. In what ways are language and learning related?

3. What is content literacy?

4. What does it mean to use language to learn?

5. What are some constructive influences on reading to learn?

6. How does schema influence comprehension and learning?

The classroom is a crucible, a place where the special mix of *teacher, student,* and *text* come together to create wonderfully complex human interactions that stir the minds and spirits of learners. Some days, of course, are better than others. The things that you thought about doing and the classroom surprises that you didn't expect fall into place. A creative energy imbues teaching and learning.

Sometimes, however, lessons limp along. Others just bomb—so you cut them short. The four or so remaining minutes before the bell rings are a kind of self-inflicted wound. Nothing is more unnerving than waiting for the bell to ring when students don't have anything meaningful to do.

Consider a science teacher's reflection on the way things went in one of her classes. "Something was missing," she explains. "The students aren't usually as quiet and passive as they were today. Excuse the pun, but the chemistry wasn't there. Maybe the text assignment was too hard. Maybe I could have done something differently. Any suggestions?" This teacher, like most good teachers, cares about what she does. She wants to know how to improve her craft. She knows that when the chemistry is there, teaching is its own reward.

Good teachers bring sensitivity and a spirit of reflective inquiry to their teaching. They care about what they do and how they do it. As Eliot Eisner (1985) aptly put it:

> Teaching can be done as badly as anything else. It can be wooden, mechanical, mindless, and wholly unimaginative. But when it is sensitive, intelligent, and creative—those qualities that confer upon it the status of an art—it should, in my view, not be regarded, as it so often is by some, as an expression of

unfathomable talent or luck but as an example of humans exercising the highest
levels of their intelligence. (p. 77)

To be a teacher today means exercising the highest levels of intelligence
in coping with difficult issues: the curriculum, content delivery, school climate,
classroom control, dropout rates, accountability, children and youth at risk of
failure, and racial, social, and cultural diversity, to name a few. There is unre-
lenting pressure on teachers to respond to problems of all types. What is abun-
dantly clear is that as important as academic content is, there's more to being
an artful teacher than having a rich and deep understanding of a subject.

Academic content, nevertheless, is the *raison d'être* for most teachers
who are wedded to a discipline. Yet it is much more difficult to teach somebody something than merely to know that something: "The teacher of the
American Revolution has to know both a great deal about the American
Revolution and a variety of ways of communicating the essence of the
American Revolution to a wide variety of students, in a pedagogically interesting way" (Shulman 1987). What to teach and how to teach it are nagging
problems for classroom teachers. For some, using texts to teach content contributes to the problem. For others, showing students how to learn with texts
is part of the solution.

Why bring learners and texts together in the classroom? Texts, after all,
are but one medium for learning academic content. What is the value of texts
in the content areas?

While we're not suggesting that texts are the only source for learning or
that they should be, they will continue to be indispensable tools for constructing knowledge; sharing the experiences, ideas, and feelings of others;
and developing new insights and perspectives. Learning how to teach with
texts contributes significantly to the way you think about teaching, learning,
and curriculum. Throughout this book, we invite you to examine content area
teaching practices, and the assumptions underlying those practices, in the
light of promising strategies for text learning and active student engagement.

All too often, academic texts are viewed as sacred canons, authoritative
sources of knowledge by which the information in a field is transmitted from
generation to generation of learners. The expression "learning *from* texts" has
been used widely in content area reading, as if a text were indeed a canon to
be mastered rather than a tool for learning and constructing meaning. The
preposition *from* suggests a one-way act in which meaning flows from A (the
text) to B (the reader). The shift in meaning from *from* to *with* is subtle but dramatic (Tierney & Pearson 1992). It places the act of reading to learn squarely in
the context of a human transaction between two parties rather than being a
transmission of information from one party to another. Learning *with* texts suggests that readers have much to contribute to the process as they interact with
texts to make meaning and construct knowledge.

Although texts come with the territory, using them to help students acquire content doesn't work well for many teachers. Teaching with texts is

more complex than it appears on the surface. Whether you're a novice or a veteran teacher, using texts effectively requires the willingness to explore instructional alternatives and to move beyond assigning and telling.

BEYOND ASSIGNING AND TELLING

Your own personal history as a student, we wager, has etched into your memory an instructional blueprint that teachers in your past probably followed: *Assign* a text to read (usually with questions to be answered) for homework; then, in subsequent lessons, *tell* students through question-and-answer routines what the material they read was about, explaining the ideas and information that the students encountered in print. The dominant interactional pattern between teacher and students during the class presentation of assigned material often involves calling on a student to answer a question, listening to the student's response, and then evaluating or modifying the student's response (Alvermann & Moore 1991). Such is the ebb and flow of assign-and-tell instructional routines in content area classrooms.

There's more to teaching with texts than assigning and telling. Assigning and telling are common but uninspired teaching practices that bog students down in the mire of passive learning. Assign-and-tell, more often than not, dampens active involvement in learning and denies students ownership of and responsibility for the acquisition of content. Teachers place themselves, either by design or by circumstance, in the unenviable position of being the most active participant during classroom interactions with students.

No wonder John Goodlad (1984) portrays textbook assignment, lecture, and recitation (a form of oral questioning in which teachers already know the answers to the questions they ask) as the dominant activities in the instructional repertoire of many content area teachers. Goodlad and his research associates conclude from a monumental study of schools that "the data from our observations in more than 1000 classrooms support the popular image of a teacher standing in front of a class imparting knowledge to a group of students" (p. 105). His team of researchers found that the prevalence of assign-and-tell practices increases steadily from the primary to the senior high school years and that teachers often "outtalk" students by a three-to-one ratio.

Try to recall what it was like when you were in school. Well-intentioned teachers, more likely than not, assigned texts to be read as homework, only to find that for one reason or another many of the students didn't quite grasp what they were assigned to read. Some didn't read the material at all. Others read narrowly, to answer questions assigned for homework. Still others may have got tangled in text, stuck in the underbrush of facts and details. So class time was spent transmitting information that wasn't learned well from texts in the first place.

Imparting knowledge in this fashion reminds Brozo and Simpson (1991) of a poster hanging on a colleague's door. The poster "satirically depicts teaching as a teacher with a spigot for a mouth opening into a funnel attached to the top of a child's head. The idea is that knowledge flows from teachers and fills students' heads much like water into a bucket" (p. 6). When teachers impart knowledge with little attention to how a learner acquires that knowledge, students soon become nonparticipants in the academic life of the classroom. Assign-and-tell practices not only result in passive reading but also influence the way students view themselves in relation to texts. The "Calvin and Hobbes" cartoon here has Calvin thinking of himself as "informationally impaired."

Shifting the burden of learning from teachers' shoulders to students' is in large measure what this book is about. What does it mean to teach with texts? Why teach with texts? How does text-related teaching prepare students to learn how to learn in content area disciplines? The answers to these questions lie in understanding the relationships that exist among language, literacy, and learning. Throughout the book, we invite you to explore the role that language and literacy play in learning and constructing knowledge.

Content area classrooms are filled with the potential of human activity, interaction, and transaction. Language, and its many uses, is often the vehicle by which teachers, students, and authors communicate with one another. Human beings think *with* language. Yet it's easy to lose sight of, or take for granted, the role that language and literacy play in teaching and learning.

Calvin and **Hobbes**   **by Bill Watterson**

Source: "Calvin and Hobbes," copyright © 1992 Bill Watterson. Reprinted with permission of Universal Press Syndicate. All rights reserved.

LANGUAGE, CONTENT LITERACY, AND LEARNING

Imagine what classrooms would be like without talk. Try getting through a class period or an entire school day in silence. Not impossible, but difficult, isn't it?

The uses of language in content area classrooms, however, involve more than talk. Although verbal interactions between students and teachers serve learning well in various instructional contexts, other modes of language are also crucial to learning. Imagine, for example, what learning would be like without texts. Texts? Our hunch is that it's far easier for you to envision teaching and learning without texts than without talk.

Yet a *text,* by its very nature, is language—written language. Written text may be fixed in typesetter's ink on a conventional printed page, or it may be on a computer screen in an electronic environment. Text, whether it's printed or electronic, may consist of a single word, sentence, paragraph, page, chapter, or text screen. Writers of texts communicate with readers in the same way that speakers use language to communicate with listeners. Language is language, whether it's spoken, written, signed, or represented visually.

Teaching with texts requires its fair share of strategy. But it involves more than assigning pages to be read, lecturing, or using questions to check whether students have read the material the night before. To use texts strategically, you must first be aware of the powerful bonds that link language to content literacy and learning.

Content Literacy in Perspective

Content literacy—the ability to use reading and writing to learn subject matter in a given discipline—is a relatively new concept that holds much potential for students' acquisition of content (McKenna & Robinson 1990). To understand better what it means to be content-literate in a discipline, examine the general construct of the term *literacy* and how it is used in today's society.

Literacy is a strong cultural expectation in the United States and other technologically advanced countries. Society places a heavy premium on literate behavior and demands that its citizens acquire literacy for personal, social, academic, and economic success. But what does it mean to be literate?

Literacy is a term whose meaning fluctuates from one context to another. It may, for example, be used to describe how knowledgeable a person is in a particular subject. What do you know about computers and how to use them? Are you *computer-literate*? In the same vein, the term *cultural literacy* refers to what an educated person should know about the arts, literature, and other determinants of culture.

The most common use of the term *literacy* has been to denote one's ability to read and write a language. In the past century, the term has undergone variations in meaning. It has been used to depict the level of competence in reading and writing—*functional literacy*—that one needs to survive in society; one's lack of education—*illiteracy*—manifested in an inability to read and write a language; and one's lack of a reading habit—*aliteracy*—especially among those who have the ability to read and write but choose not to.

The more researchers inquire into literacy and what it means to be literate, the more complex and multidimensional the concept becomes. Literacy is situational. In other words, a person may be able to handle the literacy demands of a task in one situation or context but not in another. Hence *workplace literacy* refers to the situational demands placed on workers to read and write effectively (Mikulecky 1990). These demands vary from job to job. *Family literacy* is used to describe how family interactions influence the language competence of young children (Taylor 1983). Because the environments for learning literacy vary from family to family, some young children enter school more literate than others.

Suppose you were to accompany Darryl, a sophomore at Warren Harding High, through a typical school day. Toward the end of his first-period American history class, where the students have been studying the events leading up to the Bay of Pigs invasion during John F. Kennedy's presidency, the teacher calls on Darryl to read aloud to the class a textbook section describing Fidel Castro's overthrow of the Cuban dictator Fulgencio Batista:

> Latin America was a special target for aid from the United States because the Soviet Union had recently gained a foothold there. In 1959 an uprising led by Fidel Castro succeeded in overthrowing the Cuban dictator, Fulgencio Batista. Many Americans applauded Castro's success, believing he would bring democracy to Cuba. Castro, however, quickly established a Communist-style dictatorship with strong ties to the Soviet Union.
>
> When Kennedy took office, a plan to overthrow Castro was already in the works. The plan called for an invasion of Cuba by a group of anti-Castro Cuban refugees trained and financed by the Central Intelligence Agency (CIA). Kennedy gave the green light for the plan to proceed. (Boyer & Stuckey, 1996, pp. 491–492)

Darryl reads the text quickly, completing the reading just as the bell rings. He grabs his stuff from the desk and hurries off to biology, where the class has been involved in a study of microorganisms. Five minutes into the lesson, the teacher reinforces a point she is making during her lecture by asking Darryl to read about euglenoids:

> The **euglenoids,** members of phylum Euglenophyta, are protists that have traits of both plants and animals. They are like plants because they contain chlorophyll and undergo photosynthesis. However, euglenoids have no cell walls. Instead of a cell wall, euglenoids have a layer of flexible, interlocking protein fibers inside the cell membrane. Euglenoids are similar to animals because they

are responsive and move by using one or two flagella for locomotion. Euglenoids have a contractile vacuole that expels excess water from the cell through an opening. They reproduce asexually by mitosis. (Biggs, Emmeluth, Gentry, Hays, Lundgren, & Mollura, 1991, p.275)

Darryl navigates his way through the euglenoid passage, occasionally faltering on words like *flagella* as he reads. When asked to tell the class what the passage is about, he gropes for a word or two: "I dunno. Eugenoids [*sic*] or something." His teacher manages a smile, corrects the pronunciation of *euglenoids,* and proceeds to explain what Darryl read to the class.

Mercifully, the period ends. Darryl heads for Algebra 2, his favorite class. Where the teacher assigns students to read this passage on an alternative definition of a *function:*

Since a function has the property that exactly one second component is related to each first component, an alternative definition of a function is the following. A *function* is a rule that associates with each element of one set exactly one element of another set.

Functions are often denoted by letters, such as *f, g,* and *h.* If the function defined by the rule y = 2x is called *f,* the following "arrow notation" can also be used to define the *function:*

$$f: x \rightarrow 2x$$

This is read "*f* is the function that associates with a number x the number 2x." (Dolciani, Graham, Swanson, & Sharron, 1992, p. 84)

Darryl handles the task with more purpose and confidence than he exhibited in the reading tasks from the previous classes. Why? you might wonder.

Darryl's scenario illustrates how demanding it is to switch gears from content area text to content area text. What demands do the various texts place on Darryl's ability to read? What demands does the task—reading aloud to the class—place on Darryl? What other factors besides the nature of the text and of the task are likely to affect his content literacy?

As you might surmise, a variety of classroom-related factors influence one's content literacy in a given discipline, some of which are the reader's prior knowledge of, attitude toward, and interest in the subject; the reader's purpose; the language and conceptual difficulty of the material; the assumptions the author makes about his or her audience of readers; the way the author organizes ideas; and the teacher's beliefs about and attitude toward the use of texts.

To be literate in content area classrooms, students must learn how to use reading and writing to explore and construct meaning in the company of authors, other learners, and teachers. Using reading and writing in the classroom to help students think and learn with texts doesn't require specialized training on the part of content teachers. Much of what we have to offer in this book is common sense, supported by research and experience, applied to teaching and learning. Nor does the pursuit of content literacy diminish the teacher's role as a subject matter specialist. To help students become literate in a given discipline does not mean to teach students *how to read or write.* Instead, reading and writing are tools that they use to construct knowledge— to discover, clarify, and extend meaning—in a given discipline. Using language to learn underscores students' meaning-making, thought-producing capabilities. To this end, every teacher has a role to play.

Using Language to Learn

Language helps a learner make sense of the world, understand, and be understood. As a result, language and meaning cannot be severed from one another. Language isn't language unless meaning-making is involved. Oral language, without meaning, is mere prattle—a string of senseless speech sounds. Written language, without meaning, is a cipher of mysterious markings on paper.

Language allows human beings to think and to be thoughtful. Terry Anderson demanded books of his captors to keep his mind from decaying. He fought for the right to engage in dialogue and thought, not only with other hostages, but also with authors. Helping learners be thoughtful with texts means engaging them in meaning-making activities. Students need to know how to produce and interact with texts in order to discover, organize, retrieve, and elaborate on content. Students who are literate in a given discipline are more likely to learn with texts if they are aware of and use strategies.

We are fond of a story that Bill Bernhardt (1977) reprints in the book *Just Writing.* The story is from the diary of an African slave named Olaudah Equiano whose master was a ship's captain. Equiano was mystified by the relationship that his master had with books:

> I had often seen my master employed in reading and I had a great curiosity to talk to the books as I thought [he] did. . . . For that purpose I have often taken up a book and have talked to it and then put my ears to it, when alone, in hope it would answer me; and I have been very much concerned when I found it remained silent. (From *Interesting Narrative of Olaudah Equiano,* 1789)

Equiano was on the right track. He intuitively recognized that reading is a language process—that it involves a dialogue between reader and author— but his strategies for engaging the mind in that dialogue were inappropriate. For many students today, reading for meaning is as mysterious a process as it was for Equiano more than 200 years ago. And texts remain as silent.

Learning with texts is a strategic act. To put into perspective how language works to facilitate learning, read "How to Ruin an Association" in Box 1.1.

Box 1.1

How to Ruin an Association

Once upon a time, the Midtown Chapter was one of the most active chapters in the association. It was a smooth-running, efficient organization that enjoyed great prestige in the community.

Then one day, things began to change. One of the members said to himself, "No one will miss me. I have so many other things to do, I think I'll drop out of the chapter's activities."

So hx bxgan to avoid chaptxr functions. Hx rxfusxd to accxpt his rxsponsibil-itixs, and thx chaptxr had to limp along with onx lxss mxmbxr. Of coursx, thx chaptxr could gxt along without him, but it mxant that onx of thx rxmaining mxmbxrs had to doublx up and do twicx as much work as bxforx.

Thxn, onx morx mxmbxr dxcidxd to givx up his sharx of chaptxr activitixs. This mxant thzt two mxmbxrs hzd to do doublx duty.

Thxn z third mxmbxr droppxd jut, znd thrxx jf thx jthxrs hzd tj wjrk hzrdxr thzn xvxr.

Thxn z fjurth drjppxd jut, znd mjrx jf qhz rxmzining zctivx mxmbxrs sqzrqxd wjrking hzrdxr thzn xvxr.

Zs qimx wxnq jn, mzny mjrx jf qhx chzptxr mxmbxrs ljsq inqxrxsq, znd prxqqy sjjn qhx chzptxr wzs bxing run by jnly z fxw mxmbxrs, znd iq ljjkxd likx qhis: Qkj kzqxx kzjxq jxk jzkxqk kqjz xjq kzjx xjz. Zkxq kqx zkkxq, kjz zkzxjqk zkk xkkq x xkziq kzjxq.

Reflect on your reading of "How to Ruin an Association." Did the progressive substitution of letters disrupt your efforts to comprehend the passage? Probably not, at least not until the final paragraph. Perhaps your fluency—that is, your ability to read at a conversational pace—slowed down with each succeeding paragraph, but chances are you were still able to engage in a meaningful dialogue with the author of the text.

From a strategic point of view, a reader's main goal is to make sense of what is read. To do this, readers interact with text by making use of prior knowledge as well as of their knowledge and expectations of written language. Students who struggle with the reading process often are unaware of the *role the reader plays* in comprehending and learning with texts. A strategic reader's mind is alive with questions, *cognitive questions,* as Frank Smith (1988) calls them. Although cognitive questions vary from reader to reader, they allow the strategic reader to interact with the content of the communication: What is this text about? What is the author trying to say? What is going to happen next? What does the author mean? So what? Such questions help the reader anticipate meaning; search for information; reject, modify, or confirm educated guesses; and infer from and elaborate on the content of the author's text.

The last paragraph of "How to Ruin an Association" is challenging. As a reader, you are acutely aware that you may be in trouble, that the text is no longer making sense as you struggle to make meaning.

What strategies do you use to get out of trouble? Do you reread? Do you make use of the way the author organizes his ideas in the text by asking yourself, "What is the thesis or main point of the passage, and how does the author develop it?" Do you try to figure out the author's system for making letter substitutions? Do you attempt to use syntactic and semantic knowledge to make sense of the last lines of text? Do you ask somebody for help?

The last paragraph of "How to Ruin an Association" is difficult for several reasons. The sheer number of letter substitutions within words significantly affects most readers' ability to use letter-sound information. So you're left to other resources. You may have reread the first sentence of the concluding paragraph more than once, using a system of letter substitution, the syntax, and the prior knowledge you bring to the text to translate the sentence from print to speech as follows:

> As time went on, many more of the chapter members lost interest, and pretty soon the chapter was being run by only a few members, and it looked like this:

Your reading of the lines that follow the colon may pose what seems to be an insurmountable task. No longer can you rely on the mechanics and form of written language to make sense. But as a strategic reader, you recognize that you do have an important resource—your prior knowledge—to construct a meaningful ending.

As a result, you may have inferred from the last paragraph that *it* and *this* in the phrase "and it looked like this" refer respectively to the chapter and the chaotic, disorganized string of markings that follow the colon. Hence, you may have drawn an analogy between the chapter and the disorganized, chaotic string of letters. Some of you may also have reasoned: Since the text starts out in a storylike manner—"Once upon a time . . ."—the ending must signal the moral of the story. In your own words, then, what is the moral of the story? Any reasonable response provides an ending to the text.

Reading, as you might surmise, is a constructive process in which readers need not be word-perfect to comprehend a text effectively. Immature readers tend to approach reading as if it were a word-perfect, "roll-your-eyes-over-the-print" act. What they must recognize, however, is that reading is an active process that takes place *behind* the eyes. The meaning of a text resides not in the print itself but in the interactions and transactions that take place between the reader and the text. A content-literate student knows how to make meaning with texts.

THINKING WITH TEXTS
AND CONSTRUCTING MEANING

How people acquire and construct knowledge is the subject of cognition. Coming to know has been a source of study, mainly within the tradition of philosophic inquiry, for centuries. In Plato's *Theaetetus,* written over 2000 years ago, Socrates engages in a dialogue on the subject of knowledge. In response to the question "What is the thinking process?" Socrates explains, "I have a notion that, when the mind is thinking, it is simply talking to itself, asking questions and answering them. . . . So I should describe thinking as discourse, and judgment as a statement pronounced, not aloud to someone else, but silently to oneself."

Thinking with texts invites a covert discourse, one that takes place inside the head, between the reader and the author. What Socrates had to say about thinking raises issues that are as relevant today as they were more than 2000 years ago. Today, however, thinking and knowing are the subject of inquiry from the perspective of many disciplines, including psychology, hermeneutics, semiotics, artificial intelligence, and literary analysis. Throughout the twentieth century in particular, cognition has been explored within the context of psychological inquiry: How does the mind work when people use language to comprehend and learn?

In the past century, thousands of research studies have been conducted to shed light on the cognitive processes associated with comprehension and learning. Yet a popular writer like Robert Fulghum puts the mysteries of cognition in terms a layperson can understand as he reflects on a teaching incident in his life.

Fulghum, the author of *All I Really Need to Know I Learned in Kindergarten* and other books, has a knack of discovering elemental truths in ordinary, everyday events and experiences. One such discovery came when he was teaching a beginning drawing class and had prepared a presentation on the impact of brain research on the process of art. To make his points as illustrative as possible, he used pictures and anatomy charts of the brain and even brought a cantaloupe to class, tossing it around from student to student, so that they would get some sense of the size of the brain.

The brain, however, remained abstract to his students until one class member, whose father was a research neurosurgeon at a medical school, volunteered to bring a human brain to class. So she did. When the brain arrived, the students asked Fulghum for his thoughts on the matter.

What did Fulghum think? He responded to the class's query by noting that the brain is made up of raw meat; that he had some understanding of how it works from a mechanical standpoint, likening it to a motor; and that the brain is all chemistry and electricity. Fulghum then shifted his response from the brain as a physical organ—"a lump of meat"—to its wondrous workings:

This three-pound raw-meat motor . . . contains all the limericks I know, a recipe for how to cook a turkey, the remembered smell of my junior-high locker room, all my sorrows, the ability to double-clutch a pickup truck, the face of my wife when she was young, formulas like $E = MC^2$, and $A^2 + B^2 = C^2$, the Prologue to Chaucer's *Canterbury Tales,* the sound of the first cry of my first-born son, the cure for hiccups, the words to the fight song of St. Olaf's College, fifty years' worth of dreams, how to tie my shoes, the taste of cod-liver oil, an image of Van Gogh's "Sunflowers," and a working understanding of the Dewey Decimal System. It's all there in the MEAT. (Fulghum 1989, p. 41)

Fulghum's classroom experience serves as a springboard for reflection as he celebrates the uniqueness of the brain as a meaning-making organ:

Look around and see the infinite variety of human heads. . . . And know that on the inside such differences are even greater—what we know, how we learn, how we process information, what we remember and forget, our strategies for functioning and coping. . . .

From a practical point of view, day by day, this kind of information makes me a little more patient with the people I live with. I am less inclined to protest, "Why don't you see it the way I do?" and more inclined to say, "You see it *that* way? Holy cow! How amazing!" (pp. 42–43)

Robert Fulghum captures the constructive nature of learning and suggests that people negotiate meaning in life based on their store of memories: everything that they have ever sensed, experienced, and learned. From a cognitive perspective, psychologists have used constructs such as *long-term memory, cognitive structure, schema,* and *prior knowledge* to characterize how people store and organize knowledge in memory. The brain actively seeks, selects, organizes, stores, and, when necessary, retrieves and uses information about the world (Smith 1988). The prior knowledge that students bring to learning has important implications for content area reading. These implications are supported by a *schema-theoretic view* of reading and language comprehension.

Schema, Comprehension, and Learning

Students are in a strategic position to learn with texts whenever they use prior knowledge to construct meaning for new material that they are studying. To this extent, schema reflects the experiences, conceptual understandings, attitudes, values, skills, and strategies a reader brings to a text situation. *Schema* is the technical term used by cognitive scientists to describe how people organize and store information in their heads. Given Fulghum's anecdote, a cognitive psychologist would say that Fulghum accessed various *schemata* (the plural of *schema*) in fondly recalling information-laden events, skills, and experiences in his life.

Schema activation is the mechanism by which people access what they know and match it to the information in a text. In doing so, they build on the meaning they already bring to the reading situation. Indeed, schemata have been called "the building blocks of cognition" (Rumelhart 1982) because they represent elaborate networks of information that people use to make sense of new stimuli, events, and situations.

In ordinary conversation, the language by which people communicate doesn't often pose problems for comprehension. In academic content areas, however, the reader needs to be familiar with the language of a discipline, or the text will begin to create trouble for the reader. Bransford and Stein (1984) make this clear with the passage in Box 1.2.

The passage may pose a comprehension problem if readers do not know enough about Pete or his goal. Pete, it turns out, is an astronomer, and his goal is to call into question current theories about the formation of the solar system based on data collected from a NASA spaceship's voyage to Venus. Does this information help you to better comprehend the letter? Maybe. Yet Bransford and Stein (1984) point out, "Most people feel that [information about Pete's goal] helps comprehension to some extent. However, unless they are knowledgeable about astronomy, they are unable to make many inferences about the letter" (p. 54). For example, what is the relationship, if any, between the high density of the isotopes of argon and theories of the formation of the solar system? To answer the question requires that readers make an inferential leap by using what they know to fill in gaps in the information presented in the letter.

How Schema Influences Comprehension and Learning

Schemata, as you might surmise, greatly influence reading comprehension and learning. When a match occurs between students' prior knowledge and text material, schema functions in at least three ways.

First, schema provides a framework for learning that allows readers to *seek and select* information that is relevant to their purposes for reading. In the process of searching and selecting, readers are more likely to *make inferences* about the text. Inferences occur in situations where you *anticipate* content and *make predictions* about upcoming material or, as we just suggested, *fill in gaps* in the material during reading.

Second, schema helps readers *organize* text information. The process by which you organize and integrate new information into old facilitates the ability to *retain and remember* what you read. A poorly organized text is difficult for readers to comprehend. We'll illustrate this point in more detail when we discuss the influences of text structure on comprehension and retention in later chapters.

And third, schema helps readers *elaborate* information. When you elaborate what you have read, you engage in a cognitive process that involves deeper levels of insight, judgment, and evaluation. You are inclined to ask, "So what?" as you engage in conversation with an author.

Box 1.2

Letter to Jim

Dear Jim,

Remember Pete, the guy in my last letter? You'll never guess what he did last week. First, he talked about the importance of mass spectrometers. He then discussed the isotopes of argon 36 and argon 38 and noted that they were of higher density than expected. He also cited the high values of neon found in the atmosphere. He has a paper that is already written, but he is aware of the need for further investigation as well.

Love,
Sandra

Source: Reprinted from J. D. Bransford & B. S. Stein (1984). *The ideal problem solver: A guide to improving thinking, learning, and creativity.* New York: W. H. Freeman and Co. Copyright © 1984 by W. H. Freeman and Company. Used with permission.

A Schema-Based Demonstration

To illustrate these cognitive processes in action, we will use a workshop activity.

In workshops for content teachers, we occasionally read the short story "Ordeal by Cheque" by Wuther Crue (first published in *Vanity Fair* magazine in 1932). The story is extraordinary in that it is told entirely through the bank checks of the Exeter family over a 28-year span. The workshop participants interact in small groups, and each group is assigned the task of constructing the meaning of the story. At first glance, the groups don't know what to make of their task. "You must be kidding!" is a typical response. At this point, we engage the groups in a prereading activity to activate prior knowledge, declare the purposes for reading, and arouse interest in the story. We assign them the activity in Box 1.3, which depicts in chart form the essential bits of information contained on the first eight checks of the story. Group members collaborate as they respond to the task of answering the three questions that accompany the chart: What is the story about? Who are the main characters and what do you know about them? What do you predict will happen in the remainder of the story?

We invite you to analyze the information in the chart.

Are you able to construct what has taken place so far in the story? What inferences did you make about the characters?

Here are some typical responses to these questions:

"A baby boy was born. He's named after his father."

"The Exeters must be 'fat cats.' The old man's loaded."

"He spends $83 for toys in 1903! He probably bought out the toy store."

Box 1.3

Prereading Activity for "Ordeal by Cheque"

Here are the essential bits of information contained in the first few checks of the story:

Entry date:	Paid to:	Amount:	Signed by:
8/30/03	A baby shop	$ 148.00	Lawrence Exeter
9/2/03	A hospital	100.00	Lawrence Exeter
10/3/03	A physician	475.00	Lawrence Exeter Sr.
12/10/03	A toy company	83.20	Lawrence Exeter Sr.
10/6/09	A private school for boys	1250.00	Lawrence Exeter Sr.
8/6/15	A military academy	2150.00	Lawrence Exeter Sr.
9/3/21	A Cadillac dealer	3885.00	Lawrence Exeter Sr.
9/7/21	An auto repair shop	228.75	Lawrence Exeter Sr.

What is the story about? How would you describe the main characters? What do you think will happen in the remainder of the story?

"Lawrence Jr. must be a spoiled brat!"

"Yeah, how can any kid born with a silver spoon in his mouth not turn out spoiled?"

"Let's not jump to conclusions. Why is he spoiled?"

"Look, the family sent him to a military academy after he screwed up at the private school."

"No, no. It was fashionable in those days to send your child first to a private school until he was old enough for military school. The rich sent their children to exclusive schools—it's as simple as that."

"Maybe so, but the kid is still a spoiled brat. His father buys him a Cadillac, probably for graduation from the academy, and four days later, it's in the body shop for repair."

"The father indulges his son. I wonder what will happen to Junior when he has to make it on his own?"

This demonstration illustrates that readers not only read the lines to determine what an author says but also read between the lines to infer meaning and beyond the lines to elaborate the message. Now read "Ordeal by Cheque" in its entirety on pages 20–23. As you read, you will undoubtedly find yourself raising questions, predicting, searching for relationships among the pieces of information contained in each check, inferring, judging, and elaborating.

What the Demonstration Tells Us

The statements made about Lawrence Exeter and his son are the result of schema activation. We often ask workshop participants to examine the basis for their initial suppositions about the father and the son in the story. Some speak with authority, citing knowledge and beliefs about how the rich live. Others express their inferences about the Exeters as hunches that need to be pursued as more information is revealed in the story.

The activity also activates the workshop participants' prior knowledge of stories. Some use their story schema to establish a setting and identify a problem around which the remainder of the story will revolve. Based on the information from the chart in Box 1.3, what appears to be the problem in the story? And how do you predict it will be resolved?

The 15 or so minutes that it takes to complete the prereading activity is time well spent. Not only do participants have a framework in which to construct meaning for the story, but their expectations have also been raised about the content of the checks they have yet to read. The predictions they make for the remainder of the story, though general, often suggest that they have surmised the author's intent.

The insights into comprehension presented here will be developed in succeeding chapters within the framework of instructional alternatives related to content area reading. What these insights tell the classroom teacher is this: Readers must "work" with print in an effort to explore and construct meaning. Reading is first and foremost a conversation, a give-and-take exchange, between the reader and the author of the text. However, the burden of learning is always on the reader. There are times when a text may be too difficult for students to handle on their own. In situations where text is difficult, teachers are in a strategic position to guide students' reading through various forms of instructional activity. Scaffolding learning with texts, then, is a primary responsibility of the teacher—one that we explore throughout this book.

INSTRUCTIONAL SCAFFOLDING

When texts serve as tools for learning in content area classrooms, teachers have a significant role to play. That role can be thought of in a metaphorical way as "instructional scaffolding." One of the benchmarks of content-literate

Ordeal by cheque

BY WUTHER CRUE

LOS ANGELES, CALIF. *Apr. 18th* 19 *10* No. _____
HOLLYWOOD STATE BANK 90-984
6801 SANTA MONICA BOULEVARD
PAY TO THE ORDER OF *City Bicycle Co.* $52.50
Fifty two ——————— 50/ DOLLARS
Lawrence Exeter Sr.

LOS ANGELES, CALIF. *Aug. 30th* 19 *03* No. _____
HOLLYWOOD STATE BANK 90-984
6801 SANTA MONICA BOULEVARD
PAY TO THE ORDER OF *Goosie Gander Baby Shoppe* $48.50
One hundred & forty eight ——— 50/ DOLLARS
Lawrence Exeter

LOS ANGELES, CALIF. *Aug. 26th* 19 *15* No. _____
HOLLYWOOD STATE BANK 90-984
6801 SANTA MONICA BOULEVARD
PAY TO THE ORDER OF *Columbia Military Acad.* $2,150.00
Twenty-one hundred & fifty ——— XX DOLLARS
Lawrence Exeter Sr.

LOS ANGELES, CALIF. *Sept 2nd* 19 *03* No. _____
HOLLYWOOD STATE BANK 90-984
6801 SANTA MONICA BOULEVARD
PAY TO THE ORDER OF *Hollywood Hospital* $100.00
One hundred ——————— XX DOLLARS
Lawrence Exeter

LOS ANGELES, CALIF. *Sept 3rd* 19 *21* No. _____
HOLLYWOOD STATE BANK 90-984
6801 SANTA MONICA BOULEVARD
PAY TO THE ORDER OF *Hollywood Cadillac Co.* $3,885.00
Thirty eight hundred & eighty five XX DOLLARS
Lawrence Exeter Sr.

LOS ANGELES, CALIF. *Oct. 3rd* 19 *03* No. _____
HOLLYWOOD STATE BANK 90-984
6801 SANTA MONICA BOULEVARD
PAY TO THE ORDER OF *Dr. David M. McCoy* $476.00
Four hundred & seventy five ——— XX DOLLARS
Lawrence Exeter Sr.

LOS ANGELES, CALIF. *Sept. 7th* 19 *21* No. _____
HOLLYWOOD STATE BANK 90-984
6801 SANTA MONICA BOULEVARD
PAY TO THE ORDER OF *Wilshire Auto Repair Service* $288.76
Two hundred & eighty-eight ——— 76/ DOLLARS
Lawrence Exeter Sr.

LOS ANGELES, CALIF. *Dec 19th* 19 *03* No. _____
HOLLYWOOD STATE BANK 90-984
6801 SANTA MONICA BOULEVARD
PAY TO THE ORDER OF *California Toyland Co.* $83.20
Eighty Three ——————— 20/ DOLLARS
Lawrence Exeter, Sr.

LOS ANGELES, CALIF. *Oct. 15th* 19 *21* No. _____
HOLLYWOOD STATE BANK 90-984
6801 SANTA MONICA BOULEVARD
PAY TO THE ORDER OF *Stanford University* $339.00
Three hundred & thirty-nine ——— XX DOLLARS
Lawrence Exeter Sr.

LOS ANGELES, CALIF. *Oct. 6th* 19 *09* No. _____
HOLLYWOOD STATE BANK 90-984
6801 SANTA MONICA BOULEVARD
PAY TO THE ORDER OF *Palisades School for Boys* $1,250.00
Twelve hundred & fifty ——— XX DOLLARS
Lawrence Exeter, Sr.

LOS ANGELES, CALIF. *June 1st* 19 *23* No. _____
HOLLYWOOD STATE BANK 90-984
6801 SANTA MONICA BOULEVARD
PAY TO THE ORDER OF *Miss Daisy Windsor* $25,000.00
Twenty-five thousand ——— XX DOLLARS
Lawrence Exeter Sr.

Los Angeles, Calif. *June 9th* 19 *23* No. ____
HOLLYWOOD STATE BANK 90-984
6801 SANTA MONICA BOULEVARD
PAY TO THE ORDER OF *French Line, Ile de France* $ *585.00*
Five hundred + eighty-five ———— XX DOLLARS
Lawrence Exeter Sr.

Los Angeles, Calif. *Aug. 23rd* 19 *23* No. ____
HOLLYWOOD STATE BANK 90-984
6801 SANTA MONICA BOULEVARD
PAY TO THE ORDER OF *Banque de France* $ *5,000.00*
Five thousand ———— XX DOLLARS
Lawrence Exeter Sr.

Los Angeles, Calif. *Feb. 13th* 19 *26* No. ____
HOLLYWOOD STATE BANK 90-984
6801 SANTA MONICA BOULEVARD
PAY TO THE ORDER OF *University Club Florists* $ *76.50*
Seventy-six ———— 50/ DOLLARS
Lawrence Exeter Sr.

Los Angeles, Calif. *June 22nd* 19 *26* No. ____
HOLLYWOOD STATE BANK 90-984
6801 SANTA MONICA BOULEVARD
PAY TO THE ORDER OF *University Club Florists* $ *312.75*
Three hundred + twelve ———— 75/ DOLLARS
Lawrence Exeter Sr.

Los Angeles, Calif. *Aug. 11th* 19 *26* No. ____
HOLLYWOOD STATE BANK 90-984
6801 SANTA MONICA BOULEVARD
PAY TO THE ORDER OF *Riviera Heights Land Co.* $ *56,000.00*
Fifty-six Thousand ———— XX DOLLARS
Lawrence Exeter Sr.

Los Angeles, Calif. *Oct. 30th* 19 *26* No. ____
HOLLYWOOD STATE BANK 90-984
6801 SANTA MONICA BOULEVARD
PAY TO THE ORDER OF *Renaissance Interior Decorators* $ *22,000.00*
Twenty-two thousand ———— XX DOLLARS
Lawrence Exeter Sr.

Los Angeles, Calif. *Nov. 18th* 19 *26* No. ____
HOLLYWOOD STATE BANK 90-984
6801 SANTA MONICA BOULEVARD
PAY TO THE ORDER OF *Beverly Diamond + Gift Shoppe* $ *678.45*
Six hundred + seventy-eight ———— 45/ DOLLARS
Lawrence Exeter Sr.

Los Angeles, Calif. *Nov. 16th* 19 *26* No. ____
HOLLYWOOD STATE BANK 90-984
6801 SANTA MONICA BOULEVARD
PAY TO THE ORDER OF *Hawaii Steamship Co.* $ *560.00*
Five hundred + sixty ———— XX DOLLARS
Lawrence Exeter Sr.

Los Angeles, Calif. *Nov. 21st* 19 *26* No. ____
HOLLYWOOD STATE BANK 90-984
6801 SANTA MONICA BOULEVARD
PAY TO THE ORDER OF *Lawrence Exeter, Junior* $ *200,000.00*
Two hundred thousand ———— XX DOLLARS
Lawrence Exeter Sr.

Los Angeles, Calif. *Nov. 22nd* 19 *26* No. ____
HOLLYWOOD STATE BANK 90-984
6801 SANTA MONICA BOULEVARD
PAY TO THE ORDER OF *Ambassador Hotel* $ *2,250.00*
Twenty-two hundred + fifty ———— XX DOLLARS
Lawrence Exeter Sr.

Los Angeles, Calif. *Dec. 1st* 19 *26* No. ____
HOLLYWOOD STATE BANK 90-984
6801 SANTA MONICA BOULEVARD
PAY TO THE ORDER OF *University Club Florists* $ *183.50*
One hundred + eighty-three ———— 50/ DOLLARS
Lawrence Exeter Sr.

Los Angeles, Calif. *Feb. 18* 19 *27* No. ____
HOLLYWOOD STATE BANK 90-984
6801 SANTA MONICA BOULEVARD
PAY TO THE ORDER OF *Cocoanut Grove Sweet Shoppe* $ *27.00*
Twenty seven ———— DOLLARS
Lawrence Exeter Jr.

LOS ANGELES, CALIF. July 16 19 27 No.____
HOLLYWOOD STATE BANK 90-984
6801 SANTA MONICA BOULEVARD
PAY TO THE ORDER OF Parisian Gown Shoppe $925.00
Nine hundred twenty five ————— DOLLARS
Lawrence Exeter, Jr.

LOS ANGELES, CALIF. Aug. 30 19 29 No.____
HOLLYWOOD STATE BANK 90-984
6801 SANTA MONICA BOULEVARD
PAY TO THE ORDER OF Tony Spagoni $126.00
One hundred, twenty six ———— DOLLARS
Lawrence Exeter, Jr.

LOS ANGELES, CALIF. Dec. 1 19 27 No.____
HOLLYWOOD STATE BANK 90-984
6801 SANTA MONICA BOULEVARD
PAY TO THE ORDER OF Anita Lingerie Salon $750.00
Seven hundred, fifty ————— DOLLARS
Lawrence Exeter, Jr.

LOS ANGELES, CALIF. May 25 19 30 No.____
HOLLYWOOD STATE BANK 90-984
6801 SANTA MONICA BOULEVARD
PAY TO THE ORDER OF University Club Florists $87.00
Eighty seven ————— DOLLARS
Lawrence Exeter, Jr.

LOS ANGELES, CALIF. April 1 19 28 No.____
HOLLYWOOD STATE BANK 90-984
6801 SANTA MONICA BOULEVARD
PAY TO THE ORDER OF Parisian Gown Shoppe $1,150.00
Eleven hundred fifty ————— DOLLARS
Lawrence Exeter, Jr.

LOS ANGELES, CALIF. May 28 19 30 No.____
HOLLYWOOD STATE BANK 90-984
6801 SANTA MONICA BOULEVARD
PAY TO THE ORDER OF Broadway Diamond Co. $575.00
Five hundred, seventy five ———— DOLLARS
Lawrence Exeter, Jr.

LOS ANGELES, CALIF. Nov. 1 19 28 No.____
HOLLYWOOD STATE BANK 90-984
6801 SANTA MONICA BOULEVARD
PAY TO THE ORDER OF Moderne Sportte Shoppe $562.00
Five hundred, sixty two ———— DOLLARS
Lawrence Exeter, Jr.

LOS ANGELES, CALIF. Nov. 13 19 30 No.____
HOLLYWOOD STATE BANK 90-984
6801 SANTA MONICA BOULEVARD
PAY TO THE ORDER OF Miss Flossie Wentworth $50,000.00
Fifty thousand ————— DOLLARS
Lawrence Exeter, Jr.

LOS ANGELES, CALIF. July 1 19 29 No.____
HOLLYWOOD STATE BANK 90-984
6801 SANTA MONICA BOULEVARD
PAY TO THE ORDER OF The Bootery $45.25
One hundred, forty-five 25/100 ——— DOLLARS
Lawrence Exeter, Jr.

LOS ANGELES, CALIF. Nov. 14 19 30 No.____
HOLLYWOOD STATE BANK 90-984
6801 SANTA MONICA BOULEVARD
PAY TO THE ORDER OF Wall & Smith, attys. at Law $525.00
Five hundred twenty five ———— DOLLARS
Lawrence Exeter, Jr.

LOS ANGELES, CALIF. Aug. 23 19 29 No.____
HOLLYWOOD STATE BANK 90-984
6801 SANTA MONICA BOULEVARD
PAY TO THE ORDER OF Tony Spagoni $126.00
One hundred, twenty six ——— DOLLARS
Lawrence Exeter, Jr.

LOS ANGELES, CALIF. Nov. 15 19 30 No.____
HOLLYWOOD STATE BANK 90-984
6801 SANTA MONICA BOULEVARD
PAY TO THE ORDER OF Mrs. Lawrence Exeter, Jr. $5000.00
Five thousand ————— DOLLARS
Lawrence Exeter, Jr.

Source: "Ordeal by Cheque" by Wuther Crue. Courtesy *Vanity Fair.* Copyright © 1932 (renewed 1960, 1988) by the Condé Nast Publications, Inc. Reprinted by permission.

students, as we suggested earlier, is that they know how to learn with texts independently. Yet many students in today's diverse classrooms have trouble handling the conceptual demands inherent in reading material when left to their own devices to learn with text. A gap often exists between the ideas and relationships they are studying and their prior knowledge, interests, attitudes, cultural background, language proficiency, and/or reading ability. In a nutshell, instructional scaffolding allows teachers to support readers' efforts to make sense of texts while showing them how to use strategies that will, over time, lead to independent learning.

Used in construction, scaffolds serve as supports, lifting up workers so that they can achieve something that otherwise would not have been possible. In teaching and learning contexts, scaffolding means helping learners to do what they cannot do at first (Bruner 1986). Instructional scaffolds support text learners by helping them achieve literacy tasks that would otherwise have been out of reach. Applebee (1991) explains that instructional scaffolding provides the necessary support that students need as they attempt new tasks; at the same time, teachers model or lead the students through effective strategies for completing these tasks. Providing the "necessary support" often means understanding the diversity that exists among the students in your class, planning active learning environments, and supporting students' efforts to learn through the use of instructional activities, cooperative learning groups, and authentic texts beyond the textbook—all of which are explored more closely in the chapters that follow.

 ## LOOKING BACK, LOOKING FORWARD

In this chapter, we invited you to begin an examination of content area teaching practices, and the assumptions underlying those practices, in the light of promising instructional alternatives for text learning and active student involvement. Teachers play a critical role in helping students realize a potentially powerful use of language: learning with texts. Learning with texts is an active process. Yet assigning and telling are still common teaching practices and often have the unfortunate consequence of dampening students' active involvement in learning. To shift the burden of learning from teacher to student requires an understanding of the importance of the relationships that exist among language, content literacy, and learning. As a result, we explored the role that language and literacy play in the acquisition of content knowledge. Using language to learn with texts is what content area reading is all about. Instead of teaching students how to read or write, we use reading and writing as tools to construct knowledge—to discover, to clarify, and to make meaning—in a given discipline.

Content literacy, then, underscores the situational demands placed on students to use reading and writing to learn subject matter. Content teachers are in a strategic position to show students how to use the reading and writing strategies that are actually needed to construct content knowledge.

Perhaps the single most important resource in learning with texts is a reader's prior knowledge. Therefore, we explored some of the influences and processes underlying reading to learn in content classrooms. In particular, we emphasized the role that schema plays in comprehension. Schema or prior knowledge allows readers to (1) seek and select, (2) organize text information, and (3) elaborate the information encountered in texts.

Instructional scaffolding is a concept used throughout this book. Instructional scaffolding supports text learners in achieving literacy tasks that would otherwise be out of reach.

In the next chapter, the spotlight is on learners in diverse classrooms. Content area teachers face enormous challenges in today's student population. How do you succeed with texts in classrooms where students may be at risk of failure, who may show little interest in learning with or without texts, who may come from different cultural backgrounds, and who may speak English with limited proficiency? What conditions are necessary to make learning with texts an integral part of inclusive classrooms?

 **MINDS-ON**

1. Review the passages read by Darryl in American history, biology, and algebra 2 class. In small groups, create lists of the varying situational demands that each text selection places on Darryl's ability to read. Discuss possible factors besides the nature of the text and of the task that are likely to affect his content literacy. How are Darryl's attitude and willingness to be an active learner affected by these factors? What might the teachers of these various classes have done to create a more student-centered learning experience?

2. Focus on the elements of a student-centered curriculum. Obviously, the teacher's beliefs and instructional approach play a large role in permitting students to become actively involved in an ongoing lesson, but what visible signs of student involvement would exist in the physical environment of the classroom? Just by looking, would it be possible to detect a classroom where student-centered lessons are the norm? If so, what physical evidence would be present, and what would that evidence indicate to you, the observer?

3. Imagine that during lunch, several teaching colleagues comment that since many students in their courses "can't read," these teachers rarely use books. They argue that students learn content just as well through audiovisual aids and discussions.

Divide a small group of six class members into two smaller groups of three: one representing the teachers who believe books are unnecessary and one representing those who believe books are essential. For ten minutes, role-play a lunchtime debate on the pros and cons of using reading in content areas. After the time has elapsed, discuss the arguments used by the role players. Which did you find valid, and with which did you disagree?

4. Your supervisor observes a lesson in which you use a large block of time for students to read. Afterward, the supervisor says that you should assign reading as homework, rather than "wasting" valuable class time. She adds that if you continue with lessons like this, your students will be lucky to finish one or two books over the entire year. Consequently, you request a meeting with the supervisor. What arguments might you bring to this meeting to help convince her of the validity of your approach?

HANDS-ON

1. With a small group, examine the following well-known passage and attempt to supply the missing words. Note that all missing words, regardless of length, are indicated by blanks in the passage.

Besides, Sir, we shall not fight our battles alone. There is a just God, who presides over the destinies of nations, who will raise up friends to fight our _____ for us. The battle, Sir, is not to the strong alone: it is to the vigilant, the active, the _____. Besides, Sir, we have no election. If we were base enough to desire it, it is now too late to retire from the contest.

There is no _____, but in submission or slavery. Our chains are forged. Their _____ may be heard on the plains of Boston! The war is inevitable—and let it come—I repeat, Sir, let it come! It is in vain, Sir, to extenuate the matter. Gentlemen may cry, "Peace! Peace!" But there is no peace. The war has actually begun!

The next gale that sweeps from the North will bring to our ears the clash of resounding _____! Our brethren are already in the field! Why stand we here idle? What is it that the Gentlemen wish? What would they have? Is life so _____, or peace too _____, as to be purchased at the price of chains and _____? Forbid it, Almighty God! I know not what _____ others may take, but as for me, give me _____ or give me death!

After you have filled in the blanks, discuss the processes by which decisions on possible responses were made and any problems encountered. How did prior knowledge of the passage's topic assist your reading process? Compare your experience with this passage to your reading of

"How to Ruin an Association" in Box 1.1 of the text. (After you have completed this experiment, review Patrick Henry's speech at the end of the "Hands-On" section in Chapter 5.)

In what ways was your experience similar to that of a student who attempts to decipher a content passage but who has little background knowledge of its content?

2. Bring the following materials to class: a large paper bag, five paper plates, four buttons, three cardboard tubes, scraps of material, six pipe cleaners, three sheets of construction paper, scissors, tape, and a stapler. Your instructor will silently give each group a written directive to create a replica of a living creature (cat, dog, rhinoceros, aardvark, etc.) with *no* verbal communication permitted.

   After your group has constructed its creature, list the communication difficulties, and discuss how each was overcome. Finally, have a spokesperson from each group share these difficulties with the rest of the class.

3. Rewrite Lewis Carroll's poem "Jabberwocky" using "real" words.

Jabberwocky

'Twas brillig, and the slithy toves
Did gyre and gimble in the wabe;
All mimsy were the borogoves,
And the mome raths outgrabe.

"Beware the Jabberwock, my son!
The jaws that bite, the claws that catch!
Beware the Jubjub bird and shun
The frumious Bandersnatch!"

He took his vorpal sword in hand:
Long time the manxome foe he sought—
So rested he by the Tumtum tree,
And stood awhile in thought.

And, as in uffish thought he stood,
The Jabberwock, with eyes of flame,
Came whiffling through the tulgey wood,
And burbled as it came!

One, two! One, two! And through and through
The vorpal blade went snicker-snack!
He left it dead, and with its head
He went galumphing back.

Compare your efforts with those of other members of your small group, and discuss the following questions:

a. Why are there differences in the translations?

b. Does your translation change the intended meaning of the poem?

c. Do the differences affect your enjoyment of the poem?

d. What personal experiences and prior knowledge that you brought to your reading of the poem may have influenced your translation?

SUGGESTED READINGS

Alvermann, D. E., & Moore, D. W. (1991). Secondary school reading. In R. Barr, M. L. Kamil, P. Mosentha, & P. D. Pearson (Eds.), *Handbook of reading research* (2nd ed.). New York: Longman.

Anderson, R. C. (1994). Role of the reader's schema in comprehension, learning, and memory. In R. Ruddell, M. Ruddell, & H. Singer (Eds.), *Theoretical models and processes of reading* (4th ed.) (pp. 469–482). Newark, DE: International Reading Association.

Brooks, J., & Brooks, M. (1993). *The case for constructivist classrooms.* Alexandria, VA: Association for Curriculum and Supervision Development.

Goodlad, J. (1984). *A place called school.* New York: McGraw-Hill.

Graves, M., & Graves, B. (1994). *Scaffolding reading experiences: Designs for student success.* Norwood, MA: Christopher-Gordon.

Jackson, P. W., & Haroutunian-Gordon, S. (Eds.). (1989). *From Socrates to software: The teacher as text and the text as teacher,* Eighty-Eighth Yearbook of the National Society for the Study of Education, Part 1. Chicago: University of Chicago Press.

Marshall, N. (1996). The students: Who are they and how do I reach them? In D. Lapp, J. Flood, & N. Farnan (Eds.), *Content area reading and learning: Instructional strategies* (pp. 27–38). Needham Heights, MA: Allyn and Bacon.

McAloon, N. M. (1994). Content area reading: It's not my Job! *Journal of Reading, 37,* 332–334.

McKenna, M. C., & Robinson, R. D. (1990). Content literacy: A definition and implications. *Journal of Reading, 34,* 184–186.

Menke, D. J., & Davey, B. (1994). Teachers' views of textbooks and text reading instruction: Experience matters. *Journal of Reading, 37,* 464–470.

Moje, E. B. (1996). "I teach students, not subjects": Teacher-student relationships as contexts for secondary literacy. *Reading Research Quarterly, 31,* 172–195.

Moore, D. W. (1996). Contexts for literacy in secondary schools. In D. J. Leu, C. K. Kinzer, & K. A. Hinchman (Eds.), *Literacies for the twenty-first century: Research and practice* (pp. 15–46). Chicago: National Reading Conference.

O'Brien, D. G., Stewart, R. A., & Moje, E. B. (1995). Why content literacy is difficult to infuse into the secondary school: Complexities of curriculum, pedagogy, and school culture. *Reading Research Quarterly, 30,* 442–463.

Palincsar, A (1994). Reciprocal teaching. In A. Purves (Ed.), *Encyclopedia of English studies and language arts,* Vol. 2 (pp. 1020–1021). New York: Scholastic.

Paris, S. G., Lipson, M. Y., & Wixon, K. K. (1994). Becoming a strategic reader. In R. Ruddell, M. Ruddell, & H. Singer (Eds.), *Theoretical models and processes of reading* (4th ed.) (pp. 788–810). Newark, DE: International Reading Association.

Pearson, P. D., & Fielding, L. (1991). Comprehension instruction. In R. Barr, M. Kamil, P. Mosenthal, & P. D. Pearson (Eds.), *Handbook of reading research: Volume II* (pp. 815–860). New York: Longman.

Rosenshine, B., & Meister, C. (1992). The use of scaffolds for teaching higher-level cognitive strategies. *Educational Leadership, 49* (7), 26–33.

Schumm, J. S., Vaughn, S., & Saumell, L. (1992). What do teachers do when the textbook is tough: Students speak out. *Journal of Reading Behavior, 24,* 481–503.

Sizer, T. R. (1984). *Horace's compromise: The dilemmas of the American high school today.* Boston: Houghton Mifflin.

Sizer, T. R. (1992). *Horace's school: Redesigning the American High School.* Boston: Houghton Mifflin.

Tierney, R. J., & Pearson, P. D. (1992). Learning to learn from text: A framework for improving classroom practice. In E. K. Dishner, T. W. Bean, J. E. Readence, & D. W. Moore (Eds.), *Reading in the content areas: Improving classroom instruction.* Dubuque, IA: Kendall-Hunt.

Woodward, A., & Elliott, D. L. (1990). Textbook use and teacher professionalism. In D. L. Elliot & A. Woodward (Eds.), *Textbooks and schooling in the United States,* Eighty-Ninth Yearbook of the National Society for the Study of Education, Part 1 (pp. 178–193). Chicago: University of Chicago Press.

2

Strategy Instruction in Diverse Classrooms

Effective teaching involves in-depth knowledge of both the students and the subject matter.

—Gloria Ladson-Billings, *The Dreamkeepers: Successful Teachers of African-American Children*

Organizing Principle

Teaching with texts is all the more challenging in today's classrooms, where the range of linguistic, cultural, and academic diversity has been increasing steadily since the 1960s. The growing diversity in the student population is often reflected in the way learners think about themselves as readers and writers. More often than not, students of diverse backgrounds are caught in a cycle of school failure that contributes to marginal achievement and a sense of helplessness and frustration with content literacy activities. Traditional approaches to instruction aren't reaching diverse learners in ways that make a difference in their academic development. Arguably, what may have worked in classrooms 10, 15, or 20 years ago isn't working well today. As a result, many teachers are in transition as they reconsider instructional beliefs and practices that neither are culturally responsive nor meet students' academic needs. They are shying away from traditional approaches in favor of strategies that reach diverse learners in ways that support literacy and learning in content area classrooms.

Students of diverse backgrounds are often placed in low-ability groups where instruction is based on a limited, watered-down version of the curriculum. The strengths they bring to learning situations typically go untapped. However, the trend away from "tracking" students by ability, the movement toward inclusive classrooms, and the increasing number of students whose first language is not English demand instruction that is strategic, with high learning expectations for all students.

When asked, "What do you teach?" do you respond, "I teach social studies (or math or science or physical education or any one of the subject areas in the school curriculum"? Or do you say, "I teach students"? The distinction is a subtle but important one. Today's teacher is a teacher of all kinds of students, with different language and cultural backgrounds and academic needs. As Ladson-Billings suggests, great teachers know as much and care as much about their students as their subject matter.

How can teachers be responsive to the differences in their classrooms while maintaining high standards for content literacy and learning? Becoming more aware of and understanding some of the key linguistic, cultural, and academic differences between mainstream and nonmainstream students is an important first step. The organizing principle of this chapter builds on teachers' awareness of differences: **One of the important ways that teachers respond to classroom diversity is to scaffold instruction so that students become aware of and competent with learning strategies.**

Take a moment to study and reflect on the important ideas and relationships depicted in the chapter overview. Use the "Frame of Mind" questions, in conjunction with the chapter overview, to anticipate the content and structure of the chapter. Before reading, ask yourself, "How knowledgeable am I about the ideas targeted in the overview? What do I expect to learn from my study of this chapter?"

Chapter Overview

STRATEGY INSTRUCTION IN DIVERSE CLASSROOMS

CLASSROOM DIVERSITY

DIFFERENCES AMONG STUDENTS

LANGUAGE   **CULTURE**   **ACHIEVEMENT**

SCAFFOLDING INSTRUCTION FOR STUDENTS WHO STRUGGLE WITH TEXTS

Metacognition   Strategy Instruction

STRATEGIES

Comprehension   Vocabulary

QARs   Reciprocal   Concept of   Vocabulary
              Teaching   Definition (CD)   Self-Selection
                                  Word Maps   (VSS)

Think-Alouds   Vocabulary-Building Strategies

1. Why are classrooms more diverse today than they were several decades ago?

2. What are some of the cultural and linguistic variables that students from different racial and ethnic backgrounds bring to classroom learning situations?

3. Why are low-achieving students at risk in text learning situations?

4. How can a teacher scaffold instruction in ways that make students aware of and competent in the use of strategies for text learning?

5. What is *metacognition,* and why is it important for diverse learners to develop metacognitive knowledge and skills?

6. How do think-alouds, QARs, and reciprocal teaching provide instructional support for students who have difficulty answering questions and comprehending text?

7. How do concept of definition (CD), vocabulary self-selection (VSS), and vocabulary-building strategies help students develop strategies for understanding unfamiliar concepts encountered during reading?

We began our teaching careers in the 1960s in a suburban high school just outside of Albany, New York, during the height of the civil rights movement and the Vietnam War. The times were tumultuous in the wake of great social change. Practically every facet of American society was open to critical examination, if not reform, including the nation's schools. The landmark 1954 U.S. Supreme Court case *Brown* v. *Board of Education of Topeka* ruled that "separate but equal" schools were unconstitutional and laid the groundwork for educational reform in the 1960s. The civil rights movement fueled the legislative agenda of President Lyndon Johnson's Great Society. The Civil Rights Act of 1964 prohibited discrimination in public institutions on the basis of race, color, religion, or national origin. Also in 1964, the Economic Opportunity Act resulted in educational programs, such as Head Start and Upward Bound, that are still in existence today. In 1965, the Elementary and Secondary Education Act (ESEA) established compensatory educational programs (Title 1) to provide educational opportunities for low-income students from minority backgrounds. In addition, the Bilingual Education Act of 1967 made it possible for schools to receive federal funding for minority groups who were non-English-speaking.

Despite the social and educational reforms taking place in the 1960s, it was business as usual at the high school where we taught. The school seemed impervious to change. To the best of our recollection, there were only three or four African-American students enrolled in the high school, even though the school district was adjacent to the city of Albany, where there is a large African-American community. In a student body of more than 1000 students, there were no Hispanic Americans, no Asian Americans, and no students for whom English was a second language. Nor were there support services for low-achieving students or students with learning disabilities. Instead, students were "tracked" according to academic ability. As new teachers, we were assigned mostly classes with low-achieving students.

One of our students during our first year of teaching did mechanical work whenever our car needed repair. He was one of the "forgotten" students at school who went largely unnoticed, except when he got into trouble. As it turned out, he dropped out of school and went to work at his uncle's garage. To this day, we recall how he and others of his academic status would do everything in their power to disrupt a class whenever we tried to introduce any topic that required reading and writing. The more we urged them to learn with texts, the more they resisted.

Teachers who have worked with low-achieving students are no strangers to resistant learners. Mary Krogness (1995), a veteran teacher of 29 years, wrote a book about the resistant adolescent learners she taught in a metropolitan area school district. These seventh and eighth graders were all too often overage, underprepared, and weighted down with emotional baggage. Nearly all were students of color. They scored low on intelligence and achievement tests and were tracked in basic skills classes for most of their academic lives. Yet Krogness observed that her students were smart in ways not recognized or valued in school: They could "read" people—gauge their feelings and interpret attitudes, actions, reactions, tone of voice, and body language. The challenge for Krogness became that of showing her students how to use their "street smarts" to analyze texts and interpret current events. Her aim, as she put it, was "to hook my students on talking, reading, and writing, to immerse them in language and give them plenty of practice in doing what they'd learned not to like or feel good about" (p. 5). Krogness's students are noticeably different from those she taught two decades earlier.

Changes in the racial and ethnic composition of our country's public school population have been dramatic. A case in point: Just outside Washington, D.C., in northern Virginia, there is a school district that just 30 years ago was attended primarily by white students from middle- and working-class families. However, school integration, immigration, its close proximity to Washington, and changing housing patterns have transformed the community into a multicultural area. The student population is racially, linguistically, and culturally diverse. For example, of the 1478 students enrolled at the high school, approximately 30 percent are white, 29 percent are Hispanic, 23 percent are African American, and 18 percent are Asian. About half of the students speak English as a second language. Of this group, 23 percent participate in an intensive English as a second language (ESL) program apart from the regular curriculum. The remaining second-language students speak English with enough proficiency to be mainstreamed into the regular academic program (Sturtevant 1992).

About one-third of all students at the high school receive free or reduced-price lunches and are classified as economically disadvantaged by federal funding standards. Moreover, the student population tends to be highly mobile. According to the principal of the high school, the school loses and gains about one-third of its total population every year because of the large number of parents employed by the military or the federal government (Sturtevant 1992).

Many schools have dramatic shifts in the student population in a relatively short period of time. Thirty-three of the nation's largest urban schools enroll more students from minority backgrounds than from mainstream backgrounds. But diversity cannot and should not be associated only with urban schools. Classrooms throughout the United States have been changing steadily over the past three decades, although perhaps not as dramatically as the classrooms in the northern Virginia high school cited.

Significant demographic shifts in the population have resulted in a society that is increasingly diverse. For whatever reason, students of diverse backgrounds—that is to say, students who may be distinguished by their ethnicity, social class, language, or achievement level—often struggle in their academic programs. As Wang, Reynolds, and Walberg (1994–1995) put it, these students have unusual needs and challenge teachers to the limits of their commitment, insights, and skill. However, the more that teachers develop understanding, attitudes, and strategies related to student diversity, the better equipped they will be to adapt instruction to the differences in their classrooms.

CLASSROOM DIVERSITY

Changes in the racial and ethnic composition of our country's public school population have been dramatic. Although total school enrollment declined by 2 percent between 1976 and 1988, the proportion of ethnic and language minorities increased by 23 percent (Lara 1994). Data from the U.S. Bureau of the Census show that nearly one-third of America's public school students come from minority backgrounds and that 15 percent of our total population has a non-English-speaking background. Based on population predictions for the twenty-first century, the trend toward increased classroom diversity should continue. By the year 2020, one of two public school students will be from a minority background, and the number of children living in poverty will increase by 37 percent. Schools will, in all likelihood, serve 5.4 million more children living in poverty in 2020 than they served in 1988 (Au 1993).

Not only are classrooms becoming more linguistically, culturally, and economically diverse, but they are also changing academically. The achievement needs of students contribute to the complexity of classroom diversity. Within classrooms, achievement levels may vary substantially—and often do. As schools move away from the practice of tracking students according to past performance or disabilities, the achievement differences increase and are magnified in "regular" classrooms. As one teacher noted, "With the exception of an AP class (advanced placement for the most talented students in a subject area), I teach regular classes with kids who barely read and write and others who have no problems. Ten years ago, the difference in achievement levels wasn't as noticeable."

A different student population has made teaching more challenging and demanding than ever before. Nowhere are diverse learners more academically vulnerable than in instructional contexts that require them to engage in reading and writing. Orchestrating teaching around beliefs and assumptions that are rooted in an assign-and-tell transmission model of learning will only serve to perpetuate the cycle of failure for diverse learners. What are the alternatives? Let's take a closer look at some of the differences that students bring to class so that we can explore several approaches to strategy instruction that will make a difference in the students' learning of vocabulary and comprehension of text.

Cultural and Linguistic Differences

The school memories of teachers who grew up in the 1950s and the early 1960s are most likely to be of *monocultural* classrooms. Robert Cottrol (1990), for example, recalls:

> I grew up in the fifties, in an era when public schools, with few exceptions, presented a picture of the world that was relentlessly monocultural and, I might add, monochromatic. . . . In American history class it was possible to go through the school year learning about Washington, Jefferson, Adams, Lincoln, Roosevelt, Wilson and other great men of U.S. history, with only a pause, in February, during what was then called "Negro History Week," to spend a brief moment on George Washington Carver and his experiments on the peanut. (p. 18)

The monoculture to which Cottrol refers represents the mainstream culture in American society, a culture that is rooted in European-American beliefs, standards, and values.

The rapidly changing demography of the United States and its schools, however, is transforming our country into a society that is increasingly *multicultural*. In the northern Virginia high school alluded to earlier, Elizabeth Sturtevant (1992) studied content literacy practices in a multicultural context.

An American history teacher in her study began the school year with 29 students, but by May, the size of the class had dwindled to 18. Most of the Hispanic students in this class had moved from the school district, many returning to their home countries. Of the remaining students, there were five African Americans, two whites, three Asians (a Chinese, a Korean, and a Cambodian), two Africans (one from Ethiopia and the other from Zambia), one European (from Germany), and five Latin Americans (four from El Salvador and one from Peru). All of the immigrant students spoke English with limited proficiency but well enough to be mainstreamed into the regular classroom.

The American history teacher, born in a small all-white Ohio town, drew on his own experiences in the Peace Corps to build positive social relationships in the classroom. While in the Peace Corps, he had learned what it meant to be a member of a minority cultural group on a small Caribbean island of almost entirely black inhabitants. In class, he was sensitive to cultural and language differences, and his willingness to understand these differences enabled him to teach more effectively. For example, he recognized that "kids become distrustful" if the teacher views their culture as inferior or their language as deficient. In class discussions, he avoided correcting students' English, believing that it was more important for them to explore ideas openly and critically without fear of humiliation than to speak correct English. His sensitivity to language and dialect differences allowed his students to interact with one another and with him in the way they spoke to peers and adults in their home or community.

Language and Dialect Differences

Cultural variation in the use of language has a strong influence on literacy learning. Even though students whose first language is not English do not have full control of English grammatical structures, pronunciation, and vocabulary, they can engage in reading and writing activities (Goodman & Goodman 1978). When students use their own culturally acceptable conversational style to talk and write about ideas they read in texts, they are likely to become more content-literate and to improve their literacy skills. Au and Mason (1981), for example, describe how minority Hawaiian learners improved their reading abilities when they were allowed to use their home language to talk about texts.

Language *differences* should not be mistaken for language *deficits* among culturally diverse students. Many of the low-achieving high school students in the rural Georgia classroom that Dillon (1989) studied were African Americans who spoke a dialect commonly referred to as black dialect or black English vernacular. Black dialect is acquired through family interactions and participation in the culture of the community. The teacher in Dillon's study, "Appleby," had much success in leading text-related discussions because of his sensitivity to his students' dialect as a tool for communication in the class. As Dillon put it, "Appleby allowed students to use dialect in his classroom because they were more comfortable with it and more effective communicators" (p. 245).

Shouldn't students from minority backgrounds learn to use standard American English? The question is a rhetorical one. As teachers, our stance toward the use of standard American English is critical. Standard American English, often thought of as the "news broadcast–type" English used in the conduct of business, is the language of the dominant mainstream culture in American society—the "culture of power," according to Delpit (1986, 1988). Delpit explains that the rules and codes of the culture of power, including the rules and codes for language use, are acquired by students from mainstream backgrounds through interaction with their families. Minority students, however, whose families are outside the mainstream culture, do not acquire the same rules and codes. If students are going to have access to opportunities in mainstream society, schools must acquaint students from minority backgrounds with the rules and codes of the culture of power. Not making standard American English accessible to students from minority backgrounds puts them at a disadvantage in competing with their mainstream counterparts.

Although it is important for culturally diverse learners to receive explicit instruction in the use of standard American English, *when* and *under what circumstances* become critical instructional issues. All students should understand how cultural contexts influence what they read, write, hear, say, and view. Language arts classes are probably the appropriate place to provide explicit instruction in the functional use and conventions of standard American English. Although becoming proficient in standard American English may be an important school goal for all students, it should not be viewed as a prerequisite for literate classroom behavior (Au 1993). When it is viewed as a prerequisite, teachers deny students the opportunity to use their own language as a tool for learning. Increasing their command of standard American English, in and of itself, will not improve students' ability to think critically, "since students' own languages can serve just as well for verbal expression and reasoning" (p. 130).

Students' Funds of Knowledge

The powerful role that culture plays in shaping students' behavior and their knowledge of the world often goes unnoticed in classrooms. Understanding the sociocultural dynamics of home and community gives us a broader perspective on the worldviews students bring to school. Culturally and linguistically diverse students typically come from working-class families where their individual lives are inseparable from the social dynamics of the household and the community in which they live. A teacher who makes a point of understanding the home culture, ethnic background, and community of students is in a better position both to understand the kinds of knowledge that culturally diverse students bring to learning situations and to adjust the curriculum to their sociocultural strengths.

Luis Moll (1994) contends that much is to be gained from understanding the "social networks" of the households in a cultural group. These networks are crucial to families, who often engage in exchanging "funds of knowledge." These funds of knowledge may represent occupationally related skills and information that families share with one another as a means of economic survival. Moll argues that the social and cultural resources that students bring to school—their funds of knowledge—are rarely tapped in classroom learning contexts. Using the community's rich resources and funds of knowledge builds on one of students' greatest assets: the social networks established within a cultural group. One such resource is its people. Moll puts it this way: "One has to believe that there are diverse types of people that can be helpful in the classroom even though they do not have professional credentials. Wisdom and imagination are distributed in the same way among professional and nonprofessional groups" (p. 194).

In a middle-level classroom, Mexican-American students in Tucson, Arizona, engage in a study of construction that includes inquiry into the history of dwellings and different ways of building structures. The students have access to a wide array of reading materials from the library to focus their investigation: trade books, magazines, newspapers, reference resources, and many other sources. The teacher builds on students' reading by inviting parents and community members to speak to them about their jobs in the construction industry. For example, a father visits the class to describe his work as a mason.

Showing interest in students' home cultures and ethnic backgrounds builds trust in the classroom. Jackson (1994) believes that building trust with students of diverse backgrounds is a culturally responsive strategy that is often overlooked. One way to create trust may be as simple as learning students' names and pronouncing them correctly and perhaps have them share the unique meanings and special significance of their first names. Teachers may also invite them to research and share information about their family's ethnic background, using questions suggested by Covert (1989): What generation in the United States do you represent? Are you and your siblings the first of your family to be born in this country? Were you born abroad? Where did you or your ancestors migrate from? What made them wish to come here? Does your immediate or extended family practice ethnic or cultural customs that you or they value or identify with? Do you or your relatives speak your ethnic group's language? What occupations are represented in your family background?

Ways of Knowing

Heath (1983) reminds us that it is crucially important to be aware that students from diverse cultural backgrounds may bring different ways of knowing, different styles of questioning, and different patterns of interaction to school. For example, different cultures may have different attitudes, expectations, and assumptions about the value of reading and writing and what it means to be a reader and writer. Alicia, a Latino student, didn't want to be a "schoolgirl." To be a schoolgirl meant always having her head in a book, always doing homework. However, Alicia had little trouble getting involved in school activities that revolved around meaningful, collaborative literacy activities such as tutoring younger students and writing social studies texts for them (Heath & Mangiola 1991).

Different cultures may place a different emphasis and value on various cognitive activities and styles of questioning. Some societies, for example, emphasize memorization and analytic thinking over the ability to experiment or to make predictions (Fillmore 1981). The cognitive styles of culturally diverse students may differ. Heath (1983) discovered that African-American students experienced academic difficulty in their classrooms partly because of their lack of familiarity with the kinds of questions they were expected to answer in school. For example, based on family interaction patterns in the African-American community that she studied, Heath found that students were not familiar with school questions asking them to describe or identify the attributes of objects or concepts. The students were much more familiar with analogy-type questions comparing one object or concept with another. When teachers became aware of the differences between the kinds of questions they asked and the kinds of questions familiar to the students, they were able to make adjustments in their questioning style. As a result, the teachers noticed a marked contrast in their students' participation and interest in lessons.

Ways of knowing are intertwined with ways of interacting and learning. Rather than place emphasis on individual competition, some cultural groups prize group interaction, helping one another, and collaborative activity. Reyes and Molner (1991), for example, suggest that cooperative learning is more "culturally congruent" with students from Mexican-American backgrounds. The research support for cooperative classroom strategies, especially in diverse learning situations, is impressive (Little Soldier 1989; Slavin 1987). In some minority groups, there appears to be a cultural match between learning style and cooperative instructional practices.

The World Wide Web on the Internet is an excellent medium for learning more about cultural diversity and instruction that is culturally relevant. The Web also provides exciting opportunities for students to learn about cultural differences and engage in multicultural activities. The Web sites highlighted in Box 2.1 provide teachers and/or students with access to a wealth of instructional resources.

Second-Language Learners

Immigrant students vary in their use of English as a second language. Some may have little or no proficiency in the use of English (*NEP*: non-English-proficient). Others may have limited English skills (*LEP*: limited-English-proficient). These students are placed in bilingual and English as a second language (ESL) programs until they are proficient enough in English to be mainstreamed into the regular curriculum.

Box 2.1

Nothing but Net: Multicultural Resources for Teachers and Students

Chicano! Homepage (teaching materials)
www.pbs.org/chicano/

Indigenous People's Lit. (many cultures)
www.indians.org/welker/framenat.htm

A Line in the Sand (cultural information, authentic perspective)
hanksville.phast.umass.edu:8000/cultprop/

Walk a Mile in My Shoes (excellent source for getting started)
www.wmht.org/trail/explor02.htm

MultiCultural Pavilion (student research and reading material)
curry.edschool.Virginia.EDU/go/multicultural/

Mancala (African strategy game)
imagiware.com/mancala.cgi

Kid's Window (stories in Japanese)
kiku.stanford.edu:80/KIDS/kids_home.html

Martin Luther King, Jr. (in-depth study of Martin Luther King, Jr.)
www.seattletimes.com/mlk/index.html

Miracle of the White Buffalo (many articles on topic plus links)
www.bossnt.com/page16.html

Global Sch.-Connected Clrm. (cultural interchanges)
www.gsh.org/class/default.html

KIDPROJ (multi-language activities and projects)
www.kidlink.org:80/KIDPROJ/

NickNacks Telecollaborate (global classroom)
www1.minn.net:80/~schubert/NickNacks.html#anchor100100

Intercultural E-mail (e-mail site for partner classes)
www.stolaf.edu/network/iecc/

China the Beautiful (art and history)
www.chinapage.com/china.html

Jewish Culture and History
www.igc.apc.org/ddickerson/judaica.html

Japan Links
www.geocities.com/Tokyo/4220/japanlinks.html

Tales of Wonder (folk tales from 14 countries and links)
itpubs.ucdavis.edu/richard/tales

Multicultural Book Review (listing of literature)
www.isomedia.com/homes/jmele/hompage.html

Once mainstreamed into the regular curriculum, second-language learners often struggle with content area texts. In schools where tracking still persists as an organizational tool, a disproportionate number of second-language learners have been placed in lower-track classrooms, even though the notion that students learn best with others of similar achievement levels has not been supported by research (Allington 1983; Oakes 1985).

Box 2.2

Nothing but Net: ESL Resources for Teachers and Students

Useful Resources, Lesson Plans and Teaching Materials
www.ling.lancs.ac.uk/staff/visitors/keji/teacher.htm

Optical Illusion (instructional units and ideas for ESL students)
www.darkwing.uoregon.edu/

Dave's ESL Cafe (activities for students)
www.pacificnet.net/~sperling/eslcafe.html

The Virtual Tourist (finds www locations familiar to an ESL student)
www.vtourist.com/webmap/

Web 66 (helps find schools with ESL students)
www.web66.com

In mainstream classes, reading textbooks is one of the most cognitively demanding, context-reduced tasks that language-minority students will encounter (Cummins 1994). Some students may become frustrated by texts because of issues related to background knowledge. According to Kang (1994):

> Some information or concepts in textbooks may presuppose certain background knowledge that native speakers may take for granted but that may be different or lacking in some ESL students. Culture-specific background knowledge developed in students' native country, community, or home may affect their comprehension, interpretation, and development of social, cultural, historical, and even scientific concepts. Even if students possess the background knowledge presumed for a particular text, they may not be able to activate it to relate and organize new information. (p. 649)

The vocabulary load of content area textbooks is also a problem for some second-language learners. The academic language of texts is not the language of conversational speech. If students have limited literacy skills in their own native language, they will obviously experience a great deal of frustration and failure with English texts. Moreover, if students are good readers in their native language but have minimal proficiency in English, the language barrier may inhibit them from making effective use of their literacy skills.

If you are interested in lesson plans and teaching materials or in having students engage in ESL-related Internet projects and activities, you may want to visit the sites listed in Box 2.2.

Achievement Differences

How students achieve or fail to achieve is often attributed to such factors as motivation, self-concept, prior knowledge of the subject, and their ability to read, to study, and to communicate effectively through oral and written language. Low-achieving students are said to be "at risk" of school failure (Slavin 1989). Their school lives are characterized by poor attendance, retention in grade, high dropout rates, and behavior problems. The term *at risk* can easily become a shibboleth that labels and separates one class of students (of low socioeconomic status) from another (of the middle class), although this is not necessarily the case. Middle-class students may also be at risk of low achievement and failure. Frank Macchiarola (1988), former superintendent of schools in New York City, explains that many students, particularly those who come from suburban communities, middle-class neighborhoods, or college-educated parents, disengage from active participation in the classroom and only go through the motions of getting a high school diploma.

For some low-achieving students, reading is a painful reminder of a system of schooling that has failed them. They wage a continual battle with reading as an academic activity. The failure to learn to read has contributed to these students' alienation from school. Alienated students often view teachers as uncaring and "the system" as unfair and ineffective (Wehlage & Rutter 1986). Other low-achieving students may have strategies for reading that are inappropriate for academic learning. As a result, their participation in reading-related activities is marginal. Getting through the reading task to answer homework questions is often the only reason they read at all.

Unsuccessful readers can often be found "hiding out" in classrooms. That is to say, they have developed a complex set of coping strategies to avoid reading or being held accountable for reading (Brozo 1990a). These coping behaviors include avoiding eye contact with the teacher, engaging in disruptive classroom behavior, forgetting to bring books to class, and seeking help from friends. Hiding out perpetuates a cycle of failure ensuring that the unsuccessful reader will remain helpless in text-related learning situations. The difference between successful and unsuccessful readers usually rests in their knowledge of strategies: how to use them, when to use them, and why. Effective readers know how to approach a text and make plans for reading. They also know how to locate and summarize important points, organize, and even get out of jams when they run into trouble with difficult texts.

"Learned helplessness," or a student's perception of an inability to overcome failure, is one of the chief culprits in unsuccessful reading and low achievement in content area classrooms (Vacca & Padak 1990). Unsuccessful readers often falter in reading tasks because they lack knowledge of and control over the strategies needed for effective text learning. As Marie, an immigrant student from El Salvador explains, "Books scare me" (Sturtevant 1992).

Learned Helplessness

Low-achieving students often feel helpless in text-related learning situations because they are unaware of their own reading processes. They are at risk in reading situations because they command a limited repertoire of strategies.

Often they aren't sure *what* strategies are important in particular reading tasks or *how* or *when* to use the strategies that they do possess. In addition, they have trouble recognizing *why* they read or what reading is for. Rarely do unsuccessful readers consider what their role should be as readers. Rather than take an active role in constructing meaning, they often remain passive and disengaged.

Poor self-image contributes to a sense of helplessness. Students who are at risk in text-related learning situations do not feel competent as readers and display little confidence in their ability to make meaning with texts. They hide out, avoiding reading at all costs, because they believe that they can't learn with texts successfully. As a result, they are often ambivalent about the act of reading and fail to value what reading can do for them. For one reason or another, they have alienated themselves from the world of print.

June (1995), for example, recorded the reading ambivalence of African-American students about a multicultural literature anthology, *African-American Literature: Voices in a Tradition.* At first, the students showed "proprietary interest" in the book and expressed appreciation that a textbook highlighted their literary and cultural traditions. The stories were modern and related to everyday life and concerns. However, June observed that when it came to actually reading stories from the book, the students' interest and enthusiasm faded. Some failed to bring the book to class or even to take it out of their book bags. Class discussions stalled because too many of the students hadn't done the assigned readings. One student expressed the sentiments of many in the class:

> I particularly don't like to read. . . . If I pick up a letter from one of my relatives from Arizona say, if that letter's ten pages long, I put it back down. . . . I think the students are interested in the textbook . . . but like I said I can't stand reading. If there was another way for me to get that information from the textbook, I'll use that other way. (p. 486)

Students who are ambivalent about reading won't read for the sake of reading. However, when the teacher in the literature class began to involve students in the stories through role play and other strategies of engagement, they participated in reading more willingly and actively. The more social, collaborative, and interactive teachers make reading, the less ambivalent students will be about the act of reading itself.

Students with Disabilities

Students with physical, learning, or emotional disabilities are also at risk in regular classrooms. These students, who may have been placed in self-contained special-education classes and resource rooms several years ago, are now being mainstreamed into regular classrooms. The passage of the Education for All Handicapped Children Act (Public Law 194–42) in 1975, requiring all students with disabilities to be educated in the least restrictive environment, was reauthorized in 1990 and is now known as the Individuals with Disabilities Education Act (IDEA) (Public Law 101-476).

IDEA has paved the way for state departments of education and school districts to move toward *full inclusion* in public schools. Advocates of full inclusion envision schools and classrooms as learning communities in which all children and youth with differences will be served by the regular curriculum. According to Sapon-Shevin (1994), a leading proponent of inclusive classrooms, the goal of full inclusion "is to give teachers the skills they need to work with heterogeneous classrooms [where] differences are not just accepted, but expected" (p. 1).

To learn more about special needs and students who are challenged, visit the Web sites in Box 2.3.

That there is greater diversity in language, culture, and achievement in U.S. classrooms today than at any previous time in our history makes teaching all the more demanding. Schools with diverse student populations have begun to provide teachers professional development workshops that focus, for the most part, on developing cultural understanding and an awareness of academic differences. An analysis of these workshops illustrates that they have been successful in helping sensitize teachers to differences but have been ineffective in changing their instructional practices (Sleeter 1990). Efforts to help teachers understand cultural and academic diversity are laudable, but teachers continue to say, "'OK, I now know how nonmainstream students differ from mainstream students, but how can I change my delivery of instruction to address these differences?"' (Jackson 1994, p. 298).

We address in various chapters of this book many of the changes in instructional delivery that teachers must make as they respond to the literacy needs of diverse learners. These changes revolve around strategies that are *cognitive, metacognitive,* and *social-collaborative.* Cognitive strategies, as we illustrated in Chapter 1, allow students to construct meaning as they use various thinking skills and processes to read, write, and talk about texts. Metacognitive strategies involve students in making plans for text learning, monitoring comprehension, and evaluating how well they have accomplished their goals as learners. Social and collaborative strategies, as we examine in Chapter 6, underscore the importance of talk in the classroom and collaborative interactions among students as they engage in cooperative learning activities.

Many diverse learners lack the strategies needed to learn effectively with texts. They struggle with reading, writing, and talking to learn content in classrooms. Although some students who struggle with reading may have developed *fluency,* the ability to read print smoothly and automatically, they

Box 2.3

Nothing but Net: Instructional Resources for Students Who Have Special Needs

Deaf World Web
deafworldweb.org/

A Basic Dictionary of ASL (sign language) Terms
home.earthlink.net/

The Global School House Resources for Special Student Populations
www.gsn.org/

Special Education Resources on the Internet (SERI)
www.hood.edu/

Internet Resources for Special Educators
www.interactive.net/

The Council for Exceptional Children
www.cec.sped.org/

Autism Resources
web.syr.edu/

Scotter's Low Vision Land
www.community.net/

Attention Deficit Disorder
www.ns.net/

Family Village
www.familyvillage.wise.edu/

Orton Dyslexia Society
ods.org/

Learning Disabilities Association of America
205.164.116.200/LDA/index.html

may not know what to do with texts beyond just saying the words. One of the dilemmas students face is that few effectively learn how and when to use strategies to explore and construct meaning during tasks that require literacy.

SCAFFOLDING INSTRUCTION FOR STUDENTS WHO STRUGGLE WITH TEXT

The challenge that lies ahead is to create classrooms that are responsive to and supportive and nurturing of all kinds of diversity. A key change in the delivery of instruction that would make a difference in the content literacy of all learners, especially students from diverse backgrounds, is to scaffold their use of various strategies for text learning. Scaffolding instruction allows teachers to help diverse learners negotiate meaning and overcome difficulties in text-related learning situations.

In Chapter 1, we introduced the concept of instructional scaffolding as a way of guiding students in their development as independent learners. Scaffolding, as you may recall, serves to support students as they engage in various tasks that require reading, writing, and discussion. It gives them a better chance to be successful in handling the linguistic and conceptual demands inherent in content area texts than if they are left to their own devices. Providing literacy supports for students, however, doesn't necessarily mean telling them, "You should do it this way in my class." Scaffolding instruction goes beyond imperatives. A diverse learner needs not only exhortation but also a good model or two. A key feature of instructional scaffolding is the demonstration and modeling of strategies that students need to be successful with content area texts. To scaffold instruction effectively, teachers need to understand the role that metacognition plays in comprehension and learning.

Metacognition and Learning

Metacognition involves awareness of, knowledge about, regulation of, and ability to control one's own cognitive processes (Brown, Bransford, Ferrara, & Campione 1983; Flavell 1976, 1981). Simply, it is our ability to think about and control our own learning.

Metacognition, as it applies to reading, has two components. The first is metacognitive *knowledge;* the second is *regulation.* Metacognitive knowledge includes self-knowledge and task knowledge. Self-knowledge is the knowledge students have about themselves as learners. Task knowledge is the knowledge they have about the skills, strategies, and resources necessary for the performance of cognitive tasks. The second component, self-regulation, involves the ability to monitor and regulate comprehension through strategies and attitudes that capitalize on metacognitive knowledge (Baker & Brown 1984). Self- and task knowledge and self-regulation are tandem concepts. The former are prerequisites for the latter. Together, self-knowledge, task knowledge, and self-regulation help explain how maturing readers can begin to assume the lion's share of the responsibility for their own learning.

As teachers, we have metacognition in our particular subject areas. Translating our metacognition into lessons that students understand is the crux of content area teaching. Science teachers, for example, have a metacognition of science. They have knowledge about themselves as scientists, they have knowledge of the tasks of science, and they have the ability to monitor and regulate themselves when conducting experiments, writing results, or reading technical material. Science teachers can monitor and regulate themselves because they know how to perform a set of core process strategies. They know how to observe, classify, compare, measure, describe, organize information, predict, infer, formulate hypotheses, interpret data, communicate, experiment, and draw conclusions. These are the same strategies a student taking a science course is expected to learn. A science teacher's job is to get students to think like scientists. The best way for students to learn to think like scientists is to learn to read, experiment, and write like scientists (L. Baker 1991).

Showing students how to think like scientists, historians, literary critics, mathematicians, health care professionals, artists, or auto mechanics puts them on the road to independent learning. To be independent learners, students need to know the whats, whys, hows, and whens of strategic reading and thinking. They should know enough about knowing to recognize the importance of (1) using a variety of strategies to facilitate comprehension and learning, (2) analyzing the reading task before them, (3) reflecting on what they know or don't know about the material to be read, and (4) devising plans for successfully completing the reading and for evaluating and checking their progress in accomplishing the task (Brown 1978).

Teachers need to know if students know enough about their own reading and learning strategies to approach content area text assignments flexibly and adaptively. Different text assignments may pose different problems for the reader to solve. For this reason, when assigned text material, students must be aware of the nature of the reading task and the way to handle it. Is the student sophisticated enough to ask questions about the reading task? To make plans for reading? To use and adapt strategies to meet the demands of the text assignment? Or does a student who struggles with text approach every text assignment in the same manner—plowing through with little notion of why, when, or how to read the material? Plowing through cumbersome text material just once is more than students who struggle with reading can cope with. The prospect of rereading or reviewing isn't a realistic option for them. However, teachers are in a position to show students that working with the material doesn't necessarily entail the agony of slow, tedious reading.

To be in command of their own reading, students must know what to do when they run into trouble. This is what comprehension monitoring and self-regulation are all about. Do students have a repertoire of strategies within reach to get out of trouble if they become confused or misunderstand what they reading?

The experienced reader responds to situations in text in much the same way that the experienced driver responds to situations on the road. Reading and driving become fairly automatic processes until something happens. As Milton (1982) notes, "Everything is fine for experienced drivers as long as they are in familiar territory, the car operates smoothly, they encounter no threat from other drivers, weather, road conditions, or traffic. . . . But, let even one factor become problematic, and drivers shift more attention to the process of driving" (p. 23).

And so it goes for the reader who suddenly gets into trouble with a text assignment. Attention shifts from automatic processing to strategies that will help the learner work out of the jam. The problem encountered may parallel the driver's: unfamiliar territory or getting temporarily lost. However, in the learner's case, it is the text, procedure, or problem that is unfamiliar and difficult. It doesn't take much to get lost in the author's line of reasoning, the text organization, the scientific process, or a mathematical formula.

Other problems that may disrupt smooth reading are a concept too difficult to grasp, word identification, or the inability to identify the important ideas in the text. These problems represent major roadblocks that, if left unattended, may hamper the reader's attempts to get the gist of the text passage or to construct meaning. It is in problem situations such as these that metacognitive processes play an important role in learning with text.

Linda Baker (1991) recommends six questions for students to ask themselves when they read to help monitor their comprehension:

1. Are there any words I don't understand?

2. Is there any information that doesn't agree with what I already know?

3. Are there any ideas that don't fit together because I can't tell who or what is being talked about?

4. Are there any ideas that don't fit together because I can't tell how the ideas are related?

5. Are there any ideas that don't fit together because I think the ideas are contradictory?

6. Is there any information missing or not clearly explained? (p. 10)

One way to help diverse learners think about what they do when they read is to have them take the inventory in Box 2.4. Vincent Miholic (1994) developed the inventory from the body of research on metacognitive strategies. "Correct" responses to each item on the inventory are marked with a +, while "incorrect" responses are marked with a –. Teachers who use the inventory with a class should be sure to cover the + and – row.

Not only does the inventory pique students' curiosity about strategic learning, but it also gives them a concrete idea of important strategies. Miholic (1994) suggests that the inventory invites students to become aware of the knowledge they need in order to apply strategies to various text-learning situations. In addition, it serves as a vehicle for modeling and demonstration. He warns against emphasizing scores on the inventory. It should be used more as a springboard to create strategy awareness through discussion.

Scaffolding Students' Use of Strategies

Strategy instruction helps students who struggle with text become aware of, use, and develop control over learning strategies (Brown & Palincsar 1982). Explicit teaching provides an alternative to blind instruction. In blind instructional situations, students are taught what to do, but this is where instruction usually ends. Although directed to make use of a set of procedures which will improve studying, students seldom grasp the rationale or payoff underlying a particular study strategy. As a result, they attempt to use the strategy with little basis for evaluating its success or monitoring its effectiveness. Explicit instruction, however, attempts not only to show students *what* to do, but also *why, how,* and *when.* Pearson (1982b) concludes that such instruction helps "students develop independent strategies for coping with the kinds of comprehension problems they are asked to solve in their lives in schools" (p. 22).

Strategy instruction has four components: *assessment, awareness, modeling and demonstration,* and *application.*

By way of analogy, teaching students to be strategic readers provides experiences similar to those needed by athletes who are in training. To perform well with texts, students must understand the rules, rehearse, work on technique, and practice. A coach (the teacher) is needed to provide feedback, guide, inspire, and share the knowledge and experiences that she or he possesses.

Assess What Students Know How to Do

The assessment component of strategy instruction is tryout time. It gives the teacher an opportunity to determine the degree of knowledge the students have about a strategy under discussion. Moreover, assessment yields insight into how well the students use a strategy to handle a reading task. For these reasons, assessing the use of a strategy should occur in as natural a context as possible.

Assessment can usually be accomplished within a single class period if these steps are followed:

1. Assign students a text passage of approximately 1000–1500 words. The selection should take most students 10 to 15 minutes to read.

2. Direct students to use a particular strategy. For example, suppose that the strategy involves writing a summary of a text selection. Simply ask students to do the things they normally do to read a passage and then write a summary of it. Allow adequate time to complete the task.

3. Observe the use of the strategy. Note what students do. Do they underline or mark important ideas as they read? Do they appear to skim the material first to get a general idea of what to expect? What do they do when actually constructing the summary?

4. Ask students to respond in writing to several key questions about the use of the strategy; for example: What did you do to summarize the passage? What did you do to find the main ideas? Did you find summarizing easy or difficult? Why?

Create Strategy Awareness

Assessment is a springboard to making students aware of the *why* and *how* of a study strategy. During the awareness step, a give-and-take exchange of

Box 2.4

Metacognitive Reading Awareness Inventory

There's more than one way to cope when you run into difficulties in your reading. Which ways are best? Under each question here, put a checkmark beside *all* the responses you think are effective.

1. What do you do if you encounter a word and you don't know what it means?
+ a. Use the words around it to figure it out.
+ b. Use an outside source, such as a dictionary or expert.
+ c. Temporarily ignore it and wait for clarification.
− d. Sound it out.

2. What do you do if you don't know what an entire sentence means?
+ a. Read it again.
− b. Sound out all the difficult words.
+ c. Think about the other sentences in the paragraph.
− d. Disregard it completely.

3. If you are reading science or social studies material, what would you do to remember the important information you've read?
− a. Skip parts you don't understand.
+ b. Ask yourself questions about the important ideas.
+ c. Realize you need to remember one point rather than another.
+ d. Relate it to something you already know.

4. Before you start to read, what kind of plans do you make to help you read better?
− a. No specific plan is needed; just start reading toward completion of the assignment.
+ b. Think about what you know about the subject.
+ c. Think about why you are reading.
− d. Make sure the entire reading can be finished in as short a period of time as possible.

5. Why would you go back and read an entire passage over again?
+ a. You didn't understand it.
− b. To clarify a specific or supporting idea.
+ c. It seemed important to remember.
+ d. To underline or summarize for study.

ideas takes place between teacher and students. As a result, students should recognize the *rationale* and *process* behind the use of a strategy. To make students more aware of a learning strategy, consider the following activities:

1. Discuss the assessment. Use your observations and students' reflective responses to the written questions.

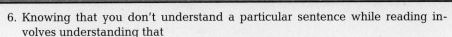

6. Knowing that you don't understand a particular sentence while reading involves understanding that
+ a. the reader may not have developed adequate links or associations for new words or concepts introduced in the sentence.
+ b. the writer may not have conveyed the ideas clearly.
+ c. two sentences may purposely contradict each other.
– d. finding meaning for the sentence needlessly slows down the reader.

7. As you read a textbook, which of these do you do?
+ a. Adjust your pace depending on the difficulty of the material.
– b. Generally, read at a constant, steady pace.
– c. Skip the parts you don't understand.
+ d. Continually make predictions about what you are reading.

8. While you read, which of these are important?
+ a. Know when you know and when you don't know key ideas.
+ b. Know what it is that you know in relation to what is being read.
– c. Know that confusing text is common and usually can be ignored.
+ d. Know that different strategies can be used to aid understanding.

9. When you come across a part of the text that is confusing, what do you do?
+ a. Keep on reading until the text is clarified.
+ b. Read ahead and then look back if the text is still unclear.
– c. Skip those sections completely; they are usually not important.
+ d. Check to see if the ideas expressed are consistent with one another.

10. Which sentences are the most important in the chapter?
– a. Almost all of the sentences are important; otherwise, they wouldn't be there.
+ b. The sentences that contain the important details or facts.
+ c. The sentences that are directly related to the main idea.
– d. The ones that contain the most details.

Source: Reprinted with permission of the International Reading Association and Vincent Miholic (1994), "An Inventory to Pique Students' Metacognitive Awareness," *Journal of Reading, 38* (2), 84–86.

2. Set the stage by leading a discussion of *why* the strategy is useful. What is the payoff for students? How does it improve learning?

3. Engage in activities that define the rules, guidelines, or procedures for being successful with the strategy.

4. Have students experience using the strategy by practicing the rules or procedures on a short selection from the textbook.

Awareness provides students with a clear picture of the learning strategy. The *why* and *how* are solidly introduced, and the road has been paved for more intensive modeling and demonstration of the strategy.

Model and Demonstrate Strategies

Once the *why* and a beginning sense of the *how* are established, the students should receive careful follow-up in the use of the strategy. Follow-up sessions are characterized by demonstration through teacher modeling, explanations, practice, reinforcement of the rules or procedures, and more practice. The students progress from easy to harder practice situations, and from shorter to longer text selections. The following activities are recommended:

1. Use an overhead transparency to review the steps students should follow.

2. Demonstrate the strategy. Walk students through the steps. Provide explanations. Raise questions about the procedures.

3. As part of a demonstration, initiate a *think-aloud* procedure to model how to use the strategy. By thinking aloud, the teacher shares with the students the thinking processes he or she uses in applying the strategy. Thinking aloud is often accomplished by reading a passage out loud and stopping at key points in the text to ask questions and/or provide prompts. The questions and prompts mirror the critical thinking required to apply the strategy. Once students are familiar with the think-aloud procedure, encourage them to demonstrate and use it during practice sessions. Later in the chapter we explain in more detail the role that think-alouds play in modeling strategies.

4. Reinforce and practice the strategy with trial runs using short selections from the textbook. Debrief the students with questions after each trial run: Did they follow the steps? How successful were they? What caused them difficulty? Have them make learning-log entries. Often, a short quiz following a trial run shows students how much they learned and remembered as a result of using the study strategy.

The demonstration sessions are designed to provide experience with the strategy. Students should reach a point where they have internalized the steps and feel in control of the strategy.

Apply Strategies

The preceding components of strategy instruction should provide enough practice for students to know *why*, *how*, and *when* to use the study strategies that have been targeted by the teacher for emphasis. Once students have made generalizations about strategy use, regular class assignments should encourage its application. Rather than assign for homework a text selection accompanied by questions to be answered, frame the assignment so that students will have to apply certain study strategies.

COMPREHENSION STRATEGIES

Readers who struggle with texts are usually unaware of strategies that will help them construct meaning. Teachers can use *think-alouds*, *reciprocal teaching*, and *question-answer relationships* (QARs) to scaffold students' use of comprehension strategies.

Using Think-Alouds to Model Comprehension Strategies

In think-alouds, teachers make their thinking explicit by verbalizing their thoughts while reading orally. Davey (1983) explains that this process helps readers clarify their understanding of reading and their understanding of how to use strategies. Students will more clearly understand the strategies after a teacher uses think-alouds because they can see how a mind actively responds to thinking through trouble spots and constructing meaning from the text.

Davey (1983) suggests five basic steps when using think-alouds. First, select passages to read aloud that contain points of difficulty, ambiguities, contradictions, or unknown words. Second, while orally reading and modeling thinking aloud, have students follow silently and listen to how trouble spots are thought through. Third, have students work with partners to practice think-alouds by taking turns reading short, carefully prepared passages and sharing thoughts. Fourth, have students practice independently, using a checklist as shown in Figure 2.1 to involve all students while verifying use of the procedures. Finally, to provide for transfer, integrate practice with other lessons, and provide occasional demonstrations of how, why, and when to use think-alouds.

Five points that can be made during think-alouds are showing how

1. To develop hypotheses by making predictions.

2. To develop images by describing pictures forming in one's head from the information being read.

3. To link new information with prior knowledge by sharing analogies.

4. To monitor comprehension by verbalizing a confusing point.

5. To regulate comprehension by demonstrating strategies.

Let's look at how each of these points can be modeled in a middle school earth science class.

While I was reading, how did I do? (Put an X in the appropriate column.)			
	Not very much	A little bit	Much of the time	All of the time
Made predictions	_____	_____	_____	_____
Formed pictures	_____	_____	_____	_____
Used "like-a"	_____	_____	_____	_____
Found problems	_____	_____	_____	_____
Used fix-ups	_____	_____	_____	_____

FIGURE 2.1   **Checklist for Self-Evaluation of Think-Alouds**

Source: From "Think Aloud—Modeling the Cognitive Processes of Reading Comprehension," by Beth Davey, *Journal of Reading,* October 1983. Copyright © 1983 by the International Reading Association. All rights reserved. Used by permission.

Develop Hypotheses by Making Predictions

Teachers might model how to develop hypotheses by making predictions from the title of a chapter or from subheadings within the chapter. Suppose you were teaching with an earth science text. You might say, "From the heading 'How Minerals Are Used,' I predict that this section will tell about things that are made out of different minerals." The text continues:

> Some of the most valuable minerals are found in ores. An **ore** is a mineral resource mined for profit. For example, bauxite (BAWK-sight) is an ore from which aluminum is taken. Iron is obtained from the ore called hematite (HEE-muh-tight). Bauxite and hematite are metallic minerals.
>
> Metallic minerals are metals or ores of metals. Gold, iron, and aluminum are examples of metals. Metals are important because of their many useful properties.
>
> One useful property of many metals is malleability (mal-ee-uh-BIL-uh-tee). **Malleability** is the ability to be hammered without breaking. Malleability allows a metal to be hammered into thin sheets.

Develop Images

To model how to develop imaging, at this point you might stop and say, "I have a picture in my head from a scene I saw in a movie about the Old West. I see a blacksmith pumping bellows in a forge to heat up an iron horseshoe. When the iron turns a reddish orange, he picks it up with his tongs, and he hammers. The sparks fly, but slowly the horseshoe changes shape to fit the horse's hoof."

The text continues:

> Another property of many metals is ductility (duk-TIL-uh-tee). **Ductility** is the ability to be pulled and stretched without breaking. This property allows a metal to be pulled into thin wires.

Share Analogies

To model how to link new information with prior knowledge, you might share the following analogies. "This is like a time when I tried to eat a piece of pizza with extra cheese. Every time I took a bite, the cheese kept stretching and stretching into these long strings. It is also like a time when I went to the county fair and watched people make taffy. They got this glob of candy and put it on a machine that just kept pulling and stretching the taffy, but it never broke."

The text continues:

> Metals share other properties as well. All metals conduct heat and electricity. Electrical appliances and machines need metals to conduct electricity. In addition, all metals have a shiny, metallic luster.

Monitor Comprehension

To model how to monitor comprehension, you can verbalize a confusing point: "This is telling me that metals have a metallic luster. I don't know what that is. I'm also confused because I thought this section was going to be about things that are made out of different minerals. This is different from what I expected."

Regulate Comprehension

To model how to correct lagging comprehension, you can demonstrate a strategy: "I'm confused about what *metallic luster* means, and I don't know why the authors are talking about this when I expected them to talk about stuff made out of minerals. Maybe if I ignore the term *metallic luster* and keep on reading, I'll be able to make some connections to what I expected and figure it all out." The text continues:

> Very shiny metals, like chromium, are often used for decorative purposes. Many metals are also strong. Titanium (tigh-TAY-nee-um), magnesium (mag-NEE-zee-um), and aluminum are metals that are both strong and lightweight. These properties make them ideal building materials for jet planes and spacecraft.

"Oh, they're talking about properties of metals that make them especially good for making certain things, like aluminum for jets because it is strong and lightweight. Now I understand why they're talking about properties. I'll bet chrome and chromium are just about the same because I know chrome is the shiny stuff on cars. I think *metallic luster* must mean something like shiny because chromium reminds me of chrome."

Think-alouds are best used at the beginning of lessons to help students learn the whats and hows of constructing meaning with text. The next teaching strategy, *reciprocal teaching,* is an excellent follow-up to think-alouds.

Reciprocal teaching helps students learn how to apply the strategy learned during a think-aloud so that they can understand the author's message.

Using Reciprocal Teaching to Model Comprehension Strategies

When using reciprocal teaching, you model how to use four comprehension activities (generating questions, summarizing, predicting, and clarifying) while leading a dialogue (Palinscar & Brown 1984). Then students take turns assuming the teacher's role. A key to the effectiveness of this strategy is adjusting the task demand to support the students when difficulty occurs. That is, when students experience difficulty, you provide assistance by lowering the demands of the task. As the process goes on, you slowly withdraw support so that students continue learning.

When planning a reciprocal teaching lesson, there are two phases. The first phase has five steps:

1. Find text selections that demonstrate the four comprehension activities.

2. Generate appropriate questions.

3. Generate predictions about each selection.

4. Locate summarizing sentences and develop summaries for each selection.

5. Note difficult vocabulary and concepts.

In the second phase, decisions are made about which comprehension activities to teach, based on the students' needs. It also helps determine students' present facility with the activities so that you are prepared to give needed support during the process. Once students are familiar with more than one strategy, reciprocal teaching can be used to model the decision-making process about which strategy to use. Reciprocal teaching can also be used to check whether the comprehension breakdown has been repaired and if not, why not.

A middle school social studies teacher recognized that his students were having difficulty understanding important terms in their text that were central to understanding the author's message. He developed a lesson that combined thinking aloud and reciprocal teaching. The first part of his lesson used think-alouds for focusing on vocabulary when lack of understanding of key words caused comprehension to break down. He then used reciprocal teaching to scaffold the reasoning process he had modeled during the think-aloud phase of his lesson.

His first steps were to activate prior knowledge, to have students make predictions about the selection, to tell what reasoning process was going to be taught, to tell why the reasoning process was important, and to discuss when it would be used:

Teacher: Today we're going to read about the U.S. Constitution. How many of you have heard of the Constitution? [Students respond.] Look at the picture at the bottom of page 119. The caption says, "The people who came together at the Constitutional Convention knew they had an important job to do." What are they doing in the picture?

Student: There are a whole bunch of guys standing around looking at one guy writing.

Teacher: Right. Now look at page 118. What is the title of this selection?

Student: "The Constitution of the United States."

Teacher: Good. Now there's something I want you to know about this selection: There are some new terms that are important for you to figure out so that you can understand the author's message. Before we read the selection, I'm going to teach you how to figure them out so that when you come to them, you'll be able to figure them out and understand the author's message on your own.

His second step was to think out loud to model *when* the reasoning process should be used:

Teacher: I'm going to pretend that I don't know a term in this story. Watch what happens. "Articles of Confederation." Hmmm. [Teacher pretends he doesn't understand the term.] I don't know that term, but I know it is important because it is part of a subheading. I'll skip it for now because this paragraph should tell me what it is. "With independence came many problems. The United States were joined together under one government by the Articles of Confederation." Hmmm. Now I know the United States were joined or glued together by this thing. "The articles listed the powers of the central government and the powers of the states." Uh-oh, this doesn't make sense to me. I'd better go back and figure this out because I've stopped understanding.

His third step was to think out loud *how* to use the reasoning process to repair the comprehension breakdown:

Teacher: I'll sound it out. The back end looks like *nation*, so *con-fed-er-ation*. Articles of Confederation. That still doesn't tell me what it means. Let's see, the articles listed—articles like in the newspaper—stuff written down. This stuff written down was joining the states together under one government. When I joined a club, we stuck together because we wrote down a list of rules for the members. The rules told who got to do what. [Teacher reads sentences over again.] It sounds like the Articles of Confederation are a list of rules that tell what the central government gets to do and what the states get to do. That makes sense now.

His fourth step was to check how the students interpreted the information by asking them to tell or show when and how to use the reasoning process:

Teacher:	Now, how would you figure out the hard word in this sentence?
Student:	At first I'd keep on reading because it might tell you later on.
Teacher:	That's good. Sometimes when you read a little further, you are given a definition. What else did I think about when that didn't work?
Student:	Sounding out the word.
Teacher:	Sometimes that helps, too, but there is something else to try. Watch and listen again. [Repeat procedure with another term.]

His fifth step was to review the title and the pictures and ask for predictions before reading:

Teacher:	Now we're going to read the selection about the U.S. Constitution. Look at the pictures on pages 119 and 120; then read the title again. In your own words, predict what you think this selection is about. What do you expect to learn? [Students make predictions; teacher gives positive reinforcement for making predictions, jots them on the chalkboard, and then summarizes predictions.]
Teacher:	Now remember, there are difficult terms in this selection, so when you come to one, try to figure it out the way I showed you.

His sixth step was to read aloud a small portion of the text.

His seventh step was to ask a question about the content, invite students to answer, and then ask individuals to share questions they had generated:

Teacher:	My question is, Why was the United States in danger of failing?
Student:	Because they wouldn't cooperate.
Teacher:	Who wouldn't cooperate?
Student:	The states wouldn't cooperate with the central government.
Teacher:	Correct. Does anyone else have a question?

His eighth step was to summarize what had been read by identifying the gist of that paragraph and how he had arrived at that summary:

Teacher:	My summary is that the Articles of Confederation didn't give the central government enough power, so the United States was in danger of failing. I thought of that summary because "Articles of Confedera-

tion" was the subheading of this paragraph. After the paragraph told what they were, it mainly told about the problems they caused because the central government didn't have enough power, which led up to the last line, which said the United States in danger of failing. Do you have anything that should be added to my summary?

His ninth step was to check on the reasoning process to see if it was working, helping him figure out difficult terms:

Teacher: Is there an unclear meaning in this paragraph?

Student: Yes. It says the states were quarreling with each other.

Teacher: Can big pieces of land argue with each other?

Student: No.

Teacher: That's right. What is the author doing here?

Student: He's making the states act like people.

Teacher: Yes, so what does he mean?

Student: He's saying that the people living in the states were arguing, because we know two pieces of land couldn't be arguing.

Teacher: Good reasoning. Are there any other parts of this paragraph that are unclear? [No student response.]

His tenth step was to ask the students to make predictions about the next segment by using the new subheading and what they had already learned. He then selected a student to be the next "teacher."

After students took turns playing the role of teacher, his final step was to close the lesson by inviting students to summarize the content of the entire selection as well as when, why, and how to use the reasoning process.

Using Question-Answer Relationships (QARs) to Model Comprehension Strategies

The type of question asked to guide comprehension should be based on the *information readers need to answer the question.* Therefore, teachers must help students *become aware of* likely sources of information as they respond to questions (Pearson & Johnson 1978).

A reader draws on two broad information sources to answer questions: information in the text and information inside the reader's head. For example, some questions have answers that can be found directly in the text. These questions are *textually explicit* and lead to answers that are "right there" in the text.

Other questions have answers that require students to think about the information they have read in the text. They must be able to search for ideas that are related to one another and then put these ideas together in order to answer the questions. These questions are *textually implicit* and lead to "think and search" answers.

Still other questions require students to rely mainly on prior knowledge and experience. In other words, responses to these questions are more inside the reader's head than in the text itself. These questions are *schema-based* and lead to "author and you" and "on your own" answers.

"Right there," "think and search," "author and you," and "on your own" are mnemonics for question-answer relationships (Raphael 1982, 1984, 1986). Many kinds of responses can be prompted by textually explicit questions, by textually implicit questions, and by schema-based questions. However, the success that students experience when responding to a certain type of question depends on their ability to recognize the relationship between the question and its answer. Let's explore in more detail how students can be taught to be more strategic in their awareness and use of question-answer relationships.

QARs make explicit to students the relationships that exist among the type of question asked, the text, and the reader's prior knowledge. In the process of teaching QARs, you help students become aware of and skilled in using learning strategies to find the information they need to comprehend at different levels of response to the text.

The procedures for learning QARs can be taught directly to students by reading teachers and can be reinforced by content area specialists. Keep in mind, however, that students may come to your class totally unaware of what information sources are available for seeking an answer, or they may not know when to use different sources. In this case, it is worth several days' effort to teach students the relationship between questions and answers. It may take up to three days to show students how to identify the information sources necessary to answer questions. The following steps, which we have adapted for content area situations, are suggested for teaching QARs:

1. Introduce the concept of QARs by showing students a chart or an overhead transparency containing a description of the four basic question-answer relationships. (We recommend a chart that can be positioned in a prominent place in the classroom. Students may then refer to it throughout the content area lessons.) Point out the two broad categories of information sources: "in the text" and "in your head." Figure 2.2 is adapted from a chart recommended by Raphael (1986).

2. Begin by assigning students several short passages from the textbook (no more than two to five sentences in length). Follow each reading with one question from each of the QAR categories on the chart. Then discuss the differences between a "right there" question and answer, a "think and search" question and answer, an "on your own" question and answer, and an "author and you" question and answer. Your explanations should be clear and complete. Reinforce the discussion by assigning several more short text passages and asking a question for each. Students will soon begin to catch on to

Where Are Answers to Questions Found?

In the Text:

Right There

The answer is in the text. The words used in the question and the words used for the answer can usually be found in the same sentences.

Think and Search

The answer is in the text, but the words used in the question and those used for the answer are not in the same sentence. You need to think about different parts of the text and how ideas can be put together before you can answer the question.

Or

In Your Head:

On Your Own

The text got you thinking, but the answer is inside your head. The author can't help you much. So think about it, and use what you know already about the question.

Author and You

The answer is not in the text. You need to think about what you know, what the author says, and how they fit together.

FIGURE 2.2   **Introducing QARs**

the differences among the four QAR categories. The example in Box 2.5 illustrates how a science teacher in the middle grades introduced the QAR categories to her students.

3. Continue the second day by practicing with short passages, using one question for each QAR category per passage. First, give students a passage to read along with questions *and* answers *and* identified QARs. Why do the questions and answers represent one QAR and not another? Second, give students a passage along with questions and answers; this time they have to identify the QAR for each. Finally, give students passages, decide together which strategy to use, and have them write their responses.

4. Review briefly on the third day. Then assign a longer passage (75–200 words) with up to six questions (at least one each from the four QAR categories). First, have students work in groups to decide the QAR category for each question and the answers for each. Next, assign a second passage, comparable in length, with five questions for students to work on individually. Discuss their responses either in small groups or with the whole class. You may wish to work with several class members or colleagues to complete the QAR exercise in Box 2.6. It was developed by a high school English teacher as part of a short story unit.

5. Apply the QAR strategy to actual content area assignments. For each question asked, students decide on the appropriate QAR strategy and write out their answers.

Once students are sensitive to the different information sources for different types of questions and know how to use these sources to respond to questions, variations can be made in the QAR strategy. For example, you might have students generate their own questions to text assignments—perhaps two for each QAR strategy. They then write down the answers to the questions as they understand them, except that they leave one question unanswered from the "think and search" category and one from the "on your own" or "author and you" category. These are questions on which the student would like to hear the views of others. During the discussion, students volunteer to ask their unanswered questions. The class is invited first to identify the question by QAR category and then to contribute answers, comments, or related questions about the material.

A second variation involves discussions of text. During question-and-answer exchanges, preface a question by saying, "This question is *right there* in the text" or, "You'll have to *think and search* the text to answer" or, "You're *on your own* with this one" or, "The answer is a combination of the *author and you.* Think about what the author tells us and what we already know to try and come up with a reasonable response." Make sure that you pause several seconds or more for "think time." Think time, or "wait time," is critical to responding to textually implicit and schema-based questions. Gambrell (1980) found that increasing think time to five seconds or longer increases the length of student responses as well as the quality of their speculative thinking.

Once students are familiar with QARs, they can be used in combination with a variety of interactive strategies that encourage readers to explore ideas through text discussions.

Modeling comprehension strategies through think-alouds, reciprocal teaching, and QARs provides the instructional support that will help students do more than just read the words on a page. These procedures scaffold students' use of strategies that will help them read texts in a more thoughtful and thought-provoking manner. Another dimension of strategy instruction is to show diverse learners how to generate meaning for unfamiliar words and concepts that they encounter during reading.

VOCABULARY STRATEGIES

Diverse learners will often encounter an enormous number of unfamiliar words during reading that may pose comprehension problems for them. Strategy instruction, therefore, should take into account tactics and procedures that will help students build meaning for important concept terms. *Vocabulary self-collection strategy (VSS), concept of definition (CD) word maps,* and *vocabulary-building strategies* scaffold students' ability to define concepts in the context of their use.

Vocabulary Self-Collection Strategy

VSS promotes the long-term acquisition of language in an academic discipline (Haggard 1986). As a result of the repeated use of the strategy, students learn how to make decisions related to the importance of concepts and how to use context to determine what words mean. VSS begins once students read and discuss a text assignment. The teacher asks students, who are divided into teams, to nominate one word that they would like to learn more about. The word must be important enough for the team to share it with the class. The teacher also nominates a word.

Here are several suggested steps in VSS:

1. Divide the class into nominating teams of two to five students. Together the students on a nominating team decide which word to select for emphasis in the text selection.

2. Present the word that each team has selected to the entire class. A spokesperson for each team identifies the nominated word and responds to the following questions:

Box 2.5

An Introduction to QARs in a Science Class

1. Everyone has some idea of what growth means. People, plants, and animals grow. But what changes occur when a person or a plant grows? Two changes usually occur during the growth process. There is an increase in height and a gain in weight.

   Question: How many changes usually occur in the growth process?

   Answer: Two

   QAR: RIGHT THERE   ___X___

              THINK AND SEARCH   _____

              ON YOUR OWN   _____

              AUTHOR AND YOU   _____

   Rationale (developed during class discussion): This is an example of a "right there" question because the answer is easy to find and the words used to make the question are also in the answer.

2. New cells must be added as an organism grows. Cells that die or are worn away must be replaced. New cells are produced by a process called *mitosis.* During mitosis, one cell divides to become two cells.

   Question: What would happen if our cells stopped dividing?

   Answer: Our bodies would stop growing and we would eventually die because cells that died or were worn away would not be replaced.

   QAR: RIGHT THERE   _____

              THINK AND SEARCH   ___X___

              ON YOUR OWN   _____

              AUTHOR AND YOU   _____

   Rationale (developed during class discussion): The answer is in the text but harder to find. The words to the question and the answer are not in the same sentence.

3. Growth in height is not steady during the life of a human. There are times when you grow very fast. At other times, you grow slowly. Adults do not grow in height at all. Your most rapid growth took place before you were born. Rapid growth continues through the first two years of life.

a. *Where is the word found in the text?* The spokesperson reads the passage in which the word is located or describes the context in which the word is used.

b. *What do the team members think the word means?* The team decides on what the word means in the context in which it is used. They must

Question: What were the times in your life when you or someone you know grew rapidly?

Answers: My 9-year-old brother (pants needed hemming); young babies; myself at puberty; high school students

QAR: RIGHT THERE   _____

THINK AND SEARCH   _____

ON YOUR OWN   ____X____

AUTHOR AND YOU   _____

Rationale (developed during class discussion): To answer a question like this, you have to use what you know already. The answer is in your head, not the text. You're "on your own."

4. Two provisions are necessary for a tree to grow more than one kind of fruit. First, the branches of different fruit trees must be properly spliced onto the original tree. Second, the different fruit of all of the branches must belong to the same genus. Many orange trees, for example, have produced grapefruits, lemons, and limes.

Question: If you were a fruit grower, would you be able to grow bananas on an apple tree?

Answer: It's impossible. Bananas are a tropical fruit. I know that bananas and apples are not related to one another like oranges, grapefruits, and lemons, which are citrus fruits.

QAR: RIGHT THERE   _____

THINK AND SEARCH   _____

ON YOUR OWN   _____

AUTHOR AND YOU   ____X____

Rationale (developed during class discussion): To answer this question, you need to take what the author tells you and connect it to what you know. The answer is not in the text but in your head. However, you need to use information in the text and link it to what you know to respond to the question.

use information from the surrounding context and may also consult reference resources.

c. *Why did the team think the class should learn the word?* The team must tell the class why the word is important enough to single out for emphasis.

Box 2.6

QAR Awareness in an English Class

"Got your glove?" asked Glennie after a time. Scho obviously hadn't.

"You could give me some easy grounders," said Scho. "But don't burn 'em."

"All right," Glennie said. He moved off a little, so the three of them formed a triangle, and they passed the ball around for about five minutes, Monk tossing easy grounders to Scho, Scho throwing to Glennie, and Glennie burning them into Monk. After a while, Monk began to throw them back to Glennie once or twice before he let Scho have his grounder, and finally Monk gave Scho a fast, bumpy grounder that hopped over his shoulder and went into the brake on the other side of the street.

"Not so hard," called Scho as he ran across to get it.

"You should've had it," Monk shouted.

It took Scho a little while to find the ball among the ferns and dead leaves, and when he saw it, he grabbed it up and threw it toward Glennie. It struck the trunk of the apple tree, bounced back at an angle, and rolled steadily and stupidly onto the cement apron in front of the firehouse, where one of the trucks was parked. Scho ran hard and stopped it just before it rolled under the truck, and this time he carried it back to his former position on the lawn and threw it carefully to Glennie. (*From "A Game of Catch" by Richard Wilbur*)

1. *Question:* What are the three boys doing?

   Answer: _____

   QAR: _____

2. *Question:* Why did Monk throw the ball so hard to Scho?

   Answer: _____

   QAR: _____

3. *Question:* Who was throwing the ball to Monk?

   Answer: _____

   QAR: _____

4. *Question*: How would you describe Scho's throwing ability?

   Answer: _____

   QAR: _____

5. *Question:* How would you characterize Monk?

   Answer: _____

   QAR: _____

6. *Question:* Why do friends sometimes get frustrated with one another?

   Answer: _____

   QAR: _____

To introduce VSS to the students, the teacher first presents his or her nominated word to the class, modeling how to respond to the three questions. During the team presentations, the teacher facilitates the discussion, writes the nominated words on the board with their meanings, and invites class members to contribute additional clarifications of the words.

To conclude the class session, students record all the nominated words and their meanings in a section of their learning logs or in a separate vocabulary notebook. These lists may be used for review and study. As a consequence of VSS, the teacher has a set of student-generated words that can be incorporated into a variety of follow-up extension activities, some of which we will explain in Chapter 8.

Concept of Definition Word Maps

Although VSS provides opportunities to define and explore the meanings of words used in text readings, many students are not aware of the types of information that contribute to the meaning of a concept. Nor have they internalized a strategy for defining a concept based on the information available to them. In addition, words in a text passage often provide only partial contextual information for defining the meaning of a concept.

CD instruction provides a framework for organizing conceptual information in the process of defining a word (Schwartz 1988; Schwartz & Raphael 1985). Conceptual information can be organized in terms of three types of relationships: the general class or category in which the concept belongs, the attributes or properties of the concept and those that distinguish it from other members of the category, and examples or illustrations of the concept. Students from elementary school through high school can use CD to learn how to construct meaning for unknown words encountered in texts.

CD instruction supports vocabulary and concept learning by helping students internalize a strategy for defining and clarifying the meaning of unknown words. The hierarchical structure of a concept has an organizational pattern that is reflected by the general structure of a CD word map (see Figure 2.3).

In the center of the CD word map, students write the concept being studied. Working outward, they then write the word that best describes the general class or superordinate concept that includes the target concept. The answer to "What is it?" is the general class or category. Students then provide at least three examples of the concept as well as three properties by responding, respectively, to the questions "What are some examples?" and "What is it like?" Comparison of the target concept is also possible when students think of an additional concept that belongs to the general class but is different from the concept being studied. Figure 2.4 provides an example of a CD word map for the word *tiger*.

Since students use the general CD word map as a framework for defining unknown concepts that they encounter during reading, a teacher can easily combine CD instruction with VSS. Schwartz (1988) recommends a detailed

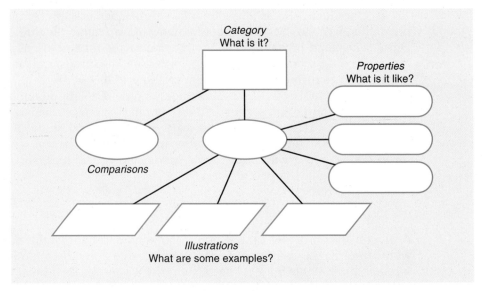

FIGURE 2.3   **A General Structure for a CD Word Map**

Source:"Learning to Learn: Vocabulary in Content Area Textbooks" by Robert Schwartz, *Journal of Reading,* November 1988. Copyright © 1988 by the International Reading Association. All rights reserved. Used by permission of the International Reading Association and Robert M. Schwartz.

plan for modeling CD with students. The plan includes demonstrating the value of CD by connecting its purpose to how people use organizational patterns to aid memory and interpretation; introducing the general structure of a CD word map, explaining how the three probes define a concept, and walking students through the completion of a word map; and applying CD to an actual text selection.

Two caveats are relevant to CD instruction: CD works best with concept words that function as nouns, but the procedure may be used, with some adaptation, with action words as well. Also, a potential misuse of CD occurs when teachers reproduce the general CD word map on the copier and expect students to define lists of words at the end of a text chapter. This is not the intent of CD instruction. Instead, students should internalize the process through demonstration and actual use, applying it as they need it in actual text learning. Ultimately, the goal of CD instruction is to have students own the strategy of defining unknown words in terms of category, property, and example relationships. (For a more detailed discussion of concept relationships, see Chapter 8.)

Vocabulary-Building Strategies

Showing diverse learners how to construct meaning for unfamiliar words encountered during reading helps them develop strategies needed to monitor comprehension and build on their own vocabularies. Demonstrating how to use

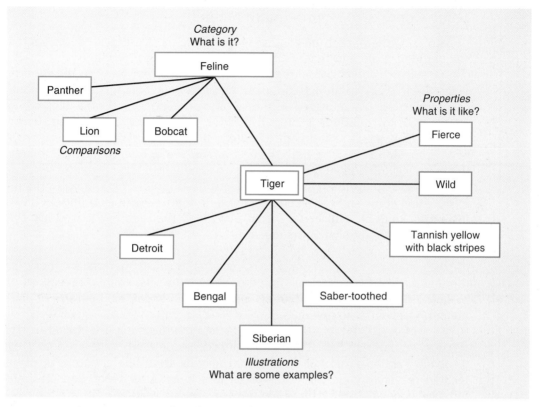

FIGURE 2.4   **A CD Map for the Word** *Tiger*

context, word structure, and the *dictionary* provides students with several basic strategies for vocabulary learning that will last a lifetime. With these strategies, students can search for information clues while reading so that they can approximate the meanings of unknown words. These clues often reveal enough meaning to allow readers who struggle with text to continue reading without "short-circuiting" the process and giving up because the text does not make sense.

You can scaffold the use of vocabulary-building strategies before assigning material to be read. If one or more words represent key concepts—and the words lend themselves to demonstration—you can model the inquiry process necessary to construct meaning. The demonstration is brief, often lasting no more than five minutes. There are three types of demonstrations that will make students aware of vocabulary-building strategies. The first is to model how to make sense of a word in the context of its use, the second involves an analysis of a word's structure, and the third combines context and word structure. Usually these demonstrations require the use of visuals such as an overhead transparency or a chalkboard. After the brief demonstration, guide students to practice and apply the strategy that you just modeled so that they can become proficient in its use.

Using Context to Approximate Meaning

Constructing meaning from context is one of the most useful strategies at the command of proficient readers. Showing readers who struggle how to make use of context builds confidence and competence and teaches the inquiry process necessary to unlock the meaning of troublesome technical and general vocabulary encountered during reading. Using context involves using information surrounding a difficult word to help reveal its meaning. Every reader makes some use of context automatically. Strategy instruction, however, is needed in cases where the text provides a *deliberate context* to help the reader with concept terms that are especially difficult. Often the text author will anticipate that certain words will be troublesome and will provide information clues and contextual aids to help readers with meaning. In these instances, students will benefit from a strategy that allows them to use the deliberate context to construct meaning.

Even though textbook authors may consciously or unconsciously use deliberate contexts for unknown words, constraints in the material itself and/or the reader's own background limit the degree to which context reveals word meaning. The teacher and students must know how context operates to limit meaning as well as to reveal it.

Deighton (1970) identified several factors that limit the use of context: (1) What a context may reveal to a particular reader depends on the reader's experience, (2) the portion of context that reveals an unfamiliar word must be located reasonably close to the word if it is to act effectively, and (3) there must be some clear-cut connection between the unfamiliar term and the context that clarifies it.

The use of context, as you have probably concluded, is mostly a matter of inference. Inference requires readers to see an explicit or implicit relationship between the unfamiliar word and its context or to connect what they know already with the unknown term. It can't be assumed that students will perceive these relationships or make the connections on their own. Most students who struggle with text just don't know how to use a deliberate context provided by an author.

Three kinds of information in particular are useful to struggling readers: *typographic, syntactic,* and *semantic* clues.

TYPOGRAPHIC CLUES   Typographic or format clues make use of footnotes, italics, boldfaced print, parenthetical definitions, pictures, graphs, charts, and the like. A typographic clue provides a clear-cut connection and a direct reference to an unknown word. Many students tend to gloss over a typographic aid instead of using it to spotlight the meaning of a difficult term. The teacher can rivet attention to these aids with minimal expenditure of class time.

For example, consider the way a science teacher modeled a strategy for revealing the meaning of the word *enzymes,* which was presented in boldfaced type in the text. Before assigning a text section titled "Osmosis in Living Cells," the teacher asked students to turn to page 241. Then he asked, "Which word in the section on osmosis stands out among the others?" The students quickly spotted the word *enzymes*. "Why do you think this word is highlighted in boldfaced type?" he asked. A student replied, "I guess it must be important." Another student said, "Maybe because it has something to do with osmosis—whatever that is." The teacher nodded approvingly and then asked the class to see if they could figure out what *enzymes* meant by reading this sentence: "Chemical substances called **enzymes** are produced by cells to break down large starch molecules into small sugar molecules."

The science teacher continued the demonstration by asking two questions: "What are enzymes?" and "What do they do?" The students responded easily. The teacher concluded the walk-through with these words: "Words that are put in large letters or boldfaced print are important. If you pay attention to them as we just did, you will have little trouble figuring out what they mean. There are four other words in boldfaced type in your reading assignment. Look for them as you read and try to figure out what they mean."

SYNTACTIC AND SEMANTIC CLUES   Syntactic and semantic clues in content materials should not be treated separately. The grammatical relationships among words in a sentence or the structural arrangement among sentences in a passage often helps clarify the meaning of a particular word.

Syntactic and semantic clues are much more subtle than typographic clues. Table 2.1 presents a summary of the most frequently encountered syntactic and semantic clues.

The chalkboard or an overhead transparency is valuable for helping students visualize the inquiry process necessary to reveal meaning. For example, if a *definition clue* is used, as in this example from Table 2.1: "Entomology is the study of insects, and biologists who specialize in this field are called entomologists"—it may be appropriate first to write the sentence on the board. During the modeling discussion, you can then show how *is* and *are called* provide information clues that will reveal meaning for *entomology* and *entomologists.* A simply strategy would be to cross out *is* and *are called* in the sentence and replace them with equal signs (=):

> Entomology ~~is~~= the study of insects, and biologists who specialize in this field ~~are called~~= entomologists.

A brief discussion will reinforce the function of the verb forms *is* and *are called* in the sentence.

The definition clue is the least subtle of the syntactic and semantic clues. However, all the clues in Table 2.1 require students to make inferential leaps. Consider one of the examples from the mood and tone clue: "The tormented animal screeched with horror and writhed in pain as it tried desperately to escape from the hunter's trap." Suppose this sentence came from a

TABLE 2.1

Syntactic and Semantic Contextual Clues

Type of Clue	Explanation	Examples[a]
1. Definition	The author equates the unknown word to the known . or more familiar, usually using a form of the verb *be*.	*Entomology* **is** the study of insects, and biologists who specialize in this field **are called** *entomologists.* A *critical review* **is** an attempt to evaluate the worth of a piece of writing.
2. Linked synonyms	The author pairs the unknown word with familiar synonyms or closely related words in a series.	Kunte Kinte was the victim of **cruel, evil,** *malevolent,* and **brutal** slave traders. The congressman from Connecticut possessed the traits of an honest and just leader: **wisdom, judgment,** *sagacity.*
3. Direct description: examples, modifiers, restatements	The author reveals the meaning of an unknown word by providing additional information in the form of appositives, phrases, clauses, or sentences.	*Example clue:* Undigested material **such as fruit skins, outer parts of grain, and the stringlike parts of some vegetables** forms *roughage.* *Modifier clues: Pictographic writing,* **which was the actual drawing of animals, people, and events,** is the forerunner of written language. *Algae,* **nonvascular plants that are as abundant in water as grasses are on land,** have often been called "grasses of many waters." *Restatement clue:* A billion dollars a year is spent on *health quackery.* **In other words, each year in the United States, millions of dollars are spent on worthless treatments and useless gadgets to "cure" various illnesses.**

TABLE 2.1 (CONTINUED)
Syntactic and Semantic Contextual Clues

Type of Clue	Explanation	Examples[a]
4. Contrast	The author reveals the meaning of an unknown word by contrasting it with an antonym or a phrase that is opposite in meaning.	You have probably seen animals perform tricks at the zoo, on television, or in a circus. Maybe you taught a dog to fetch a newspaper. **But learning tricks—usually for a reward—is very different from** *cognitive problem solving.* It wasn't a *Conestoga* like Pa's folks came in. **Instead, it was just an old farm wagon drawn by one tired horse.**
5. Cause and effect	The author establishes a cause-and-effect relationship in which the meaning of an unknown word can be hypothesized.	The *domestication* of animals probably began when young animals were caught or strayed into camps. **As a result, people enjoyed staying with them and made pets of them.** A family is *egalitarian* **when both husband and wife make decisions together and share responsibilities equally.**
6. Mood and tone	The author sets a mood (ironic, satirical, serious, funny, etc.) in which the meaning of an unknown word can be hypothesized.	A sense of *resignation* engulfed my thoughts as **the feeling of cold grayness was everywhere around me.** The *tormented* animal **screeched with horror and writhed in pain as it tried desperately to escape** from the hunter's trap.

[a] Italics denote the unknown word. Boldfaced type represents information clues that trigger context revelation.

short story about to be assigned in an English class. Assume also that many of the students would have trouble with the word *tormented* as it is used in the sentence. If students are to make the connection between *tormented* and the mood created by the information clues, the teacher will have to ask several effective clarifying questions.

The demonstration begins with the teacher writing the word *tormented* on the board. She asks, "You may have heard or read this word before, but how many of you think that you know what it means?" Student definitions are put on the board. The teacher then writes the sentence on the board. "Which of the definitions on the board do you think best fits the word *tormented* when it's used in this sentence?" She encourages students to support their choices. If none fits, she will ask for more definitions now that students have seen the sentence. She continues questioning, "Are there any other words or phrases in the sentence that help us get a feel for the meaning of *tormented*? Which ones?"

The inquiry into the meaning of *tormented* continues in this fashion. The information clues (*screeched with horror, writhed in pain, desperately*) that establish the mood are underlined and discussed. The teacher concludes the modeling activity by writing five new words on the board and explaining, "These words are also in the story that you are about to read. As you come across them, stop and think. How do the words or phrases or sentences surrounding each word create a certain feeling or mood that will allow you to understand what each one means?"

When modeling the use of context in Table 2.1, it's important for students to discover the information clues. It's also important for the teacher to relate the demonstration to several additional words to be encountered in the assignment. Instruction of this type will have a significant cumulative effect. If students are shown how to use contextual clues for two or three words each week, over the course of an academic year they will have 80 to 120 applications in the process.

Word Structure

A word itself provides information clues about its meaning. The smallest unit of meaning in a word is called a *morpheme.* Analyzing a word's structure, *morphemic analysis,* is a second vocabulary-building strategy that students can use to predict meaning. When readers encounter an unknown word, they can reduce the number of feasible guesses about its meaning considerably by approaching the whole word and identifying its parts. When students use morphemic analysis in combination with context, they have a powerful strategy at their command.

Student readers often find long words daunting. Olsen and Ames (1972) put long or polysyllabic words into four categories:

1. Compound words made up of two known words joined together. Examples: *commonwealth, matchmaker.*

2. Words containing a recognizable stem to which an affix (a prefix, combining form, or suffix) has been added. Examples: *surmountable, deoxygenize, unsystematic, microscope.*

3. Words that can be analyzed into familiar and regular pronounceable units. Examples: *undulate, calcify, subterfuge, strangulate.*

4. Words that contain irregular pronounceable units so that there is no sure pronunciation unless one consults a dictionary. Examples: *louver, indictment.*

Content vocabulary terms from categories 1 and 2 (compound words and recognizable stems and affixes) are the best candidates for instruction. You can readily demonstrate techniques for predicting the meanings of these words, because each of their isolated parts will always represent a meaning unit.

In some instances, a word from category 3 may also be selected for emphasis. However, there is no guarantee that students will bring prior knowledge and experience to words that comprise the third category. Long phonemically regular words lend themselves to syllabication. Syllabication involves breaking words into pronounceable sound units or syllables. The word *undulate,* for example, can be syllabicated (un-du-late). However, the syllable *un* is not a meaning-bearing prefix.

Many words from category 3 are derived from Latin or Greek. Students who struggle with texts will find these words especially difficult to analyze for meaning because of their lack of familiarity with Latin or Greek roots. Occasionally a word such as *strangulate* (derived from the Latin *strangulatus*) can be taught because students may recognize the familiar word *strangle*. They might then be shown how to link *strangle* to the verb suffix *-ate* (which means "to cause to become") to hypothesize a meaning for *strangulate*. Unfortunately, the verb suffix *-ate* has multiple meanings, and the teacher should be quick to point this out to students. This procedure is shaky, but it has some payoff.

Words from category 2 warrant instruction, as English root words are more recognizable, obviously, than Latin or Greek ones. Whenever feasible, teach the principles of structural word analysis using terms that have English roots. Certain affixes are more helpful than others, and knowing which affixes to emphasize during instruction will minimize students' confusion.

The most helpful affixes are the combining forms, prefixes, or suffixes that have single, invariant meanings. Deighton's (1970) monumental study of word structure has helped identify affixes that have single meanings. (See Appendix A for a summary of Deighton's findings.)

Many other commonly used prefixes have more than one meaning or have several shades of meaning. Because of their widespread use in content terminology, you should also consider these variant-meaning prefixes for functional teaching. (See Appendix B for a list of prefixes with varying meanings.)

The tables of affixes are resources for you. Don't be misled into thinking that students should learn long lists of affixes in isolation to help in analyzing word structure. This approach is neither practical nor functional. We recommend instead that students be taught affixes as they are needed to analyze the structure of terms that will appear in a reading assignment.

For example, an English teacher modeled how to analyze the meaning of *pandemonium* before students were to enounter the term in an assignment from *One Flew over the Cuckoo's Nest*. She wrote the word on the board—pan*demon*ium—underlining the English base word *demon* and asking students for several synonyms for the word. Student responses included *witch, devil, monster,* and *wicked people.*

Then she explained that *-ium* was a noun suffix meaning "a place of." "Now let's take a look at *pan.* Sheila, have you ever heard of Pan American Airlines? If you were a Pan Am passenger, name several places that you might visit." Sheila and several other students answered the question as best they could. The teacher then explained that Pan American originally specialized in flights to all places in the Americas. Further discussion centered around the word *panoramic.* Through this process, relating the known to the unknown, students decided that *pan* meant "all."

"Now, back to *pandemonium.* 'A place of all the demons.' What would this place be like?" Students were quick to respond. The demonstration was completed with two additional points. The teacher asked the class to find the place in *One Flew over the Cuckoo's Nest* where *pandemonium* was used and read the paragraph. Then she asked them to refine their predictions of the meaning of *pandemonium.* Next the teacher discussed the origin of the word—which the English poet John Milton coined in his epic poem *Paradise Lost.* Pandemonium was the capital of hell, the place where all the demons and devils congregated—figuratively speaking, where "all hell broke loose."

Using the Dictionary as a Strategic Resource

The use of context and word structure are strategies that give struggling readers insight into the meanings of unknown words. Rarely does context or word structure help learners derive precise definitions for key words. Instead, these vocabulary-building strategies keep readers on the right track so that they are able to follow a text without bogging down or giving up.

There are times, however, when context and word structure reveal little about a word's meaning. In these instances, or when a precise definition is needed, a dictionary is a logical alternative and a valuable resource for students.

Knowing when to use a dictionary is as important as knowing how to use it. A content teacher should incorporate dictionary usage into ongoing plans but should avoid a very common pitfall in the process of doing so. When asked, "What does this word mean?" the teacher shouldn't automatically reply, "Look it up in the dictionary."

To some students, "Look it up in the dictionary" is another way of saying "Don't bug me" or "I really don't have the time or the inclination to help you." Of course, this may not be the case at all. However, from an instructional perspective, that hard-to-come-by teachable moment is lost whenever we routinely suggest to students to look up a word in the dictionary.

One way to make the dictionary a functional resource is to use it to verify educated guesses about word meaning revealed through context or word structure. For example, if a student asks you for the meaning of a vocabulary term, an effective tactic is to bounce the question right back: "What do you think it means? Let's look at the way it's used. Are there any clues to its meaning?" If students are satisfied with an educated guess because it makes sense, the word need not be looked up. But if students are still unsure of the word's meaning, the dictionary is there.

When students go into a dictionary to verify or to determine a precise definition, more often than not they need supervision to make good decisions. Keep these tips in mind as you work on dictionary usage.

1. Help students determine the "best fit" between a word and its definition. Students must often choose the most appropriate definition from several. This poses a real dilemma for young learners. Your interactions will help them make the best choice of a definition and will provide a behavior model for making such a choice.

2. If you do assign a list of words to look up in a dictionary, choose them selectively: A few words are better than many. The chances are greater that students will learn several key terms thoroughly than that they will develop vague notions about a large number.

3. Help students with the pronunication key in a glossary or dictionary as the need arises. However, this does not mean that you will teach skills associated with the use of a pronunciation key in isolated lessons. Instead, it means guiding and reinforcing students' ability to use a pronunciation key as they study the content of your course.

Vocabulary development is a gradual process, "the result of many encounters with a word towards a more precise grasp of the concept the word represents" (Parry, 1993, p. 127). If this is the case, students who struggle with demanding text material will benefit from vocabulary-building strategies that make use of context clues, word structure, and appropriate uses of reference tools such as the dictionary. Johnson and Steele (1996) found that with ESL learners, the use of *personal word lists* provided excellent strategy practice and application in the use of vocabulary-building strategies.

The use of personal word lists would be of value not only to ESL students but also to all students who need explicit support in the use of vocabulary-building strategies. The personal word list technique emphasizes the need

Word	What I Think It Means	Clues (context or structure)	Dictionary Definition (if needed)
sacred	religious	they were entering a sacred building that loomed out of the night to give them what haven and what blessing they yearned for.	
vexation	displeasure	but something would come up some vexation that was like a fly buzzing around their heads.	
lurch	movement	she took a step toward the porch lurching	a sudden movement forward or sideways

FIGURE 2.5   An ESL Student's Personal Word List

Source: From "So Many Words, So Little Time: Helping College ESL Learners Acquire Vocabulary-Building Strategies." *Journal of Adolescent and Adult Literacy, 39* (5), 351. Copyright © 1996 by the International Reading Association. All rights reserved. Used by permission of the International Reading Association and Denise Johnson.

for students to self-select important concept words and incorporates key principles learned from the VSS strategy discussed earlier in the chapter. Students then complete a personal word list, which may be part of a vocabulary notebook or learning log. The personal word list is divided into four columns as illustrated in Figure 2.5. For each word entry, students list (1) the word, (2) what the word means, (3) the clues used to construct meaning for the word (context, word structure, or a combination of the two), and (4) a dictionary definition, when it is appropriate to consult the dictionary for a definition. Figure 2.5 illustrates an ESL student's personal word list entries (Johnson & Steele 1996).

LOOKING BACK, LOOKING FORWARD

Changes in the racial and ethnic composition of our student population have been dramatic. Not only are classrooms more linguistically and culturally diverse than they were in the 1960s, but they have also changed academically. The linguistic, cultural, and achievement differences of students contribute to the complexities of classroom diversity. Students of diverse backgrounds (who may be distinguished by their ethnicity, social class, language, or achievement level) often struggle in classrooms. They exhibit a learned helplessness characterized by a lack of control over reading strategies, a poor self-image, and an ambivalent attitude toward reading. As a result, diverse learners tend to avoid reading or being held accountable for reading in school. They challenge teachers to look for and experiment with instructional strategies that will actively involve them in the life of the classroom.

Teachers reach diverse learners by scaffolding instruction in ways that support content literacy and learning. Throughout this book, we explore scaffolded instruction designed to help all students learn with texts. In this chapter, we concentrated on three aspects of instructional scaffolding: metacognition, classroom discourse, and collaboration.

Metacognitive classrooms are places where students learn how to learn. We explored how to teach for metacognition so that students will be more aware of, confident in, and competent in their use of learning strategies. Scaffolded instruction includes modeling comprehension and vocabulary strategies and demonstrating their use in text learning. Think-alouds, reciprocal teaching, and question-answer relationships (QARs), vocabulary self-selection (VSS), concept of definition (CD) word maps, and vocabulary-building strategies are several learner-oriented strategies that we emphasized in this chapter.

In the next chapter, we shift our focus from learners to texts. If teachers are going to meet the academic, linguistic, and cultural needs of students, they need to reconsider the role that textbooks play in classroom learning. How do teachers move beyond the use of textbooks to provide students with authentic reading experiences by integrating a variety of trade books and electronic texts into the curriculum? We argue that trade books and electronic texts should be used interchangeably with textbooks to give students an intense and extensive involvement with subject matter.

 **MINDS-ON**

1. Picture a science class of 25 students from very diverse backgrounds—different social classes, different ethnicity, and varying achievement lev-

els. Describe some classroom strategies you might use to respond to individual differences while maintaining high standards of content literacy and learning.

2. According to Au (1993), "By the year 2020 one of two public school students will be from minority backgrounds and . . . the number of children living in poverty will increase by 37 percent." How do you believe this change will influence learning strategies in the classroom?

3. Review the opening section of this chapter, "Organizing Principle." Take turns with members of a small discussion group sharing examples of passages that demonstrated the QAR principles of (a) "right there," (b) "think and search," (c) "on your own," and (d) "author and you." How might these same principles be used with a piece of literature, a scientific explanation, or a work of art?

4. Use your knowledge of root words, suffixes, and prefixes to create five original words. Then write mock "dictionary" entries for each. Next, write a short paragraph incorporating each of the five words in their proper context. Exchange your paragraph with a partner, and see if you can determine the meanings of the original words. Discuss the semantic and structural techniques you have both used. What strategies might be used to teach the meanings of these words to someone else?

HANDS-ON

1. Bring several copies of a favorite poem or short text to class. Following the "think-aloud" guidelines in the chapter, model the checklist for self-evaluation by (a) developing hypotheses by making predictions, (b) developing images, (c) sharing analogies, (d) monitoring comprehension, and (e) regulating comprehension.

2. Using a passage from a content area text, develop one example of each of the four QAR categories: (a) "right there," (b) "think and search," (c) "on your own," and (d) "author and you."

3. For 15 minutes in a small group, discuss the topic "how technology might transform popular sports by the year 2121." After the discussion, reflect on how the unique background of each member of the group contributed to the views expressed. Did any of the following factors influence individual participation—background knowledge of sports or technology, past experience playing sports, individual understanding of sports language or technological applications, or personal definitions of "popular" sports?

What parallels might you draw with classroom lessons in which students bring cultural and linguistic differences to the learning activities?

4. Come to class prepared to share a piece of your personal "fund of knowledge"—knowledge of occupationally related skills or information that your family has passed on—with your small group. For example, you might share a passed-on craft, a skill, a family hobby, or a recipe. How did this sharing "connect" you to the group and the group to your culture?

SUGGESTED READINGS

Allington, R. L., Boxer, N. J., & Broikou, K. H. (1987). Jeremy, remedial reading and subject matter classes. *Journal of Reading, 30,* 643–645.

Au, K. H. (1993). *Literacy instruction in multicultural settings.* Orlando, FL: Harcourt Brace.

Banks, J. A. (1994). *An introduction to multicultural education.* Needham Heights, MA: Allyn & Bacon.

Blachowicz, C. (1991). Vocabulary instruction in content areas for special needs learners: Why and how? *Reading, Writing, and Learning Disabilities, 7,* 297–308.

Brozo, W. G. (1990). Hiding out in secondary content classrooms: Coping strategies of unsuccessful readers. *Journal of Reading, 33,* 324–329.

Brozo, W. G., Valerio, P. C., & Salazar, M. M. (1996). A walk through Gracie's garden: Literacy and cultural expectations in a Mexican American junior high school. *Journal of Adolescent and Adult Literacy, 40* (3), 164–170.

Buikema, J., & Graves, M. (1993). Teaching students to use content clues to infer word meanings. *Journal of Reading, 36,* 450–457.

Champion, T., & Bloome, D. (1995). Introduction to the special issues on Africanized English and education. *Linguistics and Education, 7,* 1–5.

De la Luz Reyes, M., & Molner, L. A. (1991). Instructional strategies for second-language learners in the content areas. *Journal of Reading, 35,* 96–103.

Delpit, L. (1995). *Other people's children: Conflict in the classroom.* New York: The New Press.

Delpit, L. D. (1988). The silenced dialogue: Power and pedagogy in educating other people's children. *Harvard Educational Review, 58,* 280–298.

Ehlinger, J., & Pritchard, R. (1994). Using think alongs in secondary content areas. *Reading Reseach and Instruction, 33,* 187–206.

Ezell, H., Hunsicker, S., Quinque, M., & Randolph, E. (1996). Maintanence and generalization of QAR reading comprehension strategies. *Reading Research and Instruction, 36,* 64–81.

Hiebert, E. H. (Ed.). (1991). *Literacy for a diverse society: Perspectives, practices, policies.* New York: Teachers College Press.

Johnston, P., & Winograd, P. (1990). Passive failure in reading. *Journal of Reading Behavior, 17,* 279–301.

Jimenez, R., Garcia, G., & Pearson, P. D. (1996). The reading strategies of bilingual Latina/o students who are successful English readers: Opportunities and obstacles. *Reading Research Quarterly, 31,* 90–112.

Kang, H-W, & Golden, A. (1994). Vocabulary learning and instruction in a second or foreign language. *International Journal of Applied Linguistics, 4* (1), 57–77.

Ladson-Billings, G. (1994). *The dreamkeepers: Successful teachers of African American students.* San Francisco: Jossey-Bass.

Met, M. (1994). Teaching content through a second language. In F. Genesee (Ed.), *Educating second language children* (pp. 159–182). Cambridge, England: Cambridge University Press.

Peregoy, S. F., & Boyle, O. F W. (1997). *Reading, writing, & learning in ESL: A resource book for K-12 teachers* (2nd ed.). New York: Longman.

Roller, C. M. (1996). *Variability not disability: Struggling readers in a workshop classroom.* Newark, DE: International Reading Association.

Thonis, E. W. (1996). Students acquiring English: Reading and learning. In D. Lapp, J. Flood, & N. Farnan (Eds.), *Content area reading and learning: Instructional strategies* (pp. 123–138). Needham Heights, MA: Allyn and Bacon.

Vacca, R. T., & Padak, N. D. (1990). Who's at risk in reading? *Journal of Reading, 33,* 486–489.

Walker, B. J. (1992). *Supporting struggling readers.* Markham, Ontario: Pippen Publishing.

3

Integrating Electronic Texts and Trade Books into the Curriculum

I'm all in favor of change, but there's been way too much of it lately.
—Ogden Nash

Organizing Principle

The speed at which the world of the classroom is mutating requires teachers to rethink business as usual. Technological changes, brought on by the digital forces of the computer, are transforming the way we communicate and disseminate information. Electronic texts, constructed and displayed on a computer screen, are not fixed entities cast in typesetter's print. In the Information Age, legions of new terms and concepts—*hypertext, hypermedia, CD-ROM, World Wide Web, e-mail, electronic chat rooms,* "dot-*com*"—have entered the lexicon of teachers. Highly interactive and engaging electronic texts are becoming an integral part of today's classroom.

Coupled with unprecedented opportunities for literacy learning in electronic environments is another relatively recent phenomenon that is bringing about a radical departure from traditional text experiences in the classroom. A healthy resurgence of print media has resulted in a veritable mother lode of fiction and nonfiction trade books for children and adolescents about every topic imaginable. Trade books, as distinguished from textbooks (which have "captive" audiences in school), are published for distribution to the general public through booksellers. Trade books are informative as well as entertaining. They have a built-in appeal for people of all ages. Trade books have the potential to provide students with intense involvement in a subject and the power to develop in-depth understanding in ways not imagined a few years ago.

As teachers, how will we integrate the print and electronic resources that are quickly working their way into the curriculum? How will our roles and interactions with students change as the nature and kinds of text change in our classrooms? Should textbooks be abandoned? Certainly not. Our point in this chapter, rather, is to underscore the value of integrating print and multimedia environments into the curriculum: **Trade books and electronic texts extend and enrich the curriculum.**

Chapter Overview

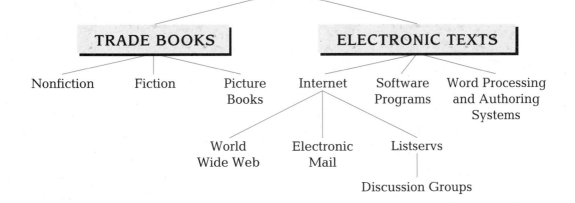

1. Why use trade books to learn subject matter?

2. Why use electronic texts?

3. What kinds of trade books can teachers use in their classrooms?

4. What kinds of electronic texts can be integrated into the curriculum?

5. How do the roles of teachers change when they make trade books and electronic texts an integral part of subject matter learning?

Textbooks are not without their problems. Not only has the quality of textbooks come under criticism but also the manner in which teachers use them to drive instruction. A predominant practice in content area teaching involves the use of one type of text—*the* textbook, often at the exclusion of other types of texts. In conventional classrooms, reading assignments come almost exclusively from textbooks, the students' primary source of information. Because of their comprehensive and encyclopedic nature, most textbooks do not treat subject matter with the breadth and depth necessary to fully develop ideas and concepts. The very nature of textbooks often restricts their use in content area classrooms.

When eleventh- and twelfth-grade students in physics classes were queried about the use of their textbook, one student in the course said flatly, "I don't mess with the textbook. It's confusing." Another responded, "I should be telling you that the text is the best way to learn information. I would tell you that [for] all of my other classes. I learn by reading, and I read a lot. [But] I just can't understand this textbook. It's way above my head." These revealing comments came from interviews that were part of a study on the use of texts in science classes (Hynd, Guzzetti, & Lay 1994). The researchers, who interviewed a mix of students in general and college-prep science classes, were struck by the similarities in the students' comments, despite assumed differences in their ability, motivation, and background. Various student comments revealed insightful perspectives, including the belief that textbooks assume too much student knowledge, textbooks need fuller explanations and more relevant examples, and textbooks should be better organized.

Textbooks provide extensive, not intensive, treatment of subject matter. No wonder students voice a concern about textbooks assuming that they know too much. Textbook authors cast a wide net in an effort to be comprehensive. As a result, they often make erroneous assumptions about what students already know in relation to the content under development. Rather than building a rich context and background for understanding difficult concepts, textbooks err on the side of providing the minimum essentials necessary for understanding before moving on to another subject. This process of distilling content to its minimal essentials, is undoubtedly associated with the second perspective voiced by students, that textbooks often do not supply full explanations.

A case in point is the Houghton Mifflin textbook *History of the United States,* which tells America's story in two volumes. The first volume is more than 700 pages long; the second is over 800 pages in length. The design of the two volumes, like many of the content area textbooks developed in the 1990s, is attractive and includes many eye-catching and instructionally helpful features throughout each chapter: black-and-white and color photos, an array of colorful visual aids (maps, tables, graphs, cartoons), and a variety of instructional aids (key terms, questions, objectives, and a capsule main idea statement for each chapter section). All of these design features serve several purposes: to support students' reading, to make learning more visual and appealing, and to break up written text into manageable chunks of writing that won't overwhelm students who may not have developed patience or persistence with long stretches of print.

The authors of *History of the United States* write in an appealing manner to capture students' interest and hold their attention. Take, for example, a passage from a subsection of text describing the Holocaust (Di Bacco, Mason, & Appy 1992, p. 433):

> People had known all along that the war was taking a terrible toll. Still, the full agony only became apparent when Allied forces entered Nazi territory and liberated dozens of concentration camps. Soldiers could not believe their eyes. They found prisoners so emaciated that they resembled living corpses. They found gas chambers, crematoriums (ovens in which bodies were burned), and thousands of corpses stacked like cordwood in boxcars and open pits. One soldier recalled:
>
>> The odors, well there is no way to describe the odors. . . . Many of the boys I am talking about now—these were tough soldiers, there were combat men who had been all the way through the invasion—were ill and vomiting, throwing up, just at the sight of this.

Much to the authors' credit, the passage they write is graphic in its description and creates a sense of horror for the atrocities that they describe. Yet despite the magnitude of the Holocaust as a historical event and its profound human and moral implications, the authors limit their coverage of the Holocaust to eight brief paragraphs as part of a comprehensive chapter on World War II. Eight paragraphs! Even though coverage of the Holocaust is cursory at best, the authors accomplish their purpose for the chapter: to chronicle events and people and to describe the major political, economic, and social forces underlying World War II.

The Holocaust coverage in *History of the United States,* we contend, illustrates the major problem with textbooks in general. They aren't designed to provide in-depth coverage. A textbook conveys a body of knowledge and is, by its very nature, comprehensive and encyclopedic. No wonder textbooks are often described as being "a mile wide and an inch deep."

In most classrooms, textbooks are more the rule than the exception. Estimates suggest that 75 to 90 percent of classrooms in the United States use textbooks almost exclusively (Palmer & Stewart 1997). The textbook has come to symbolize a shallow and superficial curriculum. Problems arise, however, when the textbook *becomes* the curriculum. In these instances, curriculum decisions often revolve around content coverage.

Time constraints in a textbook-driven curriculum are real. Teachers feel enormous pressure to cover x amount of content in x amount of time before students move on to the next chapter or unit of study. Return to the Holocaust example. If pressed for time to cover World War II in three or four weeks, an American history teacher's concern is likely to be "How can I cover World War II in the time allotted?" rather than "How do I involve students intellectually and emotionally in the people, places, events, issues, ideas, and consequences associated with World War II?" Teachers who operate under time constraints often view textbooks as efficient informational resources that support what students are studying in a particular subject at a particular time. Textbook-driven instruction relies on lecturing and other means of information-giving when content coverage is the primary purpose. The downside, from a content literacy perspective, is this: When reading merely chronicles events, students dismiss the power of text to inform and to transform their lives.

Increasing numbers of teachers are using a variety of print and nonprint media as resources for learning across the curriculum. Trade books and electronic texts are authentic alternatives to textbooks. So are magazines, newspapers, films, and any number of other print and nonprint learning tools. Unlike textbooks, which publishers distribute almost exclusively for use in schools, trade books, technology, and primary documents are preferred learning resources *outside* of school (Palmer & Stewart 1997). Trade books and electronic texts are more likely to be intrinsically motivating than textbooks. Students who absolutely refuse to read anything in schoolbooks are likely to read a book of choice, visit a Web site, or interact with multimedia on a CD-ROM. Surfing the net or curling up in a chair with a good book attracts students to the genuine uses of texts—to inform, to entertain, to solve problems, to explore—and helps them make meaningful connections to reading, writing, and discussion.

LEARNING WITH TRADE BOOKS

Trade books, rich in narrative and informational content, allow learners to interact with people, places, and ideas. Learning with trade books involves exposure to many different genres, all of which are potential sources of information for the active learner. A nonfiction or fiction trade book has the potential to be a magnifying glass that enlarges and enhances the reader's personal interaction with a subject. When teachers use textbooks and trade books in tandem, they help learners think critically about content.

Why Use Trade Books to Learn Subject Matter?

Milton Meltzer (1994) provides a writer's perspective on what it means to think critically with a text. Meltzer, a distinguished historian and biographer for young people and adults, has this to say about writing and reading history:

> My own work is confined to nonfiction, to what is commonly called "information" books. A limiting phrase, unless you ask, information about what? The young reader needs to be informed not only about how houses are built, how trucks run, how flowers grow, how birds fly, how weather is formed, how physical handicaps are overcome, but about how character is shaped and how the world works. The disasters of nature—hurricanes, floods, droughts—are worthy of attention, but so are the disasters of human society. I mean Vietnam. I mean the Holocaust. I mean poverty. Disasters created by human beings, disasters suffered by human victims. All children will encounter fundamental problems of race and class and tyranny in their lifetime. To create awareness of such issues early on is a fitting responsibility for us writers. (p. 19)

Meltzer, who has written more than 85 books, believes that writing history for children and adolescents is worthwhile if it makes them more responsive readers: If the writing, as Meltzer puts it, makes readers "more aware, deepens their feelings, broadens their experiences, enlarges their understandings—and perhaps even moves them to action" (p. 23).

Students learn at a very early age to approach textbook reading with a mind-set to find the "right" answers to questions that accompany the reading assignment. This mind-set is compounded as students move through the grades. As a result, they become less capable at reading literary and informative texts at high levels of literacy. National surveys of reading support claims that the majority of America's children and adolescents are capable of reading at a basic level of performance—reading for details, identifying main ideas, recognizing relationships among ideas. However, they have difficulty responding to texts at high levels of literacy. Results of the 1992 National Assessment of Educational Progress (NAEP) report on reading show that fewer than 5 percent of students surveyed in grades 4, 8, and 12 were able to read at an advanced level. Advanced levels of reading require students to extend, elaborate, and examine the meaning of literary and informative texts.

Trade books are likely to elicit more meaningful and thoughtful responses to literary and informative texts as students break away from the mind-set of finding answers to questions in textbook-only instruction. Reader involvement in a story, identification with characters, the potential to examine a topic in depth or explore a wide range of topics through multiple texts— all contribute to extending students' reading experiences.

McGowan & Guzzetti (1991) identify four compelling reasons to use trade books across the curriculum:

◆ *Variety*—a wide range of books consistent with student ability and interest levels

◆ *Interest*—informative, entertaining, and engaging formats and writing styles

◆ *Relevance*—connections made to students' life experience and prior knowledge

◆ *Comprehensibility*—a focus on the development of concepts and relationships among concepts

Variety

In instructional situations where teachers plan on using trade books to explore and examine a theme or topic, variety becomes an important consideration. There are numerous trade books for teachers and students to choose from dealing with important themes and topics in all content areas. Because of the wide range of books available to students, it is possible, with some advance planning and preparation, to guide students into books that will close the gap between students' reading levels and the levels of difficulty of the books. Reviews and recommendations of trade books often include appropriate age and reading levels, guidelines that may help teachers help students make good choices.

Also, exposing learners to a variety of trade books, especially nonfiction, gives them much needed practice reading informational texts (Cullinan 1993). Students need extended practice reading nonfiction texts to become proficient in the genre. The reality is that many students do not know how to read to learn with informational texts because their school experiences have been limited to textbook-only reading. For some students, the only historical, mathematics, or science materials they will ever read in a lifetime are in textbooks!

Interest and Relevance

Trade book writers are conscious not only of providing information but of entertaining readers as well—and that makes all the difference between a book and a textbook chapter on the same topic. The combination of storytelling and informing is an ancient concept that can be traced to the beginnings of the oral tradition, when storytellers were the newscasters, entertainers, and teachers who kept society intact and growing. The ancient storyteller knew that "if lore can be encoded into stories, it can be made more memorable than by any other technique" (Egan 1989, p. 282). A student can learn the dates and the names of important battles for a test covering World War II, but it takes reading books such as Aranka Siegal's *Upon the Head of the Goat: A Childhood in Hungary, 1939–1944* (1983) to begin to understand the real stories of that time period.

Certain trade books relate to students' personal needs and interests because the books are written from the viewpoint of children and adolescents. Editors categorize trade books as children's or young adults' by criteria such as the type of book (e.g., picture book, concept book, or novel), the age of the protagonist(s), and the perceived interest level of the story. Trade book selection for different age groups is often arbitrary and based on subjective criteria. But one thing is sure: People of all ages tend to be attracted to books that speak to them in some kind of personal way.

The primary motivation for including trade books in any classroom should be to capture students' attention and thus engage them in learning. Teachers in the sciences are finding that students learn better when they are actively engaged in the topic through trade books and actual experiences with scientific and mathematical concepts (Daisey 1994b).

At the beginning of a science lesson, an excerpt from a book read aloud to the class or a picture book can serve as an enjoyable preview of the lesson's contents. Trade books thus play a supporting role by introducing a part of or a perspective on the lesson that may entice students to want to know more. The verbal imagery of a text and the visual stimuli of picture books appeal to all age groups and help activate schemata that are crucial to further learning. For example, an excellent introduction to a study of the building instincts of animals and birds would be Kitchen's *And So They Build* (1993). Students might look at the detailed drawings before starting the unit and predict how each type of shelter is constructed. They might speculate on comparisons of the animals' and birds' building strategies to those of people. In addition, the teacher might read several of the examples in the book to the class and conduct a discussion of how they will be used in the forthcoming unit.

In science classes, popular books, or portions of them, may also be used in a preview to stimulate prediction and thinking about a topic. For example, the preface to Watson's *Double Helix* (1968) tells how scientists actually work. If students are familiar with the traditional scientific method, an initial reading of this book's introductory pages will inspire speculations about how the method can go awry. When the concept of objectivity (or the lack of it) in all human endeavors is discussed, students will gain valuable insight into both the *science* and the *art* of discovery and problem solving (Daisey 1996).

When students are given opportunities to interact with quality trade books, a number of things happen. Perhaps the most important is that they have a better chance of becoming lifelong learners. Textbooks alone cannot motivate students to continue their learning, particularly in the case of reluctant or academically diverse readers, who are often frustrated and defeated by textbooks in the first place. Trying to comprehend unfamiliar, difficult material in textbooks hinders some readers to the point that they quit trying altogether. Students need to be able to read trade books that capture their imagination and that appeal to their affective and cognitive needs.

Comprehensibility

Trade books help readers make sense and develop concepts in ways that are not possible with textbooks. Historical trade books, for example, help readers acquire a *framework for remembering and understanding* historical content. The same holds for content in science and in other subject areas. As Dole and Johnson (1981) indicate, popular science books—fact or fiction—provide background knowledge for science concepts covered in class and help students relate these concepts to their everyday lives.

Stories go beyond facts to get to the heart of a matter. They consider the human side of things by focusing on people and how they react to an infinite number of ideas and experiences in this world. Stories personalize ideas for readers by allowing them to experience a situation vicariously—that is, to share the thoughts of another person. People of all ages encounter aspects of human dilemmas in trade books that are not usually covered by a textbook. Readers who are invited to participate in a tale of a chimney sweep in the nineteenth century are likely to find themselves experiencing the information, instead of merely memorizing it for a test.

This is not to say that textbooks are useless. Students need diversity in the material they read so that they can compare information and make informed judgments. Though textbooks give students a broad base of information, such books cannot convey what lies below the surface. When topics are given only minimal exposure, a great deal of information is left out—information that is crucial to real learning. Levstik (1990), for example, describes young learners who were willing to delve into historical novels and other literature to find answers to questions they raised after reading their textbooks. These students expressed their interest in historical topics in terms of "needing to know" about a topic and of wanting to learn "the truth" or "what really happened." The logical source of answers to their questions and concerns was a good book.

Trade books in the content area classroom provide a variety of perspectives from which students can examine a topic. By comparing expository and narrative texts on a subject, students learn to read more critically. In other words, *reading strengthens the reading process.* Reading about a topic can dramatically improve the comprehension of related reading on the same topic. Crafton (1983) found that this was indeed the case when high school students read two different texts on the same subject. Not only did comprehension of the second text improve, but the students also read more actively. Reading experiences allow readers to construct background knowledge that they can use to comprehend other kinds of related texts.

Trade books are available to serve the needs of every student in every academic discipline. Box 3.1 provides a list of references to help teachers in selecting good books for their classrooms.

Trade Books in the Classroom: An Array of Possibilities

When students have opportunities to learn with trade books, they are in a position to explore and interact with many kinds of texts, both fiction and nonfiction.

Learning with Nonfiction Books

Informational books have blossomed in recent years to attain the level of art. It is evident in recent historical writing, for example, that really good histori-cal writers do not invent the past; instead, they give it artistic shape to con-nect with the reader (Meltzer 1988). No longer is nonfiction strictly objective in tone and literal in content; it often contains elements of fiction that flesh out the details and provide a component of entertainment in what Donelson and Nilsen (1997) call "the new journalism." This is the kind of meaty mater-ial that students can sink their teeth into and become involved in while learn-ing something about the content area, too.

The range of nonfiction books is enormous, spanning all types of topics and book designs. There are biographies and autobiographies about all sorts of people, including rock stars, writers (*Louisa May: The World and Works of Louisa May Alcott*, 1991; *Sorrow's Kitchen: The Life and Folklore of Zora Neale Hurston*, 1990), scientists (*Carl Sagan: Superstar Scientist*, 1987), or classical music composers (*Mozart Tonight*, 1991). Many of these are found in series that focus on thematic concepts or in collections that offer shorter pieces with fewer details. There are books about careers, about drugs and al-cohol (*On the Mend*, 1991) about AIDS (*Fighting Back*, 1991) and other health issues, and about manners. There are even collections of essays writ-ten with young readers in mind, such as *Busted Lives: Dialogues with Kids in Jail* (1982), by Ann Zane Shanks, which offers first-person perspectives of prison life.

Perhaps the greatest difficulty teachers face when selecting nonfiction books for the classroom is deciding which to choose from the large number available. An important thing to keep in mind is that variety is truly the spice of life where reading and learning are concerned. No one book will satisfy all readers. The point of using nonfiction trade books in the classroom is to ex-pose students to more than one point of view and in a form that is at once in-formational and readable. While a great number of nonfiction books sound like textbooks packaged in pretty covers, teachers can choose quality books that adhere to the qualifications suggested in Table 3.1.

Learning with Fiction Books

Fiction entices readers to interact with texts from a number of perspectives that are impossible to achieve in nonfiction alone. Fantasy and traditional works (e.g., folktales and myths) and historical and realistic fiction, for exam-ple, help readers step outside their everyday world for a while to consider a

Box 3.1

Trade Book Selection Guide for Children and Adolescents

The Alan Review (Assembly on Literature for Adolescents, National Council of Teachers of English). Published three times a year; articles and "Clip and File" reviews. Urbana, IL: National Council of Teachers of English.

Appraisal: Children's Science Books for Young People. Published quarterly by Children's Science Book Review Committee. Reviews written by children's librarians and subject specialists.

Association for Library Service to Children. (1995). *The Newbery & Caldecott Awards: A guide to the medal and honor books.* Chicago: American Library Association. Provides short annotations for the winners and runners-up of ALA-sponsored awards.

Book Links: Connecting Books, Libraries, and Classrooms. Published six times a year by the American Library Association to help teachers integrate literature into the curriculum; bibliographies in different genres and subjects; suggestions for innovative use in the classroom.

Booklist. Published twice monthly by the American Library Association. Reviews of children's trade books and nonprint materials (video, audio, and computer software). Approximate grade levels are given; separate listing for nonfiction books.

Books for the Teen Age. Published annually by the Office of Young Adult Services, New York Public Library. Recommendations from young adult librarians in the various branches of the New York Public Library.

Bulletin of the Center for Children's Books. Published monthly by the University of Chicago Press; detailed reviews and possible curriculum uses are noted.

Children's books: Awards and prizes. New York: Children's Book Council. Award-winning titles as well as state "Children's Choice" awards for exemplary trade books.

Christenbury, L. (Ed.). (1995). *Books for you: A booklist for senior high students* (11th ed.). Urbana, IL: National Council of Teachers of English. Provides annotations for both fiction and nonfiction written for students, organized into 50 categories.

Friedberg, J. B. (1992). *Portraying persons with disabilities: An annotated bibliography of non-fiction for children and teenagers* (2nd ed.). New Providence, NJ: Bowker. Provides comprehensive listings of nonfiction dealing with physical, mental, and emotional disabilities.

Gillespie, J. T. (1991). *Best books for junior high readers.* New Providence, NJ: Bowker. Lists more than 6000 books for young adolescents; fiction is listed by genre, nonfiction by subject.

Helbig, A., & Perkins, A. R. (1994). *This land is your land: A guide to multicultural literature for children and young adults.* Westport, CT: Greenwood Press. Provides an extensive listing of titles featuring African Americans, Asian Americans, Hispanic Americans, and Native Americans.

The Horn Book Magazine. Published six times a year by Horn Book, Inc.; articles by noted children's authors, illustrators, and critics on aspects of children's literature, including its use in the classroom. Nonfiction books are reviewed in a separate section.

International Reading Association. "Children's Choices," a list of exemplary, "reader-friendly" children's literature, is published every October in *The Reading Teacher.*

Jensen, J. L., & Roser, N. (Eds.). (1993). *Adventuring with books: A booklist for pre-K–grade 6* (9th ed.). Urbana, IL: National Council of Teachers of English. Summaries of nearly 1800 books published between 1988 and 1992, Books arranged by genre and topics within content areas.

Montenegro, V. J., O'Connell, S. M., & Wolff, K. (Eds.). (1986). *AAA's science book list, 1978–1986.* Reviews science and math books for middle and high school students. Books reviewed by experts.

Montenegro, V. J., O'Connell, S. M., & Wolff, K. (Eds.). (1988). *The best science books and materials for children.* Washington, DC: American Association for the Advancement of Science. Reviews more than 800 science and math books, graded K–9. Books reviewed by experts.

Notable children's trade books in the field of social studies. National Council for the Social Studies. Published yearly in the spring issue of *Social Education;* annotates notable fiction and nonfiction books, primarily for children in grades K–8.

Outstanding Science Trade Books for Children. National Science Teachers Association. Published each year in the spring issue of *Science and Children;* contains information consistent with current scientific knowledge, is pleasing in format and illustrations, and is nonsexist, nonracist, and nonviolent.

Rudman, M. K. (1995). *Children's literature* (3rd ed.). New York: Longman. Includes extensive annotated bibliographies of books that promote children's understanding of sensitive issues (e.g., divorce, death, siblings, heritage).

School Library Journal. Published by R. R. Bowker; articles on all aspects of children's literature, including its use in content areas; reviews by school and public librarians.

Totten, H. L., & Brown, R. W. (1995). *Culturally diverse library collections for children.* New York: Neal-Schuman. Includes annotations on Native Americans, Asian Americans, Hispanic Americans, and African Americans.

Walker, E. (Ed.). (1988). *Book bait: Detailed notes on adult books popular with young people* (4th ed.). Chicago: American Library Association. Extensive annotations of 100 books, including plot summaries and discussions of appeal for adolescents.

Williams, H. E. (1991). *Books by African-American authors and illustrators for children and young adults.* Chicago: American Library Association. Provides bibliographical information and annotations of quality literature.

Winkel, L. (Ed.). (1996). *Elementary school library collection: A guide to books and other media.* Williamsport, PA: Bordart Books. Reviews of books and other media in all subject areas for elementary and middle school students. Books rated by interest level and reading level.

TABLE 3.1

Qualifications for Choosing Quality Nonfiction Books

Genre	Essential Qualities	Organization and Scope
Informational books	Gives information and facts; relates facts to concepts; stimulates curiosity; starter," not "stopper"	From simplest to most complex; from known to unknown; from familiar to unfamiliar; from early to later developments; chronological; slight narrative for younger reader
Biography	Gives accurate, verifiable facts and authentic picture of period; subject worthy of attention	Assumes no omniscience; shows individual, not stereotype; does not ignore negative qualities of subject; focuses not only on events, but on nature of person

subject from a different point of view. By doing so, they learn something about what it means to be a human being on this planet of ours.

Ray Bradbury (1989), an acclaimed contemporary author, likens the ability to fantasize to the ability to survive. While fantasy seems an unlikely addition to the required reading list in a content area classroom, consider the possibilities for a moment. Robert C. O'Brien's *Z for Zachariah* (1975) and Louise Lawrence's *Children of the Dust* (1985) contemplate the aftermath of a nuclear holocaust and the fate of the people who are left alive. Can students really know enough about nuclear issues without considering the crises described in these books? Probably not. The facts concerning the effects of nuclear war are too large and too disconnected from our present reality to understand. Only by focusing on the possible experiences of a small group of people can readers begin to take in the ramifications of such an event.

Jane Yolen's fantasy series, which takes place on a planet called Austar IV, has much to offer readers about social conditions of modern life that need to be examined and changed. We can see ourselves more objectively when we consider our lives from the distance of these stories.

Perhaps even more unlikely in a middle or high school curriculum would be the inclusion of traditional or folk literature because of its associations with younger children; however, the protagonists of most folktales are adolescents who have much to say to today's young adults. Robin McKinley's *Beauty* (1978) and Robert Nye's *Beowulf* (1968) continue to teach readers

TABLE 3.1 (CONTINUED)

Qualifications for Choosing Quality Nonfiction Books

Style	Tone	Illustration
Imagery, figurative language,all devices; comparisons extremely useful; flawed if style is monotonous, repetitious, fragmented	Wonder, not mystery; respect; objectivity; occasional humor; fostering scientific attitude of inquiry; flawed by condescension, anthropomorphism, oversimplification, and when facts from opinions	Diagrams and drawings often clearer than photographs
Storytelling permissible for youngest reader; too muchdestroys credibility	Interest; enthusiasm; objectivity; didacticism and preaching to be avoided	Authentic

Source: From *A Critical Handbook of Children's Literature* (5th ed.), by Rebecca J. Lukens. Copyright © 1995 HarperCollins College Publishers. Reprinted by permission.

that strength of character is the crucial ingredient in changing the world. The human dimension of slavery is powerfully told in *The People Could Fly* (1985), by Virginia Hamilton, and true multicultural understanding is enhanced by her compilation of creation myths, *In the Beginning* (1988). Also, John Langstaff's *Climbing Jacob's Ladder* (1991), a compendium of African-American spirituals richly illustrated by Ashley Bryan, offers young people a further understanding of African-American history. A host of folktale collections from around the world is also readily available to add insight to the study of history, social studies, and geography. Folk literature is the "cement" or "mirror" of society (Sutherland & Arbuthnot 1986, p. 163) and thus gives readers an insider's view of a culture's beliefs and attitudes that is not found in the study of population density and manufacturing trends.

Poetry and drama also provide fascinating insight into a myriad of topics. From poetry about the rather mundane world of work in *Saturday's Children in Poems of Work* (1982) to that written about more lofty ideas, as in *Poetry of the First World War* (1988), this genre provides students with personal glimpses into the human experience of everyday life and unanswerable questions. And while the reading of drama takes a special kind of skill, it is possible to handle it well. For example, students can read Athol Fugard's *"Master Harold" . . . and the Boys* (1984) to comprehend more fully and actively the racial tensions of South Africa under apartheid. For teachers who feel uncomfortable with group plays, Murray's *Modern Monologues for*

Young People (1982) provides a forum for single-character sketches that cover a broad range of concepts.

Even cartoons have their place in the classroom, particularly when they are as well written as Art Spiegelman's *Maus: A Survivor's Tale* (1986). In this book, the story of the Holocaust is vividly told with the Nazis depicted as cats and the Jewish people as mice. Rather than detracting from the seriousness of the subject, the cartoon format lends force to the plight of the Nazis' victims.

The variety of fiction books runs the gamut of problem realism, animal realism, sports stories, mysteries, adventure stories, historical fiction, regional realism, and romance books. While many books in each of these categories have formulized plots, stereotypical characters, and overly sentimental themes, a large body of quality literature is also available. Many worthy works are found on the annual *Young Adults' Choices List,* established by research sponsored by the International Reading Association. This list reflects the diversity of young adult literature, including titles dealing with social and political issues, such as drunk driving, women's rights, death, and war.

The host of realistic fiction books available can do much to enhance and clarify the content curriculum. An author's ability to bring lifelike characters into sharp focus against a setting that smacks of real places results in compelling reading.

Learning with Picture Books

Some of the most interesting, but often overlooked, books that can be used at all grade levels are picture books. Piero Ventura's *Venice* (1987), for example, offers a wealth of information that can be gleaned both from the text and from the detailed and whimsical illustrations. This is a book for all ages, as are David Macaulay's scholarly picture books. The practical question becomes, What role do picture books play in middle and high school classrooms?

Picture books aren't just for kids anymore. Advanced technology and high-quality artistry have led to the production of unique and aesthetically pleasing books that appeal to all age groups. These books cover a wide range of subject matter and can be used to enhance any content area. Not only do the books invite students to mull over the illustrations, but they also teach lessons through the integration of pictures and text. Neal and Moore (1991) offer the following principles of using picture books with adolescents:

1. Themes of many picture books have universal value and appeal for all age levels.

2. Some of the best picture books may have been missed when students were younger or may have been published since that time.

3. Many issues demand a maturity level that young children do not possess.

4. The short format of these books facilitates incorporating picture books into lessons.

5. Our visually oriented society has conditioned students to employ pictures as comprehension aids. (pp. 290–291)

Readers construct meaning with a picture book in much the same way that they do from other types of texts, in that the readers' purposes for reading, prior knowledge, attitudes, and conceptual abilities determine in large part what and how the readers comprehend. As a result, the author's intent and the readers' purpose interact to form an interpretation. Picture books produce a variety of meanings because the illustrations enhance the story, clarify and define concepts, and set a tone for the words. (Box 3.2 lists some excellent examples of this genre.)

There are several types of picture books to consider:

♦ *Wordless books:* The illustrations completely carry the story; no text is involved. Example: *Vagabul Escapes* (1983), by J. Marol.

♦ *Picture books with minimal text:* The illustrations continue to carry the story, but a few words are used to enhance the pictures. Example: *Bored—Nothing to Do!* (1978), by Peter Spier.

♦ *Picture storybooks:* More print is involved; pictures and text are interdependent. Example: *The Moonbow of Mr. B. Bones* (1992), by J. Patrick Lewis, illustrated by Dirk Zimmer.

♦ *Books with illustrations:* These books have more words than pictures, but the illustrations remain important to the text. Example: *Kashtanka* (1991), by Anton Chekov, illustrated by Barry Moser.

A number of picture books lend themselves to use in science and math classes. Several of Mitsumasa Anno's books can be used only with older students who have a firm grasp of mathematical concepts. *Anno's Counting House* (1982), *Anno's Math Games II* (1989), and *Topsy-Turvies: Pictures to Stretch the Imagination* (1970) inspire critical analysis of the notion of sets and logical possibilities presented in the detailed illustrations. *Moja Means One: Swahili Counting Book* (1971), by Muriel and Tom Feelings, is an excellent introduction to African traditions and to learning to count in Swahili. And Macaulay's *Pyramid* (1982) is a historically accurate look at the mathematical genius of the ancient Egyptians.

Environmental issues can be explored in books such as Rylant's *When I Was Young in the Mountains* (1982), Lowe's *Walden* (1990), Van Allsburg's *Just a Dream* (1990), and Baker's wordless *Window* (1991). Each of these books provides a thought-provoking story concerning human beings and their relationship to the earth. *The Story of the Seashore* (1990), by Goodall, and *Oceans* (1990), by Simon, offer fascinating scientific information about the sea. Goodall's book is a wordless historical overview, while Simon's book

Box 3.2

Picture Books for Adolescents

Aliki. (1986). *A Medieval Feast*. New York: HarperCollins.

Anno, M. (1970). *Topsy-Turvies: Pictures to Stretch the Imagination*. New York: Weatherhill.

Anno, M. (1982). *Anno's Counting House*. New York: Philomel.

Anno, M. (1989). *Anno's Math Games II*. New York: Philomel.

Ashabranner, B. (1988). *Always to Remember: The Story of the Vietnam Veterans Memorial*. Ill. J. Ashabranner. New York: Putnam.

Baker, J. (1991). *Window*. New York: Greenwillow.

Bang, M. (1991). *Picture This: Perception and Composition*. New York: Bullfinch Press.

Bunting, E. (1994). *Smoky Night*. Orlando, FL: Harcourt Brace.

Chekov, A. (1991). *Kashtanka*. Trans. R. Pevear. Ill. B. Moser. New York: Putnam.

Edwards, M. (1982). *Alef-Bet: A Hebrew Alphabet Book*. New York: Lothrop, Lee & Shepard.

Feelings, M. (1971). *Moja Means One: Swahili Counting Book*. Ill. J. Feelings. New York: Dial.

George, J. C. (1995). *Everglades*. New York: HarperCollins.

Goodall, J. (1979). *The Story of an English Village*. New York: Atheneum.

Goodall, J. (1987). *The Story of a Main Street*. New York: Macmillan.

Goodall, J. (1990). *The Story of the Seashore*. New York: Macmillan.

Grifalconi, A. (1993). *Kinda Blue*. New York: Little, Brown.

Innocenti, R. (1991). *Rose Blanche*. New York: Stewart, Tiboria Chang.

Lewis, J. P. (1992). *The Moonbow of Mr. B. Bones*. New York: Knopf.

Lobel, A. (1981). *On Market Street*. New York: Greenwillow.

Lowe, S. (1990). *Walden*. New York: Philomel.

Macauley, D. (1973). *Cathedral*. Boston: Houghton Mifflin.

is an exquisite collection of photographs and color drawings combined with an informative and poetic text.

For history classes, Macauley's *Castle* (1978) and *Cathedral* (1973) are rich in detail, in both the text and the illustrations. Both books focus on the medieval world, and they nicely complement Aliki's *Medieval Feast* (1986) and Goodall's *Story of a Main Street* (1987) and *Story of an English Village* (1979). Aliki's book follows the preparations of a wealthy landowner's dinner for the king, and Goodall's books give wordless historical overviews from medieval times to the present. All of these books offer a profusion of information that is impossible to find in history textbooks.

Many picture books focus on the events surrounding World War II. Maruki's *Hiroshima No Pika* (1982) is a controversial book about a family's experiences

Macauley, D. (1978). *Castle*. Boston: Houghton Mifflin.

Macauley, D. (1982). *Pyramid*. Boston: Houghton Mifflin.

Macauley, D. (1988). *The Way Things Work*. Boston: Houghton Mifflin.

Mann, E. (1996). *The Brooklyn Bridge*. New York: Mikaya Press.

Marol, J. (1983). *Vagabul Escapes*. Mankato, MN: Creative Education.

Markle, S. (1995). *Outside and Inside Snakes*. New York: Macmillan.

Markle, S. (1995). *Pioneering Ocean Depths*. New York: Atheneum.

Maruki, T. (1982). *Hiroshima No Pika*. New York: Lothrop, Lee & Shepard.

Maruki, T. (1985). *The Relatives Came*. Ill. S. Gammell. New York: Bradbury.

Polacco, P. (1994). *Pink and Say*. New York: Scholastic.

Rylant, C. (1982). *When I Was Young in the Mountains*. New York: Dutton.

Rylant, C. (1984). *Waiting to Waltz: A Childhood*. Ill. S. Gammell. New York: Bradbury.

Schwartz, D. M. (1985). *How Much Is a Million?* New York: Scholastic.

Schwartz, D. M. (1989). *If You Made a Million*. New York: Lothrop, Lee & Shepard.

Seuss, Dr. (1984). *The Butter Battle Book*. New York: Random House.

Simon, R. (1990). *Oceans*. New York: Morrow Junior Books.

Spier, P. (1978). *Bored—Nothing to Do!* New York: Doubleday.

Van Allsburg, C. (1987). *The Z Was Zapped*. Boston: Houghton Mifflin.

Van Allsburg, C. (1990). *Just a Dream*. Boston: Houghton Mifflin.

Volkmer, J. A. (1990). *Song of the Chirimia: A Guatemalan Folktale*. Minneapolis: Carolrhoda.

Wisniewski, D. (1996). *Golem*. New York: Clarion.

when the atomic bombs were dropped on Japan in 1945. Innocenti's *Rose Blanche* (1991) offers a look at a young girl's discovery of a Nazi concentration camp near her home and her attempts to comfort the inmates there until she is killed by a Nazi soldier. In *The Butter Battle Book* (1984), Dr. Seuss explores the illogical nature of war and poses the question, Which country will "push the button" first? Brent and Jennifer Ashabranner's book *Always to Remember: The Story of the Vietnam Veterans Memorial* (1988) reminds readers that we must never forget the men and women who have died fighting for peace.

These picture books and countless others can be integrated into your curricular area. They can be used with older students as interesting schema builders, anticipatory sets to begin lessons, motivators for learning, read-alouds, and springboards into discussion and writing.

LEARNING WITH ELECTRONIC TEXTS

The potential for technology to make a difference in students' literacy and learning was evident in the early 1980s when computers began to play an increasingly more important role in classrooms. However, computer-related technologies a decade or so ago were primitive compared to the powerful technologies that are available today. The Internet as a technology for communication and information retrieval had little or no impact on classroom learning until recently (Mike 1996). In the 1980s, the computer's potential for classroom learning revolved mainly around its uses as a tool for word processing and as a teaching machine for computer-assisted instruction (CAI).

CAI entails the use of instructional software programs to help students to learn. CAI programs in the 1980s included the use of drills, tutorials, games, and simulations. Some computer programs, mainly simulations such as *Oregon Trail* (MECC), were engaging and interactive. But many weren't. Drill and tutorial software, for example, often provided students with dull, uninviting "electronic worksheets" to practice skills and reinforce concepts.

Times have changed, however, with the development of powerful technologies that make learning with electronic texts highly engaging and interactive. CD-ROM (compact disk, read-only memory) disks, for example, permit much larger storage capacity for text, graphics, and sound and offer tremendous retrieval capabilities not possible with floppy disks. Moreover, online learning opportunities on the Internet allow students to communicate with others throughout the world and to access significant and relevant content in ways not imagined just a few short years ago. As Rose and Fernlund (1997) explain:

> We have come a long way since those early years. We talk more about work stations than computers. A contemporary work station might combine a powerful computer with a high resolution color monitor, CD-ROM drive, a high-speed modem, scanner, speech synthesizer, digital camera/recorder, videodisc player, as well as a telecommunications link to on-line services and the Internet. (p. 160)

Today computer-related technologies create complex electronic learning environments. Reading and writing with computers allow students to access and retrieve information, construct their own texts, and interact with others. Computers run on literacy. Reinking (1995) argues that computers are changing the way we communicate and disseminate information, how we approach reading and writing, and how we think about people becoming literate. While electronic texts often enhance learning, Reinking contends that reading and writing with computers have the power to transform the way we teach and learn.

Why Use Electronic Texts?

Some of the reasons for the use of electronic texts across the curriculum parallel those associated with trade books: variety, interest, relevance, and comprehensibility. Highly engaging and interactive computer software programs—many of which provide multimedia learning environments—and the Internet make it possible for students to have access to thousands of interesting and relevant information resources. Not only is there wide access to information, but electronic texts on a relevant topic of study can help students read extensively and think critically about content central to the curriculum. In addition, text that students construct electronically can help them examine ideas, organize and report research findings, and communicate with others. *Word processing* and *authoring software* programs, for example, allow students to develop content and multimedia presentations relevant to curriculum objectives. Moreover, *electronic mail (e-mail)* has the potential to engage students in learning conversations with others within the same community or throughout the world.

We suggest a rationale for integrating electronic texts into the curriculum based on the following concepts as they apply to technology-based learning:

- *Interactivity*—students are capable of manipulating texts, and text is responsive to student's interests, purposes, and needs.

- *Communication*—telecommunication networks enhance electronic text interaction with others throughout the world.

- *Information search and retrieval*—a wide range of information resources and search capabilities enhance student research and information gathering.

- *Multimedia environments*—images, sound, and text are highly engaging and extend students' understanding.

- *Socially mediated learning*—students collaboratively construct meaning as part of literacy learning.

Interactivity

Throughout this book, we use the word *interaction* to refer to the reader's active role in learning with text. Recall from Chapter 1 that active readers engage in meaning-making whenever they interact with texts. Reinking (1995), however, points to the imprecision of the term *interaction* as it applies to printed texts. He correctly notes that the interaction between reader and printed text has a metaphorical, not literal, meaning. Reinking's point is well taken: "Printed texts are fixed, inert entities that stand aloof from the influence and needs of a particular reader (p. 22)." Yet this is not the case with electronic texts. An interactive literacy event in an electronic environment is one in which a text is responsive to the actions of the reader. Electronic texts differ from printed texts in that they have the capability to be modified and manipulated by readers according to their individual needs, interests, and purposes for reading.

Communication and Information Search and Retrieval

What better way is there to establish authentic communication than through reading and writing with computers? Digitalized technologies make it possible for students to participate in communication exchanges, searches for information, and retrieval of information from a multitude of resources throughout the world. One such technology, the Internet, offers users "a natural blend of communication and information retrieval functions incorporated within a framework that literally encompasses the world" (Mike 1996, p. 4). The Internet—also called *cyberspace,* the *information superhighway,* the *infobahn,* or simply the *Net* in popular culture—consists of a worldwide collection of computers able to communicate with each other with little or no central control. Through computers, the Internet connects people and resources. All that you need to access this vast collection of computer networks is a computer, appropriate communication software, a modem, and an account with an Internet provider.

One of the most compelling rationales for using the Internet and CD-ROM software programs is that they create multimedia environments for learning.

Multimedia Environments

Sound, graphics, photographs, video, and other nonprint media may be linked to electronic text to create a learning environment far beyond the limitations of printed texts. If students want to find out about space exploration, for example, they can access a site on the World Wide Web. They can then choose to click on the term *space shuttle* for a definition and a computer-generated model of the space shuttle, click on the highlighted word *history* for a brief overview and history of the space program, digress to an audio recording and video clip of Neil Armstrong as he sets foot on the moon, or engage in a live interview with a NASA scientist or astronaut. Later in the document, they might click on the word *projects* to find out about many of the online projects that NASA offers to students.

The concepts of hypertext and hypermedia are crucial to understanding the interactions between reader and text in a multimedia environment. *Hypertext* differs from printed text in that its structure is much less linear. If you were reading a document in a hypertext environment, you could scroll through it on a screen in a linear fashion, much as you would read a printed text paragraph by paragraph. But the hypertext format also offers a "web" of text that allows you to link to other related documents and resources on demand. When sound, graphics, photographs, video, and other nonprint media are incorporated into the hypertext format, the electronic environment is called *hypermedia.*

Socially Mediated Learning

Electronic texts create a medium for social interactions—whether we have students use the Internet to communicate or assign them to learning teams as they share a computer to access information on CD-ROM or the Web. Literacy learning with computers is social and collaborative. Students learn with electronic texts by sharing their discoveries with others. Leu (1996) underscores this type of literacy learning: "Multimedia environments, because they are powerful and complex, often require us to communicate with others in order to make meaning from them. Thus, learning is frequently constructed through social interactions in these contexts, perhaps even more naturally and frequently than in traditional print environments" (p. 163). What are the implications of socially mediated learning events in the classroom? As teachers, we need to support and encourage social interactions in electronic environments and have our students take the lead in making discoveries and sharing knowledge with other students and with us.

Electronic Texts in the Classroom: An Array of Possibilities

There are unlimited possibilities for learning with electronic texts. Access to the Internet means, quite literally, that students have at their fingertips a virtual library of electronic texts for subject matter learning. People use reading and writing almost entirely to interact with information or with other people on the Internet. With the Internet, it's possible, as suggested by Williams (1995), to engage in a variety of communication and information search and retrieval activities through use of the following: *electronic mail (e-mail)* to send and receive messages from others and to participate in discussion groups and "live" conferences; *telnet* to connect to another computer at another location and work interactively with it as if your computer were directly connected to it; *file transfer protocol (FTP)* to move files and information data from one computer to another; and the *World Wide Web,* a system for point-and-click knowledge navigation around the world to access text documents, video, images, and sound.

The Internet also provides students with CAI software, particularly CD-ROM programs, that can create multimedia environments for learning. Let's examine several of the opportunities that students have for learning with electronic texts.

Learning with Hypertext and Hypermedia

Hypertext enriches and extends any literacy learning event in the content areas. With hypertext and hypermedia, highlighted and linked texts, called *hyperlinks* (or simply *links*), enable you to move between documents in a nonlinear manner. This process is possible because in hypertext there are many "branches" or pathways that readers may choose to follow in many different orders, depending on their interests and purposes. If your students were to make a cyberspace visit to the home page of one of best science museums for young people, San Francisco's Exploratorium (http://www.exploratorium.edu/), they would be able to participate in a variety of interactive exhibits simply by selecting the links they were interested in. Suppose that several students clicked on the link *Cow's Eye Dissection.* In a second or two, the students would be transported to the cow's eye dissection demonstration site (see Figure 3.1), where they would be invited to select from several "banners" to begin the demonstration. The students may decide to link to the banner marked "Cow's Eye Primer" to participate in an interactive lesson that teaches about the parts of the eye. Or they might choose to click on "Step-by-Step: Dissecting a Cow's Eye" to begin the demonstration.

Through the use of hyperlinks, students can move to other related text or nonprint media simply by clicking on a highlighted word or icon in the document. As a result, they can "jump around" or digress to explore related branches of text at their own pace, navigating in whatever direction they choose. Jumping around in a hypertext gives a sense of freedom with text that is unattainable with printed text. The possibility for multiple digressions, according to Reinking (1997), is the defining attribute of hypertext. As he puts it, "Trying to write a hypertext means being free to digress and to assume that readers will willingly share in that same freedom. Digression can

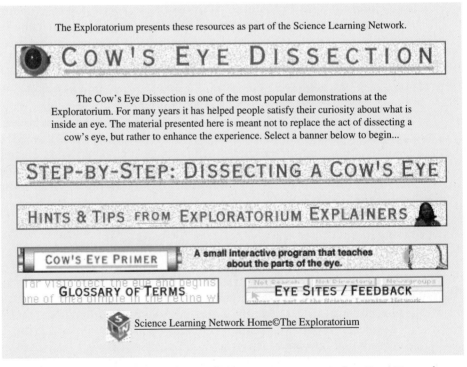

FIGURE 3.1 **Cow's Eye Dissection Home Page at the San Francisco Exploratorium's Web Site**

(http://www.exploration.edu/learning_studio/cow_eye/index.html)

be positive and enjoyable in a hypertext because there is no compulsion to stick closely to only one main idea" (p. 629).

From an instructional perspective, the branching options offered in hypertext and hypermedia serve two important functions: to scaffold students' learning experiences and to enhance and extend thinking. For readers who may struggle with text or with difficult concepts, the resources available on demand in a hypertext environment include pronunciations of key words and terms, definitions and explanations, audio versions of the text, video recordings, quick-time movies, photographs, graphics, interactive exercises, and student-centered projects. These links have the potential to arouse curiosity, stimulate interest, and reinforce and extend students' thinking about a subject.

Keep in mind, however, a cautionary note about hypertext and hypermedia learning environments. Computer software programs and the Internet are technologies that lend themselves to *extensive* explorations of information resources. A key instructional concern is to avoid the more superficial experiences with technology that are fun but do not necessarily support students' literacy learning or critical thinking about content central to the curriculum (Leu 1996). Because multimedia environments are highly engaging and seductive, student discoveries, in Leu's words, "spread like wildfire" in the classroom. Whenever you plan a lesson or unit that involves students in multimedia learning environments, you run the risk of having them ignore substantive content in favor of superficial discoveries. As a result, students might navigate multimedia environments to explore topics extensively at only a superficial level of understanding without reading and thinking deeply about a specific or single topic. How teachers scaffold intensive literacy experiences and in-depth explorations of electronic and printed texts remains a key instructional issue that we will explore throughout this book.

Online Learning with the Internet

Harry Noden (1995), a middle school teacher in Hudson, Ohio, describes an electronic conversation that he had with a teacher, Ken Blystone, from Texas. Blystone explained that he was having difficulty securing funding for Internet connections in his school district because some school administrators considered the Internet a high-tech frill rather than a substantive tool for literacy and learning. According to Noden, Blystone "approached his principal early one morning before school and asked him how much it would be worth investing to get students so excited about reading and writing that they would stand in line for the opportunity." The principal chuckled at the notion until Blystone "invited him to walk to the library. There, a half an hour before school had started, gathered around the one computer connected to the Internet, stood a large group of students . . . standing in line waiting for the opportunity to read and write" (p. 26).

World Wide Web

The Internet has been described by some as providing the "textbooks of tomorrow." And then some! The World Wide Web of the Internet is fertile ground for learning with electronic texts on every subject imaginable. Access to the Web on the Internet means access to a hypermedia system. The Web represents the universe of servers (computers) that allows text, graphics, sound, and images to be mixed together.

Alvarez (1996) describes a project called Explorers of the Universe for high school students in grades 9 through 12 enrolled in an astronomy class. In this class, the Web on the Internet became an important tool for gathering information and communicating ideas. Students worked in teams of two and three to conduct research using library resources as well as information resources on the Web. The Internet was also used as a medium to publish students' research reports, broaden their knowledge base in specific areas, and make inquiries to other students and astronomers in the field.

Alvarez notes that the Web serves a function similar to the library except that access to information resources is nearly instantaneous and students are able to contact authors of Web documents directly to clarify questions or gather additional information. The teachers involved in Explorers of the Universe used textbooks in tandem with Internet connections. They found that the textbook became a resource as opposed to a singular source of science information. Preliminary findings of the project show that students related new information to their existing world knowledge, analyzed their sources more carefully, and attempted to identify new sources of information (Alvarez 1996).

To use the Web effectively, students will need to develop expertise at navigating through the hypertext world of the Web. For students not experienced with "browsing" or "surfing" the Web, try scaffolding activities such as guided tours and scavenger hunts to familiarize beginners with how to navigate. Also, use "bookmarks" that will take students directly to locations that you want them to visit on the Web. One of the most useful resource books for literacy and learning, *Teaching with the Internet: Lessons from the Classroom* (Leu & Leu 1997), provides many suggestions for developing navigation skills and numerous Web site locations for content area study.

In Box 3.3 you will find a list of frequently visited Web sites by content area. A visit to several of these Web sites gives you insight into the possibilities for subject matter learning that await students. Information resources and Web sites can easily be integrated into units of study in your content area.

E-Mail and Discussion Groups

On the Internet, students (and teachers) can send and receive messages anywhere in the world via e-mail. E-mail messages are sent electronically from one computer to another through the use of special software. E-mail communication can generate important learning connections for students by making "reading and writing across the planet" a reality (Noden & Vacca 1994). Imagine the possibilities: On Monday, two students from Yakeala, Finland, talk to your students about minority groups in their country—the Gypsies and the Lapps. On Tuesday, students discuss the environmental problems of the Amazon jungle with students in Lima, Peru. On Wednesday, a wheelchair-bound student from Palatka, Florida, drops in to give his one- to five-star reviews of the latest video games. On Thursday, teenage refugees from Bosnia tell how most of their relatives "just disappeared" and how the young people managed to escape. On Friday, a student from Keene, New Hampshire, shares a visit from a Holocaust survivor.

These are just some of the e-mail learning events that occurred in Harry Noden's eighth grade class in the course of a week (Noden & Vacca 1994). To allow this to happen, Noden first made e-mail connections with other teachers through the use of *electronic bulletin boards,* sites where students and teachers can post ideas for exchanges and Internet projects. Leu and Leu (1997) recommend the following sites as "jumping-off points" for Internet projects:

NickNack's Telecollaborations
http://www1.minn.net:80/~schubert/
This site provides summaries of many projects.

Global SchoolNet Projects Registry
http://www.gsn.org/project/index.html
"Safe" projects are screened and lists are moderated on this very large site.

Kidlink
http://www.kidlink.org:80/KIDPROJ/
E-mail–based projects aimed at students aged 10 to 15 are featured.

Lycos
http://www.lycos.com
Use "K12 projects" for your search and you will find numerous sites to visit.

The GLOBE Program
http://www.globe.gov
This site highlights environmental science projects that connect students and scientists around the world.

In one Internet project, preservice teachers from Walsh University in Ohio engaged in e-mail exchanges with fourth graders from a local elementary school (McKeon 1997). The collaborative project revolved around "book-talks" and literature discussions. Each preservice teacher was paired with a

Box 3.3

Nothing but Net: Selected Web Sites Across the Curriculum

The Web sites that we have selected illustrate some of the possibilities for locating information resources on the Internet in various content areas. Because the Web is a fluid and continually changing medium, some of the locations listed here may no longer be in operation. (For additional Web sites in each content area, see Appendix D.)

THE ARTS

The Kennedy Center's ArtsEdge
http://www.artsedge.kennedy-center.org/artsedge.html

Asian Arts
http://www.webart.com/asianart/index.html

The Heritage of Genghis Khan
http://www.com/khan

Australian National University
http://www.ncsa.uiuc.edu/SDG/Experimental/anu-art-history/home.html

ENGLISH LANGUAGE ARTS

The English Server
http://english-server.hss.cmu.edu

National Public Radio
http://www.npr.org

PBS Web Site
http://www.pbs.org

Computer-Assisted Language Learning (CALL)
http://www.tcom.ohiou.edu/OU_Language/OU_Language.html

FOREIGN LANGUAGE

Elementary Spanish Curriculum
http://www.veen.com/Veen/Leslie/Curriculum

Reed Union School District
http://www.aboveweb.com/reed/Foreign Language.html

Woodberry Forest School Spanish Links
http://www.woodberry.org/fac/huber/spanishl.htm

Webb 66 International School Registry
http://www.66.coled.unin.edu/schools ES/Spain.html

HEALTH: IDEAS FOR HEALTH LESSONS

http://tiger.coe.missouri.edu/~kyle/edu.html

http://pe.central.vt.edu/calculatefat.html

http://pe.central.vt.edu/websitesmenu.html

http://pe.central.vt.edu/Healthlp.html

http//:www.mcrel.org/connect/lesson.html

MATHEMATICS

MathEd: Mathematics Education Resources
http://www-hpcc.astro.washington.edu/scied/math.html

21st Century Problem Solving
http://www2.hawaii.edu/suremath/home.html

MathMagic
http://forum.swarthmore.edu/mathmagic/index.html

McNair Scholar's Program
http://sonofsun.sdsu.edu/usp/mcnair

SCIENCE

EE-Link
http://www.nceet.snre.umich.edu

Digital Curriculum Lab
http://kepler.enc.org

Virtual Frog Dissection
http://george.lbl.gov/ITG.hm.pg.docs/dissect/info.html

NASA Home Page
http://www.nasa.gov

SOCIAL STUDIES

Benjamin Franklin
http://sln.fi.edu/franklin/rotten.html

Social Sciences Education (Galaxy)
http://galaxy.einet.net/galaxy/Social-Sciences/Education.html

Treasures of the Czars
http://www.times.st-pete.fl.us/Treasures/Default.html

The Egyptian Gallery
htttp://www.mordor.com/hany/egypt/egypt.html

VOCATIONAL EDUCATION

Career Mosaic
http://www.careermosaic.com

Workplace Index (EINET Galaxy)
http://galaxy.tradewave.com/galaxy/Community/Workplace.html

Business and Economy: Yahoo!
Http://www.yahoo.com/Business

The Internet's OnLine Career Center
http://occ.com

NCS Career Magazine
http://www.careermag.com/careermag

student. Throughout the semester, the e-mail partners discussed the books they were reading. These electronic conversations provided natural opportunities for the partners to engage in authentic talk about books and for the preservice teachers to blend instructional strategies into the discussion. For example, in one correspondence just prior to reading the book *A Taste of Blackberries* (Smith 1973), a preservice teacher invites his partner to make predictions about the book:

> Just to let you know before you start reading, the book is very sad and it involves people dying. I would like you to brainstorm a little bit about the name of the book and give me some guesses of what you think the story may be about. Then we will take your guesses, and after we read the book, we can find out how close you were with some of your guesses. I am really looking forward to hearing from you.

Not only was the e-mail project successful in making important learning connections during the literature discussions, but in the course of a semester, the e-mail partners got to know each other socially as they shared information and asked questions about college life, hobbies, interests, and family life.

In addition to individual messages, a person can send messages to and receive messages from groups of people by subscribing to a *mailing list* or *listserv*. These groups, often called *discussion groups,* allow students and teachers to ask questions, share information, and locate resources. In Noden's class, students received a collection of memoirs compiled by students at Hiroshima Jogakuin High School. The memoirs, written by survivors of the atomic bomb, stimulated a great deal of discussion among students, prompting them to investigate additional information sources in the library and on the Web.

Leu and Leu (1997) suggest several of the most popular mailing lists for discussion groups, including these:

Liszt Select
http://www.liszt.com
This comprehensive site contains over 50,000 lists. You can either do a search for lists in your interest area or click the Liszt Select box for a much smaller annotated list of sites.

TileNet
http://www.tile.net/tile/listserv/index.html
You can search this large site for lists alphabetically by name, host country, sponsoring organization, most popular, or subject categories.

Pitsco's Launch to Lists
http://www.pitsco.com/p/listservs.html
This site doesn't have search capabilities, but the list is focused on education.

EdWeb
http://k12.cnid.org:90/lists.html

This smaller list focuses on K–12 issues, educational technology, and education reform.

Learning with Word Processors and Authoring Systems

Reading and writing on the Internet play an important role in learning. But merely using computer-related technologies in your classrooms doesn't guarantee more effective or meaningful learning. As one teacher put it:

> Students must be good communicators. In my classroom, students whose writing skills are lacking will not spend nearly as much time on the computer as those with more competency. Does this make some students strive to be more competent so they can use the computers? Yes indeed, and that brings up a positive aspect of computers; they provide incentive and encouragement for improvement. (Jasper 1995, p. 17).

Not only do computers provide incentive for improvement, but they can also be an important tool for developing students' writing abilities.

Computers as word processors allow writers to create a text and change it in any way desired. Word processing software programs have the potential to make students more active in brainstorming, outlining, exploring and organizing ideas, revising, and editing a text.

Academic-related writing is one of the most cognitive as well as physically demanding tasks required of students in school. Computers can make writing easier by taking away some of the sheer physical demands of putting ideas on paper with a pen or pencil. This is not to say that communicating with paper and pen is less effective than with a computer. A computer, however, frees students from the laborious physical tasks associated with drafting, editing, and revising a text so that they can expend more cognitive energy on the communication itself. One of the best reasons why people use computers to write and communicate with others is that it takes a complex activity like writing and expedites the process. Suid and Lincoln (1988), somewhat "tongue in cheek," draw this analogy: "You can cook terrific meals on a wood-burning stove. But if you're like most people, you prefer a modern range. It's easier. It's faster. And it lets you do more" (p. 318). One of the things that a computer lets you do in a classroom is generate a finished and attractive text that others can read.

Student-generated texts and reports shouldn't be for the teacher's eyes only. They should be read by other students and can become "minibooks" for classroom learning. *Desktop publishing* programs, which combine text and graphics in varied arrangements, can help students produce attractive reports as part of thematic and topical units of study. Students can also design multimedia projects using hypermedia programs such as Hyperstudio, Linkway, or Hypercard. Hypermedia programs encourage active engagement with information and extend the composing process through the interaction of various media. These programs are called *authoring systems* and are often used in research projects designed by students as part of a thematic or topical unit of study.

Lapp and Flood (1995), for example, describe a middle-grade classroom where they observed small groups of students using Hyperstudio to design geology-related science projects. The students used the authoring software to help them organize their multimedia reports on a unit dealing with the causes and effects of tornadoes. One group of students located a National Geographic Society *laser disk* containing some footage of an actual tornado and used the authoring software program to incorporate the footage into their presentation. A laser disk is a computer peripheral on which large amounts of video and audio are stored. A student in another group found some photographs taken by his aunt of a tornado and the destruction it left in its wake. The student used a *scanner* to incorporate the photos into the multimedia presentation. A scanner is another peripheral used to convert pictures, texts, graphs, or charts into an image that can then be used in a computer presentation.

Authoring software allows students to develop multimedia projects and presentations that wed visual images, sound, graphics, and text. The premise underlying authoring systems is not as complicated as it may appear if you're a novice with the use of hypermedia technologies. Authoring software programs facilitate multimedia compositions and encourage students to communicate what they are learning through the construction of computer "cards" and "buttons." The student (or small group of students) creates the multimedia presentation by filling in computer cards with information (referred to as textual "fields") and with pictures, drawings, graphics, photographs, video, music, and voice messages. Buttons are then created to link the network of completed cards.

Students not familiar with authoring systems need to learn how to use hypermedia tools and peripherals to scan in photographs, create pictures and graphics, and record video and sounds. They will also need instructional support in planning, researching, and designing projects and in learning how to use authoring software effectively.

Learning with Software Programs

The proliferation of educational software programs can make it difficult for teachers to choose appropriate CAI programs for classroom use. Most of the major publishers of printed textbooks have entered the educational software market. Prentice Hall, for example, has developed highly interactive multimedia CD-ROM software in most of the content areas. One Prentice Hall program, Multimedia Math, appropriate for use in the middle grades, allows students to interact with and experience math concepts through engagement in "math investigations" and "hot pages" using a rich, three-dimensional, multisensory environment. Another of its software programs, Chemedia, designed for use in high school chemistry courses, combines videodisks with simulation software to engage students in visual explorations of interesting phenomena otherwise not available in the classroom.

In addition to software development by major publishing houses, hundreds of smaller companies, specializing exclusively in technology-related programs, have mushroomed in the past decade, inundating the educational landscape with innovative software in all content areas for all age levels. Because of the prolific development of educational software, most of the major content area education associations and societies offer program reviews in their professional journals.

Making decisions about educational software is no easy task. Rose and Fernlund (1997), speaking directly to social studies teachers, suggest asking a set of reflective questions related to CAI and multimedia use that is applicable to all content teachers who are interested in using educational software to enhance instruction. To guide the evaluation of computer-based instructional products, consider the questions posed in Box 3.4.

Learning with Electronic Books

The recent innovations in educational software have led to the development of what has been called the *electronic book.* Anderson-Inman and Horney (1997) use stringent criteria to distinguish electronic books from other forms of educational software:

- Electronic books must have electronic text presented to the reader visually.

- They must use the metaphors of a book by adapting some of the conventions associated with books, such as a table of contents, pages, and a bookmark, so that readers will feel that they are reading a book.

- They must have an organizing theme of an existing book or a central focus if it is not based on an equivalent printed book.

- They must be primarily text-centered. When media enhancements other than text are available in the software, they are incorporated primarily to support the text presentation.

Many electronic books, available on CD-ROM, make excellent reference resources. *The 1996 Grolier Multimedia Encyclopedia* (Grolier) gives readers more than 33,000 thousand articles and easy-to-use features that make searching and retrieving information uncomplicated. Many CD-ROM books are informational and focus on in-depth study of subjects. *In the Company of Whales* (Discovery Communications), intended for use in middle and high schools, provides students with well-organized informative text, pictures, action footage, and sound. The electronic text shows how whales are studied and introduces students to some of the people who study them. Still other electronic books are for recreational reading. Highly interactive storybooks

Box 3.4

Evaluating Computer-Based Educational Software: Questions to Consider

Hardware-Related Questions to Consider

1. What are the instructional tasks and levels of complexity? Do I have the necessary technology?

2. Do my computers have enough memory to run the desired software application?

3. What type of technical delivery system will be used: single computer(s) or computers attached to a local area network (LAN), or a wide area network (WAN) and/or the Internet?

4. Is the speed of the network sufficient to accomplish the instructional task in an efficient and timely manner?

Software-Related Questions to Consider

1. How does this computer program help achieve my objectives for this unit of study? Can I modify the program to fit my plans better?

2. Does my computer system have the right hardware to run this program (required memory, printers, speech synthesizer, other peripherals)?

3. Is the program easy for students to use? What preparation do students need? What preparation do I need?

4. Does the publisher offer technical assistance, free or inexpensive updates, network licenses?

5. Does the program offer multiple options for delivery? For example, can the program be used over the Internet or linked to sites on the World Wide Web (the Internet's hypertext-based environment)?

Multimedia-Use Questions to Consider

1. Do I have the necessary technology to use this multimedia package, including sufficient computer memory, a videodisk player/CD-ROM drive if needed, a large screen monitor or projection device for large class viewing?

2. What is the perspective of this commercial package? How does this viewpoint differ from other resources that I plan to have students use?

3. Is this product to be used by teachers or students? Do I want to use the entire package or select particular parts?

4. In what ways will this use of technology enhance my students' learning? How can I assess the impact on learning?

Source: From "Using Technology for Powerful Social Studies Learning," by S. A. Rose and P. M. Fernlund. *Social Education*, March 1997. Copyright © National Council for the Social Studies. Reprinted with permission.

such as *Afternoon* (Eastgate Systems) and Walt Disney's *Animated Story-books* are suitable for younger as well as older readers. In studies of interactive electronic books, researchers find that children generally respond positively to CD-ROM stories over printed versions (Matthew 1996) and that reading from electronic books increases comprehension when students read longer and more difficult narratives (Greenlee-Moore and Smith 1996).

 LOOKING BACK, LOOKING FORWARD

Trade books and electronic texts in content area classrooms extend and enrich information across the curriculum. Often textbooks are not equipped to treat subject matter with the depth and breadth necessary to develop ideas and concepts fully and engage in critical inquiry. Alternatives to the textbook, however, have the potential to capture students' interest and imagination in people, places, events, and ideas.

Whereas textbooks compress information, trade books and electronic texts provide students with intensive and extensive involvement in a subject. Trade books and electronic texts offer students a variety of interesting, relevant, and comprehensible text experiences. With trade books, students are likely to develop an interest in and an emotional commitment to the subject. Trade books are schema builders. Reading books helps students generate background knowledge and provides them with vicarious experiences. Many kinds of trade books, both nonfiction and fiction, can be used in tandem with textbooks.

Electronic texts are highly engaging and interactive. Hypertext and hypermedia make it possible to interact with text in ways not imaginable a short while ago. Text learning opportunities in electronic environments are interactive, enhance communication, engage students in multimedia, create opportunities for inquiry through information searches and retrieval, and support socially mediated learning. Reading and writing with computers has changed the way we think about literacy and learning. Whether students are navigating the Internet or interacting with innovative educational software, an array of electronic text learning experiences await them.

In the next chapter, we explore another dimension of the changing world of classrooms as we shift our attention to authentic forms of assessment in the content area classroom. Concern about assessment is one of the major issues in American education today. What role do standardized and large-scale criterion-referenced assessments play in the lives of classroom teachers? How do naturalistic forms of assessment inform instructional decisions? How can teachers use portfolios and make decisions about the texts they use? The key to assessment in content areas, as we contend in the next chapter, is to make it as authentic as possible. Let's find out how and why this is the case.

 **MINDS-ON**

1. Read this statement: "One way of thinking about a textbook is that it takes a subject and distills it to its minimal essentials. In doing so, a textbook runs the risk of taking world-shaking events, monumental discoveries, profound insights, intriguing and faraway places, colorful and influential people, and life's mysteries and processes and compressing them into a series of matter-of-fact statements." Can you think of a book you have read that opened new perspectives on a topic of which you had previously had only textbook knowledge? What do you see as the ideal balance between the use of textbooks and the use of fiction books, nonfiction books, and picture books in a content classroom?

2. To what extent do you believe students should participate in the selection of documents from Web sites for use in a content course? Would you answer this question differently for students of various ages?

3. How often have you been assigned readings outside the content textbook at any level of schooling? What types of materials did you read? What later use did the teacher make of those readings? How often have you used electronic texts as part of subject matter learning? In your estimation, did the teacher use the outside reading assignment to its full potential? If not, in what additional ways might the readings have been explored?

4. Why do many students seem to dislike doing research in a library but are enthusiastic about surfing the Net for information resurces?

 **HANDS-ON**

1. Select two texts that you would use together in the classroom. There are a variety of possibilities: a news clipping of a current event and the video coverage of that same event; a nonfiction work and a fictionalized account (novel, drama, poem, or dialogue) of the same event; the treatments of an event in an electronic text and in a textbook on the same topic. Analyze two texts by making a comparison. How are they alike? How are they different? Come to class prepared to share your analysis.

2. Select a recent news event and conduct a search for information resources on the Web. Select several resources and compare them for treatment, reliability, and accuracy. What does it mean to develop a healthy skepticism when interacting with texts on the Web?

3. Select two picture books that you might coordinate with a particular unit you now teach or with a unit you have planned or observed. Explain why you chose these particular books and how you will use them with your students. Describe the activities that will follow the initial use or reading of the book.

SUGGESTED READINGS

Bohning, G., & Radencich, M. (1989). Informational action books: A curriculum resource for science and social studies. *Journal of Reading, 32*, 434–439.

Booksearch: Recommended historical fiction. (1989). *English Journal, 79*, 84–86.

Borasi, R., Sheedy, J. R., & Siegel, M. (1990). The power of stories in learning mathematics. *Language Arts, 67*, 174–189.

Cafolla, R., Kauffman, D., & Knee, R. (1997). *World Wide Web for teachers: An interactive guide.* Needham Heights, MA: Allyn & Bacon.

Carnes, E. J. (1988). Teaching content area reading through nonfiction book writing. *Journal of Reading, 31*, 354–360.

Donelson, K. L., & Nilsen, A. P. (1997). *Literature for today's young adults* (5th ed.). New York: Longman.

Egan, K. (1989). Layers of historical understanding. *Theory and Research in Social Education, 17*, 280–294.

Gralla, P. (1996). *How the Internet works.* Emeryville, CA: Ziff-Davis.

Hahn, H. (1996). *The Internet Yellow Pages* (3rd ed.). New York: Osborne McGraw-Hill.

Leu, D. J., Jr., & Leu, D. D. (1997). *Teaching with the Internet: Lessons from the classroom.* Norwood, MA: Christopher-Gordon.

Levstik, L. S. (1990). Research directions: Mediating content through literary texts. *Language Arts, 67*, 848–853.

Miletta, M. (1992). Picture books for older children: Reading and writing connections. *Reading Teacher, 45*, 555–556.

Neal, J. C., & Moore, K. (1991). *The Very Hungry Caterpillar* meets *Beowulf* in secondary classrooms. *Journal of Reading, 35*, 290–296.

Willis, J., Stephens, E., & Matthew, K. (1996). *Technology, reading, and language arts.* Needham Heights, MA: Allyn & Bacon.

4

Making Authentic Assessments

One never steps into the same river twice.
—Ancient Chinese proverb

Organizing Principle

Making authentic assessments in content area classrooms means that students and teachers are actively engaged in an ongoing process of evaluation and self-evaluation. Instead of measuring learning by a score on a national or statewide standardized test, the learning process is combined with assessment based on an authentic task, "one in which students are required to address real-life problems" (Slater, 1994, p. 370). This kind of assessment, directly connected to teaching and the improvement of practice, is growing in popularity. It helps students and teachers make sense of how and what is taught and learned at any given time; thus it reflects the changing nature of content area instruction. As the Chinese proverb suggests, things do not remain the same; neither do students in the learning process.

Teachers who believe that assessment and instruction are mutually supportive processes understand that they must become actively involved in developing and scoring assessments, communicating with students about work for portfolios, and helping students reflect on their own performance and solve problems. These teachers want to depend on authentic measures to make decisions about instruction appropriate for each student. To understand assessment, you need to differentiate between two major, yet contrasting, approaches: a formal, standardized approach and an informal, naturalistic approach.

As depicted in the chapter overview, these major views of assessment form the base from which alternative practices, such as the use of portfolios, have emerged. Tests, observations, checklists, interviews, and inventories are some of the methods and techniques that make authentic assessments possible. Authentic assessments cut across students, texts, and teachers. That is to say, they improve your understanding of student performance and provide a basis for making instructional decisions; they provide a framework for both students and teachers to judge the difficulty of subject matter materials and reflect on learning and teaching.

Assessing for instruction should, first and foremost, provide the opportunity to gather and interpret useful information about students: their prior knowledge; their attitudes toward reading, writing, and subject matter; and their ability to use reading and writing to learn with texts. Through portfolio assessment—a process of collecting authentic evidence of student work over time—both students and teachers gather information to better reflect on, understand, and communicate those factors that affect literacy and learning and characterize an individual's performance. The organizing principle of this chapter holds that assessment should be authentic and responsive to teacher decision making. **Instructional assessment is a continuous process of gathering multiple sources of relevant information for instructional purposes.**

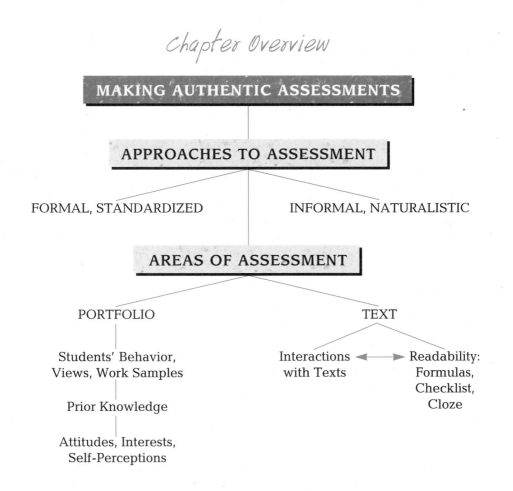

Chapter Overview

MAKING AUTHENTIC ASSESSMENTS

APPROACHES TO ASSESSMENT

FORMAL, STANDARDIZED   INFORMAL, NATURALISTIC

AREAS OF ASSESSMENT

PORTFOLIO   TEXT

Students' Behavior,   Interactions ←→ Readability:
Views, Work Samples   with Texts   Formulas,
    Checklist,
Prior Knowledge   Cloze

Attitudes, Interests,
Self-Perceptions

Frame of Mind

1. How does assessment aid in setting instructional goals?

2. How does a formal, standardized approach differ from an informal, naturalistic approach?

3. What are advantages of ongoing assessment that occurs in the natural context of the classroom?

4. What are portfolios, and what process do content teachers follow to implement them in the classroom?

5. Why do teachers have some concerns about using portfolio assessment?

6. How can teachers assess students' background knowledge?

7. Why and how should teachers assess students' attitudes toward and interests in reading?

8. How does the teacher assess students' interactions with text?

9. When and how might teachers use professional judgment in analyzing the difficulty of textbooks?

10. What are predictive measures of readability, and how do they differ from performance measures?

You are in a good position to identify and emphasize the strengths your students bring to learning situations whenever you engage in an ongoing process of assessment. This is why efforts at assessment should center on the classroom context, where the focus of assessment is not only on students but also on texts and on teacher-student-text interaction. In this sense, *diagnostic teaching* is one of the most worthwhile activities that content area teachers participate in. Nevertheless, the prospect of diagnosing is often formidable because it evokes images of expertise and specialization beyond your domain.

This need not be the case. What, then, do you need to know about students and texts to plan classroom activities better? As you go about the tasks of planning and decision making, several areas of assessment are essential. First of all, you will want to assess students' prior knowledge in relation to thematic units and specific text lessons. Moreover, you will want to assess student knowledge and use of reading strategies to learn with texts. In addition, you should consider assessing the texts you use. Each of these areas of assessment is integral to understanding some of the dynamics of the context operating in your classroom. If your purpose is to improve your understanding of that context, an informal, naturalistic approach to evaluation is likely to be more useful than a formal, standardized one.

STANDARDIZED AND NATURALISTIC APPROACHES TO ASSESSMENT

Teachers sometimes know intuitively that what they do in class is working. More often, however, information for making decisions is best obtained through careful observation of students. Their strengths and weaknesses as they interact with one another and with texts can be assessed as they participate in small groups, contribute to class discussions, respond to questions, and complete written assignments. This approach to assessment is informal and naturalistic.

A naturalistic approach to assessment has two main elements. First, it is based on the responses of the individuals directly involved. Second, it uses methods within the natural context of the classroom. These two criteria ensure that assessment will begin with classroom-centered concerns.

Naturalistic methods may include personal observation, interviews, and anecdotal records and student-selected products. The information gained from a naturalistic evaluation can be organized into a rich description or portrait of your content area classroom or into student *portfolios.* Concerns that emerge, whether about individual students or about the delivery of instructional strategies, are likely to make sense because they come directly from the classroom context and often result from teacher-student or student-student interaction.

Consider how a naturalistic approach differs from a more formal, standardized one. In Table 4.1, the two approaches are compared in several categories. Certainly there are many gray areas in an assessment, where the standardized and naturalistic approaches overlap. In this table, however, differences between the two approaches are emphasized. Traditional, formal assessments are product-oriented. They are more tangible and can be obtained at specific points in time. Naturalistic assessment is informal and process-oriented. When informal assessment is stressed, the process is ongoing and provides as much information about the reader as about the product. Together, they permit a more balanced approach that uses a combination of traditional, formal and naturalistic, informal practices. The end result is an understanding of *why* particular results are obtained in formal evaluation, which informs the *how* of the teacher decision-making process.

TABLE 4.1

Comparisons of Two Approaches to Assessment

	Standardized	Naturalistic
Orientation	Formal; developed by test publishers	Informal; developed by teachers
Administration	Testing at start or end of school year; paper-and-pencil, multiple-choice; given to groups at one seating	Continuously evolving and intermittent throughout an instructional unit; small group, one on one
Methods	Objective; standardized reading achievement tests designed to measure levels of current attainment	Classroom tests, checklists, observations, interviews, etc., designed to evaluate understanding of course content
Uses	Compare performance of one group with students in other schools, classrooms; estimate range of reading ability in a class; select appropriate materials for reading; identify students who need further diagnosis	Make qualitative judgments about students' strengths and instructional needs in reading and learning content subjects; select appropriate materials; adjust instruction when necessary
Feedback format	Reports, printouts of subtest scores; summaries of high and low areas of performance; percentiles, norms, stanines	Notes, profiles, portfolios, recommendations that evolve throughout instructional units; expansive (relate to interests, strategies, purpose for reading)

The Role of Standardized Tests

An assessment based on standardized test information is different from an assessment that evolves from naturalistic methods. A standardized reading test is more formal, may be administered at the beginning or end of the school year, and uses test methods that are considered objective. Moreover, along with the test results, schools may purchase a computer printout or report of students' strengths and weaknesses in reading subskills.

Today, public and legislative pressures for numerical scores to use in comparing school districts are resulting in more reliance on formal, large-scaled tests. Large-scaled tests usually are competency-based and not standardized according to traditional norming procedures. Many states are mandating statewide proficiency exams in math, reading, and science for fourth and ninth graders; raising standards for passing these tests; and attempting to tie financial support to each district's performance. The United States is not alone in this pursuit of ways to compare student achievement. International large-scale assessment efforts to test students worldwide often appear in newspaper headlines, citing how well, or poorly, U.S. students performed in comparison to students in other countries in a given subject. In 1997, international comparative results in mathematics and science achievement were made available for third- and fourth-grade students around the world in the IEA's Third International Mathematics and Science Study (TIMSS). We learned that Korea was the top-performing country and that Japan, the United States, Austria, and Australia also performed well.

Standardized reading tests are formal, usually machine-scorable instruments in which scores for the tested group are compared with standards established by an original normative population. The purpose of a standardized reading test is to show where students stand in relation to other students based on a single performance.

Performance on standardized reading tests can yield only rough estimates, at best, of how students will apply reading to textbooks in a particular subject. Static assessment, in which the teacher derives performance levels with scoring keys and norming tables, persists (Brozo 1990b). Yet a student who is a good reader of social studies may be a poor or mediocre reader of math or science. It's safe to say that teachers who consult standardized reading tests should do so judiciously and with reasonable expectations.

Often, standardized tests are not intended to be used to make decisions about individual students. Test publishers have developed them with a prescribed content, directions to adhere to, and a scoring arrangement to maintain a standardized analysis of the responses answered. Above all, standardized tests measure performance on a test. Hence you need to proceed with caution: Make doubly sure to understand what performance on a particular reading test means before using test results to judge the ability of a reader. A single test result, in other words, can't possibly provide a whole picture of a student's ability to interact with text because students change in the process of learning.

What Teachers Need to Know About Standardized Tests

To make sense of test information and to determine how relevant or useful it may be, you need to be thoroughly familiar with the language, purposes, and legitimate uses of standardized tests. For example, as a test user, it's your responsibility to know about the norming and standardization of the reading test used by your school district. Consult a test manual for an explanation of what the test is about, the rationale behind its development, and a clear description of what the test purports to measure. Not only should test instructions for administering and scoring be clearly spelled out, but also information related to norms, reliability, and validity should be easily defined and made available.

Norms represent average scores of a sampling of students selected for testing according to factors such as age, sex, race, grade, or socioeconomic status. Once a test maker determines norm scores, those scores become the basis for comparing the test performance of individuals or groups to the performance of those who were included in the norming sample. *Representativeness*, therefore, is a key concept in understanding student scores. It's crucial to make sure that the norming sample used in devising the reading test resembles the characteristics of the students you teach.

Norms are extrapolated from raw scores. A *raw score* is the number of items a student answers correctly on a test. Raw scores are converted to other kinds of scores so that comparisons can be made among individuals or groups of students. Three such conversions—percentile scores, stanine scores, and grade-equivalent scores—are often represented by test makers as they report scores.

Percentile scores describe the relative standing of a student at a particular grade level. For example, the percentile score of 85 of a student in the fifth grade means that his or her score is equal to or higher than the scores of 85 percent of comparable fifth graders.

Stanine scores are raw scores that have been transformed to a common standard to permit comparison. In this respect, stanines represent one of several types of standard scores. Because standard scores have the same mean and standard deviation, they permit the direct comparison of student performance across tests and subtests. The term *stanine* refers to a *sta*ndard *nine*-point scale, in which the distribution of scores on a test is divided into nine parts. Each stanine indicates a single digit ranging from 1 to 9 in numerical value. Thus a stanine of 5 is at the midpoint of the scale and represents average performance. Stanines 6, 7, 8, and 9 indicate increasingly better performance; stanines 4, 3, 2, and 1 represent decreasing performance. As teachers, we can use stanines effectively to view a student's approximate place above or below the average in the norming group.

Grade-equivalent scores provide information about reading-test performance as it relates to students at various grade levels. A grade-equivalent score is a questionable abstraction. It suggests that growth in reading progresses throughout a school year at a constant rate; for example, a student with a grade-equivalent score of 7.4 is supposedly performing at a level that is average for students who have completed four months of the seventh grade. At best, this is a silly and spurious interpretation: "Based on what is known about human development generally and language growth specifically, such an assumption [underlying grade-equivalent scores] makes little sense when applied to a human process as complex as learning to read" (Vacca, Vacca, & Gove 1995, p. 454).

Reliability refers to the consistency or stability of a student's test scores. A teacher must raise the question "Can similar test results be achieved under different conditions?" Suppose your students were to take a reading test on Monday, their first day back from vacation, and then take an equivalent form of the same test on Thursday. Would their scores be about the same? If so, the test may indeed be reliable.

Validity, by contrast, tells the teacher whether the test is measuring what it purports to measure. Validity, without question, is one of the most important characteristics of a test. If the test purports to measure reading comprehension, what is the test maker's concept of reading comprehension? Answers to this question provide insight into the *construct validity* of a test. Other aspects of validity include *content validity* (Does the test reflect the domain or content area being examined?) and *predictive validity* (Does the test predict future performance?).

Standardized test results are probably more useful at the building or district, not the classroom, level. A school, for example, may wish to compare itself in reading performance against a state or national norm. Or local districtwide norms may be compared with national norms, a process that is sometimes necessary when a district is applying for federal or state funds. In general, information from standardized tests may help screen for students who have major difficulties in reading, compare general reading-achievement levels or different classes or grades of students, assess group reading achievement, and assess the reading growth of groups of students (Allington & Strange 1980).

However, you need useful information about students' text-related behavior and background knowledge. You would be guilty of misusing standardized test results if you were to extrapolate about students' background knowledge or ability to comprehend course materials on the basis of standardized reading-test performance.

Alternatives to standardized reading assessment are found in an informal, naturalistic approach to assessment. One of the most useful tools for naturalistic inquiry is observation.

Teachers as Observers

In a standardized approach to assessment, the *test* is the major tool; in a naturalistic approach, the *teacher* is the major tool. Who is better equipped to observe students, to provide feedback, and to serve as a key informant about the meaning of classroom events? You epitomize the process of assessing students in an ongoing, natural way because you are in a position to observe and collect information continuously (Valencia 1990). Consequently, you become an observer of the relevant interactive and independent behavior of students as they learn in the content area classroom.

Observation is one unobtrusive measure that ranges from the occasional noticing of unusual student behavior to frequent anecdotal jottings to regular and detailed written field notes. Besides the obvious opportunity to observe students' oral and silent reading, there are other advantages to observation. Observing students' appearance, posture, mannerisms, enthusiasm, or apathy may reveal information about self-image. However, unless you make a systematic effort to tune in to student performance, you may lose valuable insights. You have to be a good listener to and watcher of students. Observation should be a natural outgrowth of teaching; it increases teaching efficiency and effectiveness. Instructional decisions based on accurate observations help you zero in on what and how to teach in relation to reading tasks.

However, before this can happen, you must view yourself as a participant observer and as an active researcher and problem solver. You need to systematically collect information about and samples of students' work in relation to instructional goals, with an eye to what you think best represents students' capabilities (Resnick & Resnick 1991).

Throughout the world, classroom teachers are increasingly teaching students with special needs who had previously worked with a specialist. Today's teachers are expected to meet the needs of all students. Consequently, the challenges of teaching diverse learners in the classroom may cause nonspecialist teachers to feel frustrated and unprepared. Understanding and accepting differences in students can, however, lead to effective instructional adaptations. Here's how Kim Browne, a seventh-grade teacher of language arts, used observational assessment to help deal with her "inclusion section":

> One of the most frequent questions I'm asked at parent meetings and IEP [individual educational plan] meetings is, "How does my child interact with his or her peers?" I planned to collect data on each student by using a simple observation checklist when the students are participating in their literary circles after reading *Take me out to the ball game.* I keep an index card file on each student by the class period; my focus is on peer relationships, noting any overt behavior that may be indicative of boredom or confusion, as well as cooperative interactions. Additional observations can be added to a large label stuck to the back of the card.

In addition to the basic format for time sample or interval data, Kim included two other sections: *other information,* where she noted any support the student may be receiving in or out of school or if the student is on an IEP plan and asked a specific question about this student, and *tentative conclusions,* where she made comments about what she just observed and what to focus on in the next observation. Figure 4.1 illustrates Kim's recent observation on Neil, a special needs student in her late-morning section.

To record systematic observations, to note significant teaching-learning events, or simply to make note of classroom happenings, you need to keep a notebook or index cards on hand. Information collected purposefully constitutes *field notes.* They aid in classifying information, inferring patterns of behavior, and making predictions about the effectiveness of innovative instructional procedures. As they accumulate, field notes may serve as anecdotal records that provide documentary evidence of students' interactions over periods of time.

Teachers and others who use informal, naturalistic tools to collect information almost always use more than one means of collecting data, a practice

Date: *Sept. 11, 1991* Time: Start: *11:15*   Stop: *11:25*

School: *Hadley*   Grade: *1*

Subject: *Lang. Arts*   Period: *5*

Other Information: *Neil is on an IEP that indicates A.D.D. with mild Tourette. Does Neil contribute to literary circle? Does he exhibit overt signs of Tourette or frustration?*

Time interval used: *3 min.*

Time: *11:15*   Behavior: *Neil willingly joins in a small group. He asked a question, then began to listen.*

Time: *11:18*   Behavior: *Shrugs shoulders often. Makes a frown. Contributes orally to group.*

Time: *11:21*   Behavior: *Put head down on desk. Pointed to text, laughing at what someone said.*

Conclusions if possible: *It is possible that Neil didn't fully understand what he read in Take Me Out To The Ball Game last night. Shoulder shrugging & head down may indicate confusion. He seemed to enjoy being part of literary circle.*

FIGURE 4.1   A Time Sample Observation

known as *triangulation.* This helps ensure that the information is valid and that what is learned from one source is corroborated by what is learned from another source. A fifth-grade science teacher recounted how he combined the taking of field notes with active listening and discussion to assess his students' current achievement and future needs in the subject:

> I briefly document on individual cards how students behave during experiments conducted individually, within a group, during reading assignments, during phases of a project, and during formal assessments. Knowing which students or what size group tends to enhance or distract a student's ability to stay on task helps me organize a more effective instructional environment. When students meet to discuss

their projects and the steps they followed, I listen carefully for strategies they used or neglected. I sometimes get insights into what a particular student offered this group; I get ideas for topics for future science lessons and projects or mini-lessons on time management, breaking up a topic into "chunks," and so on.

In addition to providing valid information, informal assessment strategies are useful to teachers during parent-teacher conferences for discussing a student's strengths and weaknesses. They also help build an ongoing record of progress that may be motivating for students to reflect on and useful for their other teachers in planning lessons in different subjects. And finally, the assessments themselves may provide meaningful portfolio entries from both a teacher's and a student's perspective, serving "as the essential link among curriculum, teaching, and learning" (Wilcox 1997, p. 223).

Many students want to establish a personal rapport with their teachers. They may talk of myriad subjects, seemingly unrelated to the unit. It is often during this informal chatter, however, that you find out about the students' background, problems, and interests. This type of conversation, in which you assume the role of active listener, can provide suggestions about topics for future lessons and materials and help the student's voice emerge.

Discussion, both casual and directed, is also an integral part of evaluation. You need to make yourself available, both before and after class, for discussion about general topics, lessons, and assignments. For an assessment of reading comprehension, nothing replaces one-on-one discussion of the material, whether before, during, or after the actual reading. Finally, you may even encourage students to verbalize their positive and negative feelings about the class itself as well as about topics, reading, and content area activities.

A note of caution: It's important to realize that "no matter how careful we are, we will be biased in many of our judgments" (MacGinitie 1993, p. 559). Yet teachers who observe with any sort of regularity soon discover that they are able to acquire enough information to process "in a meaningful and useful manner" (Fetterman 1989, p. 88). They can then make reliable decisions about instruction with observation and other techniques in portfolio assessment.

PORTFOLIO ASSESSMENT

One of the most exciting and potentially energizing developments in assessment is the emergence of portfolios. The use of global, alternative, balanced practices in gathering information about students, *portfolio assessment* is a powerful concept that has immediate appeal and potential for accomplishing the following purposes:

- Providing and organizing information about the nature of students' work and achievements

- Involving students themselves in reflecting on their capabilities and making decisions about their work

- Using the holistic nature of instruction as a base from which to consider attitudes, strategies, and responses
- Assisting in the planning of appropriate instruction to follow
- Showcasing work mutually selected by students and teacher
- Revealing diverse and special needs of students as well as talents
- Displaying multiple student-produced artifacts collected over time
- Integrating assessment into the daily instruction as a natural, vital part of teaching and learning
- Expanding both the quantity and the quality of evidence by means of a variety of indicators

Portfolios are vehicles for ongoing assessment. They are composed of purposeful collections that examine achievement, effort, improvement, and, most important, processes (selecting, comparing, sharing, self-evaluation, and goal setting), according to Tierney, Carter, and Desai (1991). As such, they lend themselves beautifully to instruction in content areas ranging from math and science to English, history, and health education.

Significant pieces that go into student portfolios are *collaboratively* chosen by teachers and students. Selections represent processes and activities more than products. A distinct value underlying the use of portfolios is a commitment to students' evaluation of their own understanding and personal development.

Contrasting portfolios with traditional assessment procedures, Walker (1991) submits that instead of a contrived task representing knowledge of a subject, portfolios are an "authentic" assessment that measures the process of the construction of meaning. The *students* make choices about what to include; these choices in turn encourage self-reflection on their own development, their own evaluation of their learning, and personal goal setting. Advantages of portfolios are more easily visualized when compared with traditional assessment practices as displayed in Table 4.2, adapted from Tierney, Carter, and Desai (1991, p. 44).

Adapting Portfolios to Content Area Classes

You can, by making some individual adjustments, adapt portfolios to meet your needs. Techniques such as interviewing, observing, and using checklists and inventories provide good sources of information about students in the classroom. The use of portfolios is in many ways a more practical method of organizing this type of information. Linek (1991) suggests that many kinds of data be collected for a thorough documentation of attitudes, behaviors, achievements, improvement, thinking, and reflective self-evaluation. For example, students may begin a math course with poor attitudes and may constantly challenge the validity of the content by saying things like "What are we learning this for anyway? It's got nothing to do with me and my life." If

---

TABLE 4.2

Portfolios Versus Testing:
Different Processes and Outcomes

Portfolio	Testing
Represents the range of learning activities students are engaged in.	Assesses students across a limited range of assignments which may not match what students do.
Engages students in assessing their progress and/or accomplishments and establishing ongoing learning goals.	Mechanically scored or scored by teachers who have little input.
Measures each student's achievement while allowing for individual differences between students.	Assesses all students on the same dimensions.
Represents a collaborative approach to assessment.	Assessment process is not collaborative.
Has a goal of student self-assessment.	Student assessment is not a goal.
Addresses improvement, effort, and . achievement	Addresses achievement only.
Links assessment and teaching to learning.	Separates learning, testing, and teaching.

Source: From *Portfolio Assessment in the Reading-Writing Classroom* by Tierney, Carter, and Desai. Copyright © 1991 Christopher Gordon Publishers, Inc. Reprinted by permission of Christopher-Gordon Publishers, Inc.

you provide opportunities for functional application in realistic situations, comments may change over time to "Boy, I never realized how important this was going to be for getting a job in real life!"

Much more than a folder for housing daily work, a record file, or a grab bag, a portfolio is a comprehensive profile of each student's progress and growth. In math class, whether it's arithmetic, algebra, or trig, teachers would decide with students what types of samples of student-produced work should be included. According to Stenmark (1991), a math portfolio might include samples of student-produced written descriptions of the results of practical or mathematical investigations, pictures and dictated reports by younger students, extended analyses of problem situations and investigations, reflections on problem-solving processes (see Figure 4.2), and statistical studies and graphic presentations. Still other "likely candidates for inclusion in a math portfolio are: coordinate graphs of arithmetic, algebra, and geometry; responses to open-ended questions or homework problems; group reports and photographs of student projects; copies of awards or prizes; video, audio, and computer-generated examples of student work" (p. 63). In addition to these suggestions, a math portfolio might also, in one sense, be considered a

Name: _Jeff Brandon_   Course: _Algebra II_

Grade: _9_   Date: _2-14-98_

Problem:

Little Caesar's Pizza's commercial states that a person can purchase 2 pizzas with at most 5 toppings on each pizza for $10.95. The little kid in the commercial states that there are 1,048,576 possibilities. Little Caesar's offers a choice of 12 toppings. Do you agree or disagree with the little kid? Explain.

Reflection:

For the piece on problem solving I selected the Little Caesars problem. I know I got the problem wrong, but I really liked the way I went about solving the problem. I feel my problem-solving technique is pretty accurate, but I missed one minor detail which made the answer incorrect. I spent a lot of time preparing the portfolio, and this is one portfolio where I am very proud of my problem-solving skills.

I solved this by using a smaller problem then applying it to the real problem. I first attacked this problem by writing out all of the possibilities for a smaller problem. Then I checked if using combinations would work because I knew that I couldn't count out all of the possibilities for the real problem. Then I checked and revised it. I feel that I put forth a lot of time and energy into this portfolio.

FIGURE 4.2   **A Problem-Solving Reflection for Algebra II**

Source: A Problem-Solving Reflection for Algebra II, developed by Laura Anfany and Carol Caroff, Solon High School, Solon, OH.

mathematical biography because it may contain important information about a student's attitude toward math.

Implementing Portfolios in the Classroom

To get started implementing the portfolio assessment process, certain logical steps must be taken and certain decisions need to be made:

1. *Discuss with your students the notion of portfolios as an interactive vehicle for assessment.* Explain the concept and show some examples of items that might be considered good candidates for the portfolio. Provide some examples from other fields, such as art and business, where portfolios have historically recorded performance and provided updates.

2. *Specify your assessment model.* What is the purpose of the portfolio? Who is the audience for the portfolio? How much involvement by students will be entailed? Purposes, for example, may be to showcase students' best work, to document or describe an aspect of their work over time (to show growth), to evaluate by making judgments by using either certain standards agreed on in advance or the relative growth and development of each individual, or to document the process that goes into the development of a single product, such as a unit of work on the Vietnam era or the Middle East or nutrition.

3. *Decide what types of requirements will be used, approximately how many items, and what format will be appropriate for the portfolio.* Furthermore, will students be designing their own portfolios? Will they include videos or computer disks? Or will they have a uniform look? Plan an explanation of portfolios for your colleagues and the principal; also decide on the date when this process will begin.

4. *Consider which contributions are appropriate for your content area.* The main techniques for assessing students' behavior, background knowledge, attitudes, interests, and perceptions are writing samples, video records, conference notes, tests and quizzes, standardized tests, pupil performance objectives, self-evaluations, peer evaluations, daily work samples, a collection of written work, personal progress sheets (see Figure 4.3), vocabulary-matching exercises, structured overviews, semantic maps, your own questions, freewriting, and group projects, along with checklists, inventories, and interviews.

Cherrie Jackman, a fifth-grade teacher, wanted to experiment with portfolios as an assessment tool for writing and science.

To begin this procedure in my class, I followed certain steps:

- First, I explained the concept of portfolios and discussed why they are important. We thought of how local businesses use portfolios, and how certain types of professions (architecture, art, journalism) depend on them.

- Next, I explained the purposes of our portfolio: to describe a portion of students' work over the quarter, showing how it has improved; to reflect on and evaluate their own work in writing and science; and to compile a body of work that can travel with them from year to year.

- Then we discussed the requirements for our portfolio: to select one or two pieces of work from science and writing that each student feels is representative of the best that he or she has done for the quarter; to add one piece for each subject area each quarter; and at the end of the school year, to evaluate students' overall progress.

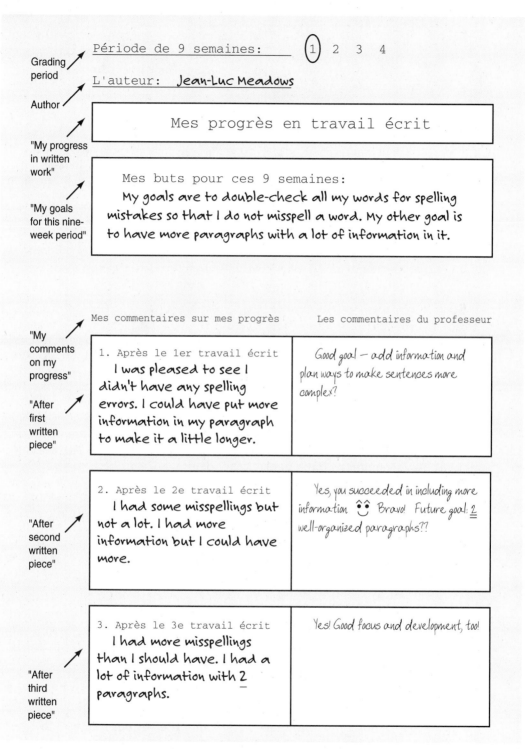

Grading period

Author

"My progress in written work"

"My goals for this nine-week period"

"My comments on my progress"

"After first written piece"

"After second written piece"

"After third written piece"

Période de 9 semaines: ____ ① 2 3 4

L'auteur: Jean-Luc Meadows

Mes progrès en travail écrit

Mes buts pour ces 9 semaines:
My goals are to double-check all my words for spelling mistakes so that I do not misspell a word. My other goal is to have more paragraphs with a lot of information in it.

Mes commentaires sur mes progrès Les commentaires du professeur

1. Après le 1er travail écrit
I was pleased to see I didn't have any spelling errors. I could have put more information in my paragraph to make it a little longer.

Good goal — add information and plan ways to make sentences more complex?

2. Après le 2e travail écrit
I had some misspellings but not a lot. I had more information but I could have more.

Yes, you succeeded in including more information ☺☺ Bravo! Future goal: 2 well-organized paragraphs??

3. Après le 3e travail écrit
I had more misspellings than I should have. I had a lot of information with 2 paragraphs.

Yes! Good focus and development, too!

FIGURE 4.3 **A Personal Progress Sheet for French II**

Source: A Personal Progress Sheet for French II, developed by Davera Potel, Solon High School, Solon, OH.

◆ I gave examples of the kinds of contributions that would be appropriate: writing samples, self-evaluations (reflections) on a particular project, semantic maps, group projects, peer evaluations—all are acceptable pieces of work to place into the portfolio.

◆ Finally, we discussed the ongoing process of conferencing that will occur in our classroom. I will meet with students on an individual basis to discuss work in progress and assist in deciding which pieces might be placed in the portfolio. Time in class will be scheduled during the week for students to write reflections, ask for peer evaluations, or hold discussions with teachers about the portfolios. Although the actual work may be done at another time (writing, science), the assessment of the work could be done during this regularly scheduled time.

Portfolios are a process! I really want students to understand that their portfolios are a work in progress. I want them to feel comfortable selecting a piece, critiquing others' work, and asking questions. I want them to feel ownership for their own work!

Two examples of Cherrie's students' contributions are a personal progress sheet on writing goals (see Figure 4.4) and a personal reflection on an experiment done in science (see Figure 4.5).

Sometimes teachers simply want to implement portfolios in one subject. Here's how Lynn Fagerholm had her fourth graders construct portfolios as ongoing assessment and direction for their language arts activities over an entire school year. By using chronological ordering as her organizer, each procedure or product was easy to identify as an outcome measure or evidence being collected for later use.

1. *Attitude assessment.* During the first week of school, students will complete the Garfield reading assessment.

2. *Tape of oral reading.* During the first week, students will also read a selection from their science or social studies textbook aloud into a tape recorder to demonstrate reading fluency.

3. *Written paragraph.* Students will compose a paragraph describing characteristics of a good reader and how well they fit that description. (This paragraph will demonstrate knowledge of reading ability and the student's ability to express ideas in written form.)

4. *Reading log.* Students will maintain a running record of all books read during the year.

5. *Genre explorations.* Students will explore the various genres and create presentations for each. These presentations should include

   • Book selected by student.

   • Complete story map.

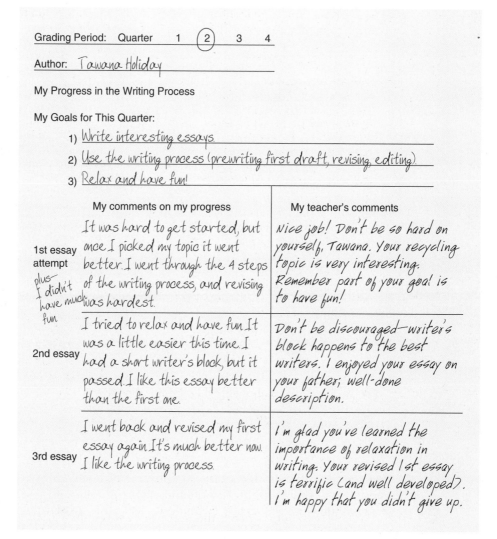

Grading Period: Quarter   1   ②   3   4

Author: Tawana Holiday

My Progress in the Writing Process

My Goals for This Quarter:

1) Write interesting essays.

2) Use the writing process (prewriting, first draft, revising, editing).

3) Relax and have fun!

	My comments on my progress	My teacher's comments
1st essay attempt plus— I didn't have much fun	It was hard to get started, but once I picked my topic it went better. I went through the 4 steps of the writing process, and revising was hardest.	Nice job! Don't be so hard on yourself, Tawana. Your recycling topic is very interesting. Remember part of your goal is to have fun!
2nd essay	I tried to relax and have fun. It was a little easier this time. I had a short writer's block, but it passed. I like this essay better than the first one.	Don't be discouraged—writer's block happens to the best writers. I enjoyed your essay on your father; well-done description.
3rd essay	I went back and revised my first essay again. It's much better now. I like the writing process.	I'm glad you've learned the importance of relaxation in writing. Your revised 1st essay is terrific (and well developed). I'm happy that you didn't give up.

FIGURE 4.4   **A Personal Progress Sheet for Writing**

- Post-it discussion forum: Student places Post-it notes with comments on relationships, personal reflections, or questions throughout the book. These are used during literature conferences held with the teacher periodically as the book is read. Teacher records the conference on a dated discussion form, noting the types of comments and questions raised by the student and the quality of the discussion.

- Project: Students may elect to present in a variety of ways (script, drama, cartoon, advertisement, book talk, poster, letter).

- Evaluation and goals: After the presentation, the student writes an evaluation of the process, the presentation, and goals for the future.

Name _Karen Manto_

Course _Science_

Grade _5_

Date _Oct. 15, 1997_

Experiment:

They're All Wet.—Determine what effect soaking seeds has on the time it takes them to sprout. In a group of four, develop an experiment using the scientific procedure. Evaluate your group from a scientific and cooperative point of view.

Reflection:

I selected the experiment "They're All Wet" as my best work in science for a number of reasons.

① My group worked very well together. Everyone was assigned a job (reader, recorder, speaker, organizer), and everyone got to talk.

② We wrote a sound hypothesis and design for our experiment because we took our time and we thought about the process.

③ We kept very good records of our observations, and then everyone participated in telling about them.

④ Even though our experiment did not prove our hypothesis, I learned many things from this experiment (see above).

Next time maybe my results will support my hypothesis, but I did learn the proper way to conduct an experiment.

FIGURE 4.5 **A Personal Reflection for Science**

6. *Quarter presentation selection.* At the end of each nine-week period, students will evaluate the contents of their portfolio and select the best presentation from that quarter. Students will write a brief paragraph explaining what sets the piece of work apart from the rest. At the end of the year, the portfolio will contain four student-selected genre explorations, along with other pieces of writing that the student considers superior or significant and wishes to include.

7. *Attitude assessment.* During the last few weeks of school, students will again take the Garfield reading attitude assessment and compare the results with those from the first week of school

8. *End-of-year assessment.* At the end of the last grading period, students will review the entire contents of their portfolios and compose a carefully written paper discussing progress made.

9. *Tape of oral reading.* Students will read a selection from the same social studies or science book used at the beginning of the year. They will compare the two recordings, listening for differences and improvements.

10. *Written paragraph.* Students will compose a written paragraph describing what a good reader is and how well they now fit that description. Afterward, they will compare this paragragh with the one written early in the year, noting differences and improvements.

Concerns of Teachers

Teachers everywhere, preschool through adult, have been engaged in the implementation of portfolio assessment as they participate in efforts to balance traditional and alternative assessment practices. For the most part, they are doing so in districts or schools in which assessment is treated as separate from the curriculum and without much, if any, formal training in alternative assessment techniques.

In a study of mathematics teachers, Cooney, Bell, Fisher-Cauble, and Sanchez (1996) interviewed and observed teachers who were attempting to implement some of the new assessment standards developed by the National Council of Teachers of Mathematics. Five major issues were of concern to teachers:

1. *Loss of predictability* creates some risk for teachers who feel more comfortable in a well-organized and predictable classroom in which there is a correct answer to every question. Also, teachers expressed concerns about being observed by administrators who won't realize what you're doing and might "mark you down because your class is kind of loud" (p. 486).

2. *Content coverage and performance on high-stakes tests* are of great concern to teachers of upper-level math courses who need to prepare students to "take the next course" and do well on standardized tests. Middle-childhood teachers, for example, are more likely to use journal writing and portfolios.

3. Students need to be trained by their teachers in *expectations for responding to open-ended questions.* Students used to being graded by the "right" answer will benefit from developing and using scoring rubrics (categories of performance response).

4. *Increased demands on time* suggest that it's a good idea to "start small and go from there" (p. 486). Until teachers actually go through the process from the beginning of the year to the end, they don't have a realistic idea of the amount of time it will take to incorporate portfolios into their classrooms.

5. *Communicating with parents* is essential, especially in terms of helping them interpret their child's grades and understand their child's assignments. Once they have a sense of what the teacher is trying to accomplish, parents can provide considerable support.

Assessing Students' Behavior and Views

Informal assessment techniques such as checklists, interviews, and content area reading inventories (discussed later in this chapter) are different from natural, open-ended observation. They often consist of categories or questions that have already been determined; they impose an a priori classification scheme on the observation process. A checklist is designed to reveal categories of information the teacher has preselected. When constructing a checklist, you should know beforehand which reading and study tasks or attitudes you plan to observe. Individual items on the checklist then serve to guide your observations selectively.

The selectivity that a checklist offers is both its strength and its weakness as an observational tool. Checklists are obviously efficient because they guide your observations and allow you to zero in on certain kinds of behavior. But a checklist can also restrict observation by limiting the breadth of information recorded, excluding potentially valuable raw data.

Figure 4.6 presents sample checklist items that may be adapted to specific instructional objectives in various content areas.

In addition to checklists, observations, and inventories, interviews should be considered part of the portfolio assessment repertoire. There are several advantages of using interviews, "be they *formal,* with a preplanned set of questions, or *informal,* such as a conversation about a book" (Valencia, McGinley, & Pearson 1990, p. 14). First, students and teachers interact in collaborative settings. Second, an open-ended question format is conducive to the sharing of students' own views. Third, it reveals to what extent students are in touch with their internal disposition toward reading subject matter material.

In general, there are several *types of interviews:* structured, semistructured, informal, and retrospective. As described by Fetterman (1989, pp. 48–50), these types blend and overlap in actual practice.

1. *Formally structured and semistructured.* Verbal approximations of a questionnaire; allow for comparison of responses put in the context of common group characteristics; useful in securing baseline data about students' background experiences.

2. *Informal.* More like conversations; useful in discovering what students think and how one student's perceptions compare with another's; help identify shared values; useful in establishing and maintaining a healthy rapport.

3. *Retrospective.* Can be structured, semistructured, or informal; used to reconstruct the past, asking students to recall personal historical information; may highlight their values and reveal information about their worldviews.

One technique developed to interview students about the comprehension process is the Reading Comprehension Interview (Wixson, Bosky, Yochum, & Alvermann 1984). Designed for grades 3 through 8, it takes about

Reading and Study Behavior	Fred	Pat	Frank	JoAnne	Jerry	Courtney	Mike	Mary
Comprehension								
1. Follows the author's message	A	B	B	A	D	C	F	C
2. Evaluates the relevancy of facts								
3. Questions the accuracy of statements								
4. Critical of an author's bias								
5. Comprehends what the author means								
6. Follows text organization								
7. Can solve problems through reading								
8. Develops purposes for reading								
9. Makes predictions and takes risks								
10. Applies information to come up with new ideas								
Vocabulary								
1. Has a good grasp of technical terms in the subject under study								
2. Works out the meaning of an unknown word through context or structural analysis								
3. Knows how to use a dictionary effectively								
4. Sees relationships among key terms								
5. Becomes interested in the derivation of technical terms								
Study Habits								
1. Concentrates while reading								
2. Understands better by reading orally than silently								
3. Has a well-defined purpose in mind when studying								
4. Knows how to take notes during lecture and discussion								
5. Can organize material through outlining								
6. Skims to find the answer to a specific question								
7. Reads everything slowly and carefully								
8. Makes use of book parts								
9. Understands charts, maps, tables in the text								
10. Summarizes information								

Grading Key: A = always (excellent)
B = usually (good)
C = sometimes (average)
D = seldom (poor)
E = never (unacceptable)

FIGURE 4.6   **Sample Checklist Items for Observing Reading and Study Behavior**

30 minutes per student to administer in its entirety. The RCI explores students' perceptions of (1) the purpose of reading in different instructional contexts and content areas, (2) reading task requirements, and (3) strategies the student uses in different contexts.

The RCI's main uses are to help identify patterns of responses (in the whole group and individuals) that then serve as guides to instruction and to analyzing an individual's flexibility in different reading activities.

Several questions on the RCI are particularly appropriate for content area reading. Although the RCI was developed for grades 3 through 8, high school teachers can make good diagnostic use of some of the questions.

Rather than an interview of each student individually, we suggest the following adaptation: Have each student keep a learning log. In these logs, students write to themselves about what they are learning. For example, they can choose to focus on problems they are having with a particular reading assignment or activity. A variation on this general purpose would be to ask students to respond to some of the more pertinent questions on the RCI—perhaps one or two at any one time over several weeks.

In relation to a particular content area textbook, examine the kinds of questions students can write about from the RCI: *

1. What is the most important reason for reading this kind of material? Why does your teacher want you to read this book?

2. Who's the best reader you know in (*content area*)? What does he/she do that makes him/her such a good reader?

3. How good are *you* at reading this kind of material? How do you know?

4. What do you have to do to get a good grade in (*content area*) in your class?

5. If the teacher told you to remember the information in this story/chapter, what would be the best way to do this? Have you ever tried (*name a strategy, e.g., outlining*)?

6. If your teacher told you to find the answers to the questions in this book, what would be the best way to do this? Why? Have you ever tried (*name a strategy, e.g., previewing*)?

7. What is the hardest part about answering questions like the ones in this book? Does that make you do anything differently?

Having students respond to these questions in writing does not deny the importance of interviewing individuals. However, it does save an enormous amount of time while providing a teacher with a record of students' perceptions of important reading tasks related to comprehension.

---

*From "An Interview for Assessing Students' Perceptions of Classroom Reading Tasks," by K. Wixson, A. Bosky, M. Yochum, and D. Alvermann, *The Reading Teacher*, January 1984. Reprinted with permission of the authors and the International Reading Association.

Another way to get at some of the same perceptions that students have about reading activities is through a questionnaire. Hahn (1984) developed a ten-item questionnaire based on modifications of a research instrument used by Paris and Meyers (1981). On the questionnaire, five items—2, 3, 4, 6, and 10—represent positive reading strategies (procedures students should use to comprehend effectively), and five items—1, 5, 7, 8, and 9—depict negative strategies (procedures that are ineffective and should be avoided); see Box 4.1.

Students who rate positive strategies as not very helpful can easily be identified when the questionnaire is scored. These students may benefit from some explicit instruction in the strategies. Also, a good point of discussion would be why the negative strategies are not helpful for effective *studying.*

Box 4.1

Questionnaire on Reading Strategies

Does it help you understand a text selection (or a story) if you . . .

1. Think about something else while you are reading?
_____ always   _____ almost always   _____ almost never   _____ never

2. Write it down in your own words?
_____ always   _____ almost always   _____ almost never   _____ never

3. Underline important parts of the selection?
_____ always   _____ almost always   _____ almost never   _____ never

4. Ask yourself questions about the ideas in the selection?
_____ always   _____ almost always   _____ almost never   _____ never

5. Write down every single word in the selection?
_____ always   _____ almost always   _____ almost never   _____ never

6. Check through the selection to see if you remember all of it?
_____ always   _____ almost always   _____ almost never   _____ never

7. Skip the parts you don't understand in the selection?
_____ always   _____ almost always   _____ almost never   _____ never

8. Read the selection as fast as you can?
_____ always   _____ almost always   _____ almost never   _____ never

9. Say every word over and over?
_____ always   _____ almost always   _____ almost never   _____ never

10. Ask questions about parts of the selection that you don't understand?
_____ always   _____ almost always   _____ almost never   _____ never

Source: Amos Hahn, "Assessing and Extending Comprehension: Monitoring Strategies in the Classroom," *Reading Horizons, 24,* 1984, pp. 225–230. By permission of Western Michigan University, College of Education.

Assessing Students' Prior Knowledge

As we mentioned in Chapter 1, one of the reasons for the recent increase in attention given to prior knowledge is the popularization of a schema-theoretic view of reading. Understanding the role of a schema in reading comprehension provides insights into why students may fail to comprehend text material. Pearson and Spiro (1982) argue that "schema inadequacies" are responsible for a great many roadblocks to reading comprehension.

Three kinds of schema-related problems can interfere with understanding. The first deals with *schema availability*. Students may lack the relevant background knowledge and information needed to comprehend a text assignment. A teacher might ask, "Does my student have the schema necessary to make sense of a particular text selection?"

A second schema inadequacy is *schema selection*. Students who have sufficient background knowledge may fail to bring it to bear as they read. For example, students may be unaware that what they already know about the selection is of any importance in the reading process. How a teacher evaluates and activates an available schema is essential to effective reading instruction in content areas.

A third type of schema inadequacy involves *schema maintenance*. Students may not be aware or skilled enough to recognize when shifts in a schema occur during reading. They may not know how or when to adapt and change schemata as a particular reading situation demands. In other words, how does a teacher help students maintain reader-text interactions during reading? The question implies that readers may have a schema available for a text selection and that it has been activated for reading. But somewhere during reading, the reading process breaks down. Students may get lost in a welter of details or bogged down in the conceptual complexity of the selection. Or they may be unable to interact with the text because of the way it is written: The author's language may be too complex, convoluted, or stylized. As a result, readers process only bits and pieces of the text and fail to grasp the author's broad message or intent.

Determining whether students possess, select, or maintain schemata helps the teacher make decisions about content area reading instruction. For example, one critical decision involves how much prereading preparation students will need for a text assignment. Another might be to decide how much background building and skill direction will be necessary. Seeking information to help make decisions such as these requires that teachers adapt and use the informal, naturalistic procedures that we have already outlined.

One assessment strategy might be to test informally the students' knowledge of the material to be learned. The teacher should construct a background knowledge inventory according to the content objectives—the major ideas and concepts—to be covered in a unit of study. The inventory or pretest can be a checklist, a short-answer quiz, or a set of open-ended essay questions. Many teachers combine short-answer questions with open-ended ones.

The pretest should not be graded; it should be discussed with the class. In fact, use the pretest to introduce students to the major concepts that will be developed in the unit. Explain why you chose to ask certain questions. Share your content objectives with the class. Students will get a sense of what they already know as a result of the discussion. But the discussion should also underscore *what students need to know* about the new material to be studied.

New and experienced teachers alike have a need to find out what their students already know about the subject matter to be taught. While Susan Courtney was doing her field experiences for her math courses before student teaching, she worked with small groups of children in fourth grade, twice a week, to teach the material requested by their teacher. Susan developed a "get to know you" activity that dovetailed with her hands-on style of assessment and instruction with manipulatives. Her goal was to diagnose the children's "comfort level with the subject matter and their background knowledge on an individual basis. I then based lessons on the information I gathered from this assessment. The checklist helped me meet the children on their instructional level—where they were, instead of where I had expected them to be." The assessment checklist in Figure 4.7 is one Susan used with her fourth-grade students studying geometry and fractions.

Alternatives to background knowledge pretesting include assessment procedures that are instructionally based. For example, the prereading plan (PreP) developed by Langer (1981) may be used to estimate background knowledge that students bring to text assignments. It is presented in Chapter 9 as a prereading activity. PreP provides the teacher with practical evaluative information about the extent to which students' language and concepts match up with the text and promote comprehension.

Assessing Students' Attitudes, Interests, and Self-Perceptions

When students learn to analyze a reading assignment by questioning what they know and don't know about the subject matter, they are taking a giant step toward self-awareness. Knowledge of *self* in relation to *texts* and reading *tasks* puts students in a strategic position to learn. Although knowledge of one's own knowledge plays an important role in this respect, a teacher needs to help students get in touch with another aspect of the *self:* their attitude toward reading. Do students value reading as a source of pleasure? As a tool for acquiring knowledge? Do they believe that reading can help them solve problems? Do they read text assignments with confidence? Or do they feel helpless when faced with a textbook assignment?

As technology advances and students become as used to CD-ROMs and computer labs as they are to worksheets, their attitude toward reading is more complex than ever. Lewis and Teale (1980) propose a multidimensional view of reading attitude, which includes such factors as (1) the value placed

Geometry

Using pattern blocks:

_____ Can identify triangles   _____ Can identify squares

_____ Can identify rhombuses   _____ Can identify trapezoids

_____ Can identify hexagons   _____ Can identify parallelograms

Using Geoboards

Can construct shapes with:

_____ right angle   _____ parallel lines

_____ quadrilateral   _____ congruent sides

_____ perpendicular lines

_____ Can give the properties of a square

_____ Can identify lines of symmetry

Fractions

_____ Knows fractional parts must be equal

_____ Can give other names for "1"

_____ Can give other names for "1/2" (generate an equivalent fraction)

_____ Can give another name for "5/4" (rename fractions greater than 1)

_____ Can add fractions with like denominators

_____ Can subtract fractions with like denominators

_____ Can add fractions with unlike but related denominators

_____ Can compare fractions with unlike but related denominators

FIGURE 4.7   **Checklist for Mathematics**

on reading as a means of gaining insight into oneself, others, and life in general; (2) the value placed on the role of reading for attaining educational or vocational success; and (3) the pleasure derived from reading. Reading attitude, based on these factors, consists of three components; a *cognitive* component (one's beliefs or opinions about reading), an *affective* component (one's evaluations of or feelings about reading), and a *behavioral* component (one's intentions to read and actual reading behavior).

Students' interests and self-concepts are interwoven into the fabric of reading attitude. What students *like* to read—their interests—influence when they read, why they read, and how often they read. Moreover, how students *view* their prior experiences with reading and reading instruction also affects their reading attitude. The perceptions they have of themselves as readers can make or break a positive attitude toward reading. McNeil (1987) puts it this way: "Learners have perceptions and feelings about themselves as readers that affect their performance. 'Learned helplessness'—the perceived inability to overcome failure—is particularly self-defeating" (p. 92). Depending on whether students view a reading task as within reach or out of their control, they will probably approach it positively or negatively.

In this book, we show how students can achieve success with textbooks. Developing a positive reading attitude is one of the keys to that success. You can influence positive attitudes toward reading through effective planning, instructional strategies that bridge the gap between students and textbooks, enthusiastic teaching, and a classroom context that supports reading and writing activity. Students may not learn to love reading in some generic sense, but they will learn to value reading as a source of information and knowledge, to believe that it can help them do well in school and everyday life, and to use reading to solve problems and develop insights.

Identifying Attitudes

Reading attitudes are not easy to identify. However, as you and students build a portfolio of evidence about their strengths and instructional needs, it would be difficult to *ignore* their attitudes, interests, and self-concepts.

Observational techniques and attitude scales are the two major means of assessing reading attitude. Indeed, observation is the method most widely used by teachers to assess reading attitudes (Heathington & Alexander 1984). Focused teacher observations in which anecdotal notes or checklists are used can be valuable in identifying and recording attitude, interests, and students' self-perception. So, too, can individual conferences with students. Any of these methods will elicit data about typical attitude-related behavior, including the following (Readence, Bean, & Baldwin 1981):

◆ Willingness to receive instruction

◆ Class participation

◆ Quality of work performed

◆ Library habits

◆ Independent reading

◆ Amount and kind of free reading

◆ Personal goals related to learning

Unfortunately, time constraints often impede continuous informal observation, especially by content area teachers who see five or six different classes each day.

An alternative or partner to observational techniques is a paper-and-pencil attitude survey. An attitude survey should meet certain requirements, such as reliability and validity and take minimal time to administer and score. Certainly, one use of an attitude survey is to document changes in student attitudes through pre- and posttest scores. The survey should be given early in the school year. Data from the assessment should give teachers a better sense of how students in a particular class approach reading in different situations. This is particularly the case when specific survey items cluster around different areas of reading activity in and out of school. By paying attention to students' *cluster scores,* teachers can begin to make plans related to their classroom reading environment. Posttesting later in the year may show that positive changes in attitude occurred for some students in conjunction with the creation of a reading environment and the application of content area reading strategies.

Awareness of the complexity of their reading attitudes can be enlightening to some students. Begin a class discussion of a survey's results by explaining how feelings toward reading may vary from situation to situation. Use the case of two students that is presented by Lewis and Teale (1980). One doesn't enjoy reading and never reads in her spare time, but she sees that reading is valuable to her in achieving success in school. The other student reads for pleasure outside school but doesn't consider reading valuable in school or for career success.

The discussion can lead to an awareness that a negative attitude may be situation-specific. With whom did the class members identify in the Lewis and Teale example? How can the teacher help? The teacher may even want to profile the class results without indicating individual scores. What can be done in this class to make reading a more positive experience?

Exploring Interests and Self-Perceptions

A textbook that appeals to students is probably high in *interestability*, a topic we'll discuss later in connection with evaluating the difficulty of a text to determine its readability. A textbook low in interestability almost always complicates instruction because students make known their lack of interest.

This does not mean that textbooks should be banished to student lockers for the entire school year. Nor does it necessarily mean that a teacher must seek out high-interest, low-vocabulary material to serve as a buffer for the textbook. Some high-interest, low-vocabulary texts have been watered down to a point where key concepts are merely mentioned rather than developed substantively.

An alternative is to help students realize that interest is not inherent in the material but is instead a state of mind (Ortiz 1983). When they express little interest in the material or say that it is boring, they may be masking what they would really like to say, that "this textbook is difficult, and I'm having trouble making sense of what I'm reading." If this is the case, adjustments can be made within the context of instruction to help the students approach the material more positively.

Ortiz (1983) recommends that students reflect on how they become involved or interested in reading material. The teacher might begin the discussion with an exaggerated circumstance: "You're locked in a telephone booth for two hours with a disconnected phone and only the telephone book to read. How would you make it interesting?" After several minutes of suggestions on making the telephone book interesting, switch the topic to textbooks: "Which part of the chapter do you usually find most interesting? Have you ever been bored by one part of a textbook and later become interested in another part? What are some things you can do to make the textbook more interesting?"

The discussion should give valuable insights to the teacher. It can lead to additional activities that will build and reinforce students' awareness of their own interest-generating capability:*

◆ Have students analyze their present reading habits. How do they decide what to read? Where does interest come from? Who controls interest?

◆ Have students select a passage that interests them from several available. Ask them to analyze why they selected a particular passage over the others. Have them read and reflect on what they found themselves doing as they read the passage that was of interest.

◆ Have students scan a table of contents and select items of interest. Analyze why they found them interesting.

◆ Have students lightly dot a passage with a pencil as they read whenever they begin to lose interest. Why?

◆ Have students read a passage they are not interested in and have them find one item they understand. Then have them find another, and so on. Evaluate how understanding relates to interest.

Although students must learn to generate interest in materials that are required for course study, the power of choice should also play a major role in content area reading. Students must have the leeway to read course-related texts of their own choosing.

---

*From "Generating Interest in Reading" by Rose Katz Ortiz, *Journal of Reading,* November 1983. Reprinted with permission of Rose Katz Ortiz and the International Reading Association.

ASSESSING TEXT DIFFICULTY

Evaluating texts and assessing students' interactions with texts are crucial tasks for content area teachers and students—and they call for sound judgment and decision making. One of the best reasons we know for making decisions about the quality of texts is that the assessment process puts you and students in touch with their textbooks. To judge well, you must approach text assessment in much the same manner as you make decisions about other aspects of content area instruction. Any assessment suffers to the extent that it relies on a single source or perspective on information rather than on multiple sources or perspectives. Therefore, it makes sense to consider evidence in the student's portfolio along with several other perspectives.

One perspective or source of information to consider is publisher-provided descriptions of the design, format, and organizational structure of the textbook along with grade-level readability designations. Another perspective is your acquired knowledge of and interactions with the students in the class. A third perspective or source of information is your own sense of what makes the textbook a useful tool. A fourth source is the student perspective, so that instructional decisions are not made from an isolated teacher perception of the student perspective. To complement professional judgment, several procedures can provide you with useful information: readability formulas, cloze procedure, readability checklists, and a content area framework for student analysis of reading assignments. The first order of business, then, if content area reading strategies are to involve students in taking control of their own learning, is to find out how students are interacting with the text.

Assessing Students' Interactions with the Text

Teacher-made tests provide another important indicator of how students interact with text materials in content areas. A teacher-made *content area reading inventory* (CARI) is an alternative to the standardized reading test. The CARI is informal. As opposed to the standard of success on a norm-referenced test, which is a comparison of the performance of the tested group with that of the original normative population, success on the CARI test is measured by performance on the task itself. The CARI measures performance on reading materials actually used in a course. The results of the CARI can give a teacher some good insights into *how* students read course material.

Administering a CARI involves several general steps. First, explain to your students the purpose of the test. Mention that it will be used for evaluation only, to help you plan instruction, and that grades will not be assigned. Second, briefly introduce the selected portion of the text to be read and give students an idea direction to guide silent reading. Third, if you want to find out how the class uses the textbook, consider an open-book evaluation, but if you want to determine students' ability to retain information, have them an-

swer test questions without referring to the selection. Finally, discuss the results of the evaluation individually in conferences or collectively with the entire class.

A CARI can be administered piecemeal over several class sessions so that
large chunks of instructional time will not be sacrificed. The bane of many
content area instructors is spending an inordinate amount of time away from
actual teaching.

A CARI elicits the information you need to adjust instruction and meet student needs. It should focus on students' ability to comprehend text and to read
at an appropriate rate of comprehension. Some authorities suggest that teachers also evaluate additional competency areas, such as study skills—skimming,
scanning, outlining, taking notes, and so forth. We believe, however, that the
best use of reading inventories in content areas is on a much smaller scale. A
CARI should seek information related to basic reading tasks. For this reason,
we recommend that outlining, note taking, and other useful study techniques
be assessed through observation and analysis of student work samples.

Levels of Comprehension

Teachers estimate their students' ability to comprehend text material at different levels of comprehension by using inventories like those in Figure 4.8
for science and Figure 4.9 for American history. These teachers wanted to assess how their students responded at literal (getting the facts), inferential
(making some interpretations), and applied (going beyond the material) levels of comprehension. At this time you can also determine a measure of reading rate in relation to comprehension.

You can construct a comprehension inventory using these steps:

1. Select an appropriate reading selection from the second 50 pages of the
   book. The selection need not include the entire unit or story but should
   be complete within itself in overall content. In most cases, two or three
   pages will provide a sufficient sample.

2. Count the total number of words in the excerpt.

3. Read the excerpt, and formulate 10 to 12 comprehension questions. The
   first part of the test should ask an open-ended question like "What was
   the passage about?" Then develop three or more questions at each level
   of comprehension.

4. Prepare a student response sheet.

5. Answer the questions, and include specific page references for discussion
   purposes after the testing is completed.

While students read the material and take the test, the teacher observes,
noting work habits and student behavior, especially of students who appear

General directions: Read pages 228–233. Then look up at the board and note the time it took you to complete the selection. Record this time in the space provided on the response sheet. Close your book and answer the first question. You may then open your textbook to answer the remaining questions.

STUDENT RESPONSE FORM

Reading time: _____ min. _____ sec.

I. *Directions:* Close your book and answer the following question: In your words, what was this selection about? Use as much space as you need on the back of this page to complete your answer.

II. A. *Directions:* Open your book and answer the following questions.

   1. An insect has six legs and a three-part body.
      a. True
      b. False
      c. Can't tell
   2. Insects go through changes called metamorphosis.
      a. True
      b. False
      c. Can't tell
   3. Most insects are harmful.
      a. True
      b. False
      c. Can't tell
   4. Bees help flowers by moving pollen from flower to flower.
      a. True
      b. False
      c. Can't tell

   B. *Directions:* Answers to these questions are not directly stated by the author. You must "read between the lines" to answer them.

   1. How is a baby cecropia moth different from a full-grown moth?
      _____
   2. Why does a caterpillar molt?
      _____
   3. What are the four stages of a complete metamorphosis?
      _____

   C. *Directions:* Answers to these questions are not directly stated by the author. You must "read beyond the lines" to answer them.

   1. Why do you suppose the caterpillar spins a long thread of silk around itself?
      _____
   2. During which season would the full-grown cecropia moth leave the cocoon? Why?
      _____
   3. Why do you think the moth leaves in that season rather than in another?
      _____

FIGURE 4.8 **Sample Comprehension Inventory in Science**

General directions: Read pages 595–600 in your textbook. Then look up at the board and note the time it took you to complete the selection. Record this time in the space provided on the response sheet. Close your book and answer the first question. You may then open your textbook to answer the remaining questions.

STUDENT RESPONSE FORM

Reading time: _____ min. _____ sec.

I. *Directions:* Close your book and answer the following question: In your own words, what was this section about? Use as much space as you need on the back of this page to complete your answer.

II. *Directions:* Open your book and answer the following questions.

1. To prevent the closing of banks throughout the country, President Roosevelt declared a national "bank holiday."
   a. True
   b. False

2. The purpose of the Social Security Act was to abolish federal unemployment payments.
   a. True
   b. False

3. The National Recovery Administration employed men between the ages of 18 and 25 to build bridges, dig reservoirs, and develop parks.
   a. True
   b. False

4. President Roosevelt established the Federal Deposit Insurance Corporation to insure savings accounts against bank failures.
   a. True
   b. False

III. *Directions:* Answers to these questions are not directly stated by the author. You must "read between the lines" to answer them.

1. Give an example how FDR's first 100 days provided relief, reform, and recovery for the nation.

_____

2. How is the Tennessee Valley Authority an example of President Roosevelt's attempt to help the poorest segment of American society?

_____

3. How did the purpose of the Civil Works Administration differ from the purpose of the Federal Emergency Relief Act?

_____

IV. *Directions:* Answers to these questions are not directly stated by the author. You must "read beyond the lines" to answer them.

1. If FDR would not have promoted his New Deal program through his fireside chats, do you think it would have been successful? Why or why not?

_____

2. Why did FDR's critics fear the New Deal? Do you think their concerns were justified? Why or why not?

_____

3. Which New Deal program would you call the most important? Why?

_____

FIGURE 4.9 **Sample Comprehension Inventory in American History**

frustrated by the test. The science and history teachers of Figures 4.8 and 4.9 allowed students to check their own work as the class discussed each question. Other teachers prefer to evaluate individual students' responses to questions first and then to discuss them with students either individually or during the next class session.

Rates of Comprehension

To get an estimate of students' rates of comprehension, follow these steps:

1. Have students note the time it takes to read the selection. This can be accomplished efficiently by recording the time in five-second intervals by using a "stopwatch" that is drawn on the board.

2. As students complete the reading, they look up at the board to check the stopwatch. The number within the circle represents the minutes that have elapsed. The numbers along the perimeter of the circle represent the number of seconds.

3. Later on, students or the teacher can figure out the students' rate of reading in words per minute.

   Example:
   Words in selection: 1500
    Reading time: 4 minutes 30 seconds
    Convert seconds to a decimal fraction. Then divide time into words.

   $$\frac{1500}{4.5} = 333 \text{ words per minute}$$

4. Determine the percentage of correct or reasonable answers on the comprehension test. Always evaluate and discuss students' rate of reading in terms of their comprehension performance.

In summary, information you glean from a CARI will help you organize specific lessons and activities. You can decide on the background preparation needed, the length of reading assignments, and the reading activities when you apply your best judgment to the information you have learned from the assessment.

Readability

There are many readability formulas that classroom teachers can use to estimate textbook difficulty. Most popular formulas today are quick and easy to calculate. They typically involve a measure of sentence length and word difficulty to determine a grade-level score for text materials. This score supposedly indicates the reading achievement level that students need to comprehend the material. Because of their ease, readability formulas are used to make judgments about materials. These judgments are global and are not intended to be precise indicators of text difficulty.

A readability formula can best be described as a "rubber ruler" because the scores that it yields are estimates of text difficulty, not absolute levels. These estimates are often determined along a single dimension of an author's writing style: sentence complexity (as measured by length) and vocabulary difficulty (also measured by length). These two variables are used to predict text difficulty. But even though they have been shown to be persistent correlates of readability, they only indirectly assess sentence complexity and vocabulary difficulty. Are long sentences always more difficult to comprehend than short ones? Are long words necessarily harder to understand than short ones? When a readability formula is used to rewrite materials by breaking long sentences into short ones, the inferential burden of the reader actually increases (Pearson 1974–1975).

And while we're examining inferential burden, keep in mind that a readability formula doesn't account for the experience and knowledge that readers bring to content material. Hittleman (1973) characterizes readability as a moment in time. He maintains that readability estimates should include the reader's emotional, cognitive, and linguistic background. A person's human makeup interacts at the moment with the topic, the proposed purposes of reading, and the semantic and syntactic structures in the material. Formulas are not designed to tap the variables operating in the reader. Our purpose, interest, motivation, and emotional state as well as the environment that we're in during reading contribute to our ability to comprehend text.

The danger, according to Nelson (1978), is not in the use of readability formulas: "The danger is in promoting the faulty assumptions that matching the readability score of materials to the reading achievement scores of students will automatically yield comprehension" (p. 622). She makes these suggestions to content area teachers (pp. 624–625):

1. Learn to use a simple readability formula as an aid in evaluating text.

2. Whenever possible, provide materials containing the essential facts, concepts, and values of the subject at varying levels of readability within the reading range of your students.

3. Don't assume that matching readability level of material to reading achievement level of students results in automatic comprehension. Remember there are many factors that affect reading difficulty besides those measured by readability formulas.

4. Don't assume that rewriting text materials according to readability criteria results in automatic reading ease. Leave rewriting of text material to the linguists, researchers, and editors who have time to analyze and validate their manipulations.

5. Recognize that using a readability formula is no substitute for instruction. Assigning is not teaching. Subject area textbooks are not designed for independent reading. To enhance reading comprehension in your subject area, provide instruction which prepares students for the assignment, guides them in their reading, and reinforces new ideas through rereading and discussion.

Within the spirit of these suggestions, let's examine a popular readability formula and an alternative, the cloze procedure.

The Fry Graph

The readability graph developed by Edward Fry (1977) is a quick and simple readability formula. The graph was designed to identify the grade-level score for materials from grade 1 through college. Two variables are used to predict the difficulty of the reading material: sentence length and word length. Sentence length is determined by the total number of sentences in a sample passage. Word length is determined by the total number of syllables in the passage. Fry recommended that three 100-word samples from the reading be used to calculate readability. The grade-level scores for each of the passages can then be averaged to determine overall readability. According to Fry, the readability graph predicts the difficulty of the material within one grade level. See Figure 4.10 for the graph and expanded directions for the Fry formula.

Cloze Procedure

The cloze procedure does not use a formula to estimate the difficulty of reading material. Originated by Wilson Taylor in 1953, a cloze test determines how well students can read a particular text or reading selection as a result of their interaction with the material. Simply defined, then, the *cloze procedure* is a method by which you systematically delete words from a text passage and then evaluate students' ability to accurately supply the words that were deleted. An encounter with a cloze passage should reveal the interplay between the prior knowledge that students bring to the reading task and their language competence. Knowing the extent of this interplay will be helpful in selecting materials and planning instructional procedures. Box 4.2 presents part of a cloze test passage developed for a health education class studying sleep.

Here is how to construct, administer, score, and interpret a cloze test.

1. Construction
   a. Select a reading passage of approximately 275 words from material that students have not yet read but that you plan to assign.
   b. Leave the first sentence intact. Starting with the second sentence, select at random one of the first five words. Delete every fifth word thereafter, until you have a total of 50 words for deletion. Retain the remaining sentence of the last deleted word. Type one more sentence

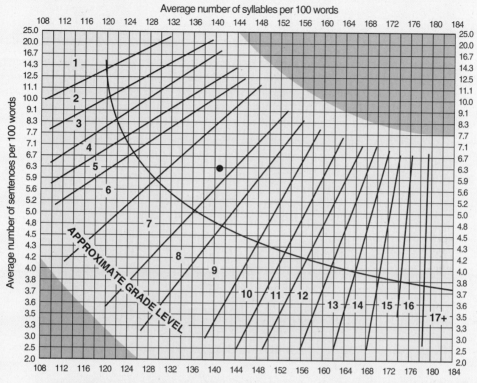

Average number of syllables per 100 words

EXPANDED DIRECTIONS FOR WORKING READABILITY GRAPH

1. Randomly select three (3) sample passages and count out exactly 100 words each, beginning with the beginning of a sentence. Do count proper nouns, initializations, and numerals.
2. Count the number of sentences in the 100 words, estimating length of the fraction of the last sentence to the nearest one-tenth.
3. Count the total number of syllables in the 100-word passage. If you don't have a hand counter available, an easy way is simply to put a mark above every syllable over one in each word; then, when you get to the end of the passage, count the number of marks and add 100. Small calculators can also be used as counters by pushing numeral 1, then pushing the + sign for each word or syllable.
4. Enter graph with *average* sentence length and *average* number of syllables; plot dot where the two lines intersect. Area where dot is plotted will give you the approximate grade level.
5. If a great deal of variability is found in syllable count or sentence count, putting more samples into the average is desirable.
6. A word is defined as a group of symbols with a space on either side; thus *1945* is one word.
7. A syllable is defined as a phonetic syllable. Generally, there are as many syllables as vowel sounds. For example, *stopped* is one syllable and *wanted* is two syllables. When counting syllables for numerals and initializations, count one syllable for each symbol. For example, *1945* is four syllables.

FIGURE 4.10   **Fry Readability Graph**

Source: Courtesy of Edward Fry, Rutgers University Reading Center.

Box 4.2

Sample Portion of a Cloze Test

Everybody sleeps—everybody, that is, except for an Italian and an Australian. These two men, according (1) twentieth-century medical literature, (2) slept at all. On (3) other hand, not long (4) the *New York Times* (5) on a professor who (6) to have fourteen hours (7) sleep a night. If (8) woke after even thirteen (9), he spent the day (10) foggy and tense. Apart (11) their sleeping patterns, though, (12) three men, according to (13) experts on such matters, (14) to be perfectly normal. (15) why, by inference, assume (16) their sleep habits were (17)? Indeed, when it comes (18) sleep, what is normal (19), by contrast, abnormal? Who's (20) say that what's perfectly natural for me might not be absurd for you?

ANSWERS:

1. to	6. had	11. from	16. that
2. never	7. of	12. these	17. abnormal
3. the	8. he	13. the	18. to
4. ago	9. hours	14. appeared	19. and
5. reported	10. feeling	15. Yet	20. to

intact. For children below grade 4, deletion of every tenth word is often more appropriate.

   c. Leave an underlined blank of 15 spaces for each deleted word as you type the passage.

2. Administration

   a. Inform students that they are not to use their textbooks or to work together in completing the cloze passage.

   b. Explain the task that students are to perform. Show how the cloze procedure works by providing several examples on the board.

   c. Allow students the time they need to complete the cloze passage.

3. Scoring

   a. Count as correct every *exact* word students apply. *Do not* count synonyms even though they may appear to be satisfactory. Counting synonyms will not change the scores appreciably, but it will cause unnecessary hassles and haggling with students. Accepting synonyms also affects the reliability of the performance criteria, since they were established on exact word replacements.

   b. Multiply the total number of exact word replacements by 2 to determine the student's cloze percentage score.

| Subject _____ |
| Period _____ |
| Teacher _____ |

Below 40 percent	Between 40 and 60 percent	Above 60 percent

FIGURE 4.11   **Headings for a Cloze Performance Chart**

    c. Record the cloze scores on a sheet of paper for each class. For each class, you now have one to three instructional groups that can form the basis for differentiated assignments (see Figure 4.11).

  4. Interpretation

    a. A score of 60 percent or above indicates that the passage can be read competently by students. They may be able to read the material on their own without guidance.

    b. A score of 40 to 60 percent indicates that the passage can be read with some competency by students. The material will challenge students if they are given some form of reading guidance.

    c. A score below 40 percent indicates that the passage will probably be too difficult for students. They will need either a great deal of reading guidance to benefit from the material or more suitable material.

The cloze procedure is an alternative to a readability formula because it gives an indication of how students will actually perform with course materials. Unfortunately, the nature of the test itself will probably be foreign to students. They will be staring at a sea of blank spaces in running text, and having to provide words may seem a formidable task. Don't expect a valid score the first time you administer the test. It's important to discuss the purpose of the cloze test and to give students ample practice with and exposure to it.

Readability Checklist

Despite the many factors to be considered in text evaluation, *teachers ultimately want texts that students will understand, be able to use, and want to use.* To help guide your assessment and keep it manageable, a checklist that focuses on *understandability, usability,* and *interestability* is useful. One such checklist is shown in Box 4.3, an adaptation of the Irwin and Davis (1980) Readability Checklist.

Box 4.3

General Textbook Readability Checklist

In the blank before each item, indicate ✓ for "yes," + for "to some extent," or x for "no" or "does not apply."

Understandability

_____ 1. Are the assumptions about students' vocabulary knowledge appropriate?

_____ 2. Are the assumptions about students' prior knowledge of this content area appropriate?

_____ 3. Are the assumptions about students' general experiential background appropriate?

_____ 4. Does the teacher's manual provide the teacher with ways to develop and review the students' conceptual and experiential background?

_____ 5. Are new concepts explicitly linked to the students' prior knowledge or to their experiential background?

_____ 6. Does the text introduce abstract concepts by accompanying them with many concrete examples?

_____ 7. Does the text introduce new concepts one at a time, with a sufficient number of examples for each one?

_____ 8. Are definitions understandable and at a lower level of abstraction than the concept being defined?

_____ 9. Does the text avoid irrelevant details?

_____ 10. Does the text explicitly state important complex relationships (e.g., causality and conditionality) rather than always expecting the reader to infer them from the context?

_____ 11. Does the teacher's manual provide lists of accessible resources containing alternative readings for the very poor or very advanced readers?

_____ 12. Is the readability level appropriate (according to a readability formula)?

Usability

External Organizational Aids

_____ 1. Does the table of contents provide a clear overview of the contents of the textbook?

_____ 2. Do the chapter headings clearly define the content of the chapter?

_____ 3. Do the chapter subheadings clearly break out the important concepts in the chapter?

_____ 4. Do the topic headings provide assistance in breaking the chapter into relevant parts?

_____ 5. Does the glossary contain all the technical terms in the textbook?

_____ 6. Are the graphs and charts clear and supportive of the textual material?

_____ 7. Are the illustrations well done and appropriate to the level of the students?

_____ 8. Is the print size of the text appropriate to the level of student readers?

_____ 9. Are the lines of text an appropriate length for the level of the students who will use the textbook?

_____ 10. Is a teacher's manual available and adequate for guidance to the teachers?

_____ 11. Are the important terms in italics or boldfaced type for easy identification by readers?

_____ 12. Are the end-of-chapter questions on literal, interpretive, and applied levels of comprehension?

Internal Organizational Aids

_____ 1. Are the concepts spaced appropriately throughout the text, rather than being too many in too short a space or too few words?

_____ 2. Is an adequate context provided to allow students to determine the meanings of technical terms?

_____ 3. Are the sentence lengths appropriate to the level of students who will be using the text?

_____ 4. Is the author's style (word length, sentence length, sentence complexity, paragraph length, numbers of examples) appropriate to the level of students who will be using the text?

_____ 5. Does the author use a predominant structure or pattern of organization (compare-contrast, cause-effect, time order, problem-solution) within the writing to assist students in interpreting the text?

(continued)

Box 4.3
(con't)

General Textbook Readability Checklist

Interest

_____ 1. Does the teacher's manual provide introductory activities that will capture students' interests?

_____ 2. Are the chapter titles and subheadings concrete, meaningful, or interesting?

_____ 3. Is the writing style of the text appealing to the students?

_____ 4. Are the activities motivating? Will they make the student want to pursue the topic further?

_____ 5. Does the book clearly show how what is being learned might be used by the learner in the future?

_____ 6. Are the cover, format, print size, and pictures appealing to the students?

_____ 7. Does the text provide positive and motivating models for both sexes as well as for other racial, ethnic, and socioeconomic groups?

_____ 8. Does the text help students generate interest as they relate experiences and develop visual and sensory images?

SUMMARY RATING

Circle one choice for each item.

The text rates highest in understandability / usability / interest.

The text rates lowest in understandability / usability / interest.

My teaching can best supplement understandability / usability / interest.

I would still need assistance with understandability / usability / interest.

STATEMENT OF STRENGTHS:

STATEMENT OF WEAKNESSES:

Source: Adapted from Judith W. Irwin and Carol A. Davis, "Assessing Readability: The Checklist Approach"(November 1980). _Journal of Reading,_ 24(2), 124–130. Copyright © 1980 by the International Reading Association. All rights reserved.Used by permission of the authors and the International Reading Association.

The domain of *understandability* provides information about how likely a given group of students is to comprehend the text adequately. It helps the teacher assess relationships between the students' own schemata and conceptual knowledge and the text information. When teachers judge textbooks for possible difficulties, it is imperative to decide whether the author has taken into consideration the knowledge students will bring to the text. The match between what the reader knows and the text will have a strong influence on the understandability of the material.

Armbruster and Anderson (1981) indicate that one way to judge the author's assumptions about students' background knowledge and experiences is to decide if enough relevant ideas are presented in a text to satisfy the author's purpose. Often, authors use headings to suggest their purposes for text passages. Convert the headings to questions. If the passage content answers the questions, the authors have achieved their purposes and the passage is *considerate.* If an author hasn't provided enough information to make a passage meaningful, the passage is *inconsiderate.*

The second major domain is *usability.* Is the text coherent, unified, and structured enough to be usable? Divided into two subsections on the Readability Checklist, this section provides information about the presentation and organization of content. It will help the teacher assess pertinent factors that will contribute to the day-to-day use of the text in teaching and the students' use in learning. These items help pinpoint for a teacher exactly what needs supplementing or what may take additional preparation time or class time to compensate.

Essentially, a teacher's response to these items is another way of deciding if a text is considerate or inconsiderate. A considerate text not only fits the reader's prior knowledge but also helps "the reader to gather appropriate information with minimal cognitive effort"; an inconsiderate text "requires the reader to put forth extra effort" to compensate for poorly organized material (Armbruster & Anderson 1981, p. 3).

The third domain, *interestability,* is intended to ascertain whether features of the text will appeal to a given group of students. Illustrations and photos may have instant appeal; students can relate to drawings and photographs depicting persons similar to themselves. The more relevant the textbook, the more interesting it may be to students.

Experiment with the Readability Checklist by trying it out on a textbook in your content area. Once you've completed the checklist, sum up your ratings at the end. Does the text rate high in understandability, usability, or interestability? Is a low rating in an area you can supplement well through your instruction, or is it in an area in which you could use more help? Also, summarize the strengths and weaknesses of the textbook. If you noted two areas in which you'd still need assistance, this text is less likely than another to meet your needs. Finally, decide how you can take advantage of the textbook's strengths and compensate for its weaknesses.

Friendliness:

How friendly is the book *Under the Sea*?

Is the index clearly organized? How?

What about the table of contents?

—big print —pictures
—it asks questions
—yes　　—space
—has page #s

Language:

How many new terms/words do you see on pages 6–10?

—lots　—only 5
—not too many
—we had some

How difficult does the author's writing look to you?

—I can't tell yet
—not too hard

Interest:

In what ways does *Under the Sea* look interesting to you?

Why?/Why not?

—It's like Epcot
—Lots of pictures
—Too many fish

Prior Knowledge:

Look at the title and the subheadings on pages 6–10. What do you already know about these topics in *Under the Sea*?

—That there are plants in the ocean
　—Kinds of fish

FIGURE 4.12　**A FLIP for Third Grade Science**

FLIP Strategy

Efforts to directly access student- or reader-based judgment have resulted in a strategy to provide students with the guidelines they need to size up reading tasks (Schumm & Mangrum 1991). Whereas checklists and formulas are designed for *teacher* use, a strategy such as FLIP (an acronym for *friendliness, language, interest,* and *prior knowledge*) is designed to engage the *reader* in estimating the level of difficulty of a given source or textbook. With teacher guidance, perhaps using an overhead projector and the think-aloud technique, students actually walk through FLIP and consider these factors:

Friendliness: How friendly is my reading assignment? *(Students look for text features such as index, graphs, pictures, summaries, and study questions)*

Language: How difficult is the language in my reading assignment? *(Students estimate the number of new terms.)*

Interest: How interesting is my reading assignment? *(Students look over the title, headings, pictures, etc.)*

Prior knowledge: What do I already know about the material covered in my reading assignment? *(Students think about the title, heading, summary, etc.)*

(pp. 121–122)

Figure 4.12 illustrates how Kristen Hecker uses a FLIP strategy to help her third graders assess the level of difficulty of *Under the Sea,* a book about different life forms living in the ocean, by Claire Llewellyn (1991). First, she asks the students to look at the pictures in the text and share what they think the book will be about with two of their classmates. Then she helps the whole class examine the tools used by the author in the book: glossary, table of contents, and index. Using an overhead projector, Kristen guides her third graders through the questions on the left side of the FLIP, making sure to record their answers, including those who don't agree with the majority.

 ## LOOKING BACK, LOOKING FORWARD

Making authentic assessments is a continuous process in which teachers and students collect and analyze information about classroom interactions and texts and themselves. Multiple methods of gathering relevant data are taken from two distinct approaches to assessment: a formal, standardized one and an informal, naturalistic one. To develop goals and objectives for teaching, you need (1) to access information about students' prior knowledge in relation to instructional units and text assignments, (2) to assess student knowledge and use of reading strategies to learn from texts, and (3) to assess materials.

An informal, naturalistic approach is a precursor to portfolio assessment. Through the use of portfolios, a more balanced approach to collecting and organizing many kinds of information can inform decision making. Careful observation of students' strengths and weaknesses as the students interact with one another and with content-specific material sheds light on the *why* as well as the *what* in teaching and learning.

In this chapter, the key terms, major purposes, and legitimate uses of standardized tests were presented. Contrasts were drawn between portfolios and testing. As teachers engage learners in a process of portfolio assessment, they make adaptations appropriate for their subject matter and consider issues that have been raised about using portfolios. Suggestions for assessing students' background knowledge included interviews, pretesting, and instructionally based strategies. Attitudes, interests, and self-perceptions rely on the interpretation of interviews, surveys, scales, and teacher observation. For insights into how students interact with text material and a measure of performance on the reading materials used in a course, teacher-made content area reading inventories were suggested.

Assessing the difficulty of text material requires both professional judgment and quantitative analysis. Text assessment takes into account various factors within the reader and the text, the exercise of professional judgment being as useful as calculating a readability formula. Teachers, therefore, must be concerned about the quality of the content, format, organization, and appeal of the material. We supplied three types of procedures for assessing text difficulty: readability formulas, the cloze procedure, and readability checklists. Finally, we offered some techniques that will help assist content area teachers reflect on their own attitudes and behaviors in the classroom and school environment.

MINDS-ON

1. You are about to teach your first class of the school year in a school whose standardized test scores have been extremely low over the past few years. Although a text has been chosen for your class, you have a wide range of auxiliary reading materials and teaching materials to choose from. You also have full authority to add and subtract from the course curriculum to meet the needs, abilities, and interests of your students. Keep in mind, however, that the superintendent is interested in improving test scores. Develop a complete plan of assessment, and give the rationale for your choices.

2. For keeping records, most portfolios of student work include a cover page, one that reflects the teacher's philosophy of assessment. With the members of your group, select a content area, and design a cover page that reflects your vision of authentic assessment.

3. Imagine that you are a new teacher, reviewing the required text you will be using in the fall. Initially, you find the book fascinating, and you are certain it will excite many of your students. Yet after analyzing the work, you discover that its readability appears to be above the reading level of most of your students. How might you use this text effectively?

4. Readability formulas are predictive measures. How do predictive measures differ from performance measures in helping you determine how difficult reading materials will be for your students?

HANDS-ON

1. In small groups, evaluate a standardized reading test frequently used at the secondary level. If possible, perform this evaluation by examining a copy of the technical manual that accompanies each standardized test. Consider questions such as What is the declared validity of the test? Its reliability? Its norming population? Its passage content? Its passage length? What conclusions can you draw from your evaluation? Will this test meet the needs of your students?

2. Develop an observation checklist for the assessment of reading and study behavior in your content area. Compare your checklist with those developed by others in the class for similar content areas. What conclusions might you draw?

3. Each member of your group should locate one sample of text material on the same topic from these sources: an elementary content area text, a secondary content area text, a newspaper, and a popular magazine. Determine the readability of a sample passage from each by using two different readability formulas. Compare your findings by using two additional readability formulas. What conclusions can you draw from the comparison?

4. Two members of your group should be designated as observers. The other members should collaboratively attempt to solve the following mathematics problem:

   Calculate the surface area of a cylinder that is 12 inches long and 5 inches in diameter.

   Note any observations that you feel might be useful in assessing the group's performance. What types of useful information do observations like these provide?

SUGGESTED READINGS

Fry, E. (1989). Reading formulas—maligned but valid. *Journal of Reading, 32,* 292–297.

Garcia, G., & Pearson, P. D. (1994). Assessment and diversity. *Review of Research in Education, 20,* 337–391.

International Reading Association and National Council of Teachers of English. (1994). *Standards for the assessment of reading and writing.* Newark, DE: International Reading Association.

Jongsma, E., & Farr, R. (1993). A themed issue on literacy assessment. *Journal of Reading, 36,* 516–600.

Kibby, M. (1993). What reading teachers should know about reading proficiency in the U.S. *Journal of Reading, 37,* 28–41.

Moje, E., Brozo, W., & Haas, J. (1994). Portfolios in a high school classroom: Challenges to change. *Reading Research and Instruction, 33,* 275–292.

Rhodes, L. (Ed.). (1993). *Literacy assessment: A handbook of instruments.* Portsmouth, NH: Heinemann.

Tierney, R. J., Carter, M. A., & Desai, L. E. (1991). *Portfolio assessment in the reading-writing classroom.* Norwood, MA: Christopher-Gordon.

Vacca, J. L., Vacca, R. T., & Gove, M. K. (1995). *Reading and learning to read* (3rd ed.). New York: HarperCollins.

Valencia, S., Hiebert, E., & Afflerbach, P. (Eds.). (1993). *Authentic assessment: Practices & possibilities.* Newark, DE: International Reading Association.

Valencia, S., McGinley, W., & Pearson, P. D. (1990). Assessing reading and writing. In G. Duffy (Ed.), *Reading in the middle school* (pp. 124–153). Newark, DE: International Reading Association.

Wiggins, G. (1993). Assessment to improve performance, not just monitor: Assessment reform in the social sciences. *Social Science Record, 30,* 5–12.

Wolf, K., & Siu-Runyan, Y. (1996). Portfolio purposes and possibilities. *Journal of Adolescent and Adult Literacy, 40,* 30–37.

Content Literacy Connections

PART 2

5

Bringing Students and Texts Together

To win without risk is to triumph without glory.
—Pierre Corneille

Organizing Principle

Teachers who rethink business as usual do so because they are committed to responding to the fast-paced changes that are occuring in their professional lives: Students are changing. Classrooms are changing. Theories of what it means to teach and learn are changing. Even notions of what constitutes a text are changing. Computers are quickly redefining what counts as literacy, and the rapid growth of the trade book industry for children and adolescents is changing the way content area teachers think about text learning in classrooms. As a result, bringing students and texts together is one of the important content literacy connections to be made in content area classsrooms.

Bringing students and texts together, however, is not without its risks or its rewards. Without risks, teaching often lacks adventure and innovation. Adventuresome teachers have enough confidence in themselves to experiment with instructional practices, even if they are uncertain of the outcomes. They are willing to go out on a creative limb and then reflect on what they do and why. If there is such a thing as glory in teaching, it often accompanies the teacher who dares to depart from the norm.

When students use literacy to learn, there's little room for assign-and-tell practices, passive learning, or students sitting in straight rows with little opportunity for interaction. Teachers who create active learning environments in their classrooms know that something not worth doing isn't worth doing well. This is especially true of passive text learning. Showing students how to use literacy to learn is worth doing—and worth doing well. The time it takes to plan literacy experiences will get you the results you want: active and purposeful learning of text materials. Planning gives you a blueprint for making decisions. The blueprint may be for a core text assignment or for multiple reading experiences involving a variety of printed and electronic texts. The organizing principle underscores the importance of active text learning in content area classrooms: **Bringing learners and texts together involves plans and practices that result in active student engagement and collaboration.**

How teachers plan lessons and units of study is the cornerstone of content literacy and learning. As you prepare to read this chapter, ask yourself why "the classroom context"—the physical, psychological, and social environments that evolve from the interactions among teachers, students, and texts—is at the top of the chapter overview.

Chapter Overview

BRINGING STUDENTS AND TEXTS TOGETHER

THE CLASSROOM CONTEXT

CREATING ACTIVE LEARNING ENVIRONMENTS

Organizing a Core Text Lesson

Planning an
Instructional Framework

Prereading   Postreading

Reader-Text Interactions

Organizing a Thematic Unit

Planning a
Thematic Unit

Creating an Inquiry/Research Focus

Finding and Investigating Problems

Library   Electronic
Resources   Resources

Human Resources

1. How can content area teachers organize instruction so that students will become actively engaged in reading and writing? Why do students need structure?

2. What is involved in designing an instructional framework for a core text assignment?

3. How does planning a thematic unit help the teacher coordinate instructional activities and texts?

4. How do teachers create an inquiry/research focus for thematic units?

Good teachers know their subject matter. A colleague's professional competence is often judged by how well informed and up-to-date she or he is in a particular field. Good teachers also know that an intimate knowledge of a subject isn't in itself a sure ticket to success in the classroom. Another aspect of professional competence lies in getting content across to students.

Getting content across is always a challenging task. The challenge is more pronounced than ever when texts become tools for learning. Bringing learners and texts together isn't easy, but neither is it impossible.

Assign-and-tell practices are deeply rooted in the culture of American schools. A teacher shouting a reading assignment to students as they hustle out the door at the end of the period probably happens more than we would like to admit. Under these conditions, the reading assignment is often purposeless. Why read it? The answer students give too frequently is "Because it was assigned." The only real purpose for such reading is to get through the material. Getting through is the prime motivation when the assignment lacks any consideration of where students are going and how they will get there.

Answering questions at the end of the selection is an important part of the getting-through syndrome. A favorite ploy of some students is to give the teacher a three-liner: an answer to a question that fills up three lines on a sheet of paper. Whether or not the response is thoughtful or fully developed, three lines suffice.

The class discussion that follows such an assignment usually slips quickly away from the students to the teacher. If the students can't or won't learn the material through reading, they'll get it through lecture or other means.

Mark Twain wrote in *Life on the Mississippi,* "I'll learn him or I'll kill him!" The same principle applies in spirit to assign-and-tell practices in classrooms. If students learn anything, they learn that they don't have to read course material because there are alternative routes to acquiring the information. The end result is passive reading or no reading at all.

Texts should be an important part of the *classroom context* in which teaching and learning occur. The interactions and transactions among teachers, students, and texts form the very basis for classroom communication, comprehension, and learning. To bring students and texts together requires an appreciation and understanding of the various contexts in which teaching and learning occur.

THE CLASSROOM CONTEXT

What happens in a particular class on a particular day depends on the interactions that occur between the teacher, the students, and the material being studied. The classroom context, generally speaking, includes all the factors that influence what happens during teaching and learning. These factors operate on different levels.

More than Just a Room

On one level, for example, the *physical context* influences what happens in the classroom. Space may restrict participation, depending on how a teacher interprets the situation. You see, the decision is still the teacher's to make. A math teacher explained why she permitted small-group work in one class but not in another: "Several overly rambunctious students and not enough room to spread them apart." Some teachers use their surroundings to promote learning. Bulletin boards reflect themes or topics being studied; a display area prominently arrays students' written work for others to read. Of course, some teachers remain oblivious of the physical environment that they and their students inhabit together. A room, after all, is just a room. Yet the physical environment of the classroom affects the nature and types of interactions that will occur. Straight rows of desks, for example, are conducive to classroom lectures and turn-taking routines in which students, one by one, recite answers to a teacher's questions.

A room isn't just a room for teachers who seek to make the physical environment compatible with interactive learning. Interactive learning invites thinking, reading, writing, speaking, listening, and sharing. Such classrooms are arranged for individuals rather than for the class as a whole; they welcome students as active participants rather than pigeonhole them as passive recipients (Noden & Vacca 1994). Various physical arrangements encourage interactive learning, such as the one illustrated in Figure 5.1, but they depend on the size of the room and the furniture that is available.

With the design in Figure 5.1, a class can be organized for individual, group, or whole-class activities. Students are initially assigned seats at a combination of small and large tables. However, when the students work in-

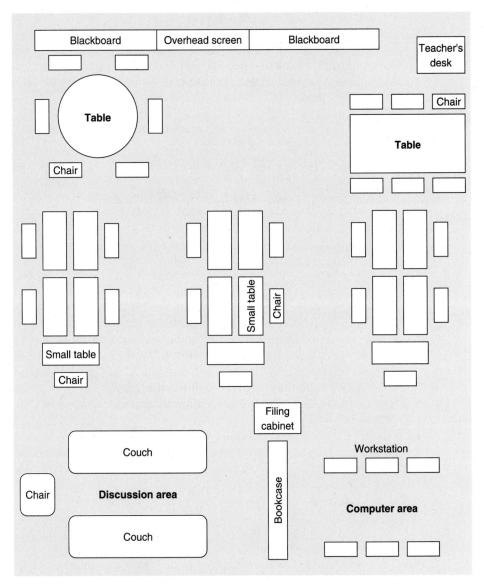

FIGURE 5.1   **A Physical Arrangement Conducive to Social Interaction in the Classroom**

dividually or in groups, they are free to abandon the assigned seating. The chalkboard (and/or overhead transparency screen) occupies a central position in the room to accommodate whole-class study.

First and foremost, interactions are social. And because they are social, interactions involve language use. The physical context, then, is necessarily tied to another dimension of the classroom: its social context.

Teacher and Students Working Together

The *social context* for learning has a tremendous effect on what happens in the classroom. The social environment depends on what the teacher and students do together. Classroom learning is as much collaborative as it is individual. It often involves on-the-spot decision making: Who gets to do what? With whom? When? Where? Because most learning situations in the classroom are face-to-face encounters, they necessarily entail language. Most instructional routines, therefore, build on a series of conversational acts between teacher and students and between students and students. These acts are governed by rules (Green & Harker 1982). Students quickly learn the rules and interact with the teacher or with other students accordingly.

In content area classrooms, communication between teacher and students, students and other students, and students and texts always occurs within a *language context*—that is, the *pragmatic,* or practical, situation in which reading, writing, talking, and listening take place.

A math teacher assigns a chapter section on the topic "angles," as well as several problems to be solved using information from the text. The context includes the students' purpose, the reading task, the set of relationships established over time between the math teacher and the students, the relationship of the students to the textbook, and all the conditions surrounding the learning situation. The context affects the way students will interact with the text and the quality of that interaction. The students' purpose, for example, will influence how they read the material. The task—reading to solve problems—also affects how students will approach the text and tackle the assignment.

Active Minds, Engaged Readers

The physical and social factors that influence the classroom context contribute heavily to the psychological and intellectual climate of content area classrooms. A healthy psychological context, as we have suggested in earlier chapters, is one that promotes student engagement. Engaged readers and writers are knowledgeable, strategic, motivated, and socially interactive. Alvermann and Guthrie (1993) put it this way: Engaged readers are architects of their own learning. They use prior knowledge and a variety of strategies to construct meaning with texts. Furthermore, they are internally motivated to succeed in learning tasks that involve literacy and choose to read and write as a way of knowing and enjoying.

Creating the physical, social, and psychological contexts for literacy is no easy matter. Yet the classroom environment is a source of study and fascination for teachers who search for meaning in what they do. Teaching is tough, complicated, and demanding work that doesn't get easier with time. However, one's teaching gets better because teachers are learners. And one of the ways a teacher learns best is through on-the-job experience. The more experienced you become at what you do, the more you develop "craft knowledge" or wisdom of practice (Leinhardt 1990).

Pathima, mathima is an old Greek expression. Loosely translated, it means, "You learn from the things that happen to you." And teachers do. The problem, of course, is that it is difficult to learn about teaching from experience if you're not tuned in to the context in which teaching and learning occur.

The development of craft knowledge about content literacy practices begins with the awareness that making the connection between literacy and learning involves a departure from assign-and-tell routines. Tuning in to the classroom context leads a teacher to ask, "How can I create active learning environments where students not only act on ideas encountered in texts but also interact with one another?" Bringing students and texts together requires that you tune in to the classroom factors and conditions that support active learning and then plan frameworks for instruction that will get you the results you seek.

Someone in the world of business once said that 90 percent of your results come from activities that consume 10 percent of your time. When this saying is applied to education, the time teachers take to plan and organize active learning environments is time well spent. Planning appropriate frameworks for instruction may include the design of *core text lessons* and *thematic units* revolving around student-centered inquiry and self-selection from an array of text possibilities. A core text lesson implies that all of the students in class are reading the same text. These lessons usually evolve from textbook assignments or from a whole-class reading of a trade book, frequently referred to as a *core book study*. A thematic unit, by contrast, suggests a departure from an exclusive focus on a core text. Units are designed around central themes or concepts and free students to pursue questions that intrigue or puzzle them in relation to the theme or topic under study. Because inquiry is at the heart of a thematic unit, students will read a wide range of texts related to the thematic explorations they are pursuing.

Lessons and units provide a blueprint for action. Whether the focus is on a core text or a thematic exploration, having a plan in advance of actual practice is just good common sense. The organization of the lesson or unit is a thread that runs through content area instruction. A game plan is essential because students respond well to structure. When reading text material, they need to sense where they are going and how they will get there. Classroom experiences without rhyme or reason lack the direction and stability that students need to grow as readers.

Lessons should be general enough to include all students and flexible enough to allow the teacher to react intuitively and spontaneously when a particular plan is put in actual practice. In other words, lessons shouldn't restrict decisions about the instruction that is in progress; instead, they should encourage flexibility and change.

Some teachers, no doubt, will argue that a lesson plan is an educational artifact and that it's too restrictive for today's learners. Yet we're convinced that "to say that lesson planning is not appropriate is to say that thinking in advance of acting is inappropriate" (Mallan & Hersh 1972, p. 41). A good lesson plan provides a framework for making decisions—nothing more, nothing less.

ORGANIZING CORE TEXT LESSONS

Teachers tend to do their planning by focusing on activities they will do with students rather than proceeding from a list of objectives to instructional activities. The preparation of core text lessons should focus on what will be happening in the classroom—for example, what the teacher will be doing and what the students will be doing. The value of imagining should not be underestimated as a planning tool. Teachers think about instruction by envisioning in their minds how classroom activities are likely to unfold for a particular group of students in a particular instructional context. This thinking through of a lesson is like playing an imaginary videotape of the lesson in which the teacher plans the questions to be asked, the sequence of instructional activity, and the adjustments to be made should something not work.

Throughout this book, we encourage you to imagine how alternative instructional strategies and activities will work and what adjustments you may have to make to meet your own particular needs and fit your own classroom context. If you have yet to teach, we invite you to imagine how you might use strategies and activities in thoughtfully planned lessons.

Planning an Instructional Framework

There's no one way to plan an effective core text lesson. The instructional framework (IF) offers the content area teacher a fairly representative approach to lesson organization (Herber 1978). Regardless of which type of plan is used, certain provisions must be made for any text-centered lesson to be effective. What the teacher does *before reading, during reading,* and *after reading* is crucial to active and purposeful reading.

The IF can help teachers envision a single lesson involving reading. A lesson doesn't necessarily take place in a single class session; several class meetings may be needed to achieve the objectives of the lesson. Nor do all the components of an IF necessarily receive the same emphasis in any given reading assignment; the difficulty of the material, students' familiarity with the topic, and your judgment all play a part when you decide on the sequence of activities you will organize. What the IF tells you is that readers need varying degrees of guidance. As we show throughout this book, there are prereading, reading, and postreading activities that will support students' efforts to make meaning and construct knowledge through integrated language use. The components of an IF can be examined in Figure 5.2.

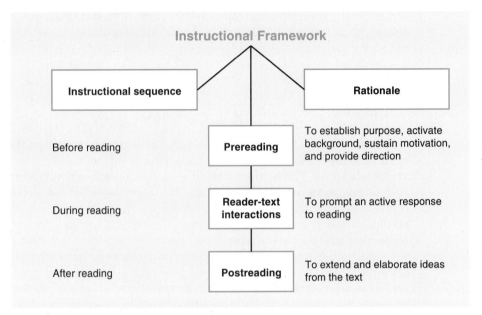

FIGURE 5.2   **The Instructional Framework (IF) in Content Areas**

Prereading

An IF that includes activity and discussion before reading reduces the uncertainty that students bring to an assignment. Prereading activities get students ready to read, to approach text material critically, and to seek answers to questions they have raised about the material. During the prereading phase of instruction, a teacher often places emphasis on one or more of the following: (1) motivating readers, (2) building and activating prior knowledge, (3) introducing key vocabulary and concepts, and (4) developing metacognitive awareness of the task demands of the assignment and the strategies necessary for effective learning.

A key factor related to motivation is activating students' interest in the text reading. However, before we take into consideration how to motivate students, we must first raise a fundamental question: Why should students be interested in this lesson? A teacher may even wish to consider whether he or she is interested in the material! If teachers are going to be models of enthusiasm for students, then the first step is to find something in the material to get really excited about. Enthusiasm—it is almost too obvious to suggest—is contagious.

Building and activating prior knowledge for a lesson and presenting key vocabulary and concepts are also essential to prereading preparation. In making decisions related to prior knowledge, it's important to review previous lessons in light of present material. What does yesterday's lesson have to do with today's? Will students make the connection to previously studied material? Sometimes several minutes of review before forging into uncharted realms of learning can make all the difference in linking new information to old. Furthermore, when deciding which vocabulary terms to single out for prereading instruction, we emphasize three questions that should be considered: What key words will students need to understand? Are all the terms equally important? Which new words carry heavy concept loads?

Prereading may also include discussions that develop an awareness of the reading task at hand and of the strategies needed to handle the task effectively. These are metacognitive discussions. Providing direction is another way of saying that students will develop task knowledge and self-knowledge about their own learning strategies. Helping students analyze the reading task ahead of them and modeling a learning strategy that students will need during reading are two metacognitive activities that quickly come to mind. Here are some general questions to ask in planning for a metacognitive discussion: What are the most important ideas in the lesson? What strategies will students need to learn these ideas? Are the students *aware* of these strategies?

An IF also includes provisions for guiding the search for meaning during reading. In other words, students need to be shown how to think with texts as they read.

Reader-Text Interactions

Teachers easily recognize the important parts of a text assignment. Most students don't. Instead, they tend to read (if indeed they read at all) every passage in every chapter in the same monotonous way. Each word, each sentence, each paragraph is treated with equal reverence. No wonder a gap often exists between the text material and the student.

The gap between text and student is especially wide in content areas where readers must interact with highly specialized and technical language. Nowhere, for example, is content literacy more challenging than in the reading of mathematics texts. Math texts are tersely written in a highly condensed system of language (Curry 1989). Students must perceive and decode mathematical symbols, construct meanings for specialized and technical vocabulary and concepts, analyze and interpret relationships, and apply interpretations to the solution of problems.

Study how two mathematics teachers adapt the lesson structure of the IF to scaffolding reader-text interactions. The first teaches prealgebra classes in a middle school. The students are studying probability, and the objective of the teacher's IF is to ensure that the class will be able to determine the probability of a simple event. As part of prereading, the students explore the questions, Why do some sporting events like football use the flipping of a coin to begin a game? Is the coin flip a fair way to decide which team will kick off? The questions tap into the students' prior knowledge and their conceptions (some naive, some sophisticated) of probability.

As part of the lesson, the teacher asks the students to use their math journals to write definitions of several terms associated with probability: *odds, chances, outcomes, events,* and *sample space.* The students' definitions are discussed as the teacher builds on what they know to arrive at a set of class definitions of the terms. He then pairs the students in "study buddy" teams and asks them to use what they already know about probability to read the assigned section from the textbook. The "study buddies" then read the text section and complete the "selective reading guide" illustrated in Box 5.1.

Together, the study buddies discuss the assigned material as they work through the guide. Selective reading guides are one way of scaffolding

Box 5.1

Using a Selective Reading Guide in Math to Scaffold Reader-Text Interactions

Page 236. Before reading, think about the ways in which we have defined *probability* in class discussion. Now compare our definitions with the one in the book. Develop in your own words a definition of *probability* based on what you know and what you have read.

Probability: _____

Page 236. Now read and define other key terms in this section.

Outcomes: _____

Events: _____

Sample space: _____

Page 236, Example 1. Read the example and answer the following:

What is the probability of rolling a 5? _____

How do you know? _____

Page 237, Example 2. Read this example slowly, and when you finish:

Define odds in favor: _____

Page 238, Example 3. Put on your thinking caps to answer the following:

What are the odds? _____

What is the difference between finding the probability and finding the odds?

_____

Pages 238–240. You're on your own!
  Complete problems 1–31 with your study buddy.

reader-text interactions by providing a "road map" to the important concepts in the material. These guides are discussed more fully in Chapter 12.

The second teacher, a high school mathematics teacher, also adapts the structure of the IF to guide students' interactions with the text and to help them make important connections between reading and mathematics. When she first started teaching, she noticed with some dismay that students almost never read the text. Nor did they talk about mathematics with one another. Therefore, she makes a conscious effort to incorporate literacy and cooperative learning principles whenever instructional situations warrant them.

One such situation occurred when her students were studying the concepts of ratio, proportion, and percentage. The focus of the lesson was a section that dealt with the development of scale drawings as an application of proportion. She initiated the lesson by having students take five minutes to write "admit slips." Admit slips are students' "tickets of admission" to the lesson. The teacher can use them in a variety of ways to find out what students are feeling and thinking as they begin the class period. A more detailed discussion of admit slips occurs in Chapter 7 within the larger context of using writing as a tool for learning subject matter.

The teacher triggered admit-slip writing with the prompt: "If you had a younger brother or sister in the sixth grade, how would you describe a scale drawing in words that he or she would understand?" Using half-sheets of paper distributed by the teacher, the students wrote freely for several minutes until instructed to "wind down" and complete the thoughts they were working on. The teacher collected the admit slips and shared a few of the students' descriptions with the class. The discussion that followed revolved around the students' conceptions of scale drawings and what it means to be "in proportion."

The teacher then formed five-member cooperative groups to guide students' interactions with the text section on scale drawings. Each team was assigned to draw a scale model of the recreation room in its "dream house." First, the teams had to decide what facilities would be included in the recreation room. Once they developed the list of facilities, the team members read the text section and discussed how to develop a scale that would fit all of the facilities into the space provided for each team at the chalkboard. The lesson concluded with the teams' describing their scale drawings. The teacher then asked the students to regroup and develop a list of the important ideas related to scale models.

Postreading

Guidance during reading bridges the gap between students and text so that students learn how to distinguish important from less important ideas, to perceive relationships, and to respond actively to meaning.

Ideas encountered before and during reading may need clarification and elaboration after reading. Postreading activities create a structure that refines

Box 5.2

Postreading Activity for a Southeast Asia Lesson

I. *Directions:* A rice farmer, a Buddhist monk, a government official, and a geographer all feel competent to speak on any of the topics listed below. Who is really best qualified? Who is the specialist in each field? On the blank line preceding each topic, place the letter of the correct specialist.

A. Rice farmer

B. Buddhist monk

C. Government official

D. Geographer

_____   1. The forested regions of Thailand

_____   2. The life of Siddhārtha Gautama

_____   3. The amount of rice exported each year

_____   4. The monsoon rains in Southeast Asia

_____   5. Harvesting rice

_____   6. The causes of suffering

_____   7. The art of meditation

_____   8. The Me Nam River Basin

_____   9. The amount of rice produced per acre

_____   10. The pagodas in Thailand

_____   11. The number of Buddhists living in Bangkok

_____   12. The virtues of a simple life

_____   13. The rice festival in Bangkok

_____   14. The Temple of the Emerald Buddha

_____   15. The attainment of Nirvana (perfect peace)

II. *Directions:* Pretend you are the rice farmer, the Buddhist monk, the government official, or the geographer. Write a paragraph revealing your professional attitude toward and opinion about the approaching monsoon season.

emerging concepts. For example, a social studies teacher who was nearing completion of a unit on Southeast Asia asked her students to reflect on their reading by using the activity in Box 5.2. The writing and follow-up discussion refined and extended the students' thinking about the ideas under study.

The questions "Who is best qualified?" and "Who is the specialist in the field?" prompted students to sort out what they had learned. The teacher provided just enough structure by listing topics from various facets of Southeast Asian culture to focus students' thinking and help them make distinctions.

Activities such as the one in Box 5.2 reinforce and extend ideas. Writing activities, study guides, and other postreading elements are springboards to thinking and form the basis for discussing and articulating the ideas developed through reading.

Some Examples of Core Text Lessons

At the Cleveland School of Science, middle-level students were assigned a text selection on how bees communicate. The text told the story of Karl von Frisch, an entomologist who had studied bees for years, and focused on his experimental observations leading to the discovery of bees' communication behavior. The teacher's objectives were to (1) involve students in an active reading and discussion of the text assignment and (2) have them experience some of the steps scientists go through when performing laboratory or field experiments. Here's how she planned her instructional activities:

I. Prereading

   A. Before introducing the text, determine what students now know about bees.
      1. Who has observed bees close up?
      2. What do you notice about bees that seems unique to them?
      3. When you see a bee, is it usually by itself or in a group?
      4. Why do you think bees swarm?

   B. Connect students' responses to these questions to the text assignment. Introduce the story and its premise.

   C. Form small groups of four students each, and direct each group to participate in the following situation:

     Karl von Frisch worked with bees for many years. He was puzzled by something he had observed again and again. When he set up a table on which he placed little dishes of scented honey, he attracted bees. Usually he had to wait hours or days for a bee to discover the feeding place. But as soon as one bee discovered it, many more came to it in a short time. Evidently, the first bee was able to communicate the news of food to the other bees in its hive.

     Pretend that you are a scientist helping von Frisch discover how bees communicate. How do they tell each other where food is located? List ten things you could do to find out the answers to this question.

   D. Have the students share their group's top five ideas with the class, and write them on the chalkboard.

II. Reader-Text Interactions

A. Assign the selection to be read in class.

B. During reading, direct students to note the similarities and differences between their ideas on the board and von Frisch's experimental procedures.

III. Postreading (Day 2)

A. Discuss the previous day's reading activity. How many of the students' ideas were similar to von Frisch's procedures? How many were different?

B. Extend students' understanding of the inquiry process that scientists like von Frisch follow. Divide the class into groups of four students to work on the following exercise:

All scientists follow a pattern of research to find answers to the questions they have about different subjects. For example, von Frisch wanted to know about how bees communicated. He (1) formed a question, (2) formulated an experiment to answer the question, (3) observed his subjects in the experiment, and (4) answered the question based on his observations.

   Now it's your turn! Tomorrow we are going on a field trip to the park to experiment with ants and food. Your first job as a scientist is to devise a question and an experiment to fit your question. After we return, you will write your observations and the answer to your question. You will be keeping notes on your experiment while we are in the park.

Question: _____

Experiment: _____

Observations: _____

Answer: _____

C. Conduct the experiment the next day at the park. Each group will be given a small amount of food to place near an existing anthill. The students will make notes and take them back to the classroom. Each group's discoveries will be discussed in class.

By way of contrast, study how a high school French teacher taught Guy de Maupassant's short story "L'Infirme" to an advanced class of language students. The story is about two men riding in a train. Henri Bonclair is sitting alone in a train car when another passenger, Revalière, enters the car. This fellow traveler is handicapped, having lost his leg during the war. Bonclair wonders about the type of life he must lead. As he looks at the handicapped man, Bonclair senses that he met him a few years earlier. He asks the man if he is not the person he met. Revalière is that man. Now Bonclair remembers that Revalière was to be married. He wonders if he got married before or after losing the leg or at all. Bonclair inquires. No, Revalière has not married, refusing to ask the girl to put up with a deformed man. However, he is on his way to see her, her husband, and her children. They are all very good friends.

The French teacher formulated five objectives for the lesson:

1. To teach vocabulary dealing with the concept of "infirmity"
2. To foster students' ability to make inferences about the reading material from their own knowledge
3. To foster students' ability to predict what will happen in the story in light of the background they bring to the story
4. To foster students' ability to evaluate their predictions once they have read the story
5. To use the story as a basis for writing a dialogue in French

Two of the activities, the *graphic organizer* and the *inferential strategy*, used in the French teacher's plan will be explained in depth in Part 3 of this book. The steps in the plan are outlined here:

I. Prereading

A. Begin the lesson by placing the title of the story on the board: "L'Infirme." Ask students to look at the title and compare it to a similar English word (or words). Determine very generally what the story is probably about. (A handicapped person.)

B. On the overhead, introduce key words used in the story by displaying a *graphic organizer:*

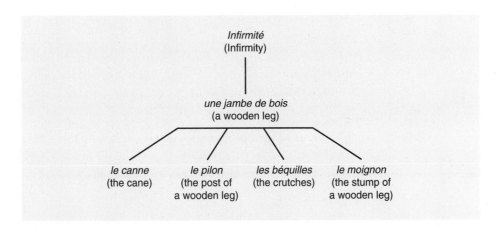

C. Use the *inferential strategy.* Ask and discuss with the class the following three sets of questions. Have the students write down their responses.
   1. *Vous avez peut-être vu quelqu'un qui est très estropié à cause de la perte d'une jambe ou d'un bras. Qu'est-ce qui traverse votre esprit? De quoi est-ce que vous vous demandez?*

(You may have seen someone who is very crippled because of the loss of a leg or an arm. When you see such a person, what crosses your mind? What do you wonder about?)

2. *Dans l'histoire, Bonclair voit ce jeune infirme qui a perdu la jambe. Qu'est-ce que vous pensez traverse son esprit?*

(In the story, Bonclair sees this crippled young man who has lost his leg. What do you think crosses his mind?)

3. *Quand vous voyez quelqu'un qui a l'air vaguement familier, qu'est-ce que vous voulez faire? Qu'est-ce que vous faites? Quels sont souvent les résultats?*

(When you see someone who looks vaguely familiar, what do you want to do? What do you do? What are often the results?)

4. *Dans cette histoire, Bonclair se souvient vaguement qu'il a fait la connaissance de cet infirme. Prédites ce qu'il fera et prédites les résultats.*

(In this story, Bonclair remembers vaguely having met this cripple. Predict what he does and the results.)

5. *Imaginez que vous êtes fiancé(e) à un jeune homme ou à une jeune femme. Puis vous avez un accident qui vous rend estropié(e). Qu'est-ce que vous feriez? Voudriez-vous se marier? Pourriez-vous compter sur l'autre de vous aimer encore?*

(Imagine that you are engaged to a young man or woman. Then you have an accident that leaves you crippled. What would you do? Would you still want to marry? Could you still expect the other to love you?)

6. *Dans notre histoire, Revalière a eu un accident juste avant son marriage. Prédites ce qu'il fera et ce qu'il comptera de la jeune fille. Prédites les résultats.*

(In our story, Revalière has had an accident just before his marriage. Predict what he did and what he expected of the young woman. Predict the results.)

II. Reader-Text Interactions

A. Assign the reading, instructing the students to keep in mind their prior knowledge and predictions.

B. Ask them to note possible changes in their predictions.

III. Postreading

A. After the reading, conduct a follow-up discussion with the class. Relate their predictions to what actually happened, noting how our background knowledge and experience of the world lead us to think along certain lines.

B. Through the discussion, note the changes and refinements in the students' predictions and when they occurred.

C. *Vocabulary exercise.* Distribute a sheet on which is reproduced a *vocabulary-context reinforcement exercise.* All vocabulary items studied in the prereading section should be listed, along with sentences from the story with blanks to be filled in with the appropriate word. There should be fewer blanks than word choices. Allow seven or eight minutes for this exercise; then ask the students to read the complete sentence (in clear French).

D. Have the class form groups of four with at least one male and one female in each group. Establish the following situation:

> *Une jeune fille vient d'être estropiée dans un accident de natation. Son fiancé lui a téléphoné. Il veut lui parler. Qu'est-ce qu'il veut lui dire? On frappe à la porte. C'est lui.*

(A young lady was recently crippled in a swimming accident. Her fiancé has called her. He wants to talk to her. What does he want to talk about? There is a knock at the door. It is he.)

1. Think together, drawing on your past knowledge and/or experience of situations like this. Write a 15- to 20-line group dialogue in French between the girl and her fiancé. What might he have to tell her? How might she react?

2. Select a boy and a girl to present the group's dialogue to the class.

The IFs that were just illustrated have the same underlying structure. Each plan provides a set of experiences designed to move students from preparation to interaction with the text to extension and elaboration of the concepts in the material under study. The IFs show how two teachers translated knowledge about content area reading into plans for active learning. Thus the IFs are working models.

How teachers imagine instructional activities in core text assignments will vary by grade level and the sophistication of the students. The same is true of developing plans for a thematic unit. In the next section, we go beyond planning core text lessons to decisions related to thematic learning involving multiple literacy experiences.

ORGANIZING THEMATIC UNITS

Thematic units organize instruction around objectives, activities, print and nonprint resources, and inquiry experiences. A thematic unit may be designed for a single discipline or may be interdisciplinary, integrating two or more content areas. In middle schools, where content area teachers are teamed in learning "communities" or "families," opportunities abound to develop interdisciplinary thematic units. Interdisciplinary units require coordination and cooperation by all of the content area teachers teamed within a learning community. Team planning helps students make connections not otherwise possible among many knowledge domains. Noden and Vacca (1994), for example, describe how a middle school teaching team organized an interdisciplinary unit around the theme of "Native Americans." They developed a four-week unit in which 130 seventh graders were "born" into one of 16 Indian tribes. The students inquired into tribal lifestyles from many disciplinary perspectives and participated in a variety of activities to understand life as a Native American both emotionally and intellectually.

Planning a Thematic Unit

The thematic unit is a planning tool that includes (1) a title reflecting the theme or topic of the unit, (2) the major concepts to be learned, (3) the texts and information sources to be studied by students, (4) the unit's instructional activities, and (5) provisions for evaluating what students have learned from the unit.

Listing Resources

Although a thematic unit may include multiple text opportunities, the textbook is not necessarily excluded from the unit. Thematic unit planning simply provides more options to coordinate a variety of information sources. In single-discipline units, prereading, reading, and postreading activities become an integral part of unit teaching. When the teacher plans a thematic unit, the mesh of activities designed to achieve content-related objectives will give students a sense of continuity, and they won't get a mishmash of unrelated experiences.

Listing texts and resources is an important part of the preparation for a single-discipline unit. One reason why a unit is so attractive a means of organization is that the teacher can go beyond the textbook—or, for that matter, bypass it. A wide array of literature, both imaginative and informational, will give students opportunities for an intense involvement in the theme under study. Trade books, electronic texts, pamphlets, periodicals, reference books, newspapers, magazines, and audiovisual materials are all potential alternative routes to acquiring information.

The Internet is quickly becoming a valuable planning resource for teachers in the development of thematic units. You can access many useful ideas for integrating electronic texts into thematic units of study. By conducting a search using the key words, "integrated technology + thematic units," you will find a number of Web sites to be explored. For example, teachers have found that one of the most interesting Web sites to visit on the Internet for unit planning ideas is "Enhancing Thematic Units with Technology: Examples of Software and Web Sites" (http://www.ed.sc.edu/caw/ THEME.HTML). The site is operated by an educator, Cheryl Wissick, for educators. It lists resources for often-taught themes, which change on a regular basis.

Many of the ideas found at the site are contributed by teachers from across the country. Not only does the site provide links to lesson plan ideas and Internet projects, it also provides a listing of software and Web sites appropriate for

This document is only a representative sample of web sites and software that could be used to enhance thematic units. If you are working on a thematic or interdisciplinary unit and use technology, I would appreciate your resources to add to this list. If you are aware of other software or web sites for the topics listed, please send me that information. I will attempt to keep the links updated whenever I have the time!!! Send any resources or comments to Cheryl Wissick.

Choose a Theme:

- Ancient Cities
- Animals
- Community Occupations
- Dinosaurs
- Environment and Ecology
- Native Americans
- Ornithology
- Social Skills
- Volcanos and Earthquakes and Canyons
- Whales

Ancient Civilizations

Web Sites related to ancient civilizations:

- Egypt Interactive
- Color Tour of Egypt
- Brief Tours in Greece
- About Greece
- Ancient City of Athens

Software related to ancient civilizations:

- Recess in Greece by Morgan Interactive
- Ancient Cities by Sumeria
- Heroic Tales: Theseus by Westwind Media
- Aesopolis by Quantum Leap
  [Return to the top]

FIGURE 5.3   **Enhancing Thematic Units with Technology: Examples of Software and Web Sites**

individual thematic units. Figure 5.3 depicts the home page for "Enhancing Thematic Units with Technology" Web site and shows the themes highlighted at the time that we accessed the site (July, 1997). The figure also lists the links to other Web sites and software appropriate for the theme, "Ancient Cities."

Determining Content Objectives

Content analysis is a major part of teacher preparation in the development of a unit of study. Content analysis results in the *what* of learning—the major concepts and understandings that students should learn from reading the unit materials. Through content analysis, the major concepts become the objectives for the unit. It doesn't matter whether these content objectives are stated in behavioral terms or not. What really matters is that you know which concepts students will interact with and develop. Therefore, it's important to decide on a manageable number of the most important understandings to be gained from the unit. This means setting priorities; it's impossible to cover every aspect of the material that students will read or be exposed to.

A middle-school science teacher's content analysis for a unit on the respiratory system yielded these major concepts to be taught:

1. Living things require oxygen.

2. Living things give off carbon dioxide.

3. Living things exchange oxygen and carbon dioxide during respiration.

4. When living things oxidize organic substances, carbon dioxide is given off.

5. When living things oxidize organic substances, energy is given off.

6. Sugars and starches are foods that store energy.

7. The respiratory system of living things is responsible for the exchange of gases.

8. Breathing is a mechanical process of living things, and respiration is a chemical process that happens in the cells of living things.

9. The body uses only a certain part of the air that it takes in during breathing.

Stating these content objectives permitted the science teacher to select texts and plan the *how* of the unit: the instructional activities.

The actual framework of thematic units will vary. For example, you might organize a unit entirely on a sequence of lessons from assignments in a single textbook. This type of organization is highly structured and is even restrictive, in the sense that it often precludes the use of various kinds of other literature rich in content and substance. However, a thematic unit can be planned so that the teacher will (1) use a single textbook to begin the unit and then branch out into multiple-text study and differentiated activities, (2) organize the unit entirely on individual or group inquiry and research, or (3) combine single-text instruction with multiple-text activities and inquiry.

Branching out provides the latitude to move from a core text lesson to independent learning activities. The move from single to multiple information sources exposes students to a variety of texts that may be better suited to their needs and interests.

A thematic unit on spatial relationships for a high school art class provides an example of how a teacher planned content objectives, activities, and materials. First, she listed the major concepts to be taught in the unit:

1. Humans are aware of the space about them as functional, decorative, and communicative.

2. Space organized intuitively produces an aesthetic result, but a reasoned organization of space also leads to a pleasing outcome if design is considered.

3. Occupied and unoccupied space have positive and negative effects on mood and depth perception.

4. The illusion of depth can be created on a two-dimensional surface.

5. The direction and balance of lines and/or forms create feelings of tension, force, and equilibrium in the space that contains them.

6. Seldom in nature is the order of objects so perfect as to involve no focal point or force or tension.

Then she developed the activities and identified the texts to be used in the unit (see Figure 5.4). As you study the figure, keep in mind that some of the text-related activities suggested will be explored later in this book.

Creating an Inquiry/Research Focus

Gathering, organizing, and sharing information are crucial to both academic success and success in our information-rich society. Inquiry should therefore play a major role in learning important content, and the process of inquiry should be woven into thematic units of study. *Standards for the English Language Arts* (1997) developed by IRA and NCTE describes the fundamental characteristics of inquiry reading as follows: "Students conduct research on issues and interests by generating ideas and questions and by posing problems. They gather, evaluate, and synthesize data from a variety of sources (e.g. print and non-print texts, artifacts, and people) to communicate their discoveries in ways that suit their purpose and audience" (p. 7).

The centerpiece of a thematic unit, therefore, is the emphasis that teachers put on inquiry and research. How teachers guide inquiry/research projects is the key to a successful unit. The process of inquiry, like the process of writing that we describe in Chapter 7, works best when it occurs in steps and stages. Clark (1987) draws on his experience as a former journalist to ease his middle-grade students into the inquiry process. The students use human resources from the community to conduct their inquiries. The students must

Text-Related Activities	Texts
1. Graphic organizer	Graham Collier, Form, Space, and Vision
2. Vocabulary and concept bulletin board	
3. Prereading	Chapter 3, Collier
4. Prereading	Chapters 6 and 7
5. Art journal	Chapters 6 and 7
6. K – W – L	Chapter 11
7. Vocabulary exercise	Chapter 3
8. Vocabulary exercise	Chapters 6 and 7
9. Vocabulary exercise	Chapter 11
10. Student's choice (list of projects for research study)	H. Botten, Do You See What I See?
	H. Helfman, Creating Things That Move
	D. McAgy, Going for a Walk with a Line
	L. Kampmann, Creating with Space and Construction
	G. LeFevre, Junk Sculpture
11. Hands-On	J. Lynch, Mobile Design
Ink dabs	
Straw painting	
Dry seed arrangement	
Cardboard sculpture	
Positive-negative cutouts	
Perspective drawing	
Large-scale class sculpture	
Mobiles	
Space frames	Calder's Universe
12. Filmstrip	
13. Field trip to studio of a sculptor	Displays of artist's works with questionnaires to be
14. Field trip to museum	filled out about them
15. Learning corner	

FIGURE 5.4   **Activities and Texts**

decide whom they will interview and what will be the focus of the inquiry. They collect data for their projects through interviews. Clark then encourages his budding researchers to write about their inquiries by using information they gather from the interviews. He identifies the following stages as part of the inquiry process that his students engage in: searching for ideas, gathering and sifting, finding a focus, building momentum, rethinking and revising, and reaching an audience. For students to be successful, Clark realizes that he must encourage inquiry through learner choice and teacher guidance.

Each stage of an inquiry/research project requires careful support by a teacher. In Box 5.3, we outline the stages and procedures for guiding inquiry/research.

When teachers simply assign and evaluate research reports, students often paraphrase whatever sources come to hand rather than actively pursue information that they are eager to share with others. Genuine inquiry is always a messy endeavor characterized by false starts, unexpected discoveries, changes in direction, and continual decision making. Too much guidance can be as dangerous as too little.

In an in-depth study of two middle school research projects, Rycik (1994) found that teachers may lose their focus on genuine inquiry as they establish procedures for guiding all students to complete a project successfully. The teachers in the study were very concerned with providing sufficient guidance, so they broke their projects down into a series of discrete steps (such as making note cards) that could be taught, completed, and evaluated separately. As the projects moved forward, the teachers gradually came to believe that mastering the procedure for each step was the primary outcome of the project, even more important than learning content information.

Rycik (1994) concluded that inquiry should not be confined to one big research paper because teachers cannot introduce and monitor the wide range of searching, reading, thinking, and writing skills that students need to complete such projects. Good researchers, like good writers, must learn their craft through frequent practice in a variety of contexts. This means that students should research from a variety of sources and express their findings for a variety of audiences in a variety of forms. Some recommendations for integrating research into the classroom routine include the following:

- Make identifying questions and problems as important in your classroom as finding answers.

- Provide frequent opportunities to compare, contrast, and synthesize information from multiple sources.

- Present findings of research in a variety of products and formats, including charts, graphs, and visual or performing arts.

- Discuss possible sources for information presented in the class or for answering questions posed by the teacher or students (e.g., personal interviews, diaries, experiments).

The research process opens the way to reading many different kinds of materials. Developing inquiry-centered projects helps students understand and synthesize what they're learning.

The teacher must carefully plan inquiry-centered projects, giving just the right amount of direction to allow students to explore and discover ideas on their own. The research process isn't a do-your-own-thing proposition, for

Box 5.3

Procedures for Guiding Inquiry/Research Projects

I. Raise questions, identify interests, organize information.

A. Discuss interest areas related to the unit of study.

B. Engage in goal setting.
   1. Arouse curiosities.
   2. Create awareness of present levels of knowledge.

C. Pose questions relating to each area and/or subarea.
   1. "What do you want to find out?"
   2. "What do you want to know about _____?"
   3. Record the questions or topics.
   4. "What do you already know about _____?"

D. Organize information; have students make predictions about likely answers to gaps in knowledge.
   1. Accept all predictions as possible answers.
   2. Encourage thoughtful speculations in a nonthreatening way.

II. Select materials.

A. Use visual materials.
   1. Trade books and encyclopedias
   2. Magazines, catalogs, directories
   3. Newspapers and comics
   4. Indexes, atlases, almanacs, dictionaries, readers' guides, computer catalogs
   5. Films, filmstrips, slides
   6. Videotapes, television programs
   7. Electronic texts: CD-ROMs, Web site documents, videodisks

B. Use nonvisual materials.
   1. Audiotapes
   2. Records
   3. Radio programs
   4. Field trips

C. Use human resources.
   1. Interviews
   2. Letters
   3. On-site visits
   4. Discussion groups
   5. E-mail
   6. Listservs

D. Encourage self-selection of materials.
   1. "What can I understand?"
   2. "What gives me the best answers?"

III. Guide the information search.

   A. Encourage active research.
     1. Reading
     2. Listening
     3. Observing
     4. Talking
     5. Writing

   B. Facilitate with questions.
     1. "How are you doing?"
     2. "Can I help you?"
     3. "Do you have all the materials you need?"
     4. "Can I help you with ideas you don't understand?"

   C. Have students keep records.
     1. Learning log that includes plans, procedures, notes, and rough drafts
     2. Book record cards
     3. Record of conferences with the teacher

IV. Consider different forms of writing.

   A. Initiate a discussion of sharing techniques.

   B. Encourage a variety of writing forms.
     1. Essay or paper
     2. Lecture to a specific audience
     3. Case study
     4. Story: adventure, science fiction, other genre
     5. Dialogue, conversation, interview
     6. Dramatization through scripts
     7. Commentary or editorial
     8. Thumbnail sketch

V. Guide the writing process.

   A. Help students organize information.

   B. Guide first-draft writing.

   C. Encourage responding, revising, and rewriting.

   D. "Publish" finished products.
     1. Individual presentations
     2. Classroom arrangement
     3. Class interaction

budding researchers need structure. Many a project has been wrecked on the shoals of nondirection. The trick is to strike a balance between teacher guidance and student self-reliance. A research project must have just enough structure to give students (1) a problem focus, (2) physical and intellectual freedom, (3) an environment in which they can obtain data, and (4) feedback situations in which to report the results of their research.

Finding and Investigating Problems

Ideally, an inquiry arises out of students' questions about the subject under study. A puzzling situation may arouse curiosity and interest. Or perhaps the teacher will provoke puzzlement through a discussion of differences in opinion, a reaction to inconsistencies in information in content material, or a response to an emotional issue. We recommend using such questions as the following to initiate research:

How is _____ different from _____? How are they alike?

What has changed from the way it used to be?

What can we learn from the past?

What caused _____ to happen? Why did it turn out that way?

What will happen next? How will it end?

How can we find out?

Which way is best?

What does this mean to you? How does this idea apply to other situations?

As a result of questioning, students should become aware of their present level of knowledge and the gaps that exist in what they know. They can use the questioning session to identify a problem. You might ask, "What do you want to find out?" During the planning stage of a research project, the emphasis should be on further analysis of each individual or group problem, breaking it down into a sequence of manageable parts and activities. The teacher facilitates by helping students clarify problems. As students progress in their research, data collection and interpretation become integral stages of the inquiry. Students will need the physical and intellectual freedom to investigate their problems. They will also need an environment—a library or media center—where they will have access to a variety of information sources, including printed material (books and encyclopedias; magazines, catalogs, directories; newspapers), nonprint materials (audiotapes; records; films, filmstrips, slides; videotapes, television programs; Internet resources, CD-ROMs), and human resources (interviews; letters; e-mail; on-site visits).

If students are conducting an inquiry on the Internet, an excellent strategy is to have them use an Internet inquiry recording sheet, as suggested by Leu and Leu (1997), to monitor and document the inquiry process that they followed. Items on the recording sheet might include the following:

1. Record any questions you asked yourself or each other when searching.

2. Explain what your search entailed (key words, Web sites, etc.).

3. Analyze your search results and draw conclusions from your data.

4. Compose a paragraph or a graphic organizer describing your results and your conclusions.

5. Prepare to share your results and conclusions with the class.

6. What discoveries did you make during this session that will help you understand or navigate in cyberspace next time?

The teacher's role throughout an Internet inquiry project is as a resource. Your questions will help the students interpret data or perhaps raise new questions, reorganize ideas, or modify plans: "How are you doing? How can I help? Are you finding it difficult to obtain information? Which ideas are giving you trouble?"

Weaving Trade Books and Electronic Texts into Thematic Units

The literature-based movement in elementary schools serves as a prototype for the use of trade books in middle and high school classrooms. In addition, technology makes it possible to access and explore information sources through CD-ROM programs, electronic books, and the Internet. Although textbooks may be used to provide an information base, the foundation for individual and group inquiry into a theme or topic is built on students' use of multiple information resources, both printed and electronic. Trade books and electronic texts are geared to students' interests and inquiry needs.

Say that in a middle-grade classroom, students are engaged in a thematic unit on the environment. What might you observe over several weeks? For starters, the teacher may conduct several whole-class lessons at the beginning of the unit using the textbook to develop a conceptual framework for individual and group investigation. As the weeks progress, however, whole-class activity is less prevalent. Instead, small groups work on research projects or in discussion teams using Gary Paulsen's *Woodsong* (1990) and *Hatchet* (1987) and Roy Gallant's *Earth's Vanishing Forests* (1991). Individual students are also working on inquiries with books such as Paul Goble's *I Sing for the Animals* (1991) and Peter Parnall's *Marsh Cat* (1991) and *The Daywatchers* (1984).

In addition, the students are conducting research online, tapping into the rich information resources of the World Wide Web. Several students investigate the Web sites of Environmental Science, the Rainforest Action Network, and the Global Recycling Network. Others are exploring software programs: Ozzie's World (Digital Impact), Zug's Adventures on Eco-Island (Zugware), Zurk's Rainforest (Soliel), and Imagination Express: Rainforest (Edmark). One or two students are navigating the pages of electronic reference books such as Grolier's Multimedia Encyclopedia (Grolier).

Toward the end of the unit, the class completes culminating activities, which may involve panel discussions, report writing, and oral presentations in which individuals or groups share knowledge gleaned from the various activities and texts. In this class, what you would observe is that everyone has something to contribute.

Brozo and Tomlinson (1986) define several steps that facilitate the uses of trade books in thematic units. We have expanded their plan to include electronic texts.

1. Identify salient concepts that become the content objectives for the unit.
   a. What are the driving human forces behind the events?
   b. What patterns of behavior need to be studied?
   c. What phenomena have affected or may affect ordinary people in the future?

2. Identify appropriate trade books, Web sites, and software that will help in the teaching of these concepts.

3. Teach the unit.
   a. Use the textbook, trade books, and electronic texts interchangeably.
   b. Use strategies such as read-aloud in which a trade book or electronic text becomes a schema builder before students read the textbook.
   c. Use trade books and electronic texts to elaborate and extend content and concepts related to the unit.

4. Follow up.
   a. Engage students in strategies and activities that involve collaboration, inquiry, and various forms of expression and meaning construction.
   b. Evaluate students' learning by observing how they interpret and personalize new knowledge.

Here are two examples of thematic units at the middle and high school levels. The first integrates trade books and Internet sites; the second combines textbook study with trade books.

Eighth-Grade Life Science: Birds—The Feathered Ones

A life science teacher in a middle school uses a textbook and literature interchangeably for a unit on birds. In his classes, students have already mastered the concept of warm-blooded animals. Birds are the first group of warm-blooded animals that the students study. Because the students have varying degrees of prior knowledge about birds, the unit is focused on a wide variety of species and the economic and aesthetic value of birds.

The students engage first in a study of the relationship between birds and reptiles. Then they explore the characteristics of birds as a class of animals and the many and varied adaptations birds have made to their environment, including adaptations for flight and migration. The students also examine the importance of birds as indicators of the health of the environment. The final phase of the unit centers on the economic and aesthetic value of birds. Figure 5.5 displays the relationships among the key concepts that students will master as a result of their studies.

The teacher weaves trade books and Internet investigations into the unit. Students engage in a variety of activities. For example, the teacher supplements textbook study with outside readings. He also requires the use of a science notebook in which students set aside a section to respond to the texts they are reading as part of the unit. The centerpiece of the unit, however, is a jigsaw group investigation of birds. (Jigsaw groups are described in Chapter

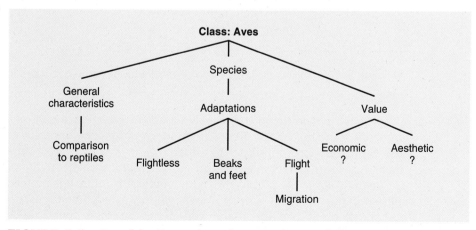

FIGURE 5.5   **Graphic Organizer for a Unit on Birds**

Box 5.4

Information Resources for a Unit on Birds

TEXTBOOK

Bierer, Loretta M., & Lein, Violetta F. (1985). *Health Life Science.* Lexington, MA: Heath, pp. 290–295.

NONFICTION

Brooks, Bruce. (1989). *On the Wing.* New York: Macmillan.

Bull, John, & Ferrand, John, Jr. (1977). *The Audubon Society Field Guide to North American Birds.* New York: Knopf.

Collins, Henry H., Jr. (1959). *Complete Field Guide to American Wildlife.* New York: Harper-Collins.

Fichter, George S. (1977). *The Changing World of Wildlife.* New York: Golden Press.

Gift of Birds. (1979). Washington, DC: National Wildlife Federation.

Harrison, Kit, & Harrison, George. (1990). *The Birds of Winter.* New York: Random House.

Life Histories: Notes on Ohio's Fish and Wildlife Species. (1985). Columbus: Ohio Department of Natural Resources, Division of Wildlife.

Project Wild: Elementary Activity Guide. (1985). Boulder, CO: Western Regional Environmental Council.

Robbins, Chandler S., Bruun, Bertel, & Zim, Herbert. (1966). *A Guide to Field Identification: Birds of North America.* New York: Golden Press.

Schutz, Walter E. (1970). *How to Attract, House, and Feed Birds.* New York: Collier.

Stokes, Donald, & Stokes, Lillian. (1987). *The Bird Feeder Book.* New York: Little, Brown.

Whitfield, Phillip. (1988). *The Macmillan Illustrated Encyclopedia of Birds.* New York: Collier.

Wood, Richard H. (1984). *Wood Notes: A Companion and Guide for Birdwatchers.* Upper Saddle River, NJ: Prentice Hall.

6.) The students participate in jigsaw groups to investigate several of the main concepts of the unit. Each group member investigates a different concept and then reports his or her findings to the group. As preparation for the report, students temporarily meet in expert groups (all of the students in an expert group are responsible for teaching the same concept to their jigsaw teammates) to share and discuss what they are investigating. Box 5.4 contains a list of information resources available to the students during their investigations.

INTERNET RESOURCES

American Birding Association
http://www.americanbirding.org

BirdBase—Fugleskue (World Birding from Norway)
http://home.sol.no/~yaffil

Birds: Our Environmental Indicators
http://www.nceet.snre.umich.edu/Curriculum/toc.html

Canadian Nature Federation
http://www.web.net/~cnf

Cats and Wildlife: A Conservation Dilemma
by John S. Coleman, Stanley A. Temple, & Scott R. Craven http://www.wisc.edu/wildlife/
extension/catfly3.htm

Cornell Lab of Ornithology
http://www.ornith.cornell.edu

Internet Flyway
http://www.netlink.co.uk/users/aw/index.html

Live: Virtual Birding on the FeederCam http://www.wbu.com/feedercam_home.htm

National Audubon Society
http://www.audubon.org

National Fish and Wildlife Foundation
http://www.nfwf.org

Peterson Online (Houghton Mifflin)
http://www.petersononline.com

Smithsonian Migratory Bird Center
http://nbhc.com/birdwg01/weeknnw1.htm

U.S. Fish and Wildlife Service
http://www.fws.gov

The teacher also uses different types of texts as part of direct instruction in the teaching of specific concepts. This approach often results in an opportunity to combine reading and writing experiences. For example, the teacher will read to the class poems about birds such as Randall Jarrell's "Bird of Night," Robert Francis's "Seagulls," and Ogden Nash's "Up from the Egg: The Confessions of a Nuthatch Avoider." After each poem, the students write in their notebooks for three minutes on how the poem made them feel. They then share their responses with others in the class. Next, the students are asked to write for another three minutes on a memory they may have associated with the poem that influenced their initial response. As another part of their response to the poem, the students choose one word that they feel summarizes the poem and write about the reasons for their choice. As a follow-up activity, the students write haiku using birds as the basic theme.

Eleventh-Grade American History: The Revolutionary War

An American history teacher designed this unit to explain the interrelatedness of the events of the Revolutionary period and their effects on later American history.

In planning the unit, the teacher constructed a graphic organizer of the major concepts and then identified literature for group and individual investigation. Notice in Figure 5.6 that she positioned key fiction and nonfiction books on the organizer in relationship to the concepts to be taught.

The literature list for the unit included the annotated bibliography in Box 5.5.

The teacher weaved literature into the unit in two ways. She had students first self-select a fiction or nonfiction book related to the American Revolution and then set up an ongoing journal. She explained to the students:

> You will keep a journal of the book that you are reading. The journal will help you record your feelings, reactions, and personal insights about the book. Decide how many pages you will read at a time. After reading each section of the book, make an entry in your journal: What moved you the most in the section? How did the section make you feel? Why do you think you felt that way? What did you learn from the reading? Be sure to include details or quotations from the book so that someone who hasn't read it would understand why you were moved by the reading.

Beth and the students decided on three due dates, each covering about one-third of the book, for turning in the journal. In class, Beth periodically put the students in "booktalk" groups to discuss their reactions to what they were reading.

In addition to keeping the journal, the students engaged in literature study through an inquiry-centered project (see Box 5.6). The inquiry allowed the class members to work in pairs to investigate a historical figure from the Revolutionary period. The inquiry resulted in a written interview that each pair of students role-played for the class.

Instructional activities within a unit may be initiated through flexible grouping patterns. Whole-class, small-group, and individual learning are all important vehicles for classroom interaction.

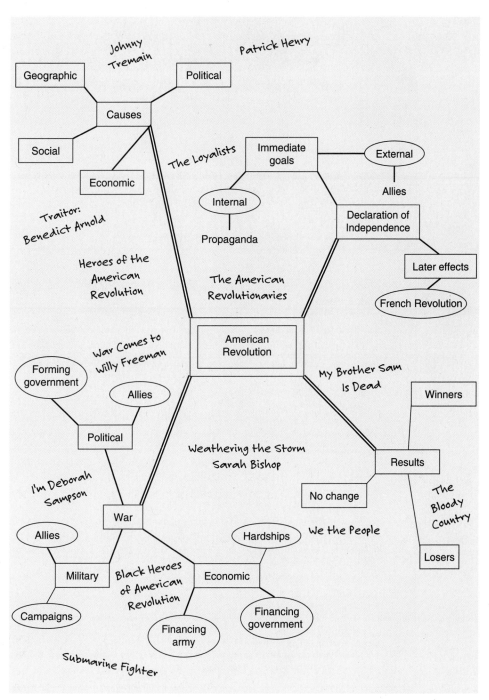

FIGURE 5.6 **Graphic Organizer for a Unit on the Revolutionary War**

Box 5.5

Annotated Bibliography for a Unit on the Revolutionary War

FICTION

Collier, James Lincoln, and Collier, Christopher. (1974). *My Brother Sam Is Dead.* New York: Four Winds.

> Tragedy strikes the Meeker family when one son joins the rebels while the rest of the family tries to stay neutral in a Tory town. Appropriate for average and developing readers.

Collier, James Lincoln, and Collier, Christopher. (1976). *The Bloody Country.* New York: Four Winds.

> Ben Buck, his family, and Joe Mountain, the family slave, while living on the western Pennsylvanian frontier during the Revolution, struggle with British soldiers, loyalists, and Indians and with Joe's growing desire for the equality proclaimed in the Declaration of Independence. Appropriate for average and developing readers.

Collier, James Lincoln, and Collier, Christopher. (1983). *War Comes to Willy Freeman.* New York: Delacorte.

> Free 13-year-old Willy Freeman risks a return to slavery as she searches for her mother in British-held New York during the Revolution. Appropriate for average and developing readers.

Forbes, Esther. (1971). *Johnny Tremain.* New York: Dell.

> Johnny Tremain, an apprentice silversmith, becomes involved in the events leading up to the Boston Tea Party and the Battle of Lexington. Appropriate for developing readers.

O'Dell, Scott. (1980). *Sarah Bishop.* Boston: Houghton Mifflin.

> After the deaths of her Tory father and rebel brother, Sarah flees her Long Island home to create a new life for herself in the wilderness. Appropriate for average readers.

NONFICTION

Campion, Nardi Reeder. (1961). *Patrick Henry: Firebrand of the Revolution.* New York: Little, Brown.

> Biography. Appropriate for developing readers.

Chidsey, Donald Barr. (1973). *The Loyalists: The Story of Those Americans Who Fought Against Independence.* New York: Crown.

> In letters, diaries, and speeches, the motivations, actions, and final treatment of the loyalists are recounted. Appropriate for advanced readers.

Clapp, Patricia. (1977). *I'm Deborah Sampson: A Soldier in the War of the Revolution.* New York: Lothrop.

> Biography. Appropriate for developing readers.

Davis, Burke. (1971). *Heroes of the American Revolution.* New York: Random House.

> Eleven concise biographies of Revolutionary War heroes, some well known (Paul Revere, Benjamin Franklin, George Washington) and some lesser known (Henry Knox, Friedrich von Steuben, George Rogers Clark). Appropriate for developing readers.

Davis, Burke. (1976). *Black Heroes of the American Revolution.* Orlando, FL: Harcourt Brace.

Davis writes about the African-American revolutionaries who are seldom mentioned in the standard text. Appropriate for the developing reader.

Evans, R. Elizabeth. (1975). *Weathering the Storm: Women of the American Revolution.* New York: Scribner.

Accounts of the Revolution drawn from the journals and diaries of 11 women. Especially interesting is the account of Deborah Sampson Gannett, who, dressed as a man, became a decorated soldier.

Evans, R. Elizabeth (1977). *The American War of Independence.* Cambridge, England: Cambridge University Press.

A short history of the Revolution. Chapter 4 looks at the war from the perspective of world politics and economics, a view usually slighted in American history texts.

Fritz, Jean. (1981). *Traitor: The Case of Benedict Arnold.* New York: Putnam.

Biography. Appropriate for developing readers.

Hilton, Suzanne. (1981). *We the People: The Way We Were, 1783–1793.* Louisville, KY: Westminster/John Knox.

Describes the life, customs, and controversies of the new country created in 1783. This new nation had no official capital, currency, or navy. Its borders had not been decided, and no one was even sure if United States was singular or plural. Appropriate for the developing reader.

Meltzer, Milton. (1987). *The American Revolutionaries: A History in Their Own Words, 1750–1800.* New York: Crowell.

Using letters, diaries, journals, memoirs, newspapers, and speeches, Meltzer describes the experience of the Revolution from a variety of viewpoints, including those of soldiers, Quakers, wives, politicians, and preachers.

Quarles, Benjamin. (1961). *The Negro in the American Revolution.* New York: Norton.

Meant for the serious historian, this book is probably too advanced for the average high school student. However, the first four pages of the preface are an excellent brief history of the interrelated military and political realities that led to the recruitment of blacks, generally slaves, by both sides. Appropriate for advanced readers or teacher resource.

Wagner, Frederick. (1963). *Submarine Fighter of the American Revolution: The Story of David Bushnell.* Binghamton, NY: Vail-Ballou Press.

The biography of David Bushnell, the inventor of the first practical submarine and of the contact underwater mine.

Box 5.6

Inquiry Project for a Unit on the Revolutionary War

Directions: Congratulations! You have been chosen to anchor the new series *TimeLine.* This show features the same type of in-depth interview as *NightLine,* except you have a time machine. You can go back in time and interview someone from the Revolution. To prevent changing the future, here are the rules:

1. Work in pairs. Both of you will do research and write the interview. Decide who will be the interviewer and who the interviewee. Decide on a historical interview date.

2. Your interviewee may be an actual historical figure (e.g., Paul Revere), or you may create a fictional eyewitness to a historical event (e.g., the Boston Tea Party).

3. Your research must be based on at least two sources, only one of which may be the encyclopedia. A bibliography must be included in the written interview turned in after presentation.

4. Presentation
   a. Introduce the interviewee and briefly tell why this person is important or interesting.
   b. Your questions must stay within your time frame. You can't ask George Washington if he wants to be president; the office doesn't exist yet. You may ask him if he would like a political office in the future.
   c. The interviewee's answers must be reasonable and based on historical facts from your research.
   d. You are encouraged to include visual aids: pictures, cartoons, maps, props, and costumes.
   e. The interview should last no less than four minutes and no more than ten minutes.

Here is a list of possible subjects, or you may choose your own.

George Washington	Haym Solomon	David Bushnell
Samuel Adams	(financier)	(submarine inventor)
Crispus Attucks	George Rogers Clark	Boston Massacre
Thomas Jefferson	John Dickinson	Boston Tea Party
John Adams	Thomas Pain	Reading and
Benjamin Franklin	John Locke	responding to the
Benedict Arnold	Jean-Jacques	Declaration of
Francis Marion,	Rousseau	Independence as a
the "Swamp Fox"	Abigail Adams	wealthy merchant or
Marquis de Lafayette	James Arnistead (spy)	planter, a poor
Charles Cornwallis	Deborah Sampson	craftsman or farmer,
(British general)	Gannett (soldier)	or a slave
Frederick North	Patrick Henry	Revolutionary battle or
(British prime	John Hancock	campaign of your
minister)	Ethan Allen	choice
King George III	Peter Zenger	Treaty of Paris

LOOKING BACK, LOOKING FORWARD

Content area teachers can plan instruction that will lead to active text learning. Students must act on ideas in print and also interact with one another when learning with texts. The instructional framework and the thematic unit provide the structure for bringing learners and texts together in content areas.

The instructional framework makes provisions for prereading, reading, and postreading instruction for core text lessons. This particular lesson structure helps teachers imagine the kinds of activity to use before, during, and after reading. A unit helps the teacher organize instructional activities around multiple texts. Unit planning gives you much more latitude to coordinate resource materials and activities. Unit activities can be organized for the whole class, small groups, or individuals. The emphasis, however, should be on inquiry-centered research projects.

In the next chapter, we explore the powerful role of talk in the curriculum. Talking to learn occurs in social collaboration—through cooperative effort. Students' interactions with one another permit them to pool knowledge, compare understandings, and share and negotiate meanings. A classroom context that encourages talk brings learners and texts together to explore and construct meaning.

 MINDS-ON

1. You have probably seen some variation of the bumper sticker "If you can read this, thank a teacher." In a small group, sitting in a circle, discuss how you feel about seeing this sticker and what you think it means. Select one member of your group to act as an observer, and use the questions that follow to record group interactions. Allow 10 to 15 minutes for discussion, and then ask the observer to share her or his list of questions and answers with the group.

   Observer's questions:

   a. Who raised questions during group discussion?

   b. Could most of the questions be answered yes or no, true or false?

   c. Who answered the questions?

   d. Who decided who would answer and when they would answer?

   e. Who kept the group on task?

   f. Did your seating arrangement change before or after the discussion?

As a group, discuss the following:

a. Did the discussion process described by the observer involve the sharing of ideas by group members with no one person asking or answering all the questions?

b. What were the advantages and disadvantages of having the discussion progress without the rigid protocol of one person deciding who would answer and when?

c. How would you contrast the effect of the seating in rows used in lecture question-and-answer sessions with the effect of the circle seating used in this discussion?

2. Join together with four or five other individuals who either teach or are planning to teach at approximately the same grade level. Imagine that you have just attended a cooperative learning workshop and you plan to incorporate what you learned into your teaching. What do you consider the single best cooperative activity for your grade level and why? Discuss how you would implement this approach with a selected topic. List any problems you expect might arise, and explain how you would solve them.

3. Recognizing that students with different abilities and interests learn differently, to what extent should a teacher attempt to organize a class so that all the students in the class will learn the same concepts and information? Would your answer be the same for a third-grade science class and a high school advanced physics class? What general guidelines can you develop as a group to help a new teacher organize learning to balance course content with individual differences? Also, what type of physical classroom design do you feel would best facilitate your philosophy?

HANDS-ON

1. Try the following experiment. Roll a standard $8\frac{1}{2}$-by-11-inch sheet of paper into a tube 11 inches long and approximately 1 inch in diameter. Then hold the tube in your left hand and, keeping both eyes open, look through the tube with your left eye. Next, place your right hand, palm toward your face, against the side of the tube approximately half the distance from your eye to the end of the tube. Angle the tube slightly so that the far end of the tube is behind your palm, and a hole should appear in your hand.

   With a small group or individually, brainstorm how you might use this experiment as a prereading activity for a science lesson on the eye.

2. Team up with two other individuals. Designate one member of your group "observer," one "reader," and one "artist." The observer's task will be to make a written record of the actions of the reader and the artist. The artist will draw a triangle described by the reader in the following instructions:

> Draw a triangle so that one side is twice as long as one of the other two. Use one of the small sides as the base, and construct the triangle so that the longest side faces the left side of the paper. Design your triangle so that the longest side is 3 inches long. Make it exactly 3 inches if you have a ruler available, or estimate the length if you do not. Finally, assign the letters *a*, *b*, and *c* to each side of the triangle, designating the longest side as *c*.

After the reader and the artist have completed the drawing, review the notes by the observer, and develop a written record of the intentions or reasons for each action previously recorded. For example, if the observer recorded that the reader turned back to reread the instructions, you might explain that the artist had forgotten a fact that he or she needed to understand.

Finally, compare observations, make a class list of the learning strategies used by each group, and discuss which are successful approaches for a number of people. From this activity, what conclusions can you draw about the role of metacognition in reading to learn?

3. Bring your favorite book, magazine, poem, or drama to class. Develop a prereading activity that would provide the rationale for using this material, and introduce this piece. (This activity can be done in small groups of five or six or with the entire class.)

Before your presentation, plan a series of entry questions and comments to match what you think others will say in response. Also, because you are introducing this material with a purpose in mind, the discussion should lead your small group to a particular point from which the next activity might begin.

Be prepared to reach that departure point by a number of alternate routes. Prereading activities and discussions often remain detached from the reading/content activity, so that a novice is tempted to say, "That's enough talking. Let's get to the real lesson." The discussion or activity must be integral to the "real" lesson.

Here is the complete passage from the exercise at the conclusion of Chapter 1:

> Besides, Sir, we shall not fight our battles alone. There is a just God, who presides over the destinies of nations, who will raise up friends to fight our battles for us. The battle, Sir, is not to the strong alone: it is to the vigilant, the active, the brave. Besides, Sir, we have no election. If we were base enough to desire it, it is now too late to retire from the contest.

There is no retreat, but in submission or slavery. Our chains are forged. Their clanking may be heard on the plains of Boston! The war is inevitable— and let it come—I repeat, Sir, let it come! It is in vain, Sir, to extenuate the matter. Gentlemen may cry, "Peace! Peace!" But there is no peace. The war has actually begun!

The next gale that sweeps from the North will bring to our ears the clash of resounding arms! Our brethren are already in the field! Why stand we here idle? What is it that the Gentlemen wish? What would they have? Is life so dear, or peace too sweet, as to be purchased at the price of chains and slavery? Forbid it, Almighty God! I know not what course others may take, but as for me, give me liberty or give me death!

SUGGESTED READINGS

Aschbacher, P. R. (1991). Humanitas: A thematic curriculum. *Educational Leadership, 49* (2), 16–19.

Clark, C., & Yinger, R. (1980). *The hidden world of teaching: Implications of research on teacher planning.* Research Series No. 77. East Lansing, MI: Institute for Research on Teaching.

Cooper, J. (1982). The teacher as decision maker. In J. Cooper (Ed.), *Classroom teaching skills.* Lexington, MA: Heath.

Fogarty, R. (1994, March). Thinking about themes: Hundreds of themes. *Middle School Journal, 25,* 30–31.

Hahn, H. (1996). *The Internet Yellow Pages* (3rd ed.). New York: Osborne McGraw-Hill.

Jacobs, H. H. (Ed.). (1989). *Interdisciplinary curriculum: Design and implementation.* Alexandria, VA: Association for Supervision and Curriculum Development.

Katz, L. G., & Chard, S. C. (1990). *Engaging children's minds: The project approach.* Norwood, NJ: Ablex.

Leu, Jr., D. J., & Leu, D. D. (1997). *Teaching with the Internet: Lesson from the classroom.* Norwood, MA: Christopher-Gordon.

Lounsbury, J. H. (Ed.). (1992). *Connecting the curriculum through interdisciplinary instruction.* Columbus, OH: National Middle School Association.

Manning, M., Manning, G., & Long, R. (1994). *Theme immersion: Inquiry-based curriculum in elementary and middle schools.* Portsmouth, NH: Heinemann.

Meinbach, A. M., Rothlein, L., & Fredericks, A. D. (1995). *The complete guide to thematic units: Creating the integrated curriculum.* Norwood, MA: Christopher-Gordon.

Moss, J. F. (1994). *Using literature in the middle grades: A thematic approach.* Norwood, MA: Christopher-Gordon.

Peterson, P., Marx, R., & Clark, C. (1978). Teacher planning, teacher behavior and student achievement. *American Education Research Journal, 15,* 413–432.

Short, K. G., & Armstrong, J. (1993). Moving toward inquiry: Integrating literature into science curriculum. *The New Advocate, 6,* 183–199.

Stevenson, C., & Carr, J. F. (Eds). (1993). *Integrated studies in the middle grades: "Dancing through walls."* New York: Teachers College Press.

Vars, G. F. (1993). *Interdisciplinary teaching in the middle grades: Why and how.* Columbus, OH: National Middle School Association.

Weaver, C., Chaston, J., & Peterson, S. (1995). *Theme exploration: A voyage of discovery.* Portsmouth, NH: Heinemann.

Talking to Learn

Talk is the sea upon which all else floats.
—James Britton

Organizing Principle

Talk is the primary means by which teachers and students communicate. Talk saturates the classroom environment. It is, to use Britton's metaphor, "the sea upon which all else floats." Without talk, it's difficult to imagine how teachers would ply their craft and how students would engage in meaningful learning. Yet talking is so much a part of our lives that we (and our students) often take for granted the role that talk plays in learning. Donald Rubin (1990), for example, compares classroom talk to the parable about fish in water: Just as fish are the least likely creatures ever to become aware of water, teachers and students hardly recognize the power of talk as a medium for learning. Because talk surrounds us and constitutes so much of what we do in the classroom, Rubin suggests that it is invisible to us much of the time. As a result, the potential to use talking to learn often goes untapped in content classrooms.

As teachers, we can make strong connections between literacy and learning when we link talking to reading and writing. Talk is a bridge to literacy and learning across the curriculum. Through the power of talk—that is to say, authentic classroom discussion—students are able to transcend the information encountered in text; and in doing so, they are in a better position to transform knowledge and make it their own. Making talk more visible in our classrooms, however, isn't an easy task. The predominant type of talk in content area classrooms usually revolves around question-answer exchanges known as *recitations,* in which students take turns answering questions with bits and pieces of information. In these exchanges, the social and psychological context for learning is dominated by teacher talk with little opportunity for students to explore and clarify ideas, think critically and creatively, and reflect on what they are learning. In this chapter, we explore what it means to teach and learn in a *response-based curriculum* and examine ways in which teachers can scaffold *text-talk* so that students engage in lively discussions about ideas they are encountering in text.

Teachers who make talk visible in their classrooms recognize that students need opportunities to talk spontaneously and to respond personally and critically to ideas they are encountering in text. Three decades ago, the London Association for the Teaching of English prepared a seminal policy document on the uses of language across the curriculum (Barnes, Britton, & Rosen 1969). The association's policy statement underscores the power of talk not only to shape a student's ideas but also to modify them by listening to others. Informal, collaborative classroom talk allows students to question; plan; express doubt, difficulty, and confusion; and experiment with new language as they connect literacy to learning. The organizing principle of this chapter highlights the connections students make: **Talking to learn helps students explore, clarify, and think about ideas and concepts they encounter in reading and writing.**

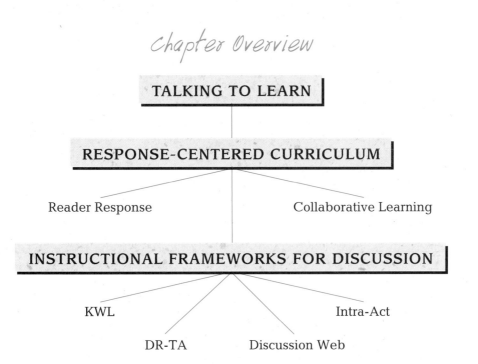

Chapter Overview

1. What is the importance of talk as a medium for literacy and learning?

2. How is recitation different from discussion as a type of classroom talk?

3. What is a response-based curriculum?

4. How can teachers plan discussions so that students actively respond to texts?

5. How can teachers engage students in cooperative learning?

6. Why and how do various instructional strategies guide reader-text interactions and encourage talking to learn?

Most students, regardless of ability, bring an important but underused resource to their classrooms, a resource that they have been developing throughout their lives to negotiate meaning and make sense of the world about them: They know how to talk. Young people talk easily and freely for a variety of aims and purposes, most of them social: to communicate, to persuade, to entertain, to inform, to learn about the world they live in. Observe students in school corridors, on the playground, or in a mall on weekends as they mingle with friends and interact with one another. Talk is something they do all the time.

Teachers are in a position to orchestrate a full range of instructional activities that promote meaningful classroom talk. Gambrell (1996) illustrates how various types of talk fall on a continuum from informal to formal modes of interaction. The model in Figure 6.1 depicts the types of informal and formal talk in relation to the range of audiences with whom individuals interact. At one end of the continuum, the most informal type of talk is inner speech (talking to oneself), and at the other end is the most formal mode of large-audience communication, broadcasting, where talk is technologically mediated as for a radio talk show or a newscast on television.

In classrooms, instructional conversations and discussions with one or more students represent less formal modes of interaction. Recitations, by contrast, are a more formal type of classroom communication. Because they are formal and directed to large groups, recitations tend to silence student voices and limit responses to one- or two-word answers.

As Douglas Barnes (1995) explains, "The kinds of participation in the classroom conversation that are supported and encouraged by a teacher signal to students what learning is required of them" (p. 2). If student talk is lim-

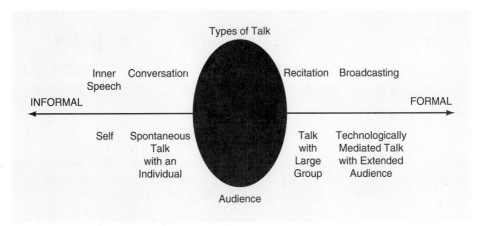

FIGURE 6.1   A Model of the Continuum of Talk

Source: From "What Research Reveals About Discussion," by Linda B. Gambrell. In Linda B. Gambrell and Janet F. Almasi (Eds.), *Lively Discussions! Fostering Engaged Reading* (Newark, DE: International Reading Association 1996), p. 28. Reprinted with permission of Linda B. Gambrell and the International Reading Association.

ited by recitations in which teachers do most of the talking, ask mostly factual questions that require one- or two-word answers, and control who takes turns answering questions, students will take their proper role to be passive nonparticipants. Lou, a student in a northern California high school, describes what it is like to be in classrooms where teachers dominate talk: "When a teacher runs the show, it's just, just kind of up to him. He has like a lecture written out and, you know, point by point. . . . A teacher kind of intimidates the students. 'Cause he's up there, you know, talking, making these complicated points and, you know, [students] just taking notes or something" (Knoeller 1994, p. 578).

Sometimes we unwittingly put students on the spot with the questions we ask during a recitation. Do you recall ever being put on the spot by a question? In that interminable second or two between question and answer, between pounding heart and short gasps for air, do you remember asking yourself, "What's *the* right answer—the one this instructor expects?" When questions are used to foster a right-answer-only atmosphere in class, they will not focus thinking about what has been read, nor will they prompt the processes by which students construct knowledge. They make the correct answer the all-important concern.

When students are on the spot, they often resort to guessing what is inside the teacher's head. One need only read Judy Blume's devastating parody of a music teacher's question to her class in Box 6.1 to appreciate how nonproductive that guessing game is.

Seeking right answers only, putting students on the spot, and reinforcing "guess what's in my head" behavior are tied to what some consider the prevalent instructional practice in American schooling, *turn taking* (Duffy

Box 6.1

Guess What's in My Head

When she finished her song she was right next to Wendy. "Wendy . . . can you tell me what was coming out of my mouth as I sang?"

"Out of your mouth?" Wendy asked.

"That's right," Miss Rothbelle told her.

"Well . . . it was . . . um . . . words?"

"No . . . no . . . no," Miss Rothbelle said.

Wendy was surprised. She can always give teachers the answers they want. Miss Rothbelle moved on. "Do you know, Caroline?"

"Was it sound?"

"Wrong!" Miss Rothbelle said, turning. "Donna Davidson, can you tell me?"

"It was a song," Donna said.

"Really Donna . . . we all know that!" Miss Rothbelle looked around. "Linda Fischer, do you know what was coming out of my mouth as I sang to the class?"

Linda didn't say anything.

"Well, Linda . . ." Miss Rothbelle said.

"I think it was air," Linda finally told her. "Either that or breath."

Miss Rothbelle walked over to Linda's desk. "That was not the correct answer. Weren't you paying attention?" She pulled a few strands of Linda's hair. . . .

She walked up and down the aisles until she stopped at my desk. . . .

"We'll see if you've been paying attention . . . suppose you tell me the answer to my question."

I had no idea what Miss Rothbelle wanted me to say. There was just one thing left that could have been coming out of her mouth as she sang, so I said, "It was spit."

"What?" Miss Rothbelle glared at me.

"I mean, it was saliva," I told her.

Miss Rothbelle banged her fist on my desk. "That was a very rude thing to say. You can sit in the corner for the rest of the period." . . .

At the end of the music period Robby Winters called out, "Miss Rothbelle . . . Miss Rothbelle . . ."

"What is it?" she asked.

"You never told us what was coming out of your mouth when you sang."

"That's right," Miss Rothbelle said. "I didn't."

"What was it?" Robby asked.

"It was melody," Miss Rothbelle said. Then she spelled it. "M-e-l-o-d-y. And every one of you should have known." She blew her pitchpipe at us and walked out of the room.

Source: Reprinted with the permission of Simon & Schuster Books for Young Readers, an imprint of Simon & Schuster Children's Publishing Division. From *Blubber* by Judy Blume. Copyright © 1974 Judy Blume.

1983). Turn taking occurs whenever the teacher asks a question or assigns a turn, the student responds, and the teacher gives feedback by correcting or reinforcing the response. Teachers often depend on turn taking to "discuss" topics under study. Yet what results is hardly a discussion at all. During turn-taking routines, questions usually forestall or frustrate classroom talk. Question-answer exchanges are brief, usually three to five seconds in duration, sometimes less, sometimes more. Rather than to characterize these question-answer exchanges as discussion, it is more appropriate to view them as recitation.

The striking feature of recitation is that the teacher's talk consists of questions. To illustrate this point, Dillon (1983, pp. 10–11) provides a transcript from a typical recitation conducted by a high school teacher of U.S. history:

Teacher:	OK, so we've kind of covered leadership and some of the things that Washington brought with it. Why else did they win? Leadership is important, that's one.
Student:	France gave 'em help.
Teacher:	OK, so France giving aid is an example of what? France is an example of it, obviously.
Student:	Aid from allies.
Teacher:	Aid from allies, very good. Were there any other allies who gave aid to us?
Student:	Spain.
Teacher:	Spain. Now, when you say aid, can you define that?
Student:	Help.
Teacher:	Define "help." Spell it out for me.
Student:	Assistance.
Teacher:	Spell it out for me.
Student:	They taught the men how to fight the right way.
Teacher:	Who taught?
Student:	The allies.
Teacher:	Where? When?
Student:	In the battlefield.
Teacher:	In the battlefield?

In these exchanges, the students take turns answering questions about the success of Washington's Revolutionary army. The eight question-answer exchanges lasted a little more than 30 seconds, or four to five seconds per exchange. Each student addressed a response to the teacher, not to other students. The nature of turn taking is such that it is forbidden for another student to jump into the exchange unless first recognized by the teacher to take a turn.

Our language and actions signal to students what their roles are to be within a lesson. Although recitation may serve legitimate educational purposes (quizzing, reviewing), it may negatively affect students' cognitive, affective, and expressive processes. Given the rules that operate during turn taking, teachers may very well increase student passivity and dependence. Furthermore, turn taking leads to a limited construction of meaning with text. Because the pace of questions is often rapid, readers hardly have the time to think about or to clarify or explore their understanding of the text. When we ask predominantly "quiz show" questions, students soon engage in fact finding rather than in thinking about the ideas the author communicates. The inherent danger to text learners is subtle but devastating: Mistaken signals may be telegraphed to students about what it means to comprehend text and what their role is as comprehenders. Finding bits and pieces of information becomes the end-all and be-all of reading.

In the remainder of this chapter, we show how you can use talk as a bridge to literacy and learning by fostering student response to text. Through discussions that are cooperative and collaborative and strategies that support text-talk, you lay the groundwork for a *response-centered* curriculum.

TOWARD A RESPONSE-CENTERED CURRICULUM

A response-centered curriculum values what students feel and think in relation to what they are reading, writing, and talking about. The hallmark of a response-centered curriculum is students' personal reactions to ideas encountered in texts. Responding to text is a reader-driven event. As students engage with texts, they construct meanings that are influenced by their own knowledge, values, and life experiences. When they share their understandings of a text in a class discussion, their own personal responses are often extended and enriched.

If you were to enter the classroom of Mary Krogness (1995, 1997), a middle school teacher in a near-urban school district, you would observe a response-centered curriculum where talk is a bridge to literacy and learning. Krogness works with students whose academic histories are characterized by low achievement and failure. The majority of the students in her classes are from minority backgrounds and score below the third stanine on achievement tests. According to Krogness (1997), the students came to her classes "expecting the teacher to do all the talking and fill 'em up each day with information, directions, and assignments; and then they pretty much expected and accepted the job of working silently and alone filling up the forty-two-minute class period" with classroom activities "that demand little original thought." The students didn't expect to talk in class in order to learn, so they relied on their teacher "to tell them what to do next, mainly because they hadn't had the experience nor had they practiced being generators of thought and questions" (pp. 28–29).

Krogness refuses to let the emotional baggage that students bring to her classes get in the way of literacy and learning. She disrupts students' expectations by making talking to learn the centerpiece of student response. As Jermaine, one of her students, puts it, "All we do in here is talk. And read and write." Students don't turn into "generators of thought" overnight. Some come to class passive and lifeless; others are threatening and disruptive and will try to derail the class whenever the opportunity arises. Yet Krogness sticks to her expectation that student response is central to learning:

> By making not my [own] but my *students'* talking central, I could begin jump-starting my kids who seriously conveyed a lack of interest in much of anything academic and help them become invested in language-making and learning. In the process of drawing everyone into the group, I could certainly help them to take control of the language and maybe even begin to take charge of their lives. . . . Listening to and watching my students . . . would help me devise projects in which talking, listening, reading, writing, and viewing were woven together into a rich fabric . . . (Krogness, 1997, p. 29).

Krogness's classes underscore the role that *reader response* plays in students' academic lives.

Fostering Reader Response Through Talking and Writing

Reader response theory has evolved from a literary tradition. As early as 1938, Louise Rosenblatt (1983) argued that *thought* and *feeling* are legitimate components of literary interpretation. A text, whether it's literary or informational, demands affective as well as intellectual response from its readers. Creating an active learning environment in which students respond personally and critically to what they are reading is an important instructional goal in a response-centered curriculum. Often in text-learning situations, a teacher will focus on what students have learned and how much. There's value in having what Rosenblatt calls an *efferent stance* as a reader. When readers assume an efferent stance, they focus attention on the ideas and information they encounter in a text. Reader response, however, is also likely to involve feelings, personal associations, and insights that are unique to the reader. When students assume an *aesthetic stance,* they shift attention inward to what is being created as part of the reading experience itself. An aesthetic response to text is driven by personal feelings and attitudes that are stirred by the reader's interactions and transactions with the text.

One way to encourage talking to learn is to take advantage of both efferent and aesthetic stances. This works well when students actively respond to what they are reading not only by talking but also by writing. One of the strategies we explore in Chapter 7, on writing to learn, is the use of *response journals.* When students combine the use of response journals with discussion, the challenge from an instructional perspective is to create an environment in which they feel free enough to respond openly. Open response is necessary to evoke students' initial feelings and thoughts. Evoking students' initial responses to a text are crucial to further exploration of the ideas they are encountering. Open responses, however, are not final responses.

For example, a history teacher divides the class into two groups and has one group read *Bearstone* (1989), by Will Hobbs, and the other read *The Cage* (1986), by Ruth Sender. These trade books have protagonists who are being held against their will in situations that are beyond their control. As the students read the books, they keep response journals in which they react to questions such as how the protagonists feel as captives of societies that discriminate against their race. When the class meets to discuss the books, students offer ideas from their response journal to generate a comparison concerning the ways in which the Jewish woman's captivity in *The Cage* during World War II differs from the contemporary American Indian boy's sense of belonging in *Bearstone.* From this discussion, students go on to explore the concept of slavery and how it changes across circumstances, societies, and historical periods.

Affect, as you can see, is a catalyst for classroom discussion. Bleich (1978) suggests that response involves both the author and the reader taking active parts in the making of meaning. Thus the initial response of "I like this" or "I hate this" becomes the springboard for other, more complex reactions. *Why* a student likes or does not like a text becomes the genesis of discussions, drama, art, and compositions that probe the reader's intentions.

A *reader response heuristic* allows students to explore their personal responses and to take those initial reactions into more analytic realms. According to Brozo (1989), the rationale behind a reader response heuristic is this: "It is through a personal connection that a text becomes meaningful and memorable" (p. 141). The following are questions that guide student responses to informational texts:

1. What aspect of the text excited or interested you the most? (The reader identifies an idea, issue, event, character, place, or any other aspect of the content that aroused strong feelings.)

2. What are your feelings and attitudes about this aspect of the text? (The reader describes and explains feelings and attitudes.)

3. What experiences have you had that help others understand why you feel the way you do? (The reader supports feelings and attitudes with personal experiences.) (Brozo 1989, p. 142)

Responses to these questions help readers consciously connect their own experiences to the content of the text. The questions can be used well in combination with writing and talking.

Student's Most Interesting Part of Text	The information about quarks was good. It was something that I didn't know before. I really thought that the names of the different types of quarks (up, down, truth, beauty, strange, and charm) were kind of weird, but these names made them easier to remember because they are so different.
Student's Feelings and Attitudes Toward Subject	The author did a good job in making all of this interesting and pretty easy to read. Quarks and their flavors and colors are kind of hard to understand when you read about them in the textbook, but I could follow this book. I think it's amazing what scientists have been able to find out about atomic particles. I especially wonder about why the universe hasn't blown up already, since the book said that it should have because of the way particles and antiparticles react. Scientists don't have the answer either. But it makes you feel a little uneasy, not knowing what holds all of this together.
Student's Personal Associations	I suppose that all of us have wondered about what keeps the universe going at some time or other. I guess what started me thinking about this was a science fiction movie that I saw that showed the world exploding into outer space. A lot of people see these kinds of shows and start to think about if that could really happen. Then, when you read about quarks, it makes you think.

FIGURE 6.2   **Reader Response Heuristic for** *Atoms, Molecules, and Quarks*

Study a student's response to a trade book titled *Atoms, Molecules, and Quarks* (1986), by Melvin Berger, presented in Figure 6.2. Students can and do become interested in and excited about scientific information when it is presented in a response-centered format.

Supporting Response Through Discussion

In a response-centered classroom, teachers and students renegotiate authority as the burden for learning shifts from teacher to student. As a result, teachers lead, but do not dominate, classroom talk, and they provide opportunities for students to participate more fully through student-led discussions. This is the case in Joan Cone's English classes.

Cone teaches in a culturally diverse high school that reformed its tracking policies by opening up senior-level English classes to all students by self-selection. Regardless of their academic history, students could choose to take college preparatory courses and even advanced-placement classes. Cone's AP class, for example, was diverse in terms of ethnicity, gender, and levels of achievement (Scholastic Assessment Test scores ranged from 750 to 1350). Given the broad range of student differences, Cone's challenge was responding to diversity while maintaining the high standards of a rigorous AP class. She experimented with a variety of instructional strategies, including student-led discussions of literature.

Christian Knoeller (1994), who studied Cone's class, notes that she allowed students to volunteer as discussion leaders. A discussion leader was responsible for raising questions and keeping the discussion moving. At times, when discussions bogged down or students had to be coached into using the text to justify their interpretations, Cone would step into the discussion to get it back on track. But she did so as a participant rather than as an authority figure. The goal was to have students engage with the text and with one another. In Cone's words:

> Besides assisting students with understanding sophisticated text, talk can create a classroom atmosphere in which the most able reader and least able reader can collaborate in making meaning and can learn from each other by sharing their insights, experiences, questions, and interpretations. . . . The emphasis [during student-led discussions] was always on asking questions, looking back in the text for substantiation, trying out interpretations, coming to agreement or living with disagreement: students creating meaning together, students teaching each other. . . . A sense of community had been established. (Knoeller 1994, p. 574)

Whether student-led or teacher-led, a discussion has certain characteristics that distinguish it from a recitation. First, discussions represent an open exchange of ideas. Second, both students and teacher ask questions. Third, students are just as likely to talk to other students as they are to respond to the teacher. And fourth, students learn to use their texts to substantiate their responses and support their interpretations.

Discussion can best be described as conversational interactions between teacher and students as well as between students. In teacher-led discussions, the teacher doesn't ask questions over long stretches of time, although questions are used judiciously throughout most discussions. As a result, discussion signifies an exchange of ideas and active participation among all parties involved.

Asking questions, even ones designed to get students to open up and share their understanding of text, doesn't always result in a good discussion or, for that matter, a bad discussion—just nondiscussion whenever students do not make sense of what they are doing or what is happening. Students stand a better chance of participating in discussion when they have a clear sense of purpose, understand the discussion task, and are given explicit directions and clear explanations.

Many of the instructional strategies in this book are necessarily tied to discussion of one kind or another. Discussion allows students to respond to text, build concepts, clarify meaning, explore issues, share perspectives, and refine thinking. But effective discussions don't run by themselves. For a discussion to be successful, a teacher has to be willing to take a risk or two.

Whenever you initiate a discussion, its outcome is bound to be uncertain, especially if its purpose is to help students think critically and creatively about what they have read. Often a teacher abandons discussion for the safety of recitation, where the outcome is far more predictable. A text discussion, however, should be neither a quiz show nor, at the opposite end of the continuum, a bull session (Roby 1987). Yet when discussions aren't carefully planned, students often feel an aimlessness or become easily threatened by the teacher's questions. Both being quizzed about text material and just shooting the bull are apt to close doors on active text learning.

Different purposes for text discussion lead to the use of different types of discussion. *Guided discussions* and *reflective discussions* provide varying degrees of structure for students to talk about text as they interact with one another.

Encouraging Text-Talk Through Guided Discussions

If your aim is to develop concepts, clarify meaning, and promote understanding, the most appropriate discussion may be *informational.* The main objective of an informational discussion is to help students grapple with issues and understand important concepts. When the discussion task is information-centered, Kindsvatter, Wilen, and Ishler (1992) suggest that teachers use a guided discussion.

In a guided discussion, the teacher provides a moderate amount of scaffolding as he or she directs students to think about what they have read through the use of questions and/or teacher-developed guide material. Because the emphasis is on content understanding and clarification, it is important to recognize the central role of the teacher in a guided discussion. Your responsibilities lie in asking questions, in probing student responses because clarifications are needed to extend thinking, in encouraging student questions, and in providing information to keep the discussion on course. The potential problem, however, is domination of the discussion. Alvermann, Dillon, and O'Brien (1988) caution that when overused, this role "can result in a discussion that more nearly resembles a lecture and frequently may confuse students, especially if they have been encouraged to assume more active roles in discussion" (p. 31).

A guided discussion can easily take a *reflective turn.* When teachers consciously shift gears from guided discussion to reflective discussion, their role in the discussion shifts.

Encouraging Text-Talk Through Reflective Discussion

A reflective discussion is different from a guided discussion in several respects. The purpose of a reflective discussion is to require students to engage in critical and creative thinking as they solve problems, clarify values, explore controversial issues, and form and defend positions. A reflective discussion, then, presumes that students have a solid understanding of the important concepts they are studying. Without a basic knowledge and understanding of the ideas or issues under discussion, students cannot support opinions, make judgments, or justify and defend positions.

The teacher's role during a reflective discussion is that of participant. As a participant, you become a group member so that you can contribute to the discussion by sharing ideas and expressing your own opinions: "Teachers can guide students to greater independence in learning by modelling different ways of responding and reacting to issues, commenting on others' points of view, and applying critical reading strategies to difficult concepts in the textbooks" (Alvermann et al. 1988, p. 31).

Creating an Environment for Discussion

Since many of the strategies in this text revolve around discussion of some sort, we offer several suggestions for creating an environment in which discussion takes place, whether in small groups or in the whole class.

First, arrange the room so that students can see each other and huddle in conversational groupings when they need to share ideas. A good way to judge how functional a classroom is for discussion is to select a discussion strategy that does not require continuous question asking. For example, in Chapter 7, we will see that brainstorming involves a good mixture of whole-class and small-group discussion. Students need to alternate their attention between the chalkboard (where the teacher or another student is writing down all the ideas offered within a specified time) and their small groups (where they might categorize the ideas) and back to the front of the room (for comparison of group categories and summarization). If students are able to participate in the various stages of brainstorming with a minimum of chair moving or other time-consuming movements, to see the board, and to converse with other students without undue disruption, the room arrangements are conducive to discussion.

Second, encourage a climate in which everyone is expected to be a good listener, including the teacher. Let each student speaker know that you are listening. As the teacher begins to talk less, students will talk more. Intervene to determine why some students are not listening to each other or to praise those who are unusually good role models for others. Accept all responses of students positively.

Try starting out with very small groups of no more than two or three students. Again, rather than use questions, have students react to a teacher-read statement ("Political primaries are a waste of time and money"). In the beginning, students may feel constrained to produce answers to questions to satisfy the teacher. A statement, however, serves as a possible answer and invites reaction and justification. Once a statement is given, set a timer or call time by your watch at two-minute intervals. During each interval, one student in the group may agree or disagree *without interruption*. After each group member has an opportunity to respond, the group summarizes all dialogue, and one person presents this summary to the class (Gold & Yellin 1982).

Third, establish the meaning of the topic and the goal of the discussion: "Why are we talking about railroad routes, and how do they relate to our unit on the Civil War?" Also, explain directions explicitly, and don't assume that students will know what to do. Many of the content area reading strategies in this book involve some group discussion. Frequently, strategies progress from independent, written responses to sharing, comparing those responses in small groups, and then pooling small-group reactions in a whole-class discussion. Without the guidance of a teacher who is aware of this process, group discussion tends to disintegrate.

Fourth, keep the focus of the discussion on the central topic or core question or problem to be solved. One way to begin discussion is by asking a question about a perplexing situation or by establishing a problem to be solved. From time to time, it may be necessary to refocus attention on the topic by piggybacking on comments made by particular students: "Terry brought out an excellent point about the Underground Railroad in northern Ohio. Does anyone else want to talk about this?" During small-group discussions, a tactic that keeps groups on task is to remind them of the amount of time remaining in the discussion.

Keeping the focus is one purpose for which teachers may legitimately question to clarify the topic. They may also want to make sure that they understood a particular student's comment: "Excuse me, would you repeat that?" Often, keeping the discussion focused will prevent the class from straying away from the task.

Fifth, support second-language learners by showing sensitivity to their literacy needs. Barton (1995) reminds teachers to simplify and clarify the language they use and to check for understanding frequently throughout classroom conversation. As we explained earlier, teachers should scaffold instruction during discussion by supporting students' use of their home languages and their own culturally acceptable conversational styles. For ESL students who are in the early stages of English acquisition, the ability to listen to talk outpaces the ability to speak the language. Yet "the student who struggles to respond in English is every bit as capable a thinker as anyone else in your classroom" (p. 348).

Finally, avoid squelching discussion. Try, for example, not to repeat questions, whether they are your own or the students'. Give students enough think time to reflect on possible answers before calling on someone or rephrasing your question. Moreover, try to avoid repeating answers or answering your own question. (One way to prevent yourself from doing the latter is to resist having a preset or "correct" answer in your own mind when you ask a question beyond a literal level of comprehension.) Do not interrupt students' responses or permit others to interrupt students' responses. Do, however, take a minute or two to summarize and bring closure to a group discussion just as you would in any instructional strategy.

Both guided and reflective discussions may be conducted with the whole class or in small groups. Small-group discussions place the responsibility for learning squarely on students' shoulders. Because of the potential value of collaborative student interactions, we examine the valuable contribution of cooperative learning in a response-centered curriculum.

Supporting Response Through Collaboration

Cooperative learning allows groups of students to pursue academic goals through collaboration. The goals of cooperative learning, therefore, are to foster collaboration in a classroom context, to develop students' self-esteem in the process of learning, to encourage the development of positive group relationships, and to enhance academic achievement (Johnson, Johnson, & Holubec 1990). Cooperative discussion groups facilitate active participation and should be a primary form of classroom organization when you are bringing learners together to respond to texts. Students produce more ideas, participate more, and take greater intellectual risks in small-group or team learning situations. A cooperative group, with its limited audience, provides more opportunity for students to contribute ideas to a discussion and take chances in the process. The students can try out ideas without worrying about being wrong or sounding dumb—a fear that often accompanies risk taking in a whole-class situation.

Many variations on cooperative team learning are possible. Several cooperative grouping patterns work well, in particular, within the context of content literacy practices and text-response discussions. The cooperative groups we describe here will give you a feel for how students might collaborate in their interactions with texts and with one another as they explore meaning and make sense of what they are reading.

Jigsaw Groups

Interdependent team learning with texts may be achieved through *jigsaw groups* (Aronson 1978). Jigsaw teaching requires students to specialize in a content literacy task that contributes to an overall group objective. Jigsaw groups are composed of students divided heterogeneously into three- to six-member teams. Each student on a team becomes an expert on a subtopic of a theme or topic that the class is reading about. Not only is the student accountable for teaching the other members of the group about his or her subtopic, but he or she is also responsible for learning the information other group members provide during the jigsaw discussions.

For example, a life science teacher in a middle school engages students in a thematic unit on the topic "birds." As part of the unit of study, he divides the class into five six-member jigsaw groups. Each member of a group is expected to become an expert on one of the following concepts in the unit: the relationship between birds and reptiles, the adaptation of various species of birds to their environment, the migration patterns of birds, the adaptation of birds for flight, the economic importance of birds, and the identification of various families and species.

As part of the jigsaw strategy, members of the different teams who share the same subtopic meet in temporary "expert groups" to discuss what they are reading and learning. Each of the expert groups has a variety of resource materials and texts made available by the teacher to help them explore and clarify their subtopics. When the members in each of the expert groups complete their tasks, they return to their jigsaw teams to teach and share what they have learned. As a jigsaw member presents his or her findings, the other members listen and take notes in preparation for a unit exam the teacher will give on the overall topic.

Student Teams Achievement Divisions (STAD)

Student teams lend themselves well to content area learning situations that combine whole-class discussion with follow-up small-group activity. The originator of STAD groups, Robert Slavin (1988), emphasizes the importance of achieving team learning goals but also recognizes that individual performance is important in cooperative groups.

STAD groups work this way: The teacher introduces a topic of study to the whole class, presents new information, and then divides the class into heterogeneous four-member groups of high-, average-, and low-achieving students to engage in follow-up team study. The goal of team study is to master the content presented in whole-class discussion. The team members help each other by discussing the material, problem solving, comparing answers to guide material, and quizzing one another to ensure that each member knows the material. The students take periodic quizzes, prepared by the teacher, following team study. A team score is determined by the extent to which each member of the team improves over past performance. A system of team awards based on how well students perform individually ensures that team members will be interdependent for learning.

Learning Circles

Johnson et al. (1990) underscore the importance of positive interdependence through a cooperative learning model. Similar to STAD, learning circles mesh whole-group study with small-group interactions and discussion. Learning circles may comprise two to six members of varying abilities who come together to share text resources and help each other learn. All of the content literacy activities that we present in this book can be adapted to the type of interdependent learning teams that are suggested by Johnson et al. However, cooperative groups don't run by themselves. You have to plan for the success of positive interdependence by teaching students how to use collaboration skills to work interdependently in teams and then facilitating the group process as students engage in discussion and interaction.

Johnson et al. (1990) suggest 18 steps for structuring learning circles, some of which are specifying content objectives, deciding on the size of the group, assigning students to groups, arranging the room, planning instructional activities and guide material to promote interdependent learning, explaining the academic task, explaining the criteria for success, structuring the division of labor within the groups, structuring individual accountability and intergroup cooperation, monitoring students' behavior, teaching the skills of collaboration, providing task assistance as needed, evaluating student learning, and assessing how well the teams functioned.

Group brainstorming, prediction, problem solving, mapping, and study strategies, all of which are to be discussed in Part 3, are easily woven into the fabric of cooperative learning circles. Coming to a group consensus on a variety of discussion tasks is an important outcome in cooperative learning groups. Students need to be shown how to engage cooperatively in consensus building as they decide what conclusions they can or cannot support as a result of their interactions with texts and one another.

Group Investigation

As we explained in Chapter 5, students can be combined in teams of two to six to collaborate on inquiry topics that interest them within the context of a thematic unit and the major concepts of study. Each group selects a topic and cooperatively plans the inquiry in consultation with the teacher. Each research team, for example, decides how to investigate the topic, which tasks each member will be responsible for, and how the topic will be reported. The groups then conduct the investigation, synthesize their findings into a group presentation, and make their presentation to the entire class. The teacher's evaluation includes individual performance and the overall quality of the group presentation.

Group Retellings

Group retellings underscore the importance of *conceptually related reading* in which each member of a cooperative group reads a different text on the same topic. For example, Wood (1987) illustrates the use of group retellings in a health class. Students of differing ability work in groups of three or more, reading timely articles or brochures on the topic of safety in the home. A magazine article might describe an eyewitness account of a home fire resulting from an electrical overload. A brochure from the local fire department might outline the precautions to take to avoid such a mishap, perhaps emphasizing the hazards associated with an overloaded circuit. A newspaper editorial might warn parents against leaving their children unattended and unfamiliar with safety hazards in the home.

After reading, each member of the group shares what he or she has read while the other members of the team listen and, at any point, share additional information and insights into the topic based on their reading. According to Wood (1987), group retellings capitalize on the pleasure derived from sharing newly learned information with a friend.

Scaffolding Collaboration Among Students

Team learning is complex, and cooperative groups don't run by themselves. Students must know how to work together and how to use techniques they have been taught. The teacher, in turn, must know about small-group processes. The practical question is, How will individual students turn into cooperative groups? Anyone who has ever attempted small-group instruction in the classroom knows the dilemma associated with the question. Many conditions can confound team learning if plans are not made in advance; in particular, teachers must scaffold instruction around such matters as the size, composition, goals, and performance criteria of small groups and the division of labor within a group.

Group Size

The principle of "least group size" operates whenever you form learning teams. A group should be just large enough to include all the skills necessary to solve a problem or complete a task. A group that's larger than necessary provides less chance for individual participation and greater opportunity for conflict. If too many students are grouped together, there's bound to be a point of diminishing returns. The group size for content area reading should range from two to six members (depending, of course, on the type of reading task). Since most small-group activities involve discussion, three- or four-member groups are probably best.

Group Composition

Homogeneous grouping is often not necessary for discussion tasks. Both intellectual and nonintellectual factors will influence a small group's performance, and the relationship between intelligence and small-group performance is often surprisingly low. Experiential and social background, interests, attitudes, and personality contribute greatly to the success of a cooperative group. Grouping solely by reading or intellectual ability shortchanges all students and robs discussion of diversity.

Students who struggle with reading shouldn't be relegated to tasks that require minimal thinking or low-level responses to content material. There is no quicker way to initiate misbehavior than to put students who find reading difficult together in a group. People learn from one another. A student whose background is less extensive than other students' can learn from them. The student who has reading difficulties needs good readers as models. Furthermore, the student who has trouble reading may in fact be a good listener and thinker who will contribute significantly to small-group discussion.

As you plan team learning situations, you should take into consideration the following critical variables: the *goals* of the cooperative group, the *tasks* in which the group is to engage, the *interdependence* of group members as they pursue goals and engage in tasks, and the *roles* and division of labor within groups.

Group Goals and Tasks

Team learning is goal-oriented. How the goals and the paths to task completion are perceived affects the amount and quality of involvement of the team members. If group goals are unclear, members' interest quickly wanes. Goals must also be directly related to the task. The conditions of the task must be clearly defined and must be understood by the individual members of the group.

Therefore, you should explain the criteria for task performance. For example, when students work with reading guides such as those that are suggested in this book, they should attempt to adhere to such criteria as the following:

1. Each student should read the selection silently and complete each item of the guide individually or with others in the group, depending on the teacher's specific directions.

2. Each item should be discussed by the group.

3. If there is disagreement on any item, a group member must defend his or her position and show why there is disagreement. This means going back into the selection to support one's position.

4. No one student should dominate a discussion or boss other members around.

5. Each member should contribute something to each group discussion.

As students work on literacy activities in their groups, the teacher can facilitate performance by reinforcing the criteria that have been established.

Positive Interdependence

Groups lack cohesiveness when learning is not cooperative but competitive and when students aren't interdependent in learning but work independently. However, since the 1970s, social scientists and instructional researchers have made great strides in understanding the problems of the competitive classroom. Researchers at Johns Hopkins University in particular (Johnson & Johnson 1987; Slavin 1988) have studied the practical classroom applications of cooperative principles of learning. The bulk of their research suggests that cooperative small-group learning has positive effects on academic achievement and social relationships. Positive interdependence can be achieved through a variety of schemes in which students are rewarded for collaborative effort (Johnson & Johnson 1990). For example, a social studies teacher attempted to have students adhere to discussion behaviors during their interactions in small groups (these discussion behaviors were basically the same as those we discussed under performance criteria). Each small group earned a performance grade for discussing text assignments in a six-week thematic unit. Here's how the group members earned their grades.

1. The teacher observed each member in the group to monitor the use of the desired discussion behaviors.

2. On Fridays, each group earned a color reward worth a given number of points: green = 1 point, blue = 2 points, black = 3 points, and red = 4 points. The color that a group earned was based on how well it had performed according to the criteria for discussion.

3. Each member of the group received the color (and the points that went with it) that the whole group earned. Therefore, if one or two members of the group did not use the appropriate discussion behaviors, the entire group got a lower point award.

4. The color for each student in the class was charted on a learning incentive chart.

5. Each week, the small groups changed composition by random assignment.

6. The points attached to each color added up over the weeks. When the unit was completed, so many points resulted in a performance grade of A, B, C, or D.

What happened as a result of the reward system? On the Monday of each week that students were randomly assigned to new groups, they immediately went to the learning incentive chart to check the color received the previous week by each of the other members in their new group. Motivation was high. Group pressure caused individual students who had not received high points the previous week to become intent on improving their performance in the new group.

GROUP ROLES AND DIVISION OF LABOR   If cooperative groups are to be successful, members must divide the work of the group and understand their different roles within the group. Therefore, consider specifying complementary and interconnected responsibilities that the group must undertake to accomplish a joint task. Johnson and Johnson (1990) define several roles, which may vary by the nature of the task, for example:

Leader: The group leader facilitates the work of the group. Leadership skills may include *giving directions* (reviewing instructions, restating the goals of the group, calling attention to time limits, offering procedures on how to complete the task most effectively); *summarizing* aloud what has been read and/or discussed; and *generating responses* by going beyond the first answer or conclusion and producing a number of plausible answers to choose from.

Reader: The reader in the group is responsible for reading the group's material aloud so that the group members can understand and remember it.

Writer-recorder: The writer-recorder records the responses of the group on paper, edits what the group has written, and makes sure the group members check for content accuracy and completeness.

Checker: The checker makes sure the group is on target by checking on what is being learned by the members. The checker, therefore, may ask individuals within the group to explain or summarize the material being discussed.

Encourager: The encourager watches to make sure that all the members in the group are participating and invites reluctant or silent members to contribute.

If students are to understand the roles and the responsibilities of each role, you will need to develop in them a knowledge and an awareness of each. Discuss each role, demonstrate appropriate behavior and responses, role-play with students, coach, and provide feedback during actual group discussions.

We believe that the main reason for the infrequent use of small groups is the frustration that teachers experience when teams lack cohesion and interdependence. Uncooperative groups are a nightmare. No wonder a teacher abandons or is hesitant to use small groups in favor of whole-class instruction, which is easier to control. Small-group instruction requires risk taking by the teacher as much as it encourages risk taking by the students.

INSTRUCTIONAL FRAMEWORKS FOR ENCOURAGING DISCUSSION

In a response-centered curriculum, teachers use instructional frameworks to guide reader-text interactions. Through the use of these frameworks, you will connect talking, listening, reading, and writing as students respond to texts and construct meaning.

The KWL Strategy

KWL is a meaning-making strategy that engages students in active text learning. The strategy creates an instructional framework that begins with what students *know* about the topic to be studied, moves to what the students *want to know* as they generate questions about the topic, and leads to a record of what students *learn* as a result of their engagement in the strategy. Follow-up activities to KWL include discussion, the construction of graphic organizers, and summary writing to clarify and internalize what has been read.

KWL may be initiated with small groups of students or the whole class. When they develop confidence and competence with the KWL strategy, stu-

K—What I Know	W—What I Want to Know	L—What I Learned and Still Need to Learn

Categories of Information
I Expect to Use

A.   E.

B.   F.

C.   G.

D.

FIGURE 6.3   **A KWL Strategy Sheet**

Source: From Donna M. Ogle, "K-W-L: A Teaching Model that Develops Active Reading in Expository Text" (February 1986). *The Reading Teacher,* 39(6), 564–570. Copyright © 1986 by the International Reading Association. All rights reserved. Used by permission of the author and International Reading Association.

dents may begin to use it for independent learning. KWL uses a strategy sheet, such as the one in Figure 6.3. The steps in KWL revolve around the completion of the strategy sheet as part of the dynamics of student response and discussion.

Steps in the KWL Strategy

Here's how the KWL strategy works.

1. *Introduce the KWL strategy in conjunction with a new topic or text selection.* Before assigning a text, explain the strategy. Donna Ogle (1992), the originator of KWL, suggests that dialogue begin with the teacher saying:

It is important to first find out what we think we know about this topic. Then we want to anticipate how an author is likely to present and organize the information. From this assignment we can generate good questions to focus on reading and study. Our level of knowledge will determine to some extent how we will study. Then as we read we will make notes of questions that get answered and other new and important information we learn. During this process some new questions will probably occur to us; these we should also note so we can get clarification later. (p. 271)

In the process of explaining KWL, be sure that students understand *what* their role involves and *why* it is important for learners to examine what they know and to ask questions about topics that they will be reading and studying.

The next several steps allow you to model the KWL strategy with a group of learners or the entire class. Some students will find it difficult to complete the KWL strategy sheet on their own. Others will avoid taking risks or revealing what they know or don't know about a topic. Others just won't be positively motivated. Modeling the KWL strategy lessens the initial risk and creates a willingness to engage in the process. Students who experience the modeling of the strategy quickly recognize its value as a learning tool.

2. *Identify what students think they know about the topic.* Engage the class in brainstorming, writing their ideas on the board or on an overhead transparency. Use the format of the KWL strategy sheet as you record students' ideas on the chalkboard or transparency. It's important to record everything that the students *think* they know about the topic, including their misconceptions. The key in this step is to get the class actively involved in making associations with the topic, not to evaluate the rightness or wrongness of the associations. Students will sometimes challenge one another's knowledge base. The teacher's role is to help learners recognize that differences exist in what they think they know. These differences can be used to help students frame questions.

3. *Generate a list of student questions.* Ask, "What do you want to know more about? What are you most interested in learning about?" As you write their questions on the chalkboard or transparency, recognize that you are again modeling for students what their role as learners should be: to ask questions about material to be studied.

When you have completed modeling the brainstorming and question-generation phases of KWL, have the students use their own strategy sheets to make decisions about what they personally think they know and what they want to know more about. Students, especially those who may be at risk in academic situations, may refer to the chalkboard or the overhead transparency to decide what to record in the first two columns.

4. *Anticipate the organization and structure of ideas that the author is likely to use in the text selection.* As part of preparation for reading, have students next use their knowledge and their questions to make predictions about the organization of the text. What major categories of information is the author likely to use to organize his or her ideas?

The teacher might ask, "How do you think the author of a text or article on _____ is likely to organize the information?" Have students focus on the ideas they have brainstormed and the questions they have raised to predict possible categories of information. As students make their predictions, record these on the board or transparency in the area suggested by the KWL strategy sheet. Then have students make individual choices on their own strategy sheets.

5. *Read the text selection to answer the questions.* As they engage in interactions with the text, the students write answers to their questions and make notes for new ideas and information in the L column of their strategy sheets. Again, the teacher's modeling is crucial to the success of this phase of KWL. Students may need a demonstration or two to understand how to record information in the L column.

Debrief students after they have read the text and have completed writing responses in the L column. First, invite them to share answers, recording these on the chalkboard or transparency. Then ask, "What new ideas did you come across that you didn't think you would find in the text?" Record and discuss the responses.

6. *Engage students in follow-up activities to clarify and extend learning.* Use KWL as a springboard into postreading activities to internalize student learning. Activities may include the construction of graphic organizers to clarify and retain ideas encountered during reading or the development of written summaries.

A KWL Illustration

In Christa Chaney's U.S. history class, students were beginning a study of the Vietnam War. Christa realized that her students would have some, if not much, prior knowledge of and attitudes toward the Vietnam War because it has remained "a strong part of our national consciousness." The students, in fact, were acutely aware of the war from recent popular movies and also from fathers and other relatives who had participated in it.

However, Christa realized that while students might know something about the Vietnam War, they had probably had little opportunity to study it from the perspective of historians. This, then, was Christa's objective as a teacher of history: to help students approach the study of the Vietnam War— and understand the social, economic, and political forces surrounding it— from a historian's perspective.

Therefore, Christa felt that the KWL strategy would be an appropriate way to begin the unit. She believed that it would help students get in touch with what they knew (and didn't know) about the Vietnam War and raise questions that would guide their interactions with the materials that they would be studying.

Christa began KWL knowing that her students were familiar with its procedures, having participated in the strategy on several previous occasions in the class. Following the six steps, the class as a whole participated in brainstorming what they knew about the war and what they wanted to know. Christa recorded their ideas and questions on an overhead transparency and encouraged students' participation by asking such questions as "What else do you know? Who knows someone who was in the war? What did he or she say about it? Who has read about the Vietnam War or seen a movie about it? What did you learn?"

As ideas and questions were recorded on the transparency, Christa asked the students to study the K column to anticipate categories of information that they might study in their textbook and other information sources that they would be using: "Do some of these ideas fit together to form major categories we might be studying?" She also asked the students to think about other wars they had studied—World Wars I and II, the U.S. Civil War, and the American Revolution: "When we study wars, are there underlying categories of information that historians tend to focus on?"

On completion of the whole-class activity, Christa invited her students to complete their strategy sheets, recording what they knew, what they wanted to find out more about, and what categories of information they expected to use.

Then, for homework, she assigned several sections from a textbook covering the Vietnam War and asked students to work on the L column on their own. Figure 6.4 shows how one student, Clayton, completed his strategy sheet.

As part of the next day's class, Christa asked the students to work in groups of four to share what they had found out about the war. They focused on the questions they had raised, as well as on new ideas they had not anticipated. When the groups completed their work, Christa brought the class together. She directed them to open their learning logs and write a summary of what they had learned from participating in KWL. Students used the L column on their strategy sheets to compose the summary. Clayton's summary is shown in Figure 6.5.

In Christa's class, the learning logs serve as a history notebook, where students can record what they are learning, using a variety of writing-to-learn activities. (We explain learning logs and their uses more fully in Chapter 7.)

A high school math teacher adapted the KWL strategy to support his students' study of the Fibonacci numbers. Fibonacci numbers (a famous sequence of numbers that have been shown to occur in nature) are the direct result of a problem posed by a thirteenth-century mathematician, Leonardo of Pisa, on the regeneration of rabbits. The teacher used a math text from an enrichment unit to clarify and extend students' understanding of the Fi-

K—What I Know	W—What I Want to Know	L—What I Learned and Still Need to Learn

U.S. lost war
protest marches
  and riots
movies made 1960s
Jungle fighting
POWs
guerrilla fighting
North and South
  fighting each
  other
U.S. soldiers
  suffered
the wall in
Washington
	Why did we go
	  to war?
	Why did we lose?
	How many soldiers
	  died?
	Who helped us?
	Who was president
	  during war?
	Whose side were
	  we on?
		Gulf of Tonkin Resolution
		  made it legal for war but
		  was not legally declared
		French helped U.S.
		Nixon withdrew troops
		  because of fighting at
		  home
		Lottery used to draft
		  soldiers
		Antiwar movement at
		  home
		55,000 Americans died plus
		  thousands of innocent
		  people
		Kennedy, Johnson, and
		  Nixon were the presidents
		Fought war to stop
		  communism

Categories of Information
I Expect to Use

A. cause   E.
B. results   F.
C. U.S. involvement G.
D. type of fighting

FIGURE 6.4   **Clayton's KWL Strategy Sheet on the Vietnam War**

bonacci numbers. The text selection, "Mathematics in Nature," illustrates the properties of the Fibonacci numbers and requires students to determine the relationships between these numbers and various phenomena in nature—for example, the leaves on a plant, the bracts on a pinecone, the curves on a seashell, or the spirals on a pineapple.

Before initiating the KWL strategy, the teacher used three props (a toy rabbit, a plant, and a pineapple) to arouse students' curiosity and to trigger

We fought the Vietnam War to stop communism. The U.S. Congress passed the Gulf of Tonkin Resolution, which said it was OK to go to war there, but the war was never declared a war—it was called just a conflict. The French and South Vietnamese people helped us, but it didn't matter. 55,000 Americans died fighting. People protested in the United States. Nixon withdrew the troops because of pressure to end the war at home.

FIGURE 6.5 **Clayton's Summary in the Learning Log**

their responses to the question "What do these items have to do with mathematics?" After some exploratory talk, he then asked students, "What do you know about mathematics and nature?" The strategy sheet in Figure 6.6 illustrates the reader-text interactions that occurred as the teacher walked students through the steps in KWL.

Directed Reading-Thinking Activity

The directed reading-thinking activity (DR-TA) fosters critical awareness by moving students through a process that involves prediction, verification, judgment, and ultimately extension of thought. The teacher guides reading and stimulates thinking through the judicious use of questions. These questions will prompt response through interpretation, clarification, and application.

The atmosphere created during a DR-TA is paramount in the strategy's success. You must be supportive and encouraging so as not to inhibit students' free participation. Never refute any predictions that students make; to do so is comparable to pulling the rug out from under them.

Think time is again important. When you pose an open-ended question, is it reasonable to pause no more than two, three, five, or even ten seconds for a response? If silence pervades the room for several seconds or more after a question has been asked, simply wait a few more seconds. Too often, the

K—What I Know	W—What I Want to Know	L—What I Learned and Still Need to Learn
planetary motion spirals 4 seasons landscaping geometric designs multiplying populations phases of the moon	What does a pineapple have to do with math? How are growth patterns in plants related to math? How is mathematics specifically related to nature? Where do bees fit in?	Pineapples have hexagons on the surface that are arranged in sets of spirals. These spirals are related to Fibonacci numbers. Fibonacci numbers found in leaf arrangement on plant The rate that bees regenerate males is related to Fibonacci numbers. Who is this Fibonacci guy? What's the big deal about the "golden ratio"?
Categories of Information I Expect to Use 1. Animals 2. Plants 3. Solar System 4. Laws of Nature		

FIGURE 6.6   **A KWL Strategy Sheet in a Math Class**

tendency is to slice the original question into smaller parts. Sometimes a teacher starts slicing too quickly out of a sense of frustration or anxiousness (after all, three seconds of lapsed time can seem an eternity in the midst of a questioning foray) rather than because of the students' inability to respond. Silence may very well be an indication that hypothesis formation or other cognitive activities are taking place in the students' heads. So wait—and see what happens.

To prepare for a DR-TA with an informational text, analyze the material for its superordinate and subordinate concepts. What do you see as relevant concepts, ideas, relationships, information in the material? The content analysis will help you decide on logical stopping points as you direct students through the reading.

For short stories and other narrative material, determine the key elements of the story: the *setting* (time and place, major characters) and the *events in the plot* (the initiating events or problem-generating situation, the protagonist's reaction to the event and his or her goal to resolve the problem, the set of attempts to achieve the goal, outcomes related to the protagonist's attempts to achieve the goal and resolve the problem, the character's reaction).

Once these elements have been identified, the teacher has a framework for deciding on logical stopping points within the story. In Figure 6.7, we indicate a general plan that may be followed or adapted for specific story lines. Notice that the suggested stopping points come at key junctures in a causal chain of events in the story line. Each juncture suggests a logical stopping point in that it assumes that the reader has enough information from at least one preceding event to predict a future happening or event.

Steps in the DR-TA

Set the climate and guide the DR-TA by the frequent use of three questions:

"What do you think?" (or "What do you think will happen next?")

"Why do you think so?" (or "What part of the story gave you a clue?")

"Can you prove it?" (or "What else might happen?")

The following may be considered general steps in the DR-TA:

1. *Begin with the title of the narrative or with a quick survey of the title, subheads, illustrations, and other expository material.* Ask, "What do you

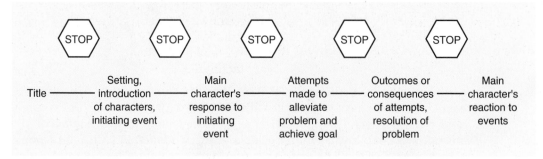

FIGURE 6.7 **Potential Stopping Points in a DR-TA for a Story Line with One Episode**

think this story (or section) will be about?" Encourage predictions. Ask, "Why do you think so?"

2. *Ask students to read silently to a predetermined logical stopping point in the text.* Have students use a 5-by-8-inch index card or a blank sheet of paper placed on the page to mark the place where they are reading to. This will also slow down those who want to read on before answering the questions.

3. *Repeat questions as suggested in step 1.* Some predictions will be refined; new ones will be formulated. Ask, "How do you know?" to encourage clarification or verification. Redirect questions.

4. *Continue silent reading to another suitable point.* Ask similar questions.

5. *Continue in this way to the end of the material.* A note of caution: Too frequent interruption of reading may detract from the focus of attention, which needs to be on larger concepts. As readers move through the DR-TA process, encourage reflection and thoughtful responses to the text.

How do you apply DR-TA to informational texts? The following steps specify the procedures.

1. *Set the purposes for reading.* Individual or group purposes are set by students based on some limited clues in material and their own background of experience.
   a. "From reading just the chapter title (subtitles, charts, maps, etc.), what do you think the author will present in this chapter (passage, next pages, etc.)?"
   b. Record speculations on the chalkboard and augment them by the query "Why do you think so?"
   c. Encourage a guided discussion. If speculations and statements of proof yield an inaccurate or weak knowledge base, review through discussion. Frequently, terminology will be introduced by students (especially those who are more knowledgeable) in their predictions. The teacher may choose to capitalize on such situations by further clarifying significant concepts in a way that enhances pupil discussion and inquiry through discovery techniques.
   d. A poll can be taken to intensify the predictive process, and a debate may naturally ensue. Additional proof may be needed from available reference books.

2. *Adjust the rate to the purposes and the material.* The teacher should adjust the amount of reading, depending on the purposes, nature, and difficulty of the reading material; skimming, scanning, and studying are involved. Students are told, "Read to find out if your predictions were

correct." The reading task may be several pages within a chapter, an entire chapter, a few passages, or some other amount of the text. If the teacher designates numerous stopping points within the reading task, the same procedures as in step 1 should be executed at each stopping point.

3. *Observe the reading.* The teacher observes the reading by assisting students who request help and noting abilities to adjust rate to purpose and material, to comprehend material, and to use word recognition strategies.

4. *Guide reader-text interactions.* Students check the purposes by accepting, rejecting, or redefining them. This can be accomplished during discussion time after students have read a predetermined number of pages or by encouraging students to rework their predictions as they read, by noting down their revised predictions and hypotheses.

5. *Extend learning through discussion, further reading, additional study, or writing.* Students and teacher identify these needs throughout the strategy.

   a. After reading, students should be asked (1) if their predictions were inaccurate, (2) if they needed to revise or reject any predictions as they read, (3) how they knew revision was necessary, and (4) what their new predictions were.

   b. Discussion in small groups is most useful in this step. A recorder, appointed by the group, can share the groups' reading-thinking processes with the total class. These should be compared with original predictions.

   c. The teacher should ask open-ended questions that encourage generalization and application relevant to students' predictions and the significant concepts presented. In any follow-up discussion or questioning, proof should always be required: "How do you know that? Why did you think so? What made you think that way?" Encourage students to share passages, sentences, and so on for further proof (Homer 1979).

A DR-TA Illustration

In an eighth-grade science class, students were engaged in a study of a textbook chapter about the light spectrum (Davidson & Wilkerson 1988). Using a DR-TA framework, the teacher guided the students' interactions with the text material. Study an excerpt of the transcript from the beginning cycle of the DR-TA in Box 6.2.

As you examine the transcript, note that teacher-student interactions are recorded in the left-hand column of the box. The teacher's questions and comments are printed in capital letters, followed by the students' responses in lowercase letters. An analysis of the DR-TA lesson as it evolved is printed in italics in the right-hand column.

The transcript shows how the students used prior knowledge to anticipate the information that the text would reveal. As they shared what they expected to find, the students engaged in analyzing their pooled ideas. Their interactions with the teacher illustrate how a DR-TA instructional framework creates a need to know and helps readers declare purposes through anticipation and prediction making.

Once the purposes were established, the teacher assigned a section of the text chapter to be read. According to Davidson and Wilkerson (1988), two observers of the lesson:

> When students read the portion of the text they were directed to read, they read that infrared waves are invisible and that they are heat waves. Discussion, involving text ideas, students' previous ideas, and their reasoning abilities, showed that they discovered that infrared light is *not* one of the hottest colors because it is not a color. They also discovered that infrared waves are hot, since they are heat waves. The text supplied literal information. The discussion facilitated concept development and critical thinking. (p. 37)

Although the students' predictions were amiss in the initial cycle of questioning, the teacher chose not to evaluate or judge the predictions. She recognized that as readers interact with the text, more often than not they are able to clarify their misconceptions for themselves.

Discussion Webs

Discussion webs encourage students to engage the text and each other in thoughtful discussion by creating a framework for students to explore texts and consider different sides of an issue in discussion before drawing conclusions. Donna Alvermann (1991) recommends discussion webs as an alternative to teacher-dominated discussions.

The strategy uses cooperative learning principles that follow a "think-pair-share" discussion cycle (McTighe & Lyman 1988). The discussion cycle begins with students' first thinking about the ideas they want to contribute to the discussion based on their interactions with the text. Then they meet in dyads to discuss their ideas with a partner. Partners then team with a different set of partners to resolve differences in perspective and to work toward a consensus about the issue under discussion. In the final phase of the discussion cycle, the two sets of partners, working as a foursome, select a spokesperson to share their ideas with the entire class.

The discussion web strategy uses a graphic display to scaffold students' thinking about the ideas they want to contribute to the discussion based on what they have read. The graphic display takes the shape of a web, as illustrated in Figure 6.8. In the center of the web is a question that is central to the reading. The question is posed in such a way that it reflects more than one point of view. Students explore the pros and cons of the question in the "no" and "yes" columns of the web—in pairs, and then in groups of four. The main goal of the four-member teams is to draw a conclusion based on their discussion of the web.

Box 6.2

Excerpt of a DR-TA Transcript from a Science Lesson on the Light Spectrum

Teacher-Student Interactions	Analysis of Lesson
I'D LIKE FOR YOU TO BEGIN BY JUST READING THIS ACTIVITY IN THIS SECTION. THEN TELL ME WHAT YOU EXPECT TO FIND IN THIS PASSAGE. YOU KNOW IT'S ABOUT LIGHT AND COLOR AND SPECTRUMS. WHAT ELSE DO YOU EXPECT THAT YOU WILL FIND?	*The teacher directs students to read a description of an activity designed to produce a sun's spectrum with a prism. The activity includes holding a thermometer in the spectrum produced, placing a fluorite substance near the spectrum, and anticipating changes.*
s: Heat WHY DO YOU SAY HEAT?	
s: Well, some of the colors are cooler.	*The student's response is based on prior knowledge which she judges will be relevant.*
DO YOU KNOW WHICH ONES WILL BE COOLER?	*The teacher encourages the student to extend the response.*
s: I think the darker ones. WHY DO YOU SAY THAT?	*Teacher asks for justification.*
s: They look cooler. THEY LOOK COOLER? OKAY.	*Teacher accepts response, recognizing that the student has, in fact, generated a question to be answered in reading the text.*
WHAT ELSE? DO YOU AGREE OR DISAGREE?	*The teacher encourages other students to analyze this hypothesis or generate a different one.*
s: Well, I agree with her on infrared and ultraviolet. They are probably the hottest colors you can get of the spectrum.	*The student's response shows that he is evaluating the other student's response. Also, he uses specific vocabulary from his prior knowledge to extend the prediction.*
ALL RIGHT. ANYBODY ELSE?	*The teacher does not make a judgment about the validity of the predictions since that is the responsibility of the students as they read and discuss.*

Teacher-Student Interactions	Analysis of Lesson
s: I think he is wrong.	*A student disagrees.*
WHY?	*Teacher asks for justification*
s: Because whenever you melt steel, steel always turns red before it turns white. When it turns white, it melts completely.	*The student analyzes the prior student's prediction and explains in terms of his own experience.*
OKAY.	
s: You can't see infrared.	*As stated, the student's response is a literal statement.*
AND HOW WOULD THAT MAKE A DIFFERENCE IN WHAT HE JUST SAID?	*The teacher assumes that there is a connection with the discussion and asks for explanation.*
s: Well, he just said that it turned red before it turned white. And you can't see white, it's just a shade. Infrared you can't see—which would be just like sunlight. You can't see sunlight. So, I think it would be hotter.	*In his extended response the student disagrees with the prior student's conclusion and explanation and uses an illustration from his prior knowledge which he feels is relevant to "prove" his point.*
YOU THINK IT WOULD BE HOTTER?	*The teacher does not point out the validity or lack of validity of either student's logic. She recognizes that both students are thinking critically and that they and others in the group will read to find clues to justify the concepts they are hypothesizing. She is consistent in her role as a facilitator of student discussion.*
OKAY.	
ANYBODY ELSE?	
WELL, LET ME GIVE YOU THIS WHOLE FIRST PARAGRAPH. I WANT YOU TO READ TO THE BOTTOM OF THE PAGE AND THEN I WANT YOU TO GO TO THE TOP OF THE NEXT PAGE. IT WILL BE THE VERY TOP PARAGRAPH. COVER UP WHAT'S BELOW IT WITH YOUR PAPER. READ THAT FAR AND THEN STOP.	
(Students read silently.)	

Source: Reprinted with permission of Jane Davidson and Bonnie Wilkerson.

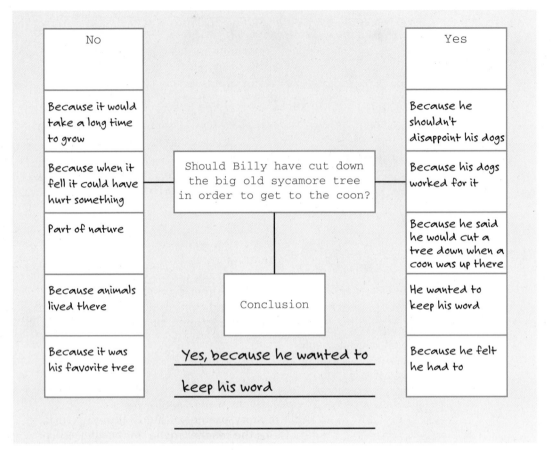

FIGURE 6.8 A Discussion Web for "Where the Red Fern Grows," by Wilson Rawls

Steps in the Discussion Web Strategy

Alvermann (1991) suggests an instructional framework for the discussion web strategy that includes the following steps:

1. *Prepare your students for reading by activating prior knowledge, raising questions, and making predictions about the text.*

2. *Assign students to read the selection and then introduce the discussion web by having the students work in pairs to generate pro and con responses to the question. The partners work on the same discussion web and take turns jotting down their reasons in the "Yes" and "No" columns. Students may use key words and phrases to express their ideas and need not fill all of the lines. They should try to list an equal number* of pro and con reasons on the web.

3. *Combine partners into groups of four to compare responses, work toward consensus, and reach a conclusion as a group.* Explain to your students that it is OK to disagree with other members of the group, but they should all try to keep an open mind as they listen to others during the discussion. Dissenting views may be aired during the whole-class discussion.

4. *Give each group three minutes to decide which of all the reasons given best supports the group's conclusion.* Each group selects a spokesperson to report to the whole class.

5. *Have your students follow up the whole-class discussion by individually writing their responses to the discussion web question.* Display the students' responses to the question in a prominent place in the room so that they can be read by others.

The level of participation in discussion web lessons is usually high. The strategy privileges students' individual interpretations of what they are reading and also allows them to formulate and refine their own interpretations of a text in light of the points of view of others. As a result, students are eager to hear how other groups reached a consensus and drew conclusions during whole-class sharing. The strategy works well with informational or narrative texts and can be adapted to the goals and purposes of most content area subjects.

A Discussion Web Illustration

Math teachers might use the discussion web to help students consider relevant and irrelevant information in story problems. Study the discussion web in Figure 6.9, noting the adaptations the teacher made. In this illustration, the students worked in pairs to distinguish relevant and irrelevant information in the story problem. They then formed groups of four to solve the problem.

Intra-Act

Intra-act lays the groundwork for reflective discussion. Pivotal to the intra-act strategy is the notion that students engage in a process of valuing as they reflect on what they have read. Hoffman (1979) suggests intra-act to provide readers with "the opportunity to experience rather than just talk about critical reading" (p. 608). According to Hoffman, students are more likely to read critically when they engage in a process of valuing. The valuing process allows students to respond actively to a text selection with thought and feeling.

The intra-act procedure can be used with a variety of reading materials—content area text assignments, historical documents, newspaper and magazine articles, narrative, and poetic material. The procedure requires the use of small groups whose members are asked to react to value statements based on the content of the text selection. There are four phases in the intra-act procedure: (1) *comprehension* (understanding of the topic under discussion),

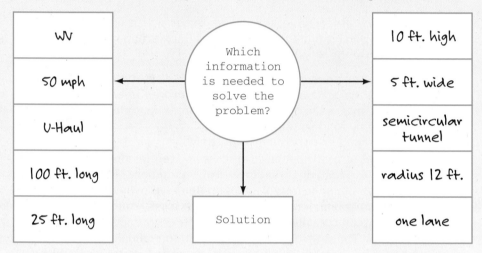

A U-Haul truck is driving through West Virginia. It is approaching a one-lane semicircular tunnel at a rate of 50 mph. The truck is 10 ft. high, 5 ft. wide, and 25 ft. long. The tunnel has a radius of 12 ft. and is 100 ft. long. Will the truck fit through the tunnel?

WV		10 ft. high
50 mph	Which information is needed to solve the problem?	5 ft. wide
U-Haul		semicircular tunnel
100 ft. long		radius 12 ft.
25 ft. long	Solution	one lane

At 2.5 ft. from the center line, the tunnel has a height of 11.7 ft., so the truck will fit.

FIGURE 6.9   **Discussion Web for a Story Problem**

(2) *relating* (connecting what has been learned about the topic to what students already know and believe), (3) *valuation* (expressing personal values and feelings related to the topic), and (4) *reflection* (reflecting on the values and feelings just experienced).

Steps in Intra-Act

Here's how intra-act works.

1. *Comprehension.* The comprehension phase promotes an understanding of the reading material to be learned. To begin this phase, the teacher follows effective prereading procedures by introducing the text reading, activating and building background knowledge for the ideas to be encountered during reading, and inviting students to make predictions and speculate on the nature of the content to be learned. Building a frame of reference for upcoming text information is crucial to the overall success of the intra-act procedure.

Prereading preparation paves the way for readers to interact with the text. Before inviting students to read the selection individually, the teacher forms small groups—intra-act teams—of four to six members. Assign a student from each group to serve as the team leader. The comprehension phase depends on the team leader's ability to initiate and sustain a discussion of the text. The team leader's responsibility is to lead a discussion by first summarizing what was read. The group members may contribute additional information about the selection or ask questions which seek clarification of the main ideas of the selection. The comprehension phase of the group discussion should be limited to seven to ten minutes.

2. *Relating.* The team leader is next responsible for shifting the discussion from the important ideas in the selection to the group's personal reactions and values related to the topic. Many times, this shift occurs naturally. However, if this is not the case, members should be encouraged by the team leader to contribute their own impressions and opinions. Discussion should again be limited to seven to ten minutes.

3. *Valuation.* Once group members have shared their personal reactions to the material, they are ready to participate in the valuation phase of the discussion. The teacher or team leader for each group distributes a game sheet. This game sheet contains a valuing exercise—a set of four declarative statements based on the selection's content. These value statements reflect opinions about the text selection and draw insights and fresh ideas from it. The purpose of the valuing exercise is to have students come to grips with what the material means to them by either agreeing (A) or disagreeing (D) with each statement. Figure 6.10 shows such a game sheet.

Study the game sheet in Figure 6.10. Note that students must first indicate on the game sheet their own reactions to the four value statements. Then, based on the previous discussion, they must predict how each of the other members of their group would respond. In the example of Figure 6.10, Joe disagreed with three of the statements. His predictions as to how other team members would respond are indicated by the circled letters underneath the individual names. Once the responding is complete, the students are ready for the reflective phase of the intra-act procedure.

4. *Reflection.* Begin the reflection phase of intra-act by scoring the game sheet. Group members take turns revealing how each responded to the four statements. As each member tells how he or she responded, the other members check whether their predictions agreed with that member's actual responses. During this phase, the teacher acts as a facilitator, noting how students responded but refraining from imposing a particular point of view on students. Instead, encourage students to reflect on what they have learned. According to Hoffman (1979), "It is very important that during this period students be allowed ample time to discuss, challenge, support and question one another's response. This interaction serves to separate opinions quickly arrived at from sound evaluative thinking" (p. 607).

Name _____
Date _____
Total Score _____
Percentage
of Correct Predictions _____

Names	Joe		Sharon		Paul		Katie	
1. Tobacco companies should be held responsible for the deaths of smokers from heart attacks and lung cancer.	A	Ⓓ	A +	D	A +	D	A −	D
2. Smokers should be able to quit. They just need to really want to.	Ⓐ	D	A +	D	A +	D	A +	D
3. The sale of cigarettes should be illegal just like the sale of cocaine or heroin.	A	Ⓓ	A +	D	A +	D	A +	D
4. The government should spend money on programs to help people stop smoking.	A	Ⓓ	A −	D	A +	D	A −	D

+: Joe's predictions were correct.
−: Joe's predictions incorrect.

FIGURE 6.10 **Joe's Game Sheet**

Intra-act will require several classroom applications before students be-come accustomed to their roles during discussion. Repeated and extensive participation in intra-act will help students become fully aware of the task de-mands of the procedure. In the beginning, we recommend that upon comple-tion of an intra-act discussion, students engage in a whole-class discussion of the process in which they participated. Help students debrief: "What did we learn from our participation in intra-act? Why must all members of a group participate? How might discussion improve the next time we use intra-act?" Questions such as these make students sensitive to the purpose of the intra-act procedure (problem solving) and the role of each reader (critical analysis).

An Intra-Act Illustration

After students in a middle school class read the article "Getting Hooked on Tobacco," four students, Joe, Sharon, Katie, and Paul, met as a group to dis-cuss their impressions. Joe, who was the group's team leader, began with a summary of the article and then gave his own reactions. Here's how Joe sum-marized the article's main ideas: "Well, basically the article says that the government says that tobacco makes you, you know, a drug addict, or something like that. It's like using cocaine or heroin. They say that people can't quit and they need more and more, so cigarettes should be like liquor and you have to get a license to sell them. The cigarette companies don't agree. Me too. I don't think a guy is going to go out and rob people just to get cigarettes. I mean, if he is that hard up, he would just quit."

After some clarifying discussion of what the article was about, the discussion shifted gears into the relating phase. Sharon reacted to the article this way: "Well, I don't think that a company should be allowed to sell stuff that kills people. And if all the people quit, the company would go out of business anyway, so it should just go out of business now because of a law."

Paul entered the conversation: "I think the guy was right that said if cigarettes were illegal the gangs would have gang wars to see who would get to sell them—just like they do with crack and cocaine right now. Besides, if people really want to kill themselves with smoking, they should be allowed. And if they don't, they should just quit. Right on the pack it says *quit*."

Katie replied, "It ain't so easy to quit. My dad tried, like, five times, and he finally had to get hypnotized to quit. And he wouldn't have started if he had to buy them from some gang or something. You get them from a store, and nobody ever asks you how old you are. Besides, who reads the warnings?"

When time for discussion was over, the valuation phase was initiated. Students were given a game sheet with these four value statements:

1. Tobacco companies should be held responsible for the deaths of smokers from heart attacks and lung cancer.

2. Smokers should be able to quit. They just need to really want to.

3. The sale of cigarettes should be illegal just like the sale of cocaine or heroin.

4. The government should spend money on programs to help people stop smoking.

Each student was asked to respond individually to the statements and then predict whether the other members of the group would agree or disagree with each statement. Joe's sheet is reproduced in Figure 6.10. From the discussion, he was pretty sure that Sharon would agree with the first statement because she had said that they "shouldn't be allowed to kill people." Similarly, he thought Paul would disagree because he thought people should "just quit." He was also pretty sure that Katie would agree since she seemed to think it was bad that you could just go into a store and buy cigarettes. He used similar reasons to predict the group members' reactions to the other statements.

As part of the reflection phase of intra-act, the group members shared what they had learned. Joe found that most of his predictions were correct. He was surprised to find out that Katie did not agree with statement 1, but she explained that, "It's not the companies' fault that they sold something that's not illegal. First, they should make it illegal; then it's the companies' fault." Other members argued that her reasoning "didn't make sense" since the tobacco companies know that cigarettes are harmful. That debate was typical of the discussion that went on in all the groups as students worked out the ways in which the ideas presented in the text fit in with their own attitudes and beliefs.

 ## LOOKING BACK, LOOKING FORWARD

Teachers connect literacy and learning when they weave together talking, listening, reading, and writing. Talking to learn is an expressive and exploratory form of classroom communication. Strategies that facilitate talking to learn help students explore, clarify, and extend ideas they encounter in text. Although classroom talk is the main medium by which students and teachers communicate, the potential for talk as a tool for learning is rarely realized in classrooms. Too often, teachers rely on a type of talk called *recitation,* expecting students to recite answers to questions. Recitation is a limiting form of oral interaction because teachers dominate classroom talk when they overuse recitation. The danger of recitation lies in signaling to students that reading is a disjointed search for bits and pieces of information.

Discussions are another type of talk that occurs in the classroom. Discussions lend themselves well to classroom talk about texts. Teachers who create a response-centered curriculum use discussion to help students respond personally and critically to text. A reader response theory of text interpretation undergirds a response-based curriculum. Response journals and and a response heuristic are often used in conjunction with discussion to engage students in text. Discussions work best when they are collaborative and cooperative.

When readers are not able to handle difficult texts on their own, a teacher supports their efforts to make meaning by *scaffolding* their interactions with texts. Various kinds of instructional strategies may be used to guide reader-text interactions. These strategies provide a structure through which students can actively engage in text response and discussion. In this chapter, several strategies that prepare students for reading, guide their interaction with texts, and help them to clarify and extend meaning were described.

KWL is a meaning-making strategy that engages students in active text learning and may be used with small groups of students or with the whole class. KWL comprises several steps that help students examine what they know, what they want to know more about, and what they have learned from reading. The directed reading-thinking activity was also described. DR-TA revolves around three guiding questions: (1) What do you think? (2) Why do you think so? (3) Can you prove it? The discussion web and intra-act strategies are based on the notion that students engage in a process of consensus building and valuing as they reflect on what they have read. Both the discussion web and intra-act lay the groundwork for reflective discussion following the reading of text material.

MINDS-ON

1. Think of the concept of "class discussion." Try to recall an example of a prior classroom situation in which enjoyable, lively "discussions" occurred. Freeze-frame this scene in your mind. Look closely at it, and jot down as many descriptive or sensory words as you can that paint this picture and make it seem real.

   Now, try to recall a prior classroom situation that was not conducive to meaningful or enjoyable class discussions. Again, freeze-frame this scene in your mind, and look at it closely. Jot down as many descriptive or sensory words as you can that paint this picture and make it seem real.

   Why and how will the instructional frameworks that you have studied help you facilitate a good environment for a class discussion?

2. With a small group, create an intra-act guide sheet for this chapter. After you have finished, discuss any insights into reading gained from this activity.

HANDS-ON

1. Without sharing perceptions, each member of your group should read this short paragraph and follow the directions that follow it.

   An artist was talking enthusiastically about one of her favorite paintings to several people visiting the gallery when a woman approached her and offered to purchase the work. The owner of the gallery removed the painting from the wall. The painting was snatched from her hands, and the woman bolted through the front door into a waiting van, which sped down the street through a nearby red light and vanished into the night.

   Using the paragraph as a reference, respond to each of the following statements, in the order presented, by circling T (for true), F (for false), or ? (for unable to determine from the paragraph). Once you have characterized a statement as true, false, or questionable, you cannot change your answer.

a. The artist talked about one of her paintings. T F?

b. The thief was a woman. T F?

c. The crime appeared to be premeditated. T F?

d. This type of theft seems unlikely. T F?

e. The owner removed the painting from the wall. T F?

f. The owner was the artist. T F?

g. The woman who bolted through the door stole the painting. T F?

h. The person who snatched the painting from the owner's hands was the artist. T F?

i. A robbery didn't occur. T F?

Discuss the variety of possible answers based on your responses.

2. Select a short informational article in a magazine or book, and duplicate copies for each member of your group. Have each member of the group create at random one of the following instructional strategies: (1) KWL (What do you *know?* What do you *want to know* more about? What did you *learn?*), (2) a directed reading-thinking activity (DR-TA), (3) intra-act, and (4) a discussion web. If there are more than four members in your group, duplicate strategies as needed.

   Using the same article, design a lesson around the strategy you have created, and make copies to share with the members of the group. As you review the four different lessons prepared by your colleagues, what comparisons and contrasts can you make between these instructional frameworks?

SUGGESTED READINGS

Alvermann, D. E. (1996). Peer-led discussions: Whose interests are served? *Journal of Adolescent and Adult Literacy, 39*, 282–289.

Alvermann, D. E., Dillon, D. R., & O'Brien, D. G. (1988). *Using discussion to promote reading comprehension.* Newark, DE: International Reading Association.

Alvermann, D. E., O'Brien, D. G., & Dillon, D. R. (1990). What teachers do when they say they're having discussions of content reading assignments: A qualitative analysis. *Reading Research Quarterly, 25*, 296–322.

Barton, J. (1995). Conducting effective classroom discussions. *Journal of Reading, 38*, 346–350.

Bayer, C. S. (1990). *Collaborative-apprenticeship learning: Language and thinking across the curriculum, K–12.* Mountain View, CA: Mayfield.

Calfee, R. C., Dunlap, K. L., & Wat, A. Y. (1994). Authentic discussion of texts in middle grade schooling: An analytic-narrative approach. *Journal of Reading, 37*, 546–556.

Carlsen, W. S. (1991). Questioning in classrooms: A sociolinguistic perspective. *Review of Educational Research, 61*, 157–178.

Carr, E. G., & Ogle, D. M. (1987). K-W-L plus: A strategy for comprehension and summarization. *Journal of Reading, 30*, 626–631.

Dillon, J. T., (1983). *Teaching and the art of questioning.* Bloomington, IN: Phi Delta Kappa.

Dillon, J. T. (1984). Research on question and discussion. *Educational Leadership, 42*, 50–56.

Dillon, J. T. (1985). Using questions to foil discussion. *Teaching and Teacher Education*, 109–121.

Gambrell, L. B., & Almasi, J. F. (Eds.). (1996). *Lively discussions! Fostering engaged reading.* Newark, DE: International Reading Association.

Gaskins, I. W., Satlow, E., Hyson, D., Ostertag, J., & Six, L. (1994). Classroom talk about text: Learning in science class. *Journal of Reading, 37*, 558–565.

Greabell, L. C., & Anderson, N. (1992). Applying strategies from the directed reading-thinking activity to a directed mathematics activity. *School Science and Mathematics, 92*, 42–44.

Johnson, D. W., Johnson, R. T., & Holubec, E. J. (1994). *The new circles of literacy: Cooperation in the classroom and school.* Alexandria, VA: Association for Supervision and Curriculum Development.

Kletzien, S. B., & Baloche, L. (1994). The shifting muffled sound of the pick: Facilitating student-to-student discussion. *Journal of Reading, 37*, 540–545.

Slavin, R. E. (1995). *Cooperative learning: Theory, research, and practice* (2nd ed.). Needham Heights, MA: Allyn & Bacon.

Vacca, J. L., Vacca, R. T., & Gove, M. K. (1995). *Reading and learning to read* (3rd ed.). New York: HarperCollins.

Vogt, M. E. (1996). Creating a response-centered curriculum with discussion groups. In L. B. Gambrell & J. F. Almasi (Eds.), *Lively discussions! Fostering engaged reading.* Newark, DE: International Reading Association.

7

Writing to Learn

We do not write in order to be understood; we write in order to understand.
—C. Day Lewis

Organizing Principle

Writing is not without its rewards and surprises. The surprises come from discovering what you want to say about a subject; the rewards lie in knowing that you crafted to satisfaction what you wanted to say. C. Day Lewis didn't sit down at his desk to write about things that were already clear in his mind. If he had, there would have been little incentive to write. Lewis used writing first to discover and clarify meaning—*to understand*—and second, to communicate meaning to others—*to be understood.*

Some of you may find it surprising to find a separate chapter in this book on the role that writing plays in content literacy and learning. In other chapters, we recommend various kinds of writing activities to scaffold students' interactions with texts. In this chapter, however, our intent is to highlight and reaffirm the powerful learning opportunities that arise whenever teachers link reading and writing in the instructional frameworks that they create.

A classroom environment that supports reading and writing provides an instructional framework in which students can explore ideas, clarify meaning, and construct knowledge. Why connect reading and writing in the content area classroom? When reading and writing are taught in tandem, the union influences content learning in ways not possible when students read without writing or write without reading. When teachers invite a class to write before or after reading, they help students use writing to think about what they will read and to explore and think more deeply about the ideas they have read.

Reading and writing have been taught in most classrooms as if they bear little relationship to each other. The result has often been to sever the powerful bonds for meaning-making that exist between reading and writing. There's little to be gained from teaching reading apart from writing. The organizing principle reflects this notion: **Writing facilitates learning by helping students explore, clarify, and think deeply about the ideas and concepts they encounter in reading.**

Chapter Overview

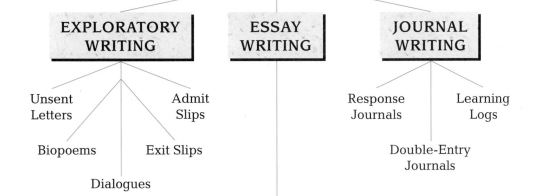

WRITING TO LEARN

READING AND WRITING TOGETHER

EXPLORATORY WRITING

ESSAY WRITING

JOURNAL WRITING

Unsent Letters

Admit Slips

Biopoems

Exit Slips

Dialogues

Response Journals

Learning Logs

Double-Entry Journals

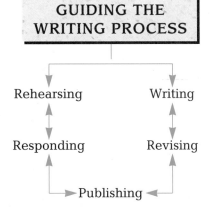

GUIDING THE WRITING PROCESS

Rehearsing

Writing

Responding

Revising

Publishing

Frame of Mind

1. Why emphasize writing to learn in content areas?

2. Why teach writing and reading together?

3. How might teachers create occasions for students to write to read, and to read to write?

4. How can teachers use exploratory writing activities to connect reading and writing?

5. How can teachers use journals to connect writing and reading?

6. How can teachers develop and evaluate essay-writing assignments?

7. Why and how do teachers guide the writing process?

Sinclair Lewis, the first American author to win a Nobel Prize for literature, said that writing is just work. It doesn't matter if "you dictate or use a pen or type or write with your toes—it is still just work." Microcomputers and word processors notwithstanding, writing isn't easy for most people. Yet for those who are successful, the process of writing—sweat and all—is enormously challenging and rewarding.

Perhaps for this reason, Allyse's mother was a bit perplexed by her daughter's writing. Allyse was 13 years old and, by all accounts, a bright student. Yet her mother was bewildered by her daughter's writing activities both in and out of school: "She'll spend hours slaving over pages to mail to an out-of-state friend but writes skimpy, simpleminded paragraphs for school assignments." When Allyse was questioned about the discrepancy in her writing, her reply was all the more confusing: "But, Mom, that's what my teachers want."

Allyse may never win a Noble Prize for literature. But she does have a need to write. Most children and adolescents do. Often, just out of sight of teachers, students will write continually to other students during the course of a school day—about classmates, teachers, intrigues, problems, parents, or just about anything else that happens to be on their minds. The topics may not be academically oriented, but they are both real and immediate to students.

In Allyse's case, writing to an out-of-state friend was so important that she was willing to struggle with a blank page to keep in touch. However, as far as school writing was concerned, she had probably psyched out what her teachers expected from her. She knew what she needed to do to get by and, most likely, to be successful. Allyse intuitively understood the role of writing in her classes and operated within that context.

Although students often engage in some form of writing in content area classrooms, few teachers use writing to its fullest potential as a tool for learning. Allyse's response to her mother's question reflects what researchers such as Judith Langer and Arthur Applebee (1987) have consistently observed to be the role of writing in content classrooms: It is mainly restricted to short responses to study questions or to taking notes in class. For example, examine in Figure 7.1 the worksheet responses of a student in a high school biology class. The students have been studying a unit on viruses. The worksheet is designed to have the class think about the life characteristics of viruses in relation to other living organisms. Notice how the spacing on the worksheet restricts the student's responses to short one- or two-sentence answers. The student provides accurate information, but just enough to satisfy the requirements of the assignment.

Characteristics of Life

1. CELLS: All living things are composed of cells.
    VIRUSES: Viruses are constructed of compounds usually associated with cells but they are not considered cells.

2. ORGANIZATION: All organisms are organized at both the molecular and the cellular level. They take in substances from the environment and organize them in complex ways.
    VIRUSES: no, they aren't organized because they don't take in substances from the environment. They just replicate, using a host cell.

3. ENERGY USE: All organisms use energy for growth and maintenance.
    VIRUSES: viruses don't use energy until they are in a cell; they do not grow they use host cells for energy.

4. RESPONSE TO THE ENVIRONMENT: All organisms respond to a stimulus. A complex set of responses is called a behavior.
    VIRUSES: they only respond when they are affecting a cell

5. GROWTH: All living things grow. Growth occurs through cell division and cell enlargement.
    VIRUSES: They don't grow

6. REPRODUCTION: All species of organisms have the ability to reproduce on their own.
    VIRUSES: it requires a host cell to reproduce.

FIGURE 7.1   **A Biology Student's Written Responses on a Worksheet**

Even though the purpose of the worksheet writing may be legitimate, students need varied and frequent experiences with writing as a tool for learning. According to Langer and Applebee (1987), "Put simply, in the whole range of academic course work, American children do not write frequently enough, and the reading and writing tasks they are given do not require them to think deeply enough" (p. 4). There are at least three good reasons for teachers to take a second look at the role of writing in their classrooms. First, writing improves thinking. Second, it facilitates learning. Third, writing is intimately related to reading.

Content area teachers usually have second thoughts about assigning writing in their classrooms because of preconceived notions of what the teaching of writing may entail. Writing isn't generally thought of as basic to thinking and learning about content fields. Nancie Atwell (1990) is quick to point out that although the role of language arts teachers is to guide students' development as writers, teachers of every discipline share in the responsibility of showing students how to think and write as scientists, historians, mathematicians, and literary critics do. When students engage in writing as a way of knowing, they are thinking on paper.

READING AND WRITING TOGETHER

There is no better way to think about a subject than to have the occasion to read and write about it. However, reading and writing don't necessarily guarantee improved thinking or learning. Students can go through the motions of reading and writing, lacking purpose and commitment, or they can work thoughtfully to construct meaning, make discoveries, and think deeply about a subject. A classroom environment for reading and writing is one that lends encouragement to students who are maturing as readers and writers and that provides instructional support so that readers and writers can play with ideas, explore concepts, clarify meaning, and elaborate on what they are learning.

Reading and writing are acts of composing because readers and writers are involved in an ongoing, dynamic process of constructing meaning (Tierney & Pearson 1983). Composing processes are more obvious in writing than in reading: The writer, initially facing a blank page, constructs a text. The text is a visible entity and reflects the writer's thinking on paper. Less obvious is the "text"—the configuration of meanings—that students compose or construct in their own minds as they read.

A good way to think about reading and writing is that they are two sides of the same coin. While the writer works to make a text sensible, the reader works to make sense from a text. As a result, the two processes, rooted in language, are intertwined and share common cognitive and sociocultural characteristics. Both reading and writing, for example, involve purpose, commitment, schema activation, planning, working with ideas, revision and rethinking, and monitoring. Both processes occur within a social, communicative context. Skilled writers are mindful of their content (the subject about which they are writing) and also of their audiences (the readers for whom they write). Skilled readers are mindful of a text's content and are also aware that they engage in transactions with its author.

The relationships between reading and writing have been a source of inquiry by language researchers since the mid-1970s (Tierney & Shanahan 1991). Several broad conclusions about the links between reading and writing can be drawn: Good readers are often good writers, and vice versa; students who write well tend to read more than those who do not write well; wide reading improves writing; and students who are good readers and writers perceive themselves as such and are more likely to engage in reading and writing on their own.

Why connect reading and writing in instructional contexts? According to Shanahan (1990), the combination of reading and writing in a classroom improves achievement and instructional efficiency. From a content area perspective, writing about ideas and concepts encountered in texts will improve students' acquisition of content more than just reading without writing. When reading and writing are taught in concert, the union fosters communication, enhances problem solving, and makes learning more powerful than if reading or writing is engaged in separately.

When teachers integrate writing and reading, they help students use writing to *think about what they will read* and to *understand what they have read*. Writing may be used to catapult students into reading. It is also one of the most effective ways for students to understand something they have read. Teachers can put students into writing-to-read or reading-to-write situations because the writing process is a powerful tool for exploring and clarifying meaning.

Donald Murray (1980) explains that writers engage in a process of exploration and clarification as they go about the task of making meaning. In Figure 7.2, Murray suggests that writers progress from exploring meaning to clarifying it as they continue to draft and shape a piece of writing. A writer's first draft is an initial attempt to think on paper. The more writers work with ideas put on paper, the more they are able to revise, rethink, and clarify what they have to say about a subject.

Santa and Havens (1991) illustrate the power of writing before and after reading with an example from a biology class. Before reading a textbook assignment on flower reproduction, students wrote before-reading entries in *learning logs* (a student resource we will explain shortly), telling what they knew about the subject they would be reading and studying. Here's an example of a student's entry:

> In this chapter I am going to learn about flower reproduction. I know that
> flowers have male and female parts. I think that these parts are in the inside
> of the flower. To see them you have to pull aside the petals. I think petals

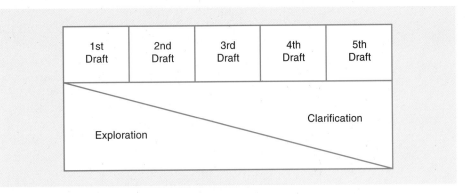

FIGURE 7.2 **Exploration and Clarification**

Source: From "Writing as Process: How Writing Finds Its Own Meaning," by Donald M. Murray in *Eight Approaches to Teaching Composition,* Donovan and McClelland (Eds). Copyright © 1980 National Council of Teachers of English. Reprinted with permission.

probably protect the reproductive parts, but I am not sure. I remember something about separate flowers for male and females, but I think many flowers have both parts on the same flower. I'm pretty sure you need to have at least two plants before they can reproduce. (p. 124)

In the biology class, students also had an occasion to write about flower reproduction after reading. In an after-reading entry, writing helps the students continue to explore and clarify meaning by focusing on what they learned and noting their misconceptions in their before-reading entries. Study the after-reading entry written by the student above:

I learned that stamens are the male parts of the flower. The stamen produces the pollen. The female part is the pistil. At the bottom of the pistil is the ovary. Plants have eggs just like humans. The eggs are kept in the ovary. I still am not sure how pollen gets to the female part. Do bees do all this work, or are there other ways to pollinate? I was right, sometimes male and female parts are on separate flowers. These are called incomplete flowers. Complete flowers have both male and female parts on the same flower. I also learned that with complete flowers just one plant can reproduce itself. So, I was partially wrong thinking it always took two plants to reproduce. (p. 124)

Occasions to write on content subjects, such as the before-reading and after-reading entries just shown, create powerful opportunities to learn content in concert with reading. Students who experience the integration of writing and reading are likely to learn more content, to understand it better, and to remember it longer. This is the case because writing, before or after reading, promotes thinking, but in different ways. Writing a summary after reading (see Chapter 10), for example, is likely to result in greater understanding and retention of important information. However, another type of writing—let's say an essay—may trigger the analysis, synthesis, and elaboration of ideas encountered in reading and class discussion.

Because writing promotes different types of learning, students should have many different occasions to write. Let's look at some ways that teachers can create occasions for students to think and learn with paper and pen.

EXPLORATORY WRITING

Exploratory writing is first-draft writing. Often, it is messy, tentative, and unfinished. Exploration of ideas and concepts may be pursued before or after reading. Writing activities that help students tap into their storehouse of memories—their prior knowledge—make excellent springboards into reading. Exploratory writing helps students collect what they know and connect it to what they will be reading. For example, some teachers combine brainstorming a topic to be studied with five or so minutes of spontaneous freewriting in which students tell what they know about the subject to be studied.

Gere (1985) describes exploratory writing as unfinished. In her words, unfinished writing is "writing that evinces thought but does not merit the careful scrutiny which a finished piece of writing deserves" (p. 4). There is value in planning unfinished writing activity in the content area classroom. The excellent monograph she edited, *Roots in the Sawdust* (1985), shows how teachers from various disciplines use and adapt exploratory writing activities in their classrooms. We have found the following to be quite useful in elementary or secondary classes.

Unsent Letters

The writing-to-learn activity known as *unsent letters* establishes a role-play situation in which students are asked to write letters in response to material being studied. The activity requires the use of imagination and often demands that students engage in interpretive and evaluative thinking. Jeremy's unsent letter to the president of the United States, written after he studied the effects of nuclear war in his social studies text, reflects both personal and informative writing.

> Dear Mr. President,
>   How is life in the White House? In school we have been studying the horrible effects of a nuclear war. The United States alone has enough nuclear weapons to wipe out 1 million Hiroshimas. The earth doesn't even have that many cities that big.
>   In a nuclear war 1.1 billion people would be killed outright, and they are the lucky ones. Another 1.1 billion would suffer from burns and radiation sickness.

1 nuclear warhead or 2 megatons is 2 million tons of TNT, imagine 15 megatons. . . .

During a nuclear war buildings and people would be instantly vaporized. The remaining people would starve to death. The radiation would be 250 rads or 1,000 medical x-rays which is enough to kill you.

After all this I hope you have learned some of the terrible facts about nuclear war. (Levine 1985, p. 44)

Unsent letters direct students' thinking with particular audiences in mind. Biopoems, by contrast, require students to play with ideas by using precise language in a poetic framework.

Biopoems

A *biopoem* allows students to reflect on large amounts of material within a poetic form. The biopoem follows a pattern that enables writers to synthesize what they have learned about a person, place, thing, concept, or event under study. For example, study the pattern suggested by Gere (1985) for a person or character:

Line 1. First name

Line 2. Four traits that describe character

Line 3. Relative ("brother," "sister," "daughter," etc.) of _____

Line 4. Lover of _____ (list three things or people)

Line 5. Who feels _____ (three items)

Line 6. Who needs _____ (three items)

Line 7. Who fears _____ (three items)

Line 8. Who gives _____ (three items)

Line 9. Who would like to see _____ (three items)

Line 10. Resident of _____

Line 11. Last name

Notice how a health education teacher adapted the preceding pattern to a writing activity in her course. The lesson was part of a unit on HIV and AIDS awareness. After the class spent several days studying the topic, the teacher introduced the biopoem strategy and explained how it could be useful in learning. She shared several biopoems from previous years that students had written on various topics. She then discussed the biopoem format and clarified any questions that students might have about writing a biopoem. She invited the students to write a biopoem using what they learned about AIDS. They could apply what they learned to a person they "invented" or to a real-life person who had the HIV virus.

Here are two of the biopoems the students wrote. The first deals with an invented person; the second, with Ervin "Magic" Johnson, a former All-Star professional basketball player who tested positive for HIV at the height of his career.

Valerie,
Thin, tired, sad, confused.
She asks: "Why me?"
       "How will I deal with this?"
       "Will I be alone?"

Valerie,
She needs love,
    support,
    care,
    and advice.

Valerie,
She fears dying,
    being alone,
    feeling rejected.

Valerie,
She would like to see a cure,
         Her family's approval,
         Friends who care.

Valerie,
Your neighbor next door
A resident of Anywhere, U.S.A.
Valerie

The Magic Man,
Born Ervin Johnson.
Strong, Brave, Outspoken, Respected
Why you?
You "the Man!" But how do you feel now:
Stupid? Confused? Lonely?
Even the Magic Man needs love, support, family.
You fear dying, rejection, loss.
Would you like to see another 10 years?
Your children grow up?
Your place in the Hall of Fame?
Resident of the world
Magic Johnson
You still "the Man!"

Dialogues

In this activity, students are asked to create an exchange between two or more persons, historical figures, or characters being studied. Beaman (1985), a high school social studies teacher, illustrated the use of dialogue as a writing-to-learn assignment. He asked his students to write a dialogue between themselves and a "friend" who wanted them to do something they were opposed to but were unsure of how to respond to because of peer pressure. Beaman suggested that students write about awkward teenage situations of peer pressure. Here's a sample dialogue between Mary and Betty:

Mary: Let's skip class and go out on the parking lot. I have some awesome dope and a new tape by the Scorpions.

Betty: I can't. I've skipped second period one too many times, and I really want to graduate. Contemporary Problems is required, and I'm afraid I may fail.

Mary: Get serious, one class missed is not going to get you an F. You need the relaxation, and besides, the Scorpions . . .

Betty: I wish I could say "yes" to you.

Mary: Say "yes" then, or are you turning into a real "school" girl?

Betty: You are pressuring me, Mary!

Mary: No pressure, just fun, come on . . .

Betty: No, I'm going to class, I do want to graduate. You can go, but I'm going to class. (Beaman 1985, p. 63)

A dialogue like this permits writers to think about conflicts and possible solutions. As an unfinished writing activity, a dialogue also provides an opportunity for students to react to ideas and to extend their thinking about the material being studied.

Foreign-language teachers adapt the use of dialogues to help their students converse in writing and then to role-play their conversations in front of the class. In the dialogue that follows, high school Spanish students wrote a dialogue about a concert they would like to see. The teacher gave them the option of working in pairs or groups of three. As part of the dialogue writing, each student had to contribute at least four lines to the conversation. The teacher also directed the students to use at least three new verbs in their dialogue and at least ten new vocabulary words. The students practiced reading their dialogues to each other while working in their groups. The teacher evaluated students on their pronunciation during the role play of the dialogues (individual accountability) and on originality, sentence structure, and grammar usage in the written dialogue (group accountability). The dialogue, as drafted by the students, follows:

Rául: ¿Te gustas el cantante Elvis Presley?

Joa Quìn: Sì, Yo fui a concìerto de Elvis. Él tenió un grande Voz.

Rául:	Yo no voy. Son Agotado
Joa Quìn:	Yo tengo un cartel y una entrada de concierto.
Rául:	Yo sìempre canto la canción "Blue suede shoes."
Joa Quìn:	Aqui vení Senorita Holtman.
Raúl:	¡Hola Senorita Holtman!
Lucía:	¡Hola, muchachos!
Joa Quìn:	Senorita Holtman, E te quedas ver la fonción de Elvis año pasado.
Lucía:	Sì, Yo me reuní muchos los jovencitos. Ellos queneron entrevistar él. fue mucho grande. Hasta Luego.

Admit Slips and Exit Slips

Admit slips and exit slips involve anonymous writing and therefore shouldn't be part of the permanent record of learning that builds over time in students' learning logs. Thus these activities should be introduced as a separate assignment and not as part of a learning-log entry.

Admit slips are brief comments written by students on index cards or half-sheets of paper at the very beginning of class. Gere (1985) recommends that these written responses be collected as tickets of admission to class. The purpose of the admit slip is to have students react to what they are studying or to what's happening in class. Students are asked to respond to a question such as

What's confusing you about _____?

What problems did you have with your text assignment?

What would you like to get off your chest?

What do you like (dislike) about _____?

The admit slips are collected by the teacher and read aloud (with no indication of the authorship of individual comments) as a way of beginning class discussion. Admit slips build a trusting relationship between teacher and students and contribute to a sense of community in the classroom.

In an Advanced Algebra class, where students had been studying complex numbers, the teacher asked the class to use admit slips to explain difficulties students had with one of their homework assignments. One student wrote, "I didn't know where to start." Several other students made similar comments. The teacher was able to use the written feedback to address some of the problems that students had with the assignment.

An *exit slip*, as you might anticipate, is a variation on the admit slip. Toward the end of class, the teacher asks students for exit slips as a way of bringing closure to what was learned. An exit slip question might require students to summarize, synthesize, evaluate, or project.

In the Advanced Algebra class, exit slips were used toward the end of the class to introduce a new unit on imaginary numbers. The teacher asked students to write for several minutes as they reflected on the question "Why do you think we are studying about imaginary numbers after we studied the discriminant?" Here's what one student wrote: "Because the discriminant can be negative and I didn't know what kind of a number $\sqrt{-1}$ was. I guessing [*sic*] it must be imaginary. Right?" The teacher was able to sort through the exit slip responses and use them to introduce the new unit.

The several minutes devoted to exit-slip writing are often quite revealing of the day's lesson and establish a direction for the next class.

JOURNAL WRITING

Because journals serve a variety of real-life purposes, not the least of which is to write about things that are important to us, they have withstood the test of time. Artists, scientists, novelists, historical figures, mathematicians, dancers, politicians, teachers, children, athletes—all kinds of people—have kept journals "to record the everyday events of their lives and the issues that concern them" (Tompkins 1990). Some journals—diaries, for example—are meant to be private and are not intended to be read by anyone but the writer. Sometimes, however, a diary makes its way into the public domain and affects readers in powerful ways. Anne Frank, probably the world's most famous child diarist, kept a personal journal of her innermost thoughts, fears, hopes, and experiences while hiding from the Nazis in World War II. Having read her diary, who hasn't been moved to think and feel more deeply about the tragic consequences of the Holocaust?

Other journals are more work-related than personal in that writers record observations and experiences that will be useful, insightful, or instructive. In more than 40 notebooks, Leonardo da Vinci recorded artistic ideas, detailed sketches of the human anatomy, elaborate plans for flying machines, and even his dreams. Novelists throughout literary history have used journals to record ideas, happenings, and conversations that have served to stimulate their imagination and provide material for their writing. Even in a professional sport such as baseball, it is not unusual for hitters to keep a log of their at-bats: who the pitcher was, what the situation was (e.g., runner on base or bases empty), what types of pitches were thrown, and what the outcome of each at-bat was.

Academic journals also serve a variety of purposes. They help students generate ideas, create a record of thoughts and feelings in response to what they are reading, and explore their own lives and concerns in relation to what they are reading and learning about. Academic journals create a context for learning in which students interact with information personally as they explore and clarify ideas, issues, and concepts under study. These journals may be used as springboards for class discussion or as mind stretchers that extend thinking, solve problems, or stimulate imagination. All forms of writing and written expression can be incorporated into academic journal writing, from doodles and sketches to poems and letters to comments, explanations, and reactions.

Three types of journals in particular have made a difference in content literacy situations: *response journals, double-entry journals,* and *learning logs.* Each of these can be used in an instructional context to help students explore literary and informational texts. Teachers who use academic journals in their classes encourage students to use everyday, expressive language to write about what they are studying, in the same way that they encourage students to use talk to explore ideas during discussion. When expressive or exploratory language is missing from students' journal writing, the students do not experience the kind of internal talk that allows them to explore and clarify meaning in ways that are personal and crucial to thinking on paper (Britton 1975).

When writing in academic journals, students need not attempt to sound "academic," even though they are writing about ideas and information of importance in various disciplines. Like the exploratory writing activities previously discussed in this chapter, journal entries need to be judged on the writer's ability to communicate and explore ideas, not on the quality of handwriting or the number of spelling and grammatical errors in the writing. Journal writing underscores informal learning. It relieves teachers of the burden of correction so that they can focus on students' thinking, and it creates a nonthreatening situation for students who may be hesitant to take risks because they are overly concerned about the mechanics of writing (e.g., handwriting, neatness, spelling, and punctuation).

Response Journals

Response journals create a permanent record of what readers are feeling and thinking as they interact with literary or informational texts. A response journal allows students to record their thoughts about texts and emotional reactions to them. Teachers may use prompts to trigger students' feelings and thoughts about a subject or may invite students to respond freely to what they are reading and doing in class. Prompts may include questions, visual stimuli, read-alouds, or situations created to stimulate thinking. An earth science teacher, for example, might ask students to place themselves in the role of a water molecule as they describe what it's like to travel through the water cycle. Examine how Mike, a low-achieving ninth grader who didn't like to write, responded in his journal entry:

> My name is Moe, its short for Molecule. I was born in a cloud when I was condensed on a dust particle. My neverending life story goes like this.

> During Moes life he had a great time boncing into his friends. He grew
> up in the cloud and became bigger and heavier. Moe became so heavy that
> one night lightning struck and he fell out of his cloud as a raindrop. He
> landed in a farmers field where this leavy plant sucked him up. Moe became
> a small section of a leave on the plant and their he absorbed sunlight and
> other things. One day a cow came by and ate Moes leave. He was now part
> of the cow.
>
> Well you can guess the rest. The farmer ate the cow and Moe became part
> of the farmer. One day the farmer was working in the field, he started sweating
> and thats when Moe escaped. He transpired into the air as a molecule again.
> Free at last he rejoined a group of new friends in a cloud and the cycle went on.

Mike's teacher was pleased by his journal entry, miscues and all. On homework questions, he usually wrote short, incoherent answers. In this entry,
however, he interacted playfully with the information in the text and demonstrated his understanding of the water cycle.

Role playing is an excellent prompt for response journal writing. A history teacher may invite students to assume the role of a historical character
and to view events and happenings from the character's perspective. In
Claudia Finley's U.S. history class, students keep a journal of events that take
place in American history from the perspective of a fictitious historical family
that each student creates. The families witness all of the events that take
place in American history and write their reactions to these events. Finley
scaffolds the journal writing assignment with the guidesheet in Figure 7.3.
Study the guidesheet, and then read several entries from one student's journal in Figure 7.4.

A high school art teacher, Ken Gessford, incorporates a sketchbook into
his courses to guide students' thinking and responses to what they are learning and studying in class. As an introduction to the sketchbook, the class discusses reasons for keeping a sketchbook, which Gessford adapted from a
model used by McIntosh (1991):

♦ What should you include in your sketchbook?

New ideas, sketches, concepts, designs, redesigns, words, notes from class, drawings to show understanding, reflections on the class, questions that you have, and
new things you've learned.

♦ When should you include entries in your sketchbook?

(1) After each class; (2) anytime an insight or a design idea or question hits you;
(3) anytime, so keep the sketchbook handy and visible in your work area.

♦ Why should you draw and write in your sketchbook?

(1) It will record your ideas and ideas you might otherwise forget; (2) it will record
and note your growth; (3) it will facilitate your learning, problem solving, idea
forming, research, reading, and discussion in class.

To help you develop your historical character, use the information that you have gained about the American colonies and your own background knowledge.

<u>Who is your character?</u>

1. What is your character's name? How old is your character? Is he or she married? (<u>Note</u>: How old were people when they married during this time?)

_____

_____

2. Who else is in your character's family? How old is each of these people? (<u>Note</u>: What happened to a lot of children during this time?)

_____

_____

3. Where does your character live?

_____

_____

4. What does your character do for a living? Is he or she rich or poor?

_____

_____

5. What religion is your character? What attitude does he or she have toward religion?

_____

_____

6. How much education does your character have?

_____

_____

7. Was your character born in the United States, Europe, or Africa? If he or she was born in Europe, in what country?

_____

_____

8. How does your character feel about people who are "different" in skin color, religion, social or economic class, or nationality?
   a. Skin color? (<u>Note</u>: This may depend on where he or she lives.)

   _____

   b. Religion?

   _____

   c. Social or economic class?

   _____

   d. Nationality?

   _____

9. How does your character feel about being part of a colony instead of living in an independent country?

_____

_____

FIGURE 7.3 **A Guidesheet for Historical Character Journals**

1770

My name is Victoria Black and I'm thirteen years old. We are a Protestant family and we attend church regularly. It's a social as well as religious occasion for us. We stay all day and my mother gossips with all of the neighbors. I've made a few friends there but usually I stay with my sister. I have long blond hair and sparkling blue eyes in my mother's words. I'm learning how to take care of the home and cook lately. My mother says it's important because soon enough I'll be married. I think she wants me to marry one of the boys from town whose father is a popular lawyer. I have an older sister Sarah who is fifteen and has just gotten married. My parents are Mathew and Elizabeth Black, they are becoming older and mother has been sick lately. We worry very much for them and say prayers daily. We live on Mander Plantation in Trenton, Pennsylvania, where my father grows cotton and some tobacco. We have many indentured servants which we treat very nicely. I've become close with a couple of them. Usually when the servants time has expired my father will give them some land to start up their lives. Because we are more north we haven't any African slaves yet. My father is planning a trip out east to buy some slaves later this month. I'm still not sure if buying people is the right thing to do but my brother told me he doesn't think they're real people. I don't know how my father feels on this, he must think it's alright. My father is very confused about what's going on with the British. He doesn't understand why the colonists think they even have a chance at fighting and winning with the British. He thinks the war will be over in no time.

FIGURE 7.4 **Historical Character Journal Entries**

◆ How should you write and draw entries in your sketchbook?

You can express yourself in sketches and drawings; in single words, questions, or short phrases; in long, flowing sentences; in designs and redesigns; in diagrams, graphs, and overlays; or in colors.

◆ Remember, the sketchbook is yours, and it reflects how perceptive you are with your ideas and how creative you are in your thought processes!

1778

I'm married now to William Brown, a new lawyer for Pennsylvania. We have two children, Mary and Richard Brown. They are still both very young, Mary is six and Richard is four and I'm expecting another soon! William is for the Revolutionary War. He feels the British are not being sensible with their laws for us. The taxation has bothered us greatly. Each week we scramble for money. Even though William is a lawyer, it's still hard to get started and receive reasonable wages. The British have also gone too far with the quartering act. We had British soldiers knock on our door last week asking for food. William was outraged. He says we have to have a revolution and win, if we want to survive and live happily. William said things are just going to get worse and worse. I don't think things could get any worse. I do worry about this war, for my brothers and William. Hopefully neither of them will be in the militia. We are already hearing of some battles, which sound awful. We are starting to go to church and pray every day now for our family and country.

1779 - 1781

William and my brothers are going to be in the militia. I'm very worried for them. William feels what he's doing is right for the country. We seem to be winning some of the battles which is surprising. The women and children from our church gather every day and pray for our brothers and husbands. We all try our hardest to stay on our feet and have enough food for everyone. Some weeks it's difficult. We feel that all of our money is going to taxes. We pray that the end will be here soon. I had a baby boy which we named Daniel Brown. It will be hard to raise these children alone. Before William goes to the militia I'm going to visit my mother, she's dying and I'd like to say goodbye to her.

Examine several of the students' sketchbook entries in Figure 7.5.

Math teachers use response journals in a variety of ways. They may invite students to write a "math autobiography" in which they describe their feelings and prior experiences as math learners. Rose (1989) suggests the following prompt for a biographical narrative in math:

Write about any mathematical experiences you have had. The narratives should be told as stories, with as much detail and description as possible. In-

<u>Van Gogh vs. Gaugin</u>

— I like Van Gogh much better
— Gaugin is nice but too showy
— I like elegance of Van Gogh
— Self portraits are really challenging
— Van Gogh — master directionalist
— Unbelievable that he (Van Gogh) had no training!

— I like looking at different artists. Even though I know these people are masters, I love their work.
— I could never do that without lots of training!!

Impressionists

— Pretty
— Watercolory
— Really masterful handling of paint. (watercolor)
— Saw them at Smithsonian.

<u>Question</u>
  When am I going to work larger?
I liked what we did on the Amiga — hope I get a chance to work with it again.

<u>Questions</u>
Why is it that I always draw late at night or early in the morning?
Shouldn't I start thinking about painting?
Will I ever understand color mixing?
Will I ever understand doing pencil directions?
Will I learn to stretch a canvas?

<u>Looking to the future</u>
— I don't use this sketchbook to do sketches — I like it more as a log
— Paint!! (probably a final problem)

FIGURE 7.5   **Entries from a Sketchbook**

clude your thoughts, reactions, and feelings about the entire experience.
(p. 24)

If students need more scaffolding than the prompt, Rose recommends having them complete and write elaborations on sentences, such as:

My most positive experience with math was _____

My background in math is _____

I liked math until _____

Math makes me feel _____

If I were a math teacher, I'd _____

The content of math journals may also include exploratory writing activities, summaries, letters, student-constructed word problems and theorem definitions, descriptions of mathematical processes, calculations and solutions to problems, and feelings about the course. Examine, for example, the journal entries in Figures 7.6 and 7.7.

In addition to prompts, consider having students engage in freewriting in their journals. Hancock (1993) provides a set of guidelines for writing freely in response journals in literature. These guidelines, with some modification, can easily be adapted to informational text. Some of the guidelines for students to consider when using response journals are the following:

◆ Write your innermost feelings, opinions, thoughts, likes, and dislikes. This is your journal. In it, feel the freedom to express yourself and your personal responses to reading.

◆ Write down anything that you are thinking about while you read. The journal is a way of recording those fleeting thoughts that pass through your mind as you interact with the book.

◆ Don't worry about the accuracy of spelling and mechanics in the journal. The content and expression of your personal thoughts should be your primary concern.

◆ Record the number of the page you were reading when you wrote your response. You might want to look back to reread and verify your thoughts.

◆ Write on only one side of your spiral notebook. Expect to read occasional interested comments from your teacher or another student on the other side.

◆ Relate what you are reading to your own experiences.

October 7

When I look at something I have to prove, the answer is always so obvious to me, I don't know what to write. This confuses me more because then I just write down one thing. Even though I understand it, no one else could. I don't use postulates & theorems because I have no idea which is which. So if you gave me a proof, I could probably prove it, but just not mathematically using big words.

FIGURE 7.6 Journal Entry in Response to the Prompt "What Goes Through Your Mind When You Do a Proof?"

9/4

How to Draw a Bisected Angle

Make an acute angle. Label it $\angle ABC$ — making Point A on one ray, B at the vertex, or point where rays meet, and C on the other ray. Now, with a compass, draw an arc of any measurement which will cross both rays. Next, use your compass to measure the distance between the two points you made by making the arc and keep the measurement locked on your protractor. Now, put the point of your compass on one of the arc points and make a slash in the middle of the angle. Do the same from the other dot on the other ray. The slash marks should cross in the center. Make a point where the slashes cross. Label it Point D. Draw a ray starting at Point B going through Point D. $\overrightarrow{BD}$ now bisects $\angle ABC$.

FIGURE 7.7   Journal Entry in Response to the Prompt "Explain to Someone How to Bisect an Angle"

♦ Ask questions while reading to help you make sense of the story or characters.

♦ Make predictions about what you think will happen as the plot unfolds. Validate or change those predictions as you proceed in the text. Don't worry about being wrong.

♦ Praise or criticize the book, the author, the style.

♦ Talk to the characters as you begin to know them. Give them advice to help them. Put yourself in their place and tell them how you would act in a similar situation.

♦ There is no limit to the type of responses you can write. These guidelines are meant to trigger, not limit, the kinds of things you write.

Teachers often make students aware of how and why to use response journals through metacognitive discussions and demonstrations. One way to demonstrate how to write an effective entry is to share with the class some past students' responses of different types. Use these demonstrations to build confidence and procedural knowledge in the use of the journal.

Double-Entry Journals

A double-entry journal is a versatile adaptation of the response journal. As the name implies, the double-entry journal allows students to record dual entries that are conceptually related. In doing so, students juxtapose their thoughts and feelings according to the prompts they are given for making the entries. To create a two-column format for the double-entry journal, have students divide sheets of notebook paper in half lengthwise. As an alternative, younger writers may need more room to write their entries than a divided page allows. They find that it is easier to use the entire left page of a notebook as one column and the right page as the other column.

Double-entry journals serve a variety of functions. In the left-hand column of the journal, students may be prompted to select words, short quotes, or passages from the text that interest them or evoke a strong response. In this column, they write the word, quote, or passage verbatim or use their own words to describe what is said in the text. In the right-hand column, the students record their reactions, interpretations, and responses to the text segments they have selected. As part of a science unit on the solar system, for example, middle-level students used double-entry journals as an occasion to explore their own personal meanings for the concept of the solar system. In the left column, they responded to the question "What is it?" In the right column, the students reflected on the question "What does it mean to you?" Study the entries that three of the students wrote in the "What is it?" column.

Then compare the three corresponding entries from the right-hand column, "What does it mean to you?"

"WHAT IS THE SOLAR SYSTEM?"

It is nine planets, along with asteroid belts, stars, black holes, etc.

It is planets and stars. Earth is the third planet from the sun. It is the only planet with water. Stars are huge many much greater that the sun in size.

The nine planets are not very interesting to me and I won't bother to go through them. But I did memorize the order of the planets by this sentance. *My very eager mother served just us nine pizzas.* Take the beginning letters to remind you of each planet.

"WHAT DOES IT MEAN TO YOU?"

The solar system is a mystery to me. I know the planets and stuff, but how did it come into being? Galileo had something to do with the solar system, but I'm not sure exactly what. I would like to find out more about it.

The solar system reminds me of a white hared scientist whose always studying the big vast opening in the sky. When I look at the sky at night I see tiny twinkling lights. People tell me that they're planets but I think they're stars. I see constellations but I don't recognize them. I am not a white hared scientist yet.

When I think about what the solar system means to me, I think about an unknown universe, which could be much larger than we think it is. I start to think about science fiction stories that I have read, alien beings and creatures that are in the universe some place.

In an eighth-grade language arts class, Harry Noden and his students were engaged in a unit on the Yukon and Jack London's *Call of the Wild* (Noden & Vacca 1994). As part of the core book study of London's classic novel about the adventures of a sled dog named Buck, Noden arranged for a sled dog team demonstration by a group of local residents who participate in dog sledding as a hobby. His class was excited by the demonstration, which took place on the school's grounds. The next day, the class used double-entry journals to reflect on the experience. In the left-hand column, they responded to the question "What did you learn from the demonstration?" In the right-hand column, they reflected on the question "How did the demonstration help you better understand the novel?" Examine some of the students' entries in Figure 7.8.

What did you learn from the demonstration?	How did the demonstration help you better understand the novel?
I learned that although dogs just look big and cudly they really can work. When people take the time they can teach there dog anything. Yet that saying also applies to life. **[Alex]**	I never realized how hard it was for Buck to pull the sled. It takes a lot of work.
It was excellent. I learned that the owners and the dogs were a family and extremely hard workers. I learned how hard a race could be and the risk involved. I'm glad I got to see the dogs and their personalities. **[Marcus]**	It proved to me how Buck needed to be treated with praise and disipline and equality. That way you get a wonderful dog and a companion for life.
I learned about how they trained their dogs and that they need as much or more love and attention as they do discipline. **[Jennifer]**	It helped me understand the book better because it showed how unique Buck is compared to the other dogs. Also what a dog-sled looks like and what Buck might have looked like. It made the story come alive more.

FIGURE 7.8 **Entries from a Double-Entry Journal Assignment for**
The Call of the Wild

Mathematics teachers have also been encouraged to use double-entry journals to help students solve word problems (Tobias 1989). In the left-hand column, a teacher might direct students to engage in "thinking out loud" as they work on a word problem. In the right-hand column, the students go about solving the problem, providing a layout of their sketches and calculations. Tobias noticed that as students began to use the two-column format to think about their problem-solving processes, they focused on posing two kinds of questions: What is making the problem difficult for me? And what could I do to make it easier for myself? Here is one student's "thinking out loud" entry in response to this problem: *A car goes 20,000 miles on a long trip, rotating its five tires (including the spare) regularly and frequently. How many miles will any one tire have driven on the road?*

> I assume there is a formula for solving this problem, but I have forgotten (if I ever knew) what it is.
>   I am being confused by the word "rotate." Simply by driving, we cause our tires to turn or "rotate" on the road. But "rotate" means something else in this problem. I had better concentrate on that.
>   I wonder how many miles each tire will have gone while in the trunk? Is this a useful approach? Let me try. (p. 52)

Tobias explains that using this unorthodox approach, trying to find the number of miles that any one tire will have traveled in the trunk of the car, is a productive way to solve the problem. In the right-hand column, the student calculated the correct answer by dividing 5 tires into 20,000 miles to get 4,000 miles per tire in the trunk. He then subtracted 4,000 miles from the total 20,000 miles driven, yielding the correct answer: Each tire, rotated onto the four on-road positions, traveled a total of 16,000 miles.

Learning Logs

Learning logs add still another dimension to personal learning in content area classrooms. The strategy is simple to implement but must be used regularly to be effective. As is the case with response and double-entry journals, students keep an ongoing record of learning *as it happens* in a notebook or looseleaf binder. They write in their own language, not necessarily for others to read but to themselves, about what they are learning. Entries in logs influence learning by revealing problems and concerns.

There is no one way to use learning logs, although teachers often prefer allowing five or ten minutes at the end of a period for students to respond to process questions such as "What did I understand about the work we did in class today? What didn't I understand? At what point in the lesson did I get confused? What did I like or dislike about class today?" The logs can be kept in a box and stored in the classroom. The teacher then reviews them during or after school to see what the students are learning and to recognize their concerns and problems. Let's take a look at how several teachers integrate logs into their instructional contexts.

Two math teachers report using learning logs with much success in their classrooms. Kennedy (1985), a middle school teacher, has designed what he calls a "writing in math" program in which learning logs are a key feature. In addition to the preceding process questions, he likes to ask students what they're wondering about. What specific questions do they have about the material being studied? He also finds that logs are effective for "making notes." According to Kennedy, the distinction between *taking* and *making* notes is central to the use of learning logs: "Taking notes is copying someone else's information; *making notes* is writing interpretive comments and personal reminders such as 'Ask about this' or just 'Why?'" (p. 61).

A high school algebra teacher introduces learning logs to her class this way:

> From time to time, I'll be asking you to write down in your logs how you went about learning a particular topic in this class. In other words, can you capture that moment when things finally made sense to you and how you felt? And can you express the frustration that might have preceded this moment? (Pradl & Mayher 1985, p. 5)

Students may at first be tentative about writing and unsure of what to say or reveal—after all, journal writing is reflective and personal. It takes a trusting atmosphere to open up to the teacher. However, to win the trust of students, teachers like the algebra teacher refrain from making judgmental or evaluative comments when students admit a lack of understanding of what's happening in class. If a trusting relationship exists, students will soon recognize the value of logs, although perhaps not as enthusiastically as one high school student:

> This journal has got to be the best thing that's hit this chemistry class. For once the teacher has direct communication with every member of the class. No matter how shy the student is they can get their lack of understanding across to the teacher. . . . These journals act as a "hot line" to and from the teacher. I feel this journal has helped me and everyone that I know in class. The only thing wrong is we should have started these on the first day of school!! In every class! (Pradl & Mayher 1985, p. 6)

The algebra teacher's students probably feel the same way about their algebra class. Here are some of the things that they do in their logs. For starters, the teacher likes to introduce a new topic by asking students to jot down their predictions and expectations of what the topic may involve. She also has her students write down their understanding of any new theorem that is introduced. After students feel that they have learned a theorem well, they use their logs to imagine how they might explain the theorem to another person, less well informed, like a younger sister or brother.

Both Kennedy and the algebra teacher use logs to have students create word problems that are then used to challenge other members of the class. Kennedy (1985) likes to have students write different kinds of word problems in their learning logs: "Sometimes I have them supply the data (for example, 'Write a problem involving the use of percent'); other times I supply the data (for example, 'Write a problem using the numbers 200, 400, and 600')" (p. 61).

In summary, most journal activities require thinking but do not demand a finished product. Students soon learn to write without the fear of making errors. However, there are times when students should know in advance that their journal entries will be read aloud in class. According to Levine (1985), this is when students often produce their best writing, because they are composing for an audience of peers. Josh, for example, an eighth grader, wrote about a lab experiment this way:

> Today in class we did a demo to try and find effective ways of recovering the solute from a solution.
>
> Several people came up with ideas as to how we could do this. A few people suggested filtering the solution, and others thought heating the solution so it evaporated would bring the solute back.
>
> First we tried filtering a copper sulfate solution but found that process didn't work. Evidently the crystals had dissolved to such an extent, that they were too small to be gathered by the filter paper.
>
> We then heated the solution and found we were far more successful than in our first try. Approximately thirteen minutes after we began heating the solution, a ring of copper sulfate crystals appeared in the bowl where the solution was. Eventually all the liquid evaporated leaving only the crystals. Quite obviously I learned that to recover the solute from a solution you can heat the solution. I also learned not to bother trying to filter the solution. (p. 45)

Journal writing allows students like Josh to express what's on their minds honestly and without pretense.

ESSAY WRITING

As useful as exploratory and journal writing are, they represent informal tools to help students explore content that they will be or are reading and studying about in class. Essay writing, by contrast, is more formal and finished. When students engage in essay writing, they become immersed in the content and are able to think more deeply about the subject they are exploring and clarifying. The purpose of writing essays, then, is to create a context in which students discover, analyze, and synthesize ideas through the process of writing.

Whereas exploratory and journal writing involves expressive, loosely written explorations of a subject, essays engage students in longer, more considered pieces of writing. Traditionally, essays have been the province of English teachers, whose students sometimes become more preoccupied with the form and organization of the essay—learning how to write a three-paragraph or five-paragraph paper—than with the exploration of content and the analysis and synthesis of ideas.

Essays have been shown to be effective writing-to-learn tools (1) when content exploration and synthesis, not form and organization, become the primary motives for the writing assignment; (2) when writing involves reading more than a single text source; and (3) when students engage in the writing process.

When students combine reading with writing essays, they think more deeply about the subject they are studying. Spivey (1984), for example, found that when writers read more than a single text source in order to write essays, they are immersed in organizing, selecting, and connecting content. Newell (1984) discovered that students who engage in essay-type writing acquire more content knowledge than students who take notes or answer study questions. Langer and Applebee (1987) concluded that when reading is combined with analytic writing, students are able to think more deeply about the key ideas and concepts they encounter during reading.

What the research on writing to learn demonstrates is that students who read to write engage in a range of reasoning processes. Essay writing creates occasions for students to discover, analyze, and synthesize ideas from multiple sources of information. The key to thoughtful student writing is to design good essay assignments. The teacher's primary concern should be how to make an assignment *explicit* without stifling interest or the spirit of inquiry. An assignment should provide more than a subject to write on.

Suppose you were assigned one of the following topics to write on, based on text readings and class discussion:

- Batiking

- The role of the laser beam in the future

- Victims of crime

No doubt, some of you would probably begin writing on one of the topics without hesitation. Perhaps you already know a great deal about the subject, have strong feelings about it, and can change the direction of the discourse without much difficulty. Others, however, may resist or even resent the activity. Your questions might echo the following concerns: "Why do I want to write about any of these topics in the first place? For whom am I writing? Will I write a paragraph? A book?" The most experienced writer must come to grips with questions such as these, and with even more complicated ones: "How will I treat my subject? What stance will I take?" If anything, the questions raise to awareness the *rhetorical context*—the *purpose, audience,* and *form* of the writing and the writer's *stance*—that most writing assignments

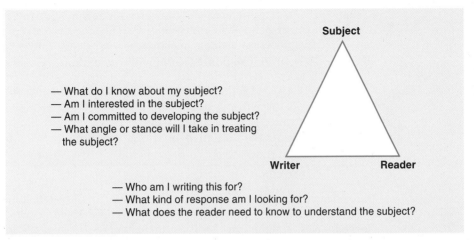

FIGURE 7.9   A Communications Triangle: Defining a Rhetorical Problem in Writing

should provide. A rhetorical context for writing allows students to assess the writer's relationship to the subject of the writing (the topic) and to the reader (the audience for whom the writing is intended). Lindemann (1982) suggests a *communications triangle* to show how the context can be defined. Some of the questions raised by the relationships among writer, subject, and reader in the communications triangle are depicted in Figure 7.9. The writer plans a response to the assignment by asking questions such as "For whom am I writing this? What do I know about my subject? How do I feel about it? What stance can I take in treating the topic?" A good essay assignment, then, *situates* students in the writing task by giving them a purpose for writing and an intended audience. It may also allude to the form of the writing and the stance the writer will take toward the topic.

Creating Lifelike Contexts for Writing

Students need to know why they are composing and for whom. One of the ways to characterize discourse, oral or written, is through its aims or purposes. As students approach an essay assignment, let them know its purpose. Is the writing aiming at personal expression? Is it to persuade? Describe? Explain? Or is it to create a text that can be appreciated in its own right for its literary or imaginative quality? These purposes are broad, to be sure, but each underscores an important aim of discourse (Kinneavy 1971).

Some essays will stimulate inquiry when they create lifelike situations in which the purpose for writing is directly tied to the audience. Instead of assigning an essay on how to batik, give students a situation to ponder:

To show that you understand how batiking works, imagine that you are giving a demonstration at an arts-and-crafts show. Describe the steps and procedures involved in the process of batiking to a group of onlookers, recognizing that they know little about the process but are curious enough to find out more.

This example creates a lifelike context, identifies a purpose and an audience, and suggests the writer's stance and a form of discourse (i.e., a position paper or demonstration). The student will not necessarily make the assumption that the teacher is the audience, even though ultimately the teacher will evaluate the written product. McAndrew (1983) portrays the reality of classroom audiences this way:

> The real audience in the classroom is the teacher. Let's admit that up front. The teacher—in his/her role as teacher-as-grader—is always and inescapably the audience for class assignments. But if we are to improve our students' writing skills, we must . . . try to create situations that allow students to experience writing to a variety of audiences even though we know, and the students know, that somewhere down the line the teacher will be the audience. (p. 49)

Essay assignments contrive situations and audiences in the context of what is being read or studied. However, they are far from trivial, nonacademic, or inconsequential. Instead, when students "become" someone else, they must look at situations in a nontraditional way. After writing, they can compare different stances on the same issue and examine the validity of the viewpoints that were taken.

Although some writing assignments may contrive situations and audiences, others should reflect real situations and audiences outside the classroom. For example, letters to the editor of the local newspaper and to political leaders, authors, and scientists can be an important part of classroom study. We will have more to say on audience identification later in this chapter when we examine the role of publication in the writing process.

Discourse Forms

Ideas can be expressed through a variety of writing forms. These discourse forms can be easily incorporated into the context of writing assignments. In Table 7.1, Tchudi and Yates (1983) provide a representative listing of some of these forms for content area writing.

Noden and Vacca (1994) provide an example of a senior-level Spanish teacher whose students were reading Spanish legends that have been handed down from one generation to another. The teacher invited the students to transform the legends they had been reading into another discourse form—a children's book, complete with illustrations. The teacher arranged to have the stories shared with English- and Spanish-speaking children in several of the elementary schools in the community. Figure 7.10 illustrates how one of the legends, "*La Dama de Piedra*" ("The Woman of Stone"), was adapted into a children's book.

TABLE 7.1

Some Discourse Forms for Content Area Writing

Journals and diaries (real or
  imaginary)
Biographical sketches
Anecdotes and stories:
  From experience
  As told by others
Thumbnail sketches:
  Of famous people
  Of places
  Of content ideas
  Of historical events
Guess who/what descriptions

Letters:
  Personal reactions
  Observations
  Public/informational
  Persuasive:
    To the editor
    To public officials
  To imaginary people
  From imaginary places
Requests
Case studies:
  School problems
  Local issues
  National concerns
  Historical problems
  Scientific issues
Songs and ballads
Demonstrations
Poster displays

Reviews:
  Books (including textbooks)
  Films
  Outside reading
  Television programs
  Documentaries

Historical "you are there"
  scenes

Science notes:
  Observations
  Science notebook
  Reading reports
  Lab reports
Written debates

Taking a stand:
  School issues
  Family problems
  State or national issues
  Moral questions

Books and booklets
Informational monographs
Radio scripts
TV scenarios and scripts
Dramatic scripts
Notes for improvised drama
Cartoons and cartoon strips
Slide show scripts
Puzzles and word searches
Prophecy and predictions
Photos and captions
Collage, montage, mobile,
  sculpture
Applications
Memos
Résumés and summaries
Poems
Plays
Stories
Fantasy
Adventure
Science fiction
Historical stories

Dialogues and conversations
Children's books
Telegrams
Editorials
Commentaries
Responses and rebuttals
Newspaper "fillers"
Fact books or fact sheets
School newspaper stories
Stories or essays for local
  papers
Proposals

Math:
  Story problems
  Solutions to problems
  Record books
  Notes and observations
Responses to literature
Utopian proposals
Practical proposals

Interviews:
  Actual
  imaginary

Directions:
  How-to
  School or neighborhood
    guide
  Survival manual
Dictionaries and lexicons
Technical reports
Future options, notes on:
  Careers, employment
  School and training
  Military/public service

Source: From *Teaching Writing in the Content Areas: Senior High School* by Stephen Tchudi and JoAnne
Yates. Copyright © 1983, National Education Association. Reprinted with permission.

La Dama de Piedra

Andrea Harrison

Había una vez, en el norte de España una francesa mala que entró en la capilla de Santiago.

1

Decidió robar el rosario de los manos de la estatua de la virgen.

2

Ella sacó el rosario sagrado y lo escondió en su bolsillo.

3

Cuando salió, un anciano apareció y le preguntó del rosario
4

La señora dijo que ella no había robado el rosario.
5

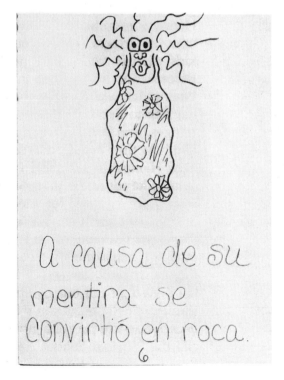

A causa de su mentira se convirtió en roca.
6

FIGURE 7.10 **Children's Book Based on a Spanish Legend**

As you can see, when students write in a particular discourse form, the work bears a stamp of authenticity.

Evaluating and Grading Essays

The paper load in classrooms where essay writing happens regularly is a persistent matter of concern for teachers. They often blanch at the prospect of grading 125 or more papers. A science teacher reacted to us in a workshop this way: "The quickest way to squelch my interest in writing to learn is to sock me with six sets of papers to correct at once." We couldn't agree more—weekends weren't made for drowning in a sea of ink.

Yet the notion of what it means to evaluate written work must be examined. "Correcting papers" is an inappropriate concept in a process approach to writing. It suggests that the teacher's role is primarily one of detecting errors and making revisions in papers. Overemphasis on error detection often telegraphs to students that correctness rather than the discovery and communication of meaning is what writing is all about. Content area teachers who view their job as an error hunt soon become, and understandably so, reluctant to devote hours to reading and "grading" papers.

The types of errors that often take the most time to detect and correct are those that involve various elements of language such as punctuation, spelling, and grammar. These elements, sometimes referred to as the *mechanics* or *form* of writing, must take a back seat to other features of writing, mainly *content* and *organization.* It's not that linguistic elements should be ignored or left unattended. However, they must be put into perspective. As Pearce (1983) explains, "If writing is to serve as a catalyst for gaining insight into course material, then content—not form—needs to be emphasized. . . . If a paper has poor content, then no amount of correcting elements of form will transform it into a good piece of writing" (p. 214). Ideas, and how they are logically and coherently developed in a paper, must receive top priority when one is evaluating and grading writing in content area classrooms.

Once writing is thought of and taught as a process, teachers can begin to deal effectively with the paper load. Although the volume of papers will inevitably increase, it is likely to become more manageable. For one thing, when provisions are made for active student responses to writing, much of the feedback that a student writer needs will come while writing is still going on. Guiding and channeling feedback as students progress with their drafts is a type of *formative* evaluation. In contrast, a *summative* evaluation takes place during the postwriting stage, usually after students have shared their finished products with one another.

Summative evaluations are often *holistic* so that a teacher can quickly and accurately judge a piece of writing based on an impression of its overall effectiveness. Thus a holistic evaluation permits teachers to sort, rank, and grade written pieces rather efficiently and effectively. Holistic scoring is organized around the principle that a written composition is judged on how successfully it communicates a message, rather than on the strengths and weaknesses of its individual features. The whole of a composition, if you will, is greater than the sum of its parts. In other words, teachers don't have to spend inordinate amounts of time enumerating and counting errors in a paper. Instead, the paper is judged for its total effect on a rater.

One type of holistic measure, *primary trait scoring,* is of particular value in content area writing situations. Primary trait scoring is tied directly to a specific writing assignment. An effective assignment, as you recall, provides a rhetorical context. The student writer's task is to respond to the special blend of purpose, audience, subject, and role specified in the assignment. Primary trait scoring helps the teacher decide how well students completed the writing task.

As a result, primary trait scoring focuses on the characteristics in a paper that are crucial to task completion. How successfully did students handle the assignment in relation to purpose, audience, subject, or role? Papers should be evaluated for these primary traits or characteristics: (1) accurate content in support of a position, (2) a logical and coherent set of ideas in support of a position, and (3) a position statement that is convincing and persuasive when aimed at an audience of fellow students.

Pearce (1983) recommends that teachers develop a *rubric* based on the primary traits exhibited in student papers. A rubric is a scoring guide. It provides a summary listing of the characteristics that distinguish high-quality from low-quality compositions. Study the rubric in Box 7.1 that Pearce developed for the following assignment: *Write a time capsule document analyzing Martin Luther King's approach to civil rights during the 1960s. Compare this approach to one taken by other Black leaders.* For this assignment, papers were evaluated for the following traits: (1) accurate and adequate content about civil disobedience, (2) a comparison of King's approach to civil disobedience with at least one other black leader's approach, and (3) a logical and organized presentation that provides evidence for any generalization made.

There are other types of holistic scoring procedures that can be used to evaluate and grade papers. For example, *analytical scales* and *checklists* can be developed to judge the quality of a piece of writing. These are explained in detail in an excellent monograph, *Evaluating Writing,* published by the National Council of Teachers of English (Cooper & Odell 1977).

Although a good essay assignment doesn't fully prepare students to engage in writing, it does give them a framework for planning and drafting. How teachers guide students through stages of the writing process ensures that students will construct meaning by exploring and clarifying ideas.

GUIDING THE WRITING PROCESS

Blank paper or an empty computer screen is the writer's call to battle. Getting started can be difficult, even terrifying. However, a good writer recognizes the difficulty of the undertaking and finds it stimulating. Writing is motivating.

Some writers come to grips with the blank page by performing one or more starting rituals. Pencils are sharpened, and the desktop is cleared of

Box 7.1

A Rubric for Grading

Paper topic: 1960s approaches to civil rights in the United States
High-quality papers contain:

An overview of civil rights or their lack during the 1960s, with three specific examples.

A statement defining civil disobedience, with three examples of how it was used and Martin Luther King's role.

At least one other approach to civil rights, with specific examples, and a comparison of this approach with King's civil disobedience that illustrates differences or similarities in at least two ways.

Good organization, well-developed arguments, few mechanical errors (sentence fragments, grammatical errors, spelling errors).

Medium-quality papers contain:

An overview of Black civil rights during the 1960s, with two specific examples.

A statement defining civil disobedience, with two examples of its use and Martin Luther King's involvement.

One other approach to civil rights, with examples, and a comparison of it with King's civil disobedience by their differences.

Good organization, few mechanical errors, moderately developed arguments.

Lower-quality papers contain:

A general statement defining civil disobedience with reference to Martin Luther King's involvement and at least one example.

One other approach to civil rights and how it differed from civil disobedience.

Fair organization, some mechanical errors.

Lowest-quality papers contain:

A general statement on who Martin Luther King was or a general statement on civil disobedience.

A general statement that not all Blacks agreed with civil disobedience.

A list of points, poor organization, many mechanical errors.

Source: From Daniel L. Pearce, "Guidelines for the Use and Evaluation of Writing in Content Classrooms" (December 1983). *Journal of Reading,* 27(3), 212–218. Copyright © 1983 by the International Reading Association. All rights reserved. Used by permission of the author and the International Reading Association.

clutter. Eventually, the first words are put on paper, and everything that has occurred to this point (all of the mental and physical gymnastics a writer goes through) and everything that will happen toward completion of the writing task can best be described as a process.

One of the teacher's first tasks is to make students aware that the writing process occurs in stages (Kirby & Liner 1981). It's the exceptional student who leaps in a single bound from a finished product in his or her head to a finished product on paper. In this book, the stages of writing are defined broadly as *prewriting, writing, rewriting,* and *postwriting.* Table 7.2 presents an overview of these stages.

By no means are the stages in the writing process neat and orderly. Few writers proceed from stage to stage in a linear sequence. Instead, writing is a back-and-forth activity. Exploring and generating ideas before writing may lead to plans for a piece of writing, but once engaged in the physical act of composing, writers often discover new ideas, reformulate plans, rewrite, and revise.

Exploring, Planning, and Organizing

What students do before writing is as important as what they do before reading. Rehearsing activity, like the prereading strategies discussed in Chapter 9, involves planning, building and activating prior knowledge, setting goals, and getting ready for the task at hand. In other words, rehearsal refers to everything that students do before putting words on paper for a first draft. The term *prewriting* is often used interchangeably with *rehearsing,* but it is somewhat misleading because students often engage in some form of writing before working on a draft. As we have shown, freewriting in journals is a good strategy for the student writer.

Rehearsal is what the writer consciously or unconsciously does to get energized—to get ideas out in the open, to explore what to say and how to say it (Graves 1978). What will I include? What's a good way to start? Who is my audience? What form should my writing take? Scaffolding rehearsing in a classroom involves any support activity or experience that motivates a student to write, generates ideas for writing, or focuses attention on a particular subject. Students can be guided to think about a topic in relation to a perceived audience and the form that a piece of writing will take. A teacher who recognizes that the writing process must slow down at the beginning will help students discover that they have something to say and that they want to say it.

Getting started on the right foot is what rehearsing is all about. Generating talk about an assignment before writing buys time for students to gather ideas and organize them for writing. Discussion before writing is as crucial to success as discussion before reading. In preparing seniors to write letters to the editor concerning the legal age for drinking in Ohio, the teacher of a course called "Problems in Democracy" asked students for their opinions:

> ### TABLE 7.2
> ## Stages in the Writing Process

Prewriting—"Getting It Out"

- Exploring and generating ideas
- Finding a topic
- Making plans (Audience? Form? Voice?)
- Getting started

Writing—"Getting It Down"

- Drafting
- Sticking to the task
- Developing fluency and coherence

Rewriting—"Getting It Right"

- Revising for meaning
- Responding to the writing
- Organizing for clarity
- Editing and proofreading for the conventions of writing, word choice, syntax
- Polishing

Postwriting—"Going Public"

- Publishing and displaying finished products
- Evaluating and grading

Source: Adapted from D. Kirby and T. Liner, *Inside Out: Developmental Strategies for Teaching Writing.* Portsmouth, NH: Boynton/Cook, 1981.

"At what age do you think people in Ohio should be permitted to drink alcoholic beverages?" The discussion among the senior students, as you might anticipate, was animated. The teacher followed the discussion by assigning a newspaper article on the legal age issue. Further discussion generated more ideas and helped students formulate a stand on the issue.

Prereading strategies, such as guided imagery, can be used effectively, with some modification, for writing situations. Let's take a closer look at several strategies that will help students rehearse for writing by gathering and organizing ideas: *brainstorming, clustering,* and *concept matrix charting*.

Brainstorming

Brainstorming permits students to examine ideas from content area lessons as rehearsal for reading or writing. In doing so, it helps them set purposes for reading or writing because it gives students problems to solve. Examine how the following two variations on brainstorming can be easily adapted to writing situations:

1. Present a concept or problem to students based on some aspect of what they have been studying. Set a time limit for brainstorming ideas or solutions. The teacher calls, "Stop," but allows *one more minute* for thinking to continue. Creative ideas are often produced under time pressure.

In a high school special education class for students with learning problems, several weeks had been spent on a unit dealing with the Civil War era. As part of their study of the Reconstruction period, students explored issues such as the rebuilding of the South and the dilemma presented by the freed slaves. One of the culminating learning experiences for the chapter on freed slaves concerned a writing activity designed to help students synthesize some of the important ideas that they had studied. As part of her introduction to the writing assignment, the teacher began the prewriting phase of the lesson with a lead-in: "Using any information that you can recall from your text or class discussion, think about what might have been some of the problems or concerns of a freed slave immediately following the Civil War. Let's do some brainstorming." As the students offered ideas related to prejudice and lack of money, homes, and food, the teacher listed them on the board. Getting ideas out in the open in this manner was the first step in her prewriting strategy. (In the next subsection, on clustering, we'll discuss how the teacher used brainstorming as a stepping-stone for students to organize ideas and make decisions about the writing assignment.)

2. Engage students in "brainwriting" (Rodrigues 1983). Here's how it works. Divide the class into cooperative groups of four or five students. Each group member is directed to jot down ideas about the writing assignment's topic on a sheet of paper. Each student then places his or her paper in the center of the group, chooses another's list of ideas, and adds to it. The group compiles the best ideas into a single list and shares them with the class. Two advantages of brainwriting are that every student contributes and there is time given to consider ideas.

Brainstorming techniques allow students to become familiar with a topic and therefore to approach writing with purpose and confidence. Often teachers combine brainstorming with another rehearsing strategy: clustering.

Clustering

To introduce the concept of clustering, the teacher should write a key word on the chalkboard and then surround it with other associated words that are offered by the students. In this way, students not only gather ideas for writing but also connect the ideas within categories of information. Teacher-led clustering provides students with an awareness of how to use this rehearsing strategy independently. Once they are aware of how to cluster their ideas around a topic, students should be encouraged to create their own clusters for writing.

In our discussion of brainstorming, we described how a special education teacher used the list of ideas generated by her students to explore the concerns of freed slaves during the post–Civil War period. This was a first step in the rehearsal phase of the writing activity. The second step was to cluster the words into meaningful associations based on student suggestions. The teacher modeled the activity by choosing as the key word the concept of *freed slaves.* She then drew a line to the upper right corner of the chalkboard and connected the key word to the word *problems.* She connected some of the words generated by students during brainstorming to the cluster. The teacher then asked what some of the results of the freed slaves' problems would be. One student volunteered the word *suffering.* The teacher wrote *suffering* in the upper left corner of the cluster and asked the students to brainstorm some examples. These examples were then connected to the cluster.

The remainder of the rehearsing session centered on discussion related to the *aid* freed slaves received and the *opportunities* that resulted from the Reconstruction years. Figure 7.11 depicts the completed cluster that the teacher and students produced on the chalkboard.

With the cluster as a frame of reference, the students were assigned to write what it would have been like to be a freed slave in the 1860s and 1870s. They were asked to consider what the form of the writing should be. Since the textbook presented a variety of primary sources (including diary entries, newspaper clippings, and death notices), the students could, if they decided, write in one of those forms. Or they could approach the writing activity as a historian would and write an account that might be read by other students as a secondary source of information (see Figure 7.12). One member of the class became so involved in the activity that he wanted his historical document to appear authentic by aging the paper. This he did by burning the edges so that it would look "historic."

Students should begin to develop their own clusters for writing as soon as they understand how to use the strategy effectively. They should feel comfortable enough to start with a basic concept or topic—written in the center of a sheet of paper—and then to let go by making as many connections as possible on the paper. Connections should develop rapidly, "radiating outward from the center in any direction they want to go" (Rico 1983, p. 35). Since there is no right or wrong way to develop a cluster, students should be encouraged to play with ideas based on what they are studying and learning in class.

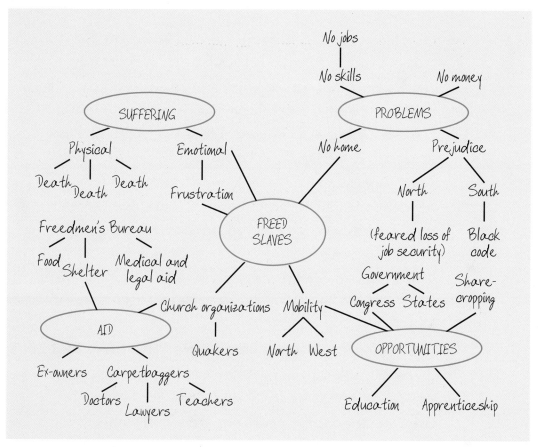

FIGURE 7.11   Cluster on the Lives of Freed Slaves in the Years After the Civil War

The value of clustering in writing shouldn't be sold short. Gabriele Rico (1983), a leading proponent of this prewriting strategy, maintains that it not only "unblocks and releases" information stored in the student writer's mind but also generates inspiration for writing. Moreover, clustering becomes a self-organizing process. According to Rico, "As you spill out seemingly random words and phrases around a center, you will be surprised to see patterns forming until a moment comes—characterized by an 'Aha!' feeling—when you suddenly sense a focus for writing" (p. 35). Students can discuss their clusters in small groups and share their plans for writing. Or as Rico recommends, they can begin to write immediately after clustering.

Concept Matrix Charting

Like clustering, a concept matrix, such as those introduced in Chapter 10, provides a way for students to organize information. However, it doesn't rely

May 3, 1866

My mane is Toby and I had been a slave for eight years before we were freed. It was good at first but them we realized there were problems.

We had great prolblems. Prejudice kept us from doing what we wanted to do. Black Codes which were suppose to help didn't help us at all. We weren't allowed to be out after dark. We weren't allowed to carry a gun. We weren't allowed to go out without a pass.

We had no food. My family had no food. My kids were all sick and there was nothing I could do to help them.

But there was some nice people. The army and Quakers helped my kids get better and they helped us get some land and food for my family. then we started a farm we grew crops and got money.

We had some opertunites. We could move to another state for a Job. We could also get an education. Some Blacks even gained Goverment positions.

FIGURE 7.12 **A Student's Writing Sample on What It Would Be Like to Be a Freed Slave**

on freely associating ideas with a key concept word. Instead, students collect and connect ideas by outlining them on a matrix. The strategy is especially appropriate for writing that relies on explanation, comparison and contrast, and description of ideas, people, events, characters, or processes.

Across the top of the matrix, as you may recall, list some of the main ideas that are to be analyzed or described in the writing assignment. Along the side of the matrix, list some of the areas in which these ideas are to be considered. As part of their rehearsing for writing, students complete the chart by jotting notes and ideas from course material, class lectures, and so on in the spaces created by the matrix.

A language arts teacher used a concept matrix as a planning tool for a writing activity that compared famous heroes from the stories that the class had read. The activity directed students to write about how the heroes (David, Hercules, and Beowulf) had approached and handled challenges. The chart in Figure 7.13 helped students reread selectively and take notes in preparation for the writing assignment.

Students in the language arts class discussed their concept matrices before engaging in writing. The concept matrix can be an effective outlining tool for writing and also has value as a study strategy in that it provides a framework on which students can organize and relate information.

Guiding the First Draft

The writing stage involves getting ideas down on paper fluently and coherently. The writer drafts a text with an audience (readers) in mind. If students are well rehearsed for writing, first drafts should develop without undue struggle. The use of in-class time for first-draft writing is as important as allotting in-class time for reading. In both cases, teachers can regulate and monitor the process much more effectively. For example, while students are writing, a teacher's time shouldn't be occupied in grading papers or attending to other unrelated chores. As Tchudi and Yates explain in *Teaching Writing in the Content Areas* (1983), teachers can do much to influence the quality of writing and learning *as* students are writing:

	David	Hercules	Beowulf
Each hero's feelings when confronted with his challenge.			
How did each hero handle his challenge?			
How did each hero react after conquering his challenge?			

FIGURE 7.13   **A Concept Matrix for "Stories About Heroes"**

When students are writing during class time, the teacher can take an active role. For example, monitor facial expressions—they often tell when a student is starting to get in a jam and needs help. Float around the class during a writing assignment, glancing at first paragraphs and rough beginnings, offering advice if it seems needed—in other words, help students get it right *while* they are writing and encourage them to solve problems the first time around. (pp. 12–13)

The writing stage, then, should be a time for conferring individually with students who are having trouble using what they know to tackle the writing task. Serve as a sounding board or play devil's advocate: "How does what we've studied in class for the past few days relate to your topic?" or "I don't quite understand what you're getting at. Let's talk about what you're trying to say." Students should also have the opportunity to confer with one another: "There are great benefits from such forms of peer collaboration as encouraging writers to bounce ideas off one another, reading draft paragraphs aloud to seek advice, pumping their friends for new advice" (Tchudi & Yates 1983, p. 17). Teacher feedback and peer collaboration underscore the importance of *response* in the writing process.

Responding and Revising

Rewriting helps students take a fresh look and rethink a paper. This is why good writing often reflects good rewriting. From a content area learning perspective, rewriting is the catalyst for clarifying and extending the concepts under study. Rewriting hinges on the feedback students receive between their first and second drafts.

Teacher feedback is always important, but it's often too demanding and time-consuming to be the sole vehicle for response. It may also lack the *immediacy* that student writers need to try out their ideas on an audience—especially if teachers are accustomed to taking home a stack of papers and writing comments on each one. The paper load soon becomes unmanageable and self-defeating. An alternative is to have students respond to the writing of other students. By working together in response groups, students can give reactions, ask questions, and make suggestions to their peers. These responses to writing in progress lead to revision and refinement during rewriting.

The purpose of peer response groups is to provide a testing ground for students to see how their writing influences a group of readers. Writers need a response to sense the kinds of changes they need to make.

Healy (1982) makes an important distinction between *response* and *evaluation.* Response involves an initial reaction to a first draft. The reaction is usually in the form of questions to the writer about the content and organization of the writing. Both teacher and student share the responsibility for responding. Evaluation, by contrast, involves a final assessment of a piece of writing that has progressed through drafts. The teacher has the primary responsibility for evaluating a finished product.

Learning to respond to writing in peer groups requires demonstrations and modeling. Response groups must be phased in gradually; students can't be expected to handle response tasks in groups without extensive modeling and coaching. Moreover, response groups shouldn't be initiated too early in the school year. After a month or two of regular writing activity, students will be more confident in their writing ability and will, in all probability, have developed some fluency in their writing. It is at this point that they are ready to be introduced to responding and rewriting situations.

 The following steps, adapted from Healy (1982) and Camp (1982), provide enough structure to shift the burden of feedback from teacher to students:

1. Discuss students' attitudes toward school writing and attempt "to shape new ones if existing attitudes are constricting or counterproductive" (Healy 1982, p. 268). For example, talk about writing as a process that occurs in stages. When students are engaged in an important writing task that will be presented to others ("published"), they shouldn't expect a finished product in one sitting. A first draft is often rough around the edges. It usually needs focus and clarity. Let students know what you value in their writing. Moreover, emphasize the importance of trying out writing on an audience before tackling a final draft. Tryouts are a time to react as readers to writing, not to nitpick over errors or to correct writing as evaluators.

2. Use the whole class as a response group to demonstrate how to give feedback to a writer. On an overhead transparency, show a paper that was written by an anonymous student from a different class. Read the paper aloud and talk about it. The goal is to practice talking about writing without posing a threat to any of the students. Camp (1982) suggests kicking off discussion with the question "If you were the teacher of this student, and you received this paper, what would you decide to teach the student *next*, so that the next paper he or she writes will be better than this one?" (p. 21). Let the students brainstorm responses. List their suggestions on the chalkboard, and then ask the class to reach a consensus on the most important points for improvement. Conclude the discussion by acknowledging that responses to content and organization have a higher priority than responses to mechanics. Writers in progress need feedback on how to set their content and organize it before attending to concerns related to spelling, capitalization, punctuation, and grammar.

3. On an overhead transparency, project another paper from a different class, and ask students to respond to the writing by making comments or raising questions. Write these on the transparency next to the appropriate section of the paper. You may find that students have difficulty with this task, so demonstrate several responses that tell what is positive about the paper: What do you as a reader like about it? What is done well?

Note the differences between *useful* and *useless* feedback. The response "This section is confusing" is of little help to the writer because it isn't specific enough. A useful response, however, is one in which the writer learns what information a reader needs: "I was confused about the Bay of Pigs invasion. Did Kennedy fail to give backup support to the commandos?" Students will soon catch on to the idea that a response gives information that helps the writer get a clear sense of the needs of the audience.

4. Form cooperative groups of three or four students. Distribute copies of a paper that was written in a different class. Also pass out a response sheet to guide the group discussion. The response sheet should contain several questions that pattern what to look for in the writing. In Figure 7.14, Camp (1982) used a response sheet to guide the response to a paper based on a personal experience.

Tchudi and Yates (1983) provide categories of questions to ask in response groups. The questions relate to *purpose, content, organization, audience, language,* and *style* and are presented in Box 7.2. Note that students shouldn't respond to more than three or four questions in any one response-group session. Choose or devise questions that are the most appropriate to the writing assignment.

```
Response Sheet: Personal Experience Writing
Writer _____
Responder _____
A. What did you like best about this paper? What worked really well?
   _____
   _____
   _____

B. What questions would you ask the writer about things in this paper that
were confusing or unclear to you?
   _____
   _____
   _____

C. Where in the paper would you like more detail? Where could the writer
show instead of tell?
   _____
   _____
   _____

D. Rate each of the following on a scale from 1 to 4. 4 is tops.
   1. Beginning _____              3. Ending _____
   2. Use of conversation _____    4. Title _____
```

FIGURE 7.14   **Sample Response Sheet**

Source: Adapted from Gerald Camp, *A Success Curriculum for Remedial Writers.* Berkeley: National Writing Project, University of California, 1982, p. 28

Box 1.2

Questions for Response Groups

Note: Do not have students ask *all* these questions (or similar ones) at every revising session. Rather, pick some questions that seem most appropriate to your assignment and have the students work on two or three each time.

PURPOSE

- Where is this writing headed? Can readers clearly tell?
- Is it on one track, or does it shoot off in new directions?
- Is the writer trying to do too much? Too little?
- Does the author seem to *care* about his/her writing?

CONTENT

- When you're through, can you easily summarize this piece or retell it in your own words?
- Can a reader understand it easily?
- Are there parts that you found confusing?
- Are there places where the writer said too much, or overexplained the subject?
- Can the reader visualize the subject?
- Does it hold your interest all the way through?
- Did you learn something new from this paper?

ORGANIZATION

- Do the main points seem to be in the right order?
- Does the writer give you enough information so that you know what he/she is trying to accomplish?
- Does the writing begin smoothly? Does the writer take too long to get started?
- What about the ending? Does it end crisply and excitingly?

AUDIENCE

- Who are the readers for this writing? Does the writer seem to have them clearly in mind? Will they understand him/her?
- What changes must the writer make to better communicate with the audience?

LANGUAGE AND STYLE

- Is the paper interesting and readable? Does it get stuffy or dull?
- Can you hear the writer's voice and personality in it?
- Are all difficult words explained or defined?
- Does the writer use natural, lively language throughout?
- Are the grammar, spelling, and punctuation OK?

Source: From *Teaching Writing in the Content Areas: Senior High School* by Stephen Tchudi and JoAnne Yates. Copyright © 1983, National Education Association. Reprinted with permission.

5. Form response groups to discuss first drafts that the students have written. Healy (1982, p. 274) recommends the following conditions for working in small groups:

- Keep the groups small—two to five at first.

- Have groups sit as far away as possible from other groups for noise control.

- Have students write the names of their response partners at the top of their original drafts.

- After response partners have heard a paper read, have them make any comments or ask the writer any questions that occur to them. The writer will note these on the paper.

- Encourage writers to ask for help with different sections of their papers.

- Have writers make all revisions on their original drafts before doing the final one. Have them staple both copies together.

A variation on these conditions is to use response sheets to guide the group discussions. They are particularly useful in the beginning, when the task of responding is still new to students. However, with enough modeling and practice, response sheets will probably not be necessary.

During the revision of the original draft, encourage students to be messy. For example, show them how to use carets to make insertions, and allow them to cross out or to cut and paste sections of text, if necessary. The use of arrows will help students show changes in the position of words, phrases, or sentences within the text.

Once feedback is given on the content and organization of a draft, response group members should work together to edit and proofread their texts for spelling, punctuation, capitalization, word choice, and syntax. Accuracy counts. Cleaning up a text shouldn't be neglected, but students must recognize that concern about proofreading and editing comes toward the end of the process.

Revising a text is hard work. Some students even think that *rewriting* is a dirty word. They mistake it for recopying—emphasizing neatness as they painstakingly transcribe from pencil to ink. They need a good rationale for going the extra mile. One solid reason is the recognition that their work will be presented to others. Publishing is an incentive for revising. As Camp (1982) explains, "The final drafts of all major writing assignments are published in some way. This final step is . . . just as essential as any of the others" (p. 41). If writing is for reading—and indeed it is—then teachers must find ways to value students' finished products.

Publishing

Kirby and Liner (1981, p. 215) give four good reasons for publishing students' written products:

1. Publishing gives the writer an audience, and the writing task becomes a real effort at communication—not just writing to please the teacher.

2. Publishing is the only reason for the writing to be important enough for the hard work of editing and proofreading.

3. Publishing involves the ego, which is the strongest incentive for the student writer to keep writing.

4. Publishing is fun.

Most students realize early in their school experience that the teacher is the only audience for their writing. When the audience is not described in a writing assignment, students typically assume that the teacher will be the sole reader. Topic-only assignments reinforce this assumption:

◆   How does the Cuban government squelch dissidents?

◆   Argue for or against smoking in public places.

◆   What causes acid rain?

We do not deny or denigrate the importance of the teacher as an audience. Neither do students. We agree with Purves (1983) that "schools, real institutions that they are, . . . should teach writing for general audiences represented by the real teacher" (p. 44).

However, when the classroom context for writing encourages a range of possible audiences for assignments (including the teacher), the purposes and the quality of writing often change for the better. This is why we called for audience-specific writing assignments early in the chapter.

When students know that their written products will be presented publicly for others to read, they develop a heightened awareness of audience. Teachers need to mine the audience resources that exist in and out of the classroom. As we just showed, response groups are one way to share writing in progress. Following are some ways to share finished products.

Oral Presentations to the Class

Reading finished papers aloud is a natural extension of peer responding to work in progress. When the writing is tied directly to content objectives, students not only have fun sharing their products but also learn a great deal from their colleagues. We recommend the frequent use of read-aloud sessions as a way of publishing so that all students will at one time or another have an opportunity to present their work.

Teachers should establish a tone of acceptance during oral presentations of original writing. The writer reads; the listeners react and respond. One variation is to establish a professional conference atmosphere in which student scientists, historians, literary critics, mathematicians, business executives, and so on convene to share knowledge with one another. Several students who have written on a related topic might even present a symposium, in which case one or two of their classmates should serve as discussants. Opportunities for learning abound when the focal point of class reaction and discussion is student-developed texts.

Class Publications

Class-produced newspapers, magazines, anthologies, and books are excellent ways to publish student writing. These vehicles of publication fit in effectively with the culmination of a unit of study. Identify a title for a class publication that reflects the theme or objective of the unit. For example, *The Civil War Chronicle,* a magazine produced by an eleventh-grade American history class, was patterned after the formats found in *Time* and *Newsweek.* A ninth-grade English class studying *To Kill a Mockingbird* put together *The Maycomb Register.* The students researched events associated with the time period of the novel (1936) and wrote a variety of local, national, and international news items related to the story. The teacher had students involved in all the phases of the newspaper's production, including typesetting and layout. She even had the paper professionally printed. To pay for the printing, the students sold the newspaper to schoolmates, parents, and neighbors.

Producing a newspaper or a magazine requires teamwork and task differentiation. We suggest that students not only participate as writers but also work in groups to assume responsibility for editing, proofreading, design, and production. The production of a class publication need not be as elaborate or expensive an activity as *The Maycomb Register.* Photocopied publications have the same effect on student writers when they see their work in print.

Room Displays

Display student writing. As Kirby and Liner (1981) point out, "A display of finished products attracts attention and stimulates talk and thinking about writing" (p. 217). Establish a reading fair during which students circulate quietly around the room reading as many papers as they can. Judy and Judy (1980) suggest that student writers provide blank sheets of paper to accompany their finished products so that readers can comment. They also recommend one-of-a-kind publications for display. These publications preserve the writing in a variety of forms (folding books, leaflets, scrolls, quartos, and folios). In their book, *Gifts of Writing,* the Judys outline numerous formats for one-of-a-kind publications.

Publishing for Real-World Audiences

Letters, community publications, commercial magazines, and national and state contests are all vehicles for real-world publishing outside the classroom and school. Letters, in particular, are valuable because there are so many audience possibilities: "Students can write everyone from school officials to administrators of policies in education, industry, and business. They can write to artists,

musicians, poets and actors to offer adulation or criticism. They can write on issues of immediate concern or long range interest" (Judy & Judy 1980, p. 119).

In addition to letters, the local newspaper, the PTA bulletin, and the
school district newsletter sometimes provide an outlet for class-related writing activity. Commercial magazines and national and state writing contests
also offer opportunities for publication. Commercial magazines and writing
contests, of course, are highly competitive. However, the real value of writing
for commercial publication lies in the authenticity of the task and the audience specification it provides.

 ## LOOKING BACK, LOOKING FORWARD

In this chapter, we focused on writing to emphasize the powerful bonds between reading and writing. Content area learning, in fact, is more within the
reach of students when writing and reading are integrated throughout the
curriculum. The two processes, both rooted in language, are intertwined and
share common cognitive and sociocultural characteristics. The combination
of reading and writing in a classroom improves achievement and instructional efficiency. When students write to learn in content area classrooms,
they are involved in a process of manipulating, clarifying, discovering, and
synthesizing ideas. The writing process is a powerful strategy for helping students gain insight into course objectives.

The uses of writing have been noticeably limited in content area classrooms. Writing has often been restricted to noncomposing activities such as
filling in the blanks on worksheets and practice exercises, writing one-para-
graph-or-less responses to study questions, or taking notes. The role of writing in content areas should be broadened because of its potentially powerful
effect on thinking and learning.

Because writing promotes different types of learning, students should
have many different occasions to write. These occasions include the use of
journals, exploratory writing activities, and essays. Journals, one of the most
versatile writing-to-learn strategies, entail students' responding to text as
they keep an ongoing record of learning while it happens, in a notebook or
loose-leaf binder. When students use response journals, double-entry journals, character journals, or learning logs, they soon learn to write without the
fear of making mechanical errors. Exploratory writing activities such as the
unsent letter place students in a role-playing situation in which they are
asked to write letters about the material being studied. Additional activities
include biopoems, dialogues, and admit and exit slips. Students can also be
assigned essays for inquiry-centered writing that is task-explicit. An explicit
assignment helps students determine the purpose, audience, and form of the
writing as well as the writer's role. Holistic scoring is recommended as a
means of evaluating and grading essays.

Writing should be thought of and taught as a process. When students are guided through a writing process, they will be in a better position to generate ideas, set goals, organize, draft, and revise. The writing process occurs in steps or stages, not necessarily in a linear sequence of events, but more as a back-and-forth activity. The stages of writing presented in this chapter included rehearsing, writing, rewriting, and postwriting. Rehearsal activities such as brainstorming, clustering, concept matrices, and discussion help students explore ideas, set purposes, and organize for writing. Rehearsal situations get students ready to write—to transcribe ideas into words on paper or on the computer screen. This step—writing—leads to an initial draft. Rewriting activities include a response by students or teachers to drafts. Feedback while writing is in progress is essential for revision. Postwriting activities involve sharing a finished product with others.

The next chapter examines the relationships between the vocabulary of a content area—its special and technical terms—and its concepts. How can a teacher help students to interact with the language of a content area and, in the process, show them how to define, clarify, and extend their conceptual knowledge?

 **MINDS-ON**

1. Each member of your group should select one of the following roles to play: (a) a language arts teacher who believes that correct mechanics are the heart of good writing, (b) a science teacher who assigns students a variety of "writing-to-learn" projects, (c) a history teacher who believes that writing is the job of the language arts department, (d) a math teacher who uses math journals to aid in students' comprehension, and (e) an administrator who lacks a philosophical view and is listening to form an opinion.

    Imagine that this group is eating lunch in the faculty lounge at a middle school where you teach. The language arts teacher turns to the science teacher and says, "My students were telling me that in the writing assignment you gave, you told them not to worry about mechanics, that you were interested mainly in their content and form. I wish you wouldn't make statements like that. After all, I'm trying to teach these kids to write correctly." Continue the discussion in each of your roles.

2. What strategies do you feel would be most useful in making writing assignments meaningful for learning?

3. Your group should divide into two teams, one pro and one con. Review each of the following five statements, and discuss from your assigned view the pros and cons of each issue. After you have discussed all five

statements, take an "agree" or "disagree" vote on each statement, and discuss what you really believe about the issue.

a. We write to discover meaning (to understand) and to communicate meaning to others (to be understood).

b. Writing is an incidental tool in learning and relatively unconnected to reading.

c. Writing to learn is a catalyst for reading and studying course material.

d. Students need to know the purpose, audience, and writer's stance for a writing assignment.

e. The stages of the writing process are so interrelated that a knowledge of them is of little practical value.

4. At the start of the chapter, we wrote, "When reading and writing are taught in tandem, the union influences content learning in ways not possible when students read without writing or write without reading." Drawing on your experience and the text, discuss some" specific examples that support this thesis.

HANDS-ON

1. In the center of a blank sheet of paper, write the name of the first color that comes to your mind. Circle that color. Let your mind wander, and quickly write down all descriptive words or phrases that come to your mind that are related to that color word. Connect the words logically, creating clusters. Next, see what images these relationships suggest to you. Write a piece (a poem, a story, or an essay) based on your clusters. Exchange papers, and in pairs, comment on

    a. The best phrase in your partner's piece

    b. What needs explanation or clarification

    c. The central idea of the piece

    With your partner, discuss how this exercise illustrates the characteristics of writing to learn.

2. Work with a partner to create a writing-process protocol. Each partner is to observe the other during the following activity and to record the characteristics of the other's process. For example, you might describe the

writer pausing, sighing, gazing off, writing hurriedly, scratching out, and erasing. At the end of the activity, share your written description with the partner you observed to see if your observations match the writer's own perceptions of the process.

For this activity, write down seven pairs of rhyming words, and then recopy the pairs, alternating words (e.g., *hot, see, not, me*). Next, give your list of rhymes to your partner, and have him or her write lines of poetry, using each word on the list as the final word in a line of the poem.

What did you learn from both observing and being observed as a writer in process?

3. Take yourself through the entire process of writing by taking part in the following activities:

   a. Brainstorm by clustering associations with the topic "writing in school."

   b. Use this cluster to write a first draft of your experiences with writing in school.

   c. Meet with a partner or a small response group. Share your draft by reading it aloud to your group. Receive formative evaluation on your piece, and respond to the writing presented by others in your response group. Make notes about possible changes that might be made in a second draft of your piece.

   d. Revise your draft.

   e. Describe for the entire class your experiences during this activity. Was this a helpful process? Discuss implications for your own teaching.

4. With a small group, create a rubric for primary trait scoring of the "writing in school" assignment in activity 3. Score your written piece using this rubric.

SUGGESTED READINGS

Applebee, A. N. (1981). *Writing in the secondary school: English and the content areas.* Urbana, IL: National Council of Teachers of English.

Atwell, N. (1989). *Coming to know: Writing to learn in the intermediate grades.* Portsmouth, NH: Heinemann.

Azzolino, A. (1990). Writing as a tool for teaching mathematics: The silent revolution. In T. Cooney, & E. Hirsh (Eds.), *Teaching and learning mathematics in the 1990's.* Reston, VA: National Council of Teachers of Mathematics.

Bright, R. (1995). *Writing instruction in the intermediate grades: What is said, what is done, what is understood.* Newark, DE: International Reading Association.

Bromley, K. (1993). *Journaling: Engagements in reading, writing, and thinking.* New York: Scholastic.

Countryman, J. (1992). *Writing to learn mathematics: Strategies that work, K-12.* Portsmouth, NH: Heinemann.

Fazio, B. (1992). Students as historians—writing their school's history. *The Social Studies, 83,* 64–67.

Fulwiler, T. (1987). *Teaching with writing.* Portsmouth, NH: Boynton/Cook.

Gere, A. R. (Ed.) (1985). *Roots in the sawdust: Writing to learn across the curriculum.* Urbana, IL: National Council of Teachers of English.

Irwin, J.W., & Doyle, M. A. (1992). *Reading/writing connections: Learning from research.* Newark, DE: International Reading Association.

Langer, J. A. (1986). Learning through writing: Study skills in the content areas. *Journal of Reading, 29,* 400–406.

Macrorie, K. (1980). *Searching writing.* Rochelle Park, NJ: Hayden.

Martin, N., D'Arcy, P., Newton, B., & Parker, R. (1976). *Writing and learning across the curriculum.* Montclair, NJ: Boynton/Cook.

Maxwell, R. (1996). *Writing across the curriculum in middle and high schools.* Boston: Allyn and Bacon.

Murray, D. (1982). *Learning by teaching.* Montclair, NJ: Boynton/Cook.

Myers, J. (1984). *Writing to learn across the curriculum.* Bloomington, IN: Phi Delta Kappa.

Santa, C., Havens, L., & Harrison, S. (1996). Teaching secondary science through reading, writing, studying, and problem-solving. In D. Lapp, J. Flood, & N. Farnan (Eds.), *Content area reading and learning: Instructional practices* (2nd ed.) (pp. 165–180). Boston: Allyn and Bacon.

Tchudi, S., & Huerta, M. (1983). *Teaching writing in the content areas: Middle school/junior high.* Washington, D.C.: National Education Association.

Tchudi, S., & Tchudi, S. (1983). *Teaching writing in the content areas: Elementary school.* Washington, D.C.: National Education Association.

Tchudi, S., & Yates, J. (1983). *Teaching writing in the content areas: Senior high school.* Washington, D.C.: National Education Association.

Wills, H. (1993). *Writing is learning: Strategies for math, science, social studies and language arts.* Bloomington, IN: Edinfo Press.

Wollman-Bonilla, J. (1991). *Response journals.* New York: Scholastic.

Instructional Strategies: Integrating Literacy and Learning

Vocabulary and Concepts

"I hope you won't take umbrage at what I tell you," she said.
"I never take umbrage," he replied
"Unless, of course, it's lying around, and no one else wants it."
HA! HA! HA! HA!
Okay, on with the story. . .

—Sally of *Peanuts* fame, reading one of her compositions to her classmates

Peanuts reprinted by permission of United Feature Syndicate, Inc.

Organizing Principle

How can anyone take umbrage at Sally's use of the word *umbrage*? She does what all of us do as we come to know words in the context of speaking, listening, writing, and reading. Language learners, like Sally, develop vocabulary and concepts by experimenting with language: using, testing, manipulating, and taking risks with words in different contexts and situations. The more experience and exposure Sally has with unfamiliar words like *umbrage,* the more familiar and meaningful they will become to her.

Such is the case not only for words encountered in everyday discourse but also for words underlying the language of academic disciplines. Vocabulary is as unique to a content area as fingerprints are to a human being. A content area is distinguishable by its language, particularly the special and technical terms that label the concepts undergirding the subject matter. Teachers know they must do something with the language of their content areas, but they often have trouble with what that something should be. Consequently, they reduce instruction to routines that have withstood time and teacher-centered practice, directing students to look up, define, memorize, and use content-specific words in sentences. Such practices divorce the study of vocabulary from an exploration of the subject matter. Learning vocabulary becomes an activity in itself—a separate one—rather than an integral part of learning academic content. The result is lack of awareness of the strong relationship between conceptual knowledge and reading comprehension. Content area vocabulary must be taught *well enough* to remove potential barriers to students' understanding of texts as well as to promote a long-term acquisition of the language of a content area. The organizing principle underscores the main premise of the chapter: **Teaching words well means giving students multiple opportunities to learn how words are conceptually related to one another in the material they are studying.**

Study the chapter overview to get a feel for the major relationships among the key concepts and strategies that we will develop in this chapter. Try to verbalize these relationships by thinking aloud: What do you predict this chapter will be about? What ideas and strategies in the chapter are familiar to you? Somewhat familiar?

Also, take the time to put yourself in a frame of mind that will enable you to approach the chapter purposefully. The "Frame of Mind" questions raise expectations of the content presented in the chapter and will help guide your search for information.

Chapter Overview

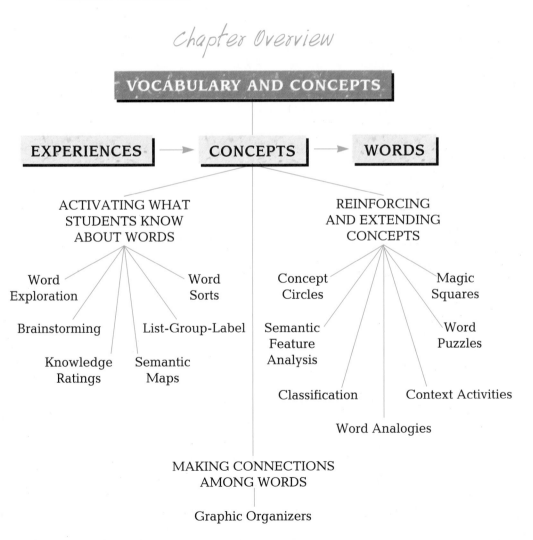

1. Why should the language of an academic discipline be taught within the context of concept development?

2. What are the relationships among experiences, concepts, and words?

3. How can a teacher activate what students know about words and help them make connections among related words?

4. How do activities for vocabulary extension help students refine their conceptual knowledge of special and technical vocabulary?

5. How do activities for vocabulary reinforcement help students associate words and definitions?

Fridays always seemed to be set aside for quizzes when we were students. And one of the quizzes most frequently given was the vocabulary test: "Look up these words for the week. Write out their definitions and memorize them. Then use each word in a complete sentence. You'll be tested on these terms on Friday."

Our vocabulary study seemed consistently to revolve around the dull routines of looking up, defining, and memorizing words and using them in sentences.

Such an instructional pattern resulted in meaningless, purposeless activity—an end in itself, rather than a means to an end. Although there was nothing inherently wrong with looking up, defining, and memorizing words and using them in sentences, the approach itself was too narrow for us to learn words in depth. Instead, we memorized definitions to pass the Friday quiz— and forgot them on Saturday.

Having students learn lists of words is based on the ill-founded conclusion that the acquisition of vocabulary is separate from the development of ideas and concepts in a content area. Teaching vocabulary often means assigning a corpus of words rather than exploring word meanings and relationships that contribute to students' conceptual awareness and understanding of a subject. Once teachers clarify the relationship between words and concepts, they are receptive to instructional alternatives.

One clarification involves the three types of reading vocabulary found in textbooks. The first type, *general vocabulary*, consists of everyday words with widely acknowledged meanings in common usage. The second, *special vocabulary*, is made up of words from everyday vocabulary that take on specialized meanings in a particular content area. The third type, *technical vocabulary*, consists of words that are used *only* in a particular area.

Box 8.1

Vocabulary Demonstration: Words in Content Areas

Directions: In each of the nine blanks, fill in the name of the content area that includes all the terms in the list below the blank.

1. _____

nationalism
imperialism
naturalism
instrumentalism
isolationist
radicalism
fundamentalist
anarchy

2. _____

forestry
ornithology
zoology
biology
entomology
botany
bacteriology
protista

3. _____

metaphor
allusion
irony
paradox
symbolism
imagery
simile

4. _____

prestissimo
adagio
larghetto
presto
allegro
largo
andante
tempo

5. _____

centimeter
milligram
deciliter
millisecond
kilometer
decimeter
kilogram
millimeter

6. _____

graffles
folutes
lesnics
raptiforms
cresnites
hygrolated
loors
chamlets

7. _____

polyunsaturated
glycogen
monosaccharide
hydrogenation
enzymes
lysine
cellulose

8. _____

octagon
hemisphere
decagon
hexagon
bisect
equilateral
quadrilateral
pentagon

9. _____

auricle
ventricle
tricuspid
semilunar
apex
mitral
aorta
myocardium

Special and technical terms are especially bothersome when they're encountered in content material. Your participation in the demonstration in Box 8.1 will illustrate why special and technical terms are likely candidates for vocabulary instruction in content areas. If your responses are similar to those of classroom teachers who have participated in this activity before, several predictable outcomes are likely.

First of all, it is relatively easy for you to identify the content areas for several of the lists. Your knowledge and experience probably trigger instant recognition. You have a good working concept of many of the terms on these easy lists. You can put them to use in everyday situations that require listening, reading, writing, or speaking. They are your words. You own them.

Second, you probably recognize words in a few of the lists even though you may not be sure about the meanings of individual words. In lists 4 and 9, for example, you may be familiar with only one or two terms. Yet you are fairly sure that the terms in lists 4 and 9 exist as words even though you may not know what they mean. Dale (1975) comments that your attitude toward these kinds of words is analogous to your saying to a stranger, "I think I've met you before, but I'm not sure." Several of the words from the lists may be in your "twilight zone"; you have some knowledge of them, but their meanings are a "bit foggy, not sharply focused." *Polyunsaturated* in list 7 is a case in point for some of us who have heard the word used in television commercials and may even have sought polyunsaturated foods at the supermarket. Nevertheless, our guess is that we would be hard pressed to define or explain the meaning of *polyunsaturated* with any precision.

Finally, in one or two cases, a list may have completely stymied your efforts at identification. There is simply no connection between your prior knowledge and any of the terms. You are probably not even sure whether the terms in one list really exist as words.

Which content area did you identify for list 6? In truth, the terms in this list represent nonsense. They are bogus words that were invented to illustrate the point that many of the content terms in textbooks look the same to students as the nonsense words in list 6 look to you. You're able to pronounce most of them with little trouble but are stymied when you try to connect them to your knowledge and experience. Students are stymied this way every day by real words that represent the key concepts of a content area.

Except for list 6, these word lists are actually taken from middle and high school textbooks. Just think for a moment about the staggering conceptual demands we place on learners daily as they go from class to class. Terminology that they encounter in content material is often outside the scope of their normal speaking, writing, listening, and reading vocabularies. Special and technical terms often do not have concrete referents; they are abstract and must be learned through definition, application, and repeated exposure.

Your participation in this demonstration leads to several points about word knowledge and concepts in content areas. The demonstration is a good reminder that every academic discipline creates a unique dialect to represent its important concepts. Teaching vocabulary in content areas is too important to be incidental or accidental. Key concept words need to be taught directly and taught well. Students shouldn't be left to their own devices or subjected to the vagaries of a look-up-and-define strategy as their only access to the long-term acquisition of the language of an academic discipline.

One can learn the definitions of special and technical terms by rote memorization without approaching a conceptual level of understanding. Looking up an unfamiliar word in a dictionary and learning it by rote is a far cry from encountering that word in reading and constructing a meaning for it based on a lifetime of prior knowledge and experience. For example, consider the term *edge.* An edge might be defined as "a 'region of abrupt change in intensity of the pattern of light waves reflected to the eye from a surface.' It should not be supposed that this kind of verbalizing would be very effective in bringing about the learning of a concept" (Gagne 1970, p. 177). Students need to experience how the word *edge* is used in a variety of contexts. They need to become aware that *edge* in this context is related to other words that help define it conceptually. Although students may be able to verbalize a dictionary definition of the word *edge,* their ability to conceptualize it and to apply it in a variety of ways may be limited.

In this chapter, we show how to teach words well in subject matter learning. Teaching words well removes potential barriers to reading comprehension and supports students' long-term acquisition of language in a content area. Teaching words well entails helping students make connections between their prior knowledge and the vocabulary to be encountered in the text and providing them with multiple opportunities to clarify and extend their knowledge of words and concepts during the course of study.

To begin, let's explore the connections that link direct experience to concepts and words. Understanding these connections lays the groundwork for teaching words, with the emphasis on learning concepts. As Anderson and Freebody (1981) suggest, "Every serious student of reading recognizes that the significant aspect of vocabulary development is in the learning of concepts, not just words" (p. 87).

EXPERIENCES, CONCEPTS, AND WORDS

Words are labels—nothing more, nothing less—for concepts. A single concept, however, represents much more than the meaning of a single word. It may take thousands of words to explain a concept. However, answers to the question "What does it mean to know a word?" depend on how well we understand the relationships among personal experiences, concepts, and words.

Concepts are learned through our acting on and interacting with the environment. Students learn concepts best through direct, purposeful experiences. Learning is much more intense and meaningful when it is firsthand. However, in place of using direct experience (which is not always possible), we develop and learn concepts through various levels of contrived or vicarious experience. According to Dale (1969), learning a concept through oral or written language is especially difficult because this kind of learning is so far removed from direct experience.

Concepts create mental images, which may represent anything that can be grouped together by common features or similar criteria: objects, symbols, ideas, processes, or events. In this respect, concepts are similar to schemata.

A concept hardly ever stands alone; instead, it is bound by a hierarchy of relationships. As a result, "most concepts do not represent a unique object or event but rather a general class linked by a common element or relationship" (Johnson & Pearson 1984, p. 33).

Bruner, Goodnow, and Austin (1977) suggest that we would be overwhelmed by the complexity of our environment if we were to respond to each object or event that we encountered as unique. Therefore, we invent categories (or form concepts) to reduce the complexity of our environment and the necessity for constant learning. For example, every feline need not have a different name; each is known as a *cat*. Although cats vary greatly, their common characteristics cause them to be referred to by the same general term. Thus to facilitate communication, we invent words to name concepts.

Consider your concept for the word *ostrich*. What picture comes to mind? Your image of an ostrich might differ from ours, depending on your prior knowledge of the ostrich or the larger class to which it belongs, known as *land birds*. Moreover, your direct or vicarious experiences with birds may differ significantly from someone else's. Nevertheless, for any concept, we organize all our experiences and background knowledge into conceptual hierarchies according to *class, example,* and *attribute* relations.

The concept *ostrich* is part of a more inclusive class or category called *land birds,* which is in turn subsumed under an even larger class of animals known as *warm-blooded vertebrates.* These class relations are depicted in Figure 8.1.

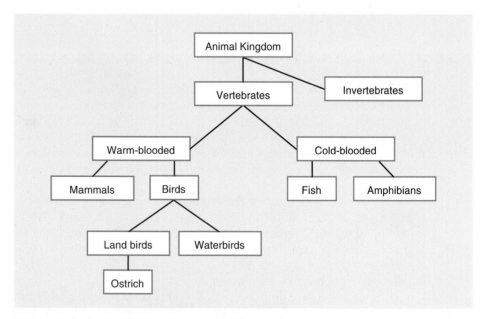

FIGURE 8.1 **Semantic Map Based on Class Relations**

In any conceptual network, class relationships are organized in a hierarchy consisting of superordinate and subordinate concepts. In Figure 8.1, the superordinate concept is *animal kingdom*. *Vertebrates* and *invertebrates* are two classes within the animal kingdom; they are in a subordinate position in this hierarchy. *Vertebrates*, however—divided into two classes, *warm-blooded* and *cold-blooded*—are superordinate to *mammals, birds, fish,* and *amphibians*, which are types or subclasses of vertebrates. The concept *land birds*, subordinate to *birds* but superordinate to *ostrich*, completes the hierarchy.

For every concept, there are examples. An *example* is a member of any concept being considered. A *nonexample*, conversely, is anything not a member of that concept. Class-example relations are complementary: Vertebrates and invertebrates are examples within the *animal kingdom*; mammals, birds, fish, and amphibians are examples of *vertebrates*; land birds are one example of *birds*; and so on.

Let's make *land birds* our target concept. What are some other examples of land birds in addition to the ostrich? *Penguin, emu,* and *rhea* are a few, as shown in Figure 8.2. We could have listed more examples of land birds. Instead, we now ask, "What do the ostrich, penguin, emu, and rhea have in common?" This question allows us to focus on their *relevant attributes*, the features, traits, properties, or characteristics common to every example of a particular group. In this case, the relevant attributes of land birds are the characteristics that determine whether the ostrich, penguin, emu, and rhea belong to the class of birds called *land birds*. An attribute is said to be *critical* if it is a characteristic that is necessary to class membership. An attribute is said to be *variable* if it is shared by some but not all examples of the class. An *irrelevant* attribute is any characteristic not shared by any examples of the class.

Thus we recognize that certain physical and social characteristics are shared by all land birds but that not every land bird has each feature. Virtually all land birds have feathers, wings, and beaks. They hatch from an egg and have two legs. They differ in color, size, habitat, and size of feet. Some

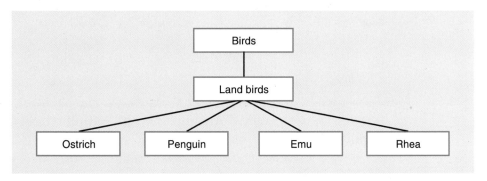

FIGURE 8.2   **Class-Example Relations of the Target Concept** *Land Birds*

land birds fly, and others, with small wings that cannot support their bodies in the air, do not. In what ways is the ostrich similar to other land birds? How is the ostrich different?

This brief discussion of the concept *ostrich* was designed to illustrate an important principle: **Teachers can help students build conceptual knowledge of content area terms by teaching and reinforcing the concept words in relation to other concept words.** This key instructional principle plays itself out in content area classrooms whenever students are actively making connections among the key words in a lesson or unit of study.

MAKING CONNECTIONS AMONG KEY CONCEPTS

At the start of each chapter, we have asked you to organize your thoughts around the main ideas in the text. These ideas are presented within the framework of a *graphic organizer*, a chart that uses content vocabulary to help students anticipate concepts and their relationships to one another in the reading material. These concepts are displayed in an arrangement of key technical terms relevant to the important concepts to be learned.

Graphic organizers may vary in format. One commonly used format to depict the hierarchical relationships among concept words is a tree diagram. Thelen (1982) illustrates a hierarchical arrangement of mathematical concepts having similar attributes and characteristics (see Figure 8.3). The concept *quadrilateral* is subordinate to *polygon*, coordinate to *triangle*, and su-

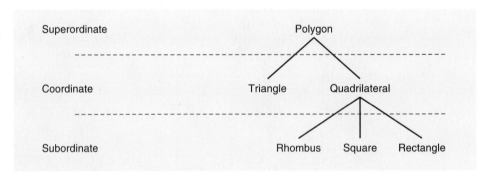

FIGURE 8.3   A Hierarchical Arrangement of Mathematical Concepts with Similar Attributes

Source: From Judith N. Thelan, "Preparing Students for Content Reading Assignments" (March 1992). *Journal of Reading,* 25(6), 544—549. Copyright © 1982 by the International Reading Association. All rights reserved. Used by permission of the author and the International Reading Association.

perordinate to *rhombus, square,* and *rectangle. Polygon* is the most inclusive concept and subsumes all of the others.

Keep in mind, the graphic organizer always shows concepts in relation to other concepts. Let's take a closer look at its construction and application in the classroom.

Constructing Graphic Organizers

Barron (1969) suggests the following steps for developing the graphic organizer and introducing the vocabulary diagram to students:

1. Analyze the vocabulary of the learning task, and list all the words that you feel are important for the student to understand.

2. Arrange the list of words until you have a scheme that shows the interrelationships among the concepts particular to the learning task.

3. Add to the scheme vocabulary terms that you believe the students understand in order to show relationships between the learning task and the discipline as a whole.

4. Evaluate the organizer. Have you clearly shown major relationships? Can the organizer be simplified and still effectively communicate the idea you consider crucial?

5. Introduce the students to the learning task by showing them the scheme, and tell them why you arranged the terms as you did. Encourage them to contribute as much information as possible to the discussion of the organizer.

6. As you complete the learning task, relate new information to the organizer where it seems appropriate.

Suppose you were to develop a graphic organizer for a text chapter in a high school psychology course. Let's walk through the steps involved.

1. *Analyze the vocabulary, and list the important words.* The chapter yields these words:

hebephrenia	neurosis	personality disorders
psychosis	schizophrenia	catatonia
abnormality	mental retardation	phobias

2. *Arrange the list of words.* Choose the word that represents the most inclusive concept, the one superordinate to all the others. Then choose the

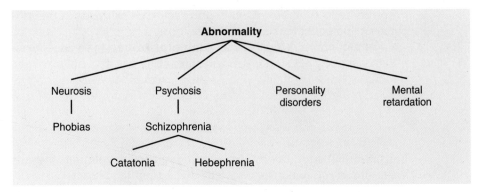

FIGURE 8.4   **Arrangement of Words in a Psychology Text**

words classified immediately under the superordinate concept, and coordinate them with one another. Then choose the terms subordinate to the coordinate concepts. Your diagram may look like Figure 8.4.

3. *Add to the scheme vocabulary terms that you believe the students understand.* You add the following terms: *antisocial, anxiety, intellectual deficit, Walter Mitty, depression, paranoia.* Where would you place these words on the diagram?

4. *Evaluate the organizer.* The interrelationships among the key terms may look like Figure 8.5 once you evaluate the vocabulary arrangement.

5. *Introduce the students to the learning task.* As you present the vocabulary relationships shown on the graphic organizer, create as much discus-

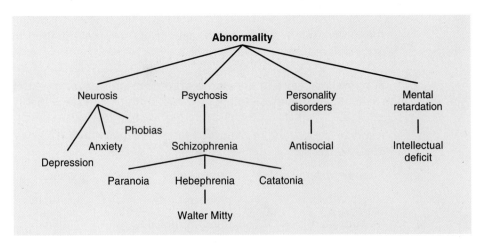

FIGURE 8.5   **Arrangement of Psychology Words After Evaluation of Organizer**

sion as possible. Draw on students' understanding of and experience with the concepts the terms label. You might have students relate previous study to the terms. For example, *Walter Mitty* is subsumed under *hebephrenia.* Students who are familiar with James Thurber's short story "The Secret Life of Walter Mitty" would have little trouble bringing meaning to *hebephrenia:* a schizophrenic condition characterized by excessive daydreaming and delusions. The discussion might also lead to a recognition of the implicit comparison-and-contrast pattern of the four types of abnormality explained in the text. What better opportunity to provide direction during reading than to have students visualize the pattern? The discussions you will stimulate with the organizer will be worth the time it takes to construct it.

6. *As you complete the learning task, relate new information to the organizer.* This step is particularly useful as a study and review technique. The organizer becomes a study guide that can be referred to throughout the discussion of the material. Students should be encouraged to add information to flesh out the organizer as they develop concepts more fully.

Use a graphic organizer to show the relationships in a thematic unit in a chapter or in a subsection of a chapter. The classroom scenario that follows provides further insight into the organizer's utility as a prereading vocabulary activity.

An eighth-grade social studies teacher constructed the organizer in Figure 8.6 for 12 pages of his text. The purpose of the graphic organizer was to introduce students to the propaganda terms used in the textbook. Before having the class read the assigned pages, the teacher placed the organizer on the board and asked students to copy it into their notebooks for future reference. Then he explained that *propaganda* is a word used to describe a way in which people try to change the opinions of others. He gave an example or two and then asked students to contribute other examples. As part of the development of the concept of *propaganda,* with the help and participation of students, he derived explanations of all the methods shown in the organizer.

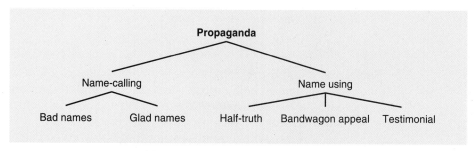

FIGURE 8.6   **A Graphic Organizer for Social Studies**

As these explanations developed, students also saw how each method related to the two categories *name-calling* and *name using.* The explanations that developed are as follows:

1. *Bad names:* calling a person an unpleasant name to make people feel angry or fearful. No facts are given about the person.

2. *Glad names:* calling a person a pleasant name to make people feel good. No facts are given about the person.

3. *Half-truth:* presenting only good or only bad information about something or someone. Only one side of the story is told.

4. *Bandwagon appeal:* telling people that "everyone is doing it" to get them to follow the crowd.

5. *Testimonial:* getting a well-known person to say he or she likes or dislikes something or someone.

The students recorded these definitions in their notebooks. At this point, they began to grasp the difference between methods and started to give examples of propaganda they saw being used in advertising. Then the teacher gave them nine sentences and asked them to identify the propaganda method used in each:

1. "Everyone in town is going to vote for Dan Ray."

2. "The present leaders are criminals and should be put in jail."

3. "She is a noble woman, capable in every way."

4. "As a football player, I know how important it is to use Brand X hair cream."

5. "The young fighter is faster than the champ and will win the fight."

6. "My opponent is a coward, afraid of solving problems."

7. "Before my TV show, I always use Brand X toothpaste."

8. "Come to the fair, and see everyone you know."

9. "The new political party is well organized. It will win the election."

Sentences 2 and 6 prompted considerable discussion about whether the method was bad names, half-truth, or both. After completing this exercise the students read the assigned pages of the text. The reading went rapidly because the students quickly recognized the different methods of propaganda cited in the textbook. The class discussion that followed was lively: the students were confident of their decisions and were eager to share them with their peers. According to the teacher, the lesson had a lasting effect on the

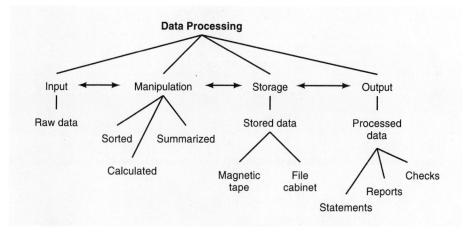

FIGURE 8.7   **A Graphic Organizer for Data Processing**

students: in subsequent lessons not dealing specifically with propaganda, they recognized the use of propaganda and shared it with the rest of the class.

So much for the testimonial of one teacher. As you study the following illustrations, consider the adaptations that you might make when developing a graphic organizer for material in your content area.

The organizer in Figure 8.7 was developed for a high school class in data processing. It introduced students to the different terms of data processing, delineating causes and effects.

An art teacher used Figure 8.8 to show relationships among types of media used in art. She used an artist's palette rather than a tree diagram. After completing the entries for paint and ceramics herself, the teacher challenged her students to brainstorm other media that they had already used or knew about and to provide examples and used the open areas on the palette to record students' associations.

 Graphic organizers are easily adapted to learning situations in the elementary grades. For class presentation, elementary teachers often construct organizers on large sheets of chart paper or on bulletin boards. Other teachers introduce vocabulary for content units by constructing mobiles they hang from the ceiling. Hanging mobiles are an interest-riveting way to attract students' attention to the hierarchical relationships among the words they will encounter. Still other elementary teachers draw pictures with words that illustrate the key concepts under study.

Showing Students How to Make Their Own Connections

Graphic organizers are prereading activities that the teacher constructs to activate prior knowledge and to show students the connections that exist

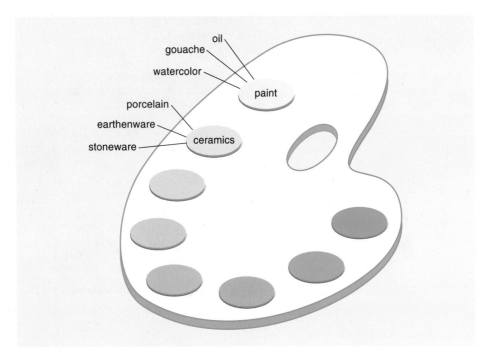

FIGURE 8.8 **A Graphic Organizer for Types of Media in Art**

among the key concepts to be studied. As such, graphic organizers are teacher-centered instructional tools that build a frame of reference for students as they approach new material. In a more student-centered adaptation of the graphic organizer, the students work in cooperative groups and organize important concepts into their own graphic representations.

To make connections effectively, students must have some familiarity with the concepts in advance of their study of the material. In addition, student-constructed graphic organizers presume that the students are aware of the idea behind a graphic organizer. If they are not, you will need to give them a rationale and then model the construction of an organizer. Exposure to teacher-constructed graphic organizers from past lessons will also create awareness and build the students' schema for the technique.

To introduce students to the process of making their own graphic organizers, follow these steps, adapted from Barron and Stone (1973):

1. Type the key words and make photocopies for students.

2. Place students in small groups of two or three students each.

3. Distribute the list of terms and a packet of 3-by-5-inch index cards to each group.

4. Have the students write each word from the list on a card. Then have them work together to decide on a spatial arrangement of the cards that depicts the major relationships among the words.

5. As students work, provide assistance as needed.

6. Initiate a discussion of the constructed organizer.

Before actually assigning a graphic organizer to students, the teacher should prepare for the activity by carefully analyzing the vocabulary of the material to be learned. List all the terms that are essential for students to understand. Then add relevant terms that you feel the students already understand and will help them relate what they know to the new material. Finally, construct your own organizer.

The form of the student-constructed graphic organizer will undoubtedly differ from the teacher's arrangement. However, this difference in and of itself should not be a major source of concern. According to Herber (1978):

> Form is not the issue; substance is, and that is demonstrated by a clear portrayal of the implicit relationships among key words. . . . Students will see things differently [from] teachers and from one another. It is good . . . for the teacher to have thought through his or her own arrangement of the words for purposes of comparison, clarification, and confirmation. (p. 149)

What is important, then, is that the graphic organizer support students' ability to anticipate connections through the key vocabulary terms in content materials.

Seniors in a calculus course participated in the construction of graphic organizers as a way of becoming familiar with key terms in a chapter on logarithmic and exponential functions and so that they were encouraged to make anticipated connections among the terms. The terms included the following:

integration	logarithmic properties
logarithmic differentiation	differentiation
natural exponential function	constructive theorem
log rule	definite integral as a function
logarithmic and exponential functions	mean value theorem for integrals
natural logarithmic function	inverse functions
second fundamental theorem of calculus	

The teacher had the students work in pairs to create a graphic display, assuring them that there were no "right answers." The students had to rely

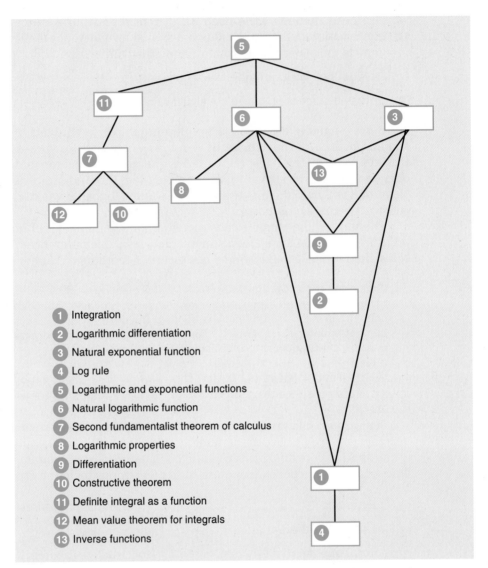

FIGURE 8.9 **A Skeletal Representation of a Graphic Organizer**

on their prior knowledge of logarithmic and exponential functions to anticipate connections. Because of the difficulty of the task, the teacher scaffolded
instruction by providing the students with the skeletal representation shown
in Figure 8.9. Even with the skeletal outline, the students differed in their
representations. These differences created enough healthy dissonance (conceptual conflict) for students to want to clarify the relationships among the
terms. Throughout the discussion of the chapter, the teacher was able to ex-

tend the lesson by referring to the activity when students encountered vocabulary terms that had been used in the organizer.

Graphic organizers activate students' prior knowledge of the vocabulary words in a text selection or unit of study. From a strategy perspective, students need to learn how to ask the question "What do I know about these words?" When you use graphic organizers prior to reading or talking about key concepts, help them build strategy awareness by exploring key terms before reading or discussion. In addition to graphic organizers, there are several instructional activities that you can use to scaffold students' exploration of words.

ACTIVATING WHAT STUDENTS KNOW ABOUT WORDS

Imagine yourself in a tenth-grade biology class in which the teacher assigns for homework a text selection titled "Darwin's Theory of Natural Selection."

In this assignment, you may encounter a variety of scientific terms. For example you come across

natural selection	competition	descendants
organism	necessities	reproduction
survival of the fittest	spores	ancestors
overpopulation	visible universe	spawn
variations	species	maturity
theory	transmit	electrons
offspring	overproduction	

The biology teacher recognizes that the vocabulary of her subject matter can create barriers to reading comprehension, and she could decide to teach the students every technical term that they will encounter in their reading of the Darwin passage. However, she knows that this approach would be impractical, time-consuming, and fairly boring. She could assign the class to look up the words and write out their definitions. But this approach, too, makes little sense to her because she knows that it often leads to rote learning and empty verbalization, which won't meet the needs of text learners. So what are some of her options?

The biology class has already studied changes in living populations through the ages. In fact, a comparison of ancient and modern organisms led to the present unit on theories of evolution. Students in the class can bring a great deal of knowledge to the Darwin passage from previous study as well as from their prior knowledge and experiences. The biology teacher knows the value of activating what the students know so that they can bring that knowledge to their reading.

Several procedures help activate what students know and help them make connections between their existing knowledge and the words they are studying.

Word Exploration

Word exploration is a *writing-to-learn* strategy that works well as a vocabulary activity. Before asking students to make connections between the words and their prior knowledge, the biology teacher asked them to explore what they knew about the concept of *natural selection* by writing in their learning logs.

A word exploration activity invites students to write quickly and spontaneously, a technique called *freewriting,* for no more than five minutes, without undue concern about spelling, neatness, grammar, or punctuation. The purpose of freewriting is to get down on paper everything that students know about the topic or target concept. Students write freely for themselves, not for an audience, so the mechanical, surface features of language, such as spelling, are not important.

Word explorations activate schemata and jog long-term memory, allowing students to dig deep into the recesses of their minds to gather thoughts about a topic. Examine one of the word explorations for the target concept *natural selection:*

> Natural selection means that nature selects—kills off—does away with the weak so only the strong make it. Like we were studying in class last time things get so competive even among us for grades and jobs etc. The homeless are having trouble living with noplace to call home except the street and nothing to eat. That's as good an example of natural selection as I can think of for now.

The teacher has several of the students share their word explorations with the class, either reading them verbatim or talking through what they have written, and she notes similarities and differences in the students' concepts. She then relates their initial associations to the concept and asks the students to make further connections: "How does your personal understanding of the idea *natural selection* fit in with some of the relationships that you see?"

Brainstorming

An alternative to word exploration, brainstorming is a procedure that quickly allows students to generate what they know about a key concept. In brainstorming, the students can access their prior knowledge in relation to the target concept. Brainstorming involves two basic steps that can be adapted easily to content objectives: (1) The teacher identifies a key concept that reflects one of the main topics to be studied in the text, and (2) students work in small groups to generate a list of words related to the concept in a given number of seconds.

These two steps help you discover almost instantly what your students know about the topic they are going to study. Furthermore, Herber (1978) suggests:

> The device of having students produce lists of related words is a useful way to guide review. It helps them become instantly aware of how much they know, individually and collectively, about the topic. They discover quickly that there are no right or wrong answers. . . . Until the students reach the point in the lesson where they must read the passage and judge whether their predictions are accurate, the entire lesson is based on their own knowledge, experience, and opinion. This captivates their interest much more than the more traditional, perfunctory review. (p. 179)

List-Group-Label

Hilda Taba (1967) suggests an extension of brainstorming that she calls "list-group-label." When the brainstorming activity is over, and *lists* of words have been generated by the students, have the class form learning teams to *group* the words into logical arrangements. Then invite the teams to *label* each arrangement. Once the list-group-label activity is completed, ask the students to make predictions about the content to be studied. You might ask, "Given the list of words and groupings that you have developed, what do you think we will be reading and studying about? How does the title of the text (or the thematic unit) relate to your groups of words? Why do you think so?"

A teacher initiated a brainstorming activity with a class of "low-achieving learners." The students, working in small groups, were asked to list in two minutes as many words as possible that were related to the Civil War. Then the groups shared their lists of Civil War words. The teacher then created a master list on the board from the individual entries of the groups. He also wrote three categories on the board—"North," "South," and "Both"—and asked the groups to classify each word from the master list under one of the categories. Here's how one group responded:

NORTH	SOUTH	BOTH
blue	gray	soldiers
Lincoln	farms	armies
Grant	Rebel	guns
factories	Booth	cannons
Yankee	slavery	Gettysburg Address

(continued)

Ford Theater	roots
victory	death
	horses
	assassination

Note that in this example, the teacher provided the categories. He recognized that students needed the additional structure to be successful with this particular task. The activity led to a good deal of discussion and debate. Students were put in the position of "authority," sharing what they knew and believed already with other class members. As a result of the activity, they were asked to raise questions about the Civil War that they wanted to have answered through reading and class discussion.

Semantic Word Maps

Semantic word maps may be used to depict spatial relationships among words. In addition, the use of semantic word maps includes brainstorming and the use of collaborative small groups, and it allows students to cluster words belonging to categories and to distinguish relationships among words. Here's how semantic mapping works:

1. The teacher or the students decide on a key concept to be explored.

2. Once the key concept is determined, the students, depending on what they have been studying and on their background knowledge and experiences, offer as many words or phrases as possible related to the concept term. These are recorded by the teacher on the chalkboard.

Once the list of terms is generated, the teacher may form small groups of students to create semantic maps and then to share their constructions in class discussion. Such was the case in a middle-grade class exploring the concept of *manufacturing*. The semantic map created by one of the small groups in the class is shown in Figure 8.10.

Teachers will need to model the construction of semantic maps once or twice so that students will get a feel for how to develop their own in small groups or individually. In Chapter 10, we will expand on the use of semantic maps as a postreading learning strategy used by students to outline content material as they study texts.

Word Sorts

Like brainstorming, word sorts require students to classify words into categories based on their prior knowledge. However, unlike in brainstorming,

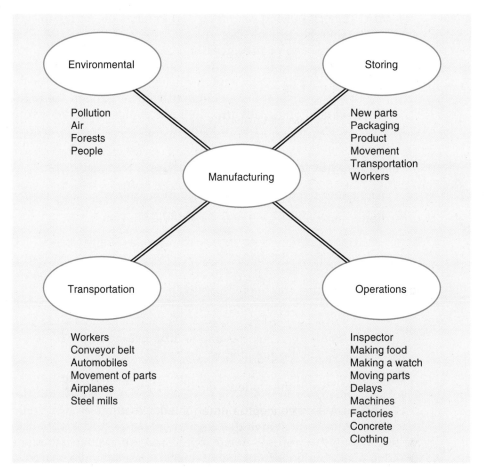

FIGURE 8.10   **A Semantic Map for the Concept** *Manufacturing*

students do not generate a list of words for a target concept. Instead, the teacher identifies the key words from the unit of study and invites the students to sort them into logical arrangements of two or more.

A word sort is a simple yet valuable activity. Individually or in small groups, students literally sort out technical terms that are written on cards or listed on an exercise sheet. The object of word sorting is to group words into different categories by looking for shared features among their meanings. According to Gillet and Kita (1979), a word sort gives students the opportunity "to teach and learn from each other while discussing and examining words together" (pp. 541–542).

Gillet and Kita (1979) also explain that there are two types of word sorts: the open sort and the closed sort. Both are easily adapted to any content area. In the closed sort, students know in advance of sorting what the main categories are. In other words, the criterion that the words in a group must share is stated. The closed sort reinforces and extends the ability to classify words, as we illustrate later in the chapter.

Open sorts prompt divergent and inductive reasoning. No category or criterion for grouping is known in advance of sorting. Students must search for meanings and discover relationships among technical terms without the benefit of any structure. For example, if you were given the following list of names, how many different arrangements could you make by grouping two or more names? You must be able to cite a reason for each arrangement.

George Washington	Susan B. Anthony
Alexander the Great	John F. Kennedy
Rembrandt	Thomas Edison
Christopher Columbus	Charles de Gaulle
Adolf Hitler	Helen Hayes
Julius Caesar	Napoleon
Cleopatra	Albert Einstein
Henry Ford	Margaret Mead

Your arrangements would probably run the gamut from the obvious (men versus women) to the less obvious (names given to foods and cities).

Word sorts can be used before or after reading. Before reading, a word sort serves as an activation strategy to help learners make predictive connections among the words. After reading, word sorts enable students to clarify and extend their understanding of the conceptual relationships.

Study how an art teacher activated what students knew about words associated with pottery making by using the word sort strategy. She asked the high school students to work in collaborative pairs to arrange the following words into possible groups and to predict the concept categories in which the words would be classified:

jordan	lead	Cornwall stone
ball	chrome	cone
antimony	slip	wheel
cobalt	scale	bisque
mortar	kaolin	stoneware
sgraffito	leather	oxidation
roka	hard	

Three categories that students formed were *types of clay*, *pottery tools*, and *coloring agents.*

Knowledge Ratings

Knowledge ratings get readers to analyze what they know about a topic Blachowicz (1986) recommends that the teacher present students with a list of vocabulary in a surveylike format and ask them to analyze each word individually as in the two examples in Figure 8.11.

"How much do you know about these words?"

From a unit on quadratic functions and systems of equations in a high school math class:

	Can Define	Have Seen/Heard	?
Exponent	X		
Intersection	X		
Domain			X
Intercept			X
Slope		X	
Parabola			X
Origin		X	
Vertex		X	
Irrationals	X		
Union		X	
Coefficient		X	

From a newspaper unit in a middle school language arts class:

	A Lot!	Some	Not Much
Wire service		X	
AP		X	
Copy		X	
Dateline	X		
Byline	X		
Caption	X		
Masthead			X
Jumpline			X
Column	X		

FIGURE 8.11   **Two Examples of Knowledge Ratings**

A follow-up discussion might revolve around questions such as these: Which are the hardest words? Which do you think most of the class doesn't know? Which are the easiest ones? Which do most of us know? Students should be encouraged within the context of the discussion to share what they know about the words. In this way, the teacher can get some idea of the knowledge the class brings to the text reading or a larger unit of study.

These procedures are all part of prereading preparation. Naturally, it would be foolhardy to use all of these procedures at one time, but one or two in combination set the stage for students to read with some confidence in their competence with the language of the text.

REINFORCING AND EXTENDING VOCABULARY KNOWLEDGE AND CONCEPTS

When students manipulate technical terms in relation to other terms, they are thinking critically. Vocabulary activities can be designed to give a class the experience of *thinking about, thinking through,* and *thinking with* the technical vocabulary of a subject.

Students need many experiences, real and vicarious, to develop word meanings and concepts. They need to use, test, and manipulate technical terms in instructional situations that capitalize on reading, writing, speaking, and listening. In having students do these things, you will create the kind of natural language environment that is needed to extend vocabulary and concept development.

You can capitalize on the four basic cognitive operations associated with learning concepts and words (Henry 1974). The first is *joining,* or bringing together. Comparing, classifying, and generalizing are examples of joining. When you ask students to explain how words are related or have them sort through word cards to group words together, you are involving them in joining.

Excluding is the second conceptual operation worth considering when you are teaching words in relation to other words. As the operation implies, students must discriminate among or reject items because they do not belong within the conceptual category. In this case, students would search through their background knowledge to distinguish examples from nonexamples or relevant attributes from irrelevant attributes as we did with the ostrich example earlier in this chapter.

The third conceptual activity or operation is *selecting.* Students simply learn to make choices and to explain why based on what they experience, know, or understand. Synonyms, antonyms, and multiple-meaning words lend themselves well to selecting.

The fourth aspect of thinking conceptually is *implying.* Are your students able to make decisions based on if-then, cause-and-effect relations among concept and words? Dupuis and Snyder (1983) suggest that implying is such a complex cognitive activity that it actually requires a combination of joining, excluding, and selecting.

As a rule of thumb, reinforcing and extending vocabulary should be completed individually by students and then discussed either in small groups or in the class as a whole. The oral interaction in team learning gives more students a chance to use terms. Students can exchange ideas, share insights, and justify responses in a nonthreatening situation. Barron and Earle (1973) suggest the following procedures for small-group discussion of reinforcement activities:

1. End small-group discussion only after the group has discussed each answer and every member of the group understands the reasons for each answer.

2. Encourage the active participation of all group members. A student who has trouble with a particular exercise can still make a valuable contribution by asking questions or asking someone to explain answers.

3. Limit talk to the particular exercise or to related questions.

4. Make sure that students use the words and their meanings in discussing the answers, rather than using letters and numbers (for example, avoid "I think the answer to number 1 is *c*").

Semantic Feature Analysis (SFA)

SFA establishes a meaningful link between students' prior knowledge and words that are conceptually related to one another. The strategy requires that you develop a chart or grid to help students analyze similarities and differences among the related concepts. As the SFA grid in Figure 8.12 illustrates, a topic or category (in this case, properties of quadrilaterals) is selected, words related to that category are written across the top of the grid, and features or properties shared by some of the words in the column are listed down the left side of the grid.

Students analyze each word, feature by feature, writing Y (yes) or N (no) in each cell of the grid to indicate whether the feature is associated with the word. Students may use a question mark (?) to suggest uncertainty about a particular feature.

As a teaching activity, SFA is easily suited to prereading or postreading. If you used it for prereading to activate what students know about words, recognize that they can return to the SFA after reading to clarify and reformulate some of their initial responses on the SFA grid.

Classification and Categorization

Closed word sorts enable students to study words by requiring them to classify terms in relation to more general concepts. Examine how a business

Directions: Determine which of these properties are found in the four quadrilaterals listed. Mark "Y" or "N" in each box.

	Parallelogram	Rectangle	Rhombus	Square
Diagonals bisect each other.				
Diagonals are congruent.				
Each diagonal bisects a pair of opposite angles.				
Diagonals form two pairs of congruent triangles.				
Diagonals form four congruent triangles.				
Diagonals are perpendicular to each other.				

FIGURE 8.12   **An SFA for Geometry**

teacher helped extend students' knowledge of concepts from an assignment on types of resources. He directed the class to classify a list of terms under the three types of resources that they had read about: natural resources, capital resources, and human resources.

tools	machinery	tractors
minerals	trees	typewriters
water	wildlife	power plants
labor	factories	buildings

Vocabulary extension exercises involving categorization require students to determine relationships among technical terms much as word sorts do. The difference lies in the amount of structure students are given to make cognitive decisions. Put another way, students are usually given four to six words per grouping and asked to do something with them. That something depends on the format used in the exercise. For example, you can give students sets of words and ask them to circle in each set the word that includes the others. This exercise demands that students perceive common attributes or examples in relation to a more inclusive concept and to distinguish superordinate from subordinate terms. Here are several sample exercises from different content areas.

SOCIAL STUDIES

Directions: Circle the word in each group that includes the others.

1. government
   council
   judges
   governor

2. throne
   coronation
   crown
   church

ENGLISH

Directions: Circle the word in each group that best includes the others.

1. satire
   humor
   irony
   parody

2. humor
   satire
   irony
   tone

GEOMETRY

Directions: Circle the word in each group that includes the others.

1. closure
   distributive
   property
   associative
   commutative

2. function
   domain
   range
   relation
   preimage

A variation on this format directs students to cross out the word that does not belong and then to explain in a word or phrase the relationship that exists among the common items.

ENGLISH

Directions: Cross out the word in each set that does not belong. On the line above the set, write the word or phrase that explains the relationship among the remaining three words.

1. _____
   drama
   comedy
   epic
   tragedy

2. _____
   time
   character
   place
   action

Concept Circles

One of the most versatile activities we have observed at a wide range of grade levels is the concept circle. Concept circles provide still another format and opportunity for studying words critically—for students to relate words conceptually to one another. A concept circle may simply involve putting words or phrases in the sections of a circle and directing students to describe or name the concept relationship among the sections. The example in Figure 8.13 is from a middle-grade science lesson.

In addition, you might direct students to shade in the section of a concept circle containing a word or phrase that *does not relate* to the words or phrases in the other sections of the circle and then identify the concept relationships that exist among the remaining sections (see Figure 8.14).

Finally, you can modify a concept circle by leaving one or two sections of the circle empty, as in Figure 8.15. Direct students to fill in the empty section with a word or two that relates in some way to the terms in the other sections of the concept circles. Students must then justify their word choice by identifying the overarching concept depicted by the circle.

As you can see, concept circles serve the same function as categorization activities. However, students respond positively to the visual aspect of manipulating the sections in a circle. Whereas categorization exercises sometimes seem like tests to students, concept circles are fun to do.

Word Analogies

Word analogies trigger critical thinking about relationships. An analogy is actually a comparison of two similar relationships: "On one side the objects are related. On the other side the objects are related in the same way. Like a mathematical equation, an analogy has equal or balanced sides" (Bellows 1980, p. 509). Students who are not familiar with the format of an analogy may have trouble reading it successfully. Therefore, teachers should give a short demonstration or two to walk students through the reading and reasoning process involved in completing an analogy.

For example, a science teacher might write on the chalkboard: "Eating: humans::photosynthesis:_____." The teacher can then point out that the colon (:) stands for *is to* and the double colon (::) stands for *as*. The class reads aloud, "Eating is to humans as photosynthesis is to _____." The students should be encouraged to complete the analogy and to explain the relationship between the items in each pair. In doing so, they will transform "Eating is to humans as photosynthesis is to plants" into a new thought pattern that may go something like this: Humans can't survive without eating, and plants can't survive without photosynthesis. Or eating and photosynthesis are essential life-sustaining processes for humans and plants, respectively.

Many types of analogies can be constructed. Several useful types for content areas are listed in Figure 8.16. Try your hand at completing each analogy by underlining the term that fits best in each blank space.

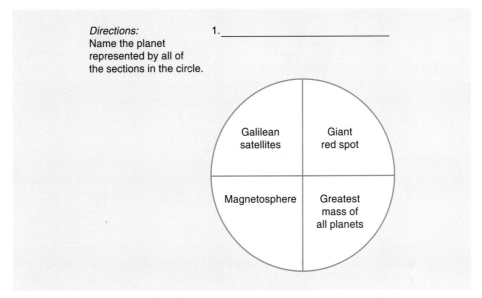

FIGURE 8.13   **An Example of the Concept Circle**

Context- and Definition-Related Activities

Artley (1975) captured the role that context plays in vocabulary learning: "It is the context in which the word is embedded rather than the dictionary that gives it its unique flavor" (p. 1072). Readers who build and use contextual knowledge are able to recognize fine shades of meaning in the way words

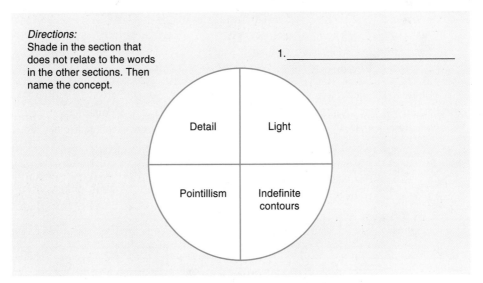

FIGURE 8.14   **A Variation on the Concept Circle**

Directions:
Add an additional
example to the circle,
and then name the
concept depicted by
the circle.

Name _____

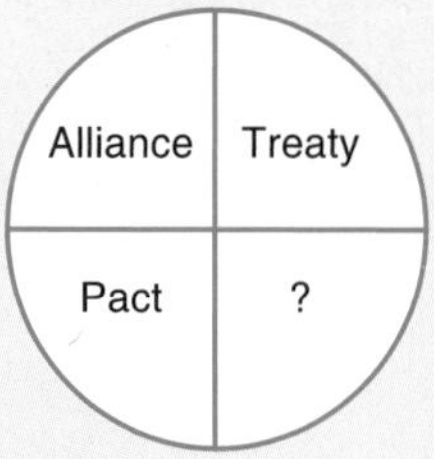

Alliance | Treaty

Pact | ?

FIGURE 8.15   **Another Variation on the Concept Circle**

are used. They know the concept behind the word well enough to use that concept in different contexts. First, we suggest several ways to reinforce and extend a student's contextual knowledge of content area terms. Then we move on to techniques to help students inquire into the meaning of an unknown word by using its context.

Modified Cloze Passages

Cloze passages (discussed in Chapter 5) can be created to reinforce technical vocabulary. However, the teacher usually modifies the procedure for teach-

1. *Part to whole*
   Clutch : transmission :: key : _____
   (starter, engine, exhaust)

2. *Person to situation*
   Lincoln : slavery :: _____ : independence
   (Jefferson, Kennedy, Jackson)

3. *Cause and effect*
   CB : radio reception :: television:_____
   (eating, homework, gym)

4. *Synonym*
   Bourgeoisie : middle class :: proletariat:_____
   (upper class, lower class, royalty)

5. *Antonym*
   Pinch : handful :: sip:_____
   (pet, gulp, taste)

6. *Geography*
   Everest : Matterhorn :: _____ Alps
   (Ozarks, Andes, Himalayas)

7. *Measurement*
   Minutes : clock :_____: temperature
   (liters, degrees, gradations)

8. *Time*
   24 hours : rotation :: 365 days:_____
   (Eastern Time, revolution, axis)

FIGURE 8.16   **Common Types of Analogies**

ing purposes. Every *n*th word, for example, needn't be deleted. The modified cloze passage will vary in length. Typically, a 200- to 500-word text segment yields sufficient technical vocabulary to make the activity worthwhile.

Should you consider developing a modified cloze passage on a segment of text from a reading assignment, make sure that the text passage is one of the most important parts of the assignment. Depending on your objectives, students can supply the missing words either before or after reading the entire assignment. If they work on the cloze activity before reading, use the subsequent discussion to build meaning for key terms and to raise expectations for the assignment as a whole. If you assign the cloze passage after reading, it will reinforce concepts attained through reading.

On completing a short lecture on the causes of the Civil War, an American history teacher assigned a cloze passage before students read the entire introduction for homework. See how well you fare on the first part of the exercise.

> *What caused the Civil War? Was it inevitable? To what extent and in what ways was slavery to blame? To what extent was each region of the nation at fault? Which were more decisive—the intellectual or the emotional issues?*
>
> Any consideration of the (1) of the war must include the problem of (2). In his second inaugural address, Abraham Lincoln said that slavery was "somehow the cause of the war." The critical word is "(3)." Some (4) maintain that the moral issue had to be solved, the nation had to face the (5), and the slaves had to be (6). Another group of historians asserts that the war was not fought over (7). In their view, slavery served as an (8) focal point for more fundamental (9) involving two different (10) of the Constitution. All of these views have merit, but no single view has won unanimous support.

(Answers can be found at the end of this chapter.)

OPIN

OPIN is a meaning-extending vocabulary strategy developed by Frank Greene of McGill University. OPIN provides another example of context-based reinforcement and extension. *OPIN* stands for *opinion* and also plays on the term *cloze*.

Here's how OPIN works. Divide the class into groups of three. Distribute exercise sentences, one to each student. Each student must complete each exercise sentence individually. Then each group member must convince the other two members that his or her word choice is the best. If no agreement is reached on the best word for each sentence, each member of the group can speak to the class for his or her individual choice. When all groups have finished, have the class discuss each group's choices. The only rule of discussion is that each choice must be accompanied by a reasonable defense or justification. Answers like "Because ours is best" are not acceptable.

OPIN exercise sentences can be constructed for any content area. Here are sample sentences from science, social studies, and home economics:

SCIENCE

1. A plant's _____ go into the soil.

2. The earth gets heat and _____ from the sun.

3. Some animals, such as birds and _____, are nibblers.

SOCIAL STUDIES

1. We cannot talk about _____ in America without discussing the welfare system.

2. The thought of _____ or revolution would be necessary because property owners would fight to hold on to their land.

3. Charts and graphs are used to _____ information.

HOME ECONOMICS

1. Vitamin C is _____ from the small intestine and circulates to every tissue.

2. Washing time for cottons and linens is eight to ten minutes unless the clothes are badly _____.

(Answers can be found at the end of the chapter.)

OPIN encourages differing opinions about which word should be inserted in a blank space. In one sense, the exercise is open to discussion, and as a result, it reinforces the role of prior knowledge and experiences in the decisions that each group makes. The opportunity to "argue" one's responses in the group leads not only to continued motivation but also to a discussion of word meanings and variations.

Context Puzzles

As we have suggested, context reinforcement encourages students to make decisions about key concept words. They must be able to recognize or apply technical terms in a meaningful context. Context reinforcement is valuable because it reinforces and extends an important skill (using context to get meaning) as well as an understanding of vocabulary terms.

Note the puzzle format used by a language arts teacher as she gave students structural clues that must be combined with context clues provided in the sentences:

Directions: Think of a word we have recently studied that fits in the blank space in each sentence below and has the same number of letters as the number of spaces provided in the corresponding line. Fill in the word on the line.

1. H __ __ D R __ __

2. A __ __ __ __ Y

3. __ __ __ U I

4. __ __ __ C O N __ __ __ __ __

5. __ O __ __ __ __

6. __ O M __ __ __

1. Charlie Brown tried to give up his _____ existence and lead a life of adventure.

2. Snoopy was in a state of _____ for weeks, showing no interest in anything.

3. Lucy showed her _____ by yawning throughout the baseball game.

4. The serious illness of Linus's grandmother left him _____; no one could comfort him.

5. The _____ in her expression was the very image of grief.

6. Such a _____ expression seems out of place on a young child.

In contrast to the puzzle format, examine several items from a high school English teacher's context reinforcement activity for his students. The teacher selected the sentences from several short stories that the class had read.

Directions: The sentences below are taken from the short stories we are studying for this unit. Using the context clues in these sentences, see if you can figure out the meanings of the italicized words. Then record the clues that helped you determine the meaning of the word.

	MEANING	CLUES
1. After hitting the ground, Arvil rose with a slightly *vexed* expression.	_____	_____
2. Because I muffed the winning point, my teammates looked at me *truculently*.	_____	_____
3. Although he had eaten well the last few months, the years of eating just enough to survive made the dog *puny* in size.	_____	_____
4. The house too was *grotesque*, painted gray, its gables hung with daggerlike icicles.	_____	_____
5. In no hurry, I *sauntered* through Grant Park, observing the people as well as the flowers.	_____	_____
6. Usually we don't like people *meddling* with our personal business.	_____	_____
7. Having traveled all the world and lived all sorts of lifestyles, he was not bound to *provincial* ideas.	_____	_____

Word Definition Puzzles

Word puzzles are helpful in reinforcing definitions. One of the best uses of these vocabulary exercises is to associate technical terms with more familiar words that convey meaning. For example, as part of a unit on geography, a social studies teacher developed a vocabulary-matching activity to help students associate technical terms in the text material with known synonyms and more familiar language. The class first completed the exercise individually and then discussed it in small groups before reading the text material.

Technical terms with multiple meanings pose problems for maturing readers. A math teacher anticipated the problem of meeting multiple-meaning words in a geometry unit she had organized. She prepared students to work with these terms through an exercise in multiple meanings.

As in the previous example, class discussion preceded reading. The math students quickly recognized that a given geometry term can refer to a different concept or different concepts outside mathematics. Here are two examples from the exercise:

1. mean   (a) signify, (b) average, (c) bad-tempered
2. point   (a) sharp end, (b) something that has a position but is not extended, (c) place or spot

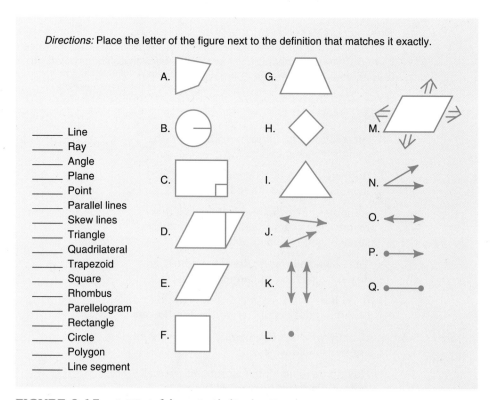

Directions: Place the letter of the figure next to the definition that matches it exactly.

_____ Line
_____ Ray
_____ Angle
_____ Plane
_____ Point
_____ Parallel lines
_____ Skew lines
_____ Triangle
_____ Quadrilateral
_____ Trapezoid
_____ Square
_____ Rhombus
_____ Parellelogram
_____ Rectangle
_____ Circle
_____ Polygon
_____ Line segment

FIGURE 8.17   **A Matching Activity in Geometry**

In addition to their value as definitional tasks, matching activities can reinforce technical vocabulary by helping students make visual associations. Notice in the example in Figure 8.17 how a math teacher reinforced technical terms from a geometry unit by having students match them with their visual counterparts.

Magic Squares

The magic square activity is by no means new or novel, yet it has a way of reviving even the most mundane matching exercise. We have seen the magic square used successfully in elementary and secondary grades as well as in graduate courses. Here's how a magic square works. An activity sheet has

Directions: Select the best answer for each of the laundering terms from the numbered definitions. Put the number in the proper space in the magic square box. If the total of the numbers are the same both across and down, you have found the magic number!

Terms

A. Durable press
B. Soil release
C. Water repellent
D. Flame retardant
E. Knitted fabrics
F. Simulated suede leather
G. Pretreating
H. Sorting
I. Care labeling

Definitions

1. Federal Trade Commission ruling that requires permanently attached fabric care instructions.
2. Fabric must maintain finish for up to 50 machine washings.
3. Ability to protect against redeposition of soil on fabrics.
4. Turn inside out to avoid snags.
5. Resists stains, rain, and dampness.
6. Special treatment of spots and stains before washing.
7. Resists wrinkling during wear and laundering.
8. Separate clothes into suitable washloads.
9. Washable suede-like fabric made from polyester.

Answer Box

A	B	C
D	E	F
G	H	I

Magic number = _____

FIGURE 8.18   **Magic Square on Care of Clothing**

two columns, one for content area terms and one for definitions or other distinguishing statements such as characteristics or examples (see Figure 8.18). Direct students to match terms with definitions. In doing so, they must take into account the letters signaling the terms and the numbers signaling the definitions. The students then put the number of a definition in the proper space (denoted by the letter of the term) in the "magic square answer box." If their matchups are correct, they will form a magic square. That is, the numerical total will be the same for each row across and each column down the answer box. This total forms the puzzle's "magic number." Students need to add up the rows and columns to check if they're coming up with the same number each time. If not, they should go back to the terms and definitions to reevaluate their answers.

The magic square exercise in Figure 8.18 is from a home economics class. Try it. Its magic number is 15. Analyze the mental maneuvers that you went through to determine the correct number combinations. In some cases, you undoubtedly knew the answers outright. You may have made several educated guesses on others. Did you try to beat the number system? Imagine the possibilities for small-group interaction.

Many teachers are intrigued by the possibilities offered by the magic square, but they remain wary of its construction: "I can't spend hours figuring out number combinations." This is a legitimate concern. Luckily, the eight combinations in Figure 8.19 make magic square activities easy to con-

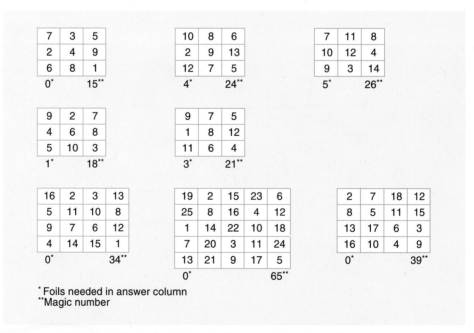

* Foils needed in answer column
** Magic number

FIGURE 8.19   **A Model of Magic Square Combinations**

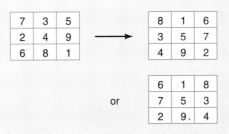

FIGURE 8.20   **Variations on Magic Square Combinations**

struct. You can generate many more combinations from the eight patterns simply by rearranging rows or columns (see Figure 8.20).

Notice that the single asterisk in Figure 8.19 denotes the number of foils or distractors needed so that several of the combinations can be completed. For example, the magic number combination of 18 requires one foil in the number 1 slot that will not match with any of the corresponding items in the matching exercise. To complete the combination, the number 10 is added. Therefore, when you develop a matching activity for combination 18, there will be ten items in one column and nine in the other, with item 1 being the foil.

Puzzles such as those described here are popular devices for reinforcing word meanings. A number of word puzzle formats work well to provide added recall and recognition of key terms.

 LOOKING BACK, LOOKING FORWARD

A strong relationship exists between vocabulary knowledge and reading comprehension. In this chapter, we provided numerous examples of what it means to teach words well: giving students multiple opportunities to build vocabulary knowledge, to learn how words are conceptually related to one another, and to learn how they are defined contextually in the material that students are studying. Vocabulary activities provide students the multiple experiences they need to use and manipulate words in differing situations. Conceptual and definitional activities provide the framework needed to study words critically. Various types of concept extension activities, such as semantic feature analysis, semantic maps, concept of definition, word sorts, categories, concept circles, word puzzles, and magic squares, reinforce and extend students' abilities to perceive relationships among the words they are studying.

In the next chapter, our emphasis turns to kindling student interest in text assignments and preparing them to think positively about what they will read. The importance of the role of prereading preparation in learning from text has often been neglected or underestimated in the content area classroom. Yet prereading activity is in many ways as important to the text learner as warm-up preparation is to the athlete. Let's find out why.

MINDS-ON

1. A few of your students come to you and ask why they aren't using dictionaries to help them learn vocabulary words as they did last year. What is your response? Justify your response.

2. Each of the following statements should be randomly assigned to members of your group. Your task with your drawn statement is to play the "devil's advocate." Imagine that you are in a conference with your child's teachers, represented by the other members of your discussion group. One member of the teaching team makes the statement you've selected, and you totally disagree. Argue to these teachers why you feel this statement is false. Members of the teaching team must respond with counter-arguments, using classroom examples for support whenever possible.

   a. Students who are interested and enthusiastic are more likely to learn the vocabulary of a content area subject.

   b. Students need to know how to inquire into the meanings of unknown words by using context analysis and dictionary skills.

   c. An atmosphere for vocabulary reinforcement is created by activities involving speaking, listening, writing, and reading.

   d. Vocabulary reinforcement provides opportunities for students to increase their knowledge of the technical vocabulary of a subject.

   e. Vocabulary taught and reinforced within the framework of concept development enhances reading comprehension.

   f. Vocabulary knowledge and reading comprehension have a strong relationship.

   Were there any statements that you had difficulty defending? If so, pose these to the class as a whole, and solicit perspectives from other groups.

3. Your principal notices that your history class spends a lot of time working in pairs and groups on vocabulary, and she doesn't see why this is neces-

sary "just to learn words." As a group, compose a letter to her explaining the importance of student interaction in learning the vocabulary of any content area.

HANDS-ON

1. The class should be organized into four groups. Two groups will represent alien life forms, and two will represent human beings. Each group meets for 15 to 20 minutes. Working separately, each alien group will create five or six statements in their own "alien" language. The humans will organize strategies for decoding the messages they will receive.

   After the time has elapsed, each alien group meets with a human group, and the aliens make their statements. If possible, the aliens will attempt to respond to the humans' questions with key words or phrases. Next, with the alien and human groups switched, the process is repeated. Finally, as a whole class, discuss your success or lack of success in translating in relation to what you have learned about vocabulary and concepts.

2. Examine the following list of vocabulary words taken from this chapter:

general vocabulary	conceptual level
technical vocabulary	concept circles
special vocabulary	word analogies
concept	OPIN
word sorts (open, closed)	context puzzles
brainstorming	word puzzles
semantic word maps	magic squares
knowledge ratings	prior knowledge
syntactic and semantic contextual aids	target concept
semantic feature analysis	cognitive operations
freewriting	joining
modified cloze passages	excluding
context	selecting
comprehension	implying

   Team with three other members of the class, and with this list of words, each create one of the following:

a. Two conceptually related activities such as a set of concept circles and a closed word sort

b. A context activity that presents the key concept words in meaningful sentence contexts

c. A semantic word map or a semantic feature analysis

Follow this activity with a discussion of the advantages and disadvantages of each approach and of the appropriate time during a unit to use each.

Answers to cloze passage: 1. causes, 2. slavery, 3. somehow, 4. historians, 5. crisis, 6. freed, 7. slavery, 8. emotional, 9. issues, 10. interpretations.
Possible answers to OPIN exercises: Science: 1. roots, 2. radiation, 3. rodents; Social Studies: 1. poverty, 2. violence, 3. organize; Home Economics: 1. absorbed, 2. soiled.

SUGGESTED READINGS

Baumann, J., & Kameenui, E. (1991). Research on vocabulary instruction: Ode to Voltaire. In J. Flood, J. M. Jensen, D. Lapp, & J. R. Squire (Eds.), *Handbook of research on teaching the English language arts.* New York: Macmillan.

Buikema, J., & Graves, M. (1993). Teaching students to use context clues to infer work meanings. *Journal of Reading, 36,* 450–457.

Blachowicz, C. L. Z. (1991). Vocabulary instruction in content classes for special needs learners: Why and how? *Reading, Writing, and Learning Disabilities, 7,* 297–308.

Blachowicz, C. L. Z., & Fisher, P. J. L. (1994). Vocabulary instruction: In A. C. Purves, *Encyclopedia of English studies and language arts.* New York: Scholastic.

Blachowicz, C. L. Z., & Fisher, P. J. L. (1996). *Teaching vocabulary in all classrooms.* Columbus, OH: Merrill.

Graves, M. F., & Slater, W. (1996). Vocabulary instruction in content areas. In D. Lapp, J. Flood, & N. Farnan (Eds.), *Content area reading and learning: Instructional strategies.* Needham Heights, MA: Allyn & Bacon.

Heimlich, J. E., & Pittelman, S. D. (1986). *Semantic mapping: Classroom applications.* Newark, DE: International Reading Association.

Kibbey, M. (1995). The organization and teaching of things and the words that signify them. *Journal of Adolescent and Adult Literacy, 39,* 208–223.

Marzano, R., & Marzano, J. (1988). *A cluster approach to elementary vocabulary instruction.* Newark, DE: International Reading Association.

McKeown, M. (1985). The acquisition of word meaning from context by children of high and low ability. *Reading Research Quarterly, 20,* 482–496.

McKeown, M., Beck, I., Omanson, R., & Pople, M. (1985). Some effects of the nature and frequency of vocabulary instruction on the knowledge and use of words. *Reading Research Quarterly, 20,* 222–235.

Nagy, W. E. (1988). *Teaching vocabulary to improve reading comprehension.* Newark, DE: International Reading Association.

Ruddell, M. R. (1994). Vocabulary knowledge and comprehension: A comprehension-process view of complex literacy relationships. In R. B. Ruddell, M. R. Ruddell, & H. Singer (Eds.), *Theoretical models and processes of reading* (4th ed.). Newark, DE: International Reading Association.

Ryder, R. (1985). Student-activated vocabulary instruction. *Journal of Reading, 28,* 254–259.

Scott, J. A., & Nagy, W. E. (1994). Vocabulary development. In A. C. Purves, *Encyclopedia of English studies and language arts.* New York: Scholastic.

Stahl, S. (1986). Three principles of effective vocabulary instruction. *Journal of Reading, 29,* 662–668.

Prior Knowledge and Interest

When the student is ready, the teacher appears.
—Anonymous

Organizing Principle

More often than not, content area teachers are perplexed by the behavior of learners who are capable of acquiring content through lecture, discussion, and other modes of classroom presentation but appear neither ready nor willing to learn with texts. The wisdom in the saying "When the student is ready, the teacher appears" is self-evident, yet teachers who want to use texts often find themselves waiting in the wings to make their appearance and wondering, "*When* is the student ready?"

Certainly, preparing students for the language of a content area, as we discussed in Chapter 8, readies them for learning with texts. The more learners connect what they know to the vocabulary of a content area, the more familiar and confident they are likely to be with the material being studied. To be ready is surely a state of mind, a mental preparation for learning, a psychological predisposition. But content area teachers know that readiness also entails an emotional commitment, an emotional stake in the ideas under scrutiny in an academic content area, and a willingness on the part of the students to *want* to engage in learning. Most students, we believe, would like to use reading to learn but don't believe that they have much chance of success. So some find any excuse to avoid reading. Others go through the motions— reading the assigned material purposelessly—to satisfy the teacher's requirements rather than their own as learners.

When are students ready? We're tempted to say, When they are willing. Students *will* want to read to learn, first and foremost, when they have developed a sense of confidence with texts. Ability alone is no guarantee that students will use reading to learn. Neither is knowledge of the subject. Competence and confidence go together like Astaire and Rogers or Laurel and Hardy. As Virgil, the ancient Roman poet, affirmed, all things are within the realm of human possibility when people have confidence in their ability to succeed. "They can," Virgil mused, "because they think they can."

Confident readers think and learn with texts, and they also think positively about the process of learning with texts. They generate interest in the task at hand; their goals are in front of them. If there is an imperative in this chapter, it is to kindle student interest in text assignments and prepare them to think positively about what they will read.

Preparing students to read can easily be neglected in a teacher's rush to cover the content of the curriculum. Yet the payoffs of prereading activation, as suggested in the organizing principle of the chapter, will make your efforts worthwhile: **Piquing interest in and raising expectations about the meaning of texts create a context in which students will read with purpose and anticipation.**

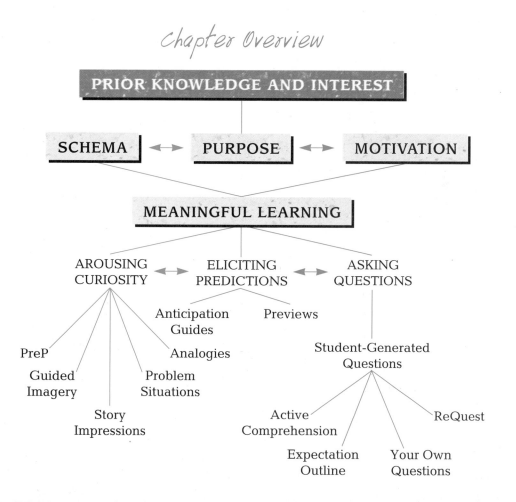

Chapter Overview

Frame of Mind

1. Why does activating prior knowledge and interest prepare students to approach text reading in a critical frame of mind?

2. How can meaningful learning be achieved with content area reading?

3. What are the relationships among curiosity arousal, conceptual conflict, and motivation?

4. How and why do prediction strategies such as previews and anticipation guides facilitate reading comprehension?

5. What is the value of student-generated questions, and how might teachers help students ask questions as they read?

6. Which prereading strategies seem to be the most useful in your content area? Least useful? Why?

Explanations of reading tend to be complex. Yet as intricate a process as reading may be, it's surely just as magical and mysterious to most of us. After all, who ever really knows a covert process—one that takes place in the head?

Huey (1908) tells a fascinating tale about the adventurer David Livingstone in Africa:

> Livingstone excited the wonder and awe of an African tribe as he daily perused a book that had survived the vicissitudes of travel. So incomprehensible, to these savages, was his performance with the book, that they finally stole it and *ate* it, as the best way they knew of "reading" it, of getting the white man's satisfaction from it. (p. 2)

The preliterate natives wanted what Livingstone had. They were so motivated by his sense of pleasure and satisfaction with texts that they wanted to exercise some control over the rather mystical and mysterious process of which they had little concept. So they acted in the only way they knew how. Eating Livingstone's book was a somewhat magical response to their uncertainty and lack of control over the process that we call reading. Teachers should be so fortunate as to have students who want to devour texts, metaphorically speaking, in the pursuit of knowledge!

Magic and uncertainty go hand in hand. According to Malinowski (1954), people resort to magic in situations where they feel they have limited control over the success of their activities. This is so in primitive cultures or in highly technological societies such as ours.

We believe an element of mystery will always be a part of reading, even though it appears to be second nature to many of us. For most teachers, reading just happens, particularly when there is a strong purpose or a need to read in the first place. However, a great deal of uncertainty pervades reading for many students. The reading process remains a mystery, a lot of hocus-pocus, to students who believe they have limited control over their chances of success with a reading assignment.

As a result, some students resort to a special kind of "magic" to achieve control over the information and concepts communicated in a text. Magic, in this case, often involves bypassing the text altogether. In its place, students may resort to memorizing class notes, reading Cliffs Notes summaries, or praying for an easy exam that doesn't require text reading.

You can do a great deal to reduce the lack of control and the uncertainty that students bring to text learning situations. You can take the mystery out of learning with texts by generating students' interest in what they are reading, convincing them that they know more about the subject under study than they think they do, helping them actively connect what they do know to the content of the text, and making them aware of the strategies they need in order to construct meaning.

The challenge content area teachers face with reading to learn is not necessarily related to students' inability to handle the conceptual and stylistic demands of academic texts. What students can do and what they choose to do are related but different instructional matters. Therefore, you need to create conditions that not only allow students to read effectively but also motivate them to want to read purposefully and meaningfully.

MEANINGFUL LEARNING, SCHEMA, AND MOTIVATION

Return to the questions: When is the student ready to read? To learn with texts? First, recognize that readiness is a conditional concept. *If,* for example, learning is to be meaningful, students must approach a reading task with purpose and commitment. Bruner (1970), a pioneer in the psychology of the mind, suggested that the mind doesn't work apart from feeling and commitment. The learner makes meaning when he or she exhibits an "inherent passion" for what is to be learned. That is to say, *if* knowledge is to be constructed, it must be put into a context of action and commitment. Willingness is the key; action, the instrument for learning.

In his book *Acts of Meaning,* Bruner (1990) champions a renewed cognitive revolution that is sensitive to meaning-making within a cultural context. How people construct meaning depends on their beliefs, mental states, intentions, desires, and commitments. Likewise, Eisner (1991) calls us to celebrate thinking in schools by reminding us that brains may be born, but minds are made. Schools do not pay enough attention to students' curiosity and imagination. As a result, students disengage from active participation in the academic life of the classroom because there is little satisfaction to be gained from it. Unless the student receives satisfaction from schoolwork, Eisner argues, there is little reason or motive to continue to pursue learning: "Thinking . . . should be prized not only because it leads to attractive destinations but because the journey itself is satisfying" (p. 40).

In exploring matters of the mind, cognitive activity cannot be divorced from emotional involvement. Schema and motivation are intertwined with students' reasons for reading. Meaningful learning with texts occurs when students reap a feeling of satisfaction with texts and a sense of accomplishment.

Two of the most appropriate questions that students can ask about a reading selection are "What do I need to know?" and "How well do I already know it?" "What do I need to know?" prompts readers to activate their prior knowledge to make predictions and set purposes. It gets them thinking positively about the reading material. "How well do I already know it?" helps readers search their experience and knowledge to give support to tentative predictions and to help make plans for reading.

As simple as these two questions may seem on the surface, maturing readers rarely *know enough* about the reading process to ask them. "What do I need to know?" and "How well do I already know it?" require *metacognitive awareness* on the part of learners. However, these two questions, when consciously raised and reflected on, put students on the road to regulating and monitoring their own reading behavior. It is never too early (or too late) to begin showing students how to set purposes by raising questions about the text.

Nevertheless, the old aphorism "You can lead a horse to water, but you can't make it drink" reflects the role that commitment and motivation play in purposeful learning. Students may be skilled in their ability to read and knowledgeable about a subject, but they may not bring that skill and knowledge to bear in a learning situation. The apathetic stares and the groans of dissatisfaction are sledgehammerlike signs that students aren't willing to attend to the learning situation at hand. It often takes more than ability to get students to open their books.

Motivation has been described by psychologists as those processes that arouse behavior, give direction or purpose to behavior, and continue to allow behavior to persist (Wlodkowski 1982). When a teacher creates conditions that allow students to establish motives for reading *within themselves,* readiness to learn is affected.

In earlier chapters, we have underscored the important role that the schema plays in meaningful learning, so we won't belabor the point here, other than to reaffirm that prior knowledge activation is inescapably bound to one's purposes for reading and learning. As students ready themselves to learn with texts, they need to approach upcoming material in a critical frame of mind for potentially meaningful but new material that they will encounter while reading. Instructional scaffolding should make readers receptive to meaningful learning by creating a reference point for connecting the given (what one knows) with the new (the material to be learned). A frame of reference signals the connections students must make between the given and the new. They need to recognize how new material fits into the conceptual frameworks they already have.

Conceptual conflicts are the key to creating motivational conditions in the classroom (Berlyne 1965). Should students be presented with prereading situations that take the form of puzzlement, doubt, surprise, perplexity, contradiction, or ambiguity, they will be motivated to seek resolution. Why? The need within the learner is to resolve the conflict. As a result, the search for knowledge becomes a driving motivational force. When a question begins to gnaw at a learner, searching behavior is stimulated; learning occurs as the conceptual conflict resolves itself.

AROUSING CURIOSITY

Arousing curiosity and activating prior knowledge are closely related instructional activities. Curiosity arousal gives students the chance to consider what they know already about the material to be read. Through your guidance, they are encouraged to make connections and to relate their knowledge to the text assignment. And further, they will recognize that there are problems—conceptual conflicts—to be resolved through reading. Arousing curiosity helps students raise questions that they can answer only by giving thought to what they read.

Creating Story Impressions

Story impressions is a prereading strategy that arouses curiosity and allows students to anticipate what stories might be about. Although teachers use story impressions with narrative text, it may also be used to create "text impressions" in content areas other than English language arts.

As a prereading activity, this strategy uses clue words associated with the setting, characters, and events in the story (the story impressions) to help readers write their own versions of the story prior to reading. McGinley and Denner (1987), originators of the strategy, describe it this way: "Story impressions get readers to predict the events of the story that will be read, by providing them with fragments of the actual content. After reading the set of clues, the students are asked to render them comprehensible by using them to compose a story of their own in advance of reading the actual tale" (p. 249).

Fragments from the story, in the form of clue words, enable readers to form an overall impression of how the characters and events interact in the story. The clue words are selected directly from the story and are sequenced with arrows or lines to form a descriptive chain. The chain of clue words triggers impressions of what the story may be about. Students then write a "story guess" that predicts the events in the story.

Study the story impressions example in Figure 9.1. It is based on *The Wretched Stone*, a children's book by Chris Van Allsburg. The book was used as a read-aloud to introduce middle-level learners to a unit on "supernatural happenings."

McGinley and Denner explain. "The object, of course, is not for the student to guess the details or the exact relations among the events and characters of the story, but to simply compare his or her own story guess to the author's actual account" (p. 250). They suggest the following steps to introduce story impressions to the class for the first time:

1. Introduce the strategy by saying to the students. "Today we're going to make up what we think this story *could* be about."

2. Use large newsprint, a transparency, or a chalkboard to show students the story chain (see the left side of Figure 9.1 for an example), saying, "Here are some clues about the story we're going to read." Explain that the students will use the clues to write their own version of the story and that after reading, they will compare what they wrote with the actual story.

3. Read the clues together, and explain how the arrows link one clue to another in a logical order. Then brainstorm story ideas that connect all of the clues in the order that they are presented, saying, "What do we think this story could be about?"

4. Demonstrate how to write a story guess by using the ideas generated to write a class-composed story that links all of the clues. Use newsprint, the chalkboard, or a transparency for this purpose. Read the story prediction aloud with the students.

5. Invite the students to read the actual story silently, or initiate a shared reading experience. Afterward, discuss how the class-composed version is like and different from the author's story.

6. For subsequent stories, use story impressions to have students write individual story predictions or have them work in cooperative teams to write a group-composed story guess.

Notice in Figure 9.2 how an American history teacher adapted story impressions to have students predict events leading up to the Boston Tea Party. In the space provided for a "text guess," try your hand at writing what you think the text will be about. Compare your guess with the one appearing at the end of this chapter.

Story Chain	Story Guess
harbor ↓ voyage ↓ crew ↓ books, instruments ↓ adventure ↓ island, water, fruit ↓ strange ↓ textured, glowing ↓ heavy, aboard ↓ fascinated, peculiar ↓ stone ↓ clumsy ↓ shrieks, fever ↓ deserted, locked ↓ danger, storm ↓ horrifying, beasts ↓ doomed ↓ lightning ↓ rescue, discovery, alert ↓ normal	A ship's crew left the harbor ~~for their~~ on a voyage. Some of the crew brought along books and instruments ~~to make it though~~ for the long journey. While sailing across the ocean, They discovered an island with strange water and fruit. They drank the water and ate the fruit. One of the crew members found a glowing stone and took it with him to the ship. They set sail, and every time the stone would glow they heard shrieks and saw horrifying beasts. The crew was doomed. Then a terrible storm hit the ship. The stone stopped glowing and everything went back to normal.

FIGURE 9.1   Story Impression for *The Wretched Stone*

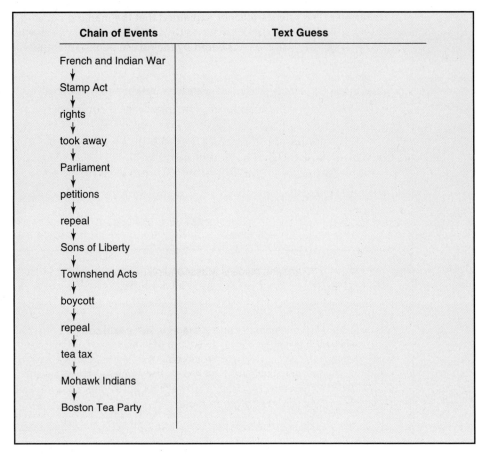

Chain of Events	Text Guess
French and Indian War ↓ Stamp Act ↓ rights ↓ took away ↓ Parliament ↓ petitions ↓ repeal ↓ Sons of Liberty ↓ Townshend Acts ↓ boycott ↓ repeal ↓ tea tax ↓ Mohawk Indians ↓ Boston Tea Party	

FIGURE 9.2   **Chain of Events Leading to the Boston Tea Party**

Establishing Problem Situations and Perspectives

Creating problems to be solved or perspectives from which readers approach text material provides an imaginative entry into a text selection. For example, the teacher's role in creating problem situations is (1) providing the time to discuss the problem, raising questions, and seeking possible solutions before reading and then (2) assigning the reading material that will help lead to resolution and conceptual development.

Collette (1973) offers an excellent example of a teachable moment that helped students get "curiouser" about reading science materials:

> An unusual fall thunderstorm killed one of two men who sought shelter under a tree. The ninth-grade students immediately were curious about the reason for the death of only one man while his companion only a couple of feet away was

unharmed. The science teacher explained that the man did not know much about the action of lightning and suggested that the pupils make a list of questions that would likely be answered by looking in books and other references. (pp. 574–575)

In addition to the teachable moment, consider keying a problem situation directly to specific text selections. For example, a social studies teacher and her students were exploring the development of early American settlements in a unit on colonial life. She presented the problem situation to her students as shown in Figure 9.3. The series of questions promoted an interest-filled discussion, putting students in a situation in which they had to rely on prior knowledge for responses.

The time is 1680, and the place is Massachusetts. Imagine that you are early European settlers. You will want to try to think as you believe they may have thought and act as they might have acted. You and your group have petitioned the Great and General Court to be allowed to form a new town. After checking to make sure you are of good character and the land is fertile and can be defended, the court says yes. It grants you a 5-mile square of land. As proprietors of this land, you must plan a town. What buildings would you put in first? Second? Third? Later? Why? How would you divide the land among the many people who want to live there? Why? As proprietors, would you treat yourselves differently from the others? Why? How would you run the government?

FIGURE 9.3   **A Problem Situation in an American History Class**

Asking the students in the social studies class to approach reading by imagining that they were early European settlers placed them in a particular role. With the role came a perspective. Creating such a perspective has its underpinnings in a schema-theoretical view of the reading process.

One of the early studies of the Center for the Study of Reading at the University of Illinois pointed to the powerful role of perspective in comprehending text (Pichert & Anderson 1977). The researchers showed just how important the reader's perspective can be. Two groups of readers were asked to read a passage about a house from one of two perspectives, that of a burglar or of a house buyer. When readers who held the perspective of a house burglar read the story about going through the house, they recalled different information from those readers who approached the story from the perspective of a house buyer.

Creating a perspective (a role) for the student is one way to get into reading. Students in these roles find themselves solving problems that force them to use their knowledge and experience.

In Figure 9.4, a high school teacher created a perspective for students before assigning a reading selection from an auto mechanics manual.

You are the only mechanic on duty when a four-wheel-drive truck with a V-8 engine pulls in for repair. The truck has high mileage, and it appears that the problem may be a worn clutch disk. What tools do you think you will need? What procedures would you follow? Put your answers to these questions under the two headings below.

Tools Needed   **Procedures**

_____   _____

_____   _____

_____   _____

_____   _____

FIGURE 9.4 **Creating a Perspective in an Auto Mechanics Class**

In preparation for reading the short story "Alas Babylon," an English teacher set up a perspective in which students' curiosity was aroused and their expectations of the story raised:

> The year is _____. We are on the verge of a nuclear disaster. Through inside sources, you hear that the attack will occur within five days. What preparations will you consider making before the nuclear attack occurs?

The class considered the orienting question. After some discussion, the teacher initiated the activity in Figure 9.5. The students formed small groups, and each group was directed to come to a consensus on the 12 activities they would choose. Those items were chosen from the list in Figure 9.5.

From the small-group discussions came the recognition that the values, beliefs, and attitudes readers bring to a text shape their perspective as much as their background knowledge of a topic. For this reason, we suggest that building the motivation for a text to be read take into account, where appropriate, an examination of values, attitudes, and controversial issues related to the subject matter.

Assuming that your town and house will not be destroyed by the bomb and that you have enough time to prepare for the attack, which 12 activities from the following list will you choose?

_____ 1. Buy a gun and ammunition to protect against looters.

_____ 2. Cash in all savings bonds and take all the money out of your checking and savings accounts.

_____ 3. Build a fireplace in your house.

_____ 4. Buy firewood and charcoal.

_____ 5. Buy extra tanks of gasoline and fill your car up.

_____ 6. Purchase antibiotics and other medicines.

_____ 7. Dig a latrine.

_____ 8. Buy lumber, nails, and various other supplies.

_____ 9. Plant fruit trees.

_____ 10. Notify all your friends and relatives of the coming nuclear attack.

_____ 11. Invest in books on canning and making candles and soap.

_____ 12. Buy a few head of livestock from a farmer.

_____ 13. Buy fishing equipment and a boat.

_____ 14. Buy seeds of several different kinds of vegetables for a garden.

_____ 15. Make friends with a farmer who has a horse and wagon.

_____ 16. Shop at antique stores for kerosene lamps and large cooking pots.

_____ 17. Buy a safe to hide your money in.

_____ 18. Buy foodstuffs.

FIGURE 9.5   **Creating a Perspective in an English Class**

Guided Imagery

Guided imagery allows students to explore concepts visually. Samples (1977) recommends guided imagery, among other things, as a means of

◆ Building an experience base for inquiry, discussion, and group work

◆ Building self-image

◆ Exploring and stretching concepts

◆ Solving and clarifying problems

◆ Exploring history and the future

◆ Exploring other lands and worlds

Guided imagery works this way: The teacher, according to Samples (1977), structures a daydream: "You use *words* to get into the process—but once there, images take over" (p. 188). Read the example in Figure 9.6; then close your eyes and do what it says.

Close your eyes . . . tell all your muscles to relax. You are entering a space capsule 10 minutes before takeoff. Soon you feel it lift off . . . you look over at your companions and check their reactions. Now you are ready to take a reading of the instrument panel. As you relay the information to ground control, it is 11 minutes into the flight . . . you settle back into your chair and tell your fellow astronauts about your thoughts . . . about what you hope to see when the vehicle lands . . . about what you might touch and hear as you explore your destination. Finally, you drift off to sleep . . . picturing yourself returning to earth . . . seeing once again your friends and relations. You are back where you started . . . tell your muscles to move . . . open your eyes.

FIGURE 9.6   **A Guided Imagery Illustration**

You may wish to have students discuss their "trips," which, of course, should parallel in some way the content of the reading selection to be assigned. In the classroom where this example was devised, students in a literature class participated in the imagery discussion before reading a short story on space travel. Discussion questions included "How did you feel just before entering the space capsule? What were the reactions of your companions? Where did your exploration take you? Were there things that surprised you on the trip? Colors? Sounds?"

Samples (1977) provides these tips as he explains the imagery strategy:

> Relaxed positions are helpful. . . . As few distractions as possible will make the first few experiences easier. A soothing but audible voice is best. For those who can't get themselves to participate, an alternative quiet activity will cut down on embarrassed giggles. Leave lots of "empty" space both in terms of specific content and time to visualize. (p. 188)

Guided imagery isn't for everyone. Some teachers will find themselves uncomfortable using it; others will not. As a prereading alternative, however, it gives you an additional option that will help students connect, in this case, what they "see" to what they will read.

Analogies

An analogy establishes a comparison or contrast between concepts familiar to the reader and unfamiliar ideas that will be encountered in text. For example, in the Hayes and Tierney (1982) study, readers compared what they already knew about the game of baseball with information from a text passage on the English sport of cricket. Activating readers' knowledge of baseball served as a frame of reference for understanding the cricket passage.

In everyday terms, analogies have often been devised as part of a verbal presentation. Analogies can be created for almost any content area. In reading a literary work, for example, an English or language arts teacher may devise an analogous situation in which students compare their approach to a problem with a problem that the protagonist of the story must resolve. Or the teacher may create an analogy around the theme of the selection. If students were to read O. Henry's story "The Gift of the Magi," they might examine their own beliefs about and understanding of giving and receiving in relation to the story's theme.

We recommend the following guidelines for constructing analogies during prereading preparation:

1. Construct an analogy for difficult text material only.

2. Devise the analogy so that it reflects the main ideas in the text to be assigned. Make sure that these ideas are prominent and easily identifiable in the analogy.

3. In the analogy, use real-life incidents, anecdotes, familiar examples, or illustrations to which the students can relate. These devices serve as a basis for comparing or contrasting what the students know already with unfamiliar material.

4. Raise a question or two in the analogy that will engage the students in thinking about the text to be read.

Study the analogy in Figure 9.7, which was prepared for a middle school science lesson on the earth's physical makeup. As the students discussed this analogy, the teacher used an orange and a facsimile of the earth as props. The discussion led to the clarification of key concept words introduced in the analogy passage. It also created the organizational framework that students needed to fit new information into existing knowledge.

Carla Mathiason (1989) tells how a sixth-grade teacher, Mrs. Johnson, used an analogy to activate prior knowledge of and interest in a text assignment on keeping the heart healthy. Mrs. Johnson's class was studying the organs of the body and their functions. Working with an overhead projector, she displayed a

> ### The Orange and the Earth
>
> The earth's physical makeup is very similar to the makeup of an orange. Sometimes an orange has one seed at its center. The earth's single central "giant seed," about 760 miles in radius, is called the *inner solid-iron core*. This inner core serves to give our planet life just as the orange's seed gives life.
>
> The earth's interior is as liquid as the interior of an orange. However, the liquid in an orange is what we call *orange juice,* while the liquid in the earth is liquid iron and is known as the *outer liquid core*. This liquid core is about 1400 miles deep. The liquid iron is confined by what is called a *rocky mantle;* the juice of the orange is confined by a white spongy cellulose material. The difference is that the white cellulose is only a small fraction of the orange's radius, while the mantle of the earth accounts for about a third of the earth's radius, about 1300 miles.
>
> As you may have guessed by now, both the orange and the earth have a crust or skin that serves to protect the interior. The earth's skin actually has two components: the *asthenosphere,* a layer of fudgelike consistency that extends about 300 miles, and the *lithosphere,* which is the earth we walk on and see. The earth's lithosphere is as thin as the skin of an orange by comparison. As you read more about the earth's physical makeup, what other comparisons can you make between the orange and the earth?

FIGURE 9.7   **Example of an Analogy**

transparency featuring a roughly sketched city map of downtown Indianapolis. Before assigning the text reading, "Keeping Your Heart Healthy," Mrs. Johnson asked the class to identify the "heart of the city on the map." As students responded, she drew a heart shape over the center of the city (see Figure 9.8). As the discussion continued, she invited the students to identify the major roadways leading into and out of the center city. As they did so, she highlighted them on the transparency. The analogy took shape as students reflected on the question "In what ways does the map remind you of the heart?"

With the analogy set, the prereading discussion was off and running. Issues were raised in terms of the familiar and the unfamiliar: the slowdown of traffic during the rush hour versus the slowing down of the blood supply by a clogging of the heart's veins and arteries; a car wreck and a heart attack. The discussion concluded with Mrs. Johnson setting the stage for reading: "Tonight, for your homework, you're going to be reading about some things that make it hard for your veins and arteries to get all the blood to the heart that it needs. Why is that important information for you to know?"

PreP

Brainstorming is a key feature of the prereading plan (PreP), which may be used to generate interest in content area reading and to estimate the levels of background knowledge that students bring to the text assignments. Judith

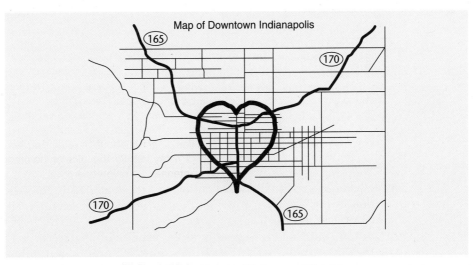

FIGURE 9.8   **Analogy of the Heart, Using a City Map**

Source: From "Activating Student Interest in Content Area Reading," by Carla Mathiason, *Journal of Reading,* December 1989. Copyright ©1989 by the International Reading Association. All rights reserved. Used by permission of the author and the International Reading Association.

Langer (1981) recommends PreP as an assessment and instructional activity that fosters group discussion and an awareness of the topics to be covered. She suggests that PreP works best with groups of about ten students.

Before beginning the PreP activity, the teacher should examine the text material for key words (which represent major concepts to be developed), phrases, or pictures and then introduce the topic that is to be read, following the three-phase plan that Langer (1981, p. 154) outlines:

1. *Initial associations with the concept.* In this first phase the teacher says, "Tell anything that comes to mind when . . ." (e.g., ". . . you hear the word *Congress*"). As each student tells what ideas initially came to mind, the teacher jots each response on the board. During this phase, the students have their first opportunity to find associations between the key concept and their prior knowledge. When this activity was carried out in a middle school class, one student, Bill, said, "Important people." Another student, Danette, said, "Washington, D.C."

2. *Reflections on initial associations.* During the second phase of PreP, the students are asked, "What made you think of . . . [the response given by a student]?" This phase helps the students develop awareness of their network of associations. They also have an opportunity to listen to each other's explanations, to interact, and to become aware of their changing ideas. Through this procedure, they may weigh, reject, accept, revise, and integrate some of the ideas that came to mind. When Bill was asked what made him think of important people, he said, "I saw them in the newspaper." When Danette was asked what made her think of Washington, D.C., she said, "Congress takes place there."

3. *Reformulation of knowledge.* In this phase, the teacher says, "Based on our discussion and before we read the text, have you any new ideas about . . . [e.g., Congress]?" This phase allows students to verbalize associations that have been elaborated or changed through the discussion. Because they have had a chance to probe their memories to elaborate on their prior knowledge, the responses elicited during the third phase are often more refined than those from the first. This time, Bill said, "Lawmakers of America," and Danette said, "U.S. government part that makes the laws."

Through observation and listening during PreP, content area teachers will find their students' knowledge can be divided into three broad levels. On one level are students who have *much* prior knowledge about the concept. These students are often able to define and draw analogies, make conceptual links, and think categorically. On another level are students who may have *some* prior knowledge. These students can give examples and cite characteristics of the content but may be unable to see relationships or make connections between what they know and the new material. On the third level are students who have *little* background knowledge. They often respond to the PreP activity with words that sound like the concept word and may attempt to make simple associations, often misassociating with the topic.

MAKING PREDICTIONS

Prediction strategies activate thought about the content before reading. Students must rely on what they know through previous study and experience to make educated guesses about the material to be read.

Why an educated guess? Smith (1988) defines predicting as the prior elimination of unlikely alternatives. He suggests:

> Readers do not normally attend to print with their minds blank, with no prior purpose and with no expectation of what they might find in the text. . . . The way readers look for meaning is not to consider all possibilities, nor to make reckless guesses about just one, but rather to predict within the most likely range of alternatives. . . . Readers can derive meaning from text because they bring expectations about meaning to text. (p. 163)

You can facilitate student-centered purposes by creating anticipation about the meaning of what will be read.

Anticipation Guides

An anticipation guide is a series of statements to which students must respond individually before reading the text. Their value lies in the discussion that takes place after the exercise. The teacher's role during discussion is to activate and agitate thought. As students connect their knowledge of the world to the prediction task, you must remain open to a wide range of responses. Draw on what students bring to the task, but remain nondirective in order to keep the discussion moving.

Anticipation guides may vary in format but not in purpose. In each case, the readers' expectations about meaning are raised before they read the text. Keep these guidelines in mind in constructing and using an anticipation guide:

1. Analyze the material to be read. Determine the major ideas—implicit and explicit—with which students will interact.

2. Write those ideas in short, clear declarative statements. These statements should in some way reflect the world that the students live in or know about. Therefore, avoid abstractions whenever possible.

3. Put these statements in a format that will elicit anticipation and prediction.

4. Discuss the students' predictions and anticipations before they read the text selection.

5. Assign the text selection. Have the students evaluate the statements in light of the author's intent and purpose.

6. Contrast the readers' predictions with the author's intended meaning.

A middle school social studies teacher prepared students for a reading assignment that contrasted the characteristics of the Northern and Southern soldiers in the Civil War. She began by writing "Johnny Reb" and "Billy Yank" in separate columns on the chalkboard. She asked students to think about what they already knew about the two soldiers: "How do you think they were alike? How were they different?" After some discussion, the teacher invited the students to participate in the anticipation activity in Figure 9.9.

Of course, each of the points highlighted in the statements was developed in the text selection. Not only did the students get a sense of the major ideas they would encounter in the text selection, but they also read to see how well they had predicted which statements more accurately represented soldiers from the South and the North during the Civil War.

A science teacher began a weather unit by introducing a series of popular clichés about the weather. He asked his students to anticipate whether the clichés had a scientific basis (see Figure 9.10).

The prereading discussion led the students to review and expand their concepts of scientific truth. Throughout different parts of the unit, the teacher returned to one or two of the clichés in the anticipation guide and suggested to the class that the textbook assignment would explain whether there was a scientific basis for each saying. Students were then directed to read to find out what the explanations were.

Johnny Reb and Billy Yank were common soldiers of the Civil War. You will be reading about some of their basic differences in your textbook. What do you think those differences will be? Before reading your assignment, place the initials JR in front of the phrases that you think best describe Johnny Reb. Place the initials BY in front of the statements that best describe Billy Yank. Do not mark statements common to both.

_____ 1. More likely to be able to read and write

_____ 2. Best able to adjust to living in open areas

_____ 3. More likely to be from a rural setting

_____ 4. More interested in politics

_____ 5. More deeply religious

_____ 6. Often not able to sign his name

_____ 7. More apt to dislike regimentation of army life

_____ 8. More likely to speak slowly

_____ 9. More probably a Native American

_____ 10. More likely to be a common man in the social order

FIGURE 9.9 **Anticipation Guide for a Civil War Lesson**

Another example of how an anticipation guide may be used as a prereading strategy is evident in a high school English teacher's presentation of Richard Brautigan's poem "It's Raining in Love." The poem is a good example of a contemporary poem that discusses love in an atypical way. It is the kind of poem that captures the way many high school students feel. Note the format used for the teacher's anticipation activity in Figure 9.11.

A health education teacher raised expectations and created anticipation for a chapter on the human immunodeficiency virus (HIV) and AIDS. Rather than prepare written statements, she conducted the anticipatory lesson as part of an introductory class discussion. She raised curiosity about the topic by asking students to participate in a strategy known as the "every-pupil response." She told the students that she would ask several questions about becoming infected with HIV. Every student was to respond to each question by giving a "thumbs up" if they agreed or a "thumbs down" if they disagreed. The class had to participate in unison and keep their thumbs up or down. After each question, the students shared their reasons for responding thumbs up or thumbs down.

Directions: Put a check under "Likely" if you feel that the weather saying has any scientific basis; put a check under "Unlikely" if you feel that it has no scientific basis. Be ready to explain your choice.

Likely   Unlikely

_____   _____   1. Red sky at night, sailors delight; red sky at morning, sailors take warning.

_____   _____   2. If you see a sunspot, there is going to be bad weather.

_____   _____   3. When the leaves turn under, it is going to storm.

_____   _____   4. If you see a hornet's nest high in a tree, a harsh winter is coming.

_____   _____   5. Aching bones mean a cold and rainy forecast.

_____   _____   6. If a groundhog sees his shadow, six more weeks of winter.

_____   _____   7. Rain before seven, sun by eleven.

_____   _____   8. If a cow lies down in a pasture, it is going to rain soon.

_____   _____   9. Sea gull, sea gull, sitting on the sand; it's never good weather while you're on land.

FIGURE 9.10   **Anticipation Guide for Clichés About Weather**

The questions were framed as follows: "Is it true that you can contract HIV by

♦ Having unprotected sex with an infected partner?"

♦ Kissing someone with HIV?"

♦ Sharing needles with an HIV-infected drug user?"

♦ Sharing a locker with an infected person?"

♦ Using a telephone after someone with HIV?"

♦ Being bitten by a mosquito?"

The "oral anticipation guide" created lively discussion as students discussed some of their preconceived notions and misconceptions about HIV and AIDS.

Directions: We have already read several poems by Richard Brautigan. Before reading "It's Raining in Love," place a check in the "You" column next to each statement that you think expresses a feeling the poet will deal with in the poem. Discuss your choices in small groups, and explain why you checked the statements you did. Then I'll assign the poem. After reading the poem, check the statements in the "Poet" column that express the feelings that the poet did deal with in his poem.

You   **Poet**

———   ———   Being in love is a painful experience.

———   ———   Boys can be just as nervous as girls when they like a member of the opposite sex.

———   ———   It is OK for a girl to call a boy and ask him out.

———   ———   It's better to be friends with members of the opposite sex than to be in love with them.

———   ———   Poetry about love must be mushy to be effective.

———   ———   Once a person has been in love, he's (or she's) much more sensitive to another person's feelings when he finds out that person likes him.

FIGURE 9.11   **Anticipation Guide for "It's Raining in Love"**

Mathematics teachers have been successful in their use of anticipation guides. In a precalculus class, the teacher introduced the activity in Figure 9.12 to begin the trigonometry section of the textbook. She created the anticipation guide to help students address their own knowledge about trigonometry and to create conceptual conflict for some of the more difficult sections of the chapter they would be studying.

Previews

Previews provide students with a frame of reference in which to understand new material. Previews should be used for difficult reading selections. Graves, Cooke, and La Berge (1983) suggested previews as a prereading strategy for difficult short stories. They found that a teacher's reading a preview to students had a significant influence on low-achieving middle school students' comprehension and recall of the stories.

The preview passage should provide much more substantive information than the brief introductory statements that usually accompany selections

Directions: Put a check under "Likely" if you feel that the statement has any mathematical truth. Put a check under "Unlikely" if you feel that it has no mathematical truth. Be ready to explain your choices.

Likely	**Unlikely**	
_____	_____	Trigonometry deals with circles.
_____	_____	Angles have little importance in trigonometry.
_____	_____	Sailors use trigonometry in navigation.
_____	_____	Angles can be measured only in degrees.
_____	_____	Calculators are useless in trigonometry.
_____	_____	Trigonometry deals with triangles.
_____	_____	Trigonometry has no application in the real world.
_____	_____	Radians are used in measuring central angles.
_____	_____	Trigonometry has scientific uses.
_____	_____	Radians can be converted to degrees.

FIGURE 9.12   **Anticipation Guide for Preconceived Notions About Trigonometry**

found in reading and literature textbooks. However, the real value of previews is that they build a frame of reference for the story by telling students a good deal about it.

To construct a preview, follow these guidelines:

1. Begin with a series of short statements and one or more questions that spark interest, provide a link between a familiar topic and the topic of the story, and encourage students to actively reflect on the theme.

2. Provide a synopsis of the story that includes key elements in the story structure (without signaling the resolution or outcome of the plot).

3. Define several key terms within the context of the preview passage.

According to Graves, Prenn, and Cooke (1985), using a preview for prereading instruction is a relatively straightforward procedure. They recommended the following steps:

1. Tell students you're going to introduce the upcoming selection.

2. Read the first few sentences of the preview.

3. Give students two or three minutes to discuss the question or questions.

4. Read the remainder of the preview.

5. Have students begin reading immediately after you complete the preview. (p. 597)

Study the example in Figure 9.13 of a preview developed for Robert Cormier's short story "In the Heat."

Have you ever heard a bell ring and immediately remember someone special? Has an aroma ever triggered a memory, either painful or pleasant? Have you ever seen an object that suddenly reminds you of a loved one? Sometimes sounds, smells, and objects can spark our dusty long-ago memories. Think for a minute. Does seeing your old Little League baseball glove bring back memories? Or how about seeing your favorite doll peering through the top of an old attic box? Can you think of any examples where sounds, smells, sights, taste, or touch can bring old memories to life? *(Pause, wait for student responses.)* Of course, just because something touches off our memories doesn't mean that what we remember will always be pleasant. Sometimes memories can be painful. But who chooses what to remember?

In the beginning of our short story, "In the Heat," the main character is a father with a difficult task ahead of him. But before he begins this most unwanted, but necessary, task, he has a flashback—the heat from the scorching summer day reminds him of a time long ago when he could hear his father yelling up the stairs to all the kids, "Hell, come on down here. Who wants to go to sleep in this heat?" Yes, in his flashback, it was his father who understood about the heat and "how a kid never wants to go to bed."

But the flashback ends quickly. Now the father of our story realizes the task at hand and all the things that must be done. He says out loud, to no one in particular, "Yes, there are other things to think about . . . Not things, really. Only one: the fact of my wife's death." *(Pause.)*

As the father prepares to go to the services, he thinks to himself, "What I dread most are the *reminders,* waiting like unexploded time bombs in unexpected places. This morning, I *discovered* one of her bobby pins on the mantel. I stared at it awhile, *remembering* last winter's fires." But the father is not concerned about *his* memories only. You see, this father has a teenage son, Richy. And the father is worried about what kind of memories Richy is going to have about his mother. Whenever Richy feels the scorching sun in the middle of summer, what will he remember about this day?

As you read this story, pay close attention to the development of the two characters: the father and Richy. Does the father need a name? Without a name, is the father still a believable character? Why or why not? Also, as you read this passage, be alert for metaphors—for example, "the sun now hemorrhaging to death" or "my heart is Hiroshima." How do these and other metaphors affect the tone of the story? The author seems to convey a great deal of sadness, but at the same time the story seems uplifting. Why do you think this is so?

FIGURE 9.13   **Preview for "In the Heat"**

If you teach (or are planning to teach) in a content area other than English, you might consider adopting the preview for nonnarrative material. The preview in Figure 9.14 was developed by a vocational education teacher for a text chapter explaining the chemistry of cosmetics. Notice that the teacher begins by *establishing the main idea* of the text to be read. She then attempts to have students *build and share background knowledge and experiences* relating to the chemicals in cosmetics that they have used. The final section of the preview helps students *make connections* between the text to be read and the knowledge they already have. *Key questions* are raised to provide students with expectations as to what is important material on which to focus attention as they read.

A knowledge of chemistry is essential to making intelligent decisions about the use of cosmetics and other products. When we think of chemistry, we often think of test tubes in a science lab with formulas bubbling and scientists experimenting. It is exactly that kind of setting where shampoos, cosmetics, perms, and hair coloring are developed. Did you ever use the wrong color or perm formula, making your hair look like a haystack? By learning some basics of chemistry, we can avoid some of those mistakes.

Chapter 32 first provides some general science information. For example, what are molecules? What is matter? The chapter then develops some important concepts about *cosmetic chemistry*. What do you need to know about mixtures and changes—physical and chemical (page 434)? What are the most common elements that you need to know about (pages 435 and 436)? Be sure that you will know how to explain pH scale (pages 436–439).

FIGURE 9.14   **Preview for "Chemistry of Cosmetics"**

Previews make excellent student writing assignments. Consider assigning students to write a preview in order to "advertise a reading assignment" for future groups of students. You might suggest that students put themselves in the shoes of the teacher or the author. The writing task might be introduced in this manner: "If you were the author of *(title of text selection)*, how would you introduce readers to the major ideas in the selection?" To accompany the written passage, students may use pictures, posters, book jackets, slogans, or bumper stickers to capture the unifying idea of the text selection and to arouse interest. As students compose, they should be aware of their audience—other students. Impress upon students that their passages will be read and used by students in future classes.

The teacher may need to model how previews are constructed as part of prewriting discussion. This may entail reflecting on a teacher-constructed passage that students had previously experienced. Which major ideas received the most prominence? Why did the teacher select these over others? Why were questions or examples included in the model passage?

STUDENT-GENERATED QUESTIONS

Teaching students to generate their own questions about material to be read is one of the major instructional goals of prereading preparation. Harry Singer (1978) contends that whenever readers are involved in asking questions, they are engaged in "active comprehension." Teachers can use an active comprehension strategy when they *ask questions that beget questions in return.* You might, for example, focus attention on a picture or an illustration from a story or book and ask a question that induces student questions in response: "What would you like to know about the picture?" In return, invite the students to generate questions that focus on the details in the picture or its overarching message.

Or you might decide to read to students an opening paragraph or two from a text selection, enough to whet their appetite for the selection. Then ask, "What else would you like to know about _____?" Complete the question by focusing attention on some aspect of the selection that is pivotal to students' comprehension. It may be the main character of a story or the main topic of an expository text.

Active comprehension questions not only arouse interest and curiosity but also draw learners into the material. As a result, students will read to satisfy purposes and resolve conceptual conflicts that they have identified through their own questions. Let us examine several additional instructional strategies for engaging students in asking questions for reading.

ReQuest

ReQuest was originally devised as a one-on-one procedure involving the student and the teacher. Yet this strategy can easily be adapted to content area classrooms to help students think as they read. ReQuest encourages students to ask their own questions about the content material under study. Self-declared questions are forceful. They help students establish reasonable purposes for their reading. Betts (1950) describes a "highly desirable learning situation" as one in which the student does the questioning: "That is, the learner asks the questions, and sets up the problems to be solved during the reading activity" (p. 450).

ReQuest fosters an active search for meaning. Manzo (1969) describes the rules for ReQuest:

> The purpose of this lesson is to improve your understanding of what you read. We will each read silently the first sentence. Then we will take turns asking questions about the sentence and what it means. You will ask questions first, then I will ask questions. Try to ask the kind of questions a teacher might ask, in the way a teacher might ask them. You may ask me as many questions as you wish. When you are asking me questions, I will close my book (or pass the book

to you if there is only one between us). When I ask questions, you close your book. . . . Any question asked deserves to be answered as fully and honestly as possible. It is cheating for a teacher to withhold information or play dumb to draw out the student. It is unacceptable for a student to answer with "I don't know," since he can at least attempt to explain why he cannot answer. If questions are unclear to either party, requests for rephrasing or clarification are in order. The responder should be ready (and make it a practice) to justify his answer by reference back to the text or to expand on background that was used to build or to limit an answer. Whenever possible, if there is uncertainty about an answer, the respondent should check his answer against the text. (pp. 124–125)

Although the rules for ReQuest were devised for one-on-one instruction, they can be adapted for the content area classroom. If you decide to use ReQuest in your class, consider these steps:

1. Both the students and the teacher silently read the same segment of the text. Manzo recommends one sentence at a time for students who have trouble comprehending what they read. However, text passages of varying length are suitable in classroom applications. For example, both teacher and students begin by reading a paragraph or two.

2. The teacher closes the book and is questioned about the passage by the students.

3. Next, there is an exchange of roles. The teacher now queries the students about the material.

4. On completion of the student-teacher exchange, the class and the teacher read the next segment of text. Steps 2 and 3 are repeated.

5. At a suitable point in the text, when the students have processed enough information to make predictions about the remainder of the assignment, the exchange of questions stops. The teacher then asks prediction questions: "What do you think the rest of the assignment is about? Why do you think so?" Speculation is encouraged.

6. Students are then assigned the remaining portion of the selection to read silently.

7. The teacher facilitates a follow-up discussion of the material.

You can modify the ReQuest procedure to good advantage. For example, consider alternating the role of questioner after each question. By doing so, you will probably involve more students in the activity. Once students sense the types of questions that can be asked about a text passage, you might also try forming ReQuest teams. A ReQuest team composed of three or four students is pitted against another ReQuest team. Your role is to facilitate the multiple action resulting from the small-group formations.

Our own experiences with ReQuest suggest that students may consistently ask factual questions to stump the teacher or other students. Such questions succeed brilliantly because you are subject to the same restrictions imposed by short-term memory as the students. That you miss an answer or two is actually healthy—after all, to err is human.

However, when students ask only verbatim questions because they don't know how to ask any others, the situation is unhealthy. The sad fact is that some students don't know how to ask questions that will stimulate interpretive or applied levels of thinking. Therefore, your role as a good questioner during ReQuest is to provide a model that students will learn from. Over time, you will notice the difference in the quality of the student questions formulated.

Expectation Outlines

Spiegel (1981) suggests the development of an expectation outline to help students ask questions about text. She recommends the expectation outline for factual material, but the strategy can be adapted to narrative studies as well. The expectation outline is developed on the chalkboard or an overhead projector transparency as students simply tell what they expect to learn from a reading selection.

If students are reading a factual selection, you may have them first take several minutes to preview the material. Then ask, "What do you think your assignment is going to be about?" Ask students to state their expectations in the form of questions. As they suggest questions, group related questions on the chalkboard or transparency. You also have the opportunity to ask students what prompted them to ask these questions in the first place. At this point, students may be encouraged to refer to the text to support their questions.

Once questions have been asked and grouped, the class labels each set of questions. Through discussion, students begin to see the major topics that will emerge from the reading. Lead them to recognize that gaps may exist in the expectation outline of the assignment. For example, you may add a topic or two to the outline about which no questions were raised. On completion of the expectation outline, students read to answer the questions generated.

For narrative materials, students may formulate their questions from the title of the selection or pictures or key words and phrases in the selection. For example, direct students to preview a story by skimming through it quickly, studying the pictures and illustrations (if any), and jotting down five to ten key words or phrases that appear to indicate the main direction of the story. As students suggest key words and phrases, write them on the board and categorize them. Then ask students to state what they expect to find out from the story. Have them raise questions about its title, setting, characters, plot, and theme. As an alternative to questions, students may summarize their expectations by writing a paragraph about the story using the key words and phrases that were jotted down and categorized.

A variation on the expectation outline is a strategy called a "asking your own questions." Here's how it works:

1. Have students listen to or read a portion of the text from the beginning of a selection.

2. Ask students to write five to ten questions that they think will be answered by the remainder of the selection.

3. Discuss some of the questions asked by the students before reading. Write the questions on the board.

4. Have students read to see if the questions are answered.

5. After reading, ask the students to explain which questions were answered, which weren't, and why not.

Strategies such as an expectation outline or asking your own questions teach students how to approach reading material with an inquisitive mind. These instructional strategies and the others presented in this chapter form a bridge between teacher-initiated guidance and independent learning behavior by students.

 ## LOOKING BACK, LOOKING FORWARD

Meaningful learning with texts occurs when students experience a sense of satisfaction with text and a feeling of accomplishment. In this chapter, the role that commitment and motivation play in purposeful learning was emphasized. Although some students may be skilled in reading and knowledgeable about the subject, they may not bring that skill and knowledge to bear in learning situations. It takes motivation, a sense of direction and purpose, and a teacher who knows how to create conditions in the classroom that allow students to establish their own motives for reading. One way to arouse curiosity about reading material is to encourage students to make connections among the key concepts to be studied. Another is to create conceptual conflict. Students will read to resolve conflicts arising from problem situations and perspectives and will use guided imagery to explore the ideas to be encountered during reading.

To reduce any uncertainty that students bring to reading material, you can help them raise questions and anticipate meaning by showing them how to connect what they already know to the new ideas presented in the text. Instructional activities involving analogies and text previews also help activate prior knowledge and interest in reading.

The questions students raise as a result of predicting will guide them into the reading material and keep them on course. Anticipation guides, ReQuest, expectation outlines, self-questioning, and previewing techniques are strategies for stimulating predictions and anticipation about the content.

 **MINDS-ON**

1. Suppose you go to the library looking for a good book to read. You see a cart with a sign: "Current Best-Sellers." Since you have little familiarity with any of the books, how will you make a selection? How will you anticipate which book is for you? Since students rarely have the opportunity to select their course textbook, what can teachers do to help students make the book "fit"?

2. Divide your small discussion group into two subgroups: individuals who are willing to take the position that all of the following statements are correct and those willing to argue that all of the statements are inaccurate. Discuss the pros and cons of each topic for five minutes. After you have finished, bring any items to the class as a whole that you feel could truly have been defended from either view, and be prepared to explain why or under what circumstances.

   a. Students are not qualified to ask their own questions about difficult content material.

   b. The old but still common practice of assigning reading in preparation for a discussion is, unfortunately, backward.

   c. Just as athletes need to warm up before a contest, readers need to warm up to get ready for text.

   d. Analyzing content vocabulary before reading is a sound instructional practice.

   e. Having students read a variety of materials on the subject matter will only confuse them.

   f. It is pointless to discuss most subjects with students before they read the text because the varied social and economic backgrounds of the students make it possible for only a few to connect any relevant personal experience to the text subject.

3. Eliot Eisner believes that brains are born but minds are made. What do you see as the teacher's role in a classroom filled with 25 brains waiting to be made into minds? Is the teacher the molder, shaper, and maker—that is, the only active partner? Is the teacher to serve as a model learner, a guide through knowledge, or a facilitator—that is, an equal but superior partner? Or do you see some happy medium? In your group, attempt

to reach a consensus on what you consider the best role for a teacher in relation to these prompts.

 HANDS-ON

1. Try the following science experiment to activate prior knowledge and to stimulate interest in reading an explanation of the formula *Force equals pressure times area.* Bring the following materials to class: one 30-gallon garbage bag, duct tape, and a dozen straws. Flatten the trash bag on a table large enough for a volunteer to lie on with his or her upper body resting on the bag. Cut four small holes about 9 inches apart along the edges of the two sides of the flattened bag that are perpendicular to the open end. Insert one straw in each opening. Next, tape each hole airtight. Tape the open end of the bag airtight as well. Ask a volunteer to lie on his or her back on top of the garbage bag on the table.

   Next, ask eight other individuals each to select one straw, and explain that they will be attempting to lift the volunteer by blowing through the straws into the sealed bag. Before proceeding, however, invite the group to pose questions, draw on their prior knowledge, and anticipate why this experiment may succeed or fail. After the group has theorized about and discussed the problem, mention that the bag will break at a pressure of 1 pound per square inch, and ask if that fact changes their predictions. Finally, have the eight individuals attempt to inflate the bag by blowing into the straws simultaneously. As they do, be sure that someone stabilizes the volunteer so that he or she does not roll off the bag.

   If the experiment works, the volunteer should rise several inches from the table. Break into small groups of five or six, and imagine that a science instructor has just used this experiment as an introduction to a chapter on the relationship between air pressure, force, and surface area. How motivated do the group members feel to read this chapter? As a group, discuss how science experiments may be used with anticipation guides, ReQuest, expectation outlines, analogies, and graphic organizers.

2. Read a journal article of your choice that pertains to any aspect or issue of content area reading. Write a preview of the article for the purpose of "advertising" the article as important reading for others in the class. Use pictures, slogans, and other means to identify the unifying ideas of the article, to stimulate interest, and to activate prior knowledge.

   Bring a copy of the article and your preview to class. Team up with a partner, share your previews, and then read each other's selected article.

Discuss how the previews enhanced your comprehension and motivated your desire to read.

3. Team with a group of four or five other students. Before the next class, each member should collect three political cartoons, each using a different newspaper, magazine, or book. These cartoons may represent current or historical political issues.

   When you return to class, share the cartoons you found, and discuss the knowledge the reader must already have in order to understand the humor. Select the one cartoon you found most enjoyable, and list the background knowledge needed to understand it. When all groups have finished discussing and selecting, have each group read and explain its favorite cartoon to the whole class. As a large group, discuss how this activity illustrates the concept of prior knowledge when reading text. If there are art majors in the class, ask them to share the role of prior knowledge in viewing artworks.

4. Bring to class a nonfiction book or magazine article on a subject you enjoy. With a partner, practice the ReQuest strategy. On completion of the activity, join with two other pairs, and as a small group, discuss the effectiveness of the questioning, the successfulness of the learning that occurred, and your perceptions of the usefulness of this activity in a content area classroom.

Text guess (by a student) for story impressions activity in Figure 9.2

Following the French & Indian War, England passed the Stamp Act to recover some of its war debts. Colonists complained that their right to vote on their own taxes had been taken away by Parliament. The Americans wrote petitions asking for the Stamp Act to be repealed. It was. Groups of colonists called the Sons of Liberty formed and carried on some rather rowdy activities. The Stamp Act was replaced by the Townshend Acts. Angry Americans boycotted all taxed products until England once again replealed the taxes-all except the tax on tea. One night a group of colonists, led by the Sons of Liberty, dressed as Mohawk Indians and threw British overboard into the Boston Harbor. This event was known as the Boston Tea Party.

SUGGESTED READINGS

Anders, P. L., & Lloyd, C. V. (1989). The significance of prior knowledge in the learning of new content-specific instruction. In D. Lapp, J. Flood, & N. Farnan (Eds.), *Content area reading and learning: Instructional strategies.* Upper Saddle River, NJ: Prentice Hall.

Anderson, R. C. (1994). Role of the reader's schema in comprehension, learning and memory. In R. B. Ruddell, M. R. Ruddell, & H. Singer (Eds.), *Theoretical models and processes of reading* (4th ed.). Newark, DE: International Reading Association.

Ash, B. H. (1992). Student-made questions: One way into a literary text. *English Journal, 81*(5), 61–64.

Bransford, J. W. (1983). Schema activation–schema acquisition. In R. C. Anderson, J. Osborn, & R. J. Tierney (Eds.), *Learning to read in American schools.* Hillsdale, NJ: Erlbaum.

Bromley, K., Irwin–De Vitis, L., & Modlo, M. (1995). *Graphic organizers: Visual strategies for active learning.* New York: Scholastic.

Crapse, L. (1995). Helping students construct meaning through their own questions. *Journal of Reading, 38,* 389–390.

Dufflemeyer, F. (1994). Effective anticipation guide statements for learning from expository prose. *Journal of Reading, 37,* 452–457.

Dufflemeyer, F., & Baum, D. (1992). The extended anticipation guide revisited. *Journal of Reading, 35,* 654–656.

Dunston, P. J. (1992). A critique of graphic organizer research. *Reading Research and Instruction, 31,* 57–65.

Gillespie, C. (1990). Questions about student-generated questions. *Journal of Reading, 34,* 250–257.

Herber, H. L. (1978). Prediction as motivation and an aid to comprehension. In *Teaching reading in content areas* (2nd ed.). Upper Saddle River, NJ: Prentice Hall.

Langer, J. A. (1982). Facilitating text processing: The elaboration of prior knowledge. In J. A. Langer & M. T. Smith-Burke (Eds.), *Reader meets author: Bridging the gap.* Newark, DE: International Reading Association.

Le Noir, W. D. (1993). Teacher questions and schema activation. *Clearing House, 66,* 349–352.

Mathiason, C. (1989). Stimulating and sustaining student interest in content area reading. *Reading Research and Instruction, 28,* 76–83.

Middleton, J. (1991). Student-generated analogies in biology. *American Biology Teacher, 53,* 42–46.

Miller, K. K., & George, J. E. (1992). Expository passage organizers: Models for reading and writing. *Journal of Reading, 35,* 372–377.

Moore, D. W., Readence, J. E., & Rickelman, R. (1988). *Prereading activities for content area reading* (2nd ed.). Newark, DE: International Reading Association.

Nolan, R. (1991). Self-questioning and prediction: Combining metacognitive strategies. *Journal of Reading, 35,* 132–138.

Ruddell, M. R. (1996). Engaging students' interest and willing participation in subject area and learning. In D. Lapp, J. Flood, & N. Farnan (Eds.), *Content area reading and learning: Instructional strategies* (2nd ed.). Needham Heights, MA: Allyn & Bacon.

Stipek, D. (1988). *Motivation to learn: From theory to practice.* Upper Saddle River, NJ: Prentice Hall.

chapter 10

Study Strategies

The process of reading is not a half-sleep, but in the highest sense, an exercise, a gymnast's struggle; that the reader is to do something for himself, must be on the alert, must himself or herself construct [meaning]—the text furnishing the hints, the clues, the start or framework.

—Walt Whitman

Organizing Principle

Walt Whitman, the great American poet, says in a few words what we have been illustrating throughout this book: Learning with text is as demanding mentally as gymnastics are physically. Reading is not a passive activity, a "half-sleep," but an active process, an exercise that takes place inside the head. The mental gymnastics that readers engage in help them use text to construct meaning. A reader who works with a text is as skillful as a gymnast who works on a balance beam or the parallel bars.

Students who study texts are self-directed, deliberate in their plans and actions, and conscious of their goals. They have reasons for studying, whether their purposes involve acquiring, organizing, summarizing, or using information and ideas. Studying a text is hard work, just as building the body through gymnastic activity is hard work. It requires readers to be disciplined and patient with print. But because they are deliberate in their plans and actions and conscious of their goals, students who study texts not only know how to work hard but also know how to work smart.

To work smart, students need to develop strategies for studying. Putting study strategies to good use is directly related to students' knowledge and awareness of what it means to study. As they become more aware of studying texts, students look for *structure*—how the important information and ideas are organized in text—in everything they read. Common sense tells us that most texts should have structure, because authors have nothing to gain and much to lose by presenting ideas aimlessly. Whitman put it well: The text furnishes "the hints, the clues, the start or framework." Good readers know how to study more effectively by using the hints and clues provided by authors and the framework of ideas embodied in the structure of the text. They use study strategies to raise questions and make plans for reading; to comprehend, make connections among the important ideas, and remember information; to summarize what they have read; and to take and make notes. The organizing principle suggests that one important aspect of studying is to show students how to use the framework of ideas in text to their advantage: **Looking for and using text structure helps students "do something" with texts in order to process and think more deeply about ideas encountered during reading.**

Chapter Overview

STUDYING TEXTS

SEARCHING FOR AND USING IMPORTANT IDEAS

Series-of-Events Chain

Network Tree   Semantic Maps

CONSTRUCTING GRAPHIC
REPRESENTATIONS   WRITING SUMMARIES

Problem-Solution   Venn
Outline   Diagram   GRASP

Comparison-Contrast
Matrix

TEXT STRUCTURE

External Organization   Internal   Story Structure
                             Organization

                             Text Patterns

MAKING AND TAKING NOTES   USING STUDY SYSTEMS

Note-Taking   Text   SQ3R
Procedure   Annotations   (Survey, Question, Read, Recite, Review)

Frame of Mind

1. What does it mean to study?

2. How are **textually** important ideas different from **contextually** important ideas?

3. How is internal text structure different from external text structure and story structure?

4. What are text patterns?

5. How do graphic representations help students make connections among important ideas?

6. How can you show students how to summarize information?

7. How can you show students how to take and make notes?

8. How can students use a study system, such as SQ3R, to preview text, raise questions, and process and reflect on ideas encountered during reading?

The poster caught our attention immediately. It had just gone up on the bulletin board in Julie Meyer's classroom. "School Daze: From A to Z" defined significant school activities in the lives of students, each beginning with a letter of the alphabet. The entry for the letter *S* just happened to be the subject of this chapter. It read, "STUDY: *Those precious moments between soap operas, movies, sports, video games, food, personal grooming, and general lollygagging when one opens one's school books—and falls asleep.*"

Though some students might agree that study is a quick cure for insomnia, few of us would deny that studying texts is one of the most frequent and predominant activities in schools today. The older students become, the more they are expected to learn with texts.

It's not uncommon to find a teacher prefacing text assignments by urging students to "study the material." And some students do. They are able to study effectively because they know what it means to *approach* a text assignment: to *analyze* the reading task at hand, to *make plans* for reading, and then to *use strategies* to suit their purposes for studying. Students who approach texts in this way achieve a level of independence because they are in charge of their own learning.

Other students, less skilled in reading and studying, wage a continual battle with texts. Some probably wonder why teachers make a big deal out of studying in the first place. For them, the exhortation to "study the material" goes in one ear and out the other. Others try to cope with the demands of study. Yet they are apt to equate studying texts with rote memorization, cramming "meaningless" material into short-term memory.

Whenever teachers urge students to study, they probably have something definite in mind. Whatever that something is, it shouldn't remain an ambiguous or unattainable classroom goal. All too often, the problem for students is that they aren't aware of what it means to study, let alone to use study strategies.

What better context than the content area classroom to teach learners what it means to be a student? The term *student,* derived from Latin, means "one who pursues knowledge."

Studying is an intentional act. Students need to establish goals for studying as much as they need to have reasons for reading. Nila B. Smith's (1959) straightforward definition of study is a simple and practical way of conceptualizing what it means to study. She explains studying as strategies that we use when our purpose is to do something with the content we have read. "Doing something" means putting strategies to good use by applying them toward purposeful ends. No wonder, then, that study is often characterized as strategic learning.

The extrinsic reason that most students give for studying is to cover the material or do well in a course. Students will tell you that they study to pass tests. Fair enough. They are quick to associate studying with memorizing information. A concept of study that includes retention has merit. But students run the risk of subscribing to a reductionist fallacy by believing that one part equals the whole or simply that memorizing is study. Too many students spend too much time using up too much energy on what often becomes their only strategy: rote memorization. Rote memorizing leads to short-lived recall of unrelated bits and pieces of information. Alternatives to rote memorization should be taught and reinforced when and where they count the most: in a content area classroom.

Studying is an unhurried and reflective process. A lack of discipline and patience with print is probably one reason why so few adolescents and young adults study effectively on their own in secondary schools or in college. A sociology instructor once met with students who were doing poorly in his class during their first semester in college. The purpose of the meeting was to discuss ways to study sociology. The students, however, soon turned the meeting into a battleground, venting their own frustrations with the course. The sociologist finally reached his own boiling point: "Listen, the bottom line is this: Studying is hard work. You can't read sociological material once and expect to 'get it' through osmosis. You should 'work' the material. Read it. And reread it. First, get the important ideas straight in your head. Make connections. And eventually you will make them a part of you."

We find ourselves agreeing with the college instructor's analysis of the "bottom line." Studying text *is* hard work. Cultivating a repertoire of study strategies for "getting the important ideas straight in your head" is essential.

Showing students how to distinguish important from less important ideas is one of the key aspects of studying texts effectively.

TEXTUALLY AND CONTEXTUALLY IMPORTANT IDEAS

To make information accessible, authors organize ideas in text. Some ideas, of course, are more important than others. Suppose you were reading a magazine article and came across the passage in Box 10.1. Read the passage; then, in the space provided, write what you think is the most important idea and why.

Box 10.1

What's the Most Important Idea in This Passage?

Standards are essential as reference points. Wise living depends upon finding a standard against which values may be measured. Consider, for example, the story about a fellow who was riding his motorcycle on a cold day. The zipper on his jacket was broken, so the rider stopped and put the jacket on backwards to shield him from the wind. A bit later, the rider had an accident and was knocked unconscious. He stayed in the hospital for weeks. The doctors said the boy wasn't hurt much in the wreck, but he was severely injured when the policeman tried to turn his head around to match his jacket. You see, a coat is supposed to zip up the front and the policeman made his judgment against that standard, which just goes to show you: If the standard is wrong, then the resulting decision will be wrong.

What is the most important idea in the passage?

_____

_____

_____

Why do you think so?

_____

_____

_____

Source: Passage from "Things Worth Keeping," by Bishop Ernest A. Fitzgerald, *Pace Magazine*, December 1987. Reprinted by permission of Ernest A. Fitzgerald.

If you were to compare your response with others' responses, what each of you wrote as the most important idea would vary. You may have written something to the effect that "standards guide the decisions we make," while someone else may have responded, "One should try not to lose one's head in an emergency." Why is there a difference? Why not a single main idea?

In their research, Moore and Cunningham (1986) classify the main ideas produced by readers according to the similarity in their responses. As a result, the researchers were able to identify nine types of main-idea response. They concluded that the term *main idea* serves as an umbrella for a *wide range of tasks* that readers engage in when they search for main ideas in a text. No wonder Pearson (1981) characterizes the concept "main idea" as an abstraction, "a polyglot of tasks and relations among ideas" (p. 124).

So what are important ideas? At least one thing is certain. What a reader identifies as the main idea may *not* be what the author intended as the main idea. The reader's purpose and the perspective that he or she brings to the text often determines the relative importance attached to what the author is saying. In this respect, the important ideas in text may vary from reader to reader and text situation to text situation (Winograd & Bridge 1986).

The distinction between *contextually* important information and *textually* important information helps the teacher understand where students are coming from when they respond to main-idea questions during discussion or writing activity. Van Dijk (1979) explains that textually important information is considered central to the text by the author. As a result, authors often showcase textually important ideas in the text organization they use.

Contextually important information, by contrast, is information that the reader considers important. In earlier chapters, we explored strategies that encourage students to use what they know to respond to text—in effect, to construct meaning that is personally or contextually important. But throughout this book, we also underscore the importance of grasping an author's intended meaning. On the road to reading maturity, students must develop flexibility in distinguishing what is textually important from what is contextually important in the texts that they read.

Authors impose structure—an organization among ideas—on their writing. Perceiving structure in text material improves learning and retention. When students are shown how to see relationships among concepts and bits of essential information, they are in a better position to respond to meaning and to distinguish important from less important ideas.

SEARCHING FOR AND USING TEXT STRUCTURE

Educational psychologists from Thorndike (1917) to Kintsch (1977) and Meyer and Rice (1984) have shown that text structure is a crucial variable in learning and memory. Likewise, for more than 50 years, reading educators have underscored the recognition and use of organization as essential processes underlying comprehension and retention (Salisbury 1934; Smith 1964; Niles 1965; Herber 1978).

The primary purpose of many content area texts is to provide users with information. To make information readily accessible, authors use external and internal structural features. *External text structure* is characterized by a text's overall instructional design—its format features. Its *internal text structure* is reflected by the interrelationships among ideas in the text as well as by the subordination of some ideas to others.

External Text Structure

Printed texts such as textbooks contain certain format features—organizational aids—that are built into the text to facilitate reading. This book, for example, contains a *preface,* a *table of contents, appendixes,* a *bibliography,* and *indexes.* These aids, along with the *title page, dedication, list of tables and illustrations,* and *glossary,* are called the *front matter* and *end matter* of a book. Of course, textbooks vary in the amount of front and end matter they contain. These aids can be valuable tools for prospective users of a textbook. Yet the novice reader hardly acknowledges their presence in texts, let alone uses them to advantage.

In addition, each chapter of a textbook usually has *introductory or summary statements, headings, graphs, charts, illustrations,* and *guide questions.*

Organizational aids, whether in electronic or printed texts, are potentially valuable—if they are not skipped or glossed over by readers. Headings, for example, are inserted in the text to divide it into logical units. Headings strategically placed in a text should guide the reader by highlighting major ideas.

Within a text, authors may use an internal structure to connect ideas logically in a coherent whole. Internal text structure might vary from passage to passage, depending on the author's purpose. These structures, or patterns of organization, within a text are closely associated with informational writing.

Internal Text Structure

Content area textbooks are written to inform. This is why exposition is the primary mode of discourse found in texts. This is not to say that some authors don't at times attempt to persuade or entertain their readers. They may. However, their primary business is to *tell, show, describe,* or *explain.* It stands to reason that the more logically connected one idea is to another, depending on the author's informative purpose, the more coherent the description or explanation is.

Patterns of organization represent the different types of logical connections among the important and less important ideas in informational material. Meyer (1975) suggests that the pattern that ties these ideas together is often

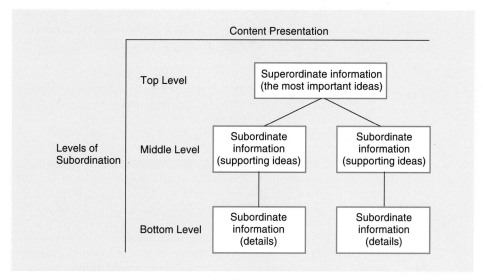

Content Presentation

| | | Superordinate information (the most important ideas) | |
|Top Level| | | |

Levels of Subordination   Middle Level   Subordinate information (supporting ideas)   Subordinate information (supporting ideas)

Bottom Level   Subordinate information (details)   Subordinate information (details)

FIGURE 10.1   **Hierarchical Relationships Between Ideas in Informational Text**

located at the "top level" of the author's content structure. She explains that an author may organize content so that there is a *hierarchical relationship* among ideas in the text passage. Therefore, the most important, or *superordinate,* ideas should be located at the top levels of the content presentation and have many supporting ideas and details below them. According to Meyer, "These top-level ideas dominate their subordinate ideas. The lower-level ideas describe or give more information about the ideas above them" (pp. 13–14). Figure 10.1 provides a general depiction of the structure of hierarchical relationships among ideas in a text passage.

The skilled reader searches for the structure of idea relationships in a text and can readily differentiate the important ideas from less important ideas in the material. Research has shown that good readers know how to look for major thought relationships (Meyer, Brandt, & Bluth 1980; Taylor 1980). They approach a reading assignment looking for a predominant *text pattern* or organization that will tie together the ideas contained throughout the text passage.

Text patterns represent the different types of logical connections among the important and less important ideas in informational material. A case can be made for five text patterns that seem to predominate in informational writing: *description, sequence, comparison and contrast, cause and effect,* and *problem and solution.*

Here are descriptions and examples of these top-level structures.

1. *Description.* Providing information about a topic, concept, event, object, person, idea, and so on (facts, characteristics, traits, features), usually qualifying the listing by criteria such as size or importance. This pattern connects

ideas through description by listing the important characteristics or attributes of the topic under consideration. Niles (1965) and Bartlett (1978) find the description pattern to be the most common textbook organization. Here is an example:

> There were several points in the fight for freedom of religion. One point was that religion and government should be kept apart. Americans did not want any form of a national church as was the case in England. Americans made sure that no person would be denied his or her religious beliefs.

2. *Sequence.* Putting facts, events, or concepts into a sequence. The author traces the development of the topic or gives the steps in the process. Time reference may be explicit or implicit, but a sequence is evident in the pattern. The following paragraph illustrates the pattern:

> John F. Kennedy was the Democratic candidate for president when in October 1960 he first suggested there should be a Peace Corps. After he was elected, Kennedy asked his brother-in-law, Sargent Shriver, to help set up a Peace Corps. In March 1961, Kennedy gave an order to create the organization. It wasn't until September that Congress approved the Peace Corps and appropriated the money to run it for one year.

3. *Comparison and contrast.* Pointing out likenesses (comparison) and/or differences (contrast) among facts, people, events, concepts, and so on. Study this example:

> Castles were built for defense, not comfort. In spite of some books and movies that have made them attractive, castles were cold, dark, gloomy places to live. Rooms were small and not the least bit charming. Except for the great central hall or the kitchen, there were no fires to keep the rooms heated. Not only was there a lack of furniture, but what there was was uncomfortable.

4. *Cause and effect.* Showing how facts, events, or concepts (effects) happen or come into being because of other facts, events, or concepts (causes). Examine this paragraph for causes and effects:

> The fire was started by sparks from a campfire left by a careless camper. Thousands of acres of important watershed burned before the fire was brought under control. As a result of the fire, trees and the grasslands on the slopes of the valley were gone. Smoking black stumps were all that remained of tall pine trees.

5. *Problem and solution.* Showing the development of a problem and one or more solutions to the problem. Consider the following example:

> The skyrocketing price of oil in the 1970s created a serious problem for many Americans. The oil companies responded to the high cost of purchasing oil by

searching for new oil supplies. This resulted in new deposits being found in some Third World nations, such as Nigeria. Oil companies also began drilling for oil on the ocean floor, and scientists discovered ways to extract oil from a rock known as *oil shale.*

Authors often showcase text patterns by giving readers clues or signals to help them figure out the structure being used. Readers usually become aware of the pattern if they are looking for the signals. A signal may be a word or a phrase that helps the reader follow the writer's thoughts. Linguists call these words *connectives,* or *ties,* because they connect one idea to another (Halliday & Hasan 1976).

Figure 10.2 shows connectives that authors use to call attention to the organizational patterns just defined.

Awareness of the pattern of *long stretches* of text is especially helpful in planning reading assignments. In selecting from the textbook a passage of several paragraphs or several pages, teachers first need to determine whether a predominant text pattern is contained in the material. This is no easy task.

Informational writing is complex. Authors do not write texts in neat, perfectly identifiable patterns. Within the individual paragraphs of a text assignment, several kinds of thought relationships often exist. Suppose an author

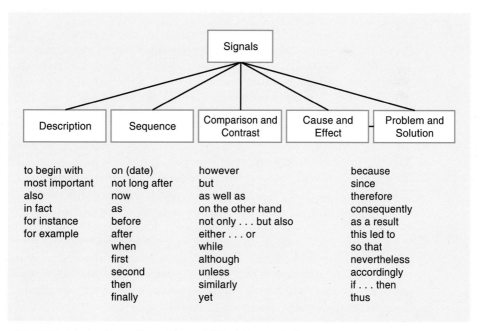

Signals				
Description	Sequence	Comparison and Contrast	Cause and Effect	Problem and Solution
to begin with	on (date)	however	because	
most important	not long after	but	since	
also	now	as well as	therefore	
in fact	as	on the other hand	consequently	
for instance	before	not only . . . but also	as a result	
for example	after	either . . . or	this led to	
	when	while	so that	
	first	although	nevertheless	
	second	unless	accordingly	
	then	similarly	if . . . then	
	finally	yet	thus	

FIGURE 10.2   **Reading Signal Words and Phrases**

begins a passage by stating a problem. In telling about the development of the problem, the author *describes* a set of events that contributed to the problem. Or perhaps the author *compares* or *contrasts* the problem under consideration with another problem. In subsequent paragraphs, the *solutions* or attempts at solution to the problem are stated. In presenting the solutions, the author uses heavy description and explanation. These descriptions and explanations are logically organized in a *sequence.*

The difficulty that teachers face is analyzing the overall text pattern, even though several types of thought relationships are probably embedded in the material. Analyzing a text for a predominant pattern depends in part on how clearly an author represents the relationships in the text.

Several guidelines follow for analyzing text patterns. First, survey the text for the most important idea in the selection. Are there any explicit signal words that indicate a pattern that will tie together the ideas throughout the passage? Second, study the content of the text for additional important ideas. Are these ideas logically connected to the most important idea? Is a pattern evident? Third, outline or diagram the relationships among the superordinate and subordinate ideas in the selection. Use the diagram to specify the major relationships contained in the text structure and to sort out the important from the less important ideas. Later in this chapter, we will explore various strategies that scaffold instruction in ways that will help students use diagrams, or *graphic representations,* to map relationships in various text patterns.

Story Structure

Most simple stories in Western culture actually aren't as simple as they might appear on the surface. Since the mid-1970s, cognitive psychologists have demonstrated how complex the underlying structure of a story can be. These psychologists have attempted to identify the basic elements that make up a well-developed story (Mandler & Johnson 1977; Thorndyke 1977; Stein & Glenn 1979). Their efforts have led to the development of several variations of *story grammar.* Just as sentence grammar provides a way of describing how sentences are constructed, story grammar helps specify the basic parts of a story and how those parts tie together to form a well-constructed story.

What do most well-developed stories have in common? Though individual story grammars may differ in their level of specificity, most researchers would agree that a narrative centers on a *setting, plot,* and *theme.* The setting introduces the main characters, or *protagonists,* and situates the characters in a time and place. The plot of a story is made up of one or more *episodes.* The intricacies of a story are often manifested in its episodic structure. A simple story has a single episode. More complex stories may have two, several, or many episodes as well as different settings. However, even a single-episode story is defined by an intricate causal chain of basic elements:

1. *An initiating event.* Either an idea or an action that sets further events in motion.

2. *An internal response.* The protagonist's inner reaction to the initiating event, in which the protagonist sets a *goal* or attempts to solve a *problem.*

3. *An attempt.* The protagonist's efforts to achieve the goal or alleviate the problem. Several attempts, some failed, may be evident in an episode.

4. *An outcome.* The success or failure of the protagonist's attempts.

5. *A resolution.* An action or state of affairs that evolves from the protagonist's success or failure to achieve the goal or alleviate the problem.

6. *A reaction.* An idea, an emotion, or a further event that expresses the protagonist's feelings about the success or failure of goal attainment or problem resolution or that relates the events in the story to some broader set of concerns.

Figure 10.3 contains an analysis of a popular short story often taught in a sophomore-level English course, "The Sniper," by Liam O'Flaherty.

Story: **"The Sniper"**
Author: **Liam O'Flaherty**

Plot	**Theme**

Episode
  Setting: The story takes place on a June night 50 years ago in Dublin, Ireland, on a rooftop near O'Connell Bridge.   The moral dilemma inherent in war.
  Character(s): Two snipers opposing one another.

Chain of Events
  Initiating event: A Republican sniper is spotted and shot by an enemy sniper. The sniper is hit in the arm, so he is unable to fire his rifle.

  Internal responses: The Republican sniper swears to himself in anger and resolves to shoot the enemy (Free Stater) sniper. He must eliminate the sniper in order to escape before morning's light.

  Attempt/outcome: The Republican sniper crawls to a new position, where he puts his cap on his rifle muzzle, raises it, and consequently draws fire from the enemy sniper. He pretends to be dead.

  Resolution: The enemy sniper falls for the trick and stands up, and the Republican sniper is able to kill him with his revolver. (The enemy's body falls to the street below.) He has survived.

  Reaction: After he takes a drink, the sniper's nerves are steadied, and he decides to look at the enemy sniper to see if he had known him before the Irish army split. He also admires him for being such a good shot. Turning the dead body over, the sniper looks into his brother's face.

FIGURE 10.3   **Story Map Analysis**

The episodic events in the story form a causal chain. Each event leads to the next one as the main character moves toward goal attainment or problem resolution. Determining the theme of a story involves moral, psychological, or philosophic judgment on the part of the reader. When readers evaluate the theme, they are making meaning or constructing knowledge. Involving students in the thematic content of stories is a personal process. Students' awareness of the theme will vary, depending on the background knowledge and experiences they bring to the story. However, a reader must learn to deal with theme in relation to the story's plot: What does the story *mean to you* in addition to what it tells? What is the author *trying to say to you* through the protagonist's actions? What do *you see* in the story, regardless of what the author may have meant?

Teachers who analyze a story's structure for setting, plot, and theme are in a better position to make decisions about instruction. According to Gillet and Temple (1982), teachers can make good use of story structure, depending on whether (1) there is access to reading materials that are written around perceivable story structures, (2) students have developed a sense of story structure (i.e., students have developed a schema for how stories are put together), and (3) students use their schema for stories to predict what is coming next in a new story. However, Beck, McKeown, McCaslin, and Burket (1979) recommend developing a *story map* before teaching a story.

A story map is a planning tool. It helps teachers analyze the story so that the questions asked during discussion will create a coherent framework for understanding and remembering the text. Therefore, a story map defines what most stories have in common: key structural elements. The analysis of the story elements of "The Sniper" in Figure 10.3 represents a story map. Suggestions are given in Table 10.1 for the kinds of questions that may be posed from the story map.

These questions allow readers to recognize and grasp the explicit and implicit elements of the story. Once students understand the general framework of the story, broader questions can be raised about the main character's motives and intentions, the theme, and conflict situations.

With informational texts, students must grasp the explicit and implicit relations in the text patterns that an author uses to structure content. When readers perceive and interact with text organization, they are in a better position to comprehend and retain information.

GRAPHIC REPRESENTATIONS

Graphic or visual representations help learners comprehend and retain *textually important information.* When students learn how to use and construct graphic representations, they are in control of a study strategy that allows them to identify what parts of a text are important, how the ideas and con-

---

TABLE 10.1
Story Map Questions

Beginning-of-Story Questions

Setting: Where does the story take place? When does the story take place? Who is the main character? What is _____ like?

Problem: What is _____'s problem? What does _____ need? Why is _____ in trouble?

Middle-of-Story Questions

Goal: What does _____decide to do? What does _____ have to attempt to do?

Attempts   What does _____ do about _____? What happens to _____?
or outcome: What will _____ do now?

End-of-Story Questions

Resolution: How has _____ solved the problem? How has _____ achieved the goal? What would you do to solve _____'s problem?

Reaction: How does _____ feel about the problem? Why does _____ do _____? How does _____ feel at the end?

Theme: What is the moral of the story? What did you learn from the story? What is the major point of the story? What does this story say about *(unusual truth)*?

---

cepts encountered in the text are related, and where they can find specific information to support more important ideas.

An entire family of teacher-directed and learner-directed techniques and strategies is associated with the use of graphic representations to depict relationships in text: word maps, semantic maps, semantic webs, graphic organizers, flowcharts, concept matrices, and tree diagrams, to name a few. Although it is easy to get confused by the plethora of labels, a rose by any other name is still a rose.

What these techniques and strategies have in common is that they help students interact with and outline textually important information. For example, when students read a text with an appropriate graphic organizer in mind, they focus on important ideas and relationships. And when they construct their own graphic organizers, they become actively involved in outlining those ideas and relationships.

Outlining helps students clarify relationships. Developing an outline is analogous to fitting together the pieces in a puzzle. Think of a puzzle piece as a separate idea and a text as the whole. A completed puzzle shows the separate identity of each idea as well as the part each idea plays in the total picture (Hansell 1978). Outlining strategies can be used effectively to facilitate a careful analysis and synthesis of the relationships in a text. They can form the basis for critical discussion and evaluation of the author's main points.

Problems arise when students are restricted by the means by which they must depict relationships spatially on paper. The word *outlining* for most of us immediately conjures up an image of the "correct" or "classic" format that we have all learned at one time or another but have probably failed to use regularly in real-life study situations. The classic form of outlining has the student represent the relatedness of information in linear form:

I. Main Idea

    A. Idea supporting I
        1. Detail supporting A
        2. Detail supporting A
           a. Detail supporting 2
           b. Detail supporting 2

    B. Idea supporting I
        1. Detail supporting B
        2. Detail supporting B

II. Main Idea

This conventional format represents a hierarchical ordering of ideas at different levels of subordination. Roman numerals signal the major or superordinate concepts in a text section; capital letters, the supporting or coordinate concepts; Arabic numbers, the supporting or subordinate details; and lowercase letters, the subsubordinate details.

Some readers have trouble using a restricted form of outlining. Initially, at least, they need a more visual display than the one offered by the conventional format. And this is where graphic representations can play a critical role in the development of independent learners.

To show students how to use and construct graphic representations, first begin by assessing how students normally outline text material. Do they have a sense of subordination among ideas? Do they have strategies for connecting major and minor concepts? Do they use alternatives to the conventional format? Make them aware of the rationale for organizing information through outlining. The jigsaw puzzle analogy—fitting pieces of information together into a coherent whole—works well for this purpose. Assessment and building awareness set the stage for illustrating, modeling, and applying the strategies.

To introduce students to various kinds of graphic representations that may be applicable to texts in your content area, Jones, Pierce, and Hunter (1988–1989) suggest some of the following steps:

1. *Present an example of a graphic representation that corresponds to the type of outline you plan to teach.* For example, suppose that a text that students will read is organized around a cause and effect text pattern. First, preview the text with the students. Help them discover features of the text that may signal the pattern. Make students aware that the title, subheads, and signal words provide them with clues to the structure of the text. Then ask questions that are pertinent to the pattern—for example, "What happens in this reading? What causes it to happen? What are the important factors that cause these effects?"

2. *Demonstrate how to construct a graphic outline.* Suppose that math students have completed reading about the differences between isosceles triangles and isosceles trapezoids. Show them how to construct a *Venn diagram* to map how they are alike and different. Next, refer to the comparison and contrast questions you raised in the preview. Walk students through the procedures that lead to the development of the Venn diagram: First, on an overhead transparency, present an example of a partially completed Venn graphic. Second, have students review the text and offer suggestions to help complete the graphic. Figure 10.4 shows a class-constructed rendering of the Venn diagram. Third, develop procedural knowledge by discussing when to use the Venn graphic and why.

3. *Coach students in the use of the graphic outline and give them opportunities to practice.* If other texts represent a particular text pattern that you have already demonstrated with the class, encourage students individually or in teams to construct their own graphic outlines and to use their constructions as the basis for class discussion.

Semantic (Cognitive) Mapping

A popular graphic representation, often called a *semantic map* or a *cognitive map*, helps students identify important ideas and shows how these ideas fit together. Teachers avoid the problem of teaching a restricted, conventional outline format. Instead, the students are responsible for creating a logical arrangement among key words or phrases that connect main ideas to subordinate information. When maps are used, instruction should proceed from teacher-guided modeling and illustration to student-generated productions.

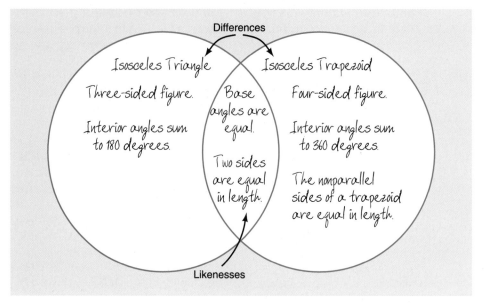

FIGURE 10.4 **Venn Diagram for Isosceles Triangle and Isosceles Trapezoid**

A semantic map has three basic components:

1. *Core question or concept.* The question or concept (stated as a key word or phrase), which establishes the main focus of the map. All the ideas generated for the map by the students are related in some way to the core question or concept.

2. *Strands.* The subordinate ideas generated by the students that help clarify the question or explain the concept.

3. *Supports.* The details, inferences, and generalizations that are related to each strand. These supports clarify the strands and distinguish one strand from another.

Students use the semantic map as an organization tool that illustrates visually the categories and relationships associated with the core question or concept under study. To model and illustrate the use of a semantic map, a middle school social studies teacher walked students through the process. The class began a unit on Ohio's early settlements. As part of the prereading discussion, four questions were raised for the class to ponder: What do you think were the three most important early settlements in Ohio? What do you think these settlements had in common? How were they different? In what ways might the location of a settlement be important to the survival of the settlers? Predictions were made and discussed and led naturally to the text assignment.

The teacher assigned the material, directing the students to read with the purpose of confirming or modifying their predictions about the early settlements.

After reading, the students formed small groups. Each group listed everything its members could remember about the settlements on index cards, with one piece of information per card.

In the center of the chalkboard, the teacher wrote "The First Ohio Settlements" and circled the phrase. She then asked students to provide the main strands that helped answer the question and clarify the concept "What were Ohio's most important early settlements?" The students responded by contrasting their predictions to the explanations in the text assignment. The teacher began to build the semantic map on the board by explaining how strands help students answer the questions and understand the main concept.

Next, she asked the students to work in their groups to sort the cards that had been compiled according to each of the settlements depicted on the semantic map. Through discussion, questioning, and think-aloud probes, the class completed the semantic map depicted in Figure 10.5.

Some teachers prefer to distinguish strands from supports through the use of lines. Notice that in Figure 10.5, a double line connects the strands to the core concept. Supports are linked to each web strand by single lines. With younger students, some teachers also recommend using different-colored chalk to distinguish one strand from another.

With appropriate modeling, explanation, and experience, students soon understand the why, what, and how of semantic maps and can begin to develop maps by themselves. We suggest that the teacher begin by providing the core question or concept. Students can then compare and contrast their individual productions in a follow-up discussion. Of course, text assignments should also be given in which students identify the core concept on their own and then generate the structures that support and explain it.

Using Graphic Representations to Reflect Text Patterns

Students can be shown how to construct maps and other types of graphic representations to reflect the text patterns authors use to organize ideas. According to Jones et al. (1988–1989), "A fundamental rule in constructing graphic representations is that the structure of the graphic should reflect the structure of the text it represents" (p. 21). For example, the semantic map of the first Ohio settlements in Figure 10.5 reflects a predominantly descriptive text pattern, but in describing the settlement of each city, the text lends itself to comparison and contrast. The teacher invites students to reorganize the heavily descriptive text into a comparison-and-contrast pattern through the use of the class-constructed semantic map. To make explicit connections that

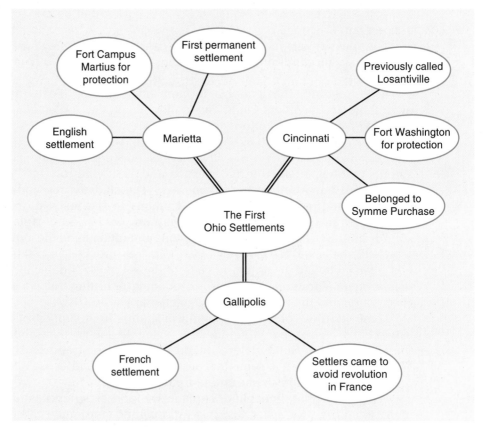

FIGURE 10.5   **Semantic Map: The First Ohio Settlements**

tie together how the settlements were alike and different, she asks guiding questions, such as "What did Marietta and Gallipolis have in common?" or "How were Marietta and Cincinnati different?"

Jones and her colleagues recommend a variety of possible graphic representations that reflect different text patterns. These "generic" outlines are illustrated in Appendix C. What follows are classroom examples of how some of these outlines might be developed in content area classrooms.

Comparison and Contrast Matrix

In addition to the Venn diagram and semantic map graphic displays, a teacher can show students how a comparison and contrast pattern serves to organize ideas in text through the use of a matrix outline. A comparison and contrast matrix shows similarities and differences between two or more things (people, places, events, concepts, processes, etc.). Readers compare and contrast the target concepts listed across the top of the matrix according to attributes, properties, or characteristics listed along the left side. Study the two examples of a comparison and contrast matrix in Figure 10.6. High school students used the biology example to outline the likenesses and differences of fungi and algae. Precalculus students used the matrix outline to compare and contrast conic sections (parabola, ellipse, and hyperbola).

Problem and Solution Outline

This graphic representation depicts a problem, attempted solutions, the results or outcomes associated with the attempted solutions, and the end result. It works equally well with narrative or informational texts to display the central problem in a story or the problem and solution text pattern. Noden and Vacca (1994) show how a world history teacher used the problem and solution outline in conjunction with a text assignment related to Wat Tyler's Rebellion, which took place in England in 1381. Wat Tyler's Rebellion was one of the first popular English movements for freedom and equality. The teacher introduced the outline in Figure 10.7 as a tool for organizing the information in the text relevant to the problem. Students first worked in pairs to complete the outline and then shared their work with the whole class. The completed outline in Figure 10.7 illustrates the thinking of two "study buddies."

Network Tree

The network tree is based on the same principle as the graphic organizers introduced in Chapter 8 and used in the chapter overviews in this book. That is to say, it represents the network of relationships that exists between superordinate concepts and subordinate concepts. It can be used to show causal information or to describe a central idea in relation to its attributes and examples. Notice how math students explored relationships in the quadratic formula by using the network tree illustrated in Figure 10.8.

Series-of-Events Chain

The series-of-events chain may be used with narrative material to show the chain of events that lead to the resolution of conflict in a story. It may also be used with informational text to reflect the sequence pattern in a text. It may include any sequence of events, including the steps in a linear procedure, the chain of events (effects) caused by some event, or the stages of something. Science and historical texts are often organized in a sequence pattern and lend themselves well to this type of graphic display. A science class, for example, might be asked to map the sequence of steps in the scientific method by using a series-of-events chain. After reading about the scientific method, students might make an outline similar to the one in Figure 10.9.

In an English class, students read an excerpt from *My Bondage and My Freedom*, by Frederick Douglass, the famous American slave, abolitionist,

	Fungi	Algae
Body structure		
Food source		
Method of reproduction		
Living environment		

a

FIGURE 10.6   Comparison and Contrast Matrices for Biology (a) and Precalculus (b)

	Parabola	Ellipse	Hyperbola
Sketch two examples			
Equation in standard form			
Special characteristics			
Foci (focal points)			
Line(s) of symmetry			

b

Problem	Who has the problem? **Peasants of England** What was the problem? **Unfair taxes and harsh labor laws** Why was it a problem? **Peasants were treated as serfs and were the lowest class of people in England.**

	Attempted Solutions	Outcomes
Solutions	1. Riots 2. Protest march on London to force a meeting with king 3. Tyler refuses to give in — makes more demands	1. Property destroyed People killed 2. King's advisers desert him; king agrees to protesters' demands 3. Tyler killed by mayor of London

End Result
King broke his promises Peasants' demands forgotten, but the rebellion inspired other popular movements for freedom and equality

FIGURE 10.7   **Problem and Solution Outline for Wat Tyler's Rebellion**

Source: Reprinted with permission from Harry Noden and Richard Vacca (1994), *Whole Language in Middle and Secondary Classrooms* (New York: HarperCollins).

and journalist. Douglass writes about the reasons for and purposes of the Negro spirituals that slaves sang and the effects that these songs had had on his life. The teacher assigned the text selection to be read in class and then divided the students into learning circles (four-member teams) to work through the sequence of events that had led to Douglass's hatred of slavery. The series-of-events chain in Figure 10.10 illustrates the work of one of the learning circles.

Appendix C illustrates additional types of graphic representations that may be adapted to different content areas. Closely associated with the use of graphic representations is an instructional scaffold known as a *text frame*.

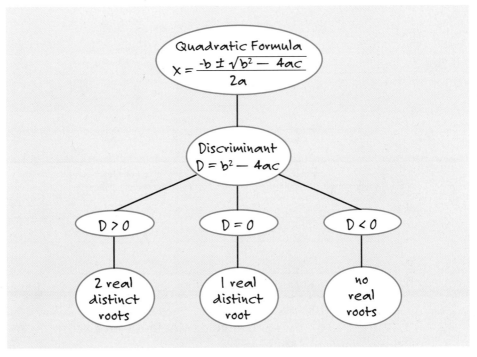

FIGURE 10.8   **Network Tree for the Quadratic Formula**

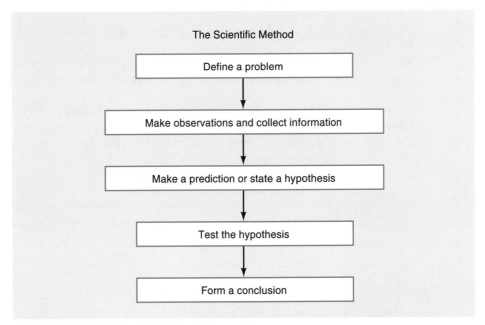

FIGURE 10.9   **Series-of-Events Chain for the Scientific Method**

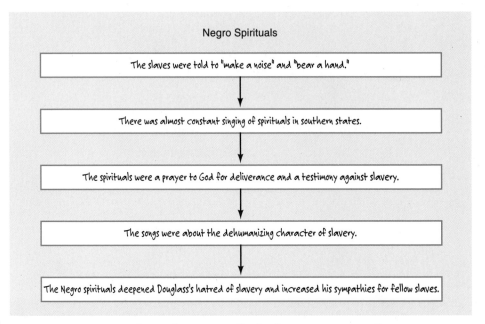

FIGURE 10.10   **Series-of-Events Chain for an Excerpt from**
My Bondage and My Freedom

Using Text Frames with Graphic Representations

Graphic representations are closely associated with text frames. Text frames are the key questions and categories of information that parallel the text patterns used by authors (Armbruster & Anderson 1985). Skilled readers are aware of these key questions and categories, and they study texts with the expectation that the authors have organized the content within the text patterns that are associated with a content area.

Along with the graphic representations, introduce students to the key questions associated with each of the frames. Beuhl (1991), for example, lists the types of questions associated with the problem and solution, cause and effect, and comparison and contrast patterns.

PROBLEM AND SOLUTION FRAME

1. What is the problem?

2. Who has the problem?

3. What is causing the problem?

4. What are the effects of the problem?

5. Who is trying to solve the problem?

6. What solutions are attempted?

7. What are the results of these solutions?

8. Is the problem solved? Do any new problems develop because of the solutions?

CAUSE AND EFFECT FRAME

1. What happens?

2. What causes it to happen?

3. What are the important elements or factors that cause this effect?

4. How are these factors or elements interrelated?

5. Will this result always happen from these causes? Why or why not?

6. How would the result change if the elements or factors were different?

COMPARISON AND CONTRAST FRAME

1. What items are being compared and contrasted?

2. What categories of attributes can be used to compare and contrast the items?

3. How are the items alike or similar?

4. How are the items not alike or different?

5. What are the most important qualities or attributes that make the items similar?

6. What are the most important qualities or attributes that make the items different?

7. In terms of the qualities that are most important, are the items more alike or more different?

Additional text-frame questions are provided in Appendix C. There are many benefits to learning how to use and construct graphic representations, not the least of which is that they make it easier for students to find and reorganize important ideas and information in the text.

In addition to using graphic outlines, teachers can scaffold students' writing of summaries to distinguish important ideas from less important ideas. Let's explore how summaries support students' interactions with text.

WRITING SUMMARIES

Summarizing involves reducing a text to its main points. To become adept at summary writing, students must be able to discern and analyze text structure. If they are insensitive to the organization of ideas and events in expository or narrative writing, students will find it difficult to distinguish important from less important information. Good summarizers, therefore, guard against including information that is not important in the text passage being condensed. Immature text learners, by contrast, tend to *retell* rather than condense information, often including in their summaries interesting but inessential tidbits from the passage. Good summarizers write in their own words but are careful to maintain the author's point of view and to stick closely to the sequence of ideas or events as presented in the reading selection. When important ideas are not explicitly stated in the material, good summary writers create their own topic sentences to reflect textually implicit main ideas.

Kintsch and van Dijk (1978) were among the first to formulate a set of basic rules for summarization based on analyses of how people summarize effectively. Others have modified and adapted these rules, but generally, students must follow these procedures:

1. *Include no unnecessary detail.* In preparing a summary, students must learn to delete trivial and repetitious information from a text passage.

2. *Collapse lists.* When a text passage includes examples, details, actions, or traits, students must learn how to condense these into broader categories of information. With frequent exposure to instructional activities such as graphic organizers, vocabulary categorization exercises, and outlining strategies, students will soon become aware that similar items of information can be encompassed by more inclusive concepts. They must learn to summarize information by collapsing a list of details and thinking of a key word or phrase that names its concept. Study the examples that Hare and Borchardt (1984) give: "If you saw a list like eyes, ears, neck, arms, and legs, you could say 'body parts.' Or, if you saw a list like ice skating, skiing, or sledding, you could say 'winter sports'" (p. 66).

3. *Use topic sentences.* Expository text sometimes contains explicit topic sentences that tell what a paragraph is about. However, if a paragraph doesn't have a topic sentence, students must learn to create their own for a summary. This is probably the most difficult demand placed on maturing learners.

4. *Integrate information.* Summarizers must learn how to use key words, phrases, and explicit and invented topic sentences to compose a summary. The first three rules help students do the basic work of summarizing. In other words, the rules *prepare* students for writing the summary. Yet when they actually put ideas into words on paper, they must integrate the information into a coherent piece of writing.

5. *Polish the summary.* Because writing often follows a composing process, students must learn to revise a *draft* of a summary into a more organized, natural-sounding piece of writing. While rethinking a summary, students will get a firmer grasp on the main points of the material and will state them clearly.

Using GRASP to Write a Summary

Teachers can show students how to summarize information through the guided reading procedure (GRP). After students have read a text passage, they turn the books face down and try to remember everything that was important in the passage. What they recall is recorded by the teacher on the chalkboard. Seize this opportune moment to show students how to delete trivial and repetitious information from the list of ideas on the board. As part of the procedure, the students are given a chance to return to the passage, review it, and make sure that the list contains all of the information germane to the text.

When this step is completed, the teacher then guides the students to organize the information using a graphic outline format. Here is where students can be shown how to collapse individual pieces of information from a list into conceptual categories. These categories can be the bases for identifying or creating topic sentences. The students can then integrate the main points into a summary.

Hayes (1989) shows how to adapt the GRP to summarizing information. As part of his instructional framework, he modeled the development and writing of an effective summary by guiding students through a procedure he labeled GRASP (guided reading and summarizing procedure). After following the initial steps of the GRP, Hayes illustrates in Figure 10.11 the information that his students remembered based on their first recollections after reading an article on the Rosetta Stone and their additions and corrections after rereading.

The students then organized the information into the following categories: importance of the Rosetta Stone, its discovery, its description, its decipherment, and the result of having made the discovery. These categories, along with the subordinate information associated with each, became the basis for writing the summary. Hayes walked the students through the summary-writing process as a whole class. First, he asked students to contribute sentences to the summary based on the outline of information that was organized on the chalkboard. Then he invited their suggestions for revising the summary into a coherent message. Figure 10.12 displays the completed summary, as revised by the class.

Polishing a Summary

As you can see from the revised summary in Figure 10.12, a good summary often reflects a process of writing *and* rewriting. Teaching students how to write a polished summary is often a neglected aspect of instruction. When students reduce large segments of text, the condensation is often stilted. It sounds unnatural. We are convinced that students will learn and understand the main points better and retain them longer when they attempt to create a more natural-sounding summary that communicates the selection's main ideas to an audience—for example, the teacher or other students. Rewriting in a classroom is often preceded by *response* to a draft by peers and teacher.

Students' First Recollections	Additions and Corrections
Found by an officer in Napoleon's army	Engineering corps
1799	Taken to British Museum, where it is today
Key to language of Egypt	Ancient
Forgotten language of Egypt	Champollion published a pamphlet
Found in mud near Rosetta	The pamphlet a tool scholars use to translate ancient Egyptian literature
Black basalt	Ancient language of Egypt had been a riddle for hundreds of years
3' 9" tall	The stone half buried in mud
Inscriptions in hieroglyphics	Demotic, the popular Egyptian language at the time
	Written with Greek letters
Jean Champollion deciphered the inscription	Champollion knew Coptic
Compared Greek words with Egyptian words in same position	Proper names
Coptic was the Egyptian language	Coptic was last stage of Egyptian language
Decree to commemorate birth of an Egyptian king	Crowning
2' 4½" wide	Carved by Egyptian priests
He knew Greek	Ptolemy V Epiphanes 203–181 B.C.

FIGURE 10.11   **Details Remembered from an Article on the Rosetta Stone**

Source: From "Helping Students Grasp the Knack of Writing Summaries," by David A. Hayes, *Journal of Reading*, November 1989. Copyright © 1989 by the International Reading Association. All rights reserved. Used by permission of the International Reading Association and David A. Hayes.

We dealt in much more detail with responding and revising in Chapter 7. Here, however, let us suggest the following:

◆   Compare a well-developed summary that the teacher has written with the summaries written by the students. Contrasting the teacher's version

The Rosetta stone provided the key for reading the ancient ~~language of Egypt. The~~

~~ancient~~ Egyptian language , which ∧ had been a riddle for hundreds of years. (An officer in

Napoleon's engineering corps) ~~found~~ the Rosetta stone ~~half buried in the~~ was found in 1799

~~mud~~ near ∧ Rosetta . The black basalt stone bore inscriptions in ancient Egyptian the Egyptian city of / by

hieroglyphics, ∧ Demotic, and ∧ Greek. The inscriptions were deciphered by Jean *in* *in*

Champollion, who with knowledge of Greek and Coptic (the last stage of the Egyptian

language) compared ~~Greek~~ words ∧ with ~~Egyptian~~ words ∧ . The inscription ~~were~~ carved in the Greek text   in the Egyptian texts   had been

by Egyptian priests to commemorate the crowning of Egyptian king Ptolemy Epiphanes,

203–181 B.C. In 1822 Champollion described the decipherment in a pamphlet which

has since been used as a tool for translating ancient Egyptian literature. The Rosetta

stone is ∧ in the British Museum. preserved / ~~kept~~

FIGURE 10.12 **The Completed Rosetta Stone Summary, as Revised**

Source: From "Helping Students Grasp the Knack of Writing Summaries," by David A. Hayes, *Journal of Reading,* November 1989. Copyright © 1989 by the International Reading Association. All rights reserved. Used by permission of the International Reading Association and David A. Hayes.

with the student productions leads to valuable process discussions on such subjects as the use of introductory and concluding statements, the value of connectives like *and* and *because* to show how ideas can be linked, and the need to paraphrase—that is, to put ideas into one's own words to convey the author's main points.

◆ Present the class with three summaries: One is good in that it contains all the main points and flows smoothly. The second is OK: It contains most of the main points but is somewhat stilted in its writing. The third is poor in content and form. Let the class rate and discuss the three summaries.

◆ Team students in pairs or triads, and let them read their summaries to one another. Student response groups are one of the most effective means of obtaining feedback on writing in progress.

◆ In lieu of response groups, ask the whole class to respond. With prior permission from several students, discuss their summaries. What are the merits of each one, and how could they be improved in content and form?

The real learning potential of summary writing lies in students' using their own language to convey the author's main ideas.

MAKING NOTES

An effective study activity for acting on and remembering material is to annotate what is read in the form of notes. Notes can be put on study cards (index cards) or in a learning log that is kept expressly for the purpose of compiling written reactions to and reflections on text readings.

Note making should avoid verbatim text reproductions. Instead, notes can be used to paraphrase, summarize, react critically, question, or respond personally to what is read. Whatever the form notes take, students need to become aware of the different types of notes that can be written and should then be shown how to write them.

Eanet and Manzo (1976) underscore the importance of making notes as a means of helping students learn what they read. They describe the different kinds of notes students can write. Several are particularly appropriate for middle-grade and secondary school students. For example, read the passage in Box 10.2. Then study each of the notes made by a high school student, shown in Figures 10.13 through 10.16.

The *summary note,* as you might surmise, condenses the main ideas of a text selection into a concise statement. Summary notes are characterized by their brevity, clarity, and conciseness. When a note summarizes expository material, it should clearly distinguish the important ideas in the author's presentation from supporting information and detail. When the summary note involves narrative material such as a story, it should include a synopsis containing the major story elements. Examine the example of a summary note from a student's note card in Figure 10.13.

The *thesis note* answers the question "What is the main point the author has tried to get across to the reader?" The thesis note has a telegramlike character. It is incisively stated yet unambiguous in its identification of the author's main proposition. The thesis note for a story identifies its theme. Study the example in Figure 10.14.

The *critical note* captures the reader's reaction or response to the author's thesis. It answers the question "So what?" In writing critical notes, the reader should first state the author's thesis, then state his or her position in relation to the thesis, and finally, defend or expand on the position taken. See Figure 10.15.

The *question note* raises a significant issue in the form of a question. The question is the result of what the reader thinks is the most germane or significant aspect of what he or she has read. See Figure 10.16.

Showing students how to write different types of notes begins with assessment; leads to awareness and knowledge building, modeling, and practice;

Box 10.2

Wild Cargo: The Business of Smuggling Animals

Unpleasantness for those trading illegally in wild animals and their products is escalating around the world. Within the past decade government after government has passed laws to restrict or prohibit the sale of wildlife seriously depleted by hunting and habitat destruction. With legal channels pinched, animal dealers have resorted to nefarious schemes to continue the flow.

Wildlife is big business. Exotic-bird collectors will pay $10,000 for a hyacinth macaw. . . . In New York I tried on a pair of trendy western boots trimmed in lizard skin. The price? "Two hundred thirty five," the clerk said, with an archness suggesting that most of his customers didn't bother to ask. . . .

These items are being sold legally. But somewhere in the dim beginnings of their trail through commerce, they may have been acquired illegally. . . .

This fascination with wildlife within the affluent nations of the world adds to the disappearance of animals in the less developed countries. In between stand the illegal traders willing to circumvent the wildlife-protection laws to satisfy the demand and their own pocketbooks. . . .

Wildlife smuggling is costing the U.S. millions of dollars to control and is denying income to the treasury of any nation that would otherwise receive duty from legal imports. It has spread diseases that would have been detected in legal quarantine periods. . . . An irreversible effect of illegal trade could be the extinction of animal species that are finding fewer and fewer places to hide.

Source: "Wild Cargo: The Business of Smuggling Animals," by Noel Grove, *National Geographic,* March 1981, pp. 290–294. Copyright © 1981 The National Geographic Society Image Collection. Reprinted by permission.

and culminates in application. First, assign a text selection and ask students to make whatever notes they wish on a separate sheet of paper. Then have the class analyze the assessment, share student notes, and discuss difficulties in making notes. Use the assessment discussion to make students aware of the importance of making notes as a strategy for learning and retention.

Next, build students' knowledge for note making by helping them recognize and define the various kinds of text notes that can be written. Eanet and Manzo (1976) recommend the following strategy: First, assign a short selection to be read in class, and then write a certain type of note on the board. Ask students how what they read on the board relates to the passage that was just assigned. Through discussion, formulate the definition and concept of the note under discussion.

As part of a growing understanding of the different types of notes, students should be able to tell a well-written note from a poorly written one.

The illegal trading of wildlife and their products is a profitable business in affluent countries around the world. The continuation of such trade threatens both developed and underdeveloped nations economically and ecologically. More recent laws are making this illegal trade much more difficult to carry out.

FIGURE 10.13   A Summary Note

Illegal wild animal trade is a very profitable business. Illegal wildlife trade is a threat to humans and their environment. More laws throughout the world can restrict this activity.

FIGURE 10.14   A Thesis Note

The trading of wildlife for high profits is something all of us will pay for ultimately. Countries are being cheated out of needed revenues. Even more important, the future of species of animals is being threatened. The money-minded traders also give little thought to the spread of disease that could be avoided by legal quarantines. All nations need to cooperate to pass stricter laws to control or prohibit the trade of life and survival for temporary luxury.

FIGURE 10.15   **A Critical Note**

(Should illegal wildlife trade be allowed to continue or, at least, be ignored, after unsuccessful attempts to stop it?) The author says that it is becoming more unpleasant for illegal traders of wildlife and their products due to more laws instituted by governments around the world. He also cites serious economic and ecological reasons not to give up the fight.

FIGURE 10.16   **A Question Note**

Have the class read a short passage, followed by several examples of a certain type of note, one well written and the others flawed in some way. For example, a discussion of critical notes may include one illustration of a good critical note, one that lacks the note maker's position, and another that fails to defend or develop the position taken.

Modeling and practice should follow naturally from awareness and knowledge building. The teacher should walk students through the process of making different types of notes by sharing his or her thought processes. Show how a note is written and revised to satisfaction through think-aloud procedures. Then have students practice note making individually and in peer groups of two or three. Peer-group interaction is nonthreatening and leads to productions that can be duplicated or put on the board, compared, and evaluated by the class with teacher direction.

To facilitate application to classroom reading tasks, we suggest that students write notes regularly in a learning log or on study cards. Save note making activities in learning logs for the latter half of a class period. The next class period then begins with a review or a sharing of notes, followed by discussion and clarification of the text material.

Notes written on study cards are an alternative to the learning log. Direct students to make study cards based on text readings. One tactic is to write questions on one side of the cards and responses to the questions on the other side. For example, ask students to convert the major subheadings of a text selection into questions, writing one question per card. The responses will probably lend themselves to summary or critical notes, depending on the questions posed. Later, students can use the study cards to prepare for a test. As part of test preparation, a student can read the question, recite the response aloud, and then review the note written earlier.

Lester (1984) offers the following tips for making notes on cards:

1. *Use ink.* Penciled notes smudge easily with repeated shuffling of the cards.

2. *Use index cards.* Index cards are more durable and can be rearranged and organized more easily than large sheets of paper.

3. *Jot down only one item per card.* Don't overload a card with more than one type of note or one piece of information.

4. *Write on one side of the card.* Material on the back of a card may be overlooked during study. (One exception is question-and-response cards.)

TAKING NOTES

Walter Pauk's response to the question "Why take notes?" is profound in its simplicity: Because we forget (1978). Over 50 percent of the material read or heard in class is forgotten in a matter of minutes. A system for taking and making notes triggers recall and overcomes forgetting.

A popular note-taking procedure, suggested by Palmatier (1973), involves the following steps: First, have students use only one side of an 8 ½-by-11-inch sheet of looseleaf paper with a legal-width margin (if necessary, the student should add a margin line 3 inches from the left side of the paper). Second, have the students take lecture notes to the right of the margin. Although no specific format for taking notes is required, students should develop a format that uses subordination and space to illustrate the organization of the material; for example, they can indent to show continuation of ideas or enumerate to show series of details. Third, have the students put labels in the left-hand margin that correspond to units of information recorded in the notes. The labels help organize the welter of information in the right-hand column and give students the chance to fill in gaps in the notes. The labeling process should be completed as quickly as possible following the original taking of notes. (See Figure 10.17.)

Once notes are taken and the labeling task is completed, students can use their notes to study for exams. For example, in preparing for a test, the student can spread out the note pages for review. One excellent strategy is to show students how to spread the pages, in order, in such a way that the lecture notes are hidden by succeeding pages and only the left-margin labels show. The labels can then be used as question stems to recall information—for example, "What do I need to know about *(label)?*" Accuracy of recall, of course, can be checked by referring to the original notes, which were concealed by overlapping the pages.

USING SQ3R AS A STUDY SYSTEM

A *study system,* as the name implies, provides students with a systematic approach for studying text. There are numerous study systems in existence, all of which work well with informational text because students make use of external and internal text structures to search for information and construct meaning. Usually, a study system involves a complex set of strategies and procedures. The mother of all study systems is *SQ3R* (the acronym stands for *survey, question, read, recite, review*). Frances Robinson (1946) originated SQ3R more than a half-century ago to help students approach text study without assistance. Numerous variations and offshoots of SQ3R have since been developed, all with the same purpose in mind: to help students study texts on their own. The steps in SQ3R are as follows:

1. *Survey.* Students preview the material to anticipate content, make plans for reading, and develop a mental framework for ideas to be encountered in the text.

Labels	Notes
Neurons are detectors that signal messages to the brain	Our eyes, ears, nose, tongue, and skin pick up messages and send them to the brain. 1. The lens of the eye focuses light on the retina, and neurons change it into a message that's carried by the optic nerves. 2. The tongue and nose work together to detect chemicals and send a message to the brain — tongue has areas for sweet, salty, sour — each area has neurons 3. The skin has neurons that detect pain, pressure, touch.

FIGURE 10.17   Note-Taking Procedure That Uses Labels and Notes

2. *Question.* Students raise questions with the expectation that they will find answers in the text.

3. *Read.* Students search for ideas and information that will answer their questions.

4. *Recite.* Students deliberately attempt to answer their questions by rehearsing aloud what they have learned and/or writing responses to the questions raised.

5. *Review.* Students review and reflect on the material by organizing and elaborating on ideas encountered in the text and rereading portions to verify or expand on responses to their questions.

There is little doubt that SQ3R and other study systems incorporate many of the accepted principles of learning with texts, including the activation of prior knowledge, the setting of purposes, and the construction of meaning. Why is it, then, that learners who are exposed to SQ3R find it difficult to use on their own? Often, they are easily frustrated, if not overwhelmed, by strict adherence to the steps in the procedure.

We suspect that a study system such as SQ3R is not used by most students because it is taught as a formula: Memorize the steps. Practice the strategies several times. Then use it for life. In other words, students are often taught what to do without enough explicit instruction to lead to independence. The key to any system's effectiveness may very well lie in how students learn to control it through selective and flexible use.

Scaffolding instruction in the use of SQ3R is essential to its effectiveness as a study system. For example, students who know how to use the survey and questioning strategies of SQ3R flexibly are in a strategic position to take charge of their own learning. Surveying is the type of cursory learning activity that helps readers make plans for reading.

To analyze the reading task and make plans, a student must ask questions such as these:

◆ What kind of reading is this?

◆ What is my primary goal or purpose?

◆ Should I try to remember details or read for the main ideas only?

◆ How much time will I devote to the reading assignment?

◆ What do I already know about the topic? What do I need to know?

In essence, questions such as these will make students aware of the purposes of a reading assignment so that they can adapt their reading and study to the task.

Surveying gives students some idea of what a text selection is about before they read it. It prepares them for what is coming. Students' tendency, of course, is to jump right into an assignment, often without rhyme or reason, and to plow through it. Not so, however, when they learn how to survey material. Surveying helps them raise questions and set purposes.

When students raise questions about content material that they survey, they are likely to examine the extent of their own uncertainty and to find out what they don't know about the information they will acquire during reading. As a result of surveying and questioning, students become involved in a search for answers during reading. However, surveying and questioning require active participation by students; this is why good as well as struggling readers have trouble previewing on their own. They need teachers who will provide explicit instruction in how to survey and activate questions. Where do you start?

Start the way a Harvard professor did. William Perry (1959) conducted an experiment with 1500 freshmen who were probably among the "finest readers in the country." He assigned a chapter from a history book, instructing the students to use their best strategies to read and study it. After approximately 20 minutes, he asked them to stop reading and answer multiple-choice questions on the details of the chapter. Not surprisingly, the vast majority of the students scored high on the test. Yet when they were asked to write a short essay summarizing the main idea of the chapter, only 15 students did so successfully. Why? Because these 15 freshmen, about 1 percent of the students in the experiment, took the time to preview the chapter before plunging into the details of the material.

Use this anecdote, as well as observations from an assessment of how students actually approach a text selection, to drive home the importance of sizing up the material before reading it. Discuss the reasons why most readers just plow through the material. And through give-and-take exchanges, begin to develop a rationale for previewing.

Surveying works well when content materials contain format features that are organizational, typographic, or visual. Text writers use these aids as guideposts for readers.

Certain organizational features, such as introductions and summaries, give readers valuable clues to the overall structure of a text or the important ideas that they will encounter. Surveying not only creates a general impression but also helps readers distinguish the forest from the trees. Heads and subheads, for example, give students a feel for the overall theme or structure of the material so that they have a sense of the sequence of ideas in the text.

Key words may also be highlighted in the text and should be singled out for discussion. Key terms in a business text may lead to questions such as these: "What do you think the author means by *values*? What does *budgeting* mean? What does it have to do with *financial planning*?" Open-ended questions such as these help readers focus their attention on the material; they also illustrate the value of predicting and anticipating content.

Typographic and visual aids, especially in electronic texts, are valuable devices for surveying. In advance of reading, to get a general outline—an agenda, so to speak—of what to expect, students can survey chapter titles;

headings and subheadings; words, phrases, or sentences in special type; and pictures, diagrams, illustrations, charts, and graphs.

An author, for example, has a definite purpose in mind in using visual aids to enhance text material. In some cases, an aid is used to expand on a concept developed in the main text. In other cases, a graphic may be inserted to serve as an example or an illustration of an idea the writer has introduced.

Visual aids, particularly charts and tables, also help readers by summarizing and organizing information. Moreover, many aids, such as photographs and drawings, are experience builders in the sense that they add a reality dimension to expository material.

In general, students should learn and follow these steps when surveying:

1. Read the title. Convert it into a question.

2. Read the introduction, summary, and questions. What seem to be the author's main points?

3. Read the heads and subheads. Convert them into questions.

4. Read any print in special type. Why are certain words, phrases, or sentences highlighted?

5. Study visual materials such as pictures, maps, and diagrams. What do the graphics tell you about the chapter's content?

The teacher demonstrates how to survey and then models effective surveying and questioning behavior. This approach entails walking students through the process. Select several text pages, and develop transparencies that annotate the types of questions students should ask while surveying. Then share the overhead transparencies with the class, explaining the reasons for your annotations. You might then have students move to another text section and take turns asking the kinds of questions that you modeled, paying attention to the organizational, typographic, and visual aids in the material. Finally, as the students develop awareness, have them raise their own questions while previewing.

Once students survey a text and raise questions, they engage in an active search for information to find answers to their questions. This is the reading phase of SQ3R. Students' concepts of reading, however, may not match what it means to actively search for information. Help your students become flexible readers by letting them in on one of the great secrets of study-type reading: *Studying text doesn't mean reading each word, each sentence, each paragraph, each section of a text with equal reverence.* Awareness of what it means to read flexibly is essential knowledge that students must possess to study texts independently. They need to know when to *skim* quickly over text; when to *slow down* for careful reading; when to *read selectively*, skipping segments of text that do not pertain to their information search; and when to *reread.*

Build knowledge of what it means to be a flexible reader by engaging in process talks. A process talk develops insights into literacy processes. Initiate a process talk around flexible reading. Ask students, "What does it mean to be flexible?" Use their ideas, and apply them to reading. Ask, "What do you think it means to be a flexible reader?" Introduce talk around the concepts of skimming, careful reading, selective reading, and rereading. For example, ask, "What does it mean to skim a stone on a pond? Or to skim on ice or snow when ice skating or skiing?" *Skimming*, as it applies to reading, involves glancing quickly over the material to see what it is about. Discuss when it's appropriate for students to skim text quickly. Show them the importance of reading the first sentence (usually a topic statement or important idea) of every paragraph. In this way, they will get a good (albeit superficial) feel for what the text is about. Then have students skim an entire text selection rapidly—in no more than one or two minutes. Encourage them to zip through every page and not to get bogged down on any one section or subsection. The students must then reconstruct what they have skimmed. Ask them to recall everything that they have read. You and they will be amazed at the quantity and quality of the recalls.

Other concepts related to flexible reading should also be explored in a similar manner. Introduce students to the notion of adjusting the rate (or speed) at which they read to their purposes for reading. If they come across a text selection that has difficult and unfamiliar concepts, they will need to slow down, read carefully, and reread to construct meaning. If they are familiar with a text topic, they should increase their rate of reading accordingly.

As students find answers to their questions, strategies for the recite and review phases of SQ3R assume prominence in the study system. If information is to be memorable and meaningful, students must rehearse aloud (literally "rehear") or write about what they are learning. Direct them to develop study cards or use a learning log to write responses to questions. If students use a learning log to record information, have them set up a double-entry format in which they put questions in one column and responses in another. As noted earlier, if they use study cards, have them put the question on one side of the card and a response to the question on the other side. It's important for them to write responses in their own words rather than copying from the text. Also, consider having students team with a study buddy to share what they have learned with one another.

Review is an opportunity to reflect on what was read. Usually students review what they have learned by organizing and elaborating ideas encountered during reading. They can write summaries or critical notes or construct graphic representations to depict text relationships. Or they can respond personally to what they have read by considering questions such as these: What aspect of the text interested you the most? What are your feelings and attitudes about this aspect of the text? What experiences have you had that help others understand why you feel the way you do?

Ultimately, what students need to learn from SQ3R demonstrations is that they do not have to use all of the phases of the study system to study text effectively. They will blend aspects of SQ3R into a system of learning, choosing those study strategies best suited to themselves and the subject they're studying. A system for studying text evolves gradually within each learner. Maturing readers need to make the transition from teacher-centered guidance to self-control and regulation of their own reading and studying.

Students need to learn how to become text-smart. Being text-smart is comparable to being street-smart. It's knowing how to stay out of trouble; it's knowing when and when not to take shortcuts; it's knowing how to survive and triumph over the everyday cognitive demands that are a natural part of classroom life.

Becoming a student requires time and patience. Studying is a process that is learned inductively through trial and error and the repeated use of different strategies in different learning situations. And this is where teachers have a role to play. Through the instructional support you provide, students discover that some strategies work better for them than others in different learning situations.

LOOKING BACK, LOOKING FORWARD

Teaching students how to study texts involves showing them how to become independent learners. In this chapter, we used the role that text structure plays to illustrate how you can teach students to use learner-directed strategies that involve constructing graphic representations, writing summaries, making and taking notes, and using SQ3R as a study system.

How authors organize their ideas is a powerful factor in learning with texts. Because authors write to communicate, they organize ideas to make them accessible to readers. A well-organized text is a considerate one. The text patterns that authors use to organize their ideas revolve around description, sequence, comparison and contrast, cause and effect, and problem and solution. The more students perceive text patterns, the more likely they are to remember and interpret the ideas they encounter in reading.

Graphic representations help students outline important information that is reflected in the text patterns that authors use to organize ideas. The construction of graphic representations allows students to map the relationships that exist among the ideas presented in text. This strategy is a valuable tool for comprehending and retaining information.

Students who engage in summarizing what they have read often gain greater understanding and retention of the main ideas in text. Students need to become aware of summarization rules and to receive instruction in how to use these rules to write and polish a summary.

Notes are part of another useful strategy for studying text. Making notes allows students to reflect on and react to important ideas in text.

A study system, such as SQ3R, provides students with a systematic approach to studying a text. SQ3R is a complex set of steps and procedures that is often taught as a formula rather than as a flexible set of strategies. Teachers can move beyond teaching SQ3R or other study systems as a formula by providing demonstrations on how to use various strategies within the system, giving students practice with the strategies, and supporting flexible, independent use.

In the next chapter, we examine the role that study guides play in content literacy. A study guide is teacher-developed and provides instructional support for content understanding of text material.

 **MINDS-ON**

1. A member of the board of education has been quoted as saying that she is opposed to "spoon-feeding" high school students. After a board meeting one evening, you have an opportunity to talk with her. You explain that there is a difference between "spoon-feeding" students and scaffolding instruction. As a group, discuss how you might justify supporting students' studying through the use of techniques such as graphic representations, summaries, and note taking.

2. Following an in-service program on using graphic representations, you notice that some teachers in your building are preparing a semantic map or graphic organizer for every assignment, while others, who say they don't have time, never use them. Your principal asks you, as a member of a team, to prepare a one-page sheet of guidelines for the use of graphic representations in which you suggest when, why, and how various graphic displays should be used. What would you include in this guide?

3. Imagine that your group is team-teaching an interdisciplinary unit on the Civil War. Each member of your group should select (a) a content area and (b) one of the text patterns described in this chapter (sequence, comparison and contrast, problem and solution, cause and effect, or description). After reviewing some materials on the art, history, music, politics, science, mathematics, and literature of the Civil War, discuss how you might make use of a selected text pattern to teach a concept.

4. As part of an effort to improve school achievement in content area subjects, the curriculum director of your school system has suggested implementing a mandatory study skills course for all high school freshmen. As a team, compose a memo explaining why and how studying can be effec-

tively taught when content area teachers are also involved in the delivery of instruction.

HANDS-ON

1. Design a semantic map for a science lesson on the characteristics of the planets. Create what you consider the most effective design for that specific content.

2. Using either problem and solution, cause and effect, or comparison and contrast, construct a graphic for a passage from an informational text. Share your representation with members of your group, and discuss how some topics seem appropriate for one specific organizational pattern while others might be organized in a variety of ways.

3. Distribute one card to each member of the class. Ask the students to write down the name of an individual they believe has made a significant contribution to society. Emphasize that the contribution may be in either a specific area of knowledge (art, music, science, literature, politics) or a nonspecific area such as acts of humanitarianism or environmental activism.

   Next, announce that the task of the class will be to create clusters of cards with names that have a common focus. Give each student in the class three minutes to find one partner whose card name relates to his or her own. Then have each team of partners locate another team whose names can be classified together. Explain that, if necessary, groups may redefine their common focus to create clusters. As a whole class, share the focus categories developed by each group.

   Finally, repeat the process, but do not allow any group to use the same common focus. Discuss how this activity relates to the process of outlining.

4. Imagine that one of your colleagues asks students to write summaries of what they are reading in class but does not provide explicit instruction on how to summarize a text effectively. You have observed that many of her students are frustrated by the task or are simply copying summaries written by other students. With one other member of your group, create a dialogue in which you discuss some instructional alternatives that will lead to having students write summaries effectively. As a group, discuss the suggestions you found effective and recommend some others that might have been included.

5. In a small group, read a short selection from a current news story, magazine article, or textbook selection. Write examples of the different kinds

of notes that can be made from the text. Compare your group's notes with those of other groups, and discuss the different thinking tasks each type of note required, as well as the further use of each note in a classroom teaching situation.

6. In a small group, compile a list of study strategies that the group members use as well as the purposes for which they are used. Categorize the strategies into different groupings according to their perceived purposes. Display the strategies on an overhead or a chalkboard for a discussion of commonalities and suggestions for studying texts.

SUGGESTED READINGS

Anderson, T. H., & Armbruster, B. B. (1991). The value of taking notes during lectures. In R. F. Flippo & D. C. Cacverly (Eds.), *Teaching reading and study strategies at the college level.* Newark, DE: International Reading Association.

Anderson, V., & Hidi, S. (1998–1989). Teaching students to summarize. *Educational Leadership, 4,* 26–29.

Armbruster, B. B., & Anderson, R. C. (1981). Research synthesis on study skills. *Educational Leadership, 19,* 154–156.

Armbruster, B. B., Anderson, T. H., & Ostertag, J. (1987). Does text structure/summarization instruction facilitate learning from expository text? *Reading Research Quarterly, 22,* 331–346.

Devine, T. G. (1991). Studying: Skills, strategies, and systems. In J. Flood, J. M. Jensen, D. Lapp, & J. R. Squire (Eds.), *Handbook of research on teaching the English language arts.* New York: Macmillan.

Garner, R., & Gillingham, M. (1987). Students' knowledge of text structure. *Journal of Reading Behavior, 29,* 247–259.

Heimlich, J. E., & Pittleman, S. D. (1986). *Semantic mapping: Classroom applications.* Newark, DE: International Reading Association.

Hill, M. (1991). Writing summaries promotes thinking and learning across the curriculum—but why are they so difficult to write? *Journal of Reading, 34,* 536–539.

Hoffman, J. (1992). Critical reading/thinking across the curriculum: Using I-charts to support learning. *Language Arts, 69,* 121–127.

Jackson, F. R., & Cunningham, J. W. (1994). Investigating secondary content teachers' and preservice teachers' conceptions of study strategy instruction. *Reading Research and Instruction, 34,* 111–135.

Jones, B. F., Palincsar, A. S., Ogle, D. M., & Carr, E. G. (1987). *Strategic teaching and learning: Cognitive instruction in content areas.* Alexandria, VA: Association of Supervision and Curriculum Development.

Jones, B. F., Pierce, J., & Hunter, B. (1988). Teaching students to construct graphic representations. *Educational Leadership, 46,* 20–25.

Pearson, J. W., & Santa, C. M. (1995). Students as researchers of their own learning. *Journal of Reading, 38,* 462–469.

Peresich, M. L., Meadows, J. D., & Sinatra, R. (1990). Content area cognitive mapping for reading and writing proficiency. *Journal of Reading, 34,* 424–432.

Santa, C. M. (1988). *Content reading including study systems.* Dubuque, IA: Kendall/Hunt.

Simpson, M. L. (1984). The status of study strategy instruction: Implications for classroom teachers. *Journal of Reading, 28,* 136–142.

Wade, S. E., Trathen, W., & Schraw, G. (1990). An analysis of spontaneous study strategies. *Reading Research Quarterly, 25,* 147–166.

Winograd, P. N. (1984). Strategic difficulties in summarizing text. *Reading Research Quarterly, 19,* 404–425.

Study Guides

There's no limit to how complicated things can get. . . .
—E. B. White

Organizing Principle

Growth *in* reading. Growth *through* reading. These are two themes that run throughout this book. From the very first day that a child picks up a book, he or she is reading to learn and learning to read. It's a two-way street from the beginning and a dual process that never ends. When the famous German author and philosopher Johann Wolfgang von Goethe was in his eighties, he is attributed with having said, "The dear people do not know how long it takes to learn to read. I have been at it all my life and cannot say that I have reached the goal." Reading is an act of maturity. And every teacher that a student encounters has the potential to contribute in a significant way to the reading maturity of students within the context of subject matter instruction.

As children read to learn and learn to read, they become more fluent, and their ability to handle the mechanics of the process becomes more automatic. But that doesn't necessarily mean that learning with texts gets easier as readers grow older. To paraphrase E. B. White, there's no limit to how complicated reading can get. This is particularly so if the ideas we encounter are beyond our knowledge or experience.

Teachers can contribute to literacy and learning as they teach subject matter. Although the raison d'être of content area literacy is to show students how to learn with texts independently, many students may have trouble handling the conceptual demands inherent in difficult texts. This is often the case, for example, when they have difficulty responding to and thinking about what they're reading at high levels of comprehension. Our task, then, is to help students experience what it is to respond to difficult texts. The organizing principle of this chapter reflects one of the most basic approaches to scaffolding difficult material: **Study guides provide the kind of instructional support that allows students to interact with and respond to difficult texts in meaningful ways.**

As the Chapter Overview shows, you will learn about several types of study guides. The first type, a *three-level guide,* reflects the concept of levels of comprehension. *Pattern guides* and *concept guides* are similar to three-level guides but make a concerted effort to help students recognize the organizational and conceptual structure underlying the author's text. The *selective reading guide* models the way a strategic reader responds to text that is difficult to read. You can devise other types of reading guides to scaffold students' learning; the ones that you will read about in this chapter reflect some of the possibilities for guided instruction.

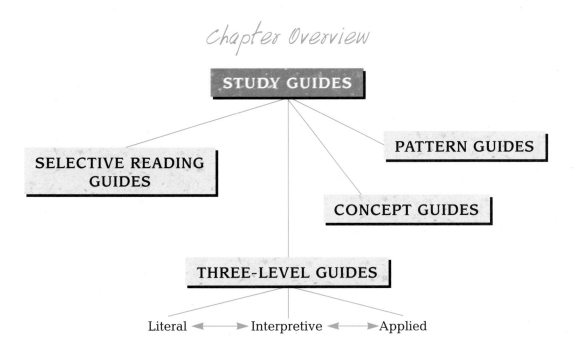

Chapter Overview

STUDY GUIDES

SELECTIVE READING GUIDES

PATTERN GUIDES

CONCEPT GUIDES

THREE-LEVEL GUIDES

Literal ◄───► Interpretive ◄───► Applied

Frame of Mind

1. Why and when should you use study guides?

2. What is a three-level guide?

3. What is a pattern guide, and how is it similar to and different from a three-level guide?

4. What is a concept guide, and how is it similar to and different from three-level and pattern guides?

5. What is a selective reading guide, and how can you use it to model flexible reading?

6. How can you use and adapt different kinds of study guides in your content area?

Study guides simplify difficult text for students. As a result, study guides, used appropriately, can make learning with texts easier for students. That doesn't mean less challenging, however; just the opposite is intended. You should use study guides precisely because the text material is difficult and important enough to warrant scaffolding.

Why will the judicious use of study guides make learning easier? The conceptual load of academic texts is often greater than the levels of reading that students bring to the reading task. As a result, students experience difficulty comprehending what they read. The whole idea of a study guide is to provide enough instructional support and direction for students to learn with texts. In the process of doing so, they will gain confidence. Over time, study guides contribute to the development of strategies that lead to independent reading and learning.

Some teachers consider the use of study guides tantamount to spoon-feeding. Maybe it is. However, spoon-feeding doesn't necessarily mean that you are giving the content away. It means that you simplify the tough sledding that is ahead for students when the information in text appears too overwhelming to read on their own. Without some simplification, students' only alternative is often to avoid textbooks altogether.

What exactly is a study guide? It has sometimes been likened to a "worksheet"—something students complete after reading, usually as homework. But study guides do more than give students work to do. As the name implies, a study guide scaffolds students' understanding of academic content *and* the literacy and thinking processes needed to comprehend and learn with texts. Guides, like worksheets, may consist of questions and activities related to the instructional material under study. The difference is that students respond to the questions and activities in the study guide *as* they read the text, not after. Because a study guide accompanies reading, it provides instructional support as students need it. Moreover, a well-developed study guide not only influences content acquisition but also prompts higher-order thinking.

Study guides are firmly grounded in the here and now, helping students comprehend texts better than they would if left to their own resources. Over time, however, text learners should be weaned from this type of scaffolding as they develop the maturity and the learning strategies to interact with difficult texts without guide material. With this caveat in mind, let's explore the use of study guides that scaffold learning at different levels of understanding.

THREE-LEVEL GUIDES

Because reading is a thoughtful process, it embraces the idea of levels of comprehension. Readers respond to meaning at various levels of abstraction and conceptual difficulty. Figure 11.1 shows the different levels of comprehension.

At the *literal level,* students *read the lines* of the content material. They stay with print sufficiently to get the gist of the author's message. In simple terms, a literal recognition of that message determines what the author says. Searching for important literal information isn't an easy chore, particularly if readers haven't matured enough to know how to make the search or, even worse, haven't determined why they are searching in the first place. Most

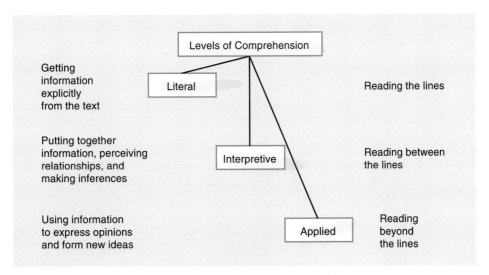

FIGURE 11.1 **Levels of Comprehension**

students can and will profit greatly from being shown how to recognize the essential information in the text.

Knowing what the author says is necessary but not sufficient in constructing meaning with text. Good readers search for conceptual complexity in material. They read at the *interpretive level—between the lines.* They focus not only on what authors say but also on what authors mean by what they say. Herber (1978) clarifies the difference between the literal and interpretive levels this way: "At the literal level readers identify the important information. At the interpretive level readers perceive the relationships that exist in that information, conceptualizing the ideas formulated by those relationships" (p. 45).

The interpretive level delves into the author's intended meaning. How readers conceptualize implied ideas by integrating information into what they already know is part of the interpretive process. Recognizing the thought relationships that the author weaves together helps readers make inferences that are implicit in the material.

From time to time throughout the book, you have probably been trying to read us—not our words but us. And in the process of responding to our messages, you probably raised questions similar to these: "So what? What does this information mean to me? Does it make sense? Can I use these ideas for content instruction?" Your attempt to seek significance or relevance in what we say and mean is one signal that you are reading at the *applied level.* You are reading *beyond the lines.*

Reading at the applied level is undoubtedly akin to discovery. It underscores the constructive nature of reading comprehension. Bruner (1961) explains that discovery "is in its essence a matter of rearranging or transforming evidence in such a way that one is enabled to go beyond the evidence so reassembled to additional new insights" (p. 21). When students respond to text at the applied level, they know how to synthesize information—and to lay that synthesis alongside what they know already—to express opinions about and to draw additional insights and fresh ideas from content material.

The levels-of-comprehension model lends itself well to the preparation of guide material to scaffold reader-text interactions. A three-level guide provides the scaffold from which students can interact with difficult texts at different levels. One of the best ways to become familiar with the three-level guide as an instructional scaffold is to experience one. Therefore, we invite your participation in the following demonstration.

First, preview the three-level guide in Figure 11.2; next, read "The Case of the Missing Ancestor" (pp. 440–441), which originally appeared in *Silver Burdett Biology* (1986). Then complete the three-level guide as you read the text or after reading.

Several comments are in order on your participation in the three-level guide demonstration. First of all, note that the three-level format gave you a "conscious experience" with comprehension levels as a process (Herber 1978). Note also that as you walked through the process, you responded to and manipulated the important explicit and implicit ideas in the material.

You may have sensed the relatedness of ideas as you moved within and among the levels.

Why did we direct you first to preview the guide and then to read the material? Because surveying helps create a predisposition to read the material. As you recall from Chapter 10, previewing helps reduce the reader's uncertainty about the material to be read. You know what is coming. When we asked you to read the guide first, we hoped to raise your expectations about the author's message. By encountering some of the ideas before reading, you are in a better position to direct your search for information in the reading material that may be relevant.

You probably noted also that the declarative statements did not require you to produce answers to questions. Rather, you had to make decisions among likely alternatives; it's easier to recognize possible answers than to produce them.

Notice, too, that in a very positive way, the statements can serve as springboards for discussion and conversation about the content. Were students to react to guides *without* the opportunity to discuss and debate responses, the instructional material would soon deteriorate into busywork and paper shuffling.

A final comment: Your maturity as a reader is probably such that you didn't need structured guidance for this selection, particularly at levels I and II. If you make the decision that certain segments of your text can be handled without reading guidance, don't construct guide material. A three-level guide is a means to growth in reading and growth through reading. It is not an end in itself.

Constructing Three-Level Guides

Don't be misled by the apparent discreteness of comprehension levels. Don't, as Dale (1969) pronounced, suffer from "hardening of the categories." The term *levels* implies a cognitive hierarchy that may be more apocryphal than real. A reader doesn't necessarily read first for literal recognition, then interpretation, and finally application—although that may appear to be a logical sequence. Many readers, for instance, read text for overarching concepts and generalizations first and then search for evidence to support their inferences.

It is very important to recognize that in reading, levels are probably interactive and inseparable. Nevertheless, the classroom teacher attempts to have students experience each aspect of the comprehension process as they read content material. In doing so, students adapt strategies as they interact with the material. They get a feel for the component processes within reading comprehension. They come to sense in an instructional setting what it means to make inferences, to use information as the basis for those inferences, and to rearrange or transform acquired understandings into what they know already in order to construct knowledge.

I. *Directions:* Check the statements that you believe say what the author says. Sometimes, the exact words are used; at other times, other words may be used.

_____ 1. The Germans discovered the fossilized remnants of the Neanderthal man and the Heidelberg man.

_____ 2. Charles Dawson found a human skull in a gravel pit in Piltdown Common, Sussex.

_____ 3. Charles Dawson was a professional archaeologist.

_____ 4. The fossil, labeled *Eoanthropus dawsoni,* became known as the Piltdown man.

_____ 5. The discovery of the Piltdown man was acclaimed as an important archaeological find.

_____ 6. Dental evidence regarding the Piltdown man was ignored.

II. *Directions:* Check the statements that you feel represent the author's *intended* meaning.

_____ 1. The English scientific community felt left out because important fossils had been found in other countries.

_____ 2. Good scientific practices were ignored by the people working with the Piltdown fossils.

_____ 3. Many scientists said that Piltdown was important because they wanted England to be important.

_____ 4. Dawson wanted to make himself famous, so he constructed a hoax.

III. *Directions:* Check the statements you agree with, and be ready to support your choices with ideas from the text as well as your own knowledge and beliefs.

_____ 1. Competition in scientific research may be dangerous.

_____ 2. Scientists, even good ones, can be fooled by poorly constructed hoaxes.

_____ 3. People often see only what they want to see.

_____ 4. A scientific "fact" is not always correct just because many scientists believe strongly in it; theories are always open to question.

FIGURE 11.2 **Three-Level Guide**

THE CASE OF THE MISSING ANCESTOR

From the mid-1800s to the early 1900s, Europeans were actively searching for early ancestors. The Germans dug up the fossilized remnants of Neanderthal man and Heidelberg man. The French discovered not only ancient bones but also cave paintings done by early humans.

England, Charles Darwin's home, had no evidence of ancient ancestors. English scientists—both professionals and amateurs—began searching for fossils. Scarcely a cave was left unexplored, scarcely a stone was left unturned. Many scientists asked workers in gravel pits to watch for fossils.

In 1912, Charles Dawson, a part-time collector of fossils for the British Museum, wrote to Dr. Arthur Smith Woodward, keeper of the Natural History Department at the British Museum. Dawson claimed that a human skull he had found in a gravel pit in Piltdown Common, Sussex, "would rival Heidelberg man." Soon Woodward was digging in the gravel pit with Dawson and other eager volunteers. They found a separate jaw that, though apelike, included a canine tooth and two molars, worn down as if by human-type chewing. Flints and nonhuman fossils found at the same dig indicated that the finds were very old.

Despite arguments by some scientists that the jaw came from a chimpanzee or an orangutan, the discoverers reconstructed the skull and connected the jaw to it. They named the fossil *Eoanthropus dawsoni*, Dawson's "Dawn man," and said that it was much older than Neanderthal man. The find came to be known as Piltdown man.

The finds were X-rayed. One dental authority was suspicious of the canine; he said it was too young a tooth to show such wear. However, such contrary evidence was ignored in the general surge of enthusiasm. So the Piltdown man was acclaimed as an important find, a human in which the brain had evolved more quickly than the jaw.

Beginning in the 1940s, the bones were subjected to modern tests. It is now believed that the skull was from a modern human and the jaw was from a modern ape, probably an orangutan. The animal fossils and flints were found to be very old, but not the types that have been found in England. Apparently, they had been placed in the gravel pit to make the finds more convincing. Why were the scientists and others fooled so easily? Perhaps the desire to find an "ancestor" may have interfered with careful scientific observation.

If the study guide were to be used with every text assignment every day, it would soon be counterproductive. One math teacher's evaluation of a three-level guide crystallizes this point: "The students said the guide actually helped them organize the author's ideas in their minds and helped them understand the material. I think the guide was successful, but I would not use it all the time because many of the assignments don't lend themselves to this type of activity." The three-level guide is only one instructional aid that helps students grow toward mature reading and independent learning.

Merlin the magician doesn't wave his magic wand to ensure the effectiveness of three-level guides. They are facilitative only when students know how to work in groups and know how to apply techniques that have been taught clearly. The heart of the matter is what the teacher does to make guided reading work.

Finally, we urge you also to consider guides as tools, not tests. Think of each statement in a study guide as a prompt that will initiate student discussion and reinforce the quality of the reader's response to meaning in text material.

There is no set of procedures for constructing three-level guides. Before constructing a guide, however, the teacher has to decide: What are the important ideas that should be emphasized? What are the students' competencies? What depth of understanding are the students expected to achieve? What is the difficulty of the material?

Having made these decisions, you may wish to consider these guidelines:

1. Begin construction of the guide at level II, the interpretive level. Analyze the text selection, asking yourself, "What does the author mean?" Write down in your own words all inferences that make sense to you and that fit your content objectives. Make sure your statements are written simply and clearly. (After all, you don't want to construct a guide to read the guide.)

2. Next, search the text for the propositions and explicit pieces of information needed to support the inferences you have chosen for level II. Put these into statement form. You now have level I, the literal level.

3. Decide whether you want to add a distractor or two to levels I and II. We have found that a distractor maintains an active response to the information search, mainly because students sense that they cannot indiscriminately check every item and therefore must focus their information search more carefully.

4. Develop statements for level III, the applied level. Such statements represent additional insights or principles that can be drawn when relationships established by the author are combined with other ideas outside the text selection itself but inside the heads of your students. In other words, help students connect what they know already to what they read.

5. Be flexible and adaptive. Develop a format that will appeal to you and your students. Try to avoid crowding too much print on the study guide.

Using Three-Level Guides

The format of the three-level guide should vary. The classroom examples that follow serve only as models. As you study them, think of ways that you will be able to adapt and apply the three-level construct to your content materials.

Guides are extremely useful adjuncts in the study of literature. A three-level guide can be easily adapted to dramatic, narrative, and poetic forms of literature. For example, note in Figure 11.3 (pp. 444–445) how a ninth-grade English teacher used a three-level guide for Shakespeare's *Romeo and Juliet*. The class was at the tail end of its study of the play, and the guide helped students pull together some of the important points related to the climactic action of the final act. Moreover, the statements at levels II and III of the guide helped students reflect on possible inferences and themes that emerge from the action.

The simplicity of Figure 11.4 (p. 446) speaks for itself. A middle-grade teacher constructed it as part of a health unit. Notice how she uses QARs as cues to direct students' responses. Students completed the guide individually and then discussed their responses in small groups.

As we have shown, one important way to guide comprehension is through three-level guides, which a teacher constructs to bridge the gap between students' competences and the difficulty of the text material. As you consider adapting three-level guides to content area materials, keep these summarizing points in mind. First, the three-level guide stimulates an active response to meaning at the literal, interpretive, and applied levels. It helps readers acquire and construct knowledge from content material that might otherwise be too difficult for them to read. Second, levels of comprehension interact during reading; in all probability, the levels are inseparable in mature readers. Nevertheless, for instructional purposes, it is beneficial to have students experience each level in order to get a feel for the component processes involved in comprehending. And third, three-level guides will help students develop a good sense of the conceptual complexity of text material.

In the next section, we consider another type of study guide: pattern guides.

PATTERN GUIDES

Text patterns, as we explained in Chapter 10, are difficult for maturing readers to discern, but once students become aware of the importance of organization and learn how to search for relationships in text, they are in a better

I. *Literal level:* Check the items that explicitly represent some of the important details and actions in the last part of the play.

_____ 1. The reason Friar Laurence marries Romeo and Juliet is to bring the families of Montague and Capulet together.

_____ 2. Friar Laurence believes words of wisdom will help Romeo deal with his banishment.

_____ 3. Juliet gives the ring to the Nurse to give to Romeo as a sign of her love.

_____ 4. Lady Capulet believes marriage to Paris will take care of all of Juliet's sorrows.

_____ 5. Paris goes to Juliet's grave nightly to place flowers.

_____ 6. Prince Escalus says that he is the one to blame for the deaths because he did not act decisively enough.

II. *Interpretive level:* Several statements are listed below that may represent what the playwright means. If you think any of the statements are reasonable inferences and conclusions, put a check on the line provided. Be prepared to support your answers by citing parts of the play.

_____ 1. Romeo would be alive if the apothecary had obeyed the law.

_____ 2. Lord and Lady Capulet are to blame for Juliet's death because they forced her into marriage.

_____ 3. If Prince Escalus had punished the Montagues and Capulets earlier, the entire tragedy would not have happened.

FIGURE 11.3 Three-Level Guide for *Romeo and Juliet*

position to use information more effectively and to comprehend material more thoroughly.

A pattern guide helps students perceive and use the major text relationships that predominate in the reading material. Although the three-level guide focuses on a recognition of the relevant information in the material, text organization is implicit.

For example, an eighth-grade social studies class read a text assignment, "Today's Stone Age Elephant Hunters" (Beebe 1968), as part of a unit on

_____   4. Romeo's impulsiveness, rashness, immaturity, and emotionalism caused him problems.

_____   5. A 14-year-old is not capable of true love.

_____   6. Romeo did not want to kill Paris.

III. *Applied level:* To apply what you read means to take information and ideas from what you have read and connect them to what you already know. If you think the statements below are supported by statements in section II and by your own previous experience or study, place a check in the blank provided. Be sure you have good reasons to justify your answers if you are called on to do so.

_____   1. People who live by the sword die by the sword.

_____   2. People in positions of power must take responsibility for the actions of those under them.

_____   3. A person cannot change the role that fate has ordained for him or her.

_____   4. The most important thing in life is love. It is even worth dying for.

_____   5. No person has the right to take his or her own life.

_____   6. Nothing is worth dying for.

_____   7. Our own personalities shape our lives, and we can shape our personalities by the choices we make.

_____   8. Events outside our control shape our lives.

FIGURE 11.3   *(continued)*

primitive cultures in the modern world. The text explains how pigmy hunters from the western Congo hunt and kill elephants for food as well as for cultural rituals associated with young hunters' rights of passage into manhood. To get a feel for how a text pattern guide scaffolds the reader's recognition of text relationships, read the excerpt from "Today's Stone Age Elephant Hunters" and then complete the text pattern guide in Figure 11.5 (pp. 448–449).

Notice how part I of the guide helps you to recognize the temporal sequence of events associated with the elephant hunt. The sequence then

I. Right There! What did the author say?

Directions: Place a check on the line in front of the number if you think a statement can be found in the pages you read.

_____ 1. Every human being has feelings or emotions.

_____ 2. Research workers are studying the effects on the body of repeated use of marijuana.

_____ 3. You should try hard to hide your strong emotions such as fear or anger.

_____ 4. Your feelings affect the way the body works.

_____ 5. You are likely to get angry at your parents or brothers or sisters more often than at other people.

II. Think and Search! What did the author mean?

Directions: Check the statements below that state what the author was trying to say in the pages you read.

_____ 1. Sometimes you act in a different way because of the mood you are in.

_____ 2. Your emotional growth has been a continuing process since the day you were born.

_____ 3. The fact that marijuana hasn't been proved to be harmful means that it is safe to use.

_____ 4. Each time you successfully control angry or upset feelings, you grow a little.

III. On Your Own! Do you agree with these statements?

Directions: Check each statement that you can defend.

_____ 1. Escaping from problems does not solve them.

_____ 2. Decisions should be made on facts, not fantasies.

_____ 3. Getting drunk is a good way to have fun.

FIGURE 11.4   **Three-Level Guide for a Health Lesson**

forms the basis for the interpretive and applied levels of comprehension. The guide helps the reader focus not only on explicit text relationships but also on important ideas implicit in the text.

How, then, might you scaffold the search for text patterns in reading materials as you teach your content? First, you should try to keep to a minimum the number of patterns that students are to identify and use. Second, your goal should be to guide students to recognize a single pattern that predominates over long stretches of print, even though you recognize that individual paragraphs and sentences are apt to reflect different thought relationships within the text selection.

Constructing Pattern Guides

As you can see, a pattern guide is a variation of the three-level guide. The difference between the two lies in the literal level: Rather than have students respond to relevant information per se, you can create guide material that allows them to experience how the information fits together. Research and experience (Vacca 1975, 1977; Herber 1978) indicate that the following teaching sequence works well in content area classes:

1. Examine a reading selection and decide on the predominant pattern used by the author.

2. Make your students aware of the pattern and how to interpret the author's meaning as part of the total lesson.

3. Provide guidance in the process of perceiving organization through a pattern guide followed by small-group or whole-class discussion.

4. Provide assistance in cases where your students have unresolved problems concerning the process or the content under discussion.

This sequence is deductive. Once you decide that a particular text selection has a predominant pattern, share your insights with the class. Perceiving text organization is undoubtedly one of the most sophisticated activities that readers engage in. Chances are that most readers will have trouble recognizing text organization independently. By discussing the pattern before they read, students will develop a frame of reference that they can apply during reading. From a metacognitive point of view, discussing the pattern and why the reader should search for relationships is a crucial part of the lesson.

The pattern guide itself tears the text organization apart. The students' task, then, is really to piece together the relationships that exist within the predominant pattern. Interaction among class members as they discuss the guide heightens their awareness of the pattern and how the author has used it to structure information. Students learn from one another as they share their perceptions of the relationships in the reading selection.

I. What is the sequence?

Directions: The pigmy hunter follows ten steps in hunting and killing an elephant. Some of the steps are given to you. Decide which steps are missing, and write them in the spaces provided. The pigmy hunter

1. takes the trail of an elephant herd.

2. _____

3. selects the elephant he will kill.

4. _____

5. moves in for the kill.

6. _____

7. _____

8. pulls out the spear.

9. _____

10. cuts off _____

II. What did the author mean?

Directions: Check the statements that you think suggest what the author was trying to say.

_____ 1. The pigmy hunter is smart.

_____ 2. The pigmy hunter uses instinct much as an animal does.

_____ 3. The pigmy hunter is a coward.

III. How can we use meanings?

Directions: Based on what you read and what you know, check the statements you agree with.

_____ 1. A person's ingenuity ensures survival.

_____ 2. Where there's a will, there's a way.

_____ 3. There are few differences between primitive and civilized people.

FIGURE 11.5 Pattern Guide for "Today's Stone Age Elephant Hunters"

TODAY'S STONE AGE ELEPHANT HUNTERS
B. F. Beebe

Some pigmies of the western Congo use a system of concealing their scent when hunting elephants. Few of these little jungle dwellers hunt elephants but those that do have chosen about the most dangerous way to secure food in today's world.

Hunting is done by a single man using a spear with a large metal spearhead and thick shaft. After taking the trail behind an elephant herd the hunter pauses frequently to coat his skin with fresh elephant droppings for several days until he had lost all human scent.

Closing on the herd the pigmy selects his prey, usually a young adult. He watches this animal until he is aware of its distinctive habits—how often it dozes, eats, turns, wanders out of the herd, and other individual behavior.

Then he moves toward his prey, usually at midday when the herd is dozing while standing. The little hunter moves silently between the elephant's legs, braces himself and drives the spear up into the stomach area for several feet. The elephant snaps to alertness, screaming and trying to reach his diminutive attacker. Many pigmy hunters have lost their lives at this moment, but if the little hunter is fast enough he pulls out the spear to facilitate bleeding and ducks for safety.

Death does not come for several days and the hunter must follow his wounded prey until it stops. When the elephant falls the pigmy cuts off the tail as proof of his kill and sets off for his village, which may be several days away by now.

The final step in the teaching sequence should not be neglected. As students work on or discuss a pattern guide, provide feedback that will keep them going, will clarify and aid in rethinking the structure of the material, and will get students back into the material. Combining information is an important intellectual act requiring analysis followed by synthesis. It isn't enough, in most cases, to exhort students to "read for cause and effect" or "study the sequence." You must show them how to perceive organization over long stretches of print. Pattern guides will help you do this.

As you consider developing a pattern guide, you may find it useful to follow these three steps:

1. Read through the text selection, identifying a predominant pattern.

2. Develop an exercise in which students can react to the structure of the relationships represented by the pattern.

3. Decide on how much guidance you want to provide in the pattern guide. If it suits your purposes, you may develop sections of the guide for the interpretive and applied levels. Or you may decide that these levels can be handled adequately through questioning and discussion once students have sensed the author's organization through the guided reading activity.

Pattern guides help students follow relationships among ideas. Pattern guides are most suitable for informational materials, where a predominant pattern of organization is likely to be apparent.

Using Pattern Guides

Note the variations in the first two classroom examples of pattern guides. Each was developed by a teacher to help students recognize the cause and effect pattern. In presenting the guides to their classes, the teachers followed the four-step teaching sequence just outlined. Study each illustration as a model for preparing your own guides based on causes and effects.

The students in an auto mechanics class—part of a high school vocational arts program—were described by the teacher as "nonreaders." Most activities in the course were hands-on, as you might expect, and although the students had a textbook, they seldom used it.

But the auto mechanics teacher felt that the textbook section on transmissions warranted reading because of the relevance of the material. To help the students follow the author's ideas about causes and effects, the teacher constructed the pattern guide in Figure 11.6.

The students worked in pairs to complete the guide. When some had trouble locating certain effects in the assignment, the teacher told them what page to study. As a result of the guided recognition of cause and effect, the teacher felt that the students would be better able to handle interpretation and application through class discussion followed by a hands-on activity.

A middle school teacher prepared a matching activity to illustrate the cause and effect pattern for students who were studying a unit titled "The American Indian: A Search for Identity." One reading selection from the unit material dealt with Jenny, an adolescent member of the Blackfoot tribe, who commits suicide.

The teacher asked, "Why did Jenny take her life?" The question led to prereading discussion. The students offered several predictions. The teacher then suggested that the reading assignment was written in a predominantly cause and effect pattern. He discussed this type of pattern, and the students contributed several examples. Then he gave them the pattern guide in Figure 11.7 to complete as they read the selection.

The class read for two purposes: to see whether their predictions were accurate and to follow the cause and effect relationships in the material. Notice

Directions: In your reading assignment on transmissions, find the causes that led to the effects listed. Write each cause in the space provided.

1. Cause:_____
   Effect: Grinding occurs when gears are shifted.
2. Cause:_____
   Effect: Car speed increases but engine speed remains constant while torque is decreasing.
3. Cause:_____
   Effect: Car makers changed over to synchronizing mechanisms.
4. Cause:_____
   Effect: Helical gears are superior to spur gears.
5. Cause:_____
   Effect: Some cars cannot operate correctly with three-speed transmissions and require extra speeds.
6. Cause:_____
   Effect: Most manuals have an idler gear.
7. Cause:_____
   Effect: All cars require some type of transmission.

FIGURE 11.6   **Pattern Guide for Power Mechanics**

that the social studies teacher included page numbers after the causes listed on the guide. These helped students focus their attention on the relevant portions of the text. First, the students read the selection silently; then they worked in groups of four to complete the pattern guide.

A final example, the comparison and contrast pattern guide in Figure 11.8 shows how the format of a guide will differ with the nature of the material (in this case, narrative) and the teacher's objectives. In Figure 11.8, juniors in an English class used the pattern guide to discuss changes in character in the story "A Split Cherry Tree."

Adapt pattern guide formats to match the major organizational structures in your content materials. If you do so, students will begin to develop the habit of searching for organization in everything they read.

CONCEPT GUIDES

Concept guides extend and reinforce the notion that concepts are hierarchically ordered in informational material, that some ideas are subordinate to others.

Directions: Select from the causes column at the left the cause that led to each effect in the effects column at the right. Put the letter of each effect next to its cause in the space provided.

Causes	**Effects**
_____ 1. Jenny takes an overdose of pills (p. 9).	a. Unemployment rate for the Blackfeet is about 50 percent.
_____ 2. The buffalo herds have been destroyed, and hunger threatens (p. 10).	b. The first victim of this life is pride.
_____ 3. Native Americans remain untrained for skilled jobs (p. 10).	c. Blackfeet have become dependent on whites' help for survival.
_____ 4. The temperature reaches 50 degrees below zero (p. 10).	d. Blackfeet turn to liquor.
_____ 5. There are terrible living conditions (no jobs, poor homes, and so on) (p. 10).	e. Native Americans are robbed of their self-confidence.
_____ 6. Pride and hope have vanished from the Blackfeet (p. 11).	f. They are always downgraded.
_____ 7. Because we're Native Americans (p. 12).	g. Eighty percent of the Blackfeet must have governmental help.
_____ 8. The old world of the Native Americans is crumbling and the new world of the whites rejects them (p. 13).	h. *Hope* is a word that has little meaning.
_____ 9. The attitude of the Bureau of Indian Affairs (p. 13).	i. She kills herself.

FIGURE 11.7   **Pattern Guide for "The American Indian: A Search for Identity"**

Directions: Consider Pa's attitude (how he feels) toward the following characters and concepts. Note that the columns ask you to consider his attitudes toward these things twice--the way he is at the beginning of the story (pp. 147-152) and the way you think he is at the end of the story. Whenever possible, note the page numbers where this attitude is described or hinted at.

Characters and Concepts	Pa's Attitude at the Beginning of the Story	Pa's Attitude at the End of the Story
Punishment Dave Professor Herbert School His own work His son's future Himself		

FIGURE 11.8   **Pattern Guide for "A Split Cherry Tree"**

Main idea–detail relationships can be described as a distinct pattern of organization. Herber (1978) explained the main idea pattern this way.

> "Main idea" is sometimes identified as an additional organizational pattern. True, it is a pattern, but . . . its construct is so broad that it subsumes each of the other patterns. For example, a *cause* might be the "main idea" of a paragraph and the *effects,* the "details"; or a *comparison* might be the "main idea" and the *contrasts,* the "details"; or a stated objective might be the "main idea" and the *enumeration* of steps leading to that objective, the "details." (p. 78)

The point, of course, is that in any pattern of organization, there are likely to be certain concepts that are more important than others.

This is why students need to be shown how to distinguish important information (the main ideas of a passage) from less important information (the details). Three-level guides and pattern guides do this to some degree. The concept guide also serves this purpose.

Baker (1977) claimed that concept guides help students associate and categorize subordinate information under major concepts. Therefore, the first step in constructing a concept guide is to analyze the text material for the main ideas. Then identify less inclusive concepts and relevant propositions that support each main idea.

Figure 11.9 presents an example of a concept guide.

Part I of the concept guide is similar to the literal-level task in a three-level guide. In part II of the guide, however, students are required to categorize information under coordinate concepts related to India's economy, which makes them aware that some ideas are more important than others. The reader associates specific pieces of information and then groups them together to aid conceptual learning and retention. The culmination of this activity leads to part III in the concept guide. Students are asked to support major ideas (superordinate concepts) that are integral to the content material.

There are many modifications that you can make in developing concept guides for your content area. Here two sample guides are described.

A high school photography instructor wanted his students to distinguish between two important concepts related to picture composition: the rules of composition and the techniques of composition. Note how the concept guide in Figure 11.10 achieves this purpose.

Figure 11.11 shows how a seventh-grade social studies teacher modified the concept guide to fit his content objectives. This guide provoked a good deal of discussion among the students. The teacher extended students' thinking after they discussed their responses to the guide by asking them to circle the numbers of the concepts in part II that they felt described life in the United States today. Students worked in small groups and had to support their decisions with specific reasons; thus the concept guide became a springboard for thoughtful conversation and discussion. Comprehension processes will develop in situations that require not only active responding but also interaction among the respondents.

INDIA'S ECONOMY

I. *Directions:* Check each of the following statements that you think is true, based on what you have learned from your textbook reading, outside reading, class discussions, and lectures.

_____ 1. Approximately 10 percent of India's people are *subsistence farmers* enjoying *private land ownership*.

_____ 2. One of India's *government programs* is the attempt to increase agriculture production.

_____ 3. Since India became independent in 1947, *land reform* has been instituted to give the peasants more land.

_____ 4. The Indian government has attempted to speed up industrialization through *five-year plans*.

_____ 5. Because of a lack of necessary *capital* to finance industrial growth, India has had to borrow money.

_____ 6. India lacks the necessary *mineral resources* needed for industrial growth.

_____ 7. India's major *agricultural products* include rice, wheat, jute, tea, sugarcane, and cotton.

_____ 8. The average annual *per capita income* in India is about $70,000.

_____ 9. Cotton and textile industries produce the largest number of *manufactured products* in India.

_____ 10. India generally has an *unfavorable balance of trade*.

_____ 11. India's *major exports* include burlap and tea; its *major imports* include rice and various foodstuffs.

II. *Directions:* Take each of the underlined words and phrases from Part I and place each under the heading to which it most closely relates. Place a check next to any word or phrase listed under more than one heading.

Agriculture   Industry   Trade   Standard of Living

III. *Directions:* Based on the information just organized and your own knowledge, check any of the following statements for which you can give an example.

_____ 1. Economic growth is determined largely by private enterprise.

_____ 2. Government has a strong influence over theeconomy.

_____ 3. Industrial production is a major source of a nation's wealth.

_____ 4. To maintain a favorable balance of trade, a country must export more than it imports.

FIGURE 11.9   Concept Guide on India's Economy

"PICTURE COMPOSITION"

I. *Directions:* As you read Chapter 12 in the textbook (pages 135–152), check the statements below that are specifically supported by the reading.

_____   1. Composition may be defined as a pleasing arrangement of subject matter in the picture area.

_____   2. Light is to the photographer as paint is to the artist.

_____   3. There are no fixed rules that will ensure good composition in every picture.

_____   4. There are only principles that may be applied to help achieve pleasing composition.

_____   5. Pictures should never tell a story.

_____   6. Simplicity is the secret of many good pictures.

_____   7. Choose a subject that will lend itself to a simple, pleasing arrangement.

_____   8. Check your camera angle carefully.

_____   9. Camera angle is unimportant.

_____   10. Poor background and foreground are errors of amateur photographers.

_____   11. The "Golden Section" is a subject placement guide.

_____   12. In photo composition, one should pay heed to balance.

_____   13. Two subjects of different sizes should be farther apart than two subjects of equal size.

_____   14. There are four basic line forms in photography.

_____   15. Use horizontal lines to show peace and tranquillity.

_____   16. Vertical lines show strength and power.

_____   17. The diagonal line is said to represent action, speed, and movement.

_____   18. The Hogarth Curve is said to be the most beautiful line in the world.

II. Categorize the statements you have checked under one of these column headings:

Rules of Composition   Techniques

FIGURE 11.10   **Concept Guide for "Picture Composition"**

THE INCAS OF PERU: "ENLARGING THE EMPIRE"

I. *Directions:* Read the chapter "Enlarging the Empire" in your textbook. As you read, check the statements below that say what the author said.

_____ 1. Unlike the nation as a whole, the capital housed no commoners.

_____ 2. The general, finding himself near an area with many villagers, ordered his men to rob the villagers of their gold and jewelry and burn the fields.

_____ 3. These assignments did provide the necessary labor for public works, and they also took troublemakers away from their own people for a while.

_____ 4. By means of this pyramid of authority, orders were transmitted to all parts of the empire.

_____ 5. Such methods and policies were a new experience for commoners. But their lives did not change much.

_____ 6. Crimes against the state were the most serious and were punishable by death.

_____ 7. Noblemen received special food, fine clothing, and many wives.

_____ 8. Panchacutec would quickly promote to important positions men who were able and trustworthy.

_____ 9. The people wanted to barter for extra food and goods with their neighbors, instead of traveling all the way to the marketplace in Cuzco.

II. *Directions:* Place the number of each statement you checked in the box next to the concept that it supports. A statement may be used more than once.

Concepts	**Supporting ideas**
1. Great empires are highly organized.	_____
2. Some people are more privileged than others.	_____
3. Unnecessary destruction during war should be avoided.	_____
4. Societies run smoothly when people are busy.	_____
5. Rewards and punishments keep people in control.	_____

FIGURE 11.11   Concept Guide for "Enlarging the Empire"

SELECTIVE READING GUIDES

Selective reading guides show students how to think with print. The effective use of questions combined with signaling techniques helps model how readers interact with text when reading and studying.

Cunningham and Shablak (1975) were among the first to discuss the importance of guiding students to respond selectively to text. They indicate that content area teachers can impart tremendous insight into *how* to acquire text information through a selective reading guide:

> The teacher begins . . . by determining the overall purpose for a particular reading assignment. Second, he selects those sections of the reading which are necessary to achieve this purpose.
>
> Most important . . . he eliminates from the assignment any and all sections that are irrelevant to the purpose. Third, for those relevant sections that remain, the teacher determines, *based on his own model reading behaviors,* what a student must operationally do to achieve the purpose—step by step, section by section. (p. 381; emphasis added)

The premise behind the selective reading guide is that teachers understand how to process information from their own subject matter areas. Figure 11.12 illustrates how an English teacher developed a selective reading guide

Page 128. Read the title. Write a definition of a permissible lie. Give an example of this type of lie.
Page 128, par 1. Do you agree with this quotation? Why or why not?
Pages 128–129. Read paragraphs 2–6 slowly and carefully. What aspects of TV were borrowed from radio? Write them down. From personal experience, do you think TV reflects reality? Jot an answer down, and then continue reading.
Pages 129–130. Read paragraphs 7–15 quickly. What specific types of commercials are being discussed?
Pages 130–131. Read paragraphs 16–26 to find out the author's opinion of this type of commercial.
Page 131. Read paragraph 7. The author gives an opinion here. Do you agree?
Pages 131–133. Read to page 133, paragraph 45. You can skim this section, slowing down to read parts that are especially interesting to you. What are some current popular phrases or ideas in advertising? Think of some commercials you've seen on TV. List another word or idea or fad that's used in a lot of advertising.
Pages 133–134. Read paragraphs 45–50 quickly. Give your own example of a sex-based advertisement.
Page 134, par. 51. According to the author, what is a good test for an advertisement? Do you agree? Would most advertisements pass or fail the test? Try out a few.
Page 134, par. 52. Restate Comant's quote in your own words.
After reading the assignment, summarize what you read in 100 words or less.

FIGURE 11.12 Selective Reading Guide for "Advertising: The Permissible Lie"

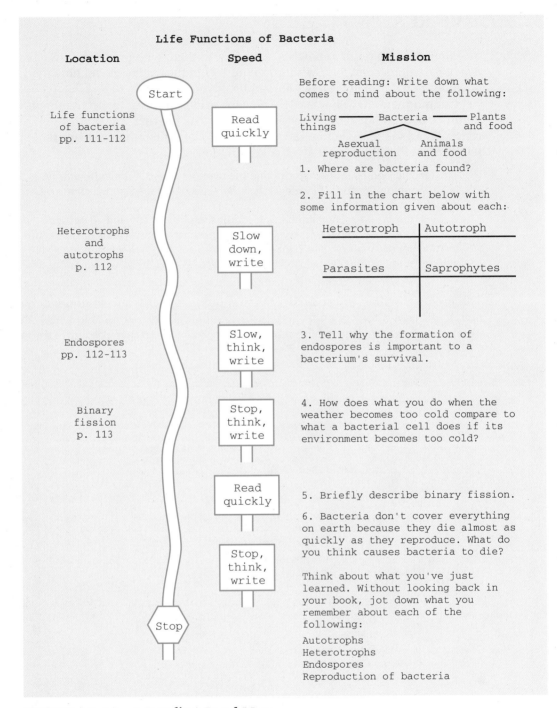

FIGURE 11.13   **A Reading Road Map**

that mixes written questions with appropriate signals for processing the material.

In elementary and middle school situations, selective reading guides have been called reading road maps (Wood 1988). For maturing readers, teachers add a visual dimension to the guide. Study the reading road map in Figure 11.13, developed by a middle school science teacher. Notice how he guides students through the life functions of bacteria by using various kinds of cues, signals, and statements. The guide provides location cues to focus students' attention on relevant segments of text, speed signals to model flexibility in reading, and mission statements that initiate tasks that help students think and learn with texts.

The examples presented in this chapter should give you some idea of how guides may be used and developed for different instructional purposes across a wide range of texts. We encourage you to develop and experiment with several study guides for potentially difficult text assignments in your content area.

 LOOKING BACK, LOOKING FORWARD

When readers are not able to handle difficult texts on their own, a teacher supports their efforts to make meaning by *scaffolding* their interactions with texts. With the use of study guides, teachers provide instructional support to allow students to interact with and respond to difficult texts in meaningful ways. We explored and illustrated four types of guides: three-level guides, pattern guides, concept guides, and selective reading guides.

Three-level guides allow readers to interact with text, constructing meaning at different levels of abstraction and conceptual complexity: literal, interpretive, and applied levels. Pattern guides help students become aware of the importance of text organization and learn how to search for relationships in text. Teachers may adapt pattern guide formats to match major organizational structures in their content materials. Concept guides are a variation of three-level guides and help readers distinguish important information from less important information. Selective reading guides show students how to think with print by modeling the reading behaviors necessary to read texts effectively.

Continuing opportunities for teachers to grow professionally are essential if the literacy practices in this book are to become part of the instructional repertoire of content area teachers. Chapter 12 offers supportive strategies for teachers who want to plan and initiate reflective, inquiry-based professional development programs in literacy and learning across the curriculum.

1. Select a popular book, film, or song that most members of your small group know. Discuss each of the following levels of comprehension communicated in that work: (a) literal (in the lines), (b) interpretive (between the lines), (c) applied (beyond the lines).

2. Some teachers believe that because literal comprehension is necessary to answering "higher-level" questions, it is unnecessary to ask literal-level questions. Do you agree? Do you think we would agree?

3. The basic premise of a study guide is to provide instructional support for students for whom the text is too difficult to handle independently. How might study guides be especially well suited to below-level students who have low self-esteem and little confidence in their ability to meet success with content material? In what ways will the purpose of meeting the individual needs of academically at-risk students be better served through their use? Provide specific examples when possible.

4. Reflect on the use of study guides in each of the content areas. Do you agree or disagree with the following statements:

   a. Study guides provide students with direction and organization for their reading.

   b. Study guides give students the chance to respond to texts in meaningful ways.

   c. Study guides are not meant to be used every day or with every reading assignment; that would reduce their effectiveness.

   d. Levels of comprehension are not as discrete as they may appear, but their division and treatment as separate entities is necessary to address each aspect of comprehension.

   e. If students become used to the support study guides offer, they will always be teacher-dependent.

5. If a study guide is offered as an independent activity, students will get little out of it; failure will be just as frequent as with the traditional question-laden worksheet. Students need to be led through the use of study guides, sometimes working independently, sometimes working together. Reflect on the role of the content teacher in designing and using study guides for learning.

HANDS-ON

1. Take a brief content area reading selection. Working as two groups, one group should prepare a selective reading guide, and the other a concept guide on the material. Meet together to share the completed products and to discuss the ways in which they are similar and dissimilar and the advantages and disadvantages of each.

2. Working in small groups or with a partner, prepare pattern guides for each of the major types of expository text organization (cause and effect, comparison and contrast, description, sequence, and problem and solution). Follow the guidelines for construction given in this chapter. The organizational pattern should guide your design and usage of the guide, so each will vary in appearance. Compare and contrast the resulting guides and frames of mind, and try to determine if one is better than the others for a particular content or organizational pattern.

3. Work together to create a three-level guide for an article from the newspaper or an educational journal. Follow the guidelines for construction presented in this chapter.

SUGGESTED READINGS

Armstrong, D. P., Patberg, J., & Dewitz, P. (1988). Reading guides: Helping students understand. *Journal of Reading, 31*, 532–541.

Bean, T. W., & Ericson, B. O. (1989). Text previews and three-level study guides for content area critical reading. *Journal of Reading, 32*, 337–341.

Brown, A. L., & Campione, J. C. (1994). Guided discovery in a community of learners. In K. McGilly (Ed.), *Classroom lessons: Integrating cognitive theory and classroom practice.* Cambridge, MA: MIT Press.

Davey, B. (1986). Using textbook activity guides to help students learn from textbooks. *Journal of Reading, 29*, 489–494.

Guthrie, J. T., McGough, K., Bennett, L., & Rice, M. E. (1996). Concept-oriented reading instruction: An integrated curriculum to develop motivations and strategies for reading. In L. Baker, P. Afflerbach, & D. Reinking (Eds.), *Developing engaged readers in school and home communities.* Hillsdale, NJ: Erlbaum.

Herber, H. L. (1978). Levels of comprehension. In *Teaching reading in content areas* (2nd ed.). Upper Saddle River, NJ: Prentice Hall.

Herber, H. L. (1985). Levels of comprehension: An instructional strategy for guiding students' reading. In T. Harris & E. Cooper (Eds.), *Reading, thinking, and concept development: Strategies for the classroom.* New York: College Entrance Examination Board.

Mooney, M. (1995). Guided reading: The reader in control. *Teaching PreK–8, 25,* 54–58.

Olson, M., & Longnion, B. (1982). Pattern guides: A workable alternative for content teachers. *Journal of Reading, 25,* 736–741.

Rosenshine, B., & Meister, C. (1992). The use of scaffolds for teaching higher-level cognitive strategies. *Educational Leadership, 49*(7), 26–33.

Wood, K. D., Lapp, D., & Flood, J. (1992). *Guiding readers through text: A review of study guides.* Newark, DE: International Reading Association.

Professional Development

Growth and Reflection in the Teaching Profession

Be not afraid of growing slowly;
Be afraid only of standing still.

—Chinese proverb

Organizing Principle

Teachers are professionals. Their preparation does not end with their initial certification but is an ongoing process, much like that of a developing reader and writer. In fact, national professional education organizations are now calling for "a continuum of professional preparation and development" (National Council for Accreditation of Teacher Education [NCATE] 1997). The "new professional teacher" is expected to demonstrate many skills, including "reflects on practice and changes methods that are not working" and "continually seeks professional growth and development" (p. 9).

To be sure, a certain amount of growth will occur naturally, as colleagues observe each other teach, share exciting and worthwhile innovations and strategies, and make decisions about instruction. Yet teachers will also need purposeful, planned support similar to that given students through instructional scaffolding. Providing necessary support to enable teachers to experience growth and reflection would mean understanding that diversity exists *among teachers* and planning for active and meaningful learning in professional communities.

Teachers at different stages in their careers are also at different levels of expertise in their craft. Simply becoming aware of what is happening in the classroom, learning to tap into their immense body of practical knowledge acquired through experience, can result in more reflective teaching and effective professional growth. Engaging in collaboration with colleagues and participating in strategies such as writing, dialogue, problem solving, technology use, and action research provide support for teachers who seek to improve their own teaching. Professional development plans, to be most useful, would be individually designed for teachers at different points in their careers.

This chapter begins with the importance of direction and purpose, collaboration, decision making, and problem solving in professional development. It also explores challenges, themes, and trends that will help teachers in their professional development and growth. Above all, it communicates a belief that powerful adult learning situations can be created: **Participating in planned, reflective, and inquiry-based professional development in content area reading leads to professional growth and improved instruction.**

Study the chapter overview. What do you already know about professional development? What do you need to learn more about?

Then use the key questions in the "Frame of Mind" section as a guide to help you interact with and respond to the chapter's ideas about professional growth and reflection.

Chapter Overview

GROWTH AND REFLECTION IN THE TEACHING PROFESSION

PURPOSES, NEEDS, GUIDELINES

THEMES, TRENDS, CHALLENGES

PROFESSIONAL DEVELOPMENT PLANS

Collaboration

Roles and Responsibilities

Lifelong Learning

Early Career

Veteran

STRATEGIES FOR SUCCESSFUL PROFESSIONAL DEVELOPMENT

Dialogue

Problem Solving

Action Research

Technology Use

Writing

Journals

Portfolios

Logs

1. Why is the new professional teacher expected to participate in continuing professional development?

2. What are some of the different purposes for engaging in professional development?

3. How are teachers' roles and responsibilities changing?

4. Select a strategy for successful professional development. How would you use it for growth and reflection?

5. In what ways are individual professional development plans different for an early-career teacher (Darby) and a veteran teacher (Mark)? In what ways are they similar?

Professional development has become synonomous with change and growth—and fortunately so. Expectations and requirements of the "new professional teacher" are changing as rapidly as today's classrooms and learners. Along with new technology, new methods, and new school structures come new roles for teachers. These roles, in turn, necessitate a major change in the way teachers view professional practice. Instead of working in isolation, new teaching professionals will come to view practice as collegial, characterized by sharing, working in teams, observing peers, and studying with colleagues (NCATE 1997).

Change takes time. Teachers who experiment with and adopt content area reading strategies are changing the nature of instruction; they are adults engaging in lifelong learning. As such, they participate in professional development for a variety of reasons and in a variety of ways. First, they may want to obtain better information and to be able to use it more rationally. Second, they may question their own beliefs, coming to a better understanding of themselves, and finding better ways of communicating with their colleagues and with parents and students. And third, they may change practice when they discover that as they engage in new experiences and pilot and reflect on new strategies, they begin to reexamine problems in teaching and learning. They inquire, thinking intuitively about alternative solutions. Professional development in content area reading involves beginning and experienced teachers in purposeful, planned change. What is the result of engaging in this worthwhile process over the long haul? Growth for teachers and students.

PURPOSES, NEEDS, AND GUIDELINES

Whose purpose should professional development programs serve? Whose needs should be met? For novice teachers, learning to teach and learning to interact with one's colleagues are important needs. More experienced teachers may want to learn what strengths each of their colleagues can contribute to a professional development plan. The district central office must take into account the implementation of new policies such as inclusion. Consider, if you will, a continuum of the various authentic purposes that drive professional development.

On one end, as illustrated in Figure 12.1, are the needs of the institution, the school district, the administrators, the schools, and the program being initiated in an individual school. On this end of the continuum reside pressing demands on administration and staff in this assessment-driven, examination-oriented age of educational reform.

Proficiency test scores and their rankings displayed district by district in the local newspaper preoccupy superintendents who must deal daily with economic and political realities, in addition to having bottom-line responsibility for meeting instructional goals. They are, without a doubt, more aware of and more accountable to multiple stakeholder groups (parents, school board members, business leaders, community advocates, and legislators) than ever before.

On the other end of the continuum are teachers who are at different stages in their careers. As Fessler and Christensen (1994) state, all teachers are at some point in their career cycle. They are at different stages of expertise in their craft and may need different types of growth and development activities. According to the *principles of professional development* recently proposed by the U.S. Department of Education (1994), high-quality professional development would ensure "the career-long development of teachers and other educators whose confidence, expectations, and actions influence the teaching and learning environment." Moreover, strategies should include concern about improving and integrating "the recruitment, selection, preparation, initial licensing, induction, ongoing development and support, and advanced certification of educators" (p. 63773).

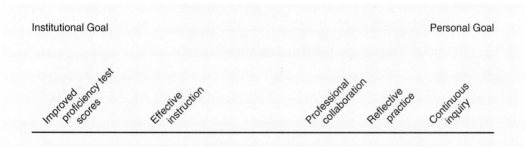

FIGURE 12.1   **Purposes of Professional Development**

The incentives appropriate for beginning teachers and for veteran, experienced teachers may be different. For teachers who are beginning their careers, praise from students, written praise, and gaining control over their instructional decisions are appropriate incentives. As you continue to grow and gain experience, designation as a master teacher along with support for classroom research is appropriate. For teachers who are frustrated following years of service, released time, aide support, and "promotion" to administration are appropriate. After many years of service, appropriate incentives become early retirement, a paid sabbatical, and various leadership opportunities.

Above all, the mission of professional development is to "prepare and support educators to help all students achieve high standards of learning and development" (U.S. Department of Education 1994, p. 63774). Thus professional development must meet all of the following criteria:

- It focuses on teachers as central to school reform yet includes all members of the school community.

- It respects and nurtures the intellectual capacity of teachers and others in the school community.

- It reflects the best research and practice in teaching, learning, and leadership.

- It is planned principally by those who will participate in that development.

- It enables teachers to develop expertise in content, pedagogy, and other essential elements in teaching to high standards.

- It enhances leadership capacity among teachers, principals, and others.

- It requires ample time and other resources that enable educators to develop their individual capacity and to learn and work together.

- It promotes commitment to continuous inquiry and improvement embedded in the daily life of schools.

- It is driven by a coherent long-term plan that incorporates professional development among a broad set of strategies to improve teaching and learning.

- It is evaluated on the basis of its impact on teacher effectiveness, student learning, leadership, and the school community, and this evaluation guides subsequent professional development efforts.

PROFESSIONAL THEMES, TRENDS, AND CHALLENGES

"The complexity of teaching is well recognized: a teacher makes over 3,000 non-trivial decisions daily" (Danielson 1996, p. 2). As professional development moves away from the training model, a focus on helping teachers make sense of this complexity within the context of their own experiences is emerging. Teachers have an immense body of practical knowledge acquired through experience, yet many are explicitly unaware of this and hence fail to tap it to further their professional growth.

Examination of this practical knowledge should be continuous and can be demanding, as the process of change and growth is not easy. Another trend is a lessening of reliance on outside experts and an increased call for teachers to engage in reflective inquiry, resulting in better teaching.

Better teaching can "mean that the teacher *knows* more about what teaching is and how it best works for him or her, is more *aware* of what is happening in the classroom as he or she teaches, and is more purposeful in the pedagogical *decisions* that he or she makes" (Baird 1992, p. 33). Simply becoming aware of the myriad aspects of one's daily practice as a teacher can be a powerful professional growth tool, and collaboration can help make it successful.

Collaboration

"Relationships with colleagues are an important element of teachers' contribution to the school and district. Professional educators are generous with their expertise and willingly share materials and insights, particularly with those less experienced than they" (Danielson 1996, p. 113). The essence of collaboration is conversation—colleagues sitting down together and engaging in serious dialogue about the "stuff" of teaching.

Whether the topic is schoolwide activities, common curricular themes, an article from a professional publication, or their own personal journal entries, the activity of teachers sharing ideas and insights with one another is a powerful one. The rapport and trust that grow between individuals break down the walls of isolation that can exist when teachers work alone in their individual classrooms. Teachers exchange roles and become learners from each other, gaining from each other's perspectives and expertise. Just as we try to realize the potential of our students by maximizing their strengths, so can we, as teachers, grow as professionals by learning from each other. This can and should be an ongoing process—across experience levels and subjects taught.

Creating partnerships is not simply a matter of goodwill. True collaboration creates a sense of connectedness that brings with it responsibility. Nevertheless, collaboration is a powerful trend in professional development today. When teachers make connections, they form a community, thereby counteracting the isolation that pervades the teaching profession. For "when teachers are engaged together in thinking aloud about their work and its consequences," the results are a greater sense of professionalism and a stronger and more cohesive instructional program (Griffin 1991, p. 250). There is also some risk, as veteran teachers know.

In a grant-funded, three-year professional development project in Seattle, Washington, a group of high school teachers get together monthly. They read, discuss, and plan for an interdisciplinary humanities curriculum. One challenge noted by the teachers is learning to confront the inevitable conflicts that arise "as the community emerges. People must interact directly with colleagues they may previously have chosen to avoid . . . [and] confront different perspectives about subject matter and teaching that dwell in the same hallway. The process is not easy or comfortable, but . . . [it is] painfully necessary" (Wineburg & Grossman 1998, p. 353).

Lifelong Learning

"Continuing development is the mark of a true professional, an ongoing effort that is never completed. Educators committed to attaining and remaining at the top of their profession invest much energy in staying informed and increasing their skills. They are then in a position to exercise leadership among colleagues" (Danielson 1996, p. 115).

One of the skills we try to foster in our students is that of becoming lifelong learners. Often we fail to include ourselves in that community of learners. By modeling those habits of learning, though, we not only guide our students but also enrich the personal and professional knowledge base from which we teach. Whatever career stage a teacher is in, there are new insights and perspectives to be gained to enliven, reinspire, and deepen one's commitment to the profession. For, as Griffin (1991) says, "development indicates forward motion, links activities and events in coherent ways, considers people as individuals at varying stages of expertise, and focuses attention on working toward an end in view, a vision of the possible" (p. 247).

At the very least, professional developers who want to improve professional development in content area reading according to these concepts would involve teachers at different career stages in program planning. The perceived usefulness of the planned activity is important and will depend on the group's mix of experiences and career stages. Both the second-year teacher still sorting out the curriculum in social studies and the veteran down the hall going through the motions need and deserve to have relevant activities for professional growth.

Recasting Roles and Responsibilities

As school reform efforts become part of the daily way of life for educators, so does the notion of change as it applies to the daily activities of teachers in schools. No longer can teachers go into their rooms, close the doors, and interact with only their own students throughout the day. Schools are opening up, not only for students, but for teachers, administrators, parents, and university personnel as well. "In almost all schools, many opportunities exist for educators to assume additional responsibilities, thereby enhancing the culture of the entire school" (Danielson 1996, p. 113).

Teachers can extend their duties and responsibilities beyond their classroom doors. "Professional educators [can] make many contributions to the life of a school" (Danielson 1996, p. 113). Schools and districts undertaking major projects increasingly include teachers in the design, planning, and implementation of these new ideas. Such activities often require a considerable investment of time and mental energy. When viewed as authentic professional growth opportunities, however, professional educators find the time to become involved. In addition to the personal knowledge and experience gained through participation, teachers are able to interact with one another on a level different from the classroom, thereby making an additional contribution to education.

As school-based and university-based personnel attempt collaboration and engage in lifelong learning, their roles begin to change. Initiatives of school and college collaboration in systemic reform through strategic intervention require teachers, administrators, and faculty who are willing to explore new roles and responsibilities. These explorations link educators from prekindergarten through adult education in the reform of education. In recently recast roles, educators may be doing any or all of the following:

- Defining performance indicators and authentic performance tasks

- Developing portfolios of assessment techniques

- Networking with colleagues in other schools, districts, and colleges around the world through technology

- Modeling teaching strategies and demonstrating their usefulness in performance-based assessments

- Redesigning curriculum around constructivism, interdisciplinary teams, inclusion, and reflective practice

Constructivism, in which learning is viewed as the learner's process of constructing knowledge and personal meaning from new experiences, has very direct implications for teaching and learning in the classroom and in professional development. Taking responsibility for one's own learning, building shared understandings, and using reader response techniques in classrooms, in which meaning is constructed socially, affect how teachers conceptualize their own roles and design their own professional development. Teachers' engaging in the process of reflection, self-examination, and problem solving in efforts to inquire into their own practice represents a fundamental change. Collectively, these themes, trends, and challenges occurring in the midst of school reform dictate the importance of *doing what works* in professional development.

STRATEGIES FOR SUCCESSFUL PROFESSIONAL DEVELOPMENT

There is no blueprint for staff development. Instead, a number of successful professional growth and development opportunities and approaches embrace the principles of current reform efforts. They are "serious and systematic, . . . engaging a group of professional educators who work together, a staff, in activities designed specifically to increase the power and authority of their shared work" (Griffin 1991, p. 244).

Teachers who want a successful content area reading program in their schools need more than knowledge and enthusiasm if this important aspect of instruction is to become a reality. Certain support strategies can be used to increase success as colleagues engage in what can best be described as a process of change. When teachers work together to grow professionally, support is essential for change to occur in the school. During professional development, relevant experiences, such as those listed in Table 12.1, need to be provided by teachers and for teachers who want to grow in their ability to deliver content area reading strategies.

TABLE 12.1

Support Strategies

◆ Regularly scheduled meetings with a predictable pattern

◆ Discussion of research theory and literature with other teachers

◆ Modeling a strategy with peers

◆ Microteaching lessons in follow-up sessions (lesson demonstrations)

◆ Peer coaching (co-workers give feedback to one another as they use strategies with their classes)

◆ Guided practice (a facilitator leads participants in trying out strategies)

◆ Structured feedback sessions (a facilitator elicits participant response after a strategy is tried)

◆ Peer support teams (co-workers share the ups and downs that accompany change)

◆ Mentor and lead-teacher models

◆ On-site and off-site consultants

◆ Telephone hotlines

◆ Visiting functional sites in either one's own or another building

---

Source: From "Staff Development," by Jo Anne L. Vacca and Holly Genzen. In S. Wepner, J. Feeley, and D. Strickland (Eds.), *The Administration and Supervision of Reading Programs* (2nd ed.). Copyright © 1995 Teachers College Press. Used with permission.

"Show me what to do on Monday morning" is a legitimate demand. Often, however, this concern is misinterpreted to mean that classroom teachers are antitheoretical and antiresearch. What teachers are actually saying is, "Show me how to improve my craft. Let me experience the process first, and if it makes sense, let's discuss why it works." Let us explore some of the most effective strategies for professional growth and reflection.

Using writing, dialogue, problem solving, technology, and action research is congruent with a reflective stance that *teachers* rather than experts hold the knowledge necessary to improve teaching. Teachers can and do become aware of their intuitive knowledge through the process of reflection. "Reflection promotes knowledge on practice, which is the heart of professional growth" (Vacca, Vacca, & Bruneau 1997, p. 445).

Writing

Writing is a major strategy that teachers can use to grow professionally; writing engages teachers in a process of reflection and self-examination. Writing can be a powerful tool for expressing individual reflection and response. In her 1989 book *Writing to Grow: Keeping a Personal-Professional Journal,* Mary Louise Holly discusses the use of journals, diaries, and logs by educators "to explore and grow from experience and reflection on practice" (p. 5). In writing, you explore connections between teaching and professional development; you identify and think about your own circumstances and how your experiences influence and shape your teaching and professional development. Holly studied seven teachers and their explorations of their joys and frustrations expressed through their writing in diaries, journaling, and meetings and seminar groups.

Journals

Waldron (1994) studied five art teachers (grades K–12) who kept *journals* for three months. The art teachers, who ranged in experience from 3 to 20 years, were given journal notebooks, but the format for their entries was intentionally left unstructured so that they could articulate their insights in their own voices. Waldron analyzed the entries for the kinds of thoughts and concerns that novice and veteran art teachers had about their experience; samples of these entries are displayed in Box 12.1. She also wanted to find out what stages the art teachers had passed through in their engagement with reflection on practice. Had teachers been able to articulate previously unexpressed concerns about their individual practice? The researcher contacted the teachers individually once a week to answer their questions about the process, to address any personal concerns, and to offer them consistent encouragement to continue making entries systematically and thoughtfully.

Box 12.1

Thoughts About Teaching Expressed in Journals

Diane, 16 years' experience:

2/18—The drawing unit is making me feel good. The students love what we've been working on—I keep stressing our goals and what we are focusing on so they *know why* they are doing *what* they are doing. I've always been told what a successful teacher I am, but it has only been lately that I've felt clear about what I'm really doing.

Yet there are days that I want to get out so bad I can't stand it. Not so much the kids, but all the other "stuff"—especially the lack of respect for teachers, the constant "blaming" for kids and their lack of education, the moronic treatment of teachers by administrators. We really are not treated as professional adults. It makes me *MAD!!* We are not allowed to leave the building, we are talked down to, we have to "report in" for everything like children. Sometimes I feel the students have more rights than teachers.

Claire, 3 years' experience:

3/22—You know—how does a person do it?—Teach I mean? It seems like you get very little feedback when you're doing good—but they don't hesitate to tell you when you are bad.

4/8—When I make art I spend a lot of time on one project and do fewer projects with more time invested. When I teach, I am still trying out a variety of different approaches because I'm so new—I don't think what I am doing is good enough yet. (Hmmm—I think the same about my art!) I feel like I can always improve—I expect good craft from my students and I do good craft myself.

Source: From *Reflective Practice in Art Education: An Inquiry Model for Staff Development,* by Deborah Z. Waldron. Copyright © 1994 by Deborah Z Waldron. Reprinted by permission.

These teachers reported that getting used to keeping journals was a slow process. Some initial entries had been conversational; others were more self-critical, asking lots of questions. One teacher who had already been thinking about her teaching "questioned, analyzed, and began resolving issues for herself." The journal writing seemed "to bring things to consciousness" for the writers. One wrote, "Revelations come and go and sometimes you are lucky enough to be holding a pen in your hand when one strikes you" (Waldron 1994, p. 105).

Journals can serve teachers well as a personal and professional growth tool. This technique, however, requires both time and patience to cultivate. For example, even a 12-week period seemed to be an insufficient amount of time. But the journal entries remained consistent in length and depth. They seemed to accomplish the purpose of "explicating thoughts for the participants" (Waldron 1994, p. 105).

Learning Logs

A *learning log* is a content area journal in which students are asked to record observations, speculations, discoveries, questions, and reflections on the learning events occurring in the classroom or in their reading. Learning logs are also becoming popular in courses taken by teachers who are continuing their education through their school districts or local universities. Usually assigned to be kept in a notebook or loose-leaf binder over the duration of a course, the log becomes an ongoing record of learning as it happens for an individual student, in this case a practicing teacher.

Two teachers, each with approximately five years of experience, wrote regularly in their logs as part of the requirements for a course they were taking on the theory and practice of teaching reading. Mitzi, a seventh-grade mathematics teacher, devoted several entries to preparation for the major course assignment, an inquiry paper.

> I'm leaning toward doing my inquiry paper on the integration of language arts and technology into the math curriculum. My school district recently adopted a new math program that promotes critical thinking and problem solving, and asks children to respond to questions in written form on a regular basis. . . . It is vital that educators do not downplay all of the different ways that the language arts curriculum is used on a regular basis.

Bob, who teaches health in two middle schools, wrote this as the semester drew to a close:

> Tonight as I read over the final draft of my learning log, I'm glad I took the time to reflect on a regular basis. Having the opportunity to write down my thoughts and ideas helped me to clarify my own philosophy on teaching and learning; it feels good to articulate my understanding of different topics.

Portfolios

For both beginning and veteran teachers, another powerful technique that focuses on writing is the development of *portfolios*. A natural bridge from preservice education to the first years of teaching, portfolios are also practical for teachers in mid-career. As purposeful collections of information involving collaboratively chosen artifacts, portfolios can serve teachers in much the same way they do students. For example, portfolios are valuable in evaluating the progress of learners in the classroom. Teachers can use portfolios to assess their own progress in implementing a program, incorporating portfolios into their planning process.

Content area teachers are encouraged to view their diverse students as active readers and writers while meeting their special learning needs. What better way to understand the developmental nature of students than for teachers to be involved themselves in the development of their own portfolios? As Graves (1992) states, "We need more policy-makers, administrators, and teachers who know portfolios *from the inside*. Their decisions about portfolio use must include the reality of living and growing with the process of keeping one" (p. 5; italics in the original).

The person responsible for professional development might meet with teachers to discuss their expectations of personal portfolio development. Dates can be set for periodic sharing and for the "final" portfolios to be presented (although, ideally, a portfolio would be continued throughout a teacher's career). What are appropriate pieces to include in a portfolio? Some items that could be part of this portfolio are "journal entries, letters to colleagues, anecdotal writing, formal writing, written plans for classroom lessons, levels-of-use checklists, and script tapes" (George, Moley, & Ogle 1992, p. 54).

The group would meet periodically to share the material from their portfolios and the experiences they have had in selecting this material. "This experience gives educators first-hand experience with a strategy they may be using with their students and also encourages teachers to look at their own continuing development" (Vacca & Genzen 1995, p. 150).

Dialogue

Another major strategy for teachers seeking professional growth is engaging in collegial dialogue. Sharing in meaningful conversation with professional colleagues works well with writing techniques such as keeping journals and logs and developing a portfolio.

In her study, Waldron (1994) combined journal writing with dialogue sessions to engage the five visual arts teachers in systematic reflection over 12 weeks. Her intent was to describe the processes of reflective teaching and collegial dialogue of in-service art teachers. To find out how teachers think about their episodes of practice—how they make sense of them and how they learn from them—she invited them to five seminar sessions, each lasting 90 minutes. Sometimes their written entries addressed personal concerns about individual practice and reactions to aspects of the collegial dialogue in seminar sharing sessions. According to one experienced teacher, "I've found I'm reflecting more carefully and slowing down my high-speed chase through the days." Another reported that she enjoyed the gatherings, but "I still find it hard to find the time to write it all down." The first two seminar sessions were spent establishing rapport and group identity, telling stories, and discussing many topics. As the teachers grew comfortable with one another, they focused more on common situations, ideas, and solutions. The dialogue sessions were useful in exploring concerns, frustrations, and personal and professional issues identified by both early-career and veteran art teachers, often in their journals. Frustrations expressed by early-career art teachers dealt more often with "constraints they felt to be directed at them personally which infringed upon their time, while veteran art teachers were more often frustrated by outward directed concerns, those that interacted with the school, community, and field" (p. 129). Waldron concludes that changes were evident in the teachers' growth in the *process* of engaging in collegial dialogue.

As teachers interact in group meetings over time and try to make sense of their experiences, they grow in several ways. According to Clemente (1992), who observed teachers in a two-year school/university urban-change project, they talked about expanding their own roles and taking curricular risks. The teachers clearly supported one another in this urban school system as they gained new perspectives on their roles. Furthermore, as the teachers interacted in meetings over time, their people-to-people skills seemed to improve. Several of the teachers showed movement toward the level of introspective questioning. As one teacher said, "Am I doing what I am supposed to be doing? Now I question everything I do" (p. 183). During the informal meetings, where participants gathered to talk about their classroom practice, frustrations were vented. These were sessions where teachers chose to work with others who had similar philosophies as a means of improving their teaching practices. These "situational aspects" were "supportive oases of confidence, trust, rapport, and friendship" (p. 185).

Where teachers were philosophically similar to each other, there was less confrontation and better communication. "In these situations . . . communication . . . went smoothly because there was a basis of trust and confidence in one another" (p. 191). Clemente's work corroborates Holly's (1989) findings that the increased opportunity to interact with other teachers, regardless of the setting, is perceived as beneficial by teachers, who viewed their colleagues as valuable resources. By engaging in a common conversation, teachers can begin to see themselves as professionals working toward a single goal—the improvement of teaching and learning.

Problem Solving

By engaging in mutual inquiry or problem solving, teachers reflect on their own practice, which strengthens teaching ability. In fact, classroom decision making from a reflective viewpoint *requires* concrete problem solving. Reflection enables content area reading teachers to consider what works in their classrooms as they attempt to solve day-to-day problems.

One time-tested inquiry model is action planning. Before implementing the basic steps in action planning, it's important to decide as a committee or team how to get at the needs, concerns, and interests of the larger teaching staff. Box 12.2 is an example of an assessment survey for content area reading.

Once the survey results are analyzed, the faculty team follows some rather explicit procedures to develop an action plan that looks like this:

    I. Define the Problem

       A. The problem as we understand it:

         Large vocabulary and concept load in high school textbooks

Box 12.2

Survey of Needs and Concerns

Please number in order of importance the areas in which you feel you need additional help to teach content through reading. Then answer each question as completely as possible.

_____ Determining the reading difficulty level of my content area materials

_____ Guiding students to comprehend their reading assignments

_____ Developing questions for a reading assignment

_____ Reinforcing technical vocabulary by providing opportunities for repeated use

_____ Developing vocabulary skills that will help students unlock the meaning of words independently

_____ Planning instruction so that students know how to approach their reading assignments

_____ Differentiating reading assignments in a single textbook to provide for a range of reading abilities

_____ Guiding students to read graphs, charts, maps, and illustrations

_____ Teaching key vocabulary terms before students meet them in an assignment

_____ Showing students how to read content materials critically

_____ Teaching students how to outline text material

_____ Developing a unit that coordinates instructional resources and materials

1. What is your area of greatest concern about your delivery of instruction in content area reading?

2. What is your area of least concern?

B. The following people are involved in the problem:

Teachers in selecting and teaching vocabulary terms and students who act uninterested

C. Other factors relevant to the problem:

Pressures to get through the content and produce acceptable test scores

D. One aspect of the problem we need to change:

Finding more effective ways of teaching vocabulary to students

II. Plan for Change

  A. Exactly what are we trying to accomplish?

  Find better ways to use social studies and history subject matter as a natural context for the development of students' vocabularies

  B. What behavior is implied?

  History and social studies teachers will identify key words, show students interrelationships, preteach, and guide students. Students will understand and use strategies they are shown.

  C. Who is going to do it?

  Each team member will meet with several other teachers to get their input, then come back to the team. Eventually most of the history and social studies staff and their students will be involved.

  D. Can it be done?

  Yes. There is every reason to expect support from the staff because the problem is a real one and we all expect improvement.

  E. What tangible evidence will indicate change?

  Teachers will be meeting to share vocabulary strategies, and students will be observed improving their vocabularies in class and using this knowledge and skill in tests.

III. Take Action Steps

  A. Actions that need to be taken
       1. Discussions with and memo to faculty
       2. Selecting consultant
       3. Arranging workshops for faculty with and without consultant
       4. Formative evaluations of progress
       5. Concerted effort in classroom vocabulary instruction
       6. Postassessment of teachers, consultant, students; summative evaluation compiled

  B. For each action: Persons responsible/Timing/Necessary resources
       1. Team and principal/January/School office budget
       2. Team and faculty/January/Team requesting money from district staff-development committee
       3. Principal/February/Principal
       4. Team and principal/February, March/Released time for workshops budgeted; consultant

5. Team and faculty/April/Materials reproduced
6. Team, principal, and planning committee/May/Principal; report disseminated

Technology Use

Learning to use technology has revolutionized the way educators access information and communicate with each other. With technology, teachers can choose to address specific individual interests or classroom needs and receive almost instant feedback. They can

♦ Infuse technology into teaching practices in different subjects

♦ Investigate skills students will need to function in the twenty-first century

♦ Design a classroom or school Web page

♦ Meet people in the news or in certain occupations

♦ Connect with students and teachers in other communities

There is, quite literally, a whole world of professional development opportunities available to today's teacher on the Internet. The path to professional growth can be as simple as an e-mail correspondence with a colleague or two to share ideas and lesson plans. More extensive connections can also be established by exploring the educational offerings of numerous Web sites and their accompanying links. Nearly every professional organization, journal, and magazine also has a site on the Internet that can provide teachers with valuable resources and references. In addition, the Internet is a good place to look for grant and funding information for K–12 programs in many subject areas.

Most of the major online service providers (such as America Online) have entire sections dedicated to teachers and education. Listservs and conversation exchange areas are set up for educators to interact. On the World Wide Web itself, a spring 1998 search on the term "education K–12" resulted in 132,275 entries, and "classroom teaching" brought 511,182 entries from which to select! Curricular references can also be found by searching on other relevant terms, such as "social studies teaching," "physical education," and "health education." Box 12.3 provides a sampling of the Web sites, mailing lists, and newsgroups available on the Internet for professional growth, lesson planning, and conversations with colleagues.

The Internet is, indeed, an appropriate starting point for building cross-disciplinary connections also, as the information can be collected so easily and quickly. Teachers can work independently, learning in areas of specific interest to themselves, or they can interact with colleagues across disciplines, grade levels, and geographic areas. The possibilities are endless.

Action Research

Action research is enjoying a resurgence in popularity through the teacher-as-researcher movement. When classroom teachers pursue action research, they investigate questions that they themselves have generated about teaching and learning. Beginning with the questions "What do I think?" and "How will I know?" teacher-researchers gather evidence in their classrooms to test their hypotheses and then evaluate their results (Gove & Kennedy-Calloway 1992). While it's probably true that "all good teachers participate in teacher research because they reflect about students' learning (and their own)" (Patterson & Shannon 1993, p. 8), it's not often that they do so as part of planned professional development.

One systematic, commonsense procedure that we've found effective is to begin by designing an inquiry plan such as the one in Figure 12.2 on page 485. In this particular plan, developed by Gary, an experienced sixth-grade teacher in a suburban school district, the focus of concern is the newly mandated process of inclusion: teaching diverse learners with diverse needs in the same classroom. A critical issue throughout education, inclusion is a good example of a topic that cuts across all subject areas and that relates to both the classroom learning level and the school organizational level.

The main benefit to working through several drafts of the plan, first individually and then with colleagues, is that it helps build confidence in the teacher-researcher. Before much time had elapsed, for example, Gary found himself immersed in conducting the action research. By the time he revised his inquiry plan, he was moving from step 3 to step 4 in the action research process:

1. Identify a problem or situation.
2. Formulate specific research questions.
3. Determine the method and procedure for investigating the question.
4. Carry out research; collect data.
5. Look at the data; analyze them; draw conclusions.
6. Make decisions based on the results of the research.

Action research, as a strategy for professional development, incorporates the first three strategies of empowerment: writing, dialogue, and problem solving. It can be especially helpful to content area teachers who try many of the instructional strategies suggested in this book. They gain experience with innovations while receiving support from colleagues, changing their own teaching, and growing professionally.

Box 12.3

Nothing but Net: Resources, Mailing Lists, and Newsgroups for Professional Growth

INFORMATION AND PLANNING RESOURCES

Classroom Connect Jump Station
http://www.classroom.net/classroom/edulinks.html
Useful planning resources, including chat rooms, instructional resources, a teacher contact database.

Eisenhower National Clearinghouse
http://www.enc.org/
Resources in science and math, including lesson plans, resource sites, a math/science search engine, publications, and answers to questions.

Global SchoolNet Foundation Home Page
http://www.gsn.org/
Connects teachers and students from around the world, especially for project-related learning.

K–12 Kaleidoscope
http://www.schoolnet.ca/adm/staff/
Organized around major curricular areas and useful for instructional ideas.

Lesson Plans and Resources for Social Studies Teachers
http://www.csun.edu/~hcedu013/index.html
Contains lesson plans, Internet resources, and links to many useful sites.

PBS Teacher Connex
http://www.pbs.org/tconnex/index.html
Provides information, lesson plans, and links to Internet sites related to television programs appearing on the Public Broadcasting Service stations.

Teachers Helping Teachers
http://www.pacificnet.net/~mandel/
For teachers to share teaching tips and innovative, instructional ideas.

LISTSERVS/MAILING LISTS

Discussion Groups for Curricular Issues
K12ASSESS-L
mailserv@lists.cua.edu
Issues related to educational assessment, grades K–12.

SCHOOL-L
listserv@listserv.hea.ie
A forum for primary and secondary school discussion.

MIDDLE-L
listserv@postoffice.cso.vivc.edu
A forum for anyone interested in middle schools.

Discussion Groups for Language Arts
KIDLIT-L
listserv@bingvmb.bitnet
Children's literature.

TAWL
listserv@listserv.arizona.edu
Whole language.

WAC-L
listserv@vmd.cso.vivc.edu
Writing across the curriculum.

Discussion Groups for Mathematics
MATHSED-L
listserv@deakin.edu.au

NCTM-L
listproc@sci-ed.fit.edu

Discussion Groups for Science
CYBERMARCH-NET
majordomo@igc.apc.org
Environmental education.

IMSE-L
listserv@uwf.cc.uwf.edu
Sponsored by the Institute for Math and Science Education.

T321-L
listserv@mizzou1.missouri.edu
Science in elementary schools.

TIMS-L
listserv@uicvm.uic.edu
Sponsored by the Teaching Integrated Mathematics and Science (TIMS) Project.

Discussion Groups for Social Studies
CIVNET
listserv@listserv.syr.edu
Teaching civics.

SOCSTUD-L
mailserv@hcca.ohio.gov
Teaching social studies.

SS435-L
listserv@ualtavm.bitnet
Teaching social studies in the elementary grades.

TAMHA
listserv@cms.cc.wayne.edu
Teaching American history.

(continued)

Box 123 (cont'd)

Nothing but Net: Resources, Mailing Lists, and Newsgroups for Professional Growth

NEWSGROUPS

Language Arts
Language Arts Curriculum in K–12 Education
k12.lang.art

Writing Instruction in Computer-Based Classrooms
comp.edu.compostion

Math Education
k12.chat.teacher
Discussion among teachers in grades K–12.

k12.ed.math
Mathematics curriculum in grades K–12.

pnet.school.k-12
Mathematics curriculum in grades K–12.

pnet.school.k-5
Mathematics curriculum in grades K–5.

Science Education
k12.ed.science
Science curriculum in K–12 education.

misc.education.science
Issues related to science education.

k12.chat.teacher
Discussion among teachers in grades K–12.

Social Studies Education
Social Studies and History Curriculum in K–12 Education
k12.ed.soc-studies

PROFESSIONAL DEVELOPMENT PLANS

Professional development activities will naturally vary over the course of a teacher's career, as one's professional focus and interests move from internal to external with years of experience. An early-career teacher, for example, might spend more time and energy trying out various techniques in the class-

Action Research: Teachers identifying and answering their most pressing questions, finding solutions, and engaging in practice-centered inquiry

Name: _Gary Hargrove_

Planning Your Study:

1. What is being studied in your field? _Inclusion, graded vs nongraded, assessment, portfolios_

2. What are you interested in studying? _Inclusion_

3. How do you choose to go about it? _(see below)_

Inquiry Plan

Purpose	Research Questions	Procedures
1. To determine the positive effects of inclusive schooling 2. To determine how an inclusive classroom in sixth and seventh grades can be organized to benefit the teachers and the students	1. How do teachers provide a supportive environment in which students with "regular" and special needs can grow together? 2. What types of teaching strategies and approaches should be used to ensure success? 3. In what ways do the students interact in the classroom? 4. How are sixth- and seventh-grade teachers currently adjusting to the new program?	Interview teachers involved in the process of inclusion Interview students in inclusive classrooms Observe classrooms in the morning and afternoon over a three-week period Interview teachers who have never dealt with inclusion

FIGURE 12.2   **An Inquiry Plan for Action Research**

room and dealing with classroom management issues. A 15-year veteran teacher, by contrast, might be looking for alternative ways to contribute to the profession or otherwise dealing with burnout issues. There are a number of successful strategies for growth and reflection in the teaching profession. With some planning, they can be used to benefit teachers at all points throughout their career. Let's see how two teachers, one a novice and one a veteran, put together individual plans for professional development.

Entry-Year Fourth-Grade Teacher

Darby is a first-year teacher in a fourth-grade classroom. Her *primary* concern is gaining a sense of mastery and comfort with being "in charge"—not only of all the daily operations of her classroom but also of the educational life of her students! The journal could be her most indispensable tool to make sense of it all. By keeping a notebook on her desk, Darby can write down random thoughts, concerns, questions, and reflections whenever she has the chance. Reading the entries every so often can provide Darby with insight into her own thinking as a teacher. If she can find a like-minded colleague (maybe even a veteran teacher) with whom to share the discoveries revealed in her journal, it can initiate conversations, furnish each teacher with fresh perspectives, and generate new ideas to use in the classroom.

Darby's special curricular interest is math. By joining a professional organization, like the National Council of Teachers of Mathematics, she can stay abreast of current thinking in the field, as well as learn practical, often hands-on, ideas for her teaching. Subscribing to a teacher's journal or magazine can also keep Darby connected with the larger field of education without being overwhelming.

Many organizations sponsor workshops and conferences throughout the year. By attending even one a year, Darby would renew and recharge her energy and enthusiasm. She would interact with fellow teachers, view the latest in curriculum materials, and pick up lots of ideas for her classroom.

Darby will soon begin making application to the state university for admission into the new middle-childhood education program. As part of her course requirements, she may well be engaged in doing learning logs, using technology to access information, and planning to begin action research.

Veteran Art Teacher

Mark, an art teacher, has taught at every level, K–12, but is currently at a middle school. Throughout his 19-year career, Mark, who has a master's degree in curriculum and instruction, has kept a journal. Though his entries were sometimes far between, he always remembered to record his thoughts, plans, and reflections on the first workday of the school year as a way to center himself and reconnect to the work at hand. Rereading these entries gives Mark an idea of how his perspective has evolved over the years. He often discusses his thinking with several colleagues with whom he has worked for many years. They've grown together.

Mark has also maintained an active membership in a number of professional organizations during his career, including both state- and national-level art education associations. These connections have given him a broader perspective on his field and allowed him to both learn from and share with colleagues, by attending and presenting at conferences and subscribing to publications. The state association provides Mark with a close network of supportive colleagues and lots of practical teaching ideas. The national association enriches Mark's interest in the more academic scholarly theory and research side of art education and keeps him in tune with the national issues and scope of the field.

Mark began by simply attending one state conference a year, early in his career. Then, after earning his master's degree over a four-year period, he tried presenting a session at the state conference and then attended a national conference in San Diego. The next step was to write a proposal and become a presenter at the national level. All these activities became avenues for Mark to grow as a teacher and a professional.

Mark has found four other avenues that keep him "charged" and excited about teaching. One is taking part in a small group of middle school teachers who set out to collaborate on developing a project that would break down disciplinary boundaries. They initiated an entirely new curriculum opportunity for their school—a school garden. They have researched interdisciplinary connections, organized school and community people to plan and build the garden, and worked together to gather resources and support for the project. His art students even covered an entire outside wall of the school with a garden mural.

A second avenue for Mark is serving as a mentor for fieldwork and student teaching interns from a nearby university's teacher education program. He tries to take one student a semester, spending extra time during and after the regular school day talking with and listening to his mentee. Mark attends one or two meetings a year at the university in connection with his responsibilities and has become friendly with several of his counterparts from other local school districts.

Third, Mark has explored the possibilities of grant writing. Funds are available from numerous sources for creative and innovative curriculum programs for students. Mark has discovered that writing grants has provided him with an unanticipated benefit: He has had to articulate his beliefs about education, his goals for the art education of his students, and his own perspective on teaching, thereby clarifying *why* he does what he does. He has written many grants and received some, but he has learned a lot about himself and teaching in the process, regardless of the outcome.

Fourth, Mark recently discovered for himself the benefit of "primary source" professional development. He participated in a workshop on Mayan archaeology, for educators, on-site in Belize. Being *in* the environment while studying it, and learning how to transmit that knowledge to students, truly made a difference. Firsthand experiences of this kind are both personally and professionally enriching. Mark prepared for this experience by reading and studying about the Maya and the rain forest. One source he used was the online program Mayaquest. This interactive curriculum, used in many classrooms, involved the contributions of Mayan experts in a number of fields and provided Mark with extensive background information, both for himself as a professional and for use with his students in the classroom.

The next step for Mark, as he nears the last phase of his teaching career, is to share what he has learned with others. This he can do by continuing to mentor novice teachers or by starting a study group in which the members simply discuss concerns they have—perhaps using their own journals. He can write articles for the publications he has read for years. And he can continue to attend and present at conferences—to inspire his newer colleagues to continue their own learning as they foster the learning of their students.

 ## LOOKING BACK, LOOKING FORWARD

We have focused in this chapter on growth and reflection in the teaching profession as a developmental, continuing process for content area teachers. To attract and retain good teachers who will incorporate content area reading into their instructional repertoires, professional growth opportunities are designed on the principles of lifelong learning and planned change. They are the result of collaborative inquiry—among teachers, administrators, specialists, and consultants—who reflect on their own practice.

Professional development programs with clear purposes are more likely to be perceived as relevant by the participants. Hence planners of professional development may deal with a range of purposes, from improved proficiency test scores to teachers' becoming reflective practitioners.

We can learn from what works. Many effective programs are described in reports and brochures. Recurring characteristics of these programs are incorporated into the guidelines and principles of professional development. In planning for professional development, where opportunities for reflection and inquiry are highly valued, there are a number of strategies for successful professional development. Building on teachers' orientation to learning as adults, their experiences, and their career stage, we proposed five strategies: *writing* for a personal sense of purpose, *dialoguing* and *problem solving* with colleagues, *using technology* for information and communication, and inquiring through *action research.*

Finally, we illustrated through two teachers, Darby and Mark, ways in which strategies that promote growth and reflection can be integrated into individual plans for professional development whether early or later in one's teaching career.

 ## MINDS-ON

1. Imagine that you are part of a committee in charge of planning a professional development program for teachers in your building. Considering

the wide range of experience levels among the teachers, what different types of growth and development activities might you devise to meet individual needs?

2. Reflect on a time when you teamed with one or more teachers on a project. What were some of the benefits to students and teachers derived from the collaboration? What were some of the drawbacks?

3. How do professionals in various fields improve their craft through reflection? In what way can reflection enhance a teacher's professional growth? How might portfolios, journals, diaries, and learning logs aid in this process?

4. Examine the following professional development needs: (a) to obtain better information and to be able to use it more rationally, (b) to reconsider one's own beliefs in order to come to a better understanding of oneself, and (c) to explore alternative strategies for improving one's teaching and learning. Where would you place your own professional needs, and how do they compare with those of others in your group?

 HANDS-ON

1. As part of a program for professional development, the administration at your school has decided to encourage teachers to develop professional portfolios. You have been asked to participate on a committee to develop guidelines for the items that might be included. Some colleagues have suggested journal entries, letters to colleagues and students, anecdotal writing, formal writing, lesson plans, checklists, and videotapes of lessons. What would you add to and delete from this list? Why?

2. Team with several people in the class who teach or will be teaching in your content area. Together, complete the "Survey of Needs and Concerns" in Box. 12.2. Finally, develop an action plan to meet these needs.

3. Think of yourself as a teacher-researcher. Come up with a question that you believe could be answered by a classroom experiment. Conduct the experiment, and share the results with the class.

4. Define teachers' career cycles in relation to a category. You might choose levels of expertise, levels of personal needs, levels of experience, or any other category you find appropriate. Using this category, create a chart of teacher career cycles, and suggest appropriate professional development activities for each stage.

SUGGESTED READINGS

Danielson, C. (1996). *Enhancing professional practice: A framework for teaching.* Alexandria, VA: Association for Supervision and Curriculum Development.

Lieberman, A., & Miller, L. (Eds.). (1991). *Staff development for education in the '90s* (2nd ed.). New York: Teachers College Press.

Patterson, L., Santa, C., Short, K., & Smith, K. (Eds.). (1993). *Teachers are researchers: Reflection and action.* Newark, DE: International Reading Association.

Russell, T., & Munby, H. (Eds.). (1992). *Teachers and teaching: From classroom to reflection.* Bristol, PA: Falmer Press.

Affixes with Invariant Meanings

AFFIX	MEANING	EXAMPLE
Combining Forms		
anthropo-	man	anthropoid
auto-	self	autonomous
biblio-	book	bibliography
bio-	life	biology
centro-, centri-	center	centrifugal
cosmo-	universe	cosmonaut
heter-, hetero-	different	heterogeneous
homo-	same	homogeneous
hydro-	water	hydroplane
iso-	equal	isometric
lith-, litho-	stone	lithography
micro-	small	microscope
mono-	one	monocyte
neuro-	nerve	neurologist
omni-	all	omnibus
pan-	all	panchromatic
penta-	five	pentamerous
phil-, philo-	love	philanthropist
phono-	sound	phonology

photo-	light	photosynthesis
pneumo-	air, respiration	pneumonia
poly-	many	polygon
proto-	before, first in time	prototype
pseudo-	false	pseudonym
tele-	far	television
uni-	one	unicellular

Prefixes

apo-	separate or detached from	apocarpous
circum-	around	circumvent
co-, col-, com-, con-, cor-	together or with	combine
equi-	equal	equivalent
extra-	in addition	extraordinary
intra-	within	intratext
mal-	bad	malpractice
mis-	wrong	mistreatment
non-	not	nonsense
syn-	together or with	synthesis

Noun Suffixes

-ana	collection	Americana
-archy	rule or government	oligarchy
-ard, -art	person who does something to excess	drunkard, braggart
-aster	inferiority or fraudulence	poetaster
-bility	quality or state of being	capability
-chrome	pigment, color	autochrome
-cide	murder or killing of	insecticide
-fication, -ation	action or process of	classification, dramatization
-gram	something written or drawn	diagram
-graph	writing, recording, drawing	telegraph, lithograph

-graphy	descriptive science of a specific subject or field	planography, oceanography
-ics	science or art of	graphics, athletics
-itis	inflammation or inflammatory disease	bronchitis
-latry	worship of	bibliolatry
-meter	measuring device	barometer
-metry	science or process of measuring	photometry
-ology, -logy	science, theory, or study of	phraseology, paleontology
-phobia	fear	hypnophobia
-phore	bearer or producer	semaphore
-scope	instrument for observing or detecting	telescope
-scopy	viewing, seeing, or observing	microscopy
-ance, -ation, -ion, -ism, -dom, -ery, -mony, -ment, -tion	quality, state, or condition; action or result of an action	tolerance, adoration, truism, matrimony, government, sanction
-er, -eer, -ess, -ier, -ster, -ist, -trix	agent, doer	helper, engineer, countess, youngster, shootist, executrix

Adjective Suffixes

-est	most	greatest
-ferous	bearing, producing	crystalliferous
-fic	making, causing, or creating	horrific
-fold	multiplied by	fivefold
-form	having the form of	cuneiform
-genous	generating or producing	androgenous, endogenous
-ic	characteristic of	seismic, microscopic
-wise	manner, direction, or position	clockwise
-less	lacking	toothless
-able, -ible	worthy of or inclined to	debatable, knowledgeable
-most	most	innermost
-like	similar to	lifelike

-ous, -ose	possessing, full of	joyous, grandiose
-acious	tendency toward or abundance of	fallacious
-ful	full of or having the quality of	masterful, useful, armful
-aceous, -ative, -ish, -ive, -itious	pertaining to	impish, foolish, additive, fictitious

Commonly Used Prefixes with Varying Meanings

PREFIX	MEANING	EXAMPLE
ab-	from, away, off	abhor, abnormal, abdicate
ad-	to, toward	adhere, adjoin
ante-	before, in front of, earlier than	antecedent, antediluvian
anti-	opposite of, hostile to	antitoxin, antisocial
be-	make, against, to a great degree	bemoan, belittle, befuddle
bi-	two, twice	biped, bivalve
de-	away, opposite of, reduce	deactivate, devalue, devitalize
dia-	through, across	diameter, diagonal
dis-	opposite of, apart, away	dissatisfy, disarm, disjointed
en-	cause to be, put in or on	enable, engulf
epi-	upon, after	epitaph, epilogue, epidermis
ex-	out of, former, apart, away	excrete, exposition
hyper-	above, beyond, excessive	hyperphysical, hypersensitive
hypo-	under, less than normal	hypodermic, hypotension
in-, il-, im-, ir-	not, in, into, within	inept, indoors
inter-	between, among	interscholastic, interstellar
neo-	new, young	neophyte, neo-Nazi

per-	through, very	permanent, perjury
peri-	around, near, enclosing	perimeter, perihelion
post-	after, behind	postwar, postorbital
pre-	before, in place, time, rank, order	preview, prevail
pro-	before, forward, for, in favor of	production, prothorax, pro-American
ortho-	straight, corrective	orthotropic, orthopedic
re-	again, back	react, recoil
sub-, sur-, sug-, sup-	under, beneath, subordinate	subsoil, substation
super-	above, over, in addition	superhuman, superlative, superordinate
syn-	with, together	synthesis, synchronize
trans-	across, beyond, through	transatlantic, transconfiguration, transaction
ultra-	beyond in space, excessive	ultraviolet, ultramodern
un-	not, the opposite of	unable, unbind

Graphic Representations with Text Frames

Graphic representations are visual illustrations of verbal statements. Frames are sets of questions or categories that are fundamental to understanding a given topic. Here are shown nine "generic" graphic forms with their corresponding frames. Also given are examples of topics that could be represented by each graphic form. These graphics show at a glance the key parts of the whole and their relations, helping the learner to comprehend text and solve problems.

Spider Map

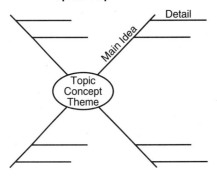

Used to describe a central idea: a thing (a geographic region), process (meiosis), concept (altruism), or proposition with support (experimental drugs should be available to AIDS victims). Key frame questions: What is the central idea? What are its attributes? What are its functions?

Used to describe the stages of something (the life cycle of a primate); the steps in a linear procedure (how to neutralize an acid); a sequence of events (how feudalism led to the formation of nation-states); or the goals, actions, and outcomes of a historical figure or character in a novel (the rise and fall of Napoleon). Key frame questions: What is the object, procedure, or initiating event? What are the stages or steps? How do they lead to one another? What is the final outcome?

Source: © 1988 North Central Regional Educational Laboratory. Reprinted with permission.

Series-of-Events Chain

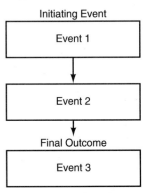

Continuum/Scale

```
|————————————————————|
Low                High
```

Used for time lines showing historical events or ages (grade levels in school), degrees of something (weight), shades of meaning (Likert scales), or ratings scales (achievement in school). Key frame questions: What is being scaled? What are the end points?

Used to show similarities and differences between two things (people, places, events, ideas, etc.). Key frame questions: What things are being compared? How are they similar? How are they different?

Compare/Contrast Matrix

	Name 1	Name 2
Attribute 1		
Attribute 2		
Attribute 3		

Problem/Solution Outline

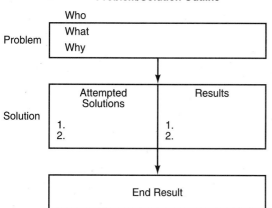

Used to represent a problem, attempted solutions, and results (the national debt). Key frame questions: What was the problem? Who had the problem? Why was it a problem? What attempts were made to solve the problem? Did those attempts succeed?

Used to show causal information (causes of poverty), a hierarchy (types of insects), or branching procedures (the circulatory system). Key frame questions: What is the superordinate category? What are the subordinate categories? How are they related? How many levels are there?

Network Tree

Human Interaction Outline

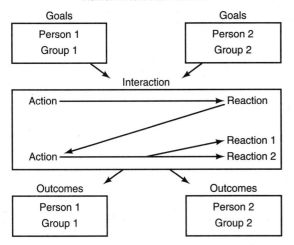

Used to show the nature of an interaction between persons or groups (European settlers and American Indians). Key frame questions: Who are the persons or groups? Did they conflict or cooperate? What was the outcome for each person or group?

Used to show the causal interaction of a complex event (an election, a nuclear explosion) or complex phenomenon (juvenile deliquency, learning disabilities). Key frame questions: What are the factors that cause X? How do they relate? Are the factors that cause X the same as those that cause X to persist?

Fishbone Map

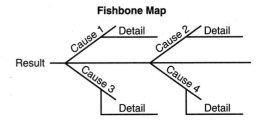

Cycle

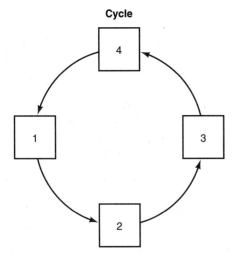

Used to show how a series of events interact to produce a set of results again and again (weather phenomena, cycles of achievement and failure, the life cycle). Key frame questions: What are the critical events in the cycle? How are they related? In what ways are they self-reinforcing?

Internet Addresses for Content Areas

The Web sites that we have selected illustrate additional possibilities for locating information resources on the Internet in various content areas. Because the Web is a fluid and continually changing medium, some of the locations listed here may no longer be in operation.

The Arts

Krannert Art
http://www.ncsa.uiuc.edu/General/UIUC/KrannertArtMuseum/
KrannertArtHome.html

Art and Architecture History Server
http://rubens.anu.edu.au

The Louvre Museum
http://mistral.enst.fr/~pioch/louvre

Bayly African Art Museum
http://www.lib.virginia.edu/dic/exhib/93.ray.aa/African.html

Asian Art Exhibit
http://www.nets.com/asianart

National Museum of Art
http://www.nmaa.si.edu

fineArt Forum Online
http://www.msstate.edu/Fineart_Online/home.html

Art Sites on the Internet
http://artsnet.heinz.cmu.edu/Artsites/Artsites.html

Art on the Net
http://www.art.net/welcome.html

Art Museums on the World Wide Web
http://www.comlab.ox.ac.uk/archive/other/museums.html

Paleolithic Cave Paintings in France
http://www.culture.fr/culture/gvpda-en.htm

Mr. Potato Head
http://winnie.acsu.buffalo.edu/potatoe

Digital Tradition Folk Song Database
http://pubweb.parc.xerox.com/digitrad

The Mammoth Music Meta-List from VIBE
http://pathfinder.com/@@U549@AAAAAAAQG7W/Vibe/mmm

The Tower Lyrics Archive
http://www.ccs.neu.edu/home/tower/lyrics.html

English Language Arts

Classics and Classical Antiquity
http://www.clark.net/pub/lschank/web/classics.html

Humanities (Galaxy)
http://www.einet.net/galaxy/Humanities.html

The Labyrinth
http://www.georgetown.edu/labyrinth/labyrinth-home.html

Science Fiction, Fantasy. Horror (Stanford)
http://akebono.stanford.edu/yahoo/Art/Literature/Science_Fiction_Fantasy_Horror

Briarwood Educational Network
http://www.briarwood.com

The Quotations Page
http://www.starlingtech.com/quotes

The C. S. Lewis WWW Home Page
http://www.cache.net/~john/cslewis/index.html

Shakespeare Web
http://www.shakespeare.com

MythText: Mythology from All Over the World
http://www.io.org/~untangle/mythtext.html

Newbery Award Winners
http://dab.psi.net/ChapterOne/children/index.html

Winnie the Pooh
http://www.infinet.com/~mimesis/Pooh/index.html

The WEB: Celebrating Children's Literature
http://www.armory.com/~web/web.html

The On-line Books Page
http://www.cs.cmu.edu/Web/books.html

Researchpaper.com
http://www.researchpaper.com/writing.html

Purdue University's On-Line Writing Lab
http://owl.trc.perdue.edu

Glossary of Poetic Terms
http://shoga.wwa.com/~rgs/glossary.html

Biographical Sketch of William Shakespeare
http://www.earthlink.net/~feiffor/bard/content/man.html

The Complete Works of William Shakespeare
http://www.the-tech.mit.edu.Shakespeare

Guide to Shakespeare resources, festivals, texts, and plays
http://www.authors.mingco.com/msub19.htm

Guide to Shakespeare's birthplace
http://www.stratford-upon-avon.co.uk/soawshst.htm

Ask the Author
http://www.ipl.org/youth/AskAuthor/

Contemporary Writing for Children and Young Adults
http://www.ucalgary.ca/~dkbrown/storcont.html

Folklore, Myth and Legend
http://www.ucalgary.ca/~dkbrown/storfolk.html

Greek Mythology
http://www.intergate.net/uhtml/.jhunt/greek_myth/

How a Book Is Made
http://www.harpercollins.com/kids/bkstepl.htm

Indigenous Peoples' Literature
http://www.indians.org/welker/framenat.html

Inkspot for Young Writers
http://www.inkspot.com/~ohi/inkspot/young.html

KIDLINK
http://www.kidlink.org/

Kidproject
http://www.kidlink.org:80/KIDPROJ/

KidPub
http://en-garde.com/kidpub/intro.html

Kindred Spirits
http://www.upei.ca/lmmi/cover.html

Language Arts and Literature
http://pen1.pen.kl2.va.us:80/~mchildre/langarts.html

Laura Ingalls Wilder Home Page
http://webpages.marshall.edu/irbyl/laura.htmlx

Lewis Carroll Home Page Illustrated
http://www.cstone.net/library/alice/carrol.html

Foreign Language

Excite Travel by city.Net
http://www.city.net/countries/spain/

Teacher Resources
http://www.tapr.org/~ird/Ludeke/teacherlinks.html

Classroom Resources
http://www.adventureonline.com/pca/*class.html

Kids Identifying and Discovering Sites
http://www.scout.cs.wisc.edu/scout/KIDS/

American Institute for Foreign Language
http://www.aifs.org/2index.htm

Mexican Newspapers
http://www.excelsior.com.mx/ *or* http://www.novedades.com.mx/

Artey Cultura Mexicana
http://www.udg.mx/cultfolk/mexico.html

Newsgroup SOC.CULTURE.MEXICAN
http://www.public.iastate.edu/~rjsalvad/scmfaq/faqindex.html

Cristina Heeren Flamenco Foundation
http://www.servicom.es/heeren/

Flamenco
http://www.red2000.com/spain/flamenco/

Recetas de España
http://www.xmission.com/~dderhak/recipes.html

Travel on Demand (TOD)
http://www.travel.com.hk/region/samermap.htm

Vocabulary Training Exercises
http://www.vokabel.com/

Links to Foreign Language Educators
http://www.erols.com/jbrennan/flteachers.htm

Linguistic Funland
http://www.linguistic-funland.com/spanlist.html

Webspañol
http://www.cyberramp.net/~mdbutler/webspan/

Ideas for Health Lessons

http://www.mcrel.org/connect/plus/nutri.html

First Aid
http://www.prairienet.org/~autumn/firstaid/

Health and Diseases
http://search-Yahoo.com/bin/search?p=health+and+literacy

Food and Nutrition
http://www.healthy.net

http://web.indstate.edu/hlthsfty/hlth221/chhome.html

School Meals
http://schoolmeals.nal.usda.gov:8001/team.html

http://www.nalusda.gov/fnic/

Mathematics

History of Mathematics
http://www-groups.dcs.st-and.ac.uk:80/~history

MegaMath
http://www.c3.lanl.gov/mega-math/welcome.html

The MathSoft Math Puzzle Page
http://www.mathsoft.com/puzzle.html

Eisenhower National Center for Mathematics and Science Education
http://www.enc.org:80/index.htm

Math Forum
http://forum.swarthmore.edu/

Math Archives
http://archives.math.utk.edu/newindex.html

About Today's Date
http://acorn.edu.nottingham.ac.uk/cgi-bin/daynum

Brain Teasers
http://www.eduplace.com/math/brain/

Fruit Game
http://www.2020tech.com/fruit/f752.html

Elementary Problem of the Week
http://forum.swarthmore.edu/sum95/ruth/elem.pow.html

The Little Math Puzzle Contest
http://www.odyssee.net/~academy/mathpuzzle/mathpuzzlecontest.html

Word Problems for Kids
http://juliet.stfx.ca/people/fac/pwang/mathpage/math1.html

Connect Four
http://www.csun.edu/~vceed009/games.html

The Hub
http://hub.terc.edu/

Mathematical Puzzles
http://thinks.com/webguide/mathpuzzles.htm

Math Games
http://www.cs.duke.edu/~jeffe/mathgames.html

Numbers and Games
http://www.cs.uidaho.edu/~casey931/conway/games.html

Board Game Using Binary Number Theory
http://www.cs.oberlin.edu/students/dhutchin/Applets/Quarto/Quarto.html

Mankala, an African board game
http://www.elf.org/mankala.html

Tower of Hanoi
http://www.cut-the-knot.com

Probability: The Birthday Problem
http://www.mste.uiuc.edu/reese/birthday/intro.html#simulation

Interactive Math Puzzles
http://mar.superlink.net/abogom

Activities for Texas Instrument calculators
http://www.TI.com

National Council of Teachers of Mathematics
http://www.NCTM.org

Educational Resources Information Center (ERIC)
http://ericir.sunsite.syr.edu/

Teacher Ideas and Activities
http://www.csun.edu/~vceed009/activities.html

Science

InterNIC Directory and Database Services
http://www.internic.net

Mars Thermal Emission Spectrometer Project
http://esther.la.asu.edu/asu_tes

Astro Web
http://stsci.edu/net-resources.html

SciEd
http://www-hpcc.astro.washington.edu/scied/science.html

Space Telescope Electronic Information Service
http://www.stsci.edu

Explorer Home Page
http://unite.ukans.edu

EcoNet
http://www.econet.apc.org/econet

Weather Browser
http://wxweb.msu.edu/weather

AIDS Patents Project
http://patents.cnidr.org

Florida Aquarium Habitats
http://www.times.st-pete.fl.us/aquarium/default.html

Penn State University
http://www.gis.psu.edu/Earth2/Earth2HTML/E2Top.html

History of the Light Microscope
http://www.duke.edu/~tj/hist/hist_mic.html

AIDS Patent Search Page
http://ds0.internic.net/aidspat/aids_search.html

U.S. Patent and Trademark Office
http://pioneer.uspto.gov

ArchNet: University of Connecticut Department of Anthropology
http://spirit.lib.uconn.edu.ArchNet/ArchNet.html

Centers for Disease Control and Prevention
http://www.cdc.gov

U.S. Department of Energy (DOE) Home Page
http://www.doe.gov

EnviroLink (EnviroLink Network)
http://envirolink.org/envirowebs.html

Enviromental Data (U.S. Geological Survey)
http://www.usgs.gov/research/environment/index.html

Collaborative Visualization Project
http://www.covis.nwu.edu

NASA Public Affairs Home Page
http://www.gsfc.nasa.gov/hqpao/hqpao_home.html

UCB Museum of Paleontology
http://ucmp1.berkeley.edu/welcome.html

Planetary Data Systems: NASA
http://stardust./jpl.nasa.gov/planets

Mt. Wilson Observatory
http://www.mtwilson.edu

The Exploratorium
http://www.exploratorium.edu

Los Alamos National Laboratory
http://www.lanl.gov/Public/Education/Welcome.html

The Learning Web (U.S. Geologic Service)
http://info.er.usgs.gov/education/index.html

Natural History Museum of England
http://www.nhm.ac.uk

Stephen Birch Aquarium-Museum
http://aqua.ucsd.edu

Global On-Line Adventure Learning
http://www.goals.com

EROS Home Page
http://sunl.cr.usgs.gov

Earthquakes
http://152.157.16.3/WWWSchools/OtherSites/CASEE/seis.html

University of Washington Geophysics Program
http://www.geophys.washington.edu/

Fish FAQs
http://www.wh.whoi.edu/homepage/faq.html

Volcano World
http://volcano.und.nodak.edu

The Field Museum
http://www.bvis.uic.edu/museum/

Dino Russ's Lair
http://denr1.igis.uiuc.edu:/isgsroot/dinos/dinos_home.html

Periodic Table of Elements
http://www.cs.ubc.ca/elements/periodic-table

James Aldridge's Resources for Chemistry Teachers
http://ramgages.onramp.net/~jaldr

HyperCard Stacks for Astronomy Studies
http://marvel.stsci.edu?exined-html/exined-home.html

Jet Propulsion Laboratory (NASA)
http://www.jpl.nasa.gov/

Weather Underground
http://groundhog.sprl.umich.edu/

Current Weather Maps/Movies
http://rs560.cl.edu/weather.index.html

American Health Association
http://www.amhrt.org

WhaleNet
http://whale.wheelock.edu/

Helping Your Child Learn Science
http://www.ed.gov/pubs/parents/Science

How Light Works
http://curry.edschool.Virginia.EDU/murray/Light/How_Light_Works.html

Smithsonian Institution's Natural History Web
http://nmnhwww.si.edu/nmnhweb.html

Cyberspace Middle School Science Fair
http://www.scri.fsu.edu/~dennisl/special/sciencefair95.html

The JASON Project
http://seawifs.gsfc.nasa.gov/scripts/JASON.html

The KinderGARDEN
http://aggie-horticulture.tamu.edu/kinder/index.html

NASA Solar System Visualization Project
http://www-pdsimage.jpl.nasa.gov/PIA

The Sea WiFS Project
http://seawifs.gsfc.nasa.gov/SEAWIFS/LIVING_OCEAN/LIVING_OCEAN.html

The Nine Planets
http://seds.lpl.arizona.edu/nineplanets/nineplanets

Ask an Expert
http://www.askanexpert.com/p/ask.html

Ask a Mad Scientist
http://128.252.223.239/~ysp/MSN/

Ask an Agriculture Expert
http://spiderweb.com/ag/

Ask an Antarctic Expert
http://icair.iac.org.nz/education/resource/askaques/askaques.htm

Ask an Animal Keeper
http://www.libertynet.org/iha/valleyforge/writeus.html

Ask an Architect
http://www.4j.lane.edu/aiab/aquestion.html

Ask an Astronaut
http://www.nss.org/askastro/home.html

Ask an Astronomer
http://www2.ari.net/home/odenwald/qadir/qanda.html

Ask an Atmospheric Expert
http://hyperion.gsfc.nasa.gov/Reading_room/ask.html

Ask a Bug Expert
http://wwworkin.com/bugdoctor.html

Ask a Dinosaur Expert
http://denr1.igis.uiuc.edu/isgsroot/dinos/rjjinput_form.html

Ask Dr. Science
http://www.ducksbreath.com/index.html

Ask an Earth Scientist
http://www.soest.hawaii.edu/GG/ASK/askanerd.html

Ask a Geologist
http://walrus.wr.usgs.gov/docs/ask-a-ge.html

Ask a Gravity Expert
http://www.physics.umd.edu/rgroups/gen_rel_the/question.html

Ask a Health Expert
http://linear.chsra.wisc.edu/chsra/chen-fu/qmail.htm

Ask a Hydrologist
http://wwwdwatcm.wr.usgs.gov/askhyd.html

Ask a Nutritionist
http://www.cornell.edu/cgi-bin/dialogs_all?nutriquest

Ask an Ocean Animal Expert
http://www.whaletimes.org/whaques.htm

Ask a Paleontology Expert
http://ucmp.berkeley.edu/museum/pals.html

Ask a Science Expert
http://www.npr.org/sfkids/resources.html

Social Studies

African Studies Web Server (University of Pennsylvania)
http://www.african.upenn.edu/African_Studies/AS.html

American Memory
http://rs6.loc.gov/amhome.html

Worlds of Late Antiquity
http://ccat.sas.upenn.edu/jod/wola.html

The World Wide Web Virtual Library: Anthropology
http://www.usc.edu/dept/v-lib/anthropology.html

Aboriginal Studies
http://coombs.anu.edu.au/WWWVL-Aboriginal.html

Asian Studies (CERN)
http://coombs.anu.edu.au/WWWVL-AsianStudies.html

China News Digest
http://www.cnd.org

City.Net
http://www.city.net

U.S. House of Representatives
http://www.house.gov

Yahoo! Business and Economy
http://www.yahoo.com/Economy

EcoWeb
http://ecosys.Drdr.Virginia.edu

Center for Egyptian Art and Archaeology
http://www.memst.edu/egypt/main.html

European Home Page
http://s700.uminho.pt/europa.html

FedWorld
http://www.fedworld.gov

Greek Mythology
http://www.intergate.net/uhtml/.jhunt/greek_myth/greek_myth.html

Legislation (Library of Congress)
http://thomas.loc.gov

Postmodern Culture
http://jefferson.village.virginia.edu/pmc/contents.all.html

Social Sciences (CERN)
http://coombs.anu.edu.au/WWWVL-SocSci.html

Government Documents (SunSITE)
http://sunsite.unc.edu/govdocs.html

Computerized Information Retrieval System: Columbus
and the Age of Discovery 1492: An Ongoing Voyage
http://www.millersv.edu/~columbus/

The U.S. Holocaust Memorial Museum
http://www.ushmm.org

The President's Cabinet
http://www.whitehouse.gov/WH/Cabinet/html/cabinet_links.html

CapWeb
http://policy.net/capweb/

The White House
http://www.whitehouse.gov

Decisions of the U.S. Supreme Court
http://www.law.cornell.edu/supct/supct.table.html

Smithsonian Institution Home Page
http://www.si.edu

U.S. Army Home Page
http://www.army.mil

U.S. Navy
http://www.ncts.navy.mil

World of Vikings
http://www.demon.co.uk/history/index.html

American Civil War Home Page
http://mirkwood.ucs.indiana.edu/acw

Civil War Letters
http://www.ucsc.edu/civil-war-letters/home.html

D-Day: The World Remembers
http://192.253.114.31/D-Day/Table_of_contents.html

Department of Interior Education and Outreach
http://www.usgs.gov/ien/doi_edu.html

American Indian
http://www.state.sd.us/state/executive/tourism/indian.html

United Nations Information
http://www.undp.org/un/index.html

Antarctica
http://icair.iac.org.nz

Argus Database
http://www.argusmap.com

Net Strategic Mapping
http://www.stratmap.com

What on Earth?
http://www.ingenius.com

Egyptian Art Gallery (EAG)
http://portal.mbnet.mb.ca/eag

National Museum of Natural History
http://www.si.edu

National Council for Social Studies
http://www.ncss.org/

History Channel
http://www.historychannel.com/index2.html

Kidsweb w/Links
http://www.npac.syr.edu/textbook/kidsweb/

Social Studies Virtual Library
http://coombs.anu.edu.au/WWWVL-SocSci.html

Computers in Social Studies
http://www.cssjournal.com/journal/

Teacher Resources
http://www.execpc.com/~dboals/

Lesson Plans/Resources
http://www.csun.edu/~hcedu013/index.html

Resources, Nebraska Department of Education
http://www.nde.state.ne.us/SS/ss.html

Resources for Teachers
http://education.indiana.edu/~socialst/

National Archives
http://www.nara.gov/

National Parks
http://www.nps.gov/

Organization of American Historians
http://www.indiana.edu/~oah/index.html

American Studies
http://www.uc.edu/~milljw/amerstud.html

American Studies
http://www.georgetown.edu/crossroads/asw/

History on the Web
http://www.TheHistoryNet.com/

World History
http://cil.andrew.cmu.edu/projects/World_History/world.html#sites

First Amendment Issues
http://apocalypse.berkshire.net/~ifas/

Feminism/Women's Studies
http://www.ibd.nrc.ca/~mansfield/feminism/

Women's Studies
http://www.mit.edu:8001/people/sorokin/women/index.html

Mayflower
http://members.aol.com/calebj/mayflower.html

Jamestown Society/History
http://www.jamestowne.org/

Eighteenth-Century Archives/Links
http://earlyamerica.com/

Salem Witch Trials
http://www.sad6.k12.me.us/salem.html

French and Indian War
http://www.kiva.net/~gorham/wolfe.html

Colonial Newspapers
http://weber.u.washington.edu/~vgillis/

Revolutionary War
http://www.uconect.net/~histnact/revwar/revwar.html

Revolutionary War
http://users.southeast.net/~dixe/amrev/index.htm

Lewis and Clark Expedition
http://www.vpds.wsu.edu/wahistcult/rasmussen.html

The Alamo
http://www.ansaldo.it/~paesani/alamo.html

Mexican War
http://members.aol.com/dmwv2/mexwar.htm

Oregon Trail
http://www.isu.edu/~trinmich/Oregontrail.html

Underground Railroad
http://www.nps.gov/undergroundrr/contents.htm

Slave Narratives
http://www.itsnet.com/home/getlost/explore.html

Civil War
http://funnelweb.utcc.utk.edu/~hoemann/cwarhp.html

Civil War links
http://www.cwc.lsu.edu/civlink.htm

Theodore Roosevelt
http://www.abcland.com/~jwiedman/tr/index.html

U.S. Imperialism
http://www.smplanet.com/imperialism/toc.html

Student Links: Twentieth Century
http://www.geocities.com/Athens/3344/

World War I
http://www.worldwar1.com/

The Roaring Twenties
http://www.users.interport.net/~ahajnal/20s.html

The Scopes Trial
http://xroads.virginia.edu/~UG97/inherit/1925home.html

Harlem Renaissance
http://members.aol.com/bonvibre/harsite.html

Rosewood Massacre
http://www.dos.state.fl.us/fgils/rosewood.htm

Richard Wright
http://www.itvs.org/programs/RW/

Langston Hughes
http://www.calpoly.edu/~mperotti/

Women's Suffrage
http://lcweb2.loc.gov/ammem/rbnawsahtml/nawshome.html

New Deal
http://newdeal.feri.org/

Franklin Roosevelt
http://www.geocities.com/Athens/4545/

World War II
http://snoopy.bunt.com/~mconrad/

Atomic Bomb
http://www.csi.ad.jp/ABOMB/index.html

Decision to Use the Atomic Bomb
http://www.peak.org/~danneng/decision/decision.html

The Holocaust
http://www.ushmm.org/education/history.html

The Holocaust
http://www.charm.net/~rbennett/l'chaim.html

Internment Camps
http://www.geocities.com/Athens/8420/main.html

Civil Rights Movement
http://www.wmich.edu/politics/mlk/

Martin Luther King Jr.
http://www-leland.stanford.edu/group/King/

Cuban Missile Crisis
http://www.ug.bcc.bilkent.edu.tr/~bayer/CMC/MAIN.HTML

Vietnam War
ftp://ftp.msstate.edu/docs/history/USA/Vietnam/vietnam.html

Vietnam War Links
http://acs.oakton.edu/%7Ewittman/warlinks.html

Watergate
http://netspace.net.au/~malcolm/wgate.htm

Ancient Mesopotamia
http://www-oi.uchicago.edu/OI/DEPT/RA/ABZU/
ABZU_REGINDX_MESO.HTML

Ancient Egypt
http://users.skynet.be/sky69900/

Greco-Roman History
http://www.perseus.tufts.edu/

Rome
http://www.indiana.edu/~romnhist/

Vocational Education

Peterson's Education Center
http://www.petersons.com

E*Span: Your OnLine Employment Connection
http://www.espan.com/

Career Resource Homepage
http://www.rpi.edu/dept/cdc/homepage.html

Catapult Career and Employment Resources
http://www.jobweb.org/catapult/catapult.html

World Wide Web Résumé Bank
http://www.careermag.com/careermag/resumes/index.html

Journal of Industrial Teacher Education
http://scholar.lib.vt.edu/ejournals/JITE/jite.html

National Center for Research in Vocational Education
http://vocserve.berkeley.edu/

Fin Aid
http://www.finaid.org/

Bibliography

Aliki. (1986). *A medieval feast.* New York: HarperCollins.

Allington, R. L. (1983). The reading instruction provided readers of differing abilities. *Elementary School Journal, 83,* 548–559.

Allington, R. L., & Strange, M. (1980). *Learning through reading in the content areas.* Lexington, MA: Heath.

Alvarez, M. C. (1996). Explorers of the universe: Students using the World Wide Web to improve their reading and writing. In B. Neate (Ed.), *Literacy saves lives* (pp. 140–145). Herts, England: United Kingdom Reading Association.

Alvermann, D. E. (1991). The discussion web: A graphic aid for learning across the curriculum. *Reading Teacher, 45,* 2, 92–99.

Alvermann, D. E., Dillon, D. R., & O'Brien, D. G. (1988). *Using discussion to promote reading comprehension.* Newark, DE: International Reading Association.

Alvermann, D. E., & Guthrie, J. (1993). Themes and directions of the National Reading Research Center. *Perspectives in Reading Research, No. 1.* Athens, GA, and College Park, MD: National Reading Research Center.

Alvermann, D. E., & Moore, D. W. (1991). Secondary school reading. In P. D. Pearson, R. Barr, M. L. Kamil, & P. Mosenthal (Eds.), *Handbook of reading research* (2nd ed.) (pp. 951–983). New York: Longman.

Anderson, R. C., & Freebody, P. (1981). Vocabulary knowledge. In J. T. Guthrie (Ed.), *Comprehension and teaching: Research perspectives* (pp. 77–117). Newark, DE: International Reading Association.

Anderson-Inman, L., & Horney, M. (1997). Electronic books for secondary students. *Journal of Adolescent and Adult Literacy, 40,* 6, 486–491.

Anno, M. (1970). *Topsy-turvies: Pictures to stretch the imagination.* New York: Weatherhill.

Anno, M. (1982). *Anno's counting house.* New York: Philomel.

Anno, M. (1989). *Anno's math games II.* New York: Philomel.

Applebee, A. N. (1991). Environments for language teaching and learning: Contemporary issues and future directions. In J. Flood, J. M. Jensen, D. Lapp, & J. R. Squire (Eds.), *Handbook of research on teaching the English language arts* (pp. 549–558). New York: Macmillan.

Armbruster, B. B., & Anderson, T. H. (1981). *Content area textbooks.* Reading Education Report No. 23. Urbana: University of Illinois Center for the Study of Reading.

Armbruster, B. B., & Anderson, T. H. (1985). Frames: Structure for informational texts. In D. H. Jonassen (Ed.), *Technology of text* (pp. 331–346). Englewood Cliffs, NJ: Education Technology Publications.

Aronson, E. (1978). *The jigsaw classroom.* Thousand Oaks, CA: Sage.

Artley, A. S. (1975). Words, words, words. *Language Arts, 52,* 1067–1072.

Ashabranner, B. (1988). *Always to remember: The story of the Vietnam Veterans Memorial.* Ill. J. Ashabranner. New York: Putnam.

Atwell, N. (1990). Introduction. In N. Atwell (Ed.), *Coming to know: Writing to learn in the intermediate grades* (pp. xi–xxiii). Portsmouth, NH: Heinemann.

Au, K. H. (1993). *Literacy instruction in multicultural settings.* Orlando, FL: Harcourt Brace.

Baird, J. R. (1992). Collaborative reflection, systematic enquiry, better teaching. In T. Russell & H. Munby (Eds.), *Teachers and teaching from classroom to reflection* (pp. 33–48). Bristol, PA: Falmer Press.

Baker, J. (1991). *Window.* New York: Greenwillow.

Baker, L. (1991). Metacognition, reading, and science education. In C. M. Santa & D. E. Alvermann (Eds.), *Science learning: Processes and applications* (pp. 12–13). Newark, DE: International Reading Association.

Baker, L., & Brown, A. (1984). Cognitive monitoring in reading. In J. Flood (Ed.), *Understanding reading comprehension* (pp. 21–44). Newark, DE: International Reading Association.

Baker, R. (1977). The effects of instructional organizers on learning and retention, content knowledge, and term relationships in ninth grade social studies. In H. Herber and R. Vacca (Eds.), *Research in reading in the content areas: Third report* (pp. 138–150). Syracuse, NY: Syracuse University Reading and Language Arts Center.

Barnes, D. (1995). Talking and learning in the classroom: An introduction. *Primary Voices K-6, 3,* 1, 2–7.

Barnes, D., Britton, J., & Rosen, H. (1969). *Language, the learner, and school.* New York: Penguin.

Barron, R. F. (1969). The use of vocabulary as an advance organizer. In H. L. Herber & P. L. Sanders (Eds.), *Research in reading in the content areas: First report* (pp. 29–39). Syracuse, NY: Syracuse University Reading and Language Arts Center.

Barron, R. F., & Earle, R. (1973). An approach for vocabulary development. In H. L. Herber & R. F. Barron (Eds.), *Research in reading in the content areas: Second report* (pp. 51–63). Syracuse, NY: Syracuse University Reading and Language Arts Center.

Barron, R. F., & Stone, F. (1973, December). *The effect of student constructed graphic post organizers upon learning of vocabulary relationships from a passage of social studies content.* Paper presented at the meeting of the National Reading Conference, Houston.

Bartlett, B. (1978). *Top-level structure as an organizational strategy for recall of classroom text.* Unpublished doctoral dissertation, Arizona State University.

Barton, J. (1995). Conducting effective classroom discussions. *Journal of Reading, 38,* 346–350.

Beaman, B. (1985). Writing to learn social studies. In A. R. Gere (Ed.), *Roots in sawdust: Writing to learn across the disciplines* (pp. 50–60). Urbana, IL: National Council of Teachers of English.

Beck, I., McKeown, M., McCaslin, E., & Burket, A. (1979). Instructional dimensions that may affect reading comprehension: Examples of two commercial reading programs. Pittsburgh: University of Pittsburgh, Language Research and Development Center.

Beebe, B. F. (1968). *African elephants.* New York: McKay.

Bellows, B. (1980). Running shoes are to jogging as analogies are to critical reading. *Journal of Reading, 23,* 507–511.

Berger, M. (1986). *Atoms, molecules, and quarks.* New York: Putnam.

Berlyne, D. E. (1965). *Structure and direction of thinking.* New York: Wiley.

Bernhardt, B. (1977). *Just writing.* New York: Teachers and Writers.

Betts, E. (1950). *Foundations of reading* (rev. ed.). New York: American Book Company.

Beuhl, D. (1991, Spring). Frames of mind. *The Exchange: Newsletter of the IRA Secondary Reading Interest Group,* pp. 4–5.

Blachowicz, C. (1986). Making connections: Alternatives to the vocabulary notebook. *Journal of Reading, 29,* 643–649.

Bleich, D. (1978). *Subjective criticism.* Baltimore: Johns Hopkins University Press.

Bransford, J. D., & Stein, B. S. (1984). *The ideal problem solver: A guide for improving thinking, learning, and creativity.* New York: Freeman.

Britton, J. (1970). *Language and learning.* London: Allen Lane.

Brown, A. L. (1978). Knowing when, where, and how to remember: A problem of metacognition. In R. Glaser (Ed.), *Advances in instructional psychology* (117–175). Hillsdale, NJ: Erlbaum.

Brown, A. L., Bransford, J. W., Ferrara, R. F., & Campione, J. (1983). Learning, remembering, and understanding. In J. Flavell & E. Markham (Eds.), *Handbook of child psychology* (pp. 393–451). New York: Wiley.

Brozo, W. G. (1989). Applying a reader response heuristic to expository text. *Journal of Reading, 32,* 140–145.

Brozo, W. G. (1990). Learning how at-risk readers learn best: A case for interactive assessment. *Journal of Reading, 33,* 522–527.

Brozo, W. G. (1992). Hiding out in secondary content classrooms: Coping strategies of unsuccessful readers. *Journal of Reading, 35,* 324–328.

Brozo, W. G., & Simpson, M. L. (1991). *Readers, teachers, learners: Expanding literacy in secondary schools.* New York: Macmillan.

Brozo, W. G., & Tomlinson, C. M. (1986). Literature: The key to lively content courses. *Reading Teacher, 40,* 288–293.

Bruner, J. (1961). The act of discovery. *Harvard Educational Review, 31,* 21–32.

Bruner, J. (1970). The skill of relevance or the relevance of skills. *Saturday Review, 53.*

Bruner, J. (1986). *Actual minds, possible worlds.* Cambridge, MA: Harvard University Press.

Bruner, J. (1990). *Acts of meaning.* Cambridge, MA: Harvard University Press.

Bruner, J., Goodnow, J., & Austin, G. (1977). *A study of thinking.* New York: Science Editions.

Camp, G. (1982). *A success curriculum for remedial writers.* Berkeley: National Writing Project, University of California.

Chekov, A. (1991). *Kashtanka.* Trans. R. Pevear. Ill. B. Moser. New York: Putnam.

Clark, R. P. (1987). *Free to write: A journalist teaches young writers.* Portsmouth, NH: Heinemann.

Clemente, R. (1992). *Teachers as meaning-makers in an educational change initiative.* Doctoral dissertation, Kent State University.

Collette, A. (1973). *Science teaching in the secondary school.* Needham Heights, MA: Allyn & Bacon.

Cooney, T., Bell, K., Fisher-Cauble, D., & Sanchez, W. (1996). The demands of alternative assessment: What teachers say. *Mathematics Teacher, 89,* 484–487.

Cooper, C. R., & Odell, L. (Eds.). (1977). *Evaluating writing.* Urbana, IL: National Council of Teachers of English.

Cottrol, R. J. (1990, Winter). America the multicultural. *American Educator, 38,* 18–21.

Covert, R. (1989). *Cultural diversity training.* Paper presented at an individual conference addressing the issues in multicultural education, Chapel Hill, NC.

Crafton, L. (1983). Learning from reading: What happens when students generate their own background knowledge. *Journal of Reading, 26,* 586–593.

Cullinan, B. E. (1993). *Fact and fiction: Literature across the curriculum.* Newark, DE: International Reading Association.

Cummins, J. (1994). The acquisition of English as a second language. In K. Spangenberg-Urbschat & R. Pritchard (Eds.), *Kids come in all languages: Reading instruction for ESL students* (pp. 36–62). Newark, DE: International Reading Association.

Cunningham, R., & Shablak, S. (1975). Selective reading guide-o-rama: The content teacher's best friend. *Journal of Reading, 18,* 380–382.

Curry, J. (1989). The role of reading instruction in mathematics. In D. Lapp, J. Flood, & N. Farnan (Eds.), *Content area reading and learning: Instructional strategies* (pp. 187–197). Upper Saddle River, NJ: Prentice Hall.

Daisey, P. (1994a). The use of trade books in secondary science and mathematics instruction: Classroom strategies. *School Science and Mathematics, 94,* 170–175.

Daisey, P. (1994b). The value of trade books in secondary science and mathematics instruction: A rationale. *School Science and Mathematics, 94,* 130–137.

Dale, E. (1969). Things to come. *Newsletter, 34,* 1–8.

Dale, E. (1975). *The word game: Improving communications.* Bloomington, IN: Phi Delta Kappa.

Danielson, C. (1996). *Enhancing professional practice: A framework for teaching.* Alexandria, VA: Association for Supervision and Curriculum Development.

Davey, B. (1983). Think aloud: Modeling the cognitive processes of reading comprehension. *Journal of Reading, 27,* 44–47.

Davidson, J. L., & Wilkerson, B. C. (1988). *Directed reading-thinking activities.* Monroe, NY: Trillium Press.

Deighton, L. (1970). *Vocabulary development in the classroom.* New York: Teachers College Press.

Delpit, L. D. (1986). Skills and other dilemmas of a progressive black educator. *Harvard Educational Review, 56,* 379–385.

Delpit, L. D. (1988). The silenced dialogue: Power and pedagogy in educating other people's children. *Harvard Educational Review, 58,* 280–298.

Di Bacco, T. V., Mason, L. C., & Appy, C. G. (1992). *History of the United States: Vol. 2. Civil War to the present.* Boston: Houghton Mifflin.

Dillon, D. R. (1989). Showing them that I want them to learn and that I care about who they are: A micro-ethnography of the social organization of a secondary low-track English-reading classroom. *American Education Research Journal, 26,* 227–259.

Dolciani, M. P., et al. (1967). *Modern school mathematics: Algebra 1.* Boston: Houghton Mifflin.

Dole, J. A., & Johnson, V. R. (1981). Beyond the textbook: Science literature for young people. *Journal of Reading, 24,* 579–582.

Donelson, K. L., & Nilsen, A. P. (1997). *Literature for today's young adults* (5th ed.). New York: Longman.

Duffy, G. G. (1983). From turn taking to sense making: Broadening the concept of reading teacher effectiveness. *Journal of Educational Research, 76,* 134–139.

Dupuis, M. M., & Snyder, S. L. (1983). Develop concepts through vocabulary: A strategy for reading specialists to use with content teachers. *Journal of Reading, 26,* 297–305.

Eanet, M., & Manzo, A. V. (1976). REAP: A strategy for improving reading/writing/study skills. *Journal of Reading, 19,* 647–652.

Egan, K. (1989). Layers of historical understanding. *Theory and Research in Social Education, 17,* 280–294.

Eisner, E. W. (1985). *The educational imagination: On the design and evaluation of school programs* (2nd ed.). New York: Macmillan.

Eisner, E. W. (1991). The celebration of thinking. *Maine Scholar, 4,* 39–52.

Feelings, M. (1971). *Moja means one: Swahili counting book.* Ill. T. Feelings. New York: Dial.

Fessler, R., & Christensen, J. (1994, February). *The teacher career cycle: A model for career-long teacher education.* Paper presented at the meeting of the American Association of Colleges of Teacher Education, Chicago.

Fetterman, D. M. (1989). *Ethnography step by step.* Thousand Oaks, CA: Sage.

Fillmore, L. W. (1981). Cultural perspectives on second language learning. *TESL Reporter, 14,* 23–31.

Flavell, J. H. (1976). Metacognitive aspects of problem solving. In L. B. Resnick (Ed.), *The nature of intelligence* (pp. 38–62). Hillsdale, NJ: Erlbaum.

Flavell, J. H. (1981). Cognitive monitoring. In P. Dickson (Ed.), *Communication skills.* Orlando, FL: Academic Press.

Fry, E. (1977). Fry's readability graph: Clarifications, validity, and extension to level 17. *Journal of Reading, 21,* 242–252.

Fugard, A. (1984). *"Master Harold" . . . and the boys.* New York: Penguin.

Fulghum, R. (1989). *It was on fire when I lay down on it.* New York: Villard Books.

Gagne, R. (1970). *The conditions of learning* (2nd ed.). Fort Worth, TX: Holt, Rinehart and Winston.

Gallant, R. A. (1991). *Earth's vanishing forests.* New York: Macmillan.

Gambrell, L. B. (1980). Think-time: Implications for reading instruction. *Reading Teacher, 33,* 143–146.

Gambrell, L. B. (1996). What research reveals about discussion. In L. B. Gambrell & J. F. Almasi (Eds.), *Lively discussions! Fostering engaged reading* (pp. 25–38). Newark, DE: International Reading Association.

George, J., Moley, P., & Ogle, D. M. (1992). CCD: A model comprehension program for changing thinking and instruction. In J. Vacca (Ed.), *Bringing about change in schools* (pp. 49–55). Newark, DE: International Reading Association.

Gere, A. R. (Ed.). (1985). *Roots in the sawdust: Writing to learn across the disciplines.* Urbana, IL: National Council of Teachers of English.

Gillet, J., & Kita, M. J. (1979). Words, kids, and categories. *Reading Teacher, 32,* 538–542.

Gillet, J., & Temple, C. (1982). *Understanding reading problems.* New York: Little, Brown.

Goble, P. (1991). *I sing for the animals.* New York: Bradbury.

Gold, P., & Yellin, D. (1982). Be the focus: A psycho-educational technique for use with unmotivated learners. *Journal of Reading, 25,* 550–552.

Goodall, J. (1979). *The story of an English village.* New York: Atheneum.

Goodall, J. (1987). *The story of a main street.* New York: Macmillan.

Goodall, J. (1990). *The story of the seashore.* New York: Macmillan.

Goodlad, J. (1984). *A place called school.* New York: McGraw-Hill.

Goodman, K., & Goodman, Y. (1978). *Reading of American children whose language is a stable rural dialect of English or a language other than English.* Washington, DC: National Institute of Education. (ERIC Document Reproduction Service No. ED 173 754)

Gove, M., & Kennedy-Calloway, C. (1992). Action research: Empowering teachers to work with at-risk students. In J. Vacca (Ed.), *Bringing about change in schools* (pp. 14–22). Newark, DE: International Reading Association.

Graves, D. (1978). *Balance to basics: Let them write.* New York: Ford Foundation.

Graves, D. (1992). Portfolios: Keep a good idea growing. In D. Graves & B. Sunstein (Eds.), *Portfolio portraits* (pp. 1–12). Portsmouth, NH: Heinemann.

Graves, M. F., Cooke, C. L., & La Berge, M. J. (1983). Effects of previewing difficult short stories on low ability junior high school students' comprehension, recall, and attitudes. *Reading Research Quarterly, 18,* 262–276.

Graves, M. F., Prenn, M. C., & Cooke, C. L. (1985). The coming attraction: Previewing short stories. *Journal of Reading, 28,* 594–597.

Green, J., & Harker, J. (1982). Reading to children: A communicative process. In J. Langer & M. T. Smith-Burke (Eds.), *Reader meets author/bridging the gap* (pp. 196–221). Newark, DE: International Reading Association.

Greenlee-Moore, M. E., & Smith, L. L. (1996). Interactive computer software: The effects on young children's reading achievement. *Reading Psychology, 17,* 43–64.

Griffin, G. A. (1991). Interactive staff development: Using what we know. In A. Lieberman & L. Miller (Eds.), *Staff development for education in the '90s* (pp. 243–258). New York: Teachers College Press.

Haggard, M. R. (1986). The vocabulary self-collection strategy: Using student interest and world knowledge to enhance vocabulary growth. *Journal of Reading, 29,* 634–642.

Hahn, A. (1984). Assessing and extending comprehension: Monitoring strategies in the classroom. *Reading Horizons, 24,* 225–230.

Halliday, M., & Hasan, R. (1976). *Cohesion in English.* London: Longman.

Hamilton, V. (1985). *The people could fly: American black folktales.* New York: Knopf.

Hamilton, V. (1988). *In the beginning: Creation stories from around the world.* Orlando, FL: Harcourt Brace.

Hancock, M. R. (1993). Exploring and extending personal response through literature journals. *Reading Teacher, 46,* 466–474.

Hansell, T. S. (1978). Stepping up to outlining. *Journal of Reading, 22,* 248–252.

Hare, V. C., & Borchardt, K. M. (1984). Direct instruction of summarization skills. *Reading Research Quarterly, 20,* 62–78.

Hayes, D. A. (1989). Helping students grasp the knack of writing summaries. *Journal of Reading, 33,* 96–101.

Hayes, D. A., & Tierney, R. T. (1982). Developing reader's knowledge through analogy. *Reading Research Quarterly, 17,* 256–280.

Healy, M. K. (1982). Using student response groups in the classroom. In G. Camp (Ed.), *Teaching writing: Essays from the Bay Area writing project* (pp. 266–290). Portsmouth, NH: Boynton Cook.

Heath, S. B. (1983). *Ways with words: Language, life, and work in communities and classrooms.* Cambridge, MA: Harvard University Press.

Heath, S. B., & Mangiola, L. (1991). *Children of promise: Literate activity in linguistically and culturally diverse classrooms.* Washington, DC: National Education Association.

Heathington, B. S., & Alexander, J. E. (1984). Do classroom teachers emphasize attitudes toward reading? *Reading Teacher, 37,* 484–488.

Henry, G. (1974). *Teaching reading as concept development.* Newark, DE: International Reading Association.

Herber, H. L. (1978). *Teaching reading in content areas* (2nd ed.). Upper Saddle River, NJ: Prentice Hall.

Hittleman, D. (1973). Seeking a psycholinguistic definition of readability. *Reading Teacher, 26,* 783–789.

Hobbs, W. (1989). *Bearstone.* New York: Atheneum.

Hoffman, J. V. (1979). The intra-act procedure for critical reading. *Journal of Reading, 22,* 605–608.

Holly, M. L. (1989). *Writing to grow: Keeping a personal-professional journal.* Portsmouth, NH: Heinemann.

Homer, C. (1979). A direct reading-thinking activity for content areas. In R. T. Vacca & J. A. Meagher (Eds.), *Reading through content* (pp. 41–48). Storrs: University Publications and the University of Connecticut Reading–Language Arts Center.

Hudson, E. (Ed.). (1988). *Poetry of the First World War.* East Sussex, England: Wayland.

Huey, E. (1908). *The psychology and pedagogy of reading.* New York: Macmillan.

Hynd, C. R., McNish, M. E., Guzzetti, B., Lay, K., & Fowler, P. (1994). *What high school students say about their science texts.* Paper presented at the annual meeting of the College Reading Association, New Orleans.

Innocenti, R. (1991). *Rose Blanche.* New York: Stewart, Tiboria, Chang.

International Association for the Evaluation of Educational Achievement. (1997). *Third international mathematics and science study.* Boston: TIMSS International Study Center, Boston College.

Irwin, J. W., & Davis, C. A. (1980). Assessing readability: The checklist approach. *Journal of Reading, 24,* 124–130.

Jackson, F. R. (1994). Seven strategies to support culturally responsive pedagogy. *Journal of Reading, 37,* 298–303.

Jasper, K. C. (1995). The limits of technology. *English Journal, 84, 6, 16–17.*

Johnson, D., & Pearson, P. D. (1984). *Teaching reading vocabulary* (2nd ed.). Fort Worth, TX: Holt, Rinehart and Winston.

Johnson, D. W., & Johnson, R. T. (1990). *Learning together and alone: Cooperative, conjunctive, and individualistic learning.* Upper Saddle River, NJ: Prentice Hall.

Johnson, D. W., Johnson, R. T., & Holubec, E. J. (1990). *Circles of learning: Cooperation in the classroom* (3rd ed.). Edina, MN: Interaction Book Company.

Johnson D. W., & Steele, V. (1996). So many words, so little time: Helping college ESL learners acquire vocabulary-building strategies. *Journal of Adolescent and Adult Literacy, 39,* 348–357.

Jones, B. F., Pierce, J., & Hunter, B. (1988–1989). Teaching students to construct graphic representations. *Educational Leadership, 46,* 4j, 20–25.

Judy, S., & Judy, S. (1980). *Gifts of writing: Creative projects with words and art.* New York: Scribner.

June, R. (1995). Culturally appropriate books call for culturally appropriate teaching. *Journal of Reading, 38,* 486.

Kang, H. (1994). Helping second language readers learn from content area text through collaboration and support. *Journal of Reading, 37,* 646–652.

Kennedy, B. (1985). Writing letters to learn math. *Learning, 13,* 58–61.

Kindsvatter, R., Wilen, W., & Ishler, M. (1992). *Dynamics of effective teaching* (2nd ed.). New York: Longman.

Kinneavy, J. L. (1971). *A theory of discourse.* Upper Saddle River, NJ: Prentice Hall.

Kintsch, W. (1977). On comprehending stories. In M. A. Just & P. A. Carpenter (Eds.), *Cognitive processes in comprehension* (pp. 360–401). Hillsdale, NJ: Erlbaum.

Kintsch, W., & van Dijk, T. (1978). Toward a model of text comprehension and production. *Psychological Review, 85,* 363–394.

Kirby, D., & Liner, T. (1981). *Inside out: Developmental strategies for teaching writing.* Portsmouth, NH: Boynton Cook.

Kitchen, B. (1993). *And so they build.* New York: Dial.

Knoeller, C. P. (1994). Negotiating interpretations of text: The role of student-led discussions in understanding literature. *Journal of Reading, 37,* 572–580.

Krogness, M. (1995). *Just teach me, Mrs. K: Talking, reading, and writing with resistant adolescent learners.* Portsmouth, NH: Heinemann.

Krogness, M. (1997). Changing voices: Working with middle schoolers. *Ohio Reading Teacher, 32,* 1, 28–31.

Langer, J. A. (1981). From theory to practice: A prereading plan. *Journal of Reading, 25,* 152–156.

Langer, J. A., & Applebee, A. N. (1987). *How writing shapes thinking.* Urbana, IL: National Council of Teachers of English.

Langstaff, J. (1991). *Climbing Jacob's ladder.* New York: Macmillan.

Lapp, D., & Flood, J. (1995). Strategies for gaining access to the information superhighway: Off the side street and on to the main road. *Reading Teacher, 48,* 432–436.

Lara, J. (1994). Demographic overview: Changes in student enrollment in American schools. In K. Spangenberg-Urbschat & R. Pritchard (Eds.), *Kids come in all languages: Reading instruction for ESL students* (pp. 9–21). Newark, DE: International Reading Association.

Lawrence, L. (1985). *Children of the dust.* New York: HarperCollins.

Leinhardt, G. (1990, March). Capturing craft knowledge in teaching. *Educational Researcher,* pp. 18–25.

Lester, J. D. (1984). *Writing research papers: A complete guide* (4th ed.). Glenview, IL: Scott, Foresman.

Leu, D. J., Jr. (1996). Sarah's secret: Social aspects of literacy and learning in a digital information age. *Reading Teacher, 50,* 162–165.

Leu, D. J., Jr., & Leu, D. D. (1997). *Teaching with the Internet: Lessons from the classroom.* Norwood, MA: Christopher-Gordon.

Levine, D. S. (1985). The biggest thing I learned but it really doesn't have to do with science. . . . *Language Arts, 62,* 43–47.

Levstik, L. S. (1990). Research directions: Mediating content through literary texts. *Language Arts, 67,* 848–853.

Lewis, J. P. (1992). *The moonbow of Mr. B. Bones.* New York: Knopf.

Lewis, R., & Teale, W. (1980). Another look at secondary school students' attitudes toward reading. *Journal of Reading Behavior, 12,* 187–201.

Lindemann, E. (1982). *A rhetoric for writing teachers.* New York: Oxford University Press.

Linek, W. M. (1991). Grading and evaluation techniques for whole language teachers. *Language Arts, 68,* 125–132.

Little Soldier, L. (1989). Cooperative learning and the Native American student. *Phi Delta Kappan, 71,* 161–163.

Llewellyn, C. (1991). *Under the sea.* New York: Simon & Schuster.

Lowe, S. (1990). *Walden.* New York: Philomel.

Macaulay, D. (1973). *Cathedral.* Boston: Houghton Mifflin.

Macaulay, D. (1978). *Castle.* Boston: Houghton Mifflin.

Macaulay, D. (1982). *Pyramid.* Boston: Houghton Mifflin.

Macchiarola, F. (1988). Values, standards, and climate in schools serving students at risk. In *School success for students at risk: Analysis and recommendations of the Council of Chief State School Officers* (pp. 13–24). Orlando, FL: Harcourt Brace.

MacGinitie, W. H. (1993). Some limits of assessment. *Journal of Reading, 36,* 556–560.

Malinowski, B. (1954). *"Magic, science and religion" and other essays.* New York: Doubleday.

Mallan, J., & Hersh, R. (1972). *No G.O.D.S. in the classroom: Inquiry into inquiry.* Philadelphia: Saunders.

Mandler, J., & Johnson, N. (1977). Remembrance of things passed: Story structure and recall. *Cognitive Psychology, 9,* 111–151.

Manzo, A. V. (1969). The ReQuest procedure. *Journal of Reading, 11,* 123–126.

Marol, J. (1983). *Vagabul escapes.* Mankato, MN: Creative Education.

Maruki, T. (1982). *Hiroshima no pika.* New York: Lothrop, Lee & Shepard.

Maruki, T. (1985). *The relatives came.* Ill. S. Gammell. New York: Bradbury.

Mathiason, C. (1989). Activating student interest in content area reading. *Journal of Reading, 33,* 170–176.

Matthew, K. (1996). What do children think of CD-ROM storybooks? *Texas Reading Report, 18,* 6.

McAndrew, D. A. (1983). Increasing the reality of audiences in the classroom. *Connecticut English Journal, 14,* 49–56.

McGinley, W. J., & Denner, P. R. (1987). Story impressions: A pre-reading/writing activity. *Journal of Reading, 31,* 248–253.

McGowan, T., & Guzzetti, B. (1991, January-February). Promoting social studies understanding through literature-based instruction. *Social Studies,* pp. 16–21.

McIntosh, M. (1991, September). No time for writing in your class? *Mathematics Teacher,* pp. 423–433.

McKenna, M., & Robinson, R. (1990). Content literacy: A definition and implications. *Journal of Reading, 34,* 184–186.

McKeon, C. (1997). *Investigating a literature-based electronic-mail collaborative.* Unpublished paper, Kent State University.

McKinley, R. (1978). *Beauty: A retelling of the story of* Beauty and the Beast. New York: HarperCollins.

McNeil, J. D. (1987). *Reading comprehension: New directions for classroom practice* (2nd ed.). Glenview, IL: Scott, Foresman.

McTighe, J., & Lyman, F. T. (1988). Cueing thinking in the classroom: The promise of theory-embedded tools. *Educational Leadership, 45,* 7, 18–24.

Meltzer, M. (1988). *Starting from home: A writer's beginning.* New York: Viking Penguin.

Meltzer, M. (1994) *Nonfiction for the classroom.* New York: Teachers College Press.

Meyer, B. J. F. (1975). *The organization of prose and its effect in memory.* Amsterdam: Elsevier North-Holland.

Meyer, B. J. F., Brandt, D., & Bluth, G. (1980). Use of top-level structure in text: Key for reading comprehension of ninth-grade students. *Reading Research Quarterly, 16,* 72–103.

Meyer, B. J. F., & Rice, E. (1984). The structure of text. In P. D. Pearson (Ed.), *Handbook of reading research* (pp. 319–352). New York: Longman.

Mike, D. G. (1996). Internet in the schools: A literacy perspective. *Journal of Adolescent and Adult Literacy, 40,* 4–13.

Mikulecky, L. (1990). Literacy for what purpose? In R. L. Venezky, D. A. Wagner, & B. S. Ciliberti (Eds.), *Toward defining literacy* (pp. 24–34). Newark DE: International Reading Association.

Milton, J. W. (1982). What the student-educator should have done before the grade: A questioning look at note-taking. In A. S. Algier & K. W. Algier (Eds.), *Improving reading and study skills* (pp. 56–71). San Francisco: Jossey-Bass.

Moll, L. C. (1994). Literacy research in community and classrooms: A sociocultural approach. In R. B. Ruddell, M. R. Ruddell, & H. Singer (Eds.), *Theoretical models and processes of reading* (4th ed.) (pp. 179–209). Newark, DE: International Reading Association.

Moore, D. W., & Cunningham, J. W. (1986). The confused world of main idea. In J. F. Baumann (Ed.), *Teaching main idea comprehension* (pp. 1–17). Newark, DE: International Reading Association.

Murray, D. M. (1980). Writing as process: How writing finds its own meaning. In T. R. Donovan & B. W. McClelland (Eds.), *Eight approaches to teaching composition* (pp. 80–97). Urbana, IL: National Council of Teachers of English.

Murray, J. (1982). *Modern monologues for young people.* New York: Plays, Inc.

Myers, J. (1984). *Writing to learn across the curriculum.* Bloomington, IN: Phi Delta Kappa.

National Council for Accreditation of Teacher Education. (1997). *Quality assurance for the teaching profession.* Washington, DC: National Council for Accreditation of Teacher Education.

Neal, J. C., & Moore, K. (1991). *The very hungry caterpillar* meets *Beowulf* in secondary classrooms. *Journal of Reading, 35,* 290–296.

Nelson, J. (1978). Readability: Some cautions for the content area teacher. *Journal of Reading, 21,* 620–625.

Newell, G. (1984). Learning from writing in two content areas: A case study/protocol analysis. *Research in the Teaching of English, 18,* 205–287.

Niles, O. (1965). Organization perceived. In H. L. Herber (Ed.), *Developing study skills in secondary schools* (pp. 36–46). Newark, DE: International Reading Association.

Noden, H. R. (1995). A journey through cyberspace: Reading and writing in a virtual school. *English Journal, 84,* 6, 19–26.

Noden, H. R., & Vacca, R. T. (1994). *Whole language in middle and secondary classrooms.* New York: HarperCollins.

Norworth, J. (1993). *Take me out to the ball game.* Ill. A. Gillman. New York: Four Winds/Macmillan.

Nye, R. (1968). Beowulf: *A new telling.* New York: Hill.

Oakes, J. (1985). *Keeping track: How schools structure inequality.* New Haven, CT: Yale University Press.

O'Brien, R. C. (1975). *Z for Zachariah.* New York: Atheneum.

Ogle, D. M. (1992). KWL in action: Secondary teachers find applications that work. In E. K. Dishner, T. W. Bean, J. E. Readence, & D. W. Moore (Eds.), *Reading in the content areas: Improving classroom instruction* (3rd ed.) (pp. 270–281). Dubuque, IA: Kendall-Hunt.

Olsen, A., & Ames, W. (1972). *Teaching reading skills in secondary schools.* Scranton, PA: Intext Educational Publishers.

Ortiz, R. K. (1983). Generating interest in reading. *Journal of Reading, 28,* 113–119.

Otto, J. H., & Towle, A. (1973). *Modern biology.* Fort Worth, TX: Holt, Rinehart and Winston.

Palinscar, A. S., & Brown, A. L. (1984). Reciprocal teaching of comprehension-fostering and comprehension-monitoring activities. *Cognition and Instruction, 1,* 117–175.

Palmatier, R. (1973). A notetaking system for learning. *Journal of Reading, 17,* 36–39.

Palmer, R. G., & Stewart, R. A. (1997). Nonfiction trade books in content area instruction: Realities and potential. *Journal of Adolescent and Adult Literacy, 40,* 630–641.

Paris, S., & Meyers, M. (1981). Comprehension monitoring, memory, and study strategies of good and poor reader. *Journal of Reading Behavior, 13,* 5–22.

Parnall, P. (1984). *The daywatchers.* New York: Macmillan.

Parnall, P. (1991). *Marsh cat.* New York: Macmillan.

Parry, K. (1993). Too many words: Learning the vocabulary of an academic subject. In T. Huckin, M. Haynes, & J. Coady (Eds.), *Second language reading and vocabulary learning* (pp. 109–129). Norwood, NJ: Ablex.

Patterson, L., & Shannon, P. (1993). Reflection, inquiry, action. In L. Patterson, C. M. Santa, K. Short, & K. Smith (Eds.), *Teachers are researchers: Reflections and action* (pp. 7–11). Newark, DE: International Reading Association.

Pauk, W. (1978). A notetaking format: Magical but not automatic. *Reading World, 16,* 96–97.

Paulsen, G. (1987). *Hatchet.* New York: Viking Penguin.

Paulsen, G. (1990). *Woodsong.* New York: Macmillan.

Pearce, D. L. (1983). Guidelines for the use and evaluation of writing in content classrooms. *Journal of Reading, 27,* 212–218.

Pearson, P. D. (1974–1975). The effects of grammatical complexity on children's comprehension, recall, and conception of certain semantic relations. *Reading Research Quarterly, 10,* 155–192.

Pearson, P. D. (1981). A retrospective reaction to prose comprehension. In C. M. Santa and B. L. Hayes (eds.), *Children's prose comprehension: Research and practice.* Newark, DE: International Reading Association.

Pearson, P. D., & Johnson, D. (1978). *Teaching reading comprehension.* Fort Worth, TX: Holt, Rinehart and Winston.

Pearson, P. D., & Spiro, R. (1982). The new buzz word in reading as schema. *Instructor, 89,* 46–48.

Perry, W. G. (1959). Students' use and misuse of reading skills: A report to the faculty. *Harvard Educational Review, 29,* 193–200.

Pichert, J. W., & Anderson, R. C. (1977). Taking different perspectives on a story. *Journal of Educational Psychology, 69,* 309–315.

Pradl, G. M., & Mayher, J. S. (1985). Reinvigorating learning through writing. *Educational Leadership, 42,* 4–8.

Purves, A. C. (1983). Teachers are real, too. *Connecticut English Journal, 14,* 43–44.

Raphael, T. E. (1982). Question-answering strategies for children. *Reading Teacher, 36,* 186–191.

Raphael, T. E. (1984). Teaching learners about sources of information for answering comprehension questions. *Journal of Reading, 27,* 303–311.

Raphael, T. E. (1986). Teaching question-answer relationships. *Reading Teacher, 39,* 516–520.

Readence, J. E., Baldwin, R. S., & Bean, T. W. (1981). *Content area reading: An integrated approach.* Dubuque IA: Kendall/Hunt.

Reinking, D. (1995). Reading and writing with computers: Literacy research in a post-typographic world. In K. A. Hinchman, D. J. Leu Jr., & C. K. Kinzer (Eds.), *Perspectives on literacy research and practice* (pp. 17–33). Chicago: National Reading Conference.

Reinking, D. (1997). Me and my hypertext: A multiple digression analysis of technology and literacy. *Reading Teacher, 50,* 626–643.

Resnick, L. B., & Resnick, D. P. (1991). Assessing the thinking curriculum: New tools for educational reform. In J. Gifford & D. O'Connor (Eds.), *Changing assessments.* Boston: Kluwer.

Reyes, M., & Molner, L. A. (1991). Instructional strategies for second-language learners in the content areas. *Journal of Reading, 35,* 96–103.

Rico, G. L. (1983). *Writing the natural way: Using right-brain techniques to release your expressive powers.* Los Angeles: Tarcher.

Robinson, F. (1946). *Effective study.* New York: HarperCollins.

Roby, T. (1968). *Small group performance.* Skokie, IL: Rand McNally.

Roby, T. (1987). Commonplaces, questions, and modes of discussion. In J. T. Dillon (Ed.), *Classroom questions and discussion* (pp. 134–169). Norwood, NJ: Ablex.

Rodrigues, R. J. (1983). Tools for developing prewriting skills. *English Journal, 72,* 58–60.

Rose, B. (1989). Writing and mathematics: Theory and practice. In P. Connolly & T. Vilardi (Eds.), *Writing to learn mathematics and science* (pp. 19–30). New York: Teachers College Press.

Rose, S. A., & Fernlund, P. M. (1997). Using technology for powerful social studies learning. *Social Education, 13,* 6, 160–166.

Rosenblatt, L. M. (1983). The literary transaction: Evocation and response. *Theory into Practice, 21,* 268–277.

Rubin, D. L. (1990). Introduction: Ways of thinking about talking and learning. In S. Hynds & D. L. Rubin (Eds.), *Perspectives on talk and learning* (pp. 1–17). Urbana, IL: National Council of Teachers of English.

Rumelhart, D. E. (1982). Schemata: The building blocks of cognition. In J. Guthrie (Ed.), *Comprehension and teaching: Research reviews* (pp. 3–26). Newark, DE: International Reading Association.

Rycik, J. A. (1994). *An exploration of student library research projects in seventh grade English and social studies classes.* Unpublished doctoral dissertation, Kent State University.

Rylant, C. (1982). *When I was young in the mountains.* New York: Dutton.

Rylant, C. (1984). *Waiting to waltz: A childhood.* Ill. S. Gammell. New York: Bradbury.

Salisbury, R. (1934). A study of the transfer effects of training in logical organization. *Journal of Educational Research, 28,* 241–254.

Samples, R. (1977). *The wholeschool book.* Reading, MA: Addison-Wesley.

Santa, C. M., & Havens, L. T. (1991). Learning through writing. In C. M. Santa & D. E. Alvermann (Eds.), *Science learning: Processes and applications* (pp. 122–133). Newark, DE: International Reading Association.

Sapon-Shevin, M. (1994, Winter). Inclusion: Public education for whom? *Education Exchange,* pp. 1, 6.

Schön, D. (1991). *The reflective turn: Case studies in and on educational practice.* New York: Teachers College Press.

Schumm, J. S., & Mangrum, C. T., II (1991). FLIP: A framework for content area reading. *Journal of Reading, 35,* 120–124.

Schwartz, R. M. (1988). Learning to learn: Vocabulary in content area textbooks. *Journal of Reading, 32,* 108–117.

Schwartz, R. M., & Raphael, T. E. (1985). Concept of definition: A key to improving students' vocabulary. *Reading Teacher, 39,* 198–204.

Sender, R. M. (1986). *The cage.* New York: Macmillan.

Seuss, Dr. (1984). *The butter battle book.* New York: Random House.

Shanahan, T. (Ed.). (1990). *Reading and writing together: New perspectives for the classroom.* Norwood, MA: Christopher-Gordon.

Siegal, A. (1983). *Upon the head of the goat: A childhood in Hungary, 1939–1944.* New York: Signet.

Simon, R. (1990). *Oceans.* New York: Morrow.

Singer, H. (1978). Active comprehension: From answering to asking questions. *Reading Teacher, 31,* 901–908.

Slater, T. (1994). Portfolios for learning and assessment in physics. *Physics Teacher, 32,* 370–373.

Slavin, R. E. (1987). Synthesis of research on cooperative learning. *Educational Leadership, 48, 5,* 72–82.

Slavin, R. E. (1988). Cooperative learning and student achievement. In R. E. Slavin (Ed.), *School and classroom organization.* Hillsdale, NJ: Erlbaum.

Slavin, R. E. (1989). Students at risk of school failure: The problem and its dimensions. In R. E. Slavin, N. L. Karweit, & N. A. Madden (Eds.), *Effective programs for students at risk.* Needham Heights, MA: Allyn & Bacon.

Sleeter, C. E. (1990). Staff development for desegregated schooling. *Phi Delta Kappan, 72,* 33–40.

Smith, D. B. (1973). *A taste of blackberries.* New York: HarperCollins.

Smith, F. (1978). *Comprehension and learning: A conceptual framework for teachers.* Fort Worth, TX: Holt, Rinehart and Winston.

Smith, F. (1988). *Understanding reading* (4th ed.). Hillsdale, NJ: Erlbaum.

Smith, N. B. (1959). Teaching study skills in reading. *Elementary School Journal, 60,* 158–162.

Smith, N. B. (1964). Patterns of writing in different subject areas. *Journal of Reading, 7,* 31–37.

Spiegel, D. L. (1981). Six alternatives to the directed reading activity. *Reading Teacher, 34,* 914–922.

Spiegelman, A. (1986). *Maus: A survivor's tale.* New York: Pantheon.

Spier, P. (1978). *Bored—nothing to do!* New York: Doubleday.

Spivey, N. M. (1984). *Discourse synthesis: Constructing texts in reading and writing.* Newark, DE: International Reading Association.

Stein, N., & Glenn, C. (1979). An analysis of story comprehension in elementary school children. In R. Freedle (Ed.), *New directions in discourse processing* (pp. 153–205). Norwood, NJ: Ablex.

Stenmark, J. K. (1991). Math portfolios: A new form of assessment. *Teaching Pre-K–8, 21,* 62–66.

Sturtevant, E. (1992). *Content literacy activities in high school social studies: Two case studies in a multicultural setting.* Unpublished doctoral dissertation, Kent State University.

Suid, M., & Lincoln, W. (1989). *Recipes for writing: Motivation, skills, and activities.* Menlo Park, CA: Addison-Wesley.

Sutherland, Z., & Arbuthnot, M. H. (1986). *Children and books* (7th ed.). Glenview, IL: Scott, Foresman.

Taba, H. (1967). *Teacher's handbook for elementary social studies.* Reading, MA: Addison-Wesley.

Taylor, B. (1980). Children's memory of expository text after reading. *Reading Research Quarterly, 15,* 399–411.

Taylor, D. (1983). *Family literacy: Young children learning to read and write.* Portsmouth, NH: Heinemann.

Taylor, W. (1953). Close procedure: A new tool for measuring readability. *Journalism Quarterly, 30,* 415–433.

Tchudi, S., & Yates, J. (1983). *Teaching writing in the content areas: Senior high school.* Washington, DC: National Education Association.

Thelen, J. (1982). Preparing students for content reading assignments. *Journal of Reading, 25,* 546–547.

Thorndike, E. (1917). Reading and reasoning: A study of mistakes in paragraph reading. *Journal of Educational Psychology, 8,* 323–332.

Thorndyke, P. (1977). Cognitive structures in comprehension and memory of narrative discourse. *Cognitive Psychology, 9,* 77–110.

Tierney, R. J., Carter, M. A., & Desai, L. E. (1991). *Portfolio assessment in the reading-writing classroom.* Norwood, MA: Christopher-Gordon.

Tierney, R. J., & Pearson, P. D. (1983). Toward a composing model of reading. *Language Arts, 60,* 568–580.

Tierney, R. J., & Pearson, P. D. (1992). A revisionist perspective on "Learning to learn from texts: A framework for improving classroom practice." In E. K. Dishner, T. W. Bean, J. E. Readence, & D. W. Moore (Eds.), *Reading in the content areas: Improving classroom instruction* (3rd ed.) (pp. 82–86). Dubuque, IA: Kendall/Hunt.

Tierney, R. J., Readence, J. E., & Dishner, E. K. (1990). *Reading strategies and practices: A compendium* (3rd ed.). Needham Heights, MA: Allyn & Bacon.

Tierney, R. J., & Shanahan, T. (1991). Research on reading-writing relationships: Interactions, transactions, and outcomes. In P. D. Pearson, R. Barr, M. Kamil, & P. Mosenthal (Eds.), *Handbook of reading research* (2nd ed.) (pp. 246–280). New York: Longman.

Tobias, S. (1989). Writing to learn science and mathematics. In P. Connolly & T. Vilardi (Eds.), *Writing to learn mathematics and science* (pp. 47–61). New York: Teachers College Press.

Tompkins, G. E. (1990). *Teaching writing: Balancing process and product.* Columbus, OH: Merrill.

U.S. Department of Education. (1994). Draft mission statement and principles of professional development. *Federal Register, 59,* 63773–63774.

Vacca, J. L., & Genzen, H. (1995). Staff development. In S. Wepner, J. Feeley, & D. Strickland (Eds.), *The administration and supervision of reading programs* (2nd ed.) (pp. 146–161). New York: Teachers College Press.

Vacca, J. L., Vacca, R. T., & Gove, M. K. (1995). *Reading and learning to read* (3rd ed.). New York: HarperCollins.

Vacca, R. T. (1975). Development of a functional reading strategy: Implications for content area instruction. *Journal of Educational Research, 69,* 108–112.

Vacca, R. T. (1977). An investigation of a functional reading strategy in seventh grade social studies. In H. L. Herber & R. T. Vacca (Eds.), *Research in reading in the content areas: Third report* (pp. 101–118). Syracuse, NY: Syracuse University Reading and Language Arts Center.

Vacca, R. T., & Padak, N. D. (1990). Who's at risk in reading? *Journal of Reading, 33,* 486–489.

Vacca, R. T., Vacca, J. L., & Bruneau, B. (1995). Teachers reflecting on practice. In J. Flood, S. B. Heath, & D. Lapp (Eds.), *Handbook for literacy educators: Research on teaching the communicative and visual arts* (pp. 445–450). Newark, DE: International Reading Association.

Valencia, S. (1990). A portfolio approach to classroom reading assessment: The whys, whats, and hows. *Reading Teacher, 43,* 338–340.

Valencia, S., McGinley, W. J., & Pearson, P. D. (1990). *Assessing reading and writing: Building a more complete picture for middle school assessment.* Champaign: University of Illinois, Center for the Study of Reading.

Van Allsburg, C. (1990). *Just a dream.* Boston: Houghton Mifflin.

van Dijk, T. A. (1979). Relevance assignment in discourse comprehension. *Discourse Processes, 2,* 113–126.

Ventura, P. (1987). *Venice: Birth of a city.* New York: Putnam.

Waldron, D. Z. (1994). *Reflective practice in art education: An inquiry model for staff development.* Doctoral dissertation, Kent State University.

Walker, B. J. (1991, February-March). Convention highlights reading assessment changes. *Reading Today,* p. 20.

Wang, M. C., Reynolds, M. C., & Walberg, H. J. (1994–1995). Serving students at the margins. *Educational Leadership, 52,* 4, 12–17.

Watson, J. (1968). *The double helix.* New York: Atheneum.

Wehlage, G. G., & Rutter, R. A. (1986). Dropping out: How much do schools contribute to the problem? *Teachers College Record, 87,* 374–392.

Wilcox, S. (1997). Using the assessment of students' learning to reshape thinking. *Mathematics Teacher, 90,* 223–229.

Williams, B. (1995). The internet for teachers. Foster City, CA: IDG Books Worldwide.

Wineburg, S., & Grossman, P. (1998). Creating a community of learners among high school teachers. *Phi Delta Kappan, 79,* 350–353.

Winograd, P. N., & Bridge, C. A. (1986). The comprehension of important information in written prose. In J. F. Baumann (Ed.), *Teaching main idea comprehension* (pp. 18–48). Newark, DE: International Reading Association.

Wixson, K. K., Bosky, A. B., Yochum, M. M., & Alvermann, D. E. (1984). An interview for assessing students' perceptions of classroom reading tasks. *Reading Teacher, 37,* 346–353.

Wlodkowski, R. J. (1982). *Motivation* (rev. ed.). Washington, DC: National Education Association.

Wood, K. D. (1987). Fostering cooperative learning in middle and secondary classrooms. *Journal of Reading, 31,* 10–18.

Wood, K. D. (1988). A guide to subject matter material. *Middle School Journal, 19,* 24–26.

Name Index

Subject Index